W9-AOI-977

WOODY LEONHARD *teaches*

Microsoft® Office 97

que®   201 West 103rd Street,
Indianapolis, Indiana 46290

Woody Leonhard

Woody Leonhard Teaches Microsoft Office 97

Copyright ©1998 by Que Publishing

All rights reserved. No part of this book shall be reproduced, stored in a retrieval system, or transmitted by any means, electronic, mechanical, photocopying, recording, or otherwise, without written permission from the publisher. No patent liability is assumed with respect to the use of the information contained herein. Although every precaution has been taken in the preparation of this book, the publisher and author assume no responsibility for errors or omissions. Neither is any liability assumed for damages resulting from the use of the information contained herein.

International Standard Book Number: 0-7897-1705-0

Library of Congress Catalog Card Number: 98-85051

Printed in the United States of America

First Printing: September 1998

00   99   98   4   3   2   1

Trademarks

All terms mentioned in this book that are known to be trademarks or service marks have been appropriately capitalized. Que Publishing cannot attest to the accuracy of this information. Use of a term in this book should not be regarded as affecting the validity of any trademark or service mark.

Executive Editor
Jim Minatel

Acquisitions Editor
Jill Byus

Development Editor
Rick Kughen

Managing Editor
Thomas F. Hayes

Project Editor
Karen A. Walsh

Technical Editor
Kyle Bryant

Copy Editor
Howard Jones

Indexers
Becky Hornyak
Cheryl Jackson

Production
Cheryl Lynch
Louis Porter, Jr.
Megan Wade

Contents at a Glance

Part I   **In the Beginning—Before You Start   1**

1   Vital Unmentionables   3
2   Precursors to Using Office   11

Part II   **Office 101   23**

3   Executive Summary   25
4   Making Office Work Your Way   41
5   Help from a Paper Clip   69

Part III   **Word 97   81**

6   Word Preliminaries   83
7   Working with Documents   105
8   Building Documents   121
9   Getting Around   137
10   Making Documents Look Good   155
11   Key Capabilities   207
12   Special Purpose Tools   227
13   On the Shoulders of Giants   253
14   Advanced Features   275

Part IV   **Outlook 98   299**

15   Outlook Preliminaries   301
16   Email   333
17   Other Outlooks   367

Part V   **Excel 97   397**

18   Excel Preliminaries   399
19   Working with Workbooks   413
20   Building Spreadsheets   427
21   Getting Around   467
22   Making Spreadsheets Look Good   479
23   Excel-lent Charts   507
24   Advanced Features   517

Part VI   **PowerPoint   547**

25   PowerPoint Preliminaries   549
26   Working with Presentations   563
27   PowerPoint's Auto Support   587
28   Making Presentations Look Better   617

Part VII   **Advanced Topics   635**

29   Tying the Parts Together   637
30   Office on the Web   667

Index   689

Table of Contents

I In the Beginning—Before You Start   1

1 Vital Unmentionables   3

Bugs   4

Viruses   6

2 Precursors to Using Office   11

Get the Latest Versions and Patches   12
   Office Service Release-1   12
   What Version of Office Do You Have?   13
   Installing SR-1 from the CD   14
   Excel Bug Patches   14
   Outlook Bug Patch… er, Outlook 98   15

Install and Update an Anti-virus Program   16

Register Your Software   17
   The Key Number   17
   Phone Registration   18

Modifying Windows to Work with Office   19
   Explorer Show Extensions   19
   Turn Off Find Fast   20

II Office 101   23

3 Executive Summary   25

Word   29

Outlook   30

Excel   31

PowerPoint   33

Components You'll Find in Some "Office"
Packages   33

Office's More Obscure Parts   35
   Office Assistant   35
   Shortcut Bar   35
   Binders   36
   OfficeArt   37
   Camcorder   37
   Photo Editor   38
   Visual Basic for Applications   38

How the Components Work Together   39

4 Making Office Work Your Way   41

Organizing My Documents   42
   A Place for Everything   45
   Customizing My Documents   45
   Creating Folders in My Documents   48
   Renaming and Deleting Folders   51
   Creating Multiple Folders in My Documents   52
   Moving Folders in My Documents   54
   Customizing My Documents   55

Backup   56
   Which Office 97 Files Need to Be Backed
   Up?   57
   How to Back Them Up   59

Starting Office   63

Making Office 97 Run Better   66
   Speed   67
   Stability   67

5 Help from a Paper Clip   69

The Office Assistant Character   70
   Toggling the Office Assistant On and Off   72
   Changing Characters   73
   Tactics   74

Less Animated Help   76
   Native Help   76
   Microsoft on the Web   79

III Word 97   81

6 Word Preliminaries   83

Crucial Changes   84
   Remove Rulers   85
   Show Paragraph Marks   88
   General Settings   90
   Disable Overstrike Mode   91
   Save Slowly   93
   The Case Against Hyperlinks   95

The Screen   97
   Title Bar   97
   Menu Bar   98
   Toolbars   99
   The Document   99
   Status Bar   100
   Vertical Scrollbar   101
   Horizontal Scrollbar   102

Adjusting Zoom   103

7 Working with Documents   105

Easy Plain Documents   106

Almost-as-Easy Fancy Documents   106

Save   110

Close   113

Open   114

Starting Over   116

Undo/Redo   117

Print   118

8 Building Documents   121

Interlude: What Is a Document, Anyway?   122
   Characters   122
   Paragraphs   122
   Sections   124
   Documents   124
   Drawing Layer   124

Deleting   125

Selecting and Moving   126

The Clipboard   128

Building a Test Document   131

9 Getting Around   137

How the Keys Work   138
   Common Keys   138
   Worthwhile Key Combinations   139

The IntelliMouse Wheel   140

Find   142

Replace   150

Go To, Good Man, Go To   154

10 Making Documents Look Good   155

Characters   156
   Font Changes from the Toolbar   157
   Font Changes from the Dialog Box   160
   Sticky Font Formatting   166

Paragraphs   169
   Paragraph Changes from the Toolbar   169
   Paragraph Changes from the Dialog Box   175
   Borders and Shading   180
   Sticky Paragraph Formatting   182

Tabs   185
Bulleted and Numbered Lists   196
Auto Bullets and Numbers   200

Sections   201

The Whole Document   202
Margins   202
Paper Size   203
Paper Source   204
Layout   204

11 Key Capabilities   207

Features You'll Use Every Day   208

Headers and Footers   208
Different First Page   211

Right-click Spell Check   214

AutoCorrect   216
When a Correct Is a Correct   217
Bending AutoCorrect to Your Own
Devices   218

Thesaurus and Dictionary   220

Symbols   221

Envelopes and Labels   222

Force a Page Break   226

12 Special Purpose Tools   227

Tables   228
Fast Pre-Fab Tables   228
Fast Free-form Tables   231
Fancy Tables   235
Odd Ways to Use Tables   236

Dates   237

Inserting Pictures   239
Clip Art   240
Freehand (AutoShapes and the Drawing
Toolbar)   244
WordArt   248
Scanned Art   249
Charts   249

Inserting Files   250

13 On the Shoulders of Giants   253

Templates and Wizards that Work   254

Doing It with Styles   257
Character Styles   258
Paragraph Styles   261

Customizing Toolbars   266

Bookmarks   269

Hyperlinks   271

14 Advanced Features   275

Page Borders   276

Watermarks   278

Drop Caps   283

Fields   284

Mail Merge   290

Macros   292

What to Avoid—If You Can   293
The Rogues' Gallery   294
The Other Half   294
Snake Oil   296

Where to Go Next   296

IV Outlook 98   299

15 Outlook Preliminaries   301

Components   302
Outlook Express Versus Outlook   303

Outlook 98 or Bust   304

Outlook 98 Installation   304
Internet Only Versus Corporate/
Workgroup   304
Installing Outlook 98 Fresh   307
Switching from Corporate/Workgroup to
Internet Only   310

Crucial Changes   311
Email Options   311
Journaling   312
Mail Delivery   312
Spelling   313

Backup   314
Daily Backups   314
AutoArchive   315
Manual Archive   319

Ancillary Programs   320
Inbox Repair Tool   320
Compacting   321

The Screens and Views   322
The Outlook Shell   322
Inbox   325
Outlook Today   328
Calendar   329
Contacts   330
Tasks, Journal, Notes   332
The Oops Switch   332

16 Email   333

Setting Up Email Accounts   334

New, Reply, Reply to All, Forward   338

Using Email Addresses   342

Adding Contacts   348

Attaching Files   351

AutoSignature   353

vCard   355

Find   357

Organize   359
Folders   359
Colors   360
Views   361
Junk Mail   361

What to Avoid—If You Can   364
WordMail   364
HTML Mail   365

17 Other Outlooks   367

Contacts   368
Creating a Contact   369
Categories   374
Copying   380

Calendar   381
Meetings   381
Events   382
Appointments   383
Recurring Activities   385
Printing Calendars   386

Tasks: It's What to Do   386

Notes   390

Journaling Phone Calls   392

Add-ins   395

V Excel 97   397

18 Excel Preliminaries   399

Terminology   400

Crucial Changes   401
AutoSave   402
Stay Put After Enter   403
Max Out the Most Recently Used List 404
Add Auditing Toolbar   405

The Screen   406
Title Bar   407
Menu Bar   407
Toolbars   407
Formula Bar   407
The Spreadsheet   407
Sheet Tabs and Scrollbar   408
Status Bar   409
Zoom   409

IntelliMouse   410

19 Working with Workbooks   413

New, Close, Open   414

Sheets   417

Undo/Redo   418

Print   418
Print Area   419
Page Sequence   420
Portrait and Landscape   422
Fit to Page   423
Gridlines   424

20 Building Spreadsheets   427

Data   428

Formulas   429
Pointing and Clicking   433
The Sum( ) Function   435
AutoSum   435
Sum( ) on the Range   436
Titles   437
Using Parentheses   439
Verifying   440
AutoCalculate   442

Entry Tricks   443
Enter and Cancel   443
Correcting Misteaks   443
Entering Functions   445
AutoComplete   446
AutoCorrect   446
AutoFill   447

Copy/Move Data   451
Simple Copy, Move   452
How Excel Pastes   454
Absolute and Relative Addresses   457

Add/Delete Rows and Columns   461

#Bad Data   464

Show Formulas   465

Comments   466

21 Getting Around   467

Worthwhile Shortcut Keys   468

Named Ranges   468

Find   471

Go To   475

Multiple Sheets   475

22 Making Spreadsheets Look Good 479

Resizing Columns and Rows 480

AutoFormat 484

Formatting Cells 486
 Number 487
 Alignment 488
 Font 493
 Border 494
 Patterns 495

Insert Picture 496

Hide Rows and Columns 497

Spell Check 498

Keep Titles Onscreen 498

Print Titles 499

Headers, Footers 501

Page Break Preview 503

23 Excel-lent Charts 507

Making a New Chart 508

Editing an Existing Chart 513

Deleting Charts 516

24 Advanced Features 517

Scenarios 518

Audit Techniques 523
 Data Validation 523
 Conditional Formatting 527

IF in a Crossfoot 529

Conditional Sums 534

PivotTables 538

VI PowerPoint 547

25 PowerPoint Preliminaries 549

A Note on Terminology 550

Crucial Changes 551

The Screen 554
 Outline View 555
 Slide View 557
 Slide Sorter View 558
 Notes Page View 559
 Slide Show 560

26 Working with Presentations 563

The View from 10,000 Feet 564

General Strategy 569

Making a New Presentation 570
 Starting AutoContent 570
 Using Pre-Fab Presentations 571
 Going It Alone 571
 Page Setup 572

Opening a Presentation 573

Save, Save As, Close, Exit 574

Organizing Slides 576

Notes and Handouts 583

Print 585

27 PowerPoint's Auto Support 587

AutoContent Wizard 588
 Wizard Options 588
 Summary Slide 591

AutoLayout/New Slide 594

Global Changes 596

Apply Design   596
Slide Master   598
Title Master   603

Footer, Date, Slide Number   606

PowerPoint Central   606

Multiple PCs   611

Pack and Go   615

28 Making Presentations Look Better   617

Charts   618

Text Boxes   622

Pictures   625

Movies and Sounds   628

Transitions and Builds   630

VII Advanced Topics   635

29 Tying the Parts Together   637

Copying, Embedding, Linking   638

Word and Outlook   639
Retrieving Names and Addresses   639
On Useful Information   643

Word and Excel   647
Copy Excel Data to Word   647
Embed a Spreadsheet in a Word
Document   651
Link to a Chart from a Word
Document   655
Which Is Best?   659

Word and PowerPoint   660

PowerPoint and Excel   665

30 Office on the Web   667

Get HTML Support   668

Open, Save on Net   669

Browse   672

Hyperlinks   674

Word Document to Web Page   677

Excel Spreadsheet to Web Page   679

PowerPoint Presentations on the Web   685

Index   689

About the Author

Woody Leonhard describes himself as "a Microsoft Office victim." A Contributing Editor at *PC Computing* magazine, prolific book author, Office add-in software developer, and electronic newsletter publisher, Woody's best known for his offbeat writing style and dead-on accurate technical content. He has earned an unprecedented six Computer Press Association awards and one American Business Press award. Woody's also a Tibetan human rights advocate, and cofounder of the Tibetan Children's Fund.

Dedication

To my loving wife Linda, who once again suffered the Book Widow Blues while I spent untold hours laboring over a hot PC. And to my son Justin, an emerging computer geek of the first degree.

Acknowledgments

As a guy who tends to look at Office through tech-colored glasses, I never would've thought of writing an introductory book had my agent, Claudette Moore, not insisted that I consider it. Thanks, Claudette. You were right. People starting out with Office need to know where the bodies are buried.

Thanks, too, to Jill, Rick, Karen, and Howard and the rest of the Que crew for their guidance and assistance in getting this book out the door. And I don't want to forget Kyle, who came up with a great tech edit.

Thanks to Jay Munro for the most excellent icons. I never looked so good!

Most of all, I want to express my admiration and appreciation to the teams at Microsoft who created, designed, wrote, and now support Office. We may have our differences at times, but the simple fact remains: Office is the most useful piece of computer software ever invented.

Tell Us What You Think!

As the reader of this book, you are our most important critic and commentator. We value your opinion and want to know what we're doing right, what we could do better, what areas you'd like to see us publish in, and any other words of wisdom you're willing to pass our way.

As the Executive Editor for the General Desktop Applications team at Macmillan Computer Publishing, I welcome your comments. You can fax, email, or write me directly to let me know what you did or didn't like about this book—as well as what we can do to make our books stronger.

Please note that I cannot help you with technical problems related to the topic of this book, and that due to the high volume of mail I receive, I might not be able to reply to every message.

When you write, please be sure to include this book's title and author as well as your name and phone or fax number. I will carefully review your comments and share them with the author and editors who worked on the book.

Fax: 317-817-7448

Email: office@mcp.com

Mail: Executive Editor

General Desktop Applications
Macmillan Computer Publishing
201 West 103rd Street
Indianapolis, IN 46290 USA

Do You Need This Book?

This isn't a normal "Intro to Office 97" book. It doesn't assume you're dumb. It won't show you ten dozen ways to save a document. You won't find tables laden with arcane key combinations that you don't have time to memorize. Most of all, it doesn't follow the Microsoft Party Line—there's no attempt to highlight the features that Microsoft's Marketing Department feels will sell more copies of Office 97. What you find here works, and works well.

Why is that important? So many of the books on store shelves simply parrot what Microsoft wants you to believe. One of the most popular Office 97 books starts with a discussion of Binders—surely among Office 97's least useful and most confusing features, but a Microsoft exclusive and thus a marketer's dream. None of the leading Office books (except this one, of course!) tell you what you need to know about Word viruses—or about keeping up-to-date on bug fixes. Most books also don't tell you about overriding ludicrous Office settings. Many books explain how pieces of Office 97 fit together, but they don't warn you about the parts that don't match up at all! That's how *Woody Leonhard Teaches Microsoft Office 97* is different. I'll give you the straight scoop and hold the sugar coating in a way that you can understand and use. Right now.

So why listen to me? Heaven knows the computer industry is full of self-appointed experts who can't tell a font from a formula. The simple fact is that I've been struggling with Microsoft Office and its predecessors for almost a decade now. I've been working with Microsoft's development teams since the days of Word 2.0. (Don't blame me for their mistakes! Sometimes they listen to me. Sometimes they don't.) I've written more than a dozen books on Office—especially Word—and Windows. I've taught hundreds of people how to use Office, and answered tough technical questions from thousands more. My electronic newsletter, WOW (Woody's Office Watch), reaches more than 50,000 people every week, and my articles in PC Computing magazine go out to more than a million.

In short, I see a lot of Office problems. Lots of things that work. Lots of things that don't. I've distilled that experience, that school-of-hard-knocks know-how, translated it into plain English, and put it into this book. Follow along and I'll get you started on the right track—and, with a bit o' luck, keep you pointed in the right direction as you pursue Office enlightenment.

I'm going to assume that Office 97 is installed on your computer, and that you know how to start the various Office components: Word, Outlook, Excel, and PowerPoint. Some of you may have received the database program Access with your copy of Office 97. Access lives in another world, unto itself; it doesn't resemble any other part of Office. I won't talk about Access in this book. Similarly, I won't be covering the ancillary programs in the Office Small Business Edition—if you're looking for help with Expedia Streets or AutoMap, this isn't the place.

DAZED AND CONFUSED?
Don't have Office 97 yet? Thinking about upgrading, but not sure whether it's worth the effort? Wondering which version of Office 97 you should buy? Skip down to Chapter 3, "Executive Summary." In the section called "Other Office Oddities," I discuss all the flavors of Office that are on the market—and the pros and cons (oy! Are there cons!) of each.

I'm also going to assume that you know how to click, drag, select text (by dragging the cursor across characters, turning them black), double-click, and right-click. I'm going to assume that you either have access to the World Wide Web, or that you can find somebody who does. Finally, I'm going to assume that you want to get the most out of Office 97 even if you have to rearrange things a bit. Don't worry. I'll show you each step, in great detail. It won't hurt a bit.

How This Book Is Organized

I've put this book together in a rather unusual way. Instead of diving straight into intensive drills with each of the Office products, I step back a bit and take a look at what you really need to do to make Office work.

Part I of *Woody Leonhard Teaches Microsoft Office 97* covers two hard, cold facts of Office life: bugs and viruses. As far as I'm concerned, if you don't protect yourself against both bugs and viruses, you're just begging for a heap of trouble. I'll show you the best defenses against Word viruses, and then I'll show you precisely how to get the latest, least buggy version of Office. Free. You'll save yourself a lot of time and frustration if you take a few simple precautions.

In Part II, I take a look at the various Office components and how they fit together, then segue into strategies for making Office an effective tool. Whether you use Office in your dorm room to tap out an occasional letter home to Mom, or you've vowed to become the alpha Office geek attached to a gazillion-dollar corporate computer network, you need to see how Office fits into what you're doing, and how you can take advantage of its capabilities to make your life easier.

I don't start hands-on work with Office components until Part III. By far the largest component of this book, Part III deals with Microsoft Word. I'll have you up and churning out documents—good looking documents—in no time. More than that, though, I show you why things work the way they do, and point out where you're bound to have problems. Much of what you learn in Part III about Word carries over to the other Office components, so any additional effort you make here is time well spent.

Part IV tackles Outlook 98. I know that it's traditional for introductory books to move from Word to Excel, but it's been my experience that many Office users spend more time with Outlook than any other piece of Office, with the possible exception of Word. And now that Microsoft has given Office a decent, stable email program and personal information manager (Outlook 97 definitely didn't meet that criterion), it's more important than ever that you learn how to take advantage of Outlook's capabilities—and avoid its quirks.

Part V takes Excel all the way up to PivotTables. I know that some people feel PivotTables are too advanced for a beginning Office user, but I say malarkey. They aren't hard at all. And if you ever hit a problem that's solved best by a PivotTable, you'll be glad you learned how to do the Pivot.

Part VI runs through PowerPoint, far enough to get a presentation going with animation and those fancy inter-slide transitions.

In Part VII, I look at Office's advanced topics. Although it's true that some of the Office applications work with others, the number of interconnections may underwhelm you—and the capabilities of the few that do work may leave you shaking your head. Don't try to connect two Office apps without reading this part. Office on the Web is also discussed in this part. Some parts of some Office apps work well on the Web. I'll show you which ones work, and how to get them going. I'll also point out the parts which—Microsoft marketing's demos to the contrary—don't work worth a hill of beans.

All in all, I hope you find this book an interesting, absorbing, occasionally funny but always dead-on accurate way to learn about the high points (and the low points!) of Office.

Conventions Used in This Book

I assume, right from the get-go, that you're an intelligent person interested in learning about Office. You needn't be a computer expert. You needn't be a typesetter or graphics designer. But you do need to have a voice inside of you, constantly asking, "Why?"

WHAT'S A GEEK?
If you're very interested in a particular topic, it would behoove you to take a gander at the Geek material. Note that these aren't limited to Computer Geek topics—you might qualify as a Font Geek or a Web Geek—so peruse the title to see whether the topic interests you.

There's an awful lot of meat in this book and very little fluff. No inscrutable cartoons. A minuscule amount of repetition. There are some funny parts, a few of which were intentional. In short, *Woody Leonhard Teaches Microsoft Office 97* is designed for people who are serious about learning what Office has to offer, although it doesn't hurt to have a sense of humor.

I've come up with three gimmicks—Geeks, Tips, and Scuttlebutts—to call your attention to parts of the book and help guide you through all this material.

WHAT'S A TIP?
When I have a tip that deserves your special attention, I'll set it aside this way. *Woody Leonhard Teaches Microsoft Office 97* comes chock full of tips, so this device is reserved for the really special tips that come along from time to time.

Most of the hands-on material comes in the guise of an exercise. I've taken great pains to ensure that Exercises include very detailed, step-by-step instructions for exploring a particular Office feature or technique. I think you'll find them fun and, in some cases, absolutely tail-saving.

WHAT'S A SCUTTLEBUTT?
Scuttlebutt material runs the gamut from Office insider gossip to catch-up material for complete novices. In any case, Scuttlebutts aren't required reading—but they can be fun.

*E*XERCISE

An Exercise on Exercises

1. Start the Exercise with Step 1.

2. If you survive, try to tackle Step 2.

3. Continue with Step 3. And so on.

One more tiny convention: When I want you to click something, I've made that something bold. So if I say, "Click **File**, and then **Open**," you should click **File**, and then **Open**. I'll also identify text that you'll see on the screen in **bold**. Anything you'll be required to type or any Web addresses will be set off in a special font that looks like this: mono. Don't worry about it. You'll catch on right away.

Woody Leonhard
Coal Creek Canyon, Colorado

In the Beginning—
Before You Start

1   Vital Unmentionables   3

2   Precursors to Using Office   11

Vital
Unmentionables

BUGS AND VIRUSES. I DON'T KNOW WHY introductory books fail to tackle bugs and viruses. Maybe the authors don't want to air dirty linen in public. Maybe publishers are afraid that Microsoft will get mad. But the simple fact is that you need to know about bugs and viruses—even before you learn how to use Office 97. Why? Because you'll waste an awful lot of time, and subject yourself to untold misery, if you don't know how to protect yourself from these unmentionables, up front.

Such is computing in the late 1990s.

Bugs

What's a bug? Good question. There's no simple answer. For the purposes of this book, we'll concentrate on "hard" bugs—errors in Word itself that will trash your documents, say, or give you incorrect answers in Excel spreadsheets.

Most beginners start out believing that Office has no bugs—that every weird thing they experience is their fault. (One fellow actually wrote to me a couple of years ago and asked how I could be so derogatory. "Mr. Gates certainly knows how to make software that works right. Look at how much money he's made!" Uh, right.) As novices gain more experience and more confidence, they flip-flop, and tend to think that every problem they encounter is due to a bug, and couldn't *possibly* be their fault. I still tend to fall in the latter category.

The truth, of course, lies somewhere in between.

Every computer program has bugs. At least, every computer program that does anything interesting. It's a simple, unfortunate, fact of life. Microsoft spends millions and millions of dollars every year wringing bugs out of Office. And they're damn good at it. By any objective measure ("bugs per line of code," "bugs per developer," "bugs per square inch"), Office comes out remarkably well. Still, there are thousands and thousands of bugs left in Office.

Don't believe it? Ah, you trusting soul! Watch while we conjure up a big, juicy bug. (Okay, okay. This is also a tricky way to get you accustomed to exercises. You caught me. What can I say?)

XERCISE

Data-destroying Word 97 Print Bug

1. Start Word 97.

2. Type a few words. Doesn't matter what you type.

3. Click **File**, then **Save**.

IGNORE THE OFFICE ASSISTANT'S PLEAS
If an obnoxious Paper Clip pops up to tell you "Before you save...," and gives you some sob story about how other people might not have Word 97, growl at it and click **Don't use suggested format**. Unfortunately, growling probably won't keep the nefarious creature from appearing at some later time, but then again you never know—and it certainly won't hurt.

4. To make this easier, let's save the document on your Windows Desktop. To do that, click the **Up one level** 🔝 button. Keep clicking that icon until the **Save in** box shows **Desktop** (see Figure 1.1).

FIGURE 1.1
Saving a
Word docu-
ment on the
Desktop.

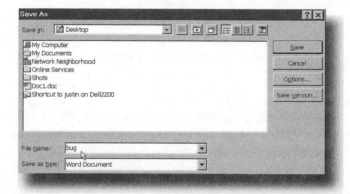

5. Down in the **File Name** box type, oh, **bug**. Click **OK**. You now have a Word 97 document called bug.doc sitting on your Desktop.

6. Type some more stuff in the document, but don't save it.

7. Switch over to the Windows Desktop. (The easiest way to do that is to click the leftmost button in the upper-right corner—the one that looks like an underline. That will minimize Word and leave you staring at the Desktop.)

8. Right-click bug.doc and choose **Print**. Wait a moment or two and bug.doc—complete with all the changes you made in Step 6—will appear on your printer.

9. Bring Word back up. (Click **Microsoft Word** on the Taskbar, down at the bottom of the screen.) Guess what? bug.doc has disappeared. But wait. It's worse than that.

10. Click **File**. bug.doc should be listed down at the bottom, next to the number 1. Click bug.doc and open it. See that? The changes you made in Step 6 were thrown away!

Microsoft, internally, tracks bugs and assigns them numbers. The worst bugs are the ones that destroy data—just like this one. They're the ones Microsoft is supposed to concentrate on, to make sure they don't appear during the test cycles, and certainly never make it all the way into a shipping product. This bug has existed at least since the release of Windows 95, back in August 1995. As of this writing, anyway, MS hadn't fixed it.

Bugs, unfortunately, rate as a way of life in Office 97—and all other major software packages, for that matter.

Viruses

As of this moment, there are more than 2,000 identified and catalogued Word viruses, and several dozen Excel viruses. Virus writing rates as a major growth industry.

What are "macro viruses?" They aren't nearly as mysterious as you probably think. A virus (in this context anyway) is a computer program that can reproduce. We tend to think of viruses as being destructive, or at least inconvenient, but those are cultural attributes that really have nothing to do with viruses. If a computer program can reproduce, it's a virus. Simple.

For the other half, a macro (in this context) is just a computer program that's attached to a Word document, Excel spreadsheet, or PowerPoint presentation. It's a bit odd to think of computer programs attached to documents. When you write to Aunt Emma, you probably don't compose a program to go along with the letter. But in many cases it's very convenient to be able to let a program hitchhike on the back of a document. Think of, oh, form letters that have programs to help you retrieve information about clients. Or spreadsheets that have special rules built-in so you don't flub a complex calculation.

Unfortunately, a few miscreants discovered that they can use Office's programmability—its macro language—to write computer viruses. By subverting a few common programming functions built into Office they found they could write programs that reproduce.

Some of the viruses, such as the original

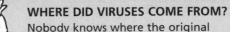

WHERE DID VIRUSES COME FROM?
Nobody knows where the original Word "macro virus," now called Concept.A, originated. We'll probably never know for sure, unless the author steps forward some day.

What we do know for sure is that there were no identified Word viruses prior to July 1995. Then, in the course of a month, a very large percentage of all the PCs at Microsoft's Redmond campus got infected. By the end of 1995, the Concept.A virus had spread to hundreds—possibly thousands—of PCs, all around the world.

Concept.A, are relatively harmless. They attach themselves to Word documents and do nothing more than propagate to other Word documents. That makes the documents a little bigger, and it leads to some strange behavior when you try to save them (Word insists on saving them as templates), but by and large Concept.A doesn't do much. When you get right down to it, the worst damage you'll suffer from a Concept.A infection is to your ego, when you have to tell your friends and coworkers that the documents you sent to them might be infected.

Other viruses aren't so nice. They have payloads that can clobber important files on your disk, wipe out most of your documents, or make Word do weird things. The most insidious viruses, called "data diddlers," make subtle changes to your documents, and leave very little evidence of their activity. You can go for months without noticing the effect of a data diddler. Once you catch the bugger, the illicit changes it's made can be impossible to track and correct. Nasty beasts.

VIRUS BIOLOGY 101

How does a macro virus reproduce? Although the details vary from virus to virus, in Word it usually goes something like this. The virus writer creates a macro—a program—that runs when you do something pretty common such as, oh, opening a document. He (and it's usually a "he") attaches that program to a document. When you open that document, the virus is "triggered" and the virus program takes over.

The virus program usually tries to make a copy of itself—a copy that will hang around, even when the infected document is long gone. If the program succeeds in making a copy of itself that will persist even after you stop and restart Word, people say that you have an "infected system."

To be truly successful as a virus, the program must in turn infect other documents. There are many ways of writing programs to ensure that an infected system will create more infected documents. Most often, the program takes over a common function inside Word itself and whenever you use that function, the program puts a copy of itself in the document that's currently open.

That's how daddy viruses make baby viruses. The worst viruses also have a payload, which runs occasionally and wreaks havoc on your machine. But the payload is just icing on the viral cake; not all viruses have destructive payloads.

So now you know how a virus can travel inside documents, and infect other documents.

It's important that you ensure Word, Excel, and PowerPoint all have their (admittedly wimpy) virus protection features turned on. And that leads us to our second exercise.

*E*XERCISE

Turn on Virus Protection

1. Start Word 97.

2. Click **Tools**, **Options**, then click the **General** tab and make sure the **Macro virus protection** box is checked (see Figure 1.2).

FIGURE 1.2
Macro virus protection in Word 97.

3. Click **File**, then **Exit**, to leave Word 97.

4. Start Excel 97.

5. Click **Tools**, **Options**, then the **General** tab, and make sure the **Macro virus protection** box is checked (see Figure 1.3).

6. Exit Excel 97 by either clicking **File**, then **Exit**, or by clicking the X in the Excel window's upper-right corner.

7. Start PowerPoint 97.

8. You'll be asked if you want to create a new presentation. Click **Cancel**. Then click **Tools**, **Options**, **General**, and make sure **Macro virus protection** is checked (see Figure 1.4).

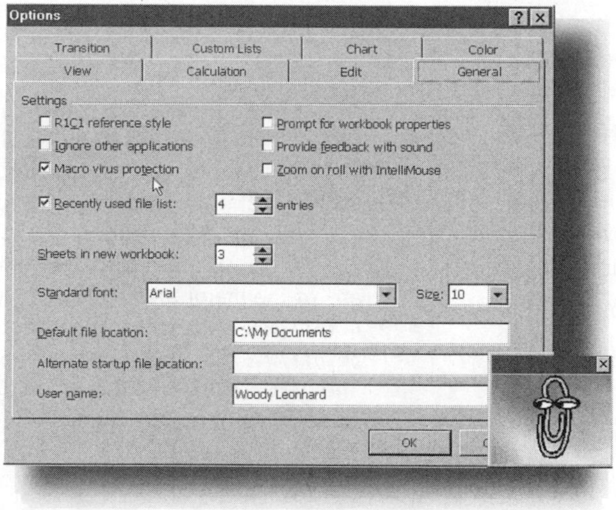

FIGURE 1.3
Macro virus protection in Excel 97.

FIGURE 1.4
Macro virus protection in PowerPoint 97.

9. Exit PowerPoint by clicking **File**, **Exit**, or by clicking the X in the upper-right corner.

There. Your first-level virus protection is in place and working. And, yes, while you were checking, I tricked you into starting three of the four major Office programs that you'll be using in this book. Outlook 98 doesn't have any virus protection, but it doesn't need any. Yet. The macro programming language that Outlook 98 uses isn't strong enough to allow the creation of viruses. I think.

Remember this exercise. Before long you'll look back on it with some degree of nostalgia. This is one of the very, very few features in Word, Excel, and PowerPoint that works more-or-less the same way in all three programs!

VIRUS INFO

There are over 2,000 known and catalogued Office macros viruses; the number's probably closer to 3,000 by the time you read this. You can get more information on macro viruses by visiting the Web pages offered by any of the major anti-virus software companies: `http://www.symantec.com/avcenter` (Norton), `http://www.nai.com/vinfo` (NAI McAfee), and `http://www.drsolomon.com` (Dr Solomon) come immediately to mind.

Precursors to Using Office

YES, I KNOW YOU WANT TO GET TO the programs. Bear with me a minute or two. There are four more things you have to do before we get started:

- Get the latest versions and patches
- Install virus-protection software
- Register your software
- Make two simple Windows modifications

If you follow the simple instructions coming up, you'll pay for this book, right off the bat. Then you can sit back and relax, secure in the knowledge that you're attacking Office like a pro, and take the rest of the book at your leisure.

Get the Latest Versions and Patches

If you're using Office 97, you may not be using the latest version of Office 97. Why is that important? Because Microsoft is constantly updating Office 97, fixing bugs, and adding important new features. If you're using the "old" version of Office 97, you'll be confronted by all sorts of headaches that simply disappear if you get the "new" version.

TRUTH IN BUG FIXING

What I'm about to tell you was accurate when I wrote this book. But fixes come at unpredictable times. (In fact, as I write this, there have been two major Excel bug fixes released by Microsoft in the past month!) That's why it's important you get the latest update information you can find. Unfortunately, you can't always trust Microsoft to give you the straight scoop—you'll see one example shortly. So I strongly suggest that you (or a friend) log on to the World Wide Web and check the site http://www.wopr.com. That's my site. I work with a bunch of people who hold Microsoft's feet to the fire—and keep the world at large apprised of our findings. We can be ornery at times, so don't be too surprised if you find us taking Microsoft to task over something. At the same time, though, if we praise a Microsoft product, the praise comes from the heart.

Office Service Release-1

In late 1997, Microsoft released The Mother of All Office 97 Bug Fixes. This free fix, called "Service Release-1" or SR-1, covers a wide variety of problems in the original Office 97. There are hundreds of fixes embodied in SR-1, many of which have to do with Office 97's stability, improvements to import and export filters, and other such arcana. The single most important reason why every Office 97 user should upgrade to SR-1? A subtle change in the Word macro language keeps a very large percentage of Word viruses from propagating when you use SR-1. You won't find that fact documented anywhere—Microsoft remains loathe to make any claims about this new feature—but the improvement rates as nothing less than spectacular.

WOODY'S OFFICE WATCH
If you really want the straight scoop delivered to your email inbox every week, subscribe to WOW, Woody's Office Watch. Yeah, *that* Woody is *this* Woody. WOW is free, and it will keep you abreast of every new development in the world of Microsoft Office. (I'll also use WOW to make updates—and corrections!—to this book.) Simply send a blank email message to wow@wopr.com. The 'bots will take care of the rest.

☞ *To learn more about Office viruses, see page 6.*

What Version of Office Do You Have?

How can you tell if you have SR-1? Unfortunately, the box Office 97 comes in isn't marked—and if you bought some old inven-

SR-1 NECESSARY BUT NOT SUFFICIENT
Yes, you need to use anti-virus software with SR-1. Virus writers caught on to the SR-1 changes shortly after the fix was released and began writing viruses that bypass the SR-1 protections days afterward. Still, SR-1 keeps more than 90% of all known Word macro viruses from infecting documents and being passed along—a remarkable achievement.

tory, you may not have SR-1, even if you bought your copy of Office 97 last week. There are two telltale signs, though. The SR-1 CD has "SR-1" printed in the upper-left corner. And, if you click **Help**, then **About**, in any of the Office applications, the app should identify itself as being SR-1 (see Figure 2.1).

FIGURE 2.1
The telltale
SR-1 sign.

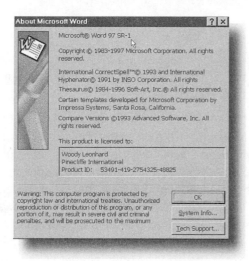

Just to make things, uh, challenging, Microsoft released two *different* products that they call SR-1. The first SR-1 (the one you don't want) is a downloadable file, available on the Microsoft Web site (`http://www.microsoft.com/office`); I call this the stunted SR-1 patch.

The second version (the one you want) consists of a completely new CD containing all of Office 97 with the SR-1 patches applied; Microsoft calls this full version the "Enterprise Update SR-1 CD." Microsoft decided to distribute two different versions simply because it's much cheaper to make a download patch available online, as opposed to mailing out loads of new CDs. I strongly recommend that you get the full Enterprise Update CD because it includes many changes that don't appear in the stunted SR-1 patch: details of the differences are on the Web at http://mcc.com.au/sr1/sr-11.htm.

If you bought your copy of Office 97—as opposed to having it bundled with a new PC—you can call Microsoft and get the full Enterprise Update SR-1 CD, free. In the USA, call 1-800-370-9272 Monday–Friday, 8 a.m. to 10 p.m. Eastern time. Outside the USA, call your local Microsoft office. Note that this phone number is specifically for Enterprise Update CDs. You'll need the CD Key number that's stuck to the back of your Office 97 CD's jewel case. If you don't have the CD Key number, follow the instructions in Exercise 2-1, which appears later in this chapter.

You should receive the CD, absolutely free, in a few days.

Installing SR-1 from the CD

When you get the CD, follow the enclosed instructions—in particular, you need to uninstall the old pre-SR-1 version of Office 97, then reinstall with this new CD. Don't worry. Your old settings will survive the indignity.

If you have an "OEM version" of Office 97—typically because you got Office 97 bundled with a new PC—your search for the Enterprise Update SR-1 CD will be considerably more difficult. Microsoft claims that the OEM (that is, your hardware manufacturer) is responsible for putting together an SR-1 CD and distributing it. Most OEMs blanch at the thought—although we hear that Dell has been very good about providing the update CD. Your best bet is to contact your hardware manufacturer and firmly request the full "Enterprise Update SR-1 CD" patch. If none is forthcoming, the stunted SR-1 patch—better than nothing—sits on the Web at http://www.microsoft.com/office/office/enhancements/sr1off97.asp.

Excel Bug Patches

Eagle-eyed Excel 97 users have found at least four significant bugs in Excel. All of the bugs show their pointed little heads when Excel is supposed to recalculate cells in a spreadsheet—that is, you change a number in a spreadsheet, and Excel is supposed to go back and recalculate everything that's changed—but for some reason Excel "forgets" to do so.

There's a simple, consolidated spreadsheet that demonstrates the recalculation bugs at `http://www.wopr.com`. If you think Excel recalculation bugs are too obscure to affect your spreadsheets, you owe it to yourself to take a look at that sample spreadsheet! Microsoft posts bug fixes as they become available. Some of them work, some of them don't.

Outlook Bug Patch... er, Outlook 98

If you're still using Outlook 97, take note! Outlook 98 incorporates hundreds—I'm tempted to say thousands—of bug fixes to the original (blecch) product. It's a free upgrade for all Office 97 users. It completely replaces Outlook 97. (Yeah, Outlook 97 was that bad.)

You may have an upgrade coupon in your Office 97 box. If so, follow the instructions there to get your free copy of Outlook 98. If not, check Microsoft's Web site `http://www.microsoft.com/outlook` for instructions on ordering or downloading the program.

WHAT TO DO IF YOU FIND A BUG?
First, make sure that the bug is replicable—try to write down a simple series of steps that demo the bug, then give the instructions to a friend and have him or her try it on a different PC. If the bug replicates, start by calling Microsoft and telling them you have the steps to "repro" a bug. Chances are pretty good Microsoft already knows about the problem, and may be able to steer you to a workaround.

Some of the time, though, the Microsoft support reps don't have the slightest idea what is causing the problem, and they're unwilling (or unable) to find somebody who can solve it. That's where WOW comes in. (See the Geek sidebar earlier in this chapter.) Simply write down your steps for replicating the problem, and send them to `ask.woody@wopr.com`. We'll take a look at it and, if it smells like a bug to us, we'll make sure the higher-ups at Microsoft have a look-see. We'll also keep you advised of any fixes Microsoft might post, and keep the world informed through WOW.

It's sad that Microsoft doesn't have a problem escalation procedure that identifies bugs and brings them to the attention of upper management—the folks at Microsoft who can bang a hand on a table, reassign some workers, and get a problem solved. Until Microsoft gets better at it, we at WOW have taken it upon ourselves to short-circuit the system. It works.

I won't even discuss Outlook 97 in this book. You really don't want to hear about it—Outlook 97 has so many problems it's best left untouched. Personally, as soon as Outlook 98 was made available, I found the Outlook 97 program on my hard drive and drove a stake through its heart. Figuratively, of course. If you don't have Outlook 98 yet, get it!

GET 'EM WHILE THEY'RE HOT
If you do nothing more than install these free upgrades, you'll have paid for the cost of this book, many times over, in saved hours (days, weeks), reduced hair-pulling, and psychiatrist's bills. Be sure you get the right upgrades!

Install and Update an Anti-virus Program

One question I hear over and over again: "Woody, which anti-virus program should I buy?" There's a simple answer: It doesn't matter which one you buy. All of the major anti-virus software packages work very well indeed. The only real difference among them is in the user interface—the part of the package that you see on the screen—and that's largely a matter of personal taste (or lack thereof). The anti-virus software companies will cite tests and reviews, trying to prove that their product is superior. But where the rubber meets the road—the ability to uncover and eliminate macro viruses—there isn't a hair's difference among them.

By all means, check the latest reviews in the magazines to see which anti-virus program seems to best meet your needs. (Personally, I look at *PC Computing*'s A-List. But I'm biased.) More than anything, though, don't let your pursuit of the ultimate anti-virus package deter you—not for a minute—in buying and installing one of the major packages.

Depending on the package you buy you'll either be forced or asked to connect to the Web immediately after installation. That's a vital step in the process. Anti-virus packages use something called a *signature file* to identify and eradicate viruses. The software manufacturers update these signature files at most weekly; some are even updated hourly. With dozens of new viruses coming to the forefront every week, you can't afford to get too far behind the curve.

GET YOUR MONEY'S WORTH
Download the latest signature file immediately, and use your anti-virus program's automatic download feature to update that signature file at least once a month—preferably once a week.

Register Your Software

If you haven't called Microsoft and registered Office 97, you should. Even if you have registered, it's a very good idea to call and make sure Microsoft has the correct mailing address and your email address. If you don't register your software—maybe you figure Uncle Bill already has enough info about you; maybe you aren't convinced it's worth the hassle—follow the other steps in this section anyway. It shows you how to get your ducks lined up just in case you have to reinstall Office 97 after some future catastrophe.

The Key Number

How many CDs do you have lying around your desk? Is the Office 97 CD among them? Good. Now a trick question: Where's the "jewel case," the little plastic doohickey your Office 97 CD came in? What, you threw it away? Yeah. Me, too. I hate the things. Just more wasted, rarely recycled plastic.

Guess what? There's a little sticker on the back of your Office 97 CD's jewel case that could be vitally important if you ever have to reinstall Office 97. Assuming you always keep all your jewel cases filed away and know precisely where your Office 97 jewel case is located at all times, you won't have any problems when the Office 97 installer program asks you for your Key Number. (That's the number printed on the sticker on the back of the jewel case.) If you're somewhat, uh, lax in that respect, here is the most important exercise you'll find in this book:

XERCISE _____

Mark Your Office 97 CD

  1. Right now, *as you're reading this book*, take a minute or two to locate your Office 97 CD and its jewel case. If you can find the jewel case, and can read the Key Number on the sticker, breathe a sigh of relief and go on to Step 6.

  2. Can't find the Key Number, eh? Well, you're in luck. There's a trick. Right-click a blank area of the Office Shortcut Bar (say, at the top). Choose **About Microsoft Office**. You should see a dialog box similar to the one in Figure 2.2.

  3. The product ID number will look something like xxxxx-111-1111111-xxxxx, or xxxxx-1111-1111111-xxxxx, where the "xxxxx"s are five-digit numbers. If the second group of numbers is three digits long, go to Step 4. If it's four digits long, go to Step 5.

FIGURE 2.2
The Secret
Key Number
dialog box.

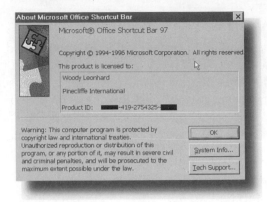

4. Your Key Number is the three digits, followed by the seven digits, in the middle of the Product ID number. So if your Product ID number is 12345-678-9012345-67890, your Key Number is 678-9012345. Go on to Step 6.

5. You have to drop one digit before you get your Key Number. The digit that gets trash-canned is the last one in the group of four. So, for example, if your Product ID number is 12345-6789-0123456-78901, your Key Number is 678-0123456.

6. Now that you have your Key Number, don't lose it! Get an indelible pen (I use a Sharpie) and write the Key Number on the top—the printed side—of your Office 97 CD. Be careful not to screw up the shiny side of the CD; that's where the program lives.

Phone Registration

With your Product ID number in hand (remember, that's the one shown in the Office Shortcut Bar's "About Microsoft Office" dialog box; see Figure 2.2) call Microsoft and make absolutely sure that you're registered, and that Microsoft has your correct address. In the USA, call 800–360–7561; outside the USA, call your local Microsoft office.

While you're on the phone with the 'Softies, ask them if you have the latest version of the various Office 97 applications. They'll be able to tell from your Product ID number. Don't be too surprised if their advice differs from mine—and if there are any discrepancies, be sure you follow the instructions at the beginning of this chapter!

Modifying Windows to Work with Office

One final step before you're ready to use Office 97 for the first time. (They didn't tell you about all these glitches when you bought Office, did they? *Heh heh heh.*) There are two little things in Windows itself that have to be changed. Even if you've been using Office since the dawn of time, you should make these changes. Don't worry, they're easy.

Explorer Show Extensions

I've been fighting Microsoft on this one for years.

When you create a new Word 97 document and give it a name such as, oh, Manifesto, Word automatically puts some extra stuff on the end of the file's name—Manifesto.doc, in this example. The .doc on the end of the file's name tells Windows (and Word, and the world, for that matter), that this is a Word document. The few characters at the end of the filename are, collectively, called a *filename extension*. Excel worksheets end with .xls. Outlook stores data in files with .pst extensions. It's a bit of old-fashioned computer gobbledygook that dates back to the earliest days of PCs and <shudder> DOS.

Somebody inside Microsoft (hi, Bill!) has decided that filename extensions are too complicated for normal people, like you and me. They want to pretend that the .doc and .xls and .pst filename extensions don't exist, and hide them from "novices" (whomever they may be). The Windows Explorer itself—whether you use Windows 95, Windows 98, or Windows NT—hides filename extensions from you. That wouldn't be so bad, except Explorer also hides filename extensions from programs like Word and Excel. (Outlook shows you filename extensions in all their glory!) And *that* wouldn't be so bad, except you can get in a whole lot of trouble if you learn that filenames have extensions, and you try to play around with them a bit. Even a little bit.

More than that, the moment you get outside the Office cocoon, you're going to bump into filename extensions—and you might as well get used to them sooner, rather than later. So here's our first Power User exercise.

*E*XERCISE

Make Explorer Show Filename Extensions

   1. Out in Windows, right-click My Computer and choose **Explore**.

   2. Click **View**, then **Folder Options** (on some machines it'll just say **Options**). Choose the **View** tab.

   3. Check the box marked **Show all files**.

4. If you're using an early version of Windows 95, uncheck the box marked **Hide MS-DOS file extensions for file types that are registered**. If you're using a later version of Windows 95, Windows NT 4, or Windows 98, uncheck the box marked **Hide file extensions for known file types** (see Figure 2.3). Click **OK** all the way back out.

FIGURE 2.3
Removing the Explorer blinders.

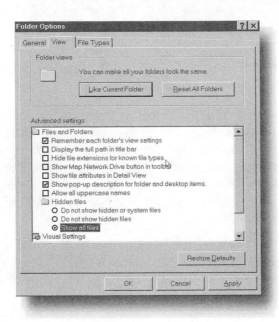

Now Windows Explorer will show you all the files on your drives; Office will show you filename extensions; and your PC's screen will match the screen shots in the rest of this book. Bet you never thought you'd be a Power User so soon in your Office career, eh?

Turn Off Find Fast

Yes, I know it's supposed to be one of Office 97's niftiest features. Hate to tell you, but on a scale from one to ten, Fast Find can barely muster a zero.

Here's how it's supposed to work: Whenever you aren't using your PC for an extended period of time, Find Fast is supposed to kick in, look at all of your documents, and create an index of every word in those documents. That way, when you want to find, say, all of your Word documents that contain the word Fubar, Find Fast will jump in, use its index, and find the documents lickety-split.

Here's what happens in the real world. You're typing along in Word 97 for a while and rest your hands for a few seconds, to let your fingers cool off. (You *are* a fast typist, aren't you?) Just as you're about to start typing again, Find Fast kicks in. The hard drive starts whirring. Lights flash. You type, type, type—and nothing appears on the screen. It's like the innards of your PC have been cryogenically treated so the little squirrel inside runs at one-hundredth its normal pace. You sit and watch the hard drive light go on and off, and sooner or later the machine unfreezes. If you're lucky.

If you're unlucky, Windows goes south, with one of those "General Protection Faults" staring at you on the screen. I've actually left my machine on overnight, only to return to a precisely arranged series of General Protection Fault messages, cascading ten deep on my lovely Windows desktop, all caused by Find Fast.

Fortunately it's easy to get rid of the beast. (Windows 98 automatically disables Find Fast if you install Win98 over the top of an existing Win95/Office setup. I guess they're learning out in Redmond. Gradually.)

XERCISE

Clobbering Find Fast

1. Go out to Windows, click **Start**, **Settings**, **Control Panel**. Then double-click the **Find Fast** icon. You'll see which drives Find Fast is currently infesting (see Figure 2.4).

FIGURE 2.4
Find Fast
surfaces.

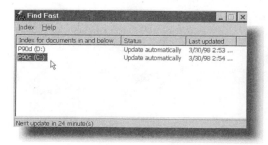

2. Click each drive, in turn, so you highlight it. Then click **Index**, **Delete Index**. Find Fast on that drive comes up for a last gasp (see Figure 2.5).

Just click **OK**, and Find Fast will never darken your door—or slow down (or crash!) your machine again.

FIGURE 2.5
Neutralizing
Find Fast.

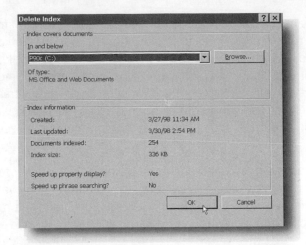

Well, that's about it for the preliminaries. With all of that under your belt, you're finally ready to start using Office 97. Easy, eh?

Office 101

3 Executive Summary   25

4 Making Office Work Your Way   41

5 Help from a Paper Clip   69

Executive
Summary

*E*ven if you aren't an executive, and can't stand summaries, you might

be interested in knowing something about the parts of this Office

97 beast that bears (and beats) you.

Microsoft Word has been around since the early days of DOS. It

was one of the first computer applications Microsoft ever sold—and

it has turned out to be the most lucrative application ever invented.

Once Windows 3.0 took off, Microsoft stopped investing in the

DOS version and turned almost all of its efforts to Word for

Windows. The folks at Microsoft believed in Windows—and Bill put

his development resources where his mouth was. Word's current

hegemony in the word processing realm can be traced directly to

Microsoft's betting on Windows—and WordPerfect's failure to back the winning Operating System horse.

The creation of Excel led to the development of Windows—not the other way around. Hard to believe nowadays, but Windows 286 was specifically invented to support Excel 1.0, and for years the demands of the Excel development team drove the people designing Windows. Around the time of Windows 3.0 the cart and horse reversed positions, but even now Excel sports innovations that the rest of the Office pack only imitate in later versions.

PowerPoint started out as a Microsoft-internal project: the people in Redmond were making so many presentations they had to come up with a package to make their lives simpler. Little did they know that they'd be creating one of the most ubiquitous time sinks on the face of the planet. PowerPoint has long suffered as Office's poor stepchild: although many smart people work on the PowerPoint team, they've never received the attention or the resources that other parts of Office have commanded.

Outlook started out on a very weak note. As I alluded to in the previous chapter, Outlook 97 (the first incarnation of Outlook) was a typical Microsoft version 1.0 product:

buggy, hard to use, and very frustrating. Still, the brilliance of including all of Office's missing links—from an address book to email to scheduling, and much more—in one package couldn't be denied. Outlook remains one of the most promising products Microsoft has ever conceived, and Outlook 98 is starting to deliver on that promise. If it doesn't already control your life, someday it probably will.

Office itself arose as a shotgun marriage between the long-established Word, the upstart Excel, and whatever else Bill could throw into the original package to make it sell. The first few versions of Office made a mockery of the terms "uniformity" and "interoperability"—each application worked its own way, the teams developing the applications rarely spoke to one another, and the whole she-bang was held together with baling wire and chewing gum. Lousy chewing gum at that.

Over the years, though, Microsoft has put a lot of effort into making the individual applications work similarly, and work together. While I wouldn't say Office has been a screaming success in either category, the fact is that learning about one Office application generally gives you a good leg up on learning the others.

Still, there are many differences between Word, Outlook, Excel, and PowerPoint—and many of those differences go straight to the core of the products. (For example, if you talk about a "template" in Word, it's very different from a template in Excel, or in PowerPoint.) So you can't always assume that the terminology stays uniform as you switch between the applications.

Some folks may disagree, but in my opinion, each of the main Office applications are best of breed. You won't find a better word processor than Word, a better spreadsheet manipulator than Excel, a presentation package that beats PowerPoint, or an all-in-one email/personal information manager that surpasses Outlook 98. Without a doubt, Office 97 is an excellent choice.

Not that Office 97 isn't without its warts! I've already talked about the bugs. Since Office sits in more offices than any other package (by, oh, an order of magnitude), it's a big target: industry pundits love to take potshots at it; virus writers love to write for it; and the chances of bugs appearing and being identified increase enormously. You can feel smug, though: you're using the best. Even if you do love to hate it. I sure do.

Let's take a thirty-second tour of each application, and put each one in perspective, particularly as they apply to this book.

Word

What's a word processor? That's a very good question indeed. Best I figure it, a word processor is a program that helps you take ideas out of your head, organize them in a somewhat linear fashion, and put them in a computer. From that point they can be printed. Or posted on the Web. Or sent to coworkers in a file. Whatever.

People get enormously frustrated over Word, for all sorts of reasons. If I had to pick the one main reason why people have problems with Word, it has to be this: Word doesn't work like a typewriter. You can't type fill-in-the-blank forms, say, and have all the blanks line up. You can't press the Tab key and watch as the platen goes *ziiiiing* over to the next tab stop. Sometimes Word gets so all-fangled confused it will keep centering lines when you don't want them centered, or make characters bold for no apparent reason.

Sometimes you'll feel like tossing your PC out the window and yearn for the good old days of the IBM Selectric typewriter. I know I do.

The people who designed Word wanted it to do much more than a typewriter—and they succeeded admirably. But in the process of making Word more than a typewriter, they had to surmount a few conceptual hurdles that are very confusing. In the end, I think it's fair to say that Word is more like a typesetting program than a typewriter—and therein lies many a difficulty.

One of the primary goals I have in writing this book is to acquaint you with the ways in which Word differs from a typewriter, and quite possibly get you to understand why Word *can't* work like a typewriter. There are hidden parts of Word that contain key pieces of information—parts of Word that Microsoft, in its infinite wisdom, has decided are too obscure for normal users. We'll "out" those hidden components, and I bet, in the end, you'll see why and how Word works the way it does—an understanding that's completely impossible if you use Word the way it's shipped.

Remember the Wizard in *The Wizard of Oz*? (The movie version anyway.) Think of me as Toto. I'm going to yank that curtain back and show you the machinations going on behind the scenes. I'll bark and growl a bit, too, while I'm at it.

Outlook

Most introductory Office books go straight from Word to Excel, and mention Outlook parenthetically, back somewhere near the fourteenth appendix. There are (at least) three reasons for this odd ordering:

- So many introductory books around today are minor updates of their Office 95 editions. Since Outlook didn't even exist in the days of Office 95, the authors threw in information about Outlook as something of a last-minute sop to the Microsoft marketing miracle.

- In the old days of Outlook 97, the product was so buggy it was hard to say anything good about it. That's changed with Outlook 98.

- Even now, Outlook has failed to capture the mindshare that it deserves. Ask most people which products are in Office, and they'll inevitably start out by mentioning Word and Excel. That's changing, too. Outlook is rapidly becoming the most-used piece of Office, particularly for wired folks who have to contend with a lot of email.

I don't want you to get the idea that Outlook 98 solves all of Office's (manifest) problems; it doesn't. On the other hand, for the vast majority of Office users—which is to say, for the vast majority of office workers with PCs—Outlook holds the potential for productivity gains on a grand scale.

Think of Outlook as a combination email program, contact manager (with an address book), calendar and group scheduling program, to-do task nagger—and all-around office organizer, with electronic sticky notes, appointment calendar, an ability to track and retrieve Office documents, even an alarm clock that warns you when you need to run to an important meeting. In other words, Outlook 98 is the catchall application that handles most business needs not met by Word, Excel, or PowerPoint. Many Office users would be well advised to keep Outlook running as their main application. Outlook 98 has a special screen called "Outlook Today" (see Figure 3.1) that is particularly well-suited to the task.

What's not to like about Outlook? My number one gripe is that it doesn't fit into the Office mold very well: it doesn't always behave like other Office applications. That makes it harder to learn in the first place, and harder to discover new features by simply poking around.

FIGURE 3.1
Outlook 98's
"Today"
mastermind
screen.

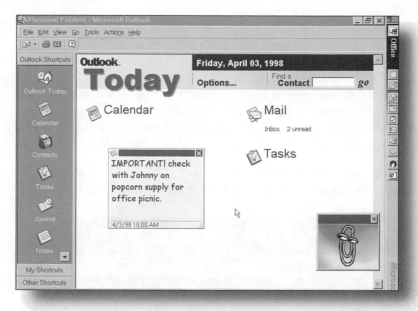

FIGURE 3.1
Outlook 98's
"Today"
mastermind
screen.

Excel

Excel is a spreadsheet program. Some of you may not be very familiar with spreadsheets, but don't let that put you off. You know how much fun it is to balance your
checkbook? Well, think of a spreadsheet as a kind of checkbook that can balance
itself, once you figure out how to put in the formulas for calculating balances. If
you've ever used a calculator for more than two minutes at a stretch, you're a good
candidate for Excel.

At its most basic, Excel has rows and columns—like an old-fashioned columnar pad,
if you've ever worked with one of those—with a built-in calculator that can be told
to calculate just about anything. The grid sits behind every spreadsheet, physically
and metaphorically, and cells on the grid hold the information you want.

But Excel reaches beyond numbers and cells. Its charting capability—where you can
turn a table of numbers into any of a gazillion different graphs—is so good it has
very nearly destroyed an entire segment of the software industry. Five years ago,
you could choose from a half-dozen well-known graphing programs. Nowadays,
the vast majority of business graphs come straight from Excel. We'll take a very
close look at how to create and manipulate graphs.

In a pinch you can also use Excel as a database program. (For that matter you can even use Excel to type business letters. Not that I would recommend it.) For simple databases—"simple" here refers to the structure of the database, not necessarily its size—Excel will suffice. And if you already know a bit about Excel, jury-rigging it to handle databases rates as one whole heck of a lot easier than learning how to use a database program, such as Access or FoxPro. At some point, though, you'll get the feeling that using Excel as a database manager is like using a shoe as an ice cream scoop.

One Excel feature that really deserves wider attention: PivotTables (see Figure 3.2). None of the introductory Office books I've seen tackle PivotTables, and that's a shame.

FIGURE 3.2
PivotTables—
an important
but often
overlooked
Excel feature.

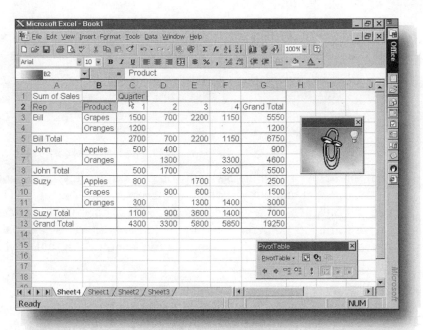

Some information naturally fits into a two-dimensional table. Say your company sells ten different products, and you want to track sales by quarter. That's easy. List products down the left side and quarters across the top, and you're done. But most information isn't so two-dimensional. If your company has a half-dozen sales people, you may be interested in sales by sales rep by quarter—or sales by rep by product. And flipping between the various spreadsheets can frequently tell you something that isn't obvious by looking at any of the static two-dimensional spreadsheets. As part of the Excel graduate course in this book, I'll show you how to set up a pivot table and use it. Even if you've never put together a spreadsheet.

PowerPoint

Few Office users ever take the time to learn how to use PowerPoint. It's almost certainly the most sink-or-swim Office application: The boss asks you to throw together a presentation, you dive into the PowerPoint cesspool... er, lagoon, push a few buttons, type some stuff, and pray that the resulting presentation looks good enough that you don't embarrass yourself. That's what I call the YAPPP approach. Yet Another PowerPoint Presentation. You kinda pray that it turns out OK.

That's a shame, really, because PowerPoint has a lot to offer. Most Office users spend a lot of time with Word. Some also put a bit of effort into learning Excel. After all, a document that looks like a second-grader's scrawl, or a spreadsheet that doesn't add up can make you look like a dunce. Few folks give PowerPoint the time investment it deserves. Once you get over the strange terminology, and figure out the tweaks (which, admittedly, don't bear much resemblance to other Office tweaks), PowerPoint can turn a mediocre presentation into a mediocre presentation that won't put people to sleep.

PowerPoint's power lies in its ability to pull together a slide-show style presentation quickly, accurately, and (if you either use the built-in templates, or know how to make your own) with a minimum of fuss. Fancy features, like wipes and fades and picture animation, can be added to presentations in no time at all. In fact, PowerPoint is so powerful that you have to use its bells and whistles in moderation: by far the largest downside to PowerPoint is that it gives you too much flash, and makes it too easy to create a presentation that outshines the subject matter.

Components You'll Find in Some "Office" Packages

Those are the four Office 97 components that we'll discuss at length in the remainder of this book. Office, though, contains other flotsam and jetsam that you'll occasionally bump into. For the sake of completeness, I'll dismiss them here.

Microsoft has a huge Office marketing staff; by and large its job is to milk the most profit possible out of Office. Fair enough. That's what a good marketing department should do. In the process of adapting Office to fit various market niches, Microsoft has come up with these flavors of Office 97:

- *Office 97 Standard Edition*. Word, Outlook, Excel, PowerPoint. You'll also get Internet Explorer (you *do* use IE 4, don't you?), the Camcorder, Photo Editor, and one free month on Microsoft Network (ho hum). Solid choice. If you're still wondering about upgrading from an earlier version of Office—well, in my opinion there's no question, as long as you have a hefty enough

PC to run it (that is, any size Pentium or a very well aspirated 486, with at least 16MB of memory, and a couple hundred megs of free hard disk space). Run out and buy Office 97. Hock your car if you have to.

- *Office 97 Professional.* All of the above, plus Access, and a stunted version of Microsoft Bookshelf called "Bookshelf Basics." That's a subset of Bookshelf that includes all of the dictionary, thesaurus, and quotations, but only "teaser" pieces of the Encyclopedia, Atlas, Chronology, Almanac, and Internet Directory. Bookshelf Basics also includes a totally dysfunctional zip code lookup routine. If you don't think you need Access (and if you're wondering, you probably don't), seriously consider buying the Standard Edition, plus Encarta 98.

- *Office 97 Developer Edition.* All of the "Pro" stuff, plus an Access run-time module (if you don't know what a run-time module is, don't worry about it), Setup Wizard (not nearly as good as WISE or InstallShield), Replication Manager, a couple of printed manuals that duplicate the online Help files, ActiveX controls, and code samples. For most people—including Office 97 developers—there isn't much here that warrants paying the extra bucks. Note that all of the macro programming languages are available directly in any version of Office (or even the component applications). If you considered buying the Developer Edition because you'd like to try writing a macro someday, forget about it. You already have everything you need.

- *Office 97 Small Business Edition, Version 1.* Word, Outlook, Excel, Microsoft Publisher 97, Automap Streets Plus, Small Business Financial Manager, one free month on Microsoft Network (yawn again). You'll only find this version on dusty back shelves, at a steep discount, or through Shady Slim's Discount Stores. Which is just as well.

- *Office 97 Small Business Edition, Version 2.* Word, Outlook 98 (yes, Outlook 98), Excel, Microsoft Publisher 98, Small Business Financial Manager 98, and Expedia Streets 98. This can be a good choice, depending on your needs. Note that there's no PowerPoint—heaven help you if you need to create a slide show—but there are good hooks between Expedia Streets (a mapping program) and Outlook 98. Small Business Financial Manager can be marginally useful, but Quicken's QuickBooks covers the same ground in a much more comprehensive way. Publisher 98 is an excellent package for producing flyers, newsletters, brochures, business cards, and the like—it's much simpler than Word, yet quite powerful. It's another good choice, although we won't cover it here.

If you bought Office 97 preinstalled on a PC, chances are good you either received the Standard Edition, or the Small Business Edition. The easy way to tell: Do you have PowerPoint? If not, you got the Small Business Edition.

That's the entire Office 97 shtick. Let's take a closer look at the lesser-known parts.

Office's More Obscure Parts

Sure Office 97 contains a handful of stellar applications—Microsoft likes to call them "best of the breed," and they probably are. But there are smaller applications that ship in most Office boxes, and many of these unsung heroes deserve more attention than they usually receive. A couple of them are complete turkeys, though, so don't get your hopes up too high.

Office Assistant

No doubt you've bumped into the little paper clip sitting in the corner of any Office program's screen. Probably bumped into it literally. Anyway, I'll have a lot to say about "that damn paper clip" in Chapter 5, "Help from a Paper Clip." Generally it's a pain in the neck, but under some conditions it can save your life. Bet you can't wait, eh?

Shortcut Bar

Back when Office 97 was first released, the Office Shortcut Bar sat at the top of the heap in the program launcher utility category. The Office Shortcut Bar (see Figure 3.3), as you may know, gives you one-click access to many Office components: you don't need to hunt around in the Start menu, or put piecemeal shortcuts on your Desktop. Unfortunately, you have to mess around with OSB to make it very useful—Microsoft stuck the wrong shortcuts on the bar, and made it reasonably difficult to get the right ones to show.

Lately, Microsoft has made the OSB obsolete. If you install Internet Explorer 4 over the top of Windows 95, or if you use Windows 98, the new version of Windows itself has a much better program launcher, located immediately to the right of the Start button. I'll have more to say about that launcher in the next section.

If you don't have Internet Explorer 4 or Windows 98, you should take a few minutes to make the Office Shortcut Bar work the way you work. See Chapter 4, "Making Office Work Your Way," for step-by-step instructions.

FIGURE 3.3
Office 97
Shortcut
Bar—rapidly
becoming
obsolete.

Binders

I don't care what you've read in other introductory books. Binders are a pain in the neck, and most users—particularly new users—should avoid them like the plague.

Office 97's Binder feature is a way to put related documents in one place and keep them all together. There are two very good reasons why you might want to use Binders:

- If you need to print both Word documents and Excel spreadsheets, interleaved, with a single header or footer. This can actually be handy if you have to put together a report where full-page Excel spreadsheets are interleaved with different Word documents, and you need to have the pages numbered continuously across both types of file. (Note that Binders won't help unless each spreadsheet, and each document, is in a separate file.) There are some similar weird circumstances where Binders can help with printing reports, but that's the main use.

- If you commonly send multiple documents to other people across your company's network, or over the Internet, and you don't know how to use a ZIP program. Binders can help you keep all the pieces together. But that's about it.

Microsoft wants you to use Binders because none of its competitors have a similar feature. (Or so MS would have you believe.) That's a silly reason to get locked into using Binders—much less to spend the time it takes to figure Binders out.

OfficeArt

Word, Excel, and PowerPoint all have drawing capabilities, ranging from pretty good to so-so. These capabilities fall under the collective rubric of *OfficeArt* even though each one works a little differently. (You Office 95 fans might know of something called *WordArt*. It's been swept into the OfficeArt camp.)

The best thing about OfficeArt? You don't have to use it. If you spend much time at all with template-based or freehand drawing, try Microsoft Draw 98. It's free to Office 97 owners. (Something else they didn't tell you about, eh?) Draw 98 includes all of the AutoShape templates you might've seen in OfficeArt, but it also has snap-to connectors that work (unlike, say, Word 97), 3D text effects, and a whole lot of additional features. Draw 98 also works with Microsoft Publisher 98 and Outlook 98.

Microsoft makes Draw 98 available free for downloading from its Web site. One irritant: the actual site has changed several times. The best way to find it is to navigate to `http://www.microsoft.com/office` and look around for Office enhancements.

Once installed, Draw 98 sits on each Office application's **Insert** menu. In Word 97, click **Insert**, **Picture**, **New Drawing**. Anywhere else, just click **Insert**, **Object**, **Microsoft Draw 98 Drawing**, and you're off to the races. Be sure you download and work with Draw 98 before shelling out the bucks for a competing product, such as Visio.

Camcorder

The Camcorder (see Figure 3.4) records everything that's happening on your PC—screens, mouse movements, sounds—so they can be played back, either on your machine or on someone else's. It's a very simple, but very effective application. Consider using it if you need to show somebody a complex series of actions and you don't want to bother trying to write it all out longhand.

FIGURE 3.4
Microsoft Camcorder recording a session.

The Office Camcorder doesn't install itself. You have to go out and find it. To do so, stick the Office 97 CD in your CD-ROM drive, right-click My Computer, choose Explore, and double-click the CD-ROM drive. Double-click the folder called \VALU-PACK, and then the folder called \MSCAM. Finally, double-click Camcordr.exe and follow the instructions. When you're done, Microsoft Camcorder will appear on the **Start/Programs** list.

Photo Editor

This rather sophisticated component of Office goes way beyond its original roots as a photo editor. In fact, Office Photo Editor will let you manipulate almost any kind of graphics file, including GIF, BMP/bitmap, WMF/Windows Metafile, JPEG, TIF/Tagged Image Files, PCD/Kodak Photo CD, and PCX/Windows Paintbrush files. If you've considered buying a package such as Adobe Photoshop, it would behoove you to take a good look at the lowly Photo Editor before shelling out the dough.

If you have a scanner, chances are very good that Photo Editor will hook right into the scanning routines, giving you a large number of options for cropping, resampling, balancing, and much more. Try using Photo Editor for a few scans and you may never go back to the manufacturer's scanning software. Plus, you get all those weird effects: embossing, posterizing, texturing, and on and on.

Check it out. **Start/Programs/Microsoft Photo Editor** will get you there.

Visual Basic for Applications

Word 97, Excel 97, and PowerPoint 97 all contain a macro programming language. I talked about it earlier, when we were looking at viruses. Although the methods used for programming each of the different applications is quite distinct, the languages in all three are very similar. They're called *Visual Basic for Applications*. As the name implies, VBA rates as a first cousin (well, maybe a second cousin, removed) to Visual Basic, the Windows programming language.

Believe it or not, if you have any of those three programs installed on your machine, you have a very powerful programming language available to you, any time. Simply click **Tools**, **Macro**, then **Visual Basic Editor** to get it going. (Outlook 98 uses a very primitive language called VBScript; it's a long, long way from VBA.)

I won't be discussing macros in this book. I was tempted to talk about the Macro Recorder—a part of Office that can be made to watch over your shoulder as you do things, and translate your actions into a macro program, which can be replayed to mimic your actions—but it's pretty hard to record a useful macro. If the macro doesn't do exactly what you thought it would, you have to dive pretty deep to figure out why. And, besides, once I start talking about macros, I find it very hard to shut up. They really can do amazing things. I made a living off them for years.

If you have a hankering to learn more about macros, I'd strongly recommend that you pick up a CD from Microsoft called Mastering Office Development. (Hint: if you have kids around the house who want to tackle a real programming language, this is a great way to start.) The CD will set you back $100 or so, but it's worth every penny, even if it does toe the Microsoft Party Line. To get the CD, which can be surprisingly hard to find, in the USA call Microsoft directly at 800-621-7930. Outside the USA, start at the Web site `http://www.microsoft.com/mastering/default.asp`, and pray.

LEARN MORE ABOUT MACROS
If you really want to learn more about macros, I suggest picking up a copy of Special Edition Using Office 97 Bestseller Edition or Using Office 97, Third Edition, both published by Que.

How the Components Work Together

You would think that Office 97, being the monolith it's marketed to be, would have all sorts of robust interconnections among its various components. Well, you'd be wrong. The fact is that each Office component grew up independently—only Outlook was born after the debut of Office as a whole—and the differences really show up when you try to tie the pieces together.

Here's a thumbnail sketch of which parts of Office 97 work with other parts, along with a little bit of heckling from Woody's Infamous Peanut Gallery:

- Excel 97 tables and charts plop into Word documents and PowerPoint presentations with little heartburn.

- Word 97 can bring names and addresses into documents from your Outlook 98 contacts list, but there are several gotchas. (I'll tell you about them toward the end of this book.) Word can also suck in a list of names from Outlook and use them to perform a mail merge (that is, Word can generate form letters and envelopes for people in your Outlook contacts database).

- It's also relatively easy to send a fax from Word via Outlook 98, out on your modem. Providing all the connections work right, anyway.

- Outlook can keep a log—called a *journal*—of all of your Word, Excel, and PowerPoint files. The journal shows you when you opened, updated, and stored away the files. That can be very handy if you get into a situation where you can remember when you did something, but not what it was. For example, "Jeez. I updated that Word document last Wednesday or Thursday, but I can't remember the name of the file."

- You can move files between Excel and Outlook. That can be handy if you want to pull your Contacts list into a spreadsheet, say.

- There's a handy, but horribly inflexible, way to turn a Word 97 outline into a PowerPoint presentation.

While the pieces of Office can work together in other ways, these are the biggies. I'll cover them in-depth—and take you through the ins and outs—toward the end of the book.

Making Office
Work Your Way

OU'LL FIND MY FAVORITE MANTRA REPEATED throughout this book: *Take Office into your own hands!* There's absolutely no reason why you should suffer along with the decisions Microsoft has made for you. Office can be changed every which way, and you'll save yourself an enormous amount of time if you'll just set it up the way that works best for you.

I'm going to start this customizing extravaganza, which will recur throughout the book, with some simple apple pie changes. Every single Office user should take these steps to make Office work better. A few minutes spent on these changes will pay off day after day as you use the product. Besides, digging through all of this is a simple way for you to get a good feel for how Office fits into Windows at large.

Organizing My Documents

Windows lets you store files—letters, faxes, invoices, memos, stories, spreadsheets, presentations, pictures, and the like—in folders. Office 97 sets up a special folder called My Documents and encourages you to store your files in that folder. While the name My Documents may strike you as a trifle cute, it's still a decent starting point to help you get organized.

ANARCHY IN THE OFFICE
Some companies force you to go along with all of Microsoft's absurd customizing decisions. There are a few tools that limit the customizing you can perform, both on Office and on Windows itself. Companies that force employees to swallow a specific collection of settings often do so in the name of Total Cost of Ownership—but their TCO calculations are frequently fallacious.

My favorite example: there are ways to keep users from changing the buttons on their Office toolbars. Microsoft created a specific set of toolbars and, dammit, Big Brother (most often in the guise of an inflexible IT department) doesn't want you to change those toolbars so they work better for you. It's all hogwash.

Big Brother will proffer an argument along the lines of, "Hey, if you change the toolbar buttons, our tech support people won't be able to help you. It'll cost us a lot of money to cover for your mistakes!"

What a crock. If you're advanced enough to change your toolbar buttons, you'll know which buttons you have, and what they do. Besides, any tech support person worth their salt should be able to work through toolbar changes. When the IT folks make decisions like this, they're lowering the IT's TCO—not yours. Just don't get fired for tinkering with the settings, OK?

Occasionally you'll find that some of the customizing recommendations in this book won't work on your machine at work. (They should work on a PC at home, though, unless you've done something weird with the installation.) If you get shut out of an important customization at work, you may well be the victim of Big Brother. I suggest you yell, real loud.

KEEPING YOUR FILES ORGANIZED

People tend to put all their Word documents in one folder, all their spreadsheets in another, graphics in yet another, and so on. You'll find it much easier to keep track of things if you keep related files together—never mind whether the files are Word documents, Excel spreadsheets, PowerPoint presentations, scanned photos, or artwork. (Outlook files tend to look after themselves; you don't need to be concerned about them at this point.)

Think about the best way to organize your information. Someone in a small business, for example, may find it easier to work with separate folders for each client. That can get a bit cumbersome if you have more than a few dozen clients, but if that's the case, you might be able to group the clients together and put each client into the appropriate group (see Figure 4.1).

FIGURE 4.1
How a typical small business person might want to arrange My Documents.

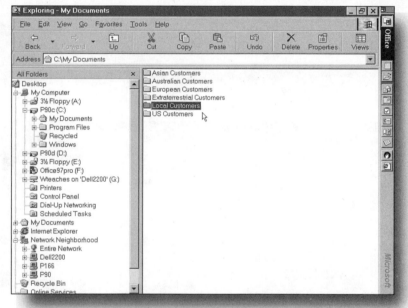

Students can group assignments in a folder and put all the folders for a specific class in yet another folder. Human Resources folks might want to use different folders for different functions—hiring, reviews, the HR manual, whatever (see Figure 4.2).

Writers could put each of their projects in a separate folder. For example, I have a folder for articles with subfolders for each feature; another folder for books, with subfolders for each book, plus separate folders for clients, accounting, and taxes—even one for my son (see Figure 4.3)!

FIGURE 4.2
An HR manager might try this arrangement.

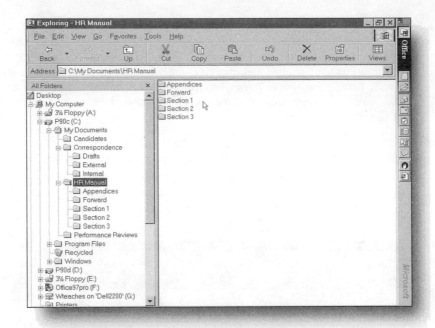

FIGURE 4.3
My My Documents.

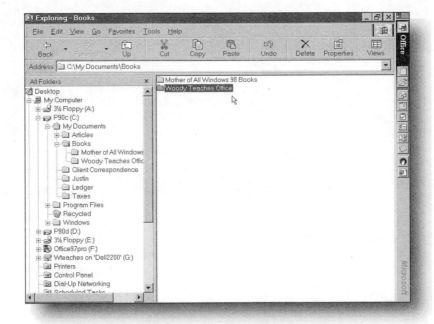

A Place for Everything

You'll save an enormous amount of time in Office 97 if you set up a place for every-thing, and keep everything in its place. (I sound like your mother, eh?) Folders can be split, combined, moved, added, and deleted as your needs change.

*E*XERCISE

Think Through My Documents

1. Forget about computers for a minute. Think about the kinds of things you need to organize. Do you work with clients? Courses? Do you put together handouts? Take out a pencil and write down the basic groups of things that drive your daily life.

2. Take a look at each of those things, in turn. Can they be broken down fur-ther? If you have clients as a major group, list all your clients. You get the idea.

3. Work out the kinks. Everyone will have some overlap between the categories. A common example: if you send invoices to clients, should all the invoices go into one giant folder, or should each invoice go into the respective client's folder? There's no right answer. Choose whatever works best for you. And remember that you can always change your mind.

Customizing My Documents

Now that you have a blueprint for My Documents, let's go through the steps neces-sary to set up your very own, customized My Documents folder.

*E*XERCISE

Get Your Bearings with Windows Explorer

1. Right-click My Computer and choose **Explore**. If you're working with a virgin Windows installation, you should see a Windows Explorer window (see Figure 4.4).

2. Take a moment to look at the screen. As you can see in Figure 4.4, it's split into two sections. The section on the left, which starts out with the lines All Folders and Desktop, is called the "left pane" (as in "window pane"—get it?). The section on the right, which starts out with My Computer and My Documents is called the right pane.

FIGURE 4.4
Windows
Explorer on a
clean
Windows 98
system.

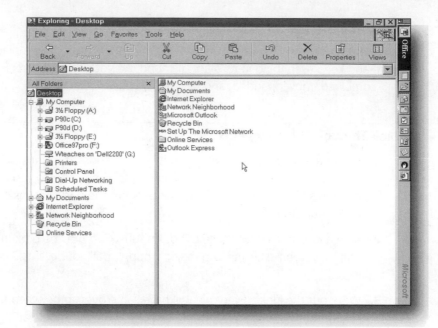

3. Move around a bit. See those plus signs in the left pane? There's one next to P90c (C:) and all the other disk drives. Clicking that plus sign *expands* the folder, showing you all the folders immediately underneath. Click the plus sign next to your C: drive (see Figure 4.5). You should see a folder called My Documents. That's the folder we need to work with.

4. In the left pane, double-click the folder called My Documents. If you haven't been using Office 97 at all, the right pane will be empty (see Figure 4.6)—in geek terminology, you don't have anything stored in the folder C:\My Documents. If you have been using Office 97, you might be surprised to discover that this is where all of those My Documents files are actually stored on your computer.

FIGURE 4.5
Exploring
down to My
Documents.

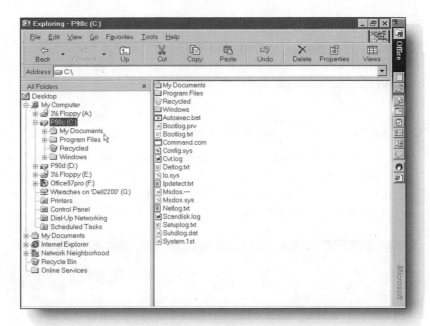

FIGURE 4.6
A clean My
Documents.

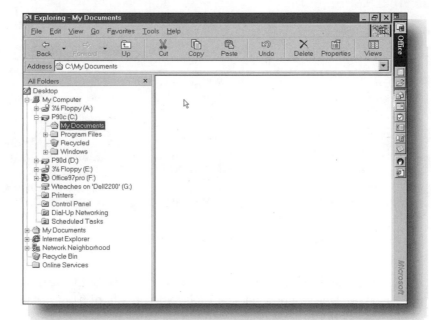

Creating Folders in My Documents

Now that you've discovered where My Documents lives, it's time to build the super-structure that will hold all your files. I'll start by showing you the simple folder-building features you have at your disposal.

*E*XERCISE _____

Create a New Folder in My Documents

1. With your Windows Explorer window looking like Figure 4.6—that is, My Documents selected in the left pane, and nothing in the right pane (with the possible exception of some old files)—right-click a blank area in the right pane. Choose **New**, then **Folder** (see Figure 4.7).

FIGURE 4.7
Creating a new folder in My Documents.

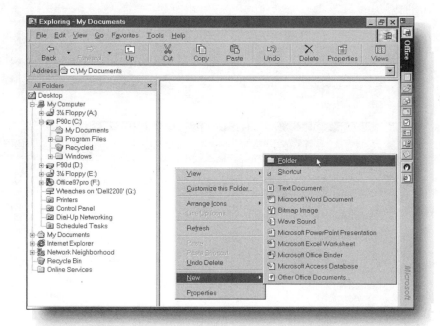

2. Windows creates a new folder and hangs it underneath My Documents. That new folder is called, uh, New Folder (see Figure 4.8). Clever, ain't it?

3. Immediately, without pressing Enter or any of the arrow keys on the keyboard, type in a new name for this folder. In a fit of pique, I typed the name (see Figure 4.9). When you're done, press the Enter key.

FIGURE 4.8
A new folder
appears.

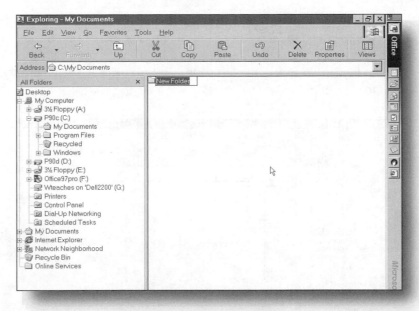

FIGURE 4.9
Naming the
new folder.

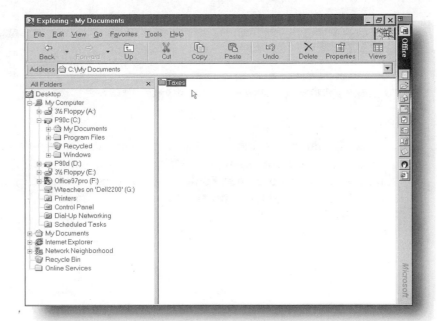

4. You've just created a new folder underneath the My Documents folder. Since you're bound to be a little skeptical at this point (hey, if I'd spent my life believing in Microsoft's Party Line, I'd be skeptical too), click the plus sign next to My Documents in the left pane (see Figure 4.10). See where the new folder sits?

FIGURE 4.10
Verifying that
the folder
Taxes now sits
underneath
My
Documents.

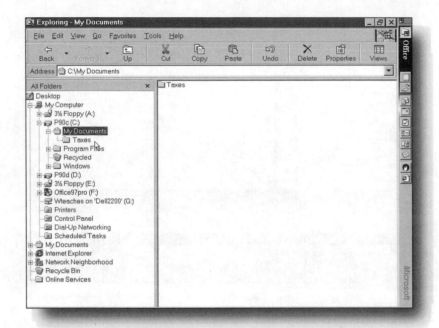

5. Fill out the rest of the folders that sit underneath My Documents. In each case, click My Documents in the left pane. Then right-click a blank space in the right pane, choose **New**, **Folder**, then type the new folder's name and press Enter. I created the folder structure you see in Figure 4.11.

FIGURE 4.11
The first level
of My
Documents
on my
machine.

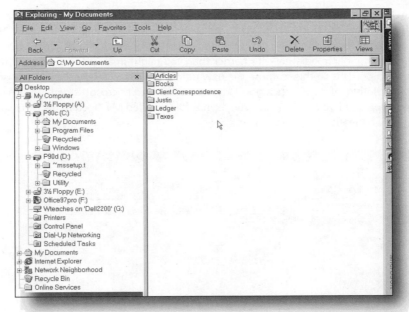

This is a good point to take a break.

Renaming and Deleting Folders

You now know how to create new folders underneath My Documents (or anywhere else on your disk drives, for that matter). What remains is fine tuning and embellishment.

XERCISE

Rename, Delete Folders in My Documents

1. It probably won't surprise you to know that you can delete a folder by clicking it and pressing the Delete key on the keyboard.

2. And if you've used Windows for more than a couple of weeks, you may already know that renaming a folder is as simple as right-clicking it, choosing **Rename** (see Figure 4.12), and typing the new name.

CAUTION

Don't rename My Documents! While it's entirely possible to change the name My Documents to anything you like—the names Letters or Work or just plain Documents come to mind immediately—it's harder than you might imagine to redirect Office's various components so they can use the new name. Until you've become quite proficient at manipulating Office 97, it's a good idea to succumb to Microsoft's naming convention and keep all of your Office documents in a folder called My Documents or in subfolders directly beneath My Documents.

FIGURE 4.12
Renaming an existing folder.

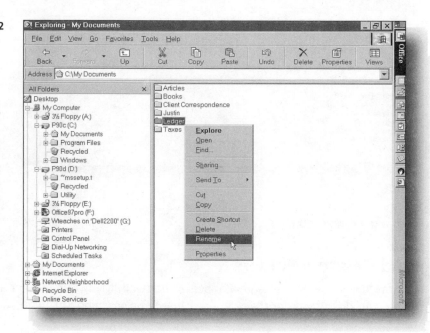

Creating Multiple Folders in My Documents

What about multiple levels of folders? For example, what if you need to have several folders underneath the Articles folder shown in Figure 4.12? Piece o' cake.

*E*XERCISE

Create Subfolders in My Documents

1. Double-click the folder under which you want to put new folders. For example, if you want to put folders under the Articles folder, double-click the Articles folder.

2. Right-click in a blank area on the right pane. Choose **New**, then **Folder**. Type in the name of the new folder, just as you did in exercise "Create a New Folder in My Documents," Step 3 (see Figure 4.13.)

FIGURE 4.13
Adding new folders underneath the Articles folder.

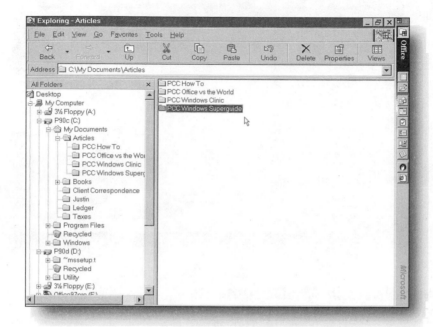

3. Follow these steps to fill in all the folders you think you'll need. Remember that folders can be nested just as deep as you like—although things can get pretty hairy, mentally, if you try to keep on top of more than five or six levels. My final My Documents looks like Figure 4.14.

SORTING FILES

Generally Windows Explorer shows folders and files in alphabetical order, with all the folders appearing above all the files. When you're adding and renaming folders, though, Explorer doesn't bother to re-sort the list until you tell it to. You can re-sort at any time by pressing F5, or by closing and restarting Windows Explorer.

FIGURE 4.14
Final configu-
ration of My
Documents
on my
machine.

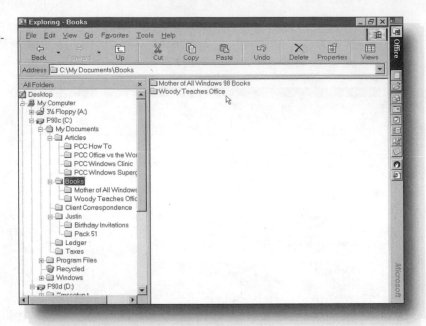

Moving Folders in My Documents

Here's one final practice exercise to show you how to move folders (and files) around once they've been created.

XERCISE

Move Folders in My Documents

1. Click and double-click around Windows Explorer until the folders you want to move appear in the right pane.

HEY WOODY, CAN'T YOU DO ALL THIS INSIDE OFFICE 97?
Yes, it's true. Inside every Office application, when you click **File**, **Open**, you have a chance to make changes to folders—add new ones, rename existing ones, even move them around. But the methods available inside Office's **File Open** box are very cumbersome: moving files from folder to folder is difficult, and you can never see the whole folder structure at once. Besides, even novice users need to know where the documents in My Documents really reside. That's why I strongly recommend that you do your heavy work outside Office, in the Windows Explorer.

2. Select the folders you want to move. To choose one folder, just click it. To choose a contiguous block of folders, click the first folder, hold down the Shift key and click the last folder. To pick and choose a bunch of folders, click the first one, hold down the Ctrl key, and keep clicking all the others.

3. Move the folders by dragging them from the right pane to the left pane (see Figure 4.15).

FIGURE 4.15
Explorer lets you move folders by dragging them— usually from the right to the left pane.

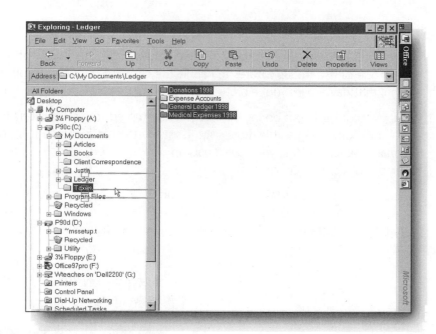

Customizing My Documents

It's time to put all of your Windows Explorer talent to work now, and create your very own customized My Documents.

*Ɛ*XERCISE

Build Your Own My Documents

1. Re-create the folder structure you traced out in Exercise 4-1. Play with it a bit. Don't be afraid to move folders around until the structure seems right to you.

2. If you already have files in My Documents, use the technique explained in the preceding Exercise to move them into the folders where they now belong. If you're bringing files over from an old machine, use Windows Explorer to move them into their correct new locations.

3. Exit Windows Explorer by clicking **File**, then **Close**, or by clicking the X in the upper-right corner.

Your Office 97 house is now in order, with My Documents ready to take on your work in your way. Next, let's take a look at what you'll need in case your disk drive ever decides to go bye-bye. Disk drives do die. Oh, my, yes they do.

Backup

Someday, somewhere—probably in some parallel universe—Microsoft will come up with one of its famous wizards to handle the chore of backing up your Office files. Until that day arrives you're pretty much on your own.

I know that backup is boring. I know you're tempted to blow right by this section and go onto something a little more sexy. Resist the temptation. I say this from bitter personal experience: Until you have a backup plan in action, you'd be a fool to do any important work in Office 97.

Fortunately, Windows 95 and 98 have good Backup routines built into the product. (Actually, Windows 95's is OK, but Windows 98's is excellent.) While you can write your own program to perform backups, the built-in Windows Backup programs work well enough for most purposes.

Regardless of what you use, or how you do it, someday a good backup will save your, uh, neck. I won't regale you with my tales of woe. Suffice it to say that having your c: drive die a day before a big assignment comes due is just about as much fun as having a root canal while being audited by the IRS *and* undergoing a digital prostate probe. Simultaneously.

SURVIVAL ON THE CORPORATE NETWORK
Those of you working at companies with local area networks should feel pretty secure if you keep your Office 97 data files on the server. (A "server" is just a hefty PC that provides services—printing, file storage, security, sometimes online access—to other machines on the network. It sounds mysterious, but it isn't.) The IT people usually back up the server religiously, but if you're not quite sure, ask!

If you keep your data on your own PC's hard drive, though, you should take a good look at what we're doing here and modify things so your backup goes to the server. That may sound complicated, but about any computer geek will no doubt do it for you, for the price of a beer and a pizza. Cheap insurance.

Putting together a good backup plan involves three steps. First, you have to figure out which files to back up. Second, you have to figure out how to get those files onto the backup drive or tape. Third, you have to use the backup process every single day.

I can help you with the first two. For the third, you're on your own.

Which Office 97 Files Need to Be Backed Up?

Office 97 uses an enormous number of different files. Most of those files can be identified by their filename extensions.

☞ *For details about filename extensions, see page 19.*

Table 4.1 shows a list of all the filename extensions Office 97 uses, what they're used for, and where those files are usually located.

Table 4.1   Office 97 Filename Extensions

Extension	Type of File	Usual Location
.doc	Word Document	c:\My Documents
.dot	Word Template	c:\Program Files\Microsoft Office
.dic	Custom Dictionary	c:\Program Files\Microsoft Office
.xls	Excel Worksheet	c:\My Documents
.xla	Excel Add-In	c:\Program Files\Microsoft Office
.xlt	Excel Template	c:\Program Files\Microsoft Office
.ppt	PowerPoint Presentation	c:\My Documents
.pot	PowerPoint Template	c:\Program Files\Microsoft Office
.mdb	Access Database	c:\My Documents
.htm	Web Document in HTML Format	c:\My Documents
.html	Web Document in HTML Format	c:\My Documents
.wiz	Office Wizard	c:\Program Files\Microsoft Office
.obd	Office Binder	c:\My Documents
.obt	Office Binder Template	c:\Program Files\Microsoft Office
.oft	Outlook Template	c:\Program Files\Microsoft Office
.pst	Outlook Data	c:\Windows\Profiles\username\Application Data\Microsoft\Office\8.5\Outlook
.acl	Office AutoCorrect Entries	c:\Windows

Windows NT puts the .acl files in the primary Windows folder, which is frequently called c:\winnt. The .pst file may hang underneath that. If you're using NT, you may have to look around for them.

IDENTIFYING OFFICE DATA FILES

Is all of this Greek to you? Don't get freaked out! That table isn't nearly as mysterious as it appears at first glance. Just take a deep breath and I'll walk you through it slowly.

We need to figure out which files on your hard drive are Office data files—those are the ones we want to back up. It ends up that you can identify all of Office's major data files if you look at the filename extension—the final few characters, after the period on the end of the filename. This table just lists the 17 filename extensions that Office 97 uses to identify its data files.

Take the table's first row. (Please.) It says that Word documents have the filename extension of .doc. (You knew that already, based on our discussion in Chapter 2, right?) So if you call a Word document, oh, Letter to Ma, its filename comes out Letter to Ma.doc. If we want to back up all of your Word documents, we'd better snag every file that has a name ending with .doc. So far so good.

The first row also says that Word documents are usually stored in c:\My Documents. That's just geek shorthand for saying they're usually stored in the folder called My Documents that sits on the c: disk drive. In fact, as you discovered in the previous section of this chapter, Word documents are usually in the My Documents folder, or in one of the folders that hang off of My Documents.

If you've done something weird and installed Office 97 in an odd folder—or *shudder,* changed the name of the My Documents folder—you may have to go searching your hard drive to see where these files got scattered. That's not terribly difficult if you use Windows File Find utility. Simply click **Start**, **Find**, **Files or Folders** (see Figure 4.16), but I won't go into the gory details. If you get in that deep, find some knowledgeable help.

If you look at Table 4.1 long enough, you'll probably come to the conclusion that what you really want to do is back up the folder called My Documents, plus the folder called Microsoft Office (which sits under the My Programs folder). You'll also want to back up all the folders underneath My Documents and Microsoft Office. You should probably pick up the .acl and .pst files, too, sitting in and under the Windows folder. That's our general strategy.

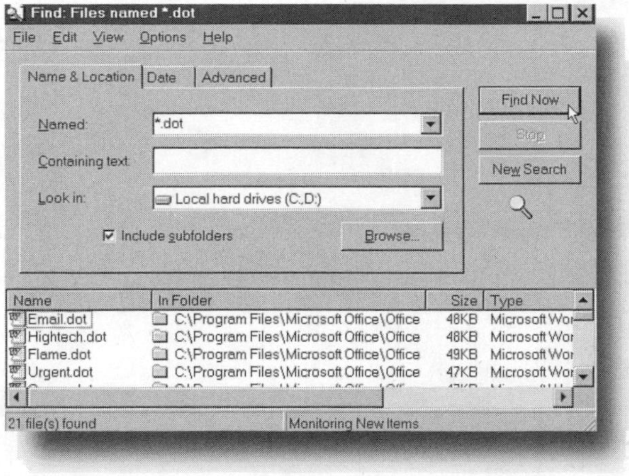

FIGURE 4.16
Using Windows File Find to find Office files.

How to Back Them Up

If you have a commercial backup program, you have all the information you need to get going. (Sorry, I can't step you through the backup program itself; each one is different.) Make sure you get c:\My Documents, c:\Program Files\Microsoft Office, and all the folders underneath them in your backups, plus the .pst file in c:\Windows\Profiles\ username\Application Data\Microsoft\Office\8.5\Outlook (Gad! What a name!), and you'll be in good shape. The .acl AutoCorrect files would be nice to have but, believe me, if your hard drive goes down you'll be thanking your lucky stars to have anything you can get.

If you don't have a commercial backup system, your next best choice is to use Windows' own Backup system. I'll step you through the Windows 98 Backup; the steps for Windows 95 are quite similar.

*E*XERCISE

Using Windows 98 Backup

1. Click **Start**, **Programs**, **Accessories**, **System Tools**. Do you see an entry called Backup? If so, go on to Step 4. If not, you'll have to install Windows Backup from your original Windows installation CD.

2. To install Windows Backup, click **Start**, **Settings**, **Control Panel**, and double-click **Add/Remove Programs**. Click the **Windows Setup** tab. Double-click **System Tools** (see Figure 4.17).

3. Check the box marked **Backup** (see Figure 4.18). Click **OK** twice. When the PC asks you to insert your Windows CD, do so, and click **OK**. Backup will be installed.

FIGURE 4.17
Changing
System Tools
in Windows
Setup.

FIGURE 4.18
Installing
Backup from
the Windows
CD.

4. Start Windows Backup by clicking **Start**, **Programs**, **Accessories**, **System Tools**, **Backup**. Windows will give you a spiel about the three steps to creating a backup (see Figure 4.19).

FIGURE 4.19
Windows has
three steps
for perform-
ing a backup.

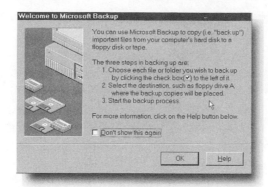

5. Select the files you want to back up. In most cases, the easiest way to do that
is to check the box next to My Documents in the left pane. Then double-click
Program Files in the left pane and check the box next to Microsoft Office in
the right pane (that selects the Microsoft Office folder under the Program Files
folder). Double-click the Windows folder in the left pane and check all .acl
files in the right pane (see Figure 4.20). Finally, click .pst files in
c:\Windows\Profiles\username\Application Data\Microsoft\Office\8.5\Outlook.

FIGURE 4.20
Select the
folders and
files you want
to back up.

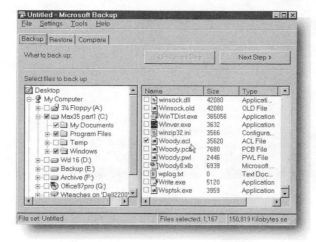

6. Click **Next Step** in the upper-right corner. Then choose a place to put the
backup files. In my case, I put backups on the e:\ drive (see Figure 4.21).

FIGURE 4.21
Choose a
backup
location.

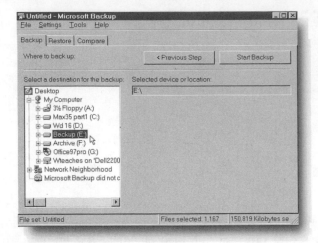

7. If you save the backup settings that you've chosen at this point, you'll be able to retrieve them again, the next time you use Windows Backup. To do so, click **File**, then **Save**. Type a name such as Office Backup (see Figure 4.22) and click **Save**.

FIGURE 4.22
Saving your
Windows
Backup set-
tings to make
it easier next
time.

8. You're now ready—finally!—to perform the backup. Just click the button marked **Start Backup**.

Now you can breathe easy. If you've followed all the nostrums up to this point, you're fully protected and ready to start using Office 97 in the real world.

Starting Office

If you've installed Internet Explorer 4.0 or later, or if you're using Windows 98, there are a few quick steps you can take to make it easier and faster to launch Office applications. (You also can get rid of the Office Shortcut bar.) And, even if you're stuck with the Office Shortcut bar, there are a few tweaks you should consider to make it work better.

XERCISE

Office Taskbar Launcher

1. Look at the Windows taskbar, immediately to the right of the Start button. Do you see a bunch of little icons there (see Figure 4.23)? It's called the Quick Launch toolbar. If so, continue with Step 2. If not, see the exercise later in the chapter.

FIGURE 4.23
The tiny Windows Quick Launch taskbar icons.

2. Let's put a little icon down there on the taskbar that will launch Word 97. Start up Windows Explorer by right-clicking My Computer and choosing **Explore**. Navigate down to the c:\Program Files\Microsoft Office folder (see Figure 4.24). See the line marked Microsoft Word? Click it once.

3. Click that Microsoft Word line and drag it down to the taskbar's Quick Launch toolbar icon box. When you've positioned the I-beam where you want it, release the mouse button. I put Microsoft Word first in the Windows Quick Launch toolbar because it's the program I use most often (see Figure 4.25).

4. Similarly, click and drag any other Office applications that you use frequently onto the Windows Quick Launch toolbar. In this case, I've put Outlook, Excel, and PowerPoint on the Quick Launch toolbar (see Figure 4.26).

5. If you make a mistake—or if you just want to delete some of the icons in the Quick Launch toolbar that you'll never use (prime candidates: Outlook Express and View Channels)—simply right-click the offending icon and choose **Delete**.

6. Test your new icons. You should be able to click once on any of them and have Windows launch the respective application.

FIGURE 4.24
The Microsoft
Word short-
cut in the
Microsoft
Office folder.

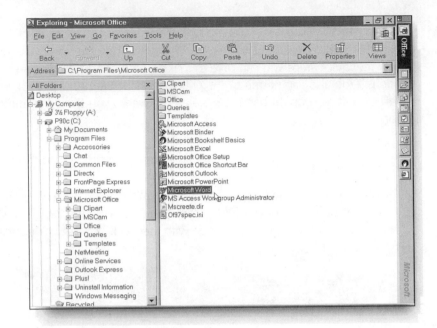

FIGURE 4.25
Dragging
Microsoft
Word onto
the Windows
taskbar.

FIGURE 4.26
Adding more
Office appli-
cations to the
Windows
taskbar.

7. Consider getting rid of the Office Shortcut bar. To do so, right-click any blank spot and choose **Exit**. When asked if you want the Office Shortcut bar to reappear the next time you start Windows, just say **No** (see Figure 4.27). The OSB will never darken your doorstop—or take up your precious screen space—again.

FIGURE 4.27
Getting rid of the Office Shortcut bar, permanently.

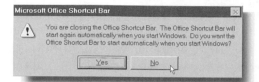

If you haven't yet upgraded to a version of Windows or Internet Explorer that supports those little icons in the Windows Quick Start toolbar, you should probably go ahead and use the Office Shortcut bar. It's better than no launcher at all. But there are some tricks. (Aren't there always?)

*E*XERCISE

Making the Office Shortcut Bar Tolerable

1. Shrink the OSB. Right-click any empty space on the Office Shortcut bar and choose **Customize**. Click the button that says **Auto Fit into Title Bar area** (see Figure 4.28).

FIGURE 4.28
Make the Office Shortcut bar shrink.

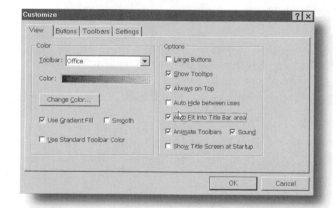

2. Grab the top of the OSB and click and drag it up onto the top of your Windows screen. You'll know that you have it shrunk as much as possible when it looks like the OSB in Figure 4.29.

FIGURE 4.29
Place the OSB in its least obtrusive position.

3. Once again, right-click an open space in the OSB, and choose **Customize**.
   Now click the **Buttons** tab. Uncheck the boxes in front of the Office applications that you don't want to appear on the OSB. Then check the boxes in
   front of the applications you want (see Figure 4.30). You can change the
   order of the buttons by clicking a specific application, then clicking the up
   and down buttons. Play with it a bit. You'll see.

FIGURE 4.30
Customizing
the buttons
on the Office
Shortcut bar.

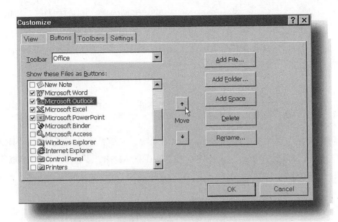

The Office Shortcut bar has quite a number of customizing options beyond the ones
I've discussed here. If you're stuck with the OSB—and don't figure you'll upgrade to
IE 4 or Windows 98 any time soon—it might behoove you to spend a little bit of time
playing with the other customizing options.

Personally, I deep-six the OSB and use the Windows Quick Launch toolbar. The screen
shots you'll see in the remainder of this book reflect that fact.

Making Office 97 Run Better

I'd like to finish this chapter with a very short discussion concerning the question I'm
asked most frequently: "Woody, how do you make Office 97 run better?"

When folks ask me that question, they usually mean one of two things: how do you
make the bloody thing run faster; or, how do you keep it from crashing so often?

Fortunately, each of those questions has a series of simple answers.

Speed

The very best way to make Office 97 run faster is to buy a faster PC. (Okay, okay. I'll wait while you finish groaning.)

The next best way to make Office 97 run faster is to get more memory. The difference between Office running on 16 MB and Office running on 64 MB will impress you mightily.

The third best way to make Office 97 run faster is to upgrade to Windows 98. You'll find that Office loads much faster and runs a tiny bit faster.

Anything else you try to do—faster hard drives, fancy video cards, souped up controllers—won't amount to a hill of beans. Spend your money on something you'll use, like a bigger screen, a second hard drive, or a tray to lower your keyboard below normal desk height.

Stability

Which brings me to the problem with crashes. Yes, it's true, if you use Office 97 hard—I mean, day in and day out—you're going to watch it crash. Sometimes the crashes turn out relatively benign: Word might freeze and swallow a few minutes' worth of typing. Pressing Ctrl+Alt+Del and rebooting Windows brings everything back to life. Sometimes, though, you won't be so lucky. That's why you have backups, eh?

The single most important way to improve Office 97's stability is to get all the fixes (such as Service Release-1) and to apply them religiously. You should do that regardless of what other stability improvement techniques you might attempt.

The next way to improve Office 97 stability is to run it on Windows 98. Yeah. It's surprising. I have, oh, maybe half the number of crashes under Windows 98 that I did under Windows 95.

The very best way to improve Office 97 stability? Use Windows NT. This is the first book I've ever written entirely with Word 97 and NT 4, and it's like the difference between night and day. I haven't had a single crash yet—knock on wood—and I haven't rebooted NT more than once a week. Simply stunning.

There. You just paid for this book. Again.

Help from a
Paper Clip

*N*o BOOK ON OFFICE 97 CAN COVER the entire product. No, not even those

1,200-page behemoths. Er, *especially* not those 1,200-page

behemoths. Office 97 has so many nooks and crannies it would take

10,000 pages or more to describe all of its nuances. Maybe 20,000.

That's why online help is built into Office itself.

There are three significant disadvantages to the help available inside

Office 97:

- The help is official help, so it parrots the Microsoft Party Line. Often that means the help you'll find explains how Office is *supposed* to work, not how it actually *does* work.

- It can be very difficult to find help on the specific topic that interests you, particularly when you don't know the technical jargon.

● Sometimes the help you find leaves you hanging in mid-air. You'll find instructions for solving part of the problem, but not all of it. Even the built-in help doesn't cover all of Office's capabilities.

Fortunately, there are some tactics you can employ to ameliorate each of those problems. I'll show you how. But first let's start with the basics.

The Office Assistant Character

Every time you start an Office application, you'll be accosted by a paper clip. He/she/it has a name: Clippit. (Cute, eh?) More than anything else, Clippit resembles the ancient oracle at Delphi. Ask it a question, and you'll get an answer. Depending on your luck and the oracle's mood, that answer could be spot-on correct, utterly unrelated to the question, or totally inscrutable (see Figure 5.1). Such is the nature of oracles.

FIGURE 5.1
Clippit answers, "Where do I want to go today?"

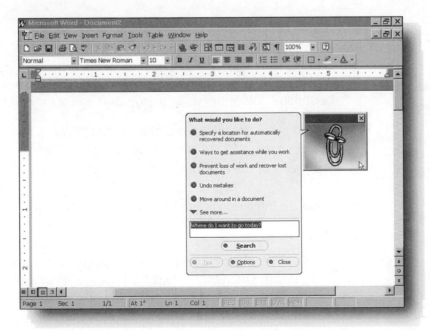

$\mathcal{E}$XERCISE

Ask the Oracle a Question

1. Start any of the Office applications.

2. Click Clippit.

3. Type a question. Any question.

4. Press Enter (or click **Search**). Did you get a reasonable answer? I didn't think so.

5. Click any of the offered topics. You'll be transported into the less-visual (and much less friendly!) Office Help system. See how it works? Click the X in the upper-right corner of the Help box to get rid of it.

BOB INVADES MICROSOFT OFFICE
Microsoft has long pioneered usability improvements in its products, and one of the best—or worst—examples has to be Microsoft's ill-fated Bob. Good ol' Bob, as you might recall, beamed a broad yellow smile, incorporated something called a social interface, and did just about nothing else. Buyers shunned Bob in droves. Tons of boxes sporting Bob's smiling face piled up in warehouses. Microsoft couldn't give 'em away.

In the end, though, Bob may steal the last laugh—at your expense. When Bob failed to get off the ground, the team that developed Bob found itself out of work, until the Office Assistant project came to the rescue. The Office Assistant—that, uh, cute little paper clip you may have seen lurking at the corner of your screen—owes its existence to Bob's demise.

Microsoft lore (possibly apocryphal) has it that the first incarnation of the Office Assistant looked like a clown, not a paper clip. Supposedly the Bob team presented an Office Bob prototype to Bill one day. Gates played around with it a bit and pronounced it good—except, "I kept wanting to strangle that damn clown."

The next time you feel like strangling the Office Assistant character, remember this: You're in good company. Bill couldn't stand it either.

Although it's considered somewhat fashionable among the Office cognoscenti to belittle the Office Assistant, sometimes ol' Clippit really hits the spot. Personally, it's the first place I go when I can't figure out why something isn't working.

The Office Assistant watches over your shoulder as you type. Whenever you click it, the character tries to figure out what you're trying to do and gives you a series of tips that may be appropriate—in true oracular tradition, you needn't even ask a question before the oracle

A SUGGESTION FOR THE FOLKS IN REDMOND

Hey, Microsoft! Why can't you make an Office Bob that sits up in the applications' title bar? It could even flop down into the menu area as long as it doesn't overlap the toolbars. You did it with the Office Shortcut bar. Why can't you do it with a paper clip?

will give you an answer. Sometimes the Office Assistant will look at what you're doing and come to the conclusion that you could be accomplishing the same thing with less work. In such circumstances, a light bulb appears in the upper-right corner of the Assistant. Click the little guy to see if he/she/it has any worthwhile tips.

Unfortunately, the Office Assistant character, aside from being cloyingly cute, frequently gets in the way. Yes, it's supposed to scoot around, moving out of the way as you type or enter data in spreadsheet cells. Yes, it's supposed to shrink to a smaller size if you don't use it for a few minutes. In practice, I find both the scooting and the shrinking to be vastly over-rated: Clippit just gets in the way, obscuring things I want to see on the screen.

Toggling the Office Assistant On and Off

That's why I usually turn the Office Assistant off. It's easy to do—just click the X in the upper-right corner of the Office Assistant's little box, and the character gets the axe (see Figure 5.2).

FIGURE 5.2
Click here to destroy Clippit.

Once the Office Assistant has been zapped, it's easy to resurrect. In fact, you have three different choices. Simply push F1, click the **Office Assistant** 🔘 button on the toolbar, or click Help, and then choose the first option (that is, Microsoft Word Help, Microsoft Outlook Help, Microsoft Excel Help, or Microsoft PowerPoint Help). Any way you go, the Office Assistant immediately springs back to life.

Changing Characters

Maybe you don't want to get rid of the little critter. That's not a bad decision, really, at least until you're accustomed to the fact that the Office Assistant is only a click away.

If you do decide to stick with the Office Assistant box, at least you can rotate the characters. When Clippit gets boring, you can switch to an Einstein clone, or a dog in a cape. (And who says Microsoft doesn't have a sense of humor?)

XERCISE _____

Changing Office Assistant Characters

1. Right-click the Office Assistant. (That'll be Clippit, if you haven't already changed it.) Choose **Choose Assistant**. You'll be transported to the Office Assistant Gallery (see Figure 5.3).

FIGURE 5.3
The Office
Assistant
Gallery.

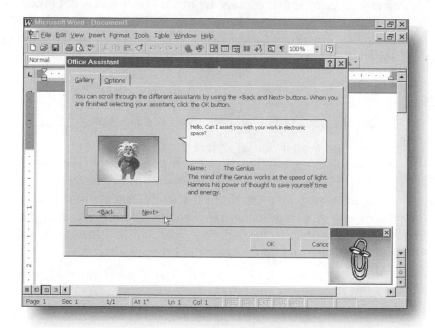

2. Click the Back and Next buttons until you find a character you like. Click **OK** and your new character will appear in the Office Assistant box.

From time to time Microsoft releases new Office Assistants and, if you have access to the Web, you can get new characters free (for the price of a download, anyway). Two of the new characters that I would recommend are Earl and Rocky. Earl, a cat of sorts, has no end of redeeming social values—a head that pops off at appropriate times, a nasty habit of sniffing his armpits, and a tongue that puts Mick Jagger to shame. Rocky, the dog, specializes in wagging his tail, pulling things out of his collar, and reading books.

Both characters will no doubt keep you moderately amused for a little while. Whether they're worth the time to download (at 2+ megabytes, these aren't tiny files) depends a lot on how easily you're amused.

As of this writing, Earl, Rocky, and other Office Assistant characters were available at `http://www.microsoft.com/office/office/enhancements/assistants .asp`. Microsoft moves around freebies like these fairly frequently, though, so if you can't find them at that address, try `http://www.microsoft.com/office`, and look around. Once you've downloaded the file, run it and the character will appear in the Office Assistant Gallery. Select your new character using the instructions in the previous exercise.

Tactics

I know of several tactics for using the Office Assistant.

First and foremost, if you don't find the answer you're looking for, try rephrasing your question, using completely different terminology. The natural language recognition routine buried in the Office Assistant isn't very natural at all, and sometimes using one wrong word can throw the whole gizmo out of whack. Remember that there's very little native understanding going on here—mostly, the Office Assistant throws away nonessential phrases ("How do I?" "Where is?") and tries to identify, and then search on, the key words in your question.

Second, you can adjust the size of the Office Assistant. If you start feeling cramped because the Office Assistant is always in the way, click a corner and drag the Assistant's window to make it smaller.

FIGURE 5.4
Making the
Rocky charac-
ter smaller.

Third, the light bulb tips shouldn't be taken as gospel. Although Microsoft has made some great strides in help technology, the Office Assistant's attempts to follow along, analyze what you're doing, and offer ideas to improve your work often fall flat on their face. If the light bulb tip you get in any particular situation doesn't seem to make sense, it probably doesn't.

Finally, you can make some crude adjustments to the Office Assistant's sensitivity (see Figure 5.5).

FIGURE 5.5
Earl shows the Office Assistant options.

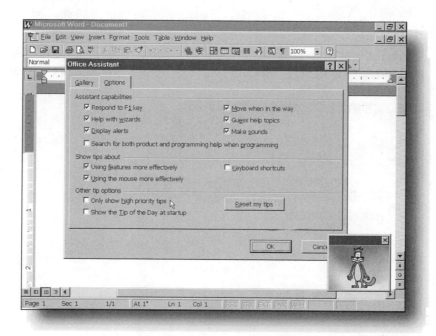

If you click the Office Assistant, then choose **Options**, you'll find several choices that may make the Office Assistant more useful to you. In particular, if you see that light bulb appearing too often—that is, the suggestions offered when the light bulb is on don't matter much to you—consider checking the box that says **Only show high priority tips**. That will keep the light bulb flashes down to a minimum. It also prevents the Office Assistant from appearing, unbidden, at strange times.

Less Animated Help

Novice Office users tend to identify the Office Assistant character with Office's built-in help. In fact, the characters are simply window dressing: they make the Office Help system a little more palatable by using friendly faces and by making a game attempt at recognizing questions posed in normal English.

The real Help system sits behind the characters' pretty faces.

Native Help

To see the real Help system, start any Office application, click **Help**, then **Contents and Index**. You'll connect directly with the mother lode (see Figure 5.6).

FIGURE 5.6
Native Help contents.

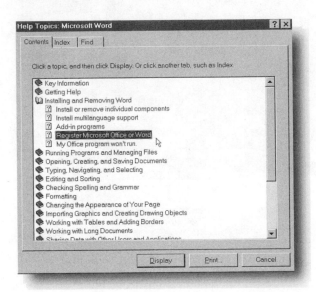

Think of the Help contents page as a table of contents, just like a book's table of contents, organizing and pointing you to the vast amount of information stored in Office's Help files. If you want to read about a general topic, this is the place to start.

If you click the **Index** tab, you'll see an index into the Help documentation (see Figure 5.7).

In my experience, the index is the weakest part of Office Help. If you look at Figure 5.6, you can see that native Help has a section on registering your Office applications. But if you look in the index, shown here in Figure 5.7, there's no reference to register or registering. None whatsoever. I rarely use the index.

FIGURE 5.7
Native Help index.

Fortunately, Office's designers have also built a full-text search capability into native Help. You can see it by clicking the **Find** tab. The first time you click that tab, Office creates a detailed database of all the important entries in the Help system (see Figure 5.8).

After the database has been built, you merely type the key word that interests you in the **Find** tab's top box. Find then scrolls through the entries in its database. You select one of the entries, and click **Display** for full information (see Figure 5.9).

FIGURE 5.8
Building the
native help
Find data-
base.

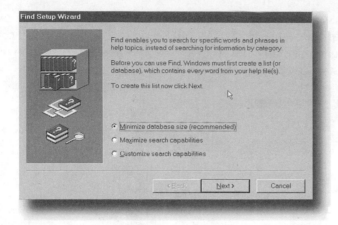

FIGURE 5.9
Using native
Help's Find
function.

As you can see in Figure 5.9, the Find function has quite a few entries for the word
"register." In general, Find is much more useful than the pre-built index.

Microsoft on the Web

While native Help has much to offer, it pales in comparison to the quantity (and, yes, quality) of information Microsoft has available, free, on the Web. To get at that information, click **Help**, then **Microsoft on the Web** (see Figure 5.10).

FIGURE 5.10
Microsoft on the Web options.

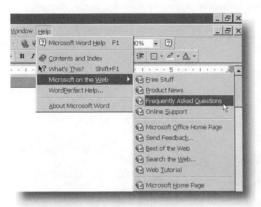

After you're acquainted with the basic functions of Office, I strongly recommend that you spend a few hours poking around Microsoft's Web site. While the site itself can be maddeningly slow and occasionally hard to navigate, you just can't beat it for Office information and support.

TIMING YOUR VISIT TO MICROSOFT'S WEB SITE
Microsoft's Web site may be the slowest one on the Internet. I've found that I can save loads of frustration visiting the site only at odd hours: early in the morning, and on workday evenings. If there's any way you can avoid working hours during the week, and evenings on the weekends, do it.

MSKB: THE ANSWER TO (ALMOST) EVERY QUESTION
Do you have a really tough question about Office 97? After you've exhausted the online Help—both via the Office Assistant and digging directly into native Help—log onto the Microsoft Knowledge Base. Bet you'll find the answer there.

Microsoft's most important source of Office information sits underneath the Microsoft on the Web/Online Support menu. Clicking that item transports you to the Microsoft Knowledge Base (known to insiders as "MSKB"), the central repository of all information about Microsoft products (see Figure 5.11).

FIGURE 5.11
Gateway to the Microsoft Knowledge Base.

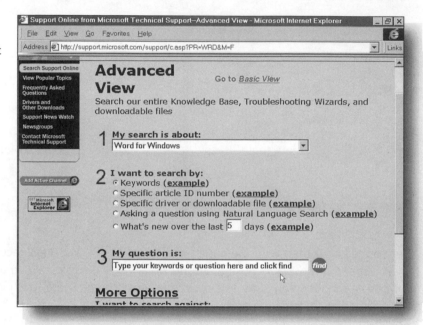

The MSKB consists of tens of thousands of articles, each one addressing a specific problem, solution, or feature of a Microsoft product. While they're written by Microsoft staff, and thus utilize some interesting euphemisms (that is, articles always say a bug is an "issue"), the MSKB is as close as you'll come to revealed truth in the Microsoft realm.

Word 97

6   Word Preliminaries 83

7   Working with Documents 105

8   Building Documents 121

9   Getting Around 137

10 Making Documents Look Good 155

11 Key Capabilities 207

12 Special Purpose Tools 227

13 On the Shoulders of Giants 253

14 Advanced Features 275

Word Preliminaries

*A*FTER A SOMEWHAT ROCKY START, Microsoft's Word for Windows has become the most-often-used computer application ever created. Considering how much it's used, you'd think it would be easy to understand, eh?

Not a chance. Not even close.

Crucial Changes

Word 97, like all the other Office applications, contains an enormous number of options. Thousands of 'em. The people who designed Word included enough options to make Word usable in every imaginable situation, from jotting short notes to rewriting the U.S. Tax Code (I wish!). Rank novices might only use Word once a week; Microsoft assumes (rightly or wrongly) that beginners don't want to understand *why* things happen—they just want to type a bit and print the result, desultory as their results may be. Microsoft chose Word's standard options for these folks. They dumbed down Word as much as they dared, and then tossed a few whizbang features on the toolbar to make it easier to demo and sell the product.

As I introduce each of the Office applications to you, I'm going to step

WHAT YOU DON'T KNOW WON'T HELP YOU...
Don't laugh. It's true. Microsoft's official position is that they have to hide all the parts of Word that will help you understand the product, because those parts are too intellectually challenging for the novice user. If you become an advanced user, so the Microsoft Party Line goes, you'll become smart enough to discover and use the hidden tools, *deus ex machina*. Literally.

(Latin lesson for today: *deus ex machina* = "god from (out of) a machine." A stage term dating to the times of Euripedes. Describes the resolution of poorly written, hideously complex plots, which could only be unraveled by the expedient of having a god drop onto the stage, via a mechanical crane, to sort things out. When Kenny in South Park avoids volcanic immolation thanks to a previously unseen Scuzzlebutt monster with a Patrick Duffy leg, you're watching *deus ex machina*, updated a little bit for the '90s. And, yep, they killed Kenny.)

Life isn't like that, of course. I don't care if you've only used Word for ten minutes, and consider yourself an unrepentant dummy, you've no doubt poked around in the menus a bit. It's as if Microsoft handed you a loaded shotgun and left you to discover the finer points of its operation by trial and error.

If you're very lucky, you may have found some non-standard settings that make your work easier. (Although you probably don't remember where they were, eh?) If you're very unlucky, you discovered the Tools/Options menu and accidentally changed something really important. Kaboom.

you through a series of crucial settings—options that will help you see what's going on and make your life a little simpler. At first some of these settings won't make much sense, and for that I apologize. By the time you get to the end of the book, I bet you'll be able to go back and see precisely why I had you change them.

YOUR MILEAGE MAY VARY
None of these settings should be considered gospel: when you get comfortable with the setting and its side-effects, by all means go ahead and change it to suit the way you work. But in the absence of strong evidence to the contrary, I think you'll find these settings most conducive to getting your work done.

I have a secondary motive for showing you each of these groups of settings. If you've been poking around a bit, you may have inadvertently changed something and not know exactly how to get everything back to normal. Forget about uninstalling and reinstalling the application—Microsoft's usual answer to weird Office behavior. Reinstalling usually doesn't change any of your settings: if they were screwed up, they'll stay screwed up. Instead, take a few minutes to go through these steps to restore your application to some semblance of sanity.

Remove Rulers

Unless you can afford a 21-inch computer screen and run Windows at some ungodly high resolution, every square inch of Word's window is precious. The less space Word itself occupies the more peerless prose you'll see on the screen. Let's start by getting rid of something you don't need: Word's rulers.

WHAT'S A VIEW?
Word supports several *views*—ways of looking at the information in a document. I always work in Page Layout view because it most closely mimics the way pages will appear on the printer. If your PC gets sluggish with large documents, you might want to consider switching to Normal view: in Normal view, Word concentrates on showing you the text in the document, but doesn't go to any great lengths to lay out the pages. That lets Word run faster, but it can also lead to surprises when you finally print the page.

*E*XERCISE

Don't Show Rulers

1. Start Word 97. Make it appear full-screen (what Microsoft calls *maximized*) by clicking the maximize icon—it's in the upper-right corner of the Word window, immediately to the left of the X icon.

2. Type a sentence or two. If you haven't changed anything in Word, your screen will look like Figure 6.1. If it doesn't look like that, don't worry. We'll go through all the settings shortly and get them reset.

FIGURE 6.1
Bone-stock
Word 97.

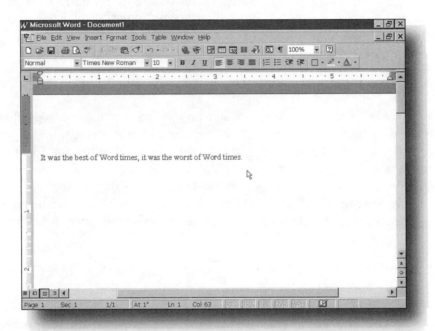

3. Click **View** and make sure **Page Layout** is checked (see Figure 6.2). Choosing Word's Page Layout view ensures that you'll see things on the screen pretty much as they will appear on your printer.

4. Click **View** and then click **Rulers** to clear away the checkmark in the Rulers box. The rulers on the top and left side will disappear from the screen (see Figure 6.2).

5. What? You want to see your rulers? No problem. To see the upper ruler (what Word calls the *horizontal ruler*, move your mouse around until the cursor is just underneath the box that says Times New Roman. You may

have to jiggle it a bit—the position you want is on or just below the dark horizontal line that separates the menus from the document itself (see Figure 6.5). Just hold the mouse there for a second and the top ruler appears. The ruler disappears after you move your pointer away.

FIGURE 6.2
Uncheck the View/Rulers box.

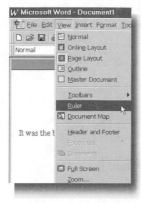

FIGURE 6.3
Hover at the top of the page if you ever need the horizontal ruler.

6. Similarly, you can see the left-side ruler (the *vertical ruler*) by hovering your mouse on the left side, near the vertical dark line (see Figure 6.4).

FIGURE 6.4
Hover on the left for the vertical ruler.

Very good. You've now reclaimed some precious screen space—and lost absolutely nothing in the process. Your eyes will thank you.

Show Paragraph Marks

I've been ranting about this one for years. If you've used Word more than a day, I bet you've hit a situation where the paragraphs don't line up correctly: suddenly all your paragraphs start centering themselves, or appear right-justified, hard up against the right margin. Maybe you typed a couple of **bold** words, and now everything you type turns to bold. Or you indented a paragraph, and now all your new paragraphs get indented. Or somehow you

- Started getting bullets (those dots on the left are called *bullets*—probably because you feel like shooting Word when they appear unbidden) like these

- And you don't know why they started,

- Or how to get rid of them.

No, you aren't going crazy. Word is supposed to work like that. But in order to understand what's going on—and I'll show you exactly what's happening, in Chapter 10, "Making Documents Look Good"—you have to be able to see a little marker that Word keeps in your document. The Redmond Gods, in their infinite wisdom, have determined that this marker is too confusing for the average reader to see—thereby condemning legions of Word users to untold hours, days, and weeks of frustration.

That little marker is called a *paragraph mark* and, as you might imagine, it simply marks the end of every paragraph. No, the marker doesn't appear on the printer when you print a document. (That's why Microsoft thinks most people would be confused if it showed up on the screen.) But if you can make that little leap of faith—that something in your document that shows up on the screen won't appear on the printer—you'll stand a fighting chance of understanding what is going on with your documents, and why. It's a small price to pay for some regained sanity.

I mean, can you imagine trying to learn how to drive a car when the car manufacturer insists that the steering wheel remain invisible?

XERCISE

Show Paragraph Marks and Tab Characters

1. If you've just finished the previous Exercise, fine. If not, start Word 97 and type in a sentence or two.

2. Click **Tools**, and then **Options**. Make sure the **View** tab is showing (click **View** if there's any question), and check the box marked **Paragraph marks** (see Figure 6.5).

3. While you're here, also check the box marked **Tab characters** (see Figure 6.5). That will let you see tabs inside your documents—another invisible character that can lead to no end of confusion.

FIGURE 6.5
The Tools, Options, View dialog box.

4. Finally, double-check all the settings on the **View** tab on your machine. Do they match the ones shown in Figure 6.5? If not, seriously consider changing the settings so they do match, particularly if you aren't quite sure what the settings mean.

5. Click OK.

Now take a look at the sentence you typed. See the backward-P character at the end of the sentence (see Figure 6.6)? That's a paragraph mark.

If you type a little more, you'll soon discover that the paragraph mark appears at the end of each paragraph—in other words, every time you press the Enter key. It doesn't appear on printouts. Click **Print** 🖨 up on the toolbar to print a page. You'll see.

FIGURE 6.6
The para-
graph mark
appears!

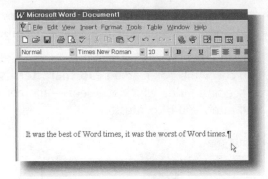

FIGURE 6.6
The para-
graph mark
appears!

PARAGRAPH AND TAB MARKS ARE VITAL

A little lesson from the School of Hard Knocks. Don't ever work on a Word document unless both paragraph marks and tabs are showing on the screen. So many things depend on both the paragraph mark and the tab character that you're literally shooting in the dark if you try to figure out what's going on without those two showing.

General Settings

You've already seen this dialog box, way back in Figure 1.2. It's the one that controls how Word responds to macros—thus potentially protecting your documents from destructive viruses.

*E*XERCISE

Set Virus Protection and the "Files" List Length

1. Make sure Word 97 is going. Click **Tools**, **Options**; then click the **General** tab.

2. Ensure that the **Macro virus protection** box is checked. It should be checked, unless you've told Word that you don't want it to watch for viruses. Regardless, make sure that it gets checked now.

3. Run the spinner on the **Recently used file list** line up as far as it will go. That should be a 9 (see Figure 6.7). This setting controls how many files Word will keep track of in its history list. The most recently used files show up on Word's **File** menu.

4. Double-check the other settings on the **General** tab. They should look a lot like those in Figure 6.7.

5. Click OK.

FIGURE 6.7
The Tools,
Options,
General
choices.

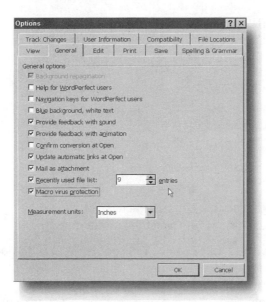

Disable Overstrike Mode

Here's another lousy decision that was made for you by the user-
friendly folks at Microsoft. Take a look at your keyboard. Somewhere,
typically to the right of the Enter key, you'll find a key marked INS or
Insert. That key can cause you no end of grief, whether you've been
using Word for a day or a decade.

As it ships right out of the box, Word 97 uses the Insert key to go into
something called Overstrike mode. The easiest way to describe
Overstrike mode is to take you through a little experiment.

*E*XERCISE

The Dread Overstrike Mode

1. You have Word 97 running, and a sentence or two (or more)
on the screen, right?

2. Use your mouse and click somewhere in the middle of one of
the sentences. Doesn't matter where.

3. Start typing. See how the stuff you type goes into the document, pushing all the words that were already there to the
right? Good.

4. Now click the **INS** or **Insert** key. Word goes into Overstrike mode—you can tell that it's in Overstrike mode because the letters **OVR** down in the lower-right corner switch from gray to black (see Figure 6.8).

FIGURE 6.8
Word 97 enters Overstrike (Overtype) mode.

5. Type some more. See that? The characters you type *replace* the characters in the sentence. That's what Overstrike mode does.

6. Click the **INS** or **Insert** key again. You should go back to normal mode. The **OVR** should go back to gray. *Whew!*

Nine hundred and ninety-nine times out of a hundred, Overstrike mode is a mistake: You accidentally click the **INS** or **Insert** key when you really wanted to click **DEL** or **Home** or some other key. And you don't discover your mistake until you've typed a sentence or two—and clobbered whatever good things might have gone before.

Fortunately, Word gives you an easy way to disable this madness.

XERCISE

Use Insert Key to, uh, Insert

1. With Word running, click **Tools**, **Options**; then click the **Edit** tab.

2. Click the box marked **Use the INS key for paste** (see Figure 6.9). Make sure the box is checked.

3. Double-check the other settings to make sure they match Figure 6.9. Click **OK** and you're done.

FIGURE 6.9
Tools Options
Edit settings.

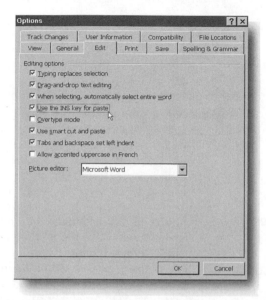

Save Slowly

Back in the not-so-good old days, Word's approach to saving documents could best be described as leisurely. Saving a small document on a floppy diskette could take ages; saving a medium-sized file on those old, slow hard drives sometimes took long enough for a quick latte break. Worst of all, Word frequently stalled completely while it was saving a document to disk—releasing the keyboard in a series of freeze-frame chops worthy of a Jackie Chan movie.

Nowadays, though, saving documents evokes much less trauma. With fast gizmos inside your PC, and smart tricks inside Windows itself, Word can usually save large files without slowing your typing or otherwise calling attention to its boorish manners.

The major problem with Fast Save occurs when something goes haywire in the middle of saving a big file—your cat chews through the power cord, or Windows turns belly-up and takes all the running programs with it. In those situations, a Fast Saved file can look like an old newspaper in the bottom of a bird cage. And be just about as useful.

I strongly recommend that you disable Fast Save. Here's how.

*E*XERCISE

Disable Fast Save

1. With Word 97 running, click **Tools**, **Options**, and then click the **Save** tab.

2. Make sure the box marked **Allow Fast Saves** is unchecked. See Figure 6.10. (Note: If you're running Office 97 Service Release-1, as I recommended in Chapter 2, "Precursors to Using Office," Microsoft has already unchecked this box. But if you're still using the original Office 97, the box is checked. Regardless, you want the box unchecked.)

3. There's another lousy setting in this Figure 6.10 dialog box. I

WHAT'S A FAST SAVE?
Normally when you save a file, Windows overwrites the older version: the whole new file gets written out to disk, replacing the older one. That can take a lot of time. Word's Fast Save updates a document by leaving the old version out on the disk, and writing *changes* to the end of the file. So, for example, a Fast Saved document might have instructions at the end that tell Word, "go back and change the second sentence to this-and-that, and then make the fourth paragraph bold." Word continues to append these instructions to the document until it figures that the changes take up more room than the original document. At that point, it rolls all of the changes into the document, gets rid of the old version, and replaces it with the new one.

This can lead to some embarrassing situations. Say you start a letter with, "My boss is a dingbat!" Later, you change your mind and modify the document to say, "My boss is wonderful!" If you Fast Save that document, your original words will be stored in the file; there will be an entry later in the file that says something like, "remove 'a dingbat' and replace it with 'wonderful.'" If somebody looks at the contents of the file, bypassing Word, they'll discover your original sentence. Oops.

A couple of years ago the mainstream computer press picked up on this idiosyncrasy. Some writers touted it as a major bug. It isn't. It's the only way Fast Save could possibly work.

don't know why, but Microsoft set things up so Word 97 users will normally save documents so old-fashioned versions of Word can read them—even if that means you lose some of the fancy new Word 97 features you've paid for. Balderdash! If the box marked **Save Word Files as** says **Word 6.0/95**

(*.doc), click that down-arrow and choose **Word Document (*.doc)**.
There. Might as well get your money's worth.

4. Again, check to make sure your other settings match those in Figure 6.10.
When you're satisfied, click **OK**.

FIGURE 6.10
Tools,
Options, Save
Settings.

The Case Against Hyperlinks

You have to admire Microsoft for one thing: When they jump on a bandwagon,
you can hear the wagon's springs squeal from the weight. When Microsoft
embraced the Internet a couple of years ago it went overboard in trying to Webify
everything in sight. That's how this final crucial change item came into existence.

In Word 97, when you type a Web address such as http://www.mcp.com, Word
takes it upon itself to convert that address into a hyperlink. A *hyperlink* is just a fancy
name for a hot button— you can click a hyperlink, and you're supposed to be transported to whatever location is mentioned in the link. In this case, if you click the
hyperlink http://www.mcp.com, Word 97 will take you to the Web site called
www.mcp.com.

Which is all well and good, if you're in a hyperlinking mood—that is, if you're looking at a document somebody else wrote, *and* it's on the screen of a machine that's
connected to the Web, *and* you don't mind having your machine go absolutely
bonkers for a couple of minutes any time you accidentally click the hyperlink.

Here's the clincher. Not only does Word turn your perfectly reasonable typed Web address and convert it into a rarely useful Web Wonderland rabbit hole, it makes the link so ugly you'd be ashamed to print it. When Word 97 identifies a hyperlink, it makes the hyperlink underlined and blue! (The old version of Word 97 also made the hyperlink bold—an assault on the senses rarely matched in modern annals of computing.)

Anyway, it's easy to turn off this nonsense, if you know the trick.

*E*XERCISE

Leave My Web Addresses Alone

1. Get Word going. If you want to see how Word mangles Web addresses, just type a simple Web address, say, `http://www.mcp.com`. See how Word 97 makes it blue and underlined (and possibly bold, if you're using an older version)? Blecch.

2. Stop the insanity by clicking **Tools**, **AutoCorrect**, **AutoFormat As You Type**, and clear the checkbox marked **Internet and network paths with hyperlinks** (see Figure 6.11).

FIGURE 6.11
Keep Word's mitts off your Web addresses.

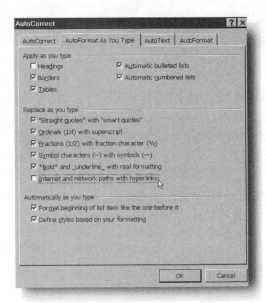

3. Double-check and make sure your settings match the ones in Figure 6.11. Again, it's all right if they're different, as long as you understand why you've changed them. Click **OK**.

Now you're ready to tackle Word on your own terms. Congratulations.

The Screen

Time for a quick guided tour around the Word screen (see Figure 6.12). No need to memorize anything, but you might want to dog-ear this page so you can refer back to it if something puzzles you in the future.

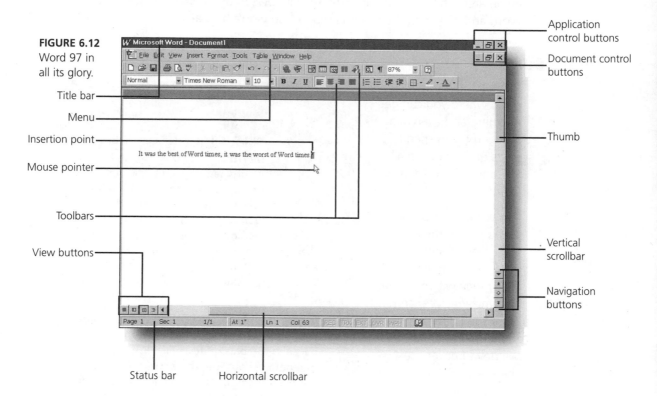

FIGURE 6.12
Word 97 in all its glory.

Title Bar

Across the top of the Word window you'll see the title bar. It's just like any other title bar you'll find in any other Windows application. You can click it and drag the Word window around, or resize the window by grabbing any of the Word window's edges.

Over on the extreme right of the title bar, the three Application Control Buttons work just like any others in Windows: from left to right, they minimize, maximize/restore (toggle between Word filling up the entire Windows Desktop, and floating the Word window on the Desktop), and shut down Word.

The flying W icon at the far left simply duplicates the functions of the Application Control Buttons. I never use it, and you probably won't either.

If you aren't familiar with all of these Windows housekeeping chores, crank up Word and play with them. Don't worry, you won't hurt anything.

Menu Bar

The next row down contains Word's menu bar. This is Word's working class bar, the place where you can get anything and everything done. You can spend years getting lost in all the options buried in Word's menus.

To the far right of the menu bar sit three Document Control Buttons. From left to right, they will minimize, maximize/restore, and close the current document, all inside Word's window. I never use them either.

The "W on a piece of paper" icon at the far left—to the left of File— replicates the functions of the Document Control Buttons. It's another button you can safely forget about.

WHAT'S THE DIFFERENCE BETWEEN A MENU BAR AND A TOOLBAR?
At first blush you'd think that Word's menu bars and toolbars have little in common: after all, a menu bar has words on it, while the toolbars have pictures on them. Click something on the menu bar and you get, well, menus. Click an icon on the toolbar, and you get actions. Surprisingly, the difference isn't nearly so clear-cut.

In fact, in a stroke of true genius, the people who designed Office 97 decided to make menu bars and toolbars quite similar. We won't go into detail about it in this book, but you can put menu items on a toolbar, and you can put icons on the menu bar. There's essentially no limitation on how you can mix and match menus and icons.

So if you've been wondering what the real difference is between the menu bar and the toolbars (a question that surely rates right up there with The Meaning of Life and Everything), you can rest easy. There really isn't any difference.

Toolbars

Below the menu bar sit two toolbars. This is where Word starts to get interesting. Toolbars exist solely to let you work faster. They're nothing but shortcuts to actions that you can perform just as well by hunting and pecking through Word's menus. If you've been mystified by the funny buttons, and wonder what all of them mean, let me warn you in advance: about half of the toolbar buttons you see in Figure 6.12 will become old friends, rather quickly. A few of the others come in handy from time to time. But lots of the toolbar buttons you see there are very esoteric. You won't use them in a hundred years. So don't get too hung up on Word's toolbar buttons, trying to decipher what those tiny pictures really mean. They don't *mean* much of anything.

Word has lots of toolbars, hidden away until you've learned how to use them. We'll work with a couple of them in subsequent chapters.

The Document

Right smack dab in the middle of the screen you'll see a mock-up of your document. When you type, Word stuffs the characters you type into your document and shows them right here on the screen.

As you get more proficient at Word, you'll want to reduce the clutter on the screen and open up as much room as possible for the document. After all, that's why we're here—the document serves as the alpha and omega of Word's existence. Everything else you see on the screen is just a means to the document's end.

Inside every document you'll find a blinking vertical line called an insertion point. This mark indicates where the next letter you type on the keyboard will appear in the document.

GIVE US OLD-TIMERS A BREAK...
If you talk to old-timers, they'll refer to either the insertion point and/or the mouse pointer as the *cursor*. That's because they spent their formative years B.M.—Before the mouse, back when the only controllable moving item on a screen was called a cursor. Forgive them.

I'm an old-timer, too, and a bit addled to boot. I try hard to use the terms insertion point and mouse pointer the way I'm supposed to—but sometimes I forget. Cut me a little slack, OK? You should always be able to tell from the context whether cursor means the Insertion Point or the mouse pointer. Think of it as an exercise for dealing with crusty old PC users, wherever they may be.

The mouse pointer, which can take on the appearance of an arrow, an I-beam pointer, or any of a dozen additional shapes, indicates where your mouse is located within the document, or on the screen.

Status Bar

Way down at the bottom of the screen, Word maintains a status bar. Some of the information shown on the status bar may interest you, from time to time. Many of the statistics shown here relate to the insertion point.

Reading from left to right:

- *Page.* This tells you the page number of the page you're looking at. This is the number that will print on that page, if you have Word print page numbers. (Sounds complicated, eh? Hang on. It gets worse.)

- *Sec.* This is the section number of the current section. Word lets you break documents (usually large documents) into sections. This tells you which section you're in.

- *x/y.* This shows you which page you're on (x), and the total number of pages in the document (y). The x here can be different from the page mentioned earlier, because Word lets you restart page numbering in each section. This x is the number you would get if you printed the document and then started counting the number of pieces of paper that come out the printer—one, two, three—stopping when you get to the current page. (Still sound complicated? Don't worry about it.)

- *At x.* This tells you, more or less, how far down the page the insertion point sits. It's a quick way of judging vertical distance without having to use that obtrusive ruler.

- *Ln x.* This tells you, more or less, which line on the page contains the insertion point.

- *Col x.* This tells you, more or less, how many characters sit to the left of the insertion point, plus one. In other words, Col 1 means there are zero characters to the left of the insertion point; Col 2 means there's one character to the left; and so on.

The **Spelling and Grammar Status**  icon on the right side of the status bar indicates that Word is all caught up with formatting and displaying the document on the screen. If Word gets behind a little bit (say, when you're typing fast), the X turns into a pencil. When Word prints, the whole icon turns into a printer,

WHAT DO YOU MEAN, MORE OR LESS? Don't take the information on the Word 97 status bar too seriously. All sorts of things can throw the numbers off. Probably the worst offender: embedded pictures—if you have pictures in your document, all bets are off for the At, Ln, and Col numbers. I've also seen situations where the page numbers (even the section numbers) don't get updated properly, so *caveat emptor, er, writor...*

counting off the pages printed. When you save a file, a pulsing diskette appears to the right of the icon. In general, if you can't figure out why Word 97 isn't responding to what you're doing, look around that **Spelling and Grammar Status**  icon. It might tell you why Word can't keep up.

Vertical Scrollbar

The scrollbar on the right side of the screen, commonly called the vertical scrollbar, helps you move through your documents. Like most Windows scrollbars, you can click the up or down arrow to move a little bit at a time, or drag the gray rectangle (it's called a *thumb*) to maneuver more quickly.

Unlike other Windows scrollbars, though, clicking the thumb tells you exactly what page you're on (see Figure 6.13). As you drag the thumb up and down, Word 97 keeps track of where you'll go in the document. Let go of the mouse button, and you're transported to the page indicated next to the thumb. Although the page numbering occasionally gets out of whack by a page or two, I rate this as one of Word's niftiest features for those of you who work with long documents.

Down at the bottom of the vertical scrollbar, below the scrolling down-arrow, sit three navigation buttons. They help you move quickly through a document. The **Select Browse Object** button in the middle of the three lets you choose what you want to search for. (Most commonly you'll be looking for specific text inside the document, but Word also lets you search for all sorts of things, for example, pictures, tables, even footnotes.) The up and down buttons let you repeat your previous search, moving toward (respectively) the top or the bottom of the document. We'll cover the Navigation Buttons at length in Chapter 9, "Getting Around."

FIGURE 6.13
The vertical scrollbar's thumb knows all, tells all.

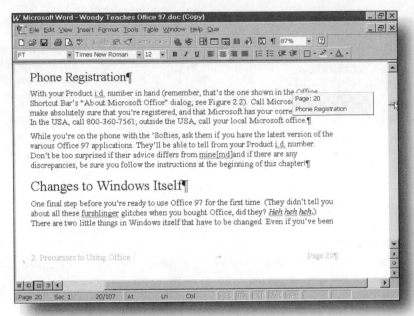

Horizontal Scrollbar

While the vertical scrollbar lets you move through the pages in your document, the horizontal scrollbar only controls the centering of the document on the screen. For most Word users it's nearly useless, once you set the zoom factor properly (see the next exercise).

On the far left of the horizontal scrollbar you'll find four icons. These let you switch quickly between Normal, Online, Page, and Outline view. If you hover the mouse pointer over these icons, a ScreenTip appears to identify each.

☞ *I talked about Normal and Page view on page 85.*

The other views are less likely to be of interest to you. Online view shows you how the page will look if it's posted on the World Wide Web. Outline view collapses the document down to an outline. All of these views can be controlled by clicking the appropriate item in the (surprise!) **View** menu.

Adjusting Zoom

There's one more setting that varies so much from computer to computer that it's hard to give general advice about it. That setting is the Zoom factor. As the name implies, it affects how much of a document appears onscreen at any given moment. I suggest that you first set the zoom following these guidelines, and then refer back here from time to time, particularly if your eyes start driving you crazy.

$\mathcal{E}$XERCISE

Adjust Word 97's Zoom

1. Start Word 97. Click **View**, and then **Zoom**. Your screen should look something like that in Figure 6.14.

FIGURE 6.14
Where the zoom factor lives.

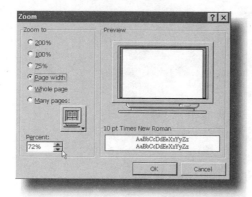

2. For a first approximation, click the button marked **Page Width**. You're trying to juggle two competing goals here: you want to show as much of the page on the screen as possible, but at the same time you want your letters to look good. If you try to show too much of the page on the screen, the letters will be too small; if you enlarge the letters so they're more readily visible you reduce the fraction of a document that will appear on the screen at any given moment.

3. Click the arrows on the **Percent** box up and down and try to find a Zoom percentage that shows the entire width of a document, but also makes the letters large enough so you can see them without straining your eyes.

4. When you're happy with the Zoom percent—for now anyway—click **OK**.

If you were lucky enough to get the entire width of the document on the screen without aggravating your myopia, there's one final step you should take: get rid of the horizontal scrollbar. It only takes up precious screen space, and if you don't need to scroll left-and-right all of the time, why put up with it?

*E*XERCISE

Ditch the Horizontal Scrollbar

1. Get Word running, and make sure you can see the entire width of the document onscreen.

2. Click **Tools**, **Options**; then click the **View** tab. Uncheck the box marked **Horizontal scroll bar** (see Figure 6.15).

FIGURE 6.15
The demise of the horizontal scrollbar.

3. Click **OK** and the horizontal scrollbar is history. Come back to this Exercise and turn it on again if you need to—say, work with an odd-sized sheet of paper.

Working with Documents

*E*VERY WORD 97 DOCUMENT HAD TO originate somewhere, right? Word documents don't exactly grow on trees. This is where I get to show you the options you have for creating new documents.

Easy Plain Documents

Every time you start Word it figures that you probably want to work with a new document, so it creates one for you, and gives that document the name Document1.

The first one's free. After that, you have to make your own. Creating a new, blank document couldn't be simpler.

*E*XERCISE

Make a New Empty Document

1. Click the **New** 🗋 icon. A new document appears.

2. Word gives the document a name like Document2, Document3, or some such. The numbers get assigned sequentially. You can see the new document's (temporary) name up on the title bar.

Almost-as-Easy Fancy Documents

Microsoft has spent an enormous amount of time and money coming up with alternatives to the plain, blank document. It pays to spend a little bit of time poking around the different kinds of documents Word offers. While Word doesn't ship from the factory with a copy of your company's next annual report on the CD, or even the term paper that's due next week, you might well find a document that can save you gobs of time and effort. And, hey, you've already paid for it!

Microsoft distributes its prefab documents in two different forms, *templates* and *Wizards*. You've probably bumped into Windows Wizards. They guide you by the hand, asking questions, helping you make choices and set options. Word Wizards behave quite similarly. If you can find a Wizard to help you through the hard spots—say, writing a résumé, or creating your first Web page—you should take the Wizard up on the offer to help. When you're done, the worst that you'll do is throw the document away.

Templates are similar to Wizards, but they're dumb. In general, they don't ask questions or guide you through options. More than anything templates resemble cookie-cutter images of documents that you can create. Because of that, templates rate as a good place to store boilerplate text and standard forms. Even though they're dumb cookie-cutter prototypes of real documents, they can still be valuable, particularly if they show you how to lay out a tricky kind of document (for example, a newsletter), or if they contain a skeleton of a document that you can readily adapt to your work.

You get to Word's templates and Wizards by clicking **File**, then **New**, and choosing the template or Wizard that interests you.

*E*XERCISE

Create a New Résumé with Word's Résumé Template

1. Click **File**, then **New**. Click the **Other Documents** tab. Pay particular attention to the thumbnail sketch in the **Preview** box over on the right. That's where Word shows you a postage-stamp size mock-up of how the new document will look.

THE OTHER 10,000,000 TEMPLATES
Microsoft has zillions and zillions of templates—and a few more Wizards—that you can use, free. There's a large collection on the Office 97 installation CD that aren't copied onto your hard drive in a "Typical" installation. To retrieve them, put the CD back in your CD drive, choose Install, and choose a Custom installation. Check all of the Word templates and you'll be in template heaven. You'll find templates to help you create dozens of business documents, legal documents, envelopes, resumes of all types, and much more.

The second big source: the Web. If you have a Web browser hooked up on your PC, the easiest way to see all of the extra templates is to click **File**, **New**, **Other Documents**, and choose **More Templates**. Word will shimmer and hum for a few minutes, and you'll end up at Microsoft's template site, `www.microsoft.com/office/enhword.asp`, on the World Wide Web.

Templates are a lot like fonts: at first you'll be tempted to gather all you can find, but sooner or later the sheer volume of them forces you to be more selective. Go for the good ones.

2. Double-click Contemporary Resume.dot (see Figure 7.1).

3. Word creates a new document based on the Contemporary Resume.dot template. Basically, it copies everything in the cookie-cutter template (the stuff you saw in the **Preview** box) into a brand new document (see Figure 7.2).

4. At this point the template has done its work. You can click on the document, type, move, or delete text—do anything you would normally do to a document.

Contrast the "dumb" template approach to the "smart" Word Wizard that also produces a résumé.

FIGURE 7.1
Choosing the
Contemporary
Resume tem-
plate in the
File Open dia-
log box.

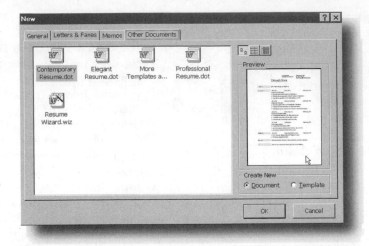

FIGURE 7.2
The text from
the template
is poured into
the new doc-
ument.

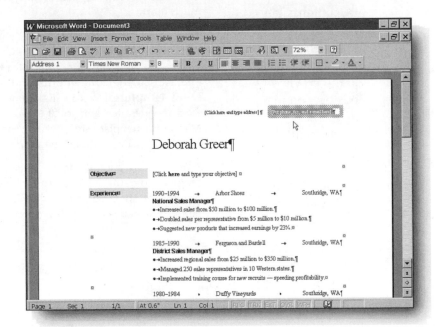

EXERCISE

Create a New Résumé with Word's Wizard

1. Click **File**, then **New**. Click the **Other Documents** tab and double-click **Résumé Wizard.wiz**. The Word Résumé Wizard kicks in (see Figure 7.3). Click **Next**.

FIGURE 7.3
Word's
Résumé
Wizard starts
with an
overview.

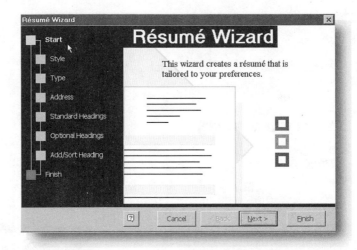

2. The Résumé Wizard asks what kind of résumé you'd like. I chose
Professional (see Figure 7.4).

FIGURE 7.4
The Résumé
Wizard offers
several differ-
ent types of
resumes.

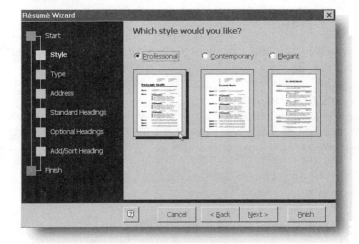

3. Next, the Wizard takes you through a series of questions about your name
and address, and which headings you want to appear in your résumé.
Choose something appropriate.

4. When you hit the final screen in the Wizard, click **Finish**. You'll be presented with a custom résumé, ready for your embellishment and shameless
puffery (see Figure 7.5).

FIGURE 7.5
The final résumé created by the Résumé Wizard.

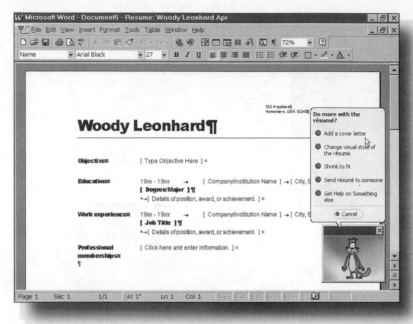

So, you ask, which is better—the Wizard or the template? Personally, I like the dumb template-generated résumé a little more than the fancy-schmancy Wizard-generated one. Just as in real life, smarter ain't necessarily better!

OTHER WAYS TO START ANEW
You aren't limited to using the **New** [image] toolbar icon for creating empty new documents. You can create a new blank document via the **File**, **New** route, by choosing **Blank Document** under the **General** tab.

Save

Save often, save well. A mantra for our times.

Although the act of saving a document may strike you as terribly simple, the nuances of selecting an appropriate file name and locating the document in a reasonable folder rate right up there with the greatest problems in biological taxonomy. Take some time and do it right!

*E*XERCISE

Save Your Résumé

1. Do you still have the résumé showing from the previous Exercise? Good. (If not, start Word, and type a few sentences.)

2. Click the **Save** 🖫 icon, or click **File** then **Save**. They both do the same thing. You should get Word's Save As dialog box, as shown in Figure 7.6.

3. Navigate around to the folder you'd like to have hold this document. Navigating, in this case, involves double-clicking on folders you want to dig into, clicking the **Up One Level** 🖃 icon to move up to a higher level folder, or clicking the down-arrow next to the **Save in** box to hopscotch around all the drives available to Word (see Figure 7.7).

WORD'S AUTOSAVE FEATURE IS A LIFESAVER

Are you really new to computers? Not to worry. We've all been there. If you're just getting your feet wet, you might think that any document you can see on your computer's screen is safely stored away inside your computer. And you'd be wrong.

At the risk of over-simplifying just a little bit, the document you see on Word's screen only exists in your PC's main memory—you know, those memory chips that look like boxy black cockroaches with silvery legs? If the power to your PC goes *kaput,* main memory craps out, and the document goes with it. From time to time you need to *save* your documents. Save is a rather strange term, but the idea behind it is quite straightforward: when you save a document, you copy it from main memory onto something else—usually a hard drive. Once it's on a hard drive, your document will stick around through power outages and almost any other calamity you can imagine (short of a crashed hard drive).

I was a little sneaky in Chapter 6, "Word Preliminaries." I glossed right over something called AutoRecover. If you followed my instructions in Chapter 6 precisely, you set up Word so it automatically saves a copy of all the open documents—that is, all the documents in main memory—every ten minutes. That way, unless you're extraordinarily unlucky, you'll never lose more than ten minutes' worth of work if the power goes out.

If you frequently make lots and lots of small changes—as, say, an editor might—you might want to think about having Word save your documents every five minutes, or even every minute. That way you'll give up control of your PC more often, letting Word come in and do its save thing, but you'll also know that you're never more than a minute or two away from a full restore, should the worst happen.

FIGURE 7.6
Saving a file
for the first
time.

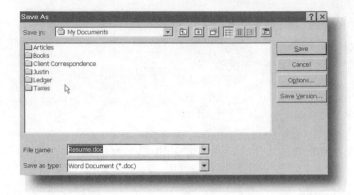

FIGURE 7.7
The drop-
down save
list for hop-
ping around
all available
drives.

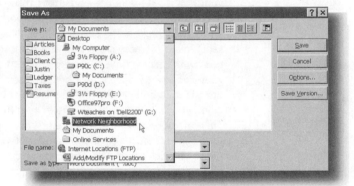

4. Type a meaningful name in the box marked **File name**. (You can use letters, numbers, spaces, and the _ underscore character, but should avoid weird characters such as * / ? – and almost anything else.) In this case, Word has guessed that I would like to call the document Résumé.doc. That sounds good to me. Click **OK** and Word saves the document to disk.

Choose that **Save** 🖫 icon from time to time as you're working. It'll keep a recent copy of your document on disk, and protect you just in case your two-year-old walks by and punches your PC's off button.

You've probably noticed that Windows in general (and Word in particular) usually shows lists of file names sorted in alphabetical order. If you're very clever in the way you assign names to your documents, Word will keep them in order for you. For example, if you commonly write letters to a client named John, you might consider ordering them by date. Thus, a letter written on January 14, 1999 could be called John 19990114.doc, and one written on February 27, 1999, could be John

19990227.doc. Simple tricks like this one can make sorting through documents much simpler in the future.

Finally, remember that the folder structure you have established isn't set in concrete.

☞ *You can change it at any time by following the instructions on page 42.*

Close

Once you're done working on a document, you can close it by clicking **File**, then **Close**. That takes it off the screen so you don't have to deal with it any more. Closing consists of two steps:

WHAT'S THE DIFF BETWEEN SAVE AND SAVE AS?
You caught me. I tried to finesse that one right by you. Sheeesh. If you save a document, and that document already has a name, Word merely copies the document from main memory onto your disk drive. But if the document doesn't have a name—and in this case, the Résumé document *didn't* have a name—Word has to ask you what to call the document, and where to put it. So instead of simply copying the document to disk, Word pops up this Save As dialog box, gets the info it needs, then copies the document to disk.

Any time you have a document open inside Word, you can tell Word that you want to save a copy of the document with a different name. That's where Save As comes in. If you click **File**, then **Save As**, Word asks you for the name and location of the new document, then copies the document from main memory to the disk. The old document—the one still on disk—isn't changed at all.

1. Word figures out if you've made any changes to the document since the last time you saved it. If there have been changes made, Word asks you if you want to save the changes. If you say yes, Word goes through the normal Save process, described in the preceding section. If you say no, Word doesn't save the document, so the copy on disk doesn't change.

2. Word then removes the document from main memory. It gets zapped off the screen. In most cases if there's another document open it takes the closed document's place.

If you shut down Word, either by clicking **File**, then **Exit**, or by clicking the X in the upper-right corner of the Word window, Word closes each currently open document, in turn, before banishing itself to that big bit-bucket in the sky.

*E*XERCISE _____

Close Resume.doc

1. In the preceding Exercise you saved Resume.doc. Make sure that it's still the document that's "on top" in the Word window.

2. To close Resume.doc, click **File**, then **Close**. There. That wasn't too difficult, was it? Heh heh heh.

Open

Word offers several methods for opening documents, ranging from quite straightforward to incredibly complex. Let's take a look at the two most common—and least difficult—methods.

*E*XERCISE _____

File Open via the Menu or Toolbar

1. Say you want to open Resume.doc, the document you closed in the preceding Exercise. You can click the **Open** 🖼 icon, click **Resume.doc**, and click **Open** (see Figure 7.8).

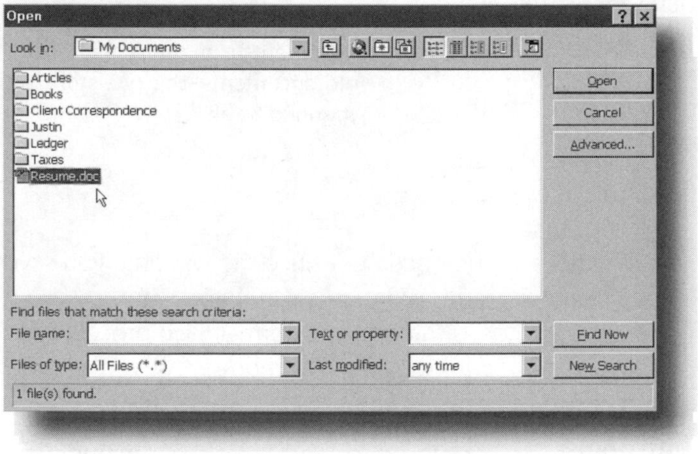

FIGURE 7.8
Resume.doc
in the File
Open dialog
box.

2. Alternatively, you can click on **File**, then **Open**, and then double-click **Resume.doc**.

If you know that you've used the document recently, though, there's a much faster way to open it. Word 97 maintains a most recently used (*MRU*) file list under the **File** menu. Opening a document from that list is very fast and easy.

To open Resume.doc from the MRU list, click **File**, slide your mouse pointer down to **1.Resume.doc**, and let go of the mouse button (see Figure 7.9). *Boom!*

FIGURE 7.9
Resume.doc
on the MRU
file list.

Word 97 includes a very powerful, comprehensive search engine, built into the product itself. That search engine can help you find, say, all the documents on your hard drive that include the phrase, "Free Bill!" or "Peter Piper picked a peck of pickled peppers."

To use the search engine, click **Open** 🖼, or click **File**, then **Open**. When you see the Open dialog box (see Figure 7.8), click the **Advanced** button. Now call up Word's built-in Help by pressing the F1 key, typing `find files`, clicking **Search**, and clicking the button marked **Find files** (see Figure 7.10).

FIGURE 7.10
Get help for
Word's File
Open search
engine from
the Office
Assistant.

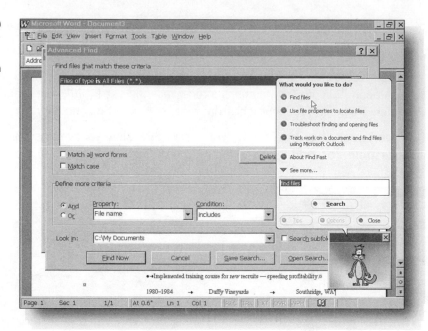

Starting Over

Have you ever screwed up something so badly that you just wanted to throw it away and start over? Word gives you that opportunity. In fact, there are two different ways to recover from disastrous flubs, if you think and plan ahead.

The easy way: Only save a document if you know it's "good." Once you have a good saved copy, make all the changes to the document that you like. If you get to the point where you want to throw away your current version and retrieve the last saved version, simply close the document (click **File**, **Close**), and when Word asks if you want to save the changes, click **No**. You can then open the old version of the document—the one you saved—as it's still on disk.

The hard way: Word will actually maintain versions of a document for you. While there's a considerable amount of overhead involved (each version is a document unto itself, and takes a fair amount of storage space), this approach gives you great flexibility, as you can retrieve any old version, at any time.

To make Word save versions of a document, click **File**, then **Save As**. When you get the Save As dialog, click **Save Version** (see Figure 7.11).

FIGURE 7.11
Setting up a
document to
save versions.

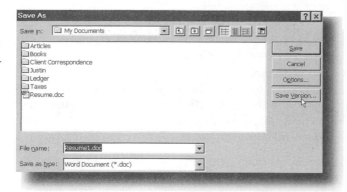

VERSIONING HELP

Word has an excellent online help article on versioning, but it's nearly impossible to find. (I never could locate it using the Office Assistant.) To see the details, click **Help**, then **Contents and Index**. Click the **Find** tab. Type `document versions`, then scroll down to the entry marked **Save multiple versions of a document in one file** and click on it. Click **Display**, and follow from there.

Undo/Redo

Word 97 contains one of the most sophisticated undo/redo capabilities you'll find in any computer program. If you ever get a hankering to throw away all your work, check first to see if you can undo the part that really gives you heartburn.

*E*XERCISE

Undo and Redo

1. Start a new document by clicking on the **New** icon.

2. Type a sentence or two.

3. Click the loopy arrow part of the **Undo** icon to undo your typing (see Figure 7.12).

FIGURE 7.12
One click to
undo the pre-
vious action.

4. *Poof!* The sentence disappears. To bring it back—"redo" in Microsoft-speak—click the loopy arrow part of **Redo** [↻ ▾].

UNDOING MULTIPLE ACTIONS

Sometimes you'll want to undo a whole bunch of actions, all at once. If that's the case, click the down-wedgie part of the **Undo** [↺ ▾] icon, and choose however many actions you want to undo. If you overshot your mark, the **Redo** [↻ ▾] has a similar feature for redoing any number of changes.

As long as you keep a file open, you can undo or redo a nearly unlimited number of steps. The undo/redo information sticks around even when you save the file. But the minute you close the file, all of that history gets tossed away. The actions available for "undo-ing" can be seen by clicking the arrow next to the **Redo** [↺ ▾] icon.

CAUTION—YOU CANNOT UNDO A SAVE

When you save a file, you write a copy of it out to disk, replacing the old copy. For that reason, you can't really undo a save. But as long as the document remains open, you can undo any actions that you've taken, and if you then save the resulting document you'll have, in effect, undone the changes made in the save.

Print

Most of the time you'll want to print a single copy of the current document, on the printer you normally use (if you have more than one printer). Word 97 has you covered.

*E*XERCISE_____

Print One Copy, Quick

1. Make sure the document you want to print is showing in Word's window.

2. Click the **Print** [🖨] icon. One copy goes straight to your printer.

Occasionally you'll want to do something a bit more complicated than run off one quick copy. Word has you covered there, too.

*E*XERCISE_____

Fancy Printing

1. Once again, make sure the document you want to print is the top one in Word's window.

2. Click **File**, then **Print** (see Figure 7.13). Your Print dialog may look different from this one, but it should be pretty close.

FIGURE 7.13
A plethora of
printing
options.

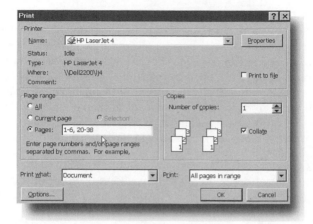

3. If you have more than one printer attached to your computer (or your network), or if you have fax software on your PC, you should choose the desired printer or fax from the options offered in the **Name** box.

4. To print the current page, or any range of pages, choose the appropriate option from the **Page range** box. In Figure 7.13, I've told Word to print pages 1 through 6, and 20 to 38. (Yes, Microsoft did screw up the wording at the bottom of the **Page range** box! Did you catch that?)

5. Choose how many copies you want to print, and whether you want the pages collated. If you print more than one copy and check the **Collate** box, Word will print the entire document, then print it a second time, and so on. If you don't check the **Collate** box, you'll get all the copies of page 1, followed by all the copies of page 2, and so on.

DUPLEX PRINTING ON A SHOESTRING
The final box, disingenuously marked **Print**, usually allows you to print all the odd pages, or all the even pages, in a document. (Again, your printer may be different.) Why would you want to do that? If you figure out the correct sequence—and believe me, it can be tricky—you can use this feature to print on the front and back of every sheet of paper, odd pages on the front and even pages on the back. Printing this way is called *duplex* printing, and it's a capability found only on very expensive printers.

SAVE TIME BY PRINTING UNCOLLATED COPIES

On most printers it's much, much faster to print copies uncollated. Why? Most printers support a command that says something like, "Print 14 copies of the following page." So if you want 14 copies of your document, Word only has to send the pages out once—with each page preceded by the "Print 14 copies of the following page" command. On the other hand, if you want those 14 copies collated, Word has to send the printer all the instructions for printing page 1, then page 2, and so on, and when the first copy of the document is done, it has to start all over again, sending page 1, page 2, etc., and that sequence is repeated 14 times.

You can play around with the other settings on the Print dialog box (refer to Figure 7.13), without fear of breaking anything, as long as you don't change the settings in the box you'll see when you click **Options**.

Building Documents

DOCUMENTS, DOCUMENTS, DOCUMENTS. I'VE BEEN talking about documents so much, you probably think I'm document eccentric. Could be. I've been accused of worse.

Most people think the term "document" has something to do with paper; after all, the memos you type, the reports you read, and the books you buy are all documents, aren't they?

Interlude: What Is a Document, Anyway?

In the computer milieu, a document has nothing to do with paper. A document is merely a computer file—a collection of ones and zeros, stored away somewhere—nothing more, nothing less.

Word 97 documents are special kinds of computer files, ones that can be read and understood by, *mirabile dictu*, Word 97. If you spend a few years working with Word documents, twist and turn and squint real hard, you'll come to the conclusion that Word documents contain very specific parts, built up like Lego toys, in a rather inflexible order. The parts go something like this.

(Latin lesson for the day: *mirabile dictu* = "wondrous/miraculous to relate." Frequently stated with tongue firmly in cheek. As in: I went to the Microsoft Web site and it recommended, *mirabile dictu!*, that I go buy the latest version.)

Characters

Characters form the basic building blocks of Word documents.

Every Word 97 document contains at least one character, and every "empty" new Word 97 document starts out with one character—the paragraph mark. (Since you followed my suggestion in Chapter 6, "Word Preliminaries," you can see the paragraph marks in your documents, right?) Yes, it's pretty weird to think of a paragraph mark as a character—usually *characters* are letters, numbers, punctuation marks, and the like. But Word's different. In fact, when it comes to understanding how Word works, paragraph marks are the *most important* characters.

Put a bunch of characters together and what do you get? Sentences? Well, maybe yes and maybe no. In fact, Word is pretty haphazard in identifying sentences. (Writers can be awfully haphazard about sentences, too!) Word has to accept sentence fragments, disembodied phrases, columns of numbers, and the like without croaking or giving the writer too much guff. It does so by pretty much ignoring sentences and moving on to the next level of aggregated characters.

Paragraphs

You know what a paragraph is, right? Miss Smith in your sixth grade grammar class taught you. In the real world, a paragraph is a collection of sentences with a unified theme, or something along those lines. (Hey, I didn't do any better in sixth grade grammar than you did.)

Microsoft's *Bookshelf 97*, part of Office 97 Professional, declares that a paragraph is

"A distinct division of written or printed matter that begins on a new, usually indented line, consists of one or more sentences, and typically deals with a single thought or topic or quotes one speaker's continuous words."

Yeah, sure. That kind of definition may keep English professors fully employed, but it doesn't do squat for a computer.

As far as Word 97 is concerned, a paragraph consists of

1. A paragraph mark

2. All the characters sitting in front of the paragraph mark, up to but not including the preceding paragraph mark (if there is one)

I really prefer that definition, don't you? It would've made my English Composition class a whole lot easier. It's also the kind of definition you—and Word—can sink your teeth into. No wishy-washy "thought or topic or quotes" stuff. A paragraph mark and the preceding characters. Period.

Because every "blank" Word document starts out with a single character—a paragraph mark—it's also true that every "blank" Word document starts out with one paragraph. There's nothing in the paragraph but a paragraph mark, but them's the breaks, eh?

Word has paragraphs nailed cold. In the next few chapters, you'll see just how staked out Word paragraphs can be.

So what's the next building block? You put a bunch of paragraphs together and what do you get, a page? Well, no, not necessarily:

THE HORRIBLE TRUTH ABOUT SECTIONS

All right, all right. I can't stand lying. The truth is that Word has relaxed the concept of section a bit, and if you're a geek (like me), you may be curious about the details. Almost all the time, sections are large parts of documents, consisting of many paragraphs. People typically use sections to separate out chapters in books, or major parts of reports. But in certain extremely unusual situations you can define a section as just part of a paragraph. That is, you can break a paragraph into more than one section. Why would you want to do that? Usually it's because you want to vary the number of newspaper-like snaking columns in a large paragraph. Sometimes it's to change the line numbering (as in a legal document, where numbers appear on each line). But it's really, really rare, and I'm going to ignore it from this point on.

Pages can have parts of paragraphs, and the paragraphs can flip-flop all over the place as you add more characters to a document, appearing first on one page and then on another.

Sections

I'm going to simplify things a bit and tell you a lie. The next basic building block in constructing Word documents is called a *section*. (No, that isn't the lie.) Sections consist of one or more paragraphs. (There. That's the lie.)

Almost all the documents you'll work with consist of just one section, and that shouldn't bother you a bit.

☞ *We'll talk about a few reasons for setting up multiple sections on page 201.*

But in almost all cases, working with sections is more hassle than it's worth.

Documents

The ultimate Word construct, the document, consists of one or more sections. Every document contains at least one character (you guessed it, a paragraph mark), and at least one paragraph.

See how these parts fit together? Each one of these components has a slightly different affect on a document, and each can be manipulated in a slightly different way. Word builds them up, piece by piece, characters turning into paragraphs, paragraphs turning into sections, as it constructs your documents. Remember that and you'll be a long way ahead of the game.

Drawing Layer

Word 97 documents have one additional component that's a bit hard to describe. It's called the drawing layer, and it floats like a ghost on top of each document. You can see right through the drawing layer. In fact, it's frequently difficult figuring out what's in the drawing layer, and what's in the document itself, underneath the drawing layer.

When you put drawings (such as, oh, clip art) in a document, they usually go in the document itself. They behave more or less like big characters—you can copy them, move them, and push them around like normal characters.

But when you start playing with Word's drawing tools (see Figure 8.1), making free-hand drawings, or putting arrows and circles on things, those drawings go in the drawing layer. They float above the text itself, and sometimes it can be maddening nailing down the floaters so they stay put.

FIGURE 8.1
Word 97's drawing tools— doorway to the drawing layer.

Now you know the complete anatomy of a Word 97 document. Let's see what kind of trouble you can get into by manipulating those parts to best effect.

DON'T OVERLOOK DRAW 98
If you do much drawing in Word, you really should get Microsoft's Draw 98. Microsoft makes Draw 98 available free for the downloading from its Web site. One irritant: The actual site has changed several times. The best way to find it is to navigate to http://www.microsoft.com/office and look around for Office enhancements. Draw 98 is vastly superior to Word's native drawing tools. It works with the rest of Office, too.

Deleting

You know how to get characters into a document: you type. (And who said Word was tough?) But how, exactly, do you get rid of them? Ends up that's pretty easy, too.

You have two choices: You can zap out characters from in front, or you can zap them from behind. If you position the mouse pointer directly in front of the characters you want to delete, then click the mouse, you can press the Del or Delete key to get rid of subsequent characters.

If you prefer sneaking up from behind, click the mouse after the character(s) you want to delete, and press the Backspace key.

Selecting and Moving

Word 97 sports a variety of tools for picking up text and moving it around in a document. The easiest is the old select-click-and-drag.

SELECTING TEXT: WHAT YOU NEED TO KNOW

If you're new to computers, *selecting* may be a foreign concept. Not to worry. You've undoubtedly seen it in action before. In Word 97, when you select something you turn it black—the characters appear white against a black background. Invariably, you select something before you do something to it—move it, delete it, something along those lines.

To select some text, just move the mouse pointer to the beginning of the text you want to select, and push the left mouse button down. Hold the button down while you swipe it across the text you want to select. It's a lot like wielding an electronic paintbrush.

If you've never selected much, practice a bit when you get to step 3 in the next Exercise. You'll be selecting like an old pro in no time.

XERCISE

Move Text by Dragging

1. Start with a new document. Click **New** if you need to.

2. Type a sentence or two.

3. Select some text near the end of the sentence (see Figure 8.2). Remember to let go of the mouse button when you're done selecting. The stuff you've selected should appear white on a black background.

FIGURE 8.2
Selecting "if you don't mind" at the end of a sentence.

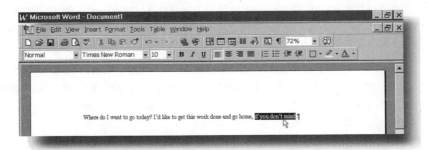

4. Move the selected text to a new location by clicking inside the selected area (that is, the area that has a black background), and dragging it to the desired location (see Figure 8.3).

FIGURE 8.3
Moving the selected text to the beginning of the sentence.

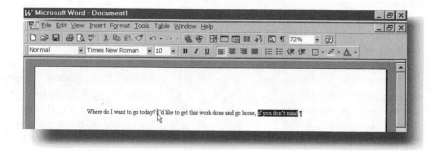

5. Finally, drop the text in its new location by letting go of the mouse button (see Figure 8.4).

FIGURE 8.4
Releasing the text in its new location.

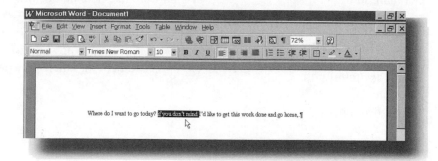

Using that basic select-click-and-drag method you can rearrange documents till the cows come home.

COPYING INSTEAD OF MOVING

If you want to copy text instead of moving it, simply hold down the Ctrl key before you start dragging. A little box with a plus sign shows up underneath the mouse pointer, and a new copy of the text will appear wherever the mouse pointer was sitting when you let go of the mouse button.

CANCELLING DRAG-AND-DROP

If you start to move or copy text using this drag-and-drop method, and you suddenly decide that you don't want to finish the job, drag the text back to where you started, or press the Esc or Escape key. That cancels out the whole thing, quickly and easily.

WORD: A SPEED DEVIL?

You can use drag and drop to move text a long way. If you drag the text to the top or the bottom of the screen, Word will scroll forward or backward in your document, only stopping when you move your mouse pointer back into the middle of the screen.

There's only one problem. Sometimes Word moves too fast! (You'll hit this problem, too, if you try to select a lot of text by moving the mouse pointer off the screen.) Yes, it's hard to believe, but sometimes Word turns into a speed devil when you least want it to. I haven't found a solution yet, aside from running on a slower computer.

Yeah. Sure.

If you select a bunch of characters and press the Del or Delete key, they'll be deleted. Another round of rocket science, eh?

SELECT FIRST

Okay, I'm being a little flippant. Sorry. There's actually an important principle sitting around here, one that may not be apparent if you haven't thought about it before. Almost always, Word wants you to act in a two-step fashion. First, you select whatever you want to change. Second, you apply the changes to whatever has been selected.

While that isn't a universal requirement, if you ever have trouble figuring out why Word won't do what you want it to do, keep it in mind. Select first. Then act.

You'd be surprised how many experienced Word users forget that simple principle.

The Clipboard

People talk about the Windows Clipboard as if it were an actual place. You move this to the Clipboard, you shove that off the Clipboard. Back and forth.

In fact, the Clipboard is just a figment of Windows' imagination. It's a convenient fiction that's been concocted to make it easier for you to visualize how Windows lets you move data back and forth within a document, and between documents and even different programs.

CLIPBOARD EXPOSED

Yes, what I'm saying is true. There is no physical location inside your computer where the Clipboard lives. It's just an imaginary thing, set up with typical programming smoke and mirrors. That may explain why you can lose stuff that's "on the Clipboard." If the application holding the information you put on the Clipboard goes south, it takes the Clipboard contents along with it.

Okay. So let's just pretend there's this thing called the Windows Clipboard. And let's pretend that you can use it from inside Word. What does the beast do for you?

First you have to realize that the Clipboard is a very, uh, limited place. It can only hold one thing at a time. If you have something in the Clipboard, and you put something else in the Clipboard, the stuff that was in there to begin with gets knocked out. That doesn't mean the Clipboard is small. Heavens no. It can hold gazillions of characters at a time. But it isn't smart enough to handle two different chunks of your documents at once.

With that warning, working with the Clipboard usually goes like this:

- You select whatever part of your Word document that you want to put on the Clipboard
- You tell Windows to copy the selected stuff onto the Clipboard
- You move to a different place in the document
- You tell Windows to take the stuff out of the Clipboard and stick it in your document at the indicated place

There's one minor variation in working with the Clipboard that's pretty common. Instead of copying the selected stuff onto the Clipboard, you can tell Word to copy it, but then delete it from inside the document. The usual method is called a *copy*. This variation is called a *cut*.

In both cases, when you copy stuff from the Clipboard into your document, it's called a *paste*.

XERCISE _____

Using the Clipboard

1. Once again, start with a clean document and type a sentence or two.

2. Select some text (see Figure 8.5).

FIGURE 8.5
Selecting text
for the
Clipboard
exercise.

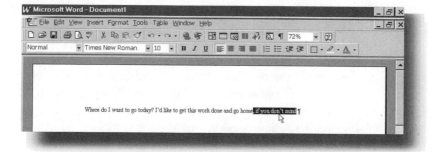

3. Let's cut the text and put it on the Clipboard. There are three easy ways to cut text: click **Edit**, then **Cut** (as shown in Figure 8.6); click the **Cut** ⚓ icon on the toolbar; or—the fastest way, once you get used to it—pressing Ctrl+X. If you've never used Ctrl+X, now's a good time to try it out.

FIGURE 8.6
Cutting the text.

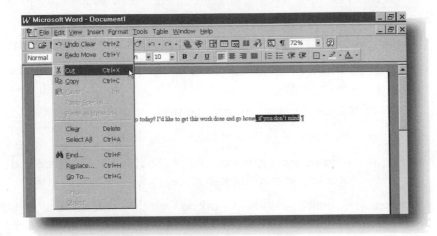

4. Move the insertion point to wherever you want the text to go. In this case (see Figure 8.7) I'm putting it in front of the question mark.

FIGURE 8.7
Relocating the insertion point to the destination.

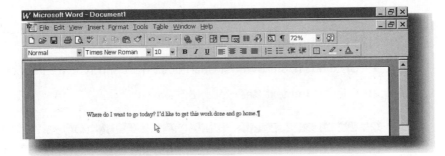

5. Now paste the text from the Clipboard into the document. There are four easy ways to paste text: click **Edit**, then **Paste** (as shown in Figure 8.8); click the **Paste** 📋 icon on the toolbar; press Ctrl+V; or, if you followed my advice in Chapter 6 to change Word's default setting, press the Ins or Insert key.

FIGURE 8.8
Pasting the
Clipboard
contents
back into the
document.

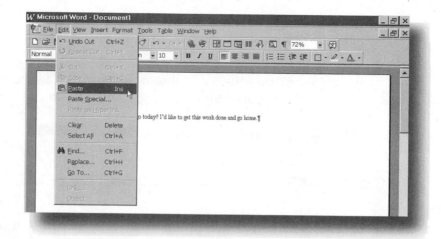

Building a Test Document

You're now in a position to put together a test document, one we can use for exercises through the remainder of this book. I won't presume to tell you what to put in your test document. But, uh, creativity counts.

*E*XERCISE

Create a Test Document

1. Start with a blank document. Type an interesting sentence or two. I've used one of my favorite passages from Mark Twain.

2. Select the text you've typed, *but not the paragraph mark* (see Figure 8.9).

FIGURE 8.9
Selecting text
in a test
document,
omitting the
paragraph
mark.

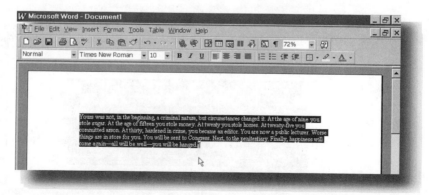

3. Copy the selected text to the Clipboard. I use Ctrl+C, but you can click **Edit**, then **Copy**, or you can click the **Copy** icon on the toolbar.

4. Put the insertion point immediately in front of the paragraph mark. Press the spacebar, then paste the Clipboard contents into the document via your favorite method (Ctrl+V, **Ins**, **Paste**, or **Edit**, **Paste**. See Figure 8.10).

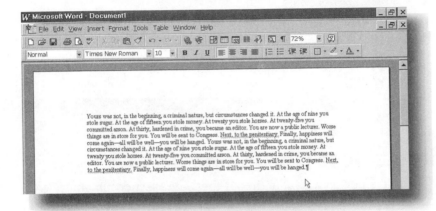

FIGURE 8.10
Making a second copy of the text in the first paragraph of the test document.

5. Repeat step 4 one more time—press the Spacebar, then copy the Clipboard contents into the paragraph.

6. Now select the whole paragraph, *including the paragraph mark* (see Figure 8.11). Copy the whole paragraph onto the Clipboard.

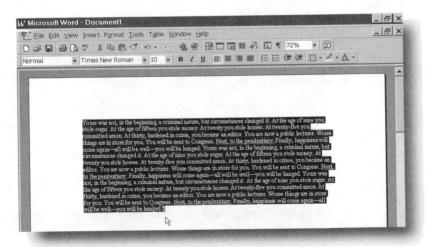

FIGURE 8.11
Copy the entire paragraph onto the Clipboard.

7. Repeatedly paste from the Clipboard back into the document. Do it 10 or 20 times, or more—whatever it takes to build a document that's three or more pages long (see Figure 8.12).

FIGURE 8.12
Paste and paste again, to bulk up the test document.

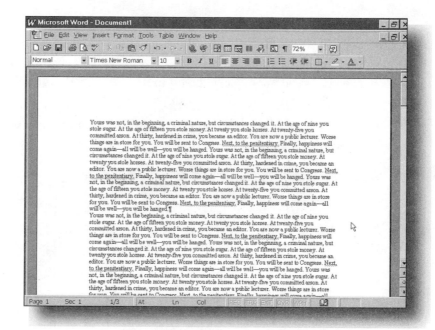

8. Save the document in the My Documents folder. Give it a name like test.doc. (Click **File**, then **Save**, type `test` in the **File name** box, click **Save**, see Figure 8.13.)

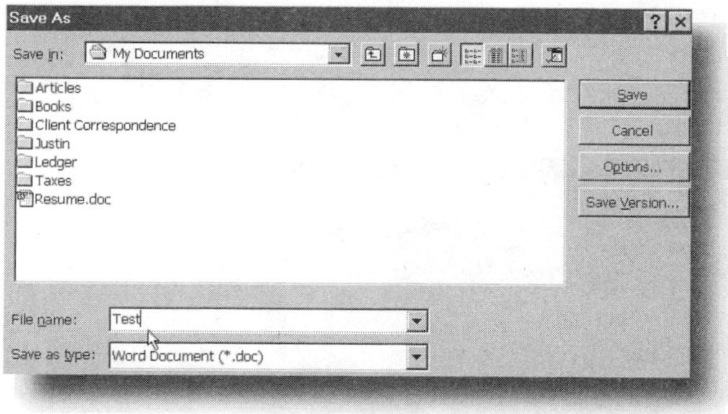

FIGURE 8.13
Saving c:\My Documents\ test.doc.

We'll use test.doc frequently. In fact, if you have resume.doc from the preceding chapter (or any other Word 97 document, for that matter) handy, we'll use it and test.doc in this interesting multiple-document exercise.

*E*XERCISE

Copying from Document to Document

1. You should have test.doc open and freshly saved from the preceding Exercise. In addition, you're going to need a second Word 97 document, such as resume.doc, which you saved in Chapter 7.

2. Open resume.doc by clicking **File**, **Open**, choosing resume.doc, and clicking **Open** (see Figure 8.14).

FIGURE 8.14
Opening resume.doc for the copying exercise.

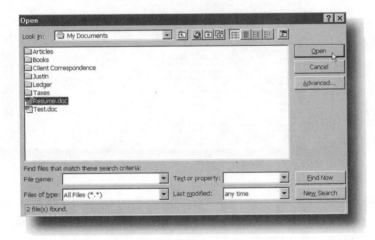

3. Word 97 now has two documents open: test.doc and resume.doc. You can verify that by clicking the **Window** menu (see Figure 8.15). Both documents should be listed.

FIGURE 8.15
Two documents are currently open.

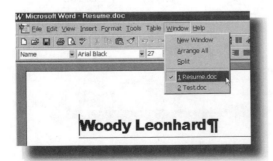

4. It's easy to flip back and forth between the two documents. Just click **Window**, then **2. Test.doc** to look at test.doc, and click **Window**, then **1. Resume.doc** to get back to resume.doc.

5. Let's copy that big, bold name from resume.doc to test.doc. Start by putting resume.doc on top (if necessary, click **Window**, then **1. Resume.doc**).

6. Select the text you want to copy. (In my case, it's **Woody Leonhard**. See Figure 8.16.)

FIGURE 8.16
Selecting the name in resume.doc.

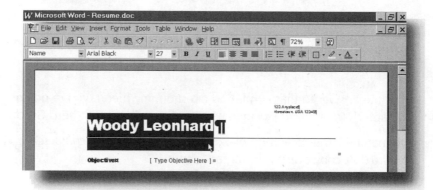

7. Copy the selected text to the Clipboard. I'll use Ctrl+C; you can pick whatever method you like.

8. Switch over to test.doc and click **Window**, then **2**. Test.doc.

9. Let's put that name at the beginning of test.doc. Position the insertion point by clicking at the beginning of test.doc (see Figure 8.17).

FIGURE 8.17
Positioning the insertion point where the pasted text should go.

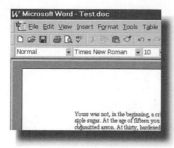

10. Now paste that big, bold name into the beginning of test.doc. I'll use Ctrl+V; you can use whichever method you like (see Figure 8.18).

FIGURE 8.18
Pasting the big, bold name into test.doc.

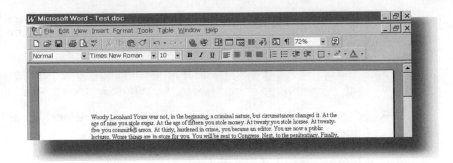

11. What the %$#@!? What happened to that big, bold name? Why is it a puny, scrunchy thing? What's going on here?

For the answer to that perplexing question, my friend, you're going to have to read Chapter 10, "Making Documents Look Good." Heh heh heh. Gotcha, didn't I?

Remember: *The paragraph mark is the most important character in Word 97.* And you didn't copy over the paragraph mark!

Getting Around

ORD 97 HAS DOZENS—MANY DOZENS—of key combinations for moving
around inside a document, selecting text, and manipulating items
that exist in documents. Truth be told, I don't know more than a
handful of people who use more than a very few key combinations.

How the Keys Work

No doubt you've already figured out the common navigation keys and how they work.

TAKE CTRL

Combining Ctrl with those keys turns them into super keys. Ctrl+↓ goes to the beginning of the next paragraph. Ctrl+↑ goes to the beginning of the preceding paragraph. Ctrl+Home goes to the start of the document. Ctrl+End goes to the end.

Common Keys

At the risk of restating the obvious:

- Arrow keys ↑ ↓
  ← → move up, down, left, or right.

- Home goes to the beginning of the current line.

- End goes to the end of the current line.

- Page Up (or PgUp) and Page Down (PgDn) go up or down a screen—*not* a page.

- Scroll Lock and Pause don't do anything.

EASY SCREEN SHOTS

From time to time you might want to take a snapshot of the Word screen, particularly if you need to show somebody how something is going wrong. Few people realize it, but you have all the tools you need built into Word. To take a shot of the entire screen, press the Print Screen key. Then click **Edit**, **Paste**, and the whole screen will appear in your document. It's a high-quality shot: people will be able to see all the details from the screen in the document. It prints pretty nicely, too.

- Print Screen (PrtScr) takes a snapshot of the current screen and puts it on the clipboard. Not exactly what you expected, eh?

If you're an extremely fast touch typist who dreads the thought of moving your fingers to the (*eek!*) mouse, you might want to run down and memorize the key combinations. You can

If you only want to take a shot of the *active* window (that is, the window that has its title bar highlighted), press Alt+Print Screen. That puts the current active window on the Clipboard. You can then paste it into your document (or any other Windows application, for that matter).

find endless lists of shortcut keys by starting the Office Assistant (that is, pressing F1), typing shortcut keys, and pressing Enter (see Figure 9.1).

FIGURE 9.1
All the short-cut keys fit to print.

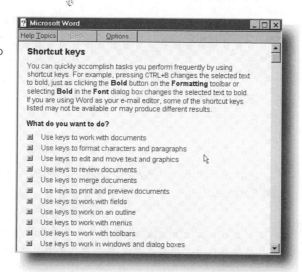

Worthwhile Key Combinations

If you're basically lazy like me and unwilling to spend hours wading through (much less memorizing) that key combination garbage, chances are good all you want to know is the important stuff.

Great. That's what I'm here for.

Here are ten key combinations most people find useful. Don't bother memorizing them. You'll remember them if you use them enough to make it worthwhile. Write these out on a yellow stick-on note and put them on your monitor, down at the bottom where they're easiest to see. Most of all, remember that they're meant to be shortcuts—if you have to search around for them, don't bother. Almost all of them have equivalents sitting under the **Edit** menu.

Key	Description
F1	Brings up the Office Assistant
Ctrl+A	Selects the whole document
Ctrl+C	Copies whatever is selected to the Clipboard

continues

continued

Key	Description
Ctrl+V	Pastes the contents of the Clipboard into the document
Ctrl+X	Cuts whatever is selected to the Clipboard
Shift+F5	Goes to the last place you were editing
Ctrl+Home	Goes to the beginning of the document
Ctrl+End	Goes to the end of the document
Print Screen	Puts a shot of the screen on the Clipboard
Alt+Print Screen	Puts a shot of the current active window on the Clipboard

You may find a few more useful key combination hidden in Word 97's darker regions, but by and large they're a pain, unless you have a photographic memory. As the saying goes, don't sweat the small stuff. And when it comes to memorizing key combinations, it's all small stuff.

The IntelliMouse Wheel

It's the scrollbar on the right side of the screen that lets you move through your documents. Click the little up or down wedgies to move a few lines at a time. Click inside the scrollbar to move a screenfull at a time. Grab the thumb and drag it to whatever page you may be interested in and let go.

☞ *I talked about the vertical scrollbar on page 101.*

Around the same time Microsoft released Office 97, the folks in Redmond came up with a redesigned mouse that promised to revolutionize navigating through Office documents. The marketers anointed it with the moniker "IntelliMouse." Some early versions of Office 97 came with the IntelliMouse inside the box—an interesting way to kick-start sales of a commodity with only questionable improvements over the plain, generic mouse attached to every PC sold in the past century or two.

Since that time, a couple of mouse manufacturers have jumped on the roller band-wagon, so you'll see wheeled rodents of various stripes on retailers' shelves.

Personally, I have a couple of IntelliMouses (IntelliMeese?), but I don't use the roller very often. It takes a little more brain power than I can muster to keep the roller going in the right direction while trying to accomplish some real work. Maybe I just haven't used it enough to get accustomed to the different feel. Whatever.

If you own an IntelliMouse, or one of its clones, you may well feel differently. In that case, you should be aware of several wheel moves that really can come in handy, in the right circumstances:

DOING WHEELIES

If you decide that you like the wheel, you can always get rid of the vertical scrollbar. That frees up a little extra space on the screen—although most people want to reclaim more space at the top and bottom of the screen rather than the right edge. Anyway, to get rid of the vertical scrollbar, click **Tools**, **Options**, **View**, and uncheck the box marked **Vertical scroll bar** (see Figure 9.2).

I *don't* recommend that you get rid of the scrollbar. If you zap it, you'll be losing Word's (nifty) show-the-page-number-when-you-click-the-thumb feature. You'll also lose the repeat Find function, which I'll describe in the next section. But, well, *de gustibus non est disputandum*, eh?

(Latin lesson for the day: *de gustibus non est disputandum* = "there is no disputing tastes." Or, as R Crumb so succinctly put it, "Diff'rent strokes for diff'rent folks, I guess.")

- Roll the wheel to go up and down, just as if you were clicking on the scrollbar.

- Click (push down on) the wheel and move the mouse up or down to scroll up and down in your document. The farther up or down you go, the faster the scrolling. Click the wheel again to stop scrolling.

- You should try zooming with the wheel—just once. (That's probably all it will take for you to give up, because you'll likely develop an advanced case of motion sickness or vertigo.) Hold down the Ctrl key and roll the wheel.

FIGURE 9.2
IntelliMouse users might want to consider removing the vertical scrollbar.

Find

Quite possibly the most powerful, and most frequently used, document navigation method, Find searches a document for characters that you specify. For example, if you want to search through a document and find every occurrence of the phrase "Party of the First Part," the Find function hops through the document, at your command, stopping each time "Party of the First Part" appears.

It's important that you understand some of Find's nuances, so I'm going to take you through several variations on the standard Find. Let's start with an easy one: bone stock Find.

XERCISE

Basic Find

1. If you still have test.doc sitting on the screen from the previous Exercise, you're in good shape. If not, open test.doc (click **File**, **Open**, click **test.doc**, click **Open**).

2. Pick a word from test.doc. Doesn't matter which one. For this example, I'm going to choose "editor." (Book editors just love it when I do that.) You're going to search for all occurrences of that word.

3. Click **Edit**, then **Find**. You should see the Find and Replace dialog box, per Figure 9.3. If you can see the screen animation, and you look closely, you'll

notice that the Find and Replace dialog box springs from the **Select Brrowse Object** 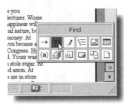 dot near the bottom of the vertical scrollbar. Word, in its inimitable way, is trying to show you that **Find and Replace** lives in that little dot.

FIGURE 9.3
The Find and Replace dialog box, which also covers Go To.

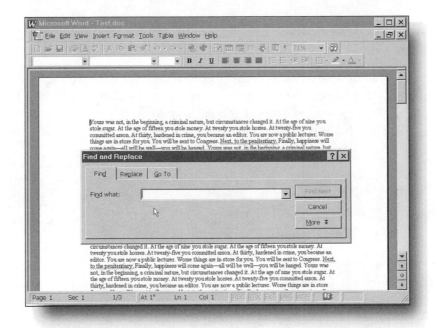

4. Let's visit **Find and Replace** where it lives. (Those of you who disabled the vertical scrollbar will have to bypass this step.) Click **Cancel** in the Find and Replace dialog box. Then click the little **Select Brrowse Object** dot, and click the **Find** pair of binoculars (see Figure 9.4). The Find and Replace dialog box (see Figure 9.3) comes back.

FIGURE 9.4
You now know where Find and Replace lives.

5. Type the word you want to find in the **Find what** box. In my case, I've typed in editor (see Figure 9.5).

FIGURE 9.5
Type the characters you want to find in the Find what box.

6. To find a match in the document, click **Find Next**. Word hops down to the first occurrence of the characters you're searching for (see Figure 9.6). Sometimes the Find and Replace dialog box will cover up the characters that Word has found. If you don't see the highlighted characters, move the box around until they become visible.

FIGURE 9.6
Word finds the characters of the word "editor."

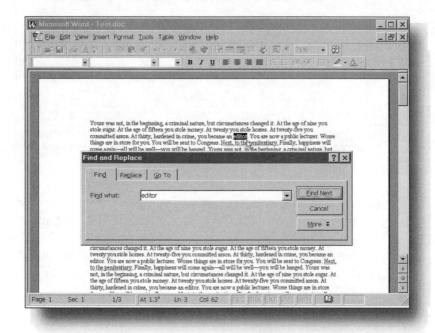

7. Notice how the Find and Replace dialog box sticks around. Go ahead and click down in the document and see how you can type, delete characters, or do just about anything while the Find and Replace dialog box just sits there.

8. Click **Find Next**. Word jumps down to the next occurrence of the characters you've typed (see Figure 9.7). Cool, eh? Hang on. It gets considerably cooler.

A LA MODE
This is one of the few Word 97 dialog boxes that lets you play around with the document while the dialog box stays on the screen. The techy term for this kind of dialog box is a *modeless* box. Don't ask me why Microsoft chose that weird terminology, but it makes a great trivia question. Enjoy this step while you can, because it'll be a long time before you see another modeless Word dialog box.

9. Let's face it. That big Find and Replace dialog box on the screen really takes over things. It's hard to see what you're doing while the box just sits there—and the box doesn't help much once you've set up the search. So click **Cancel** and get rid of the box.

FIGURE 9.7
On to the next occurrence of "editor."

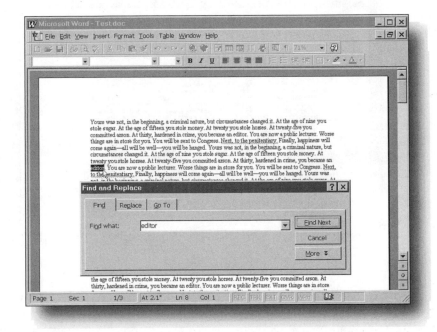

10. See the blue double-wedgie just below the **Select Browse Object** dot where **Find and Replace** lives? Move your mouse over there and let it sit (or hover) for a second or two (see Figure 9.8).

FIGURE 9.8
Next Find/GoTo on the vertical scrollbar.

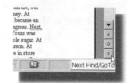

11. Guess what? To do a Find Next, you don't need that huge dialog box. All you need to know is the trick! Click that blue down double-wedgie and Word moves on to the next occurrence of your Find characters (see Figure 9.9). But wait! There's more!

FIGURE 9.9
Clicking the blue down double-wedgie propels Word to the next occurrence.

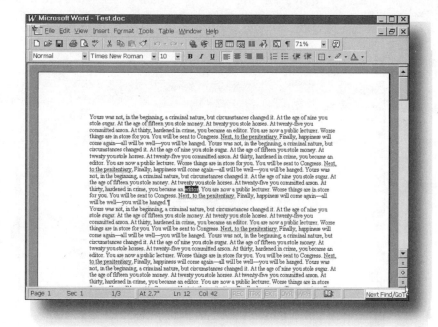

12. See the blue *up* double-wedgie, just above the **Select Browse Object** dot where **Find and Replace** lives? Can you guess what that one does? Yeah. You're pretty bright. Go ahead and click it, and watch as Word searches *backward*—toward the beginning of the document—for the text you seek (see Figure 9.10).

FIGURE 9.10
Repeating
the search,
this time
toward the
start of the
document.

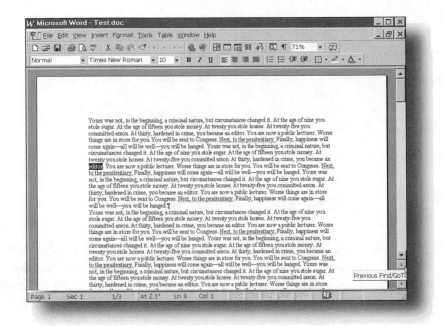

Practice that exercise a couple of times. I think you'll find it one of the best time-saving devices Word 97 has to offer.

SPEEDING UP YOUR SEARCH
When Word 97 does a search, it starts from the current location of the insertion point. So if you want to skip over a bunch of stuff—say, start your search in the middle of a document—go to the place you want to start the search and click the mouse to move the insertion point to that location.

That's the most basic kind of search Word offers. Now let's try a somewhat more complex search.

*E*XERCISE

A More Interesting Search

1. Click the **Select Browse Object** 🔲 dot where **Find and Replace** lives. You'll get the Find and Replace box, of course, as shown in Figure 9.3.

2. Click the **More** button. You'll see a variety of options, ways that Word will modify your search, to narrow it down to snag only those characters you want to find (see Figure 9.11).

FIGURE 9.11
The More
part of the
Find and
Replace dia-
log box.

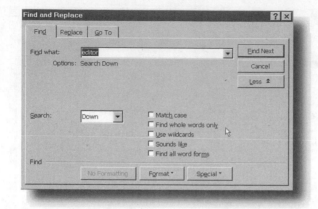

3. Look for a capitalized word in test.doc. In my case, I've chosen the word **Worse**. Type that word in the **Find what** box. Then click the checkbox marked **Match case**. Word will tell you that it's going to search down (that is, toward the end of the document), and that it will only stop when it matches the upper/lower case characters in the **Find what** box (see Figure 9.12).

FIGURE 9.12
A Match case
search in
Word's Find.

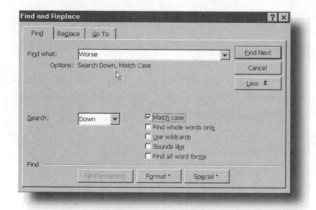

4. Click **Find Next**. Word will scan through test.doc, starting wherever the insertion point happens to be, and look for the characters in the **Find what** box, but only stop if there's an exact match on the upper/lower case characters (see Figure 9.13).

FIGURE 9.13
An exact
match for
Worse, both
upper- and
lowercase.

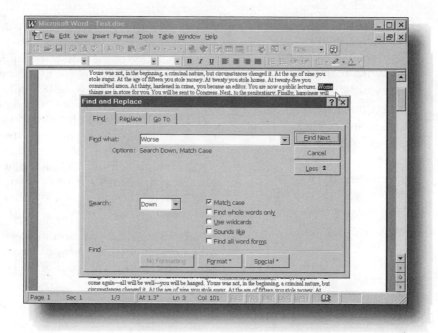

5. Try playing with this extended Find feature for a bit. I bet you'll find lots of interesting combinations. If you want to know precisely what each of those More options mean (and, believe me, they aren't exactly intuitive!) click the ? in the upper-right corner, then click the option that befuddles you (see Figure 9.14).

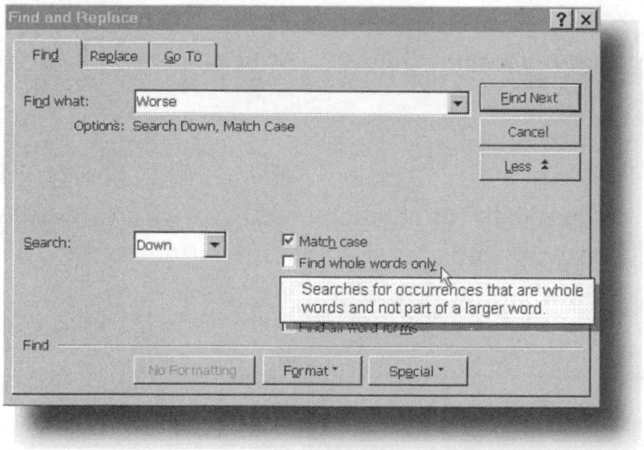

FIGURE 9.14
Immediate
help in the
Find and
Replace dia-
log box,
courtesy of
the ? icon.

In general, I haven't had much luck with the **Sounds like** and **Find all word forms** choices. In my experience, computers don't do very well at listening or verb declensions. (I'll probably hang up my keyboard when they do.) But the others work quite well. Your mileage may vary, of course.

WHAT'S A WILDCARD?
One of the most powerful Find options—and one of the hardest to figure out—is the **Use wildcards** checkbox, which lets you specify parts of words and have Word fill in the blanks. Single missing letters are represented by **?** and multiple letters are denoted *****. For example, if you ask Word to find **b?ll** it will stop on both **bill** and **bull**. If you specify **b*ll**, Word will stop on both of those, plus **blackball**.

To get a full list of wildcards that Word will recognize (and there are many of them!), click **?**, then **Use wildcards**, and click the **For more information** button.

TARGETING YOUR SEARCH

You can limit a search to a specific part of your document. Just select the text you want to search before clicking on the **Select Browse Object** ⬚ dot. Word will look through the selected text and, if it doesn't find a match, ask you if you want to continue searching the rest of the document.

To tell the truth, I've only touched the surface of all the things Find can do. If you want to look up something you've searched for recently, click the down arrow at the end of the **Find what** box. If you want to look for an oddball character—a paragraph mark, say, or any number of consecutive spaces (*white space*), click the **Special** button. You can also try playing with the **Format** button, but you'll probably want to go through the next chapter before you tackle that one.

Replace

Word 97 will not only search for characters ten ways from Tuesday, it can replace the characters it finds with other characters of your choosing. That's what the Replace function does.

*E*XERCISE

Replace

1. If it isn't already open from the preceding Exercise, open test.doc. Move to the beginning of the document either by scrolling and clicking at the beginning, or by pressing Ctrl+Home.

2. Click the **Select Browse Object** ⊡ dot where **Find and Replace** lives.
   Then click the **Replace** tab. (If you have disabled your vertical scrollbar, click
   Edit, then **Replace**.) If you can see a button marked **Less**, uncheck all the
   boxes in the lower half of the dialog box—**Match case** may be checked, if
   you're following along here closely—then click the **Less** button. (The **More**
   options in Replace match those you saw for Find, in Figure 9.11.) The dialog
   box should look like Figure 9.15.

FIGURE 9.15
The Replace
dialog box, in
abbreviated
form.

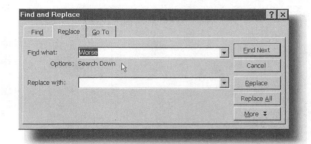

3. Choose a word or phrase you'd like to change in test.doc, and what you'd
   like to change it to. Type the former in the **Find what** box, and the latter in
   the **Replace with** box. In Figure 9.16, I chose Mark Twain's phrase **in the
   beginning** and decided to replace it with **originally**.

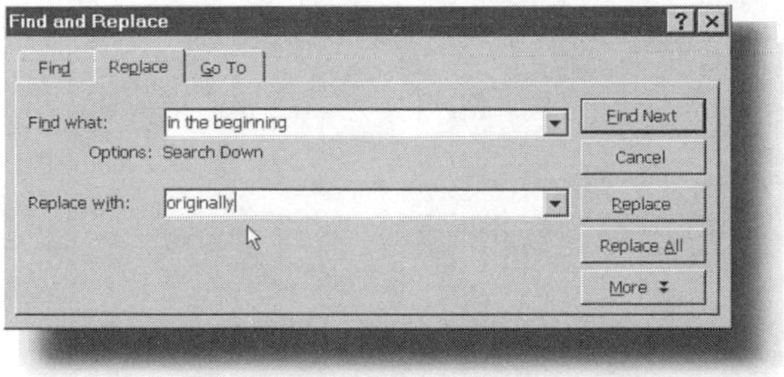

FIGURE 9.16
Replacing "in
the begin-
ning" with
"originally."

4. Click **Find Next**. Word should find the first occurrence of the characters
   you want to replace and stop there so you can consider whether you really
   want to replace them (see Figure 9.17).

5. If, upon consideration, you really do want to replace the characters—in this
   case, replace **in the beginning** with **originally**, click the **Replace** button.
   In a lightning-fast move, Word not only replaces the chosen characters, it
   moves down to the next occurrence of the characters in the **Find what** box

(see Figure 9.18). If you're not convinced that it all happened that quickly, scroll back to the first occurrence and confirm that it's been replaced.

FIGURE 9.17
Stopped at
"in the begin-
ning."

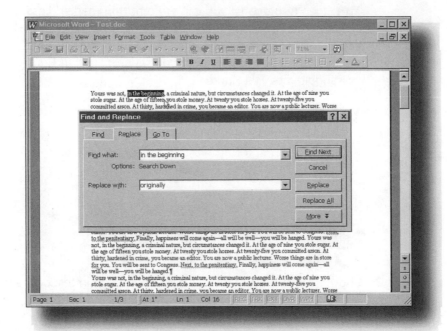

FIGURE 9.18
One replace
done, another
in progress.

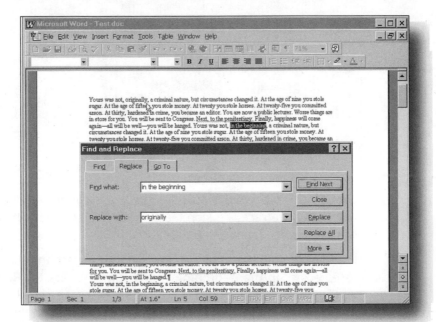

6. Continue through the document this way. If you decide that you don't want to replace a particular occurrence of the **Find what** characters, don't click the **Replace** button; just click **Find Next**.

WATCH OUT!

Be careful! **Replace All** is a mighty dangerous option. One of the first Windows books I ever wrote had an address book in it, listing products and addresses from all the major Windows-oriented hardware and software manufacturers. One of the editors at that publishing company (no, it isn't QUE!) got tired or lazy or whatever one night, and decided he didn't like my abbreviating the word "Road" as "Rd". So he did a Word **Replace All** of **Rd** to **Road**. Unfortunately, he didn't limit the replace to match case, or whole words only.

I didn't notice until the book came out. It was embarrassing to see how some hardware manufacturers offered, oh, *Video boaRoads*.

7. If, at some point, you decide you want to replace all the occurrences of the **Find what** characters, click **Replace All**. Word will do your bidding, then pop up a message that tells you how many times the string was replaced.

8. This is a good point to give test.doc a rest. Click **File**, then **Close**. When Word asks if you want to save changes, click **No**.

Replace is quite smart, in many respects. For example, it adjusts capitalization: If the word you replace is capitalized in the original document, its replacement will be capitalized as well.

STICKY SETTINGS

Word 97's Find and Replace settings are "sticky." For example, if you try to find a phrase and click the **Match case** box, the next time you do a Find, the **Match case** box will still be checked—even if you search for a different bunch of characters.

Worse, the settings are sticky across both Finds and Replaces. If you find a phrase and click the **Match case** box, the next time you do a Replace it too will have the **Match case** box checked.

Beware! Many a Word buff has gone utterly insane trying to figure out why running a Find suddenly won't find something right in front of Word's nose.

Go To, Good Man, Go To

You may have noticed there's one more tab on the Find and Replace dialog box. It's marked **Go To** and, well, it lets you Go To various places in a document (see Figure 9.19).

FIGURE 9.19
W000000000
00000 tab.

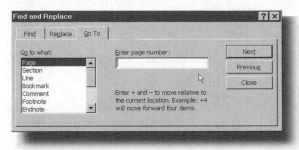

I won't go into too much detail on **Go To**, simply because it's rarely all that useful for the garden-variety Word user. If you want to go to a specific page number, you'll probably find it easier to click the vertical scrollbar's thumb and slide it to the page in question. The other things you can Go To are pretty esoteric, at least for beginners.

10

Making Documents Look Good

IN THIS CHAPTER WE'RE GOING TO TAKE a look at formatting—changing the appearance of various components of your documents. When most people say they want to learn Office, the very first thing they think about is making their Word documents look professional. So I'm going to take some extra time in this chapter (the longest chapter in the book) and make sure you get a very thorough look at the formatting options available to you, and how best to use those options.

Before we get going, I want you to tattoo this mantra on the inside of your eyelids:

Select first, then apply formatting

- If you want to change the appearance of a few characters in your document, select the characters first, then apply the new formatting.

- If you want to change a few words, select the words, then change them.

- If you want to change a few sentences, select the sentences, then change them.

- If you want to change a few paragraphs, select the paragraphs, then change them.

Word 97 just works like that. If you want to change the appearance of something, Word wants to know *what* you want to change before it applies the changes. Select first, and then apply the formatting.

I'll have one more mantra for you, later in this chapter. Both mantras are *crucial* allies in the battle to get Word to work for you, not against you.

Select first, and then apply formatting. Got it?

Characters

We'll start with Word's most fundamental component: characters. You probably know all about changing fonts, or making words bold, but bear with me. It's not quite as simple as you think.

ANOTHER HARD AND FAST RULE, EH WOODY?
Okay, okay. There are a couple of minor exceptions to the select first, then apply formatting rule. (For example, you don't have to select an entire document before you change page margins.) But the exceptions are few and far between, and I'll point them out when we discuss them.

Font Changes from the Toolbar

Exercise

Changing Fonts

1. Open test.doc.

2. Select a few words. It doesn't really matter what or where. I chose a random sentence from Mark Twain's priceless prose (see Figure 10.1).

FONTS GALORE!
If you've never played with fonts very much, you're in for a treat. Back in the good old days (say, five years ago), fonts were expensive—I once paid $119 for a font I really wanted—and many of the old fonts weren't all that good. Nowadays, fonts practically grow on trees and it's easy to find collections of excellent fonts for less than a buck apiece. Much less.

Font purists insist that there's a difference between a *font* and a *typeface,* and quibble over other terminology. They're right. But I'm going to succumb to popular lingo and use terms here the way you'll hear them used on the street.

FIGURE 10.1
First, select the text where you want the font changes to appear.

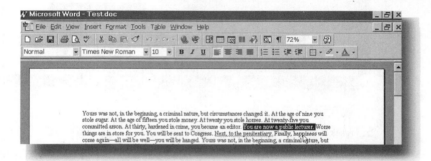

3. Change the font. The easiest way to do that is to click the down-arrow to the right of the font list, and choose a different font. In Figure 10.2 I've chosen Arial Black, a thick font frequently used for headings and posters.

4. Change the font size. With the text still selected, click the right-arrow next to the **Font size** ⌷ icon and choose a big font size. I chose 36 point in Figure 10.3. A *point* is a rather esoteric measurement, equal to one-72nd of an inch (meaning that 72-point type creates letters that are an inch tall). Suffice it to say that 36 point is pretty big (half an inch), 6 point is pretty small, and most text looks best at 10, 11, or 12 point.

FIGURE 10.2
Change the font to Arial Black.

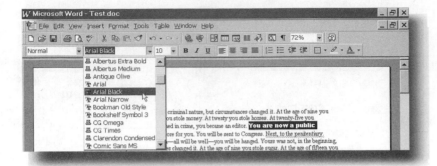

FIGURE 10.3
Boost the font size to 36 points.

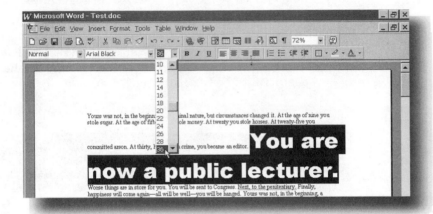

5. Make the text italic. With that same text still selected, click the **Italic** [*I*] icon. That makes the text italic, as you can see in Figure 10.4.

6. You probably won't be too surprised to discover that the **Bold** [**B**] icon turns text bold, and the

WEIRD HIGHLIGHTING MOVES
I don't know why, but when you apply highlighting to characters in Word 97, Word takes it upon itself to scoot your cursor (uh, the insertion point) to the end of the stuff that has just been highlighted. That's very distracting if you're expecting Word to act consistently—no other formatting pops the cursor off the selection. Don't let it take you by surprise.

Ah well. As Emerson said, way back in 1841, "A foolish consistency is the hobgoblin of little minds, adored by little statesmen and philosophers and divines. With consistency a great soul has simply nothing to do."

Underline ⊍ icon puts an underline under whatereryou have selected. Play with those buttons if you like.

7. Word 97 has a feature that lets you highlight text, just as if you'd run over it with a semi-transparent highlighting pen. To put a yellow highlight on the selected text, press the **Highlight** ⊘ icon (see Figure 10.5). Word 97 isn't limited to yellow highlighting, of course. (*Ach! So pedestrian!*) You can choose from a rainbow of colors by clicking the down arrow next to the **Highlight** ⊘ icon.

FIGURE 10.4
Changing over to italic.

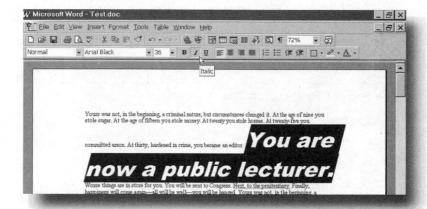

FIGURE 10.5
Adding a highlight to selected text.

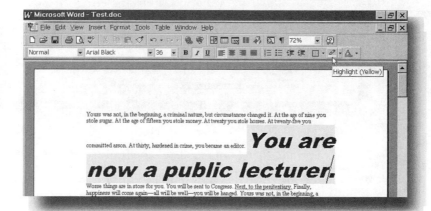

8. Finally, you can play around with Word's ability to change the color of selected text. Just click the **Font Color** ⓐ icon to get the hang of it.

9. When you're done monkeying around with all these toolbar-based font choices, close test.doc without saving changes. (That is, click **File**, then **Close**, and when Word asks if you want to save changes, click **No**.)

That's what you can do to fonts from that lower toolbar. (It probably won't surprise you too much to discover that the lower toolbar is called the *Formatting toolbar*.) It ends up that's just a small part of the Word character formatting shtick.

Font Changes from the Dialog Box

To see the whole panoply of Word character formatting choices, you have to open up the Format Font dialog box. It really should be called the Format Character dialog box, but sometimes you just have to go with the Microsoft flow.

*E*XERCISE

The Format Font Dialog Box

1. Open test.doc.

2. Select some random text. In Figure 10.6, I've selected a different sentence from Twain's writing.

FIGURE 10.6
Selecting text for major font changes.

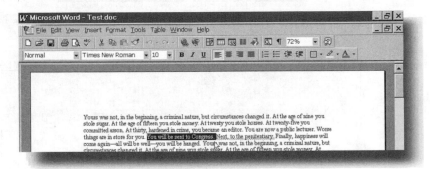

3. Click **Format**, then **Font**. You'll see the Font dialog box, shown in Figure 10.7.

4. Many of the choices in the Font dialog box mirror those available from the Formatting toolbar: font name, size, bold, italic, underline, color, and the like. The major advantage this dialog box has over the toolbar lies in its **Preview** screen: You can actually see the changes being made to your characters before those changes take effect.

FIGURE 10.7
The Font dialog box—the fount of all font changes.

5. Try one or two of the effects on offer. For example, in Figure 10.8 I've chosen both the **Shadow** and **Outline** options. Yes, the result does look just as horrible as what you see here.

FIGURE 10.8
Shadow and Outline on Times New Roman.

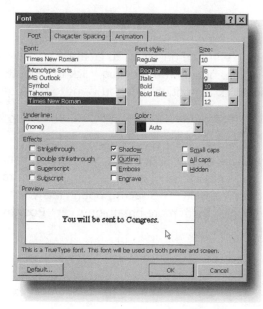

6. The one font formatting option that's worthy of mention here is **Hidden**. When you mark characters as Hidden, they don't appear on the screen, or in printouts, unless you take specific steps to unhide them. I know teachers who use hidden text to jot down answers to exams. They'll print the exams out normally to hand to students, then they'll go back and print all the hidden text (the answers) along with the questions to create a key. To learn about hidden text, or any other option in this dialog, click the **?** button in the upper-right corner, then click the option that you want to have clarified.

KERNING

The last setting you'll see in the Character Spacing dialog box says **Kerning for fonts**. Kerning is a method of squishing specific pairs of letters together. For example, you'll frequently see A and W squished together because they nestle up so nicely (see Figure 10.10). Kerning is something you can only do to specific fonts, ones that have been set up by the font manufacturer with kerning information. Most of the time you don't want to make the computer do all the extra work involved with kerning. For small fonts, it usually isn't worth the effort, as the effect of kerning is very subtle. But for larger fonts, perhaps 14 or 16 or 20 points or above, kerning can be worthwhile; it's mostly a question of what you like, and how much you're willing to slow down Word to achieve your desired effect. In the **Points and above** box you tell Word how big characters have to be before Word should worry about kerning them.

7. We've only just started working with character formatting. Click the **Character Spacing** tab (see Figure 10.9).

8. Try fiddling with these settings a bit. They can come in handy. The **Scale** setting adjusts your characters horizontally—makes them fatter or skinnier, without making them taller. The **Spacing** option lets you squish characters closer together, or give them more breathing room. **Position** makes characters superscript or subscript.

FIGURE 10.9
Adjust character spacing.

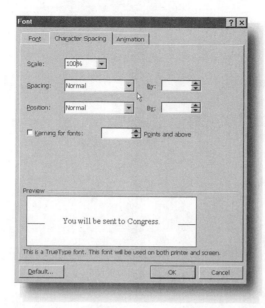

FIGURE 10.10
The letters AW in Times New Roman 72 point, unkerned (above) and kerned (below).

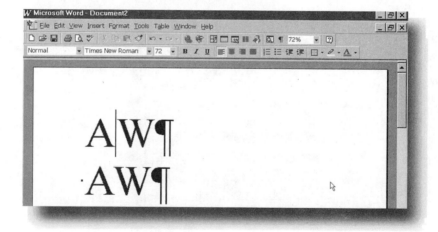

9. Now click the **Animation** tab (see Figure 10.11). Here you'll find formatting special effects—cool and colorful ways of highlighting text that will show up on the screen, but not on the printer.

FIGURE 10.11
Word 97's font anima-tion effects.

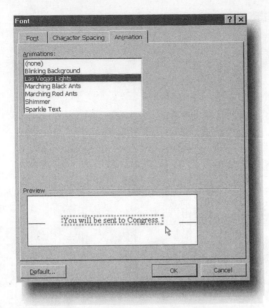

FIGURE 10.12
The quick way to change fonts in all your new blank documents.

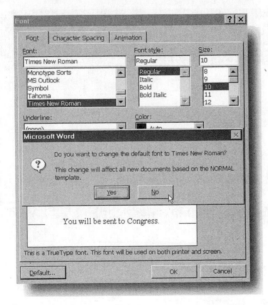

10. One last experiment before we leave this exercise. There's a fast way to get to the Font dialog box. Try it and you may get hooked. If you can see the Font dialog box right now, click **Cancel** to get out of it. Make sure you have some characters selected in test.doc, then right-click the characters. As shown in Figure 10.13, one of your choices will be Font. Click it, and the Font dialog box appears quick as a wink.

11. Close test.doc without saving your changes.

CHANGING THE DEFAULT FONT
In the lower-left corner of all three Font dialog boxes (Figure 10.8, Figure 10.9, and Figure 10.11), you'll see a button marked **Default**. That's a very powerful button with a very lousy description. If you click it, you'll get a message (see Figure 10.12) that tells you it'll change the "default font (for) all new documents based on the NORMAL template." Let me explain what that technobabble means.

Right now, with Word 97 running the way it comes straight out of the box, whenever you create a new, blank document, Word turns all the characters you type into Times New Roman font at 10 point. You can change the font around, of course, by selecting the characters you want to change and applying the changes. Still, everything starts in Times New Roman 10 point, and it takes extra effort if you want to make the primary text in all of your documents, say, Garamond 11 point.

You can change the default font—the font Word automatically uses whenever you create a new, blank document—by selecting the font here, clicking the **Default** button, and responding **Yes** to that atrociously worded message about "...all new documents based on the NORMAL template."

Note that this changes the font in the current document, and for all new, blank documents created *in the future*. It does nothing to documents that already exist.

I'm told that this is the most frequently asked question among all Word 97 users. Too bad the folks answering the phone at Microsoft have to wade through all this gobbledygook to answer the question. (Why can't Word have a Format menu item that says "Format/All new blank documents"?)

FIGURE 10.13
The right-click context menu that tunnels straight into the Font dialog box.

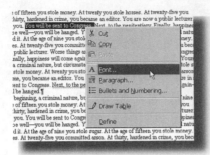

Sticky Font Formatting

By far the fastest way to write a paper or report or book is to just get the words down, then go back later and apply formatting. If you don't confuse yourself with italics here and bolds there, the words can be cranked out much more quickly and the appearance can follow much later, almost as an afterthought.

That's sure a great theory, isn't it? Truth be told, I can't work like that, and I bet you can't either. Just about everybody edits as they type.

There are three tricks for those of us who don't want to take the time to go back through what we've typed, carefully selecting the characters we want to format, then applying the formatting. Each needs to be used with a bit of understanding and caution.

XERCISE

Quick Tricks for Character Formatting

1. Open test.doc.

2. Click once inside any word, then click the **Italic** icon on the toolbar. The *whole word* turns italic. In Figure 10.14, I clicked inside the word Yours, and then clicked the

WHERE'S THE HIGHLIGHTING FORMAT IN THE FONT DIALOG BOX ?
If you were watching very carefully, you might've noticed that one of the toolbar buttons, the **Highlighting** icon, doesn't have an associated entry in the Font dialog box. In fact, it's true. There's no way to control highlighting from any Word dialog box. The only way you have to work with highlighting is from the toolbar.

It all has to do with the odd way Microsoft's programmers decided to handle highlighting. Don't get me going on that one…

Italic [I] icon. *Yours* turned italic. This is a very handy two-click trick that can save you a lot of time.

FIGURE 10.14
Click once inside a word, and the whole word gets formatted.

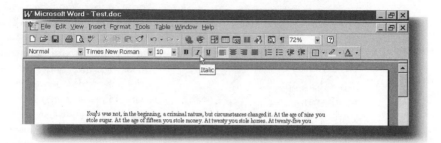

3. Click anywhere inside test.doc and start typing. After you've typed a few letters, click the **Bold** [B] bold icon, and resume typing. See how all the subsequent characters are bold? Type a few more characters, then click the **Bold** [B] icon again. That turns bold off so you can go back to typing normally.

4. Click once inside the group of bold characters you just typed in Step 3. See how the new characters come out bold, too? When you're typing in Word 97, each new character you type inherits the formatting of the immediately preceding character. The inheritance works with the font name, point size, bold, italic, underscore, color—just about everything except highlighting.

TAMING BERSERK FONTS
How many times have you been typing along when character formatting goes berserk? Suddenly your characters turn bold or italic (typically because you accidentally press the Ctrl+B or Ctrl+I key combinations, which turn text bold or italic respectively), and then everything you type from that point on comes out bold or italic. To fix the problem, select all the text that has gone haywire, click the **Bold** [B] or **Italic** [I] icon, and your typing should go back to normal.

5. Word has one more way to accomplish quick, on-the-fly formatting. I call it *character stropping*. Some people find it very helpful. Others go ballistic when they find out what's happening. To see how character stropping works, click once in a random location inside test.doc. Type a few words, then type an asterisk (a *****, or a "capital 8"). Type a few more words, then type another asterisk. See what happens? All the characters between the two asterisks turn bold, and the asterisks themselves disappear.

6. Word has one more recognized strop character. It's the _ underscore, which appears above the hyphen, to the right of the zero on your keyboard.

Again, go to a random point in test.doc. Type a few words. Then type an underscore. Type a few more words or characters and another underscore. Everything between the underscores turns italic.

WHENCE THE STROP?
Those of you who have worked much with email will recognize these strop characters as commonly used characters for adding formatting to plain text email messages. That's where Microsoft originally came up with this idea. (The term *strop* is an old programmer's word, which this old programmer used to use back in his college days. It's probably the wrong word for the concept, but I don't know of any better one.)

7. If you like these quick formatting strop characters, great! They'll save you lots of time. But if you don't like them—and many people don't—there are two things you can do. First, if you catch the problem immediately after it happens—just after you type that final asterisk or underscore—simply press the Backspace key and Word will restore what you rightfully typed. If that becomes too much of a bother, you can turn the feature off permanently by clicking **Tools**, **AutoCorrect**, then the **AutoFormat As You Type** tab, then uncheck the box marked ***Bold* and _underline_ with real formatting** (see Figure 10.15).

FIGURE 10.15
Disabling the * and _ strop characters.

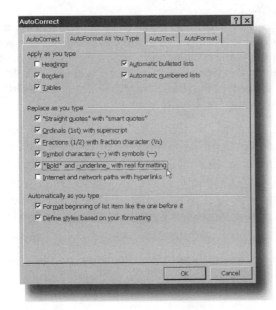

8. Good. You survived another exercise. Close test.doc and tell Word not to save the changes.

Now you know the high points about character formatting in Word.

Paragraphs

Next we'll tackle the second major component of Word documents, the paragraph. Remember that a paragraph consists of a paragraph mark, along with all the characters up to, but not including, the preceding paragraph mark. Also remember that you need to select the paragraphs you want to format before you apply the formatting.

Paragraph Changes from the Toolbar

*E*XERCISE

Paragraph Formatting on the Toolbar

1. Open test.doc.

2. Select a paragraph or two. Note that, for paragraph formatting, you don't have to select an entire paragraph—as long as you have any part of a paragraph selected it'll be changed when you apply formatting. (In fact, if there's nothing selected, the formatting will be applied to the paragraph that contains the insertion point.) In Figure 10.16 I've selected the first paragraph.

FIGURE 10.16
The first paragraph of test.doc is selected.

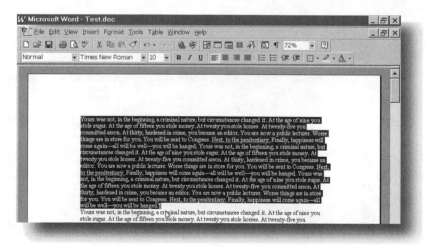

3. See up on the toolbar that the **Alighn Left** 🔳 icon has been selected? That's because this paragraph is left justified (also called *left-aligned* or *ragged right*), which means that the text lines up on the left, but flip-flops all over the place on the right.

4. Click the **Center** 🔳 icon. As you probably guessed, that's the icon for centering all the lines in a paragraph (see Figure 10.17).

FIGURE 10.17
Centering each of the lines in the paragraph.

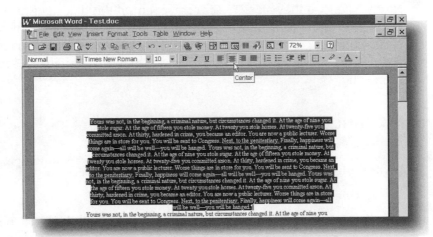

5. Now click the next icon, **Align Right** 🔳. Word will right-justify (also referred to as *right-align* or *ragged left*) the paragraphs, as shown in Figure 10.18.

FIGURE 10.18
Right alignment from the toolbar.

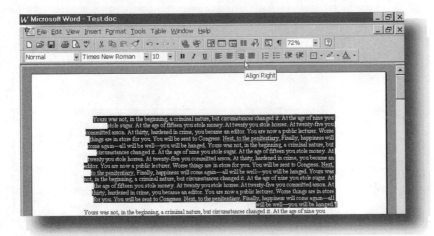

6. Finally, as you've probably guessed, the fourth icon, **Justify** [icon], makes all the lines extend fully from the left margin of the page to the right margin (sometimes called *fully justified*, sometimes just *justified*). See Figure 10.19.

FIGURE 10.19
The icon for full justification.

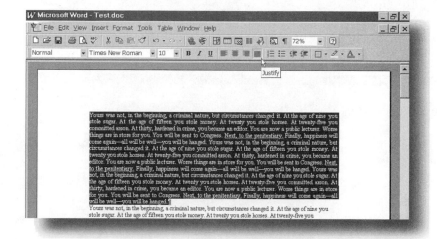

7. Now select two or three paragraphs. Click the **Numbering** [icon] button. Your selected paragraphs turn into a numbered list, as shown in Figure 10.20.

FIGURE 10.20
Creating a numbered list from the toolbar.

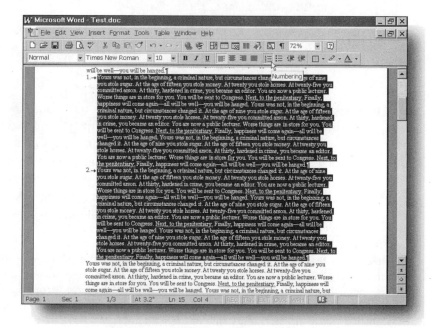

8. Click that **Numbering** 📋 icon again and the numbering disappears. With the same two or three paragraphs selected, click the next icon, **Bullets** 📋. See how the paragraphs are now bulleted, as shown in Figure 10.21?

9. This is, far and away, the most accurate way to make bulleted or numbered lists. We'll look at other methods later in this section, but they're all sloppy compared to this toolbar approach.

FIGURE 10.21
Making a bulleted list using the toolbar.

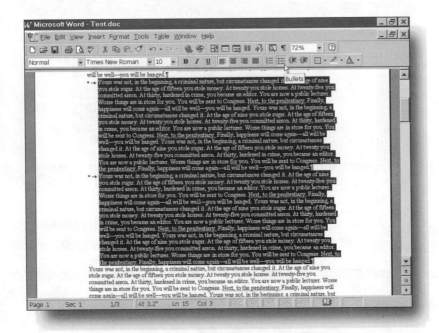

10. Click the **Bullets** 📋 icon again to remove the bulleting. Then play with the next two icons on the toolbar, **Decrease Indent** 📑 and **Increase Indent** 📑. They move the left edge of the chosen paragraphs in and out by half an inch per click (see Figure 10.22). You can move the left edge just about anyplace you like, except this button won't let you move text beyond the left margin of the paper. When you're finished with this step, leave the paragraphs flush with the rest of the document, back where you started.

ABOUT THOSE INDENTS...
Microsoft calls the distance from the paper's left margin to the left edge of the paragraph an *indent*. I find that really confusing because I use the term indent to refer only to the initial line of a paragraph. Not so with Word. In the World According to Word, the indent distance controls the entire left edge of a paragraph. Something called a *first line indent* distance affects the first line of the paragraph. We'll see that setting shortly.

FIGURE 10.22
Moving the left indent in by an inch (two clicks of the toolbar icon).

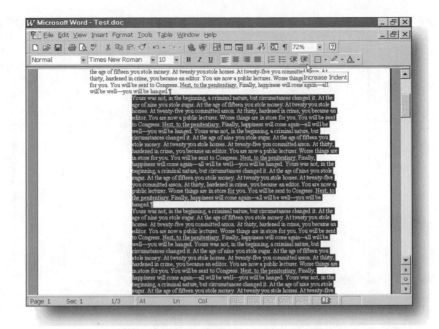

11. The next button draws lines around words, sentences, or paragraphs. Word calls such lines borders. This is a very important and powerful toy, er, tool, with a lot of options. Let's try a few of the more basic machinations. Start by selecting two or three paragraphs and simply clicking the **Outside Border** ☐▾ icon. Word draws a box all the way around the selected paragraphs (see Figure 10.23).

12. Click the **Undo** ↺▾ icon to get rid of that box. Now, with the same two paragraphs selected, click the down-arrow next to the **Outside Border** ☐▾ icon, and choose the **All Borders** ⊞ icon in the lower-left corner. Word draws independent boxes around the top and the bottom paragraphs, as shown in Figure 10.24.

13. Again, click the **Undo** ↺▾ icon to remove the boxes, uh, borders that you just inserted. Now select some random text inside test.doc and click the **Outside Border** ☐▾ icon. Word draws a rather distinctive box around the selected text, per Figure 10.25.

14. I could step you through dozens of similar examples, but you get the idea. Try selecting various combinations of words, sentences, and paragraphs and applying the various border types. I think you'll come away impressed with Word 97's extensive repertoire.

FIGURE 10.23
A single border (box) drawn around two paragraphs.

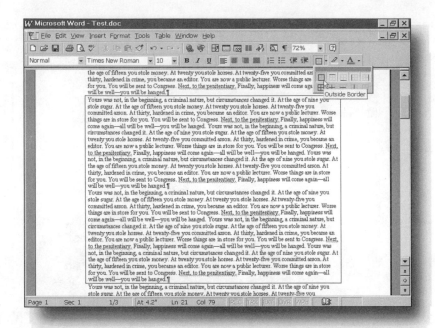

FIGURE 10.24
Use All Borders to create independent boxes around each paragraph.

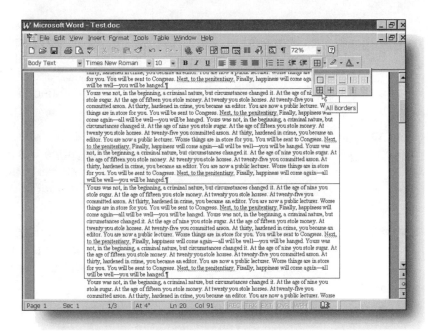

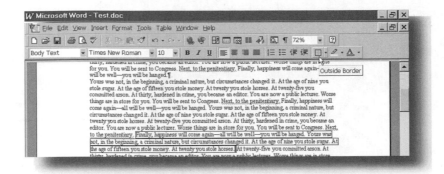

FIGURE 10.25
Boxing up
random text.

15. When you're done, close test.doc and don't save changes.

Paragraph Changes from the Dialog Box

As was the case with character formatting, Word only puts a small subset of its available options on the toolbar.

*E*XERCISE

Paragraph Formatting in the Dialog Box

1. Open test.doc. Again. Don't get too discouraged: This is going to be fun. Word can do all sorts of amazing things to paragraphs when you dig into the belly of the beast.

2. Your cursor (er, the insertion point) should be at the beginning of test.doc. That's fine for now; we'll only mess around with the first paragraph.

3. Click **Format**, then **Paragraph**. (If you're feeling your oats, you can also right-click inside that first paragraph and choose **Paragraph**.) The **Paragraph** formatting dialog box comes up, as shown in Figure 10.26.

4. Click the **Alignment** drop-down box. The choices you see there—**Left**, **Centered**, **Right**, and **Justified**—are the same choices you had on the toolbar. Ho-hum. Nothing new here.

5. The **Outline Level** box sets the heading level for the selected paragraph. That's a rather esoteric setting that only applies to outline mode, and a wonderfully conceived but nearly useless feature called Document Map (more on that in Chapter 15, "Outlook Preliminaries"). You might think that **Outline Level** would change how things appear in Word's automatically generated Table of Contents, but it doesn't. Another loser.

FIGURE 10.26
The Paragraph formatting dialog box.

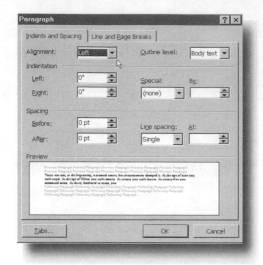

6. The **Left Indentation** box controls the distance from the left edge of the paragraph to the left margin of the page. You played with that already, when you clicked on the **Decrease Indent** and **Increase Indent** buttons. The **Right Indentation** box controls the distance from the right edge of the paragraph to the right margin of the page. You can crank that up and down for a few seconds of, uh, marginal amusement.

7. Things start getting interesting when you get to the **Special** box. (Why it's called Special I'll never know.) Here's where you adjust paragraph indentation—you know, in the old-fashioned sense of the term. It's just as easy to create indented paragraphs (regular, old fashioned indented paragraphs) as it is to create hanging indents (where the first line of the paragraph juts out to the left of the body of the paragraph). For the former, choose **First Line** in this box (see Figure 10.27); for the latter, choose **Hanging** (see Figure 10.28). The **Preview** box at the bottom of the dialog box gives you an excellent thumbnail view of what the various options look like.

8. The **Before** and **After Spacing** boxes control how much white space appears (respectively) before or after the selected paragraphs. The spacing is additive—if one paragraph has **After Spacing** of 12 points, and the next paragraph has **Before Spacing** of 24 points, there's going to be a 36 point gap (read: lots of white space) between the paragraphs. The easiest way to see this interaction is to select the first two paragraphs in test.doc and try a few different numbers for **Before** and **After** (see Figure 10.29).

FIGURE 10.27
First line
indentation
of half an
inch.

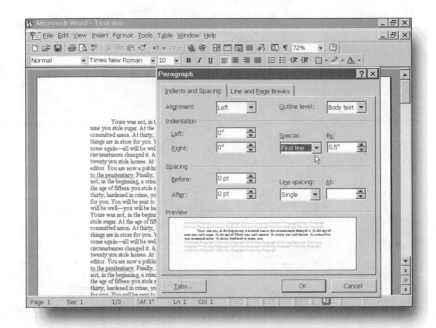

FIGURE 10.28
A hanging
indent of half
an inch.

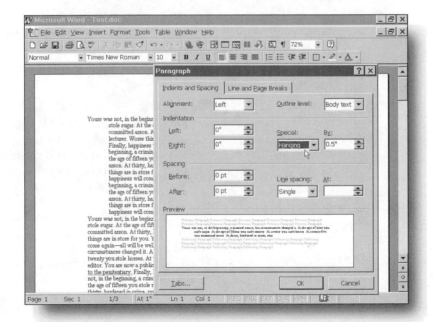

FIGURE 10.29
Before and
After Spacing
on para-
graphs is
additive.

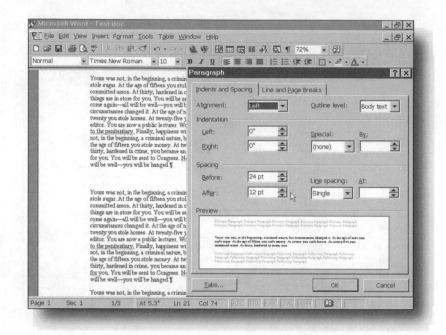

9. The **Line spacing** box on the Paragraph dialog box controls the amount of white space within the paragraphs—between the lines of the paragraph. (So, for example, if there's only one line in the paragraph this setting doesn't change anything at all!) If you use just one font, at one point size, in any given paragraph, the choices offered here— **Single** (plain old single spacing), **1.5 Lines** (frequently called 1fi spacing), **Double** (that's just double-spaced), **At Least** (where you specify a minimum distance between lines), **Exactly**

TRUTH IN LINE SPACING
The actual rules for line spacing are quite complex, and depend upon certain font characteristics. Suffice it to say that if you mix two fonts on a line, you may get different spacing on that line than on other lines in a paragraph. If you're concerned about weird line spacing inside a paragraph, try to use the **Exactly** setting. If that doesn't work and you want the full, gory details, check the *Hacker's Guide to Word for Windows, 2nd ed.*, pp 15–17. As far as I know, that's where you'll find the only accurate description of all these settings.

(for a precise, fixed distance between lines), and **Multiple** (so, for example, **3** means triple-spaced)—work pretty well and make sense (see Figure 10.30).

FIGURE 10.30
First para-
graph set to
Exactly 12
point
spacing—
note how
there's extra
white space
in that para-
graph.

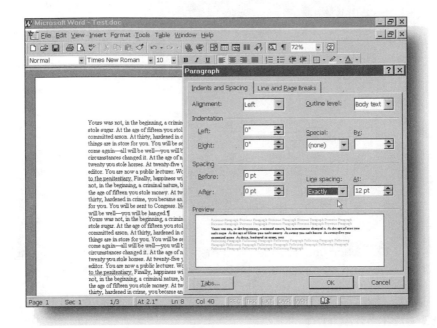

10. If you click the Paragraph dialog box's **Line and Page Breaks** tab (shown in Figure 10.31), you'll find several settings of interest. Checking **Widow/Orphan control** keeps Word from printing just one line from a paragraph on a page. Usually you don't want Word to split up a paragraph so one line dangles: It looks pretty bad when the first line of a paragraph prints at the end of a page (that's called a *widow*) or when the last line of a paragraph prints at the top of a page (an *orphan*).

11. The **Keep lines together** setting requires Word to keep all the lines in each of the selected paragraphs together—on the same page. **Keep with next** requires Word to print both the selected paragraph, and the following paragraph, together on the same page. (If you use **Keep lines together** and/or **Keep with next** to the extent that there's too much to put on a single page, Word is smart enough to effectively tell you to buzz off, and breaks the pages the way it thinks it should.) No, there's no Keep with previous setting. **Page break before** makes Word start the selected paragraph on a fresh page. The other two options are pretty esoteric, and I won't bore you with them.

FIGURE 10.31
The Line and
Page Breaks
tab.

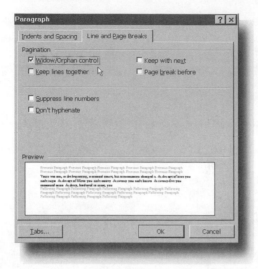

12. When you're done experimenting with paragraph formatting, close test.doc and do not save changes.

Borders and Shading

We had a taste of Word's bordering (box drawing) capability when you used the **Outside Border** ▣▾ icon earlier in this chapter. In fact, Word offers a veritable cornucopia of paragraph bordering and background shading when you click **Format**, **Borders and Shading**.

The **Borders** tab (shown in Figure 10.32) lets you choose from prebuilt borders, representing several commonly used styles, or it lets you build your own borders by clicking specific areas in the **Preview** box.

If you want to build a custom border, click in the **Preview** box on the edge where you'd like to have a line. For example, if you want a line at the right side of the paragraph, click the right side of the dummied grayed-out text in the **Preview** box.

The **Shading** tab (see Figure 10.33) has Word apply background colors or gray scales to the selected paragraphs or characters. You can even change the intensity of the color (or gray scale) by changing the setting in the **Style** box.

You'll see, if you flip back and forth between the **Borders** and **Shading** tabs, that Word keeps track of all your colorific settings and presents them to you in the **Preview** pane.

FIGURE 10.32
Word 97 lets
you draw
almost any
kind of box
around para-
graphs or
characters.

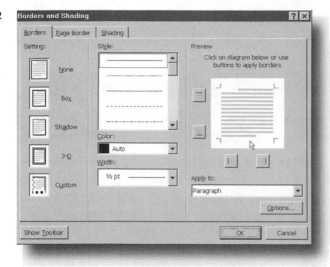

FIGURE 10.33
Both back-
ground color
and grayscale
lurk on the
Shading tab.

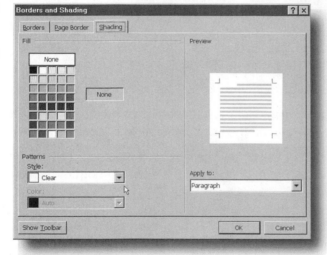

ADDING BORDERS TO PARAGRAPHS

Word has a quick way of adding borders to paragraphs. If you start a new paragraph
and type three or more equal signs, then press Enter, Word formats the previous
paragraph with a double line border on the bottom. Similarly, if you start a new
paragraph and type three or more dashes, or hyphens , and press Enter, Word formats the preceding paragraph with a single line border on the bottom. Give it a try!

Sticky Paragraph Formatting

Here's the other mantra you need to tattoo to the inside of your eyelids. (Hey, that's why you have two eyelids, isn't it?)

Paragraph formatting is in the paragraph mark

More blood, sweat, and tears have been lost to Word over that little observation than all the other hassles combined. Well, pretty close.

All paragraph formatting sits in the paragraph mark: centering, indenting, bullets, numbers, borders, line spacing, widow and orphan control, and on and on. It's all stored in the paragraph mark. When you delete a paragraph mark, the paragraph formatting disappears. *Poof!* When you move a paragraph mark, the paragraph formatting moves with it. When you copy a paragraph mark, the paragraph formatting is copied, too. When you create new paragraph marks (by pressing the Enter key), the new paragraph mark picks up the formatting of the old paragraph mark.

Let me show you what I mean about paragraph formatting sitting in the paragraph mark.

XERCISE

Paragraph Formatting's on the Mark

1. Open test.doc. Your cursor should be at the beginning of the document.

2. Apply some weird paragraph formatting to the first paragraph. In Figure 10.34 I've formatted the first paragraph with a half-inch hanging indent.

3. Now stick your cursor anywhere inside the paragraph. Press Enter. See that? The paragraph formatting settings are sticky—both of the new paragraphs have the same formatting as the old paragraph (see Figure 10.35). When you press Enter inside a paragraph, the new paragraphs both take on the formatting of the old paragraph.

TELLING LIES AGAIN, ARE WE WOODY? Okay. You caught me again. That last sentence isn't 100% true. But it's *almost* always true: When you press Enter, the new paragraph mark almost always picks up all of the formatting of the old paragraph mark. The only exception has to do with Styles, and a funny setting called **Style for following paragraph**. For now, we're going to ignore it. When you get to be a hot-shot Word expert, we'll talk about it.

FIGURE 10.34
Use Format,
Paragraph,
Special to set
a hanging
indent.

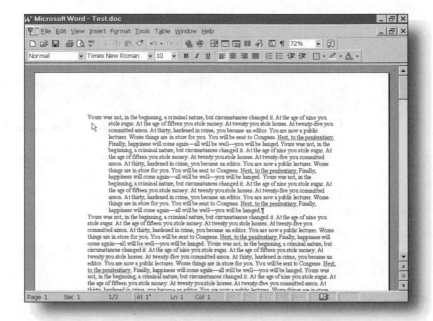

FIGURE 10.35
Press Enter
and all the
old paragraph
formatting
applies to
both the old
and new
paragraphs.

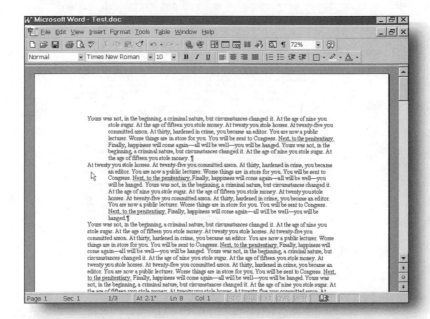

4. Select the paragraph mark at the end of the first paragraph. Copy it (with the **Copy**  button or **Ctrl+C**). Move your cursor into the middle of the first paragraph, and paste the paragraph mark. As you can see in Figure 10.36, both of the newly created paragraphs also have the same hanging indent formatting.

WHAT HAPPENS WHEN PARAGRAPH MARKS DIE?
Try deleting a paragraph mark. Note how the new, combined paragraph takes on the formatting of the first paragraph. In other words, the formatting in the deleted paragraph mark is transferred to the paragraph mark of the new, combined paragraph. Weird, huh?

FIGURE 10.36
Copying a paragraph mark also copies the formatting.

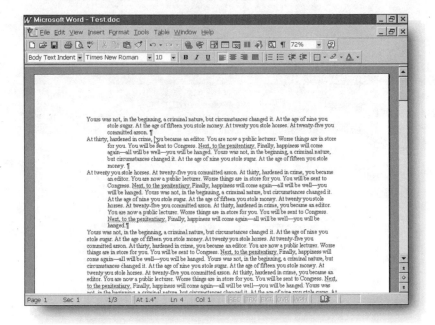

5. See how that works? Play with it a bit. Try copying parts of a paragraph, with and without a paragraph mark, into other locations in test.doc. Put your cursor immediately in front of a paragraph mark, press Enter, and verify that all the formatting in the old paragraph gets copied to the new paragraph.

6. Don't fall asleep on me. This may sound pretty trivial at the moment. But when we start talking about tab stops and bulleting/numbering in the
next sections, it'll explain all sorts of odd behavior—things that can't be explained any other way. Oh ye of little faith.

7. When you're through watching the bouncing Paragraph marks, close test.doc and do not save changes.

Once again: Paragraph formatting lives in the paragraph mark. *Ommmmmm…*

Tabs

The world of Word 97 users can be divided into two camps: those who have tried to use tab stops the way you would use them on a typewriter (perhaps to construct a fill-in-the-blanks kind of form), and those who have not. I can always identify people in the former group: their blood pressure has gone up 30 points, their faces are flushed, veins protrude from their necks, and they hurl epithets like sailors in a storm. The latter group just doesn't understand. Why do so many people hate Word? Spend an hour (or day or week) battling tab stops and you'll see.

My mission for this section is to introduce you to tab stops, tell you how (and even why) they behave so oddly, and then step you through an exercise that shows you a relatively easy way to get tab stops to behave themselves. No other introductory Office book covers this ground. Yet, at least in my experience, *every* first-time Word user bumps into these problems soon after they start using the program. Few ever figure out what's going on. You'll be one of the few.

In Word, a *tab stop* consists of a rather complex combination of two electronic concepts. First, there are the stops themselves—invisible locations on each line that you can set up to stop the progress of tab characters. Second are the tab characters, genuine characters that get placed in your document when you press the Tab key.

When Word builds a page on the screen, or on the printer, it handles tab characters in a very straightforward way. Word builds the line the way it always does and, when it hits a tab character, it moves the insertion point to the next tab stop.

*E*XERCISE _____

Intro to Tabs

1. Start with a new, blank document. If you don't have one showing, click the **New** 🗋 icon.

2. Word 97, straight out of the box, ships with tab stops set up every half inch: there's a stop at 0.5", 1.0", 1.5", 2.0", 2.5", and so on. To see that, type an **A** then press the Tab key. Type another **A** and press Tab. Do it a couple more times. Your document should look something like Figure 10.37. See how the **A**'s line up every half inch? (You might want to bring down the ruler by *hovering* your cursor just below the toolbar. Or, if you're really skeptical, print the document and use a real ruler. Go ahead. I won't be offended.)

THE SKINNY ON TAB STOPS

In the days of the typewriter, a *tab stop* consisted of a very simple combination of two mechanical devices. First, there was the stop itself—typically, a piece of metal that jutted out of the back of the typewriter, cleverly positioned so it would stop the platen at a predetermined location. If you set up tab stops every half inch, you could turn the typewriter around and see pieces of metal sticking out every half inch, ready to stop the platen (typewriter roller) dead in its tracks. The second device was a tab key. That key worked a little bit like the Spacebar, except it released the platen, sent it merrily zipping along, only to be halted when the next tab stop reared its little metallic head. The only major improvement to the tab stop came with the invention of the Selectric. On those machines the ball head, not the platen, moved along. Still, the concept was the same: a tab key that released the internal mechanism, and stop that, physically, stopped the movement.

Naturally, computers don't have metal pegs sticking out the back. (Or do they? Sometimes I wonder.) There's no way to duplicate the action of typewriter tab stops: Your monitor wouldn't appreciate being sent zinging across your desk. Computer people had to come up with a replacement to the tab stop—lots of folks wanted to use them—but the electronic version is only vaguely related to the original. Very vaguely.

3. To see how tab characters and tab stops interact, type a long word or two, press the Tab key, and type one more *a*. As you can see in Figure 10.38, that tab character lines the final a up at another half-inch hitching post.

FIGURE 10.37
Word's default tab stops are at every half inch.

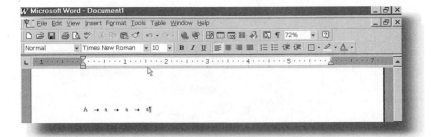

FIGURE 10.38
Tab characters always move the insertion point forward, to the next tab stop.

4. It's important that you see how Word puts this line together. It lays down the characters as you typed them. When Word hits a tab character, it zips down the line to the next tab stop. Then it continues laying down the characters you type.

5. Change the first tab stop so it appears at 1.25 inches, instead of half an inch. To do so, click **Format**, **Tabs**, type **1.25** in the box marked **Tab stop position**, and click **Set**, then **OK** (see Figure 10.39). When you set up a tab stop manually, as we just did, Word wipes out all the preceding default tab stops. So now, instead of having tab stops at 0.5", 1.0", 1.5", 2.0", 2.5", and so on, this line has tab stops at 1.25", 1.5", 2.0", 2.5", and so on.

6. Note in Figure 10.40 how the whole line has moved to the right, because the first tab character doesn't stop Word until it gets to the 1.25 inch mark.

7. Play with this document until you feel comfortable with the way Word handles tab stops and tab characters. Remember that tab characters are just characters—they can be copied, deleted, and moved from one document to another. But the tab stops are buried, invisible, in the line. When you're done, close the document and don't save changes.

FIGURE 10.39
Setting a new
tab stop at
one inch.

FIGURE 10.40
First tab stop
changed to
1.25 inches.

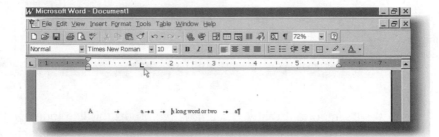

After my diatribe in the previous section, it probably won't surprise you very much to learn that *tab stop information is stored in the paragraph mark*. Think about that for a minute. It's not at all what you would expect. But it goes a long, long way toward explaining why tabs can be so infuriating!

SETTING TAB STOPS

In the old days of the typewriter tab stops were typically set up

DIFFERENT TYPES OF TABS

You might've noticed in Figure 10.39 that Word supports different tab alignments. A left-aligned tab is the kind of tab you're accustomed to. A right-aligned tab forces characters to sit to the left of the tab stop. Centered tabs center text on the tab stop. Decimal aligned tabs are usually for currency, so all the decimal points line up. The Bar tab listed in Figure 10.39 has nothing whatsoever to do with tabs. It draws a vertical line inside the paragraph, at the indicated location. It's like a Borders setting, except it's inside the paragraph. I've been railing against Microsoft about this one for years. It doesn't belong in the Tabs dialog box.

for an entire document. (Although you could, if you felt sufficiently masochistic, change tab stops at any moment.) Word doesn't work that way. Word has you set up tab stops *for each paragraph*. And it stores the tab stop information in the paragraph mark.

You can't even change tab stops for the various lines inside a paragraph. If a paragraph is ten lines long and the first line has tab stops at 1.0", 3.0", and 5.0", then *every* line in that paragraph has tab stops at 1.0", 3.0", and 5.0". Period.

XERCISE

Tab Stop Propagation

1. Start with a new, blank document.

2. Press Enter five or six times, then click back at the beginning of the document. Each of the paragraphs in this new document has "default" tab stops at 0.5", 1.0", 1.5", 2.0", and so on.

3. Type an A, press the Tab key, type another A, press the Tab key again, type a long word or two, press Tab, and type one more A. Your document should look like Figure 10.41.

FIGURE 10.41
Tab stops at the default locations.

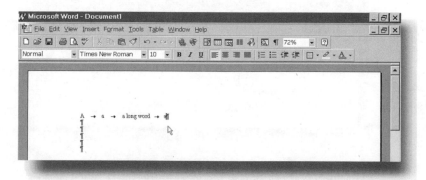

4. Change the first tab stop. Click **Format**, then **Tabs**, type 1.25 in the box marked **Tab stop position**, and click **Set**, then **OK** (refer to Figure 10.39). Again, the tab stops for this paragraph are now at 1.25", 1.5", 2.0", 2.5", and so on.

5. Now, with the insertion point sitting immediately in front of the paragraph mark on the first line, press Enter. The new paragraph will inherit the tab settings from the original, first paragraph. Verify that by typing a b, pressing the Tab key, typing another b, pressing the Tab key again, typing a long word or two, pressing Tab, and typing one more b (see Figure 10.42).

FIGURE 10.42
The effect of sticky tab stops.

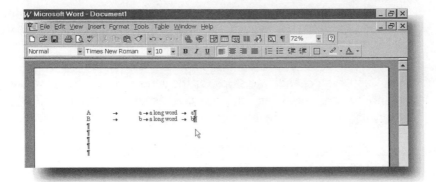

6. Move on to the next line by pushing the right arrow or down arrow. (*Don't* press the Enter key.) Try typing a c, then press Tab, type another c, press Tab, type a long word, press Tab, and type one final c. See in Figure 10.43 how the tab stop information in this paragraph hasn't changed?

FIGURE 10.43
But the original paragraphs still have the old tab stops.

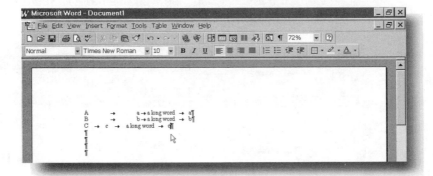

7. When you're done working with the file, close it and don't save changes.

I'd guess that 90% of the beginning Word users I know start trying to use tabs within a few weeks of discovering Word. They'll change the tab stops in one paragraph, then start pressing Enter and they can't figure out why in the world the tab stops stick. Then they wonder how to get their old tab stops back. I, personally, wasted several days (weeks?) trying to figure out how this works. Far as I know, it isn't documented anywhere. But Word has always worked this way, and it behaves very similarly with bulleted and numbered lists. We'll see that in the next section.

RULES TO LIVE BY

There are three hard and fast school-of-hard-knocks rules I've come up with for dealing with tabs. Ignore them at your own peril!

1. Don't use tabs unless you have to.

2. If you have to use tabs, press Enter many times before you start setting tab stops. That way, you can always move down in your document and pick up a "virgin" paragraph mark—one with no tab stop formatting information, other than the default tab stop every half inch—if you need one.

3. The only real way to deal with the multiple-line-single-paragraph dichotomy is to simplify the way you set up lines that will contain tab stops. I always, always set things up so each line that will contain a tab stop is one single paragraph. Sounds complicated? It isn't. Let me illustrate what I mean in this final tab stop exercise.

XERCISE

A Fill-in-the-Blanks Form

1. Start with a new blank document.

2. We're going to create a simple fill-in-the-blanks form, the kind of form you see every day. It will have slots for a name; two lines for address; city, state, and zip. Sounds like it should be easy, but it isn't. In fact, if you've tried to do this on your own, guided by those other books and Word's online help, you might think it's impossible!

3. Press Enter 8 or 10 times. You can never have too many virgin paragraph marks. Move the cursor back to the beginning of the document.

4. Type Name and press the Tab key twice. Your form should look like Figure 10.44.

FIGURE 10.44
Starting the first line of the form.

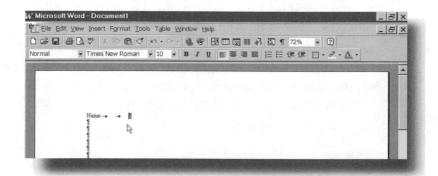

5. We want to set this line up so Name: appears on the left margin, then there's a space, and then a line where the respondent can type her name. Measuring from the left, we'll make that line begin at 1.0" and extend to the 6.0" point. There are lots of ways to draw that line, but here's the easiest.

6. Click **Format**, then **Tabs**. Type 1 in the box marked **Tab stop position**, and click **Set**, then **OK**. That puts a tab stop at 1.0", so the tab immediately after Name: will advance Word up to the 1.0" mark (see Figure 10.45).

FIGURE 10.45
Setting the
first tab stop
at one inch.

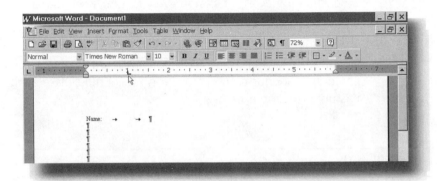

7. Now we need to draw an underline from the 1.0" point to the 6.0" location. One way to do that is to set up a tab stop at 6.0" and tell Word that we want to use an underline *leader*. A leader is just a bunch of repeated characters that lead up to a tab stop. You've no doubt seen the period used as a leader, for example, "John Smith..................800-555-1212". We'll use the underline character as a leader.

8. To do so, click **Format**, **Tabs** again. Type 6 in the box marked **Tab stop position**, click **4** (that's the underline) in the **Leader** pane, and click **Set**, then **OK** (see Figure 10.46).

9. You should see a line that looks like the one in Figure 10.47. Congratulations. You've finished the hard part.

10. Now press Enter. Remember, Word copies the tab information from the old paragraph into the new paragraph—so you now have all the tabs set up for the next line of the form. Type Address and press the Tab key twice. Your form should be taking shape, as shown in Figure 10.48.

FIGURE 10.46
Setting up a tab stop at 6 inches, with an underline leader.

FIGURE 10.47
The first line of the form, complete with the underline.

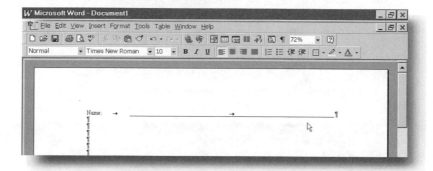

FIGURE 10.48
The Address line comes easy.

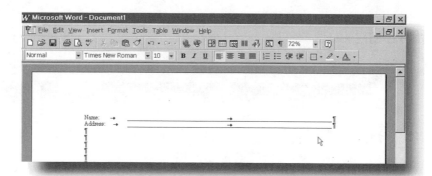

11. For the second address line, we just want a blank on the left with a line on the right, so press Enter, then press the Tab key twice (see Figure 10.49). Do you see how the inherited tab stop information can come in handy?

FIGURE 10.49
The second
address line,
with a blank
on the left.

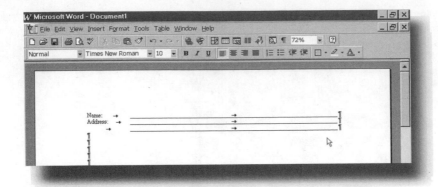

12. The next line has to hold City, State, and Zip, so we can't use the tab stops we've set up for the first three lines. Go down to the next line by pressing the right arrow or down arrow (*don't* press Enter). That puts the cursor in front of a "virgin" paragraph mark.

13. Type `City`, press Tab twice, type `State`, press Tab, type `Zip`, and press Tab one more time. Your document should look like Figure 10.50.

FIGURE 10.50
The last line
of the form
goes on.

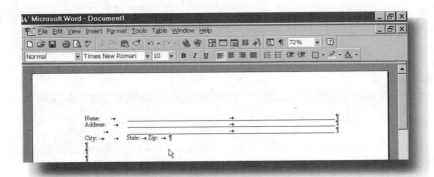

14. All that remains is setting up the tab stops for the last line. Here's how I did it. (No, you never get it right the first time. This one took a few tries, but each time I screwed up I pressed the **Undo** icon, and started over again.) Click **Format**, then **Tabs**, type 1, click **Set** (that's to put the first underline underneath all the others). Type 4, click **4** in the **Leader** pane and click **Set** (that's for the underline leading up to **State**). Type 5, click **4** in the **Leader** pane and click **Set** (that's for the underline leading up to **Zip**). Finally type 6, click **4** in the **Leader** pane and click **Set** (that's for the final underline). Click **OK**, and your form will appear as shown in Figure 10.51.

FIGURE 10.51
The finished
fill-in-the-
blanks form.

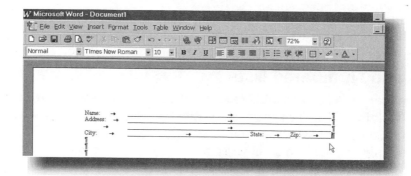

15. You really should be proud of this form. I know people who have used Word for years who haven't the slightest idea how to solve this problem. When you're done, close the document and don't save changes. (Or save it, just for bragging rights, if you like.)

There's a definite rhythm to building fill-in-the-blank forms. Figure out what you want on a line, including how many tab characters you'll need. Type those in. Then go back and use **Format**, **Tabs** to draw the lines correctly. That works pretty well.

DID YOU SEE THAT?

There's one last technique from this example I'd like to emphasize. Did you see how I greatly simplified the problem by making each line its own paragraph? That's why I say, when you use tabs, create one line per paragraph, and one paragraph per line.

AVOID TABBING WITH THE RULER

You've probably noticed that tab stops appear on Word's horizontal ruler. Some people swear the only way to work with tabs is to drop and drag them on the ruler. Personally, I get so confused by the different kinds of tabs and indents and their funny pictures on the ruler, the bizarre rules for using the ruler to create new tabs, and the poor control

SO WHEN DON'T YOU NEED TO USE TABS?

Tabs rarely rate as the easiest solution to a Word problem. If you want to indent the first line of a paragraph, don't use a tab, set the **Format, Paragraph, "Special" First line indent** value, as discussed earlier in this chapter. If you just need columns of text or pictures, use a table. (We'll discuss tables in the next chapter.) If you want to put an entire paragraph on the right edge of the page, use the **Align Right** icon.

offered by mousing tabs—how often do you want a tab at 1.01 inches?—that I gave up on tabbing with the ruler long ago. I suggest you avoid it, too.

Bulleted and Numbered Lists

Word has an amazingly thorough—although not, by any means, complete—set of tools for bulleting and numbering lists. The only difference between a numbered and a bulleted list is that Word uses the same character (the *bullet*) to start out each paragraph in a bulleted list, and it uses different characters (typically, but not always, a sequence of numbers) to start out each paragraph in a numbered list.

You might be surprised to learn that the bullets and numbers aren't real characters. You can't select them, move them, copy them, delete them, change their colors using the toolbar, or do anything else you would expect to do with real characters. Nope. Bulleting and numbering are properties of a paragraph, and as such (tell me if you've heard this one before) *they're stored in the paragraph mark*.

*E*XERCISE

Sticky Bullets

1. Start with a clean new document.

2. Type a few paragraphs and press Enter once or twice more so there will be a supply of virgin paragraph marks at the end of the document, if you ever need them. In Figure 10.52 I've typed three paragraphs and pressed Enter one extra time.

FIGURE 10.52
Setting up a document for bulleting.

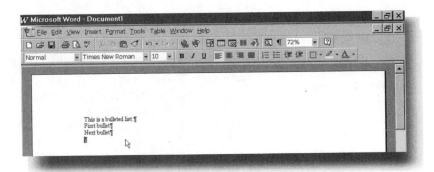

3. Select a couple of paragraphs in the document. Click the **Bullets** ⦂☰ icon on the toolbar. You'll get two bulleted paragraphs, as shown in Figure 10.53.

FIGURE 10.53
Applying bul-
lets to two of
the para-
graphs.

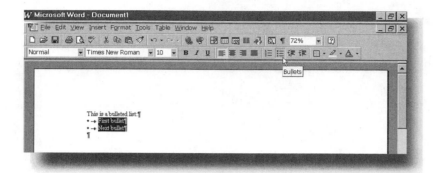

4. Put your cursor just before the paragraph mark at the end of the second bulleted paragraph. In this example, you'd put the cursor immediately after the text Next bullet.

5. Press Enter. The new paragraph is bulleted, as shown in Figure 10.54. Remember, bulleting is a formatting property of the paragraph mark, and when you press Enter, Word copies the formatting from the old paragraph mark into the new one. That's how you get a new bulleted paragraph. (If you've used Word more than a few days, I'll bet you've been wondering about that.)

FIGURE 10.54
Bulleting is
another one
of those
sticky settings
stored in the
paragraph
mark.

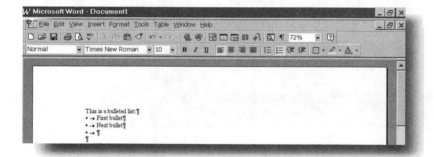

6. Fortunately, Microsoft built a bail-out sequence into this bulleting behavior. Press Enter one more time. Word 97 has the smarts to realize that you probably didn't want another bullet point, so it bails out—automatically removes the bullet from the previous (empty) paragraph, and creates a new, non-bulleted paragraph (see Figure 10.55).

7. When you're finished, close the document and do not save changes.

FIGURE 10.55
Press Enter
again,
though, and
Word bails
out of
bulleting.

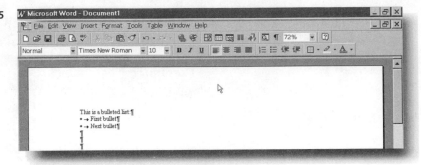

Word behaves precisely the same way with numbered lists: Numbering is a sticky paragraph formatting option, stored in the paragraph mark. If you press Enter while your cursor sits in a numbered paragraph, the next paragraph mark picks up the numbered formatting from the previous paragraph and the new paragraph is numbered, too.

Just as with bulleted lists, numbered lists will bail out if you press Enter while the cursor is in an empty numbered paragraph.

As you've probably guessed, you can apply all sorts of bullets or numbers using the **Format**, **Bullets and Numbering** dialog box. Simply select the paragraph you want to format, click **Format**, then **Bullets and Numbering**, and have at it.

Bulleting options, on the **Bulleted** tab (see Figure 10.56), run the gamut from fairly subdued to absolutely wild. If you click the **Customize** button in that dialog box, you'll have a chance to choose any character—any character at all—as your bullet.

FIGURE 10.56
The standard
bullets Word
has on offer.

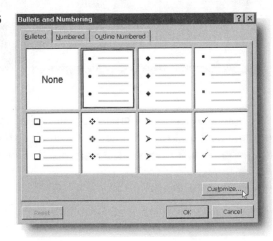

USING HAPPY FACES

Yes, I know what you're wondering. If you want to use Happy Faces as bullets, click **Customize**, then **Bullet**, scroll down to the Wingdings font, and look in the second row. You're welcome.

Similarly, the numbering options on the **Numbered** (see Figure 10.57) and **Outline Numbered** (Figure 10.58) tabs can be modified via the **Customize** button.

FIGURE 10.57
The stock
Word num-
bering
options.

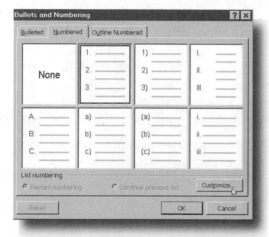

FIGURE 10.58
Word's out-
line number-
ing allows
you to create
different
kinds of
numbers at
different
levels.

WORD NUMBERING AND SUB-NUMBERING LIMITATIONS

If you work in a legal office, you're bound to be wondering, just about now, if Word can do the kind of fancy numbering and sub-numbering that so seem to enamor attorneys and judges. The short answer: probably not. (Yes, I know, WordPerfect has been doing it for years. Don't yell at me. Yell at Microsoft.) Poke around the Outline Numbered tab's Customize dialog box and give it a shot—there's an enormous array of choices there—but don't be too surprised if Word just can't handle the peculiar breed of numbering that your office requires.

Auto Bullets and Numbers

I hate it when computers think they're smarter than I am. (I particularly hate it when they *are* smarter than I am.) This is one of those situations, but if you're just starting out with Word, these automatic features may amount to more of a help than a hindrance. That's why I didn't tell you to turn them off in Chapter 6.

If you start a new paragraph, then type the number 1 followed by a tab, Word assumes that you want to start a numbered list. It swallows up the real character 1 and replaces it with the imitation-numbering-formatted paragraph you came to know in the previous section. In most cases that's what you want. In some cases, though, it's a pain.

HIT THAT BACKSPACE KEY!

If you press the Backspace key immediately after Word pulls its numbering-formatted paragraph switcheroo, you'll get your number back as a real character, and be able to continue typing without Word interfering.

Bulleting can kick in similarly if you start a paragraph with an asterisk, a dash (hyphen), a greater-than sign, or any of several combinations including -> and =>.

MORE AUTONUMBERING TRIGGERS

In fact, Word will interpret any of a large number of things as the beginning of a numbered list. Typing 1 followed by a period, a space, and some characters will do it. Ditto for an A followed by a tab, or an A followed by a period, space and characters. A closing parenthesis behaves the same way as the period. If you already have a numbered list somewhere in your document and you type a number that's close to the last number on the list, Word may pick that up, too. So if your paragraphs suddenly kick into autonumbering—a very disconcerting experience for many—realize that what you're witnessing is Microsoft trademarked Intelli-sense at work, and seriously consider turning it off.

If you like the way Word does that, more power to ya. If you want to zap the behavior out, now that you understand what's going on, click **Tools**, then **AutoCorrect**. Click the **AutoFormat As You Type** tab, and uncheck the boxes marked **Automatic bulleted lists** and **Automatic numbered lists**.

STARTING WITH A PAGE NUMBER GREATER THAN 1
Yes, it can be done, but boy is it difficult. If you want to start page numbering in a document with a number greater than one, you have to click **Insert**, **Page Numbers**, **Format** (see Figure 10.59). What a place to hide a setting, eh?

Sections

In general, I strongly recommend that beginners stay away from sections and using multiple-section documents. To tell the truth, I avoid sections, too, unless I have to change page numbering in the middle of a document. Even then I'm tempted to break the document into multiple pieces, put each piece in a separate document, and manage the page numbers in each separately.

FIGURE 10.59
The starting page number gets set in this very obscure dialog box.

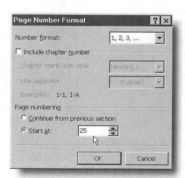

If you feel you absolutely must use multiple sections in a document, flip over to Normal view (click **View**, then **Normal**)—that way you can see the section breaks—then bring up the Office Assistant and search on **Section Breaks**. There isn't much information there, but it's more than enough to get you in all sorts of trouble. Just don't say I didn't warn you.

The Whole Document

Word gives you complete control over

- The printable area on a piece of paper (which is to say, the margins)

- Whether pages should be laid out portrait (with the short side on top) or landscape (turned sideways, with the long side on top)

- Which tray the printer should use to print the document, if it has more than one paper tray

These and several other settings are in the Page Setup dialog box. Occasionally people can actually use these settings, but all too frequently they get screwed up, and you find that you need to change the settings back so your documents look normal.

Let me step through each of the four tabs in the Page Setup dialog box and warn you about the things that can, and do, go wrong.

BE CAREFUL!
One overriding warning: If you ever change anything in the Page Setup dialog box, make sure the **Apply to** box shows **Whole document**. If that box has **This point forward** showing, it means that Word has inserted a surreptitious (and nearly invisible) section break in your document, and your only hope—short of becoming an expert in Word sections—is to make a copy of the file, open it in Normal View, and delete all the section marks.

You needn't select the entire document before applying these formatting options. They're automatically applied to the entire document, as long as the **Apply to** box shows **Whole document**.

Margins

The Page Setup dialog box's **Margins** tab (see Figure 10.60) lets you set margins— the boundaries of white space around the top and bottom of a document.

I commonly see two problems under the **Margins** tab.

First, most printers can't print all the way out to the edge of a piece of paper. Many laser printers, for example, can't print in the last quarter inch. So if the margin on any side is less than the printer allows, you'll get a nasty message every time you try to print that says, "The margins are set outside the printable area of the page. Do you want to continue?"

FIGURE 10.60
Beware of
margins that
are too small
for your
printer.

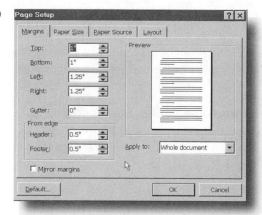

The second problem arises when someone mistakenly checks the **Mirror margins** box. That causes Word to print pages with margins that flip-flop, with odd numbered pages having different margins from even numbered pages. This is a very useful setting if you're printing both sides of each piece of paper and the printed pages will be bound into a book or stored in a binder. In most cases, though, it's just a mistake.

Paper Size

The **Paper Size** tab (see Figure 10.61) on the Page Setup dialog box controls the size of the page you see on your screen. It doesn't necessarily have anything to do with the size of the paper you'll ultimately print on.

FIGURE 10.61
Where you
control the
size of paper
Word thinks it
will print on.

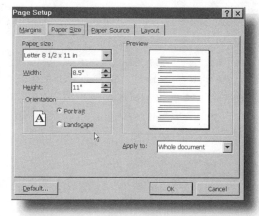

For example, if you want to design wedding invitations, you may find it advantageous to put the size of the invitation in this box, but print on normal-sized paper until you get the pages laid out precisely the way you want them. There's no requirement that these numbers match the dimensions of the physical piece of paper.

Sometimes the **Portrait** and **Landscape** buttons get messed up, particularly if you've been poking around a bit and don't really work much with portrait and landscape. If your pages suddenly start printing 90-degrees rotated from the way they should, this is where to look.

Paper Source

The **Paper Source** tab (see Figure 10.62) controls which paper bin your printer uses to print the document, assuming your printer has more than one paper bin.

FIGURE 10.62
Where the
paper comes
from.

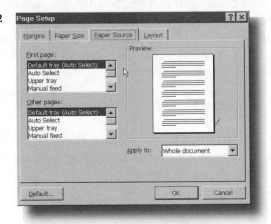

If you suddenly start getting weird error messages on your printer (typically appearing on the light panel on the front of the printer), this is one place to check. Similarly if your documents start printing on envelopes pulled from your printer's envelope feeder, chances are awfully good this setting is causing the mayhem.

Layout

The **Layout** tab (see Figure 10.63) controls all sorts of things that can, and do, go wrong.

FIGURE 10.63
If your documents get spaced out this is the place to look.

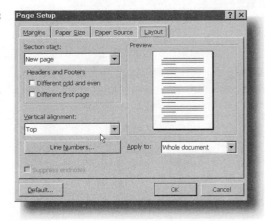

We'll talk about headers and footers in the next chapter, but this is where you tell Word if your document is to have a different header/footer for the first page (common in most kinds of manuscripts and reports), and whether there should be different headers/footers on even and odd pages (common for documents printed on both sides of the paper).

The truly bizarre setting on this dialog box is the one marked **Vertical alignment**. When Word is putting together pages in a document it looks at this setting to see how you want your paragraphs aligned, from top to bottom. If you start to get a lot of white space *between* paragraphs, it's possible that this box has been switched to **Justified**. In a worst-case situation, if you have Word keep the lines of paragraphs together, and the paragraphs are pretty long, each paragraph in a document could appear centered—centered from top to bottom—in the middle of its own page.

Ah, yes, it happens. More often than you think.

11

Key Capabilities

CONGRATULATIONS ON SURVIVING THAT formatting marathon! Next we'll tackle many of the features inside Word that will make your work easier.

Features You'll Use Every Day

In this chapter I'm going to cover a hodgepodge of the most important Word features that most people will use every day:

- Headers and footers, which print at the top and bottom of every page in a document

- Spell checking, one of Word's niftiest features, only one click away

- Using AutoCorrect to correct common mistakes and, more importantly, speed up your typing

- Getting at and using the Thesaurus, and the Dictionary if you have Office 97 Professional Edition

- Putting symbols of various types in your documents

- Printing envelopes and labels

- Forcing page breaks

By the time you're done with this chapter, you should have enough techniques under your belt to start whipping out documents like a-ringin' a bell.

Headers and Footers

Chances are pretty good you'll want a header or a footer in any document that runs longer than one page. Headers appear at the top of each page. Footers appear at the bottom. Word has a built-in toolbar that helps you with the most common kinds of text you'll want to see in your headers and footers—as you might imagine, the page number falls at the top of that list.

*E*XERCISE

A Simple Header and Footer

1. Open test.doc. (You should have one left over from Chapter 10, "Making Documents Look Good"; if not, start with a new, clean document, and type a few paragraphs of text.) If test.doc is less than one page long, copy some text and repeatedly paste it until you go over one page, then save the new test.doc (click the **Save** icon on the toolbar).

2. Click **View**, then **Header and Footer**. Word should propel your cursor up into the top margin, where the header goes, and present you with the Header and Footer toolbar (see Figure 11.1).

FIGURE 11.1
Word prepares you for creating a header.

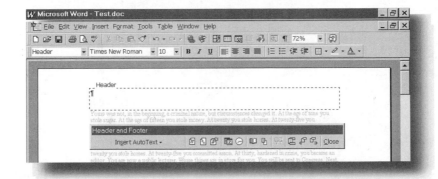

3. Type a few words, press the Tab key, type another word or two, press Tab, and type a few final words. Word should set things up so the words you typed are left-aligned, centered, and right-aligned on the page (see Figure 11.2).

FIGURE 11.2
Left-aligned, centered, and right-aligned text in the header.

4. Click the **Switch Between Header and Footer** 🖭 icon on the Header and Footer toolbar. You'll end up in the document's footer (see Figure 11.3).

FIGURE 11.3
Starting a new footer.

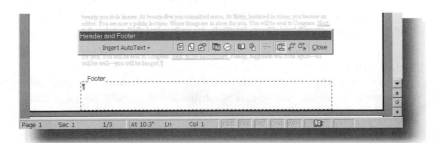

5. Press the Tab key, type `Page`, and a space, then click the **Insert Page Number** [#] icon. Then type a space, `of`, another space, and click the **Insert Number of Pages** [⊡] icon (see Figure 11.4). See how Word helps you out with these nifty features? They can be very handy, if you know they're there!

FIGURE 11.4
Using Word's
page number
and number
of pages val-
ues in the
footer.

6. Press Tab again, type `Printed`, then a space, click the **Insert Time** [⊙] icon, then the **Insert Date** [⊡] icon (see Figure 11.5).

FIGURE 11.5
Time and
date in the
footer.

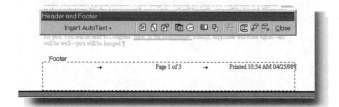

7. Click **Close** on the Header and Footer toolbar. That puts your cursor back inside the document, and your new headers and footers appear grayed out at the top and bottom of each page. Scroll through test.doc and verify that the same headers and footers (with the correct page numbers) appear on every page in the document.

8. If you want to change a header or footer, just double-click it. Word puts your cursor inside the header or footer, brings up the Header and Footer toolbar, and lets you make whatever changes you like. Note, though, that any changes you make show up on *all* the pages in the document. You can put anything you like—even pictures—in headers and footers.

GET BACK, JACK
You needn't click **Close** in the Header and Footer toolbar to get back to the document—simply double-clicking inside the document does the trick.

9. Close test.doc without saving changes.

Different First Page

Although there are many tricks you can play with headers and footers, the most important trick you're likely to need concerns headers and footers on the first page of a document.

BUT WHICH TIME IS IT?

Although you see the current date and time in test.doc right now, every time you print test.doc the time and date (and page number and total number of pages, for that matter) get updated by Word before the document is printed. All of these icons—page number, number of pages, date and time—put fields in your headers or footers. We'll talk about fields in Chapter 14, "Advanced Features," but for now suffice it to say that these fields get updated immediately prior to printing. So if you save this version of test.doc and print it a week from today, the time and date shown on the printed page will be the time and date when the document was printed.

WHY DIFFERENT?

In most documents you're going to want to have a different header (and possibly a different footer) on the first page. For example, if you put together a multiple-page letter, the first page probably wouldn't have any header at all. But the second and subsequent pages could list who the letter is from (or to), and a page number. Frequently, multiple-page memos work the same way.

Similarly, most reports won't have a header on the first page—you'll put the report title at the top of the first page and won't want the header to kick in until page two.

Word has a name for that concept: it's called Different First Page, and it frequently confuses the living daylights out of first-time Word users. I'll show you how to cope in the following Exercise.

*E*XERCISE

Different First Page Headers

1. Open test.doc. I'm going to show you the easiest way to put page numbers at the bottom of all the pages in a document, but only put the document's title on the top of the second and subsequent pages.

2. Click **File**, then **Page Setup**. Click the **Layout** tab. Then check the box marked **Different first page** (see Figure 11.6). That tells Word that you want to have different headers and footers on the first page of test.doc—different in the sense that headers and footers on the second and all subsequent pages are the same, but the header and footer on page 1 may be different. Click **OK**.

FIGURE 11.6
Setting the document to have different headers and footers on the first page.

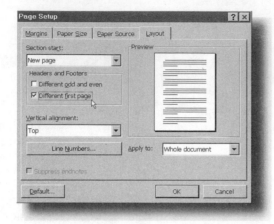

3. We don't want a header on the first page, so let's start with the second page. Scroll down to the second page of test.doc and click anywhere on the second page. Click **View**, then **Header and Footer**. Word goes to the header (this is the header for the second and subsequent pages), and shows the Header and Footer toolbar. Type something appropriate (see Figure 11.7).

FIGURE 11.7
The header for the second and subsequent pages.

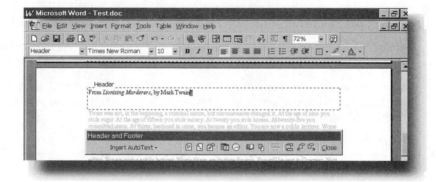

4. Click the **Switch Between Header and Footer** 🔁 icon on the Header and Footer toolbar. Word goes down to the footer for the second and subsequent pages. Type whatever you like down here. In Figure 11.8, I pressed Tab twice, typed Page, then a space, and clicked the **Insert Page Number** 📄 icon.

FIGURE 11.8
Setting up
the page
number on
the second
and subse-
quent pages.

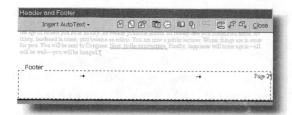

5. Click **Close** (or double-click inside the document). Now scroll through test.doc. You'll find headers and footers starting on page 2, and going for the length of the document. But you won't find hide nor hair of a header or a footer on page 1.

6. To put a footer on the first page, click once on the first page, then click **View**, then **Header and Footer**. Word puts you in the header—note how it's marked First Page Header—so click the **Switch Between Header and Footer** icon on the Header and Footer toolbar.

7. You should be in the First Page Footer. Type something interesting. In Figure 11.9, I've pressed the Tab key twice, typed Page, then a space, and clicked the **Insert Page Number** icon, the same way I put together the second (and subsequent) page footer.

FIGURE 11.9
Setting the
First Page
Footer.

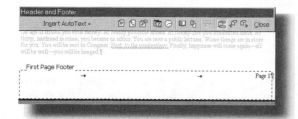

8. Click **Close** or double-click inside the document. On page 1 you should have a footer with the page number, but no header. And the other headers and footers throughout test.doc should remain unchanged.

9. Close test.doc and don't save changes.

That's how you put together professional headers and footers.

Right-click Spell Check

When you type a word that Word doesn't recognize, Word puts a red squiggly line underneath it. You can right-click a word with a squiggly red line under it and most of the time Word offers you a correctly spelled version of the word on a list. Move down to whatever spelling you like, let loose of the mouse button, and *boom!* the chosen word takes the place of the misspelled word.

Right-click spell check is a very cool feature, one that you've probably already discovered and used. But it's only the tip of the iceberg. Let's look a little deeper.

XERCISE

Spell Check on Steroids

1. Create a new document. Type something that Word's built-in dictionary won't recognize. In my case, that's easy. Word doesn't know how to correctly spell my last name (see Figure 11.10). When you type something Word doesn't recognize, it'll get a squiggly red underline.

FIGURE 11.10
Word's built-in dictionary doesn't recognize Leonhard, so it gets the squigglies.

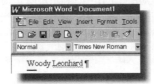

2. Right-click a word with the red squiggly underline. Word makes a guess—usually a very good guess—at what you meant. If you misspelled the word and can find the correct spelling on the list, scroll down to the correctly spelled list and let go of the mouse button. In Figure 11.11, Word guesses that I meant Leonard. I didn't, of course.

FIGURE 11.11
Word guesses Leonard. Bzzzzzzt.

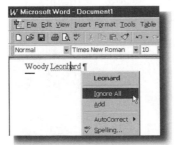

3. Each of the options listed in the right-click context menu, shown in Figure 11.11, holds interesting possibilities. The first option after the suggested correct spellings, **Ignore All**, tells Word to ignore this word throughout the current document. If you've typed a word that you aren't likely to use again in other documents, that's a good choice.

4. On the other hand, if you expect to use the word in other documents, it would be a good idea to choose **Add** (as in Figure 11.12). By doing so, you're telling Word to put this particular word in your custom dictionary. The custom dictionary is treated like other Word dictionaries, so the next time you type this particular word, it'll be in the dictionary. That way Word knows that it shouldn't receive a red squiggle.

FIGURE 11.12
This option adds the word to cus-tom.dic, your custom dictionary.

5. Ah, but what if you make a mistake? What if you put a word into your custom dictionary, and you discover that you screwed up? How do you *remove* a word from your custom dictionary?

6. It's amazingly easy, if you know the trick. Click **Tools**, **Options**, then click the **Spelling & Grammar** tab. Highlight the name of your custom dictionary (which, per Figure 11.13, is usually custom.dic), then click **Edit**. Word opens the custom dictionary and lets you add, delete, or change any of the entries. When you're done, just restart Word.

7. The next option in the right-click context menu lets you add this word to your AutoCorrect list. I'll talk about AutoCorrect in the next section, but here it's important to note what Word is offering to do. In Figure 11.14, Word offers to automatically correct the word Leonhard, turning it into Leonard, every time you type Leonhard. That may or may not be what you want to do, so make an informed decision.

FIGURE 11.13
The secret
entrance to
your custom
dictionary.

FIGURE 11.14
A quick
tunnel to
AutoCorrect,
from the
right-click
spelling con-
text menu.

8. In the final entry, Word offers to send you into the full-blown Spelling and Grammar dialog box—the same one you can get to by clicking **Tools**, then **Spelling and Grammar**. This batch-mode spell checker, where Word checks spelling for the whole document, almost always amounts to overkill; I never use it.

9. Play with right-click spell check for a bit. When you're comfortable with the options, click **File**, **Close**, and don't save changes.

Remember, you *can* fix any mistakes you make when adding items to your custom dictionary.

AutoCorrect

AutoCorrect is Word 97's number one productivity enhancer. Hands down. Learn the tricks to using AutoCorrect and you can boost your effective typing rate enormously. Some of those older Word books tell you to use a feature called AutoText. *Balderdash!* AutoCorrect has AutoText beat to smithereens. I'll show you why.

When a Correct Is a Correct

By now you've no doubt seen AutoCorrect in action. If you type "teh" Word changes it to "the"—and doesn't even bother to tell you. Here's what's happening behind the scenes. Word keeps track of what you're typing. When you press the Spacebar or type a punctuation mark, Word looks at the word you've just typed and checks to see if it has an entry for that word in the AutoCorrect list. If there's an AutoCorrect entry, whatever you typed is replaced with whatever sits in the entry.

So, for example, Word 97 has an AutoCorrect entry for "teh." That entry says "teh" should be replaced by "the." Every time you type teh, followed by a space or a punctuation mark, Word looks up "teh" in its AutoCorrect list and changes it to "the." And the change occurs very, very quickly.

XERCISE

Check Out Word's Built-in AutoCorrect Entries

1. Start with a new document.

2. Type accommodate. Note the misspelling (see Figure 11.15). I misspelled that word in a fourth-grade spelling bee, and never forgot it. Amazing how Word 97 can effectively cope with so many childhood traumas!

FIGURE 11.15
Word acom-
modates
many mis-
spellings.

3. Now type a space or a punctuation mark. Word changes acommodate to accommodate, as any, uh, accommodating program should.

4. Let's go see why. Click **Tools**, then **AutoCorrect**. At the bottom, scroll down to the entry marked **acommodate** (see Figure 11.16). That's where Word picked up on the idea that it was supposed to swap out acommodate and swap in accommodate.

5. Scroll through the list of words that Word 97 will correct for you. It's an enormous, impressive list. Thousands of words.

6. Click **Cancel** to back out of the dialog box.

FIGURE 11.16
Where the accommoda-
tion occurs.

Bending AutoCorrect to Your Own Devices

You can add your own entries to the AutoCorrect table. It's very important that you understand *these entries need not be spelling corrections!* You can put anything you like in here, and if you organize things well, you can speed up your typing enormously.

XERCISE

Make Your Own AutoCorrect Entry

1. You can keep working with the document you used in the previous exercise, or you can start a new one. Say you work for a company called Spacely Sprockets, Inc., and you type that company name a gazillion times a day.

2. Press Enter a few times, then type `Spacely Sprockets, Inc.` in the document.

3. Select **Spacely Sprockets, Inc.** (see Figure 11.17).

4. Click **Tools**, then **AutoCorrect**. Type `spac` in the **Replace** box (see Figure 11.18), then click **Add**.

5. Back out in the document, type `spac`, and press the Spacebar. See how Word 97 now "corrects" the, *ahem!*, misspelled spac into Spacely Sprockets, Inc.?

FIGURE 11.17
Selecting
Spacely
Sprockets,
Inc.

FIGURE 11.18
Adding spac
to the
AutoCorrect
list so it
comes out
Spacely
Sprockets,
Inc.

6. When you're done, delete the bogus entries you've placed in the AutoCorrect list by clicking once on each entry and clicking **Delete**. Click **OK** and close the document without saving changes.

Note how I didn't use the abbreviations sp or spa, both of which appear from time to time in various kinds of documents. (In other words, sp. as an abbreviation for spelling or space.) But spac is long enough that it shouldn't cause any confusion, yet short enough to memorize. I also could've used ssi or even something really short like s#, where the punctuation mark at the end would trigger an AutoCorrect replacement before you even press the Spacebar.

AutoText entries are a lot like AutoCorrect entries, except they require you to press the Tab key to expand. That's why they tend to be much more cumbersome than AutoCorrect entries—and why I recommend that you use AutoCorrect.

Thesaurus and Dictionary

Most Office 97 users don't realize that they have a perfectly good—well, at least a fairly adequate—Thesaurus sitting in the wings. That's true even if you bought Office 97 Standard Edition or Small Business Edition; you don't need the fancy Bookshelf to get at synonyms and antonyms.

To get to the Thesaurus, click once inside the word you want to look up, then click **Tools**, **Language**, **Thesaurus**. You'll see the Thesaurus dialog box (see Figure 11.19), and can navigate your way from there.

FIGURE 11.19
Word's relatively well-hidden Thesaurus.

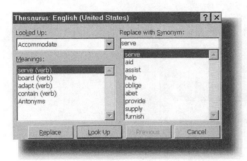

If you did buy Office 97 Professional edition, you have a pretty good dictionary at your disposal as part of Bookshelf Basics. Make sure your Office 97 Pro CD is in its drive, then right-click the word you want to look up and choose **Define** (see Figure 11.20).

QUICK THESAURUS

So why didn't Microsoft put a Thesaurus entry on this menu? Good question. I don't know the answer. Mike Craven has a free program that adds a right-click Thesaurus to Word; it's available at www.wopr.com.

You can also have Word scoot straight to the Thesaurus by clicking inside the word you want to look up, then pressing Shift+F7.

FIGURE 11.20
Definitions are one click away for Office 97 Professional users.

If your sound card is hooked up right, Bookshelf Basics will even pronounce the word for you if you click the icon that looks like a speaker.

Symbols

Word 97 Office supports an enormous variety of characters, as Dr. Seuss used to say, "On beyond zebra." Many weird characters appear in the common fonts that you're likely to have on your computer. If you install even stranger fonts, you're bound to see characters you've never even imagined—at least, not in this dimension.

To put an odd symbol in your document, first position the insertion point wherever you want the character to go. Then click **Insert**, then **Symbol** and click the **Symbols** tab. Leaf through the various fonts listed in the **Font** box (see Figure 11.21). When you spy the character that you want to put in your document, click it once and click **Insert**, or—much simpler—just double-click the character.

FIGURE 11.21 Inserting the Wingdings font's Wheel of Dharma character.

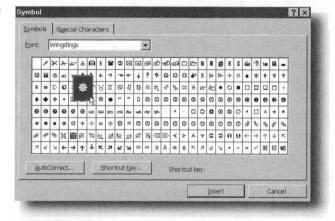

This same dialog box lets you turn a weird character into an AutoCorrect entry (so, for example, you can make the word greekpi automatically change into a Greek pi from the Symbol font), or assign a shortcut Ctrl+Alt style key combination to the character.

The **Special Characters** tab on this dialog box (see Figure 11.22) lets you insert common typesetting and page markup characters without the hunt-and-peck searching generally required to find other symbols. It's also a good place to find the shortcut key combinations that let you put those characters in your documents with a minimum of fuss, should you be so inclined.

FIGURE 11.22
Special Characters—primarily typesetting and markup characters—sit on the Special Characters tab.

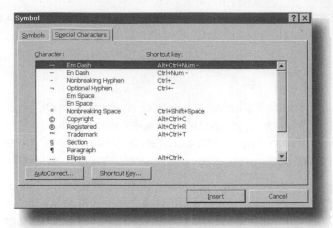

Envelopes and Labels

You'll never need to hand-address an envelope again. After you've printed your first Word envelope, it'll be faster to type an address into Word, select it, and print an envelope than it ever would be to address it by hand. Plus, if you use Word's built-in features, the envelope will get there quicker because it will include the correct POSTNET bar code.

XERCISE

Print an Envelope

1. Start with a new document. Type a name and address.

2. Click **Tools**, **Envelopes and Labels**, and then the **Envelopes** tab (see Figure 11.23). Make sure that the recipient's address (**Delivery address**) and your return address are correct.

WHAT ARE THOSE FUNNY ICONS?
The Envelopes dialog box has two funny icons, both of which look like an open book with a down-arrow to the right. When you get Outlook set up, these icons transport you to your Outlook Contacts list. The one on top sticks a Contact entry into the recipient box. The one on the bottom does the same for your return address. They can be very handy if you need to double-check an address, or swap among several different return addresses.

FIGURE 11.23
Verify addresses in the Envelopes dialog box.

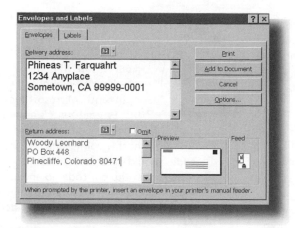

THE NAME GRAB

Word usually does a good job of snatching the name and address from an underlying document, but if it has trouble with one of yours, select the name and address before clicking **Tools**.

3. If you haven't set up Word 97 to print envelopes the way you like, click the **Options** button.

4. If you want to print a USPS POSTNET bar code on your envelopes (that's the bar code that enables automatic sorters to route your mail), click the box marked **Delivery point barcode** (see Figure 11.24). Note that Word 97 prints the POSTNET bar code immediately above the name and address of the recipient.

FIGURE 11.24
Printing envelope bar codes is just a click away.

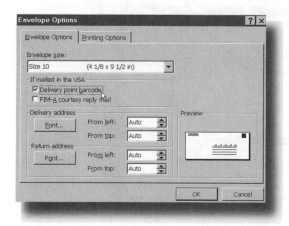

5. Chances are pretty good that Word 97 figured out how you need to feed envelopes into your printer. (Check your printer manual, but you probably need to feed them manually, possibly through a special tray.) Just to make sure Word got it right, click the **Printing Options** tab, and make any necessary changes (see Figure 11.25). Click **OK** to return to the Envelopes dialog box.

WHY DOES THE BAR CODE PRINT ABOVE THE RECIPIENT'S NAME? I've wondered about that, too. Apparently Microsoft took the U.S. Postal Service's original recommendations—several years old at this point—and decided that bar codes should go on top. In fact, the USPS doesn't require that the bar code go above the name. Their own machines put it in the lower-right corner, where the mail gods intended.

<Shameless self promotion alert> The first macro I ever wrote for Word 1.0 printed envelopes. Word's envelope features have improved greatly since then, but they still leave a lot to be desired. It's nearly impossible to put the bar code at the bottom of the envelope; you'll have a hard time printing a logo on the envelope; heaven help you if you need to change the location of the return address. If you want to see a professional envelope printer, download WOPR, Woody's Office POWER Pack, from `www.wopr.com`.

FIGURE 11.25 Sometimes Word doesn't get the paper feed options quite right.

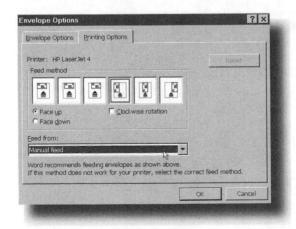

6. When you're convinced everything is set up properly, click **Print**. Don't be too surprised if the envelope doesn't turn out right the first time—it rarely does. Keep jiggling the **Printing Options** tab settings and refer constantly to your printer manual until it comes out right. It's definitely worth the effort.

7. When you're done, keep the document open. We'll use it for labels in the next exercise.

Although Word 97's label printing capabilities might not win any awards for innovative features—it's impossible to print a return address on a large label, for example—you will nonetheless discover that it handles the basics pretty well.

XERCISE

Make a Label

1. When you're back in that document with a name and address showing, click **Tools**, then **Envelopes and Labels**, and choose the **Labels** tab (see Figure 11.26).

FIGURE 11.26
Printing labels is easy and quick.

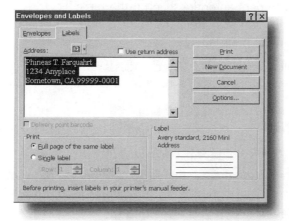

2. You have to tell Word what kind of labels you're using. To do so, click the **Options** button. You'll see the Label Options dialog box (see Figure 11.27).

3. Those numbers you see on the left side of the **Product Number** box are Avery label product numbers. There's a good reason for that. Avery helped Microsoft build this part of Word 97!

FIGURE 11.27
Choose the labels you're going to use in the Label Options dialog box.

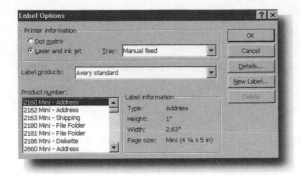

4. If you're feeling very, very lucky, you can set up your own custom label sizes by clicking on **New Label**. Yes, it can be done, but it's not something I would recommend for the faint of heart, or marginally sane. You'll have more fun watching *Barney* reruns. Don't say I didn't warn you.

5. Choose the type of label you're using, then click **OK**.

6. If you want to print an entire sheet of the same label, click **Print**. Otherwise, follow the instructions in the dialog box or ask the Office Assistant how to print labels.

7. Close the document. Don't save changes.

Force a Page Break

Amazing how something so important can be so hard to find, eh?

If you want to force a page break—that is, force Word to start putting text on a new page—put your cursor right in front of whatever is to appear on the new page, then click **Insert**, **Break**, make sure **Page break** is checked, and click **OK**.

Speaking of breaks—now's a good time to take one. When you're ready, come back and we'll start to tackle some of Word's more esoteric features in Chapter 12, "Special Purpose Tools."

Special
Purpose Tools

I'S AN ADMITTEDLY ARBITRARY DISTINCTION, but in this chapter I wanted to go over some important Word 97 features that most of you probably won't use every day:

- Word's tables
- Putting dates (and times) in documents, and why some of them change and some don't
- Putting pictures into your documents
- Combining existing documents to create new documents

Each of these features, in the right set of circumstances, at the right time, can save your tail. So play with them a bit and remember that Word can cover these problems, too.

Tables

Word 97 has several built-in methods for creating and formatting tables. The very first question you should ask is, "Why would I use Word, instead of Excel, to make tables?" The short answer: Use Word if you don't want to do any arithmetic. The minute you need to add columns of numbers, or draw fancy graphs based on calculated numbers inside tables, Word craps out completely (although it can draw excellent graphs if you have the data already crunched).

Some day Microsoft will integrate Word and Excel a bit better. When that day comes, drawing tables in Word may fade into obscurity. For now, though, Word tables are the best way to solve a wide variety of common business problems.

Fast Pre-Fab Tables

Word has a high-level menu devoted entirely to tables, so it shouldn't surprise you too much to know that there are lots and lots of table-related commands inside Word 97. Some of them actually crank out respectable looking tables very quickly.

*E*XERCISE

A Quick Table

1. Start with a new, clean document

2. Click **Table**, then **Insert Table**. You'll see the Insert Table dialog box shown in Figure 12.1.

FIGURE 12.1
A very quick
and dirty way
to create a
new table.

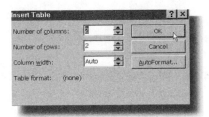

3. Click **OK** to create a new 2-column by 2-row table. Type something in the first cell of the table, press Tab to move over to column number two, type something else, press Tab again, type more, and press Tab one last time to move to the final cell, and type even more. Your screen should look like Figure 12.2.

FIGURE 12.2
A filled out
2-column by
2-row table.

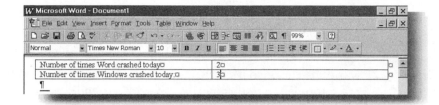

4. The easiest way to create a new row in the table: put your cursor at the end of the text in the final cell, then press the Tab key. Word adds a new row on the bottom of the table and lets you fill it in (see Figure 12.3).

FIGURE 12.3
Adding a new row is as simple as putting the cursor at the end of the last cell, and pressing Tab.

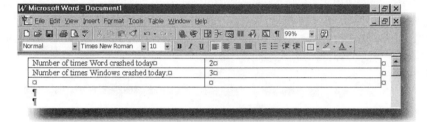

5. The table in Figure 12.3 has several components you might not be familiar with. The sunburst-like stars at the end of each cell are called *end of cell markers*. They resemble paragraph marks in that they appear on the screen, but they don't print on the printer.

6. You'll also notice starburst markers at the end of each row, after the table cell proper. These are called *end of row markers* (ingenious terminology, eh?) and they, like the end of cell markers, contain formatting information. The last end of row marker, the one at the bottom, is an *end of table marker*

WHY HAVE AN END OF CELL MARKER?
Paragraphs end with a paragraph mark, and as you know (if you survived Chapter 10, "Making Documents Look Good," anyway), Word puts paragraph formatting in the paragraph mark. Well, Word table cells end with an end of cell marker, and Word stuffs *both* paragraph and cell formatting information in the end of cell marker. It's something of a super paragraph mark.

(bet you saw that one coming). These markers aren't as mysterious as Word's paragraph marks because you can't easily copy, move, or delete them. Still, they hold important information. Treat them with respect.

7. Move the cursor so it's hovering over the last vertical line in the table. You'll see it turn into a double-headed arrow. Click and drag that last vertical line in the table; move it closer to the left (see Figure 12.4). Note how Word automatically pops a ruler up on the screen to help you align things. You also can adjust the height of rows or individual cells using this click and drag method. Play with it a bit and you'll see.

FIGURE 12.4
Click and drag any of the lines to adjust table dimensions.

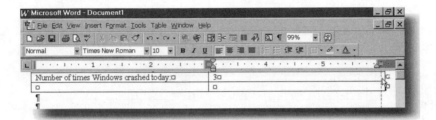

8. Let's get rid of that blank row on the end. To do so, click over in the left margin, to the left of the first blank cell. The last row should be selected, as in Figure 12.5. Then click **Table**, **Delete Rows** to delete the row.

FIGURE 12.5
Delete rows in Word tables by selecting them, then clicking Table, Delete Rows.

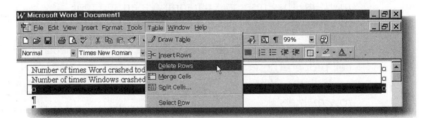

9. Try clicking on any of the **Table** menu items. You'll become immersed in the lore of Word tables.

10. When you're done, close the document and don't save changes. We'll create several more tables shortly.

Fast Free-form Tables

If you know that your table is going to be rectangular, with neat and orderly cells, and that it needs rows that are all of equal width, the **Table**, **Insert Table** method can't be beat. But if you're a bit more freewheeling, you'll probably get a kick out of this.

XERCISE

Roll Your Own Table

1. Start with a new, clean document.

2. Click **Table**, **Draw Table**. Word responds by displaying the Tables and Borders toolbar, popping up the Office Assistant with a redundant suggestion (which is repeated in the status bar), and turning your cursor into a table-drawing machine. Click to dismiss the Office Assistant, then use the mouse to draw the outer boundary of your new table (see Figure 12.6).

FIGURE 12.6
Freehand table drawing starts by defining the outer limits of the table.

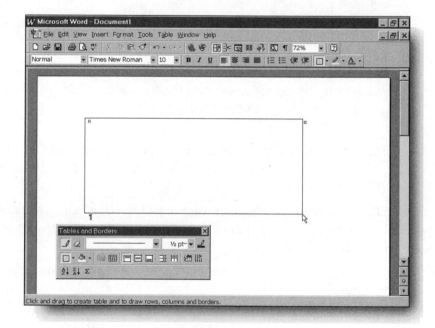

3. Use the cursor to draw a couple of vertical lines in appropriately eclectic places. As soon as you let go of the mouse button, the lines turn into vertical lines in the table, and cells appear (see Figure 12.7).

FIGURE 12.7
Simply draw
vertical lines
to define the
columns of
the table.

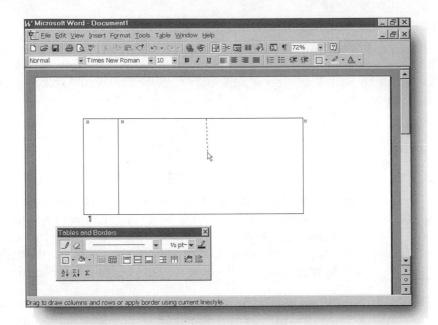

4. Now repeat the drawing motions, this time dragging left-to-right to come up with horizontal lines—the rows (see Figure 12.8). Note that these rows don't have to go all the way across the table; they can begin or end on any vertical line. Cool!

5. When you're done being creative, step back and take a look at the table you've created, freehand. In Figure 12.9 I've come up with a table that contains five cells.

6. What? You say you don't want one of the lines? Okay. Nothing to it. Simply click the **Eraser** 🔲 icon, then click the line you don't want any more (see Figure 12.10).

7. Let go of the mouse button and poof! The line disappears, just like that (see Figure 12.11).

8. Try anything you like with the new table. Type text into the cells. Move the rows and columns around. You're the boss. When you get bored, close the document and don't save changes.

FIGURE 12.8
Click and drag horizontal lines to create rows.

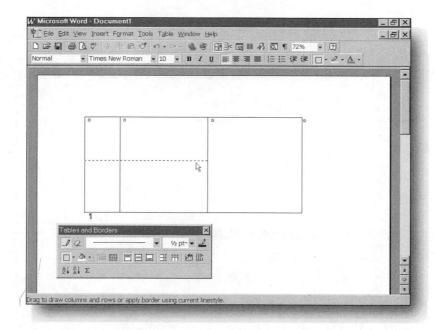

FIGURE 12.9
This freehand drawing tool gives you a lot of flexibility in creating tables.

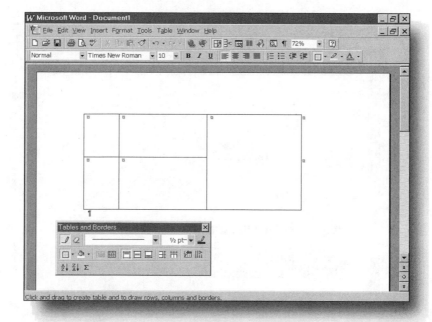

FIGURE 12.10
Click on the
Eraser and
choose a line
to erase.

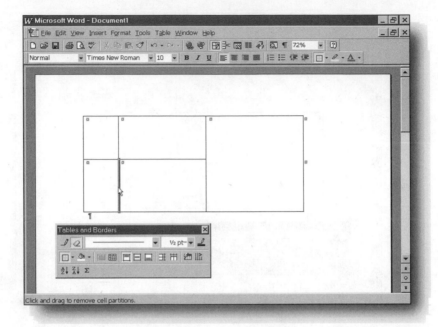

FIGURE 12.11
After the line
is selected,
release the
mouse button
and it's gone.

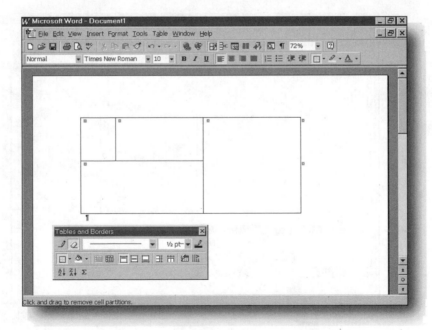

Note that the freehand drawing tool will work on any table—even tables that were originally created with the Table, Insert Table dialog box. In Figure 12.12 I've gone into just such a table, created originally as 2-column by 2-row, and added a mole's nest of odd cells. If you ever need to fabricate a bizarre table, this is the way to do it.

FIGURE 12.12
Hand-draw additional cells on a basic 2 x 2 table.

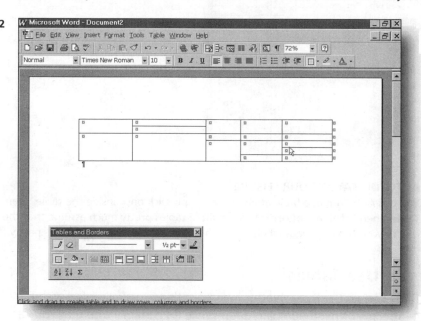

Fancy Tables

Although I can't begin to cover all the tools Word has available for drawing and modifying tables, there's one final table trick I use all the time, and I'd like to show it to you.

*E*XERCISE

AutoFormat—The Table Wizard

1. Start with a new, clean document.

2. Click **Table**, **Insert Table**, then **AutoFormat**.

3. Word will present you with a huge array of table formats (see Figure 12.13). You simply choose one, click **OK**, and start typing in data.

4. The generated tables are real tables: you can modify them any way you like, or poke around to change some of Word's formatting options.

5. When you're done, close the document and don't save changes.

FIGURE 12.13
The Professional AutoFormat table offers quite a bit of built-in formatting.

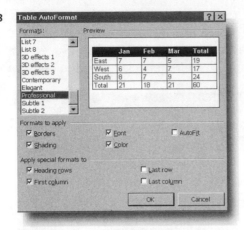

AUTOFORMAT AT YOUR LEISURE

You can AutoFormat a table at any time. Simply click once inside the table, then click **Table**, then **Table AutoFormat**. The built-in tables pretty much assume that the first row in your table includes labels for all the columns. Other than that, it's pretty flexible.

Odd Ways to Use Tables

Most people think of tables as little boxy things, usually filled with boring statistics or streams of mind-numbing data. While it's certainly true that you can use Word to put anything to sleep, it's also true that tables can solve all sorts of formatting problems.

THINK TABLES, NOT TABS

Here's a simple rule of thumb: If you're thinking of using tabs to organize a page in some way, chances are very good you can solve the problem easier, faster, and better by using tables.

One classic example: the resume. In a resume you typically want to keep headings on the left side of the page and line up detailed information indented on the right. If you try to create a resume with indents or tabs, you'll be pulling your hair out before the first resume even gets printed.

The trick is to build a big table, with two columns. The leftmost column contains the headings. The rightmost column contains text.

The people who built Word's templates used this trick. Click **File**, then **New**, go over to the **Other Documents** tab, and double-click **Professional Resume.dot** (or any of the other resumes, for that matter).

What you see is a table. It's a bit difficult to visualize because you can't see the table's gridlines, although you *can* see the end of cell markers, which should be a dead giveaway. The people who created the template hid the gridlines. Click **Table**, then **Show Gridlines,** and you'll see the whole table, as in Figure 12.14.

FIGURE 12.14
Word's pre-built resumes all use tables.

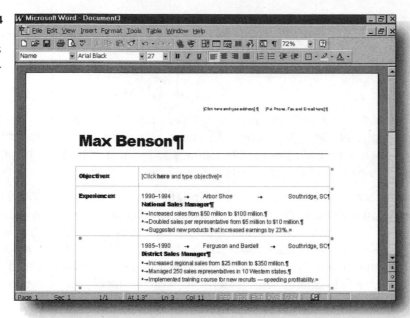

Tables have many uses. Don't get boxed in by table stereotypes. Get creative!

Dates

If you want to put the current date or time in a document, the easiest way, by far, is to simply click **Insert**, then **Date and Time**. You'll get the Date and Time dialog box, as shown in Figure 12.15.

Unfortunately, there's a little box at the bottom of the dialog box which will drive you nuts. It says **Update automatically**, and you're to be excused if you don't understand what Word means by *automatically*. It's a simple concept, hard to explain, made even more difficult because there isn't much room in the dialog box to explain what's going on.

FIGURE 12.15
Word lets you insert dates and times easily—but the Update box can really fool you.

If you don't check that box, Word puts today's current time or date in the document, and that's that. Open the document an hour, a week, or a century from now, and the date or time you'll see there will be identical to the date or time you originally put in the document. Print it next month, and you'll get this month's date. It isn't updated.

On the other hand, if you check the **Update automatically** box, Word puts something called a *field* in the document. Fields can do many things—as we'll see in Chapter 14, "Advanced Features"—but from time to time this particular field retrieves the current date or time and puts it in the document. The process of looking up the current date or time and putting it in the document is called *updating the field*. Word updates fields under several circumstances, but the two most common ones are

● When the document is opened

● Just before the document is printed

There's an easy way to see what's going on.

*E*XERCISE

Updated Dates

1. Start with a new, blank document.

2. Click **Insert**, then **Date and Time**. Choose one of the times that includes seconds, such as the one shown earlier in Figure 12.15. Make sure the **Update automatical**ly box is unchecked, and click OK. You'll see the current time in the document.

3. Press Enter a few times. Then click **Insert**, then **Date and Time**. This time, choose the same time—one that shows seconds—and check the **Update automatically** box. Click **OK**, and a later time will appear in your document (see Figure 12.16).

FIGURE 12.16
Two times in the document—the first is not updated, the second is.

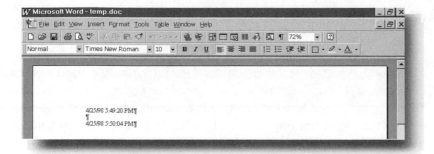

4. Now click the **Print** 🖨 icon. Watch the second time in the document. If you look very closely, you'll see it flicker, then change, immediately prior to printing (see Figure 12.17).

FIGURE 12.17
Word updates the time immediately prior to printing.

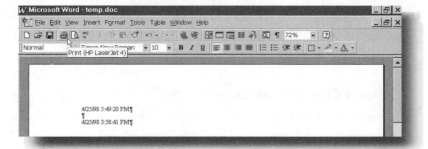

5. You can repeat that printing as often as you like. Immediately prior to printing, Word 97 updates the time on the second line—but it leaves the time on the first line intact.

6. Close the document and save changes. Call it, oh, temp.doc. Open it. See how the second time has changed again? Whenever Word opens the document, it *updates fields*—and thus updates the time on the second line.

Inserting Pictures

And now for something completely different.

Word lets you place almost any kind of computerized drawing inside your documents. These same techniques work pretty much the same way in the other Office 97 components, too, so let's take some time to explore them thoroughly.

Clip Art

The term *clip art* once referred to artwork that could be cut (thus, *clipped*) and pasted onto a sheet of paper. As far as Office is concerned, clip art is just a picture, sound, or video loop that you don't intend to change—you may move it around, resize it, chop off (*crop*) one or more of the edges, adjust the contrast or brightness, or draw a box around it, but you aren't going to change what's in the image itself, at least not from inside Office 97. That's what makes Office clip art, well, clip art. Thus, if you're creating illustrations with another program (say, using Collage to take screen shots, as I have with this book, or putting together freehand drawings with Corel Draw), those illustrations are just clip art, from Office's point of view.

☞ *Throughout this discussion of clip art, I'm going to assume that you've installed Office 97 Service Release 1, as described on page 12.*

The original version of Word 97 made inserting and working with clip art a living nightmare. The other components of Office 97 aren't so adversely affected, but using clip art in Word 97 without Service Release 1 rates right up there with self-administered prefrontal lobotomies.

Office's Clip Art Collection

Office 97 ships with a limited collection of clip art. To see it, put your Office 97 CD in the drive, click **Insert**, then **Picture**, then **Clip Art**. That brings up the Office Clip Gallery, shown in Figure 12.18.

FIGURE 12.18
The Office 97 Clip Art Gallery—limited, but occasionally useful.

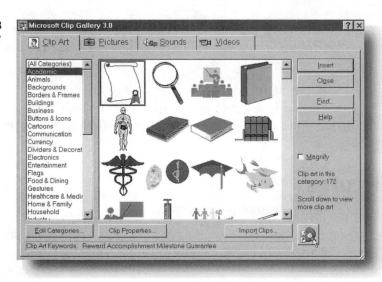

You can spend some time scrolling the pictures on offer here; when you find a picture that you want to put in your document, click **Insert**, and the picture gets transported back into your document.

I want to point out two specific features on this **Clip Art** tab. First, if you have clip art that you use all the time, it's relatively easy to import it into the Clip Gallery. Simply click the **Import Clips** button and follow the instructions from that point.

Second, Office 97 really does ship with a huge selection of clip art—it's just that you have to pop onto the Web to find it! If you have a Web connection established on your PC, click the icon in the lower-right corner—the one that looks like a globe with a magnifying glass. Wait a little while (if you do this in the middle of a business day, wait a *long* while), and you'll ultimately be rewarded with thousands and thousands of high-quality clips, free, from the Microsoft Web site (see Figure 12.19).

FIGURE 12.19
Getting to the mother lode Microsoft clip Web site is as easy as clicking a button.

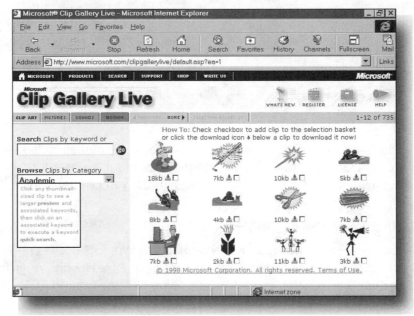

When you download clips from the Microsoft Web site, they're automatically stored on your hard drive, and added to the Clip Gallery, so if you want the same clip again, there's no need to hook up to the Web.

PUT THAT WALLET AWAY!
If you've ever thought of spending a hundred bucks (or even half that) on a clip art collection, make sure you've explored this free site first. You might be surprised how extensive a collection you already own!

Click the different tabs—**Pictures** (a collection of background patterns and photographs), **Sounds**, and **Videos**. Just for fun, click the video called **fistslam**, then click **Insert** (see Figure 12.20). After the video is back in your document, double-click it to see the animation in action.

FIGURE 12.20
The fistslam animated video clip.

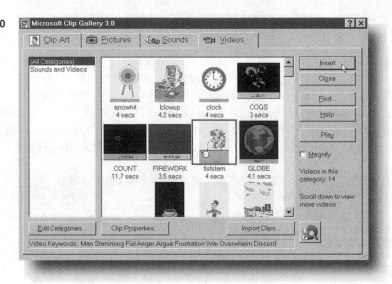

No, it's not exactly high art. And you aren't going to want animated sequences in documents that you print and send to the boss. But it is a neat trick you should shove away in the back of your mind, just in case you can use it some day.

Using Your Own Clip Art

If you ever need to put your own artwork into a Word 97 document—and artwork in this context can mean almost any kind of picture file, sounds, or animated video clips—you'll likely use the Insert Picture dialog box (see Figure 12.21). To get to it, click **Insert**, then **Picture**, and choose **From File**.

Office 97 supports a wide variety of file types. To see what kinds of files you can put into documents, click the down arrow on the **Files of Type** box and scroll through the list.

Of course, you can bring almost any picture into any Office document, if you can get it on the Clipboard. Just create the picture by whatever means, click **Edit**, then **Copy**, flip over to your Office program, and click the **Paste** 📋 icon. We'll look at one way to do that in the next Exercise.

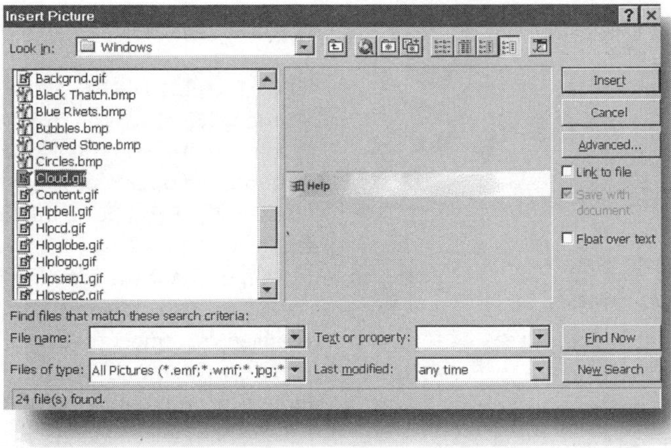

FIGURE 12.21
Office lets you insert any kind of artwork from this dialog box.

If you use the Insert Picture dialog to bring artwork into your documents, two check boxes in Figure 12.21 deserve your undivided attention:

- *Link to file.* If you check this box prior to inserting the picture, Office doesn't actually put the picture in the document. Instead, it puts a link—a pointer to the file—inside the document. On the plus side, that means your document will be much smaller— pictures tend to consume a lot of space, whereas links don't take hardly any space at all. On the minus side, it

GIMME MORE IMPORT FILTERS
Office uses small programs to bring picture files into documents. These programs are called *import filters*. They're necessary to translate from the format of the picture file into something that Office can understand. When you click the down arrow on the **Files of Type** box in the **Insert Picture** dialog box, what you're really looking at is a list of the import filters that have been made available to Office 97.

If you need to bring a particular type of file into an Office 97 document, and no import filter for that kind of file appears listed in this **Files of Type** box, try reinstalling Office, choosing a Custom install, and choosing from the import filters available there.

If that still doesn't get you the import filter you need, check the extensive collection indexed by Microsoft's Knowledge Base at www.microsoft.com/support.

means that you can't move the picture, and if you give this document to anybody else you have to give them the picture file, too. Worse, they have to reconstruct your exact file structure and put the picture file in the same folder that you used in order for the picture to work right.

FLOAT OVER TEXT GOOF FIXED
In the original version of Word 97, Microsoft checked this **Float over text** check box; you actually had to uncheck it every time you put a picture in a document to ensure that the picture went in the document itself, and not the drawing layer. Microsoft heard so many screams from irate and horribly confused customers that they were forced to back off this dumb design decision. It was the single most frequently asked question about Word 97 that *I* encountered. I can only imagine how many tens of thousands of phone calls MS Technical Support had to field.

In Service Release-1, Word is smart enough to leave **Float over text** unchecked, forcing you to check the box if you want to relegate your pictures to the twilight zone.

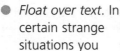 *Float over text*. In certain strange situations you might want to make the picture *float*: put the picture in the drawing layer, the ghost-like no man's land that floats over the top of Word documents. Putting the picture in the drawing layer lets you click the picture and use your mouse to position it anywhere within a document. It also lets Word automatically *wrap* text around the picture (click once on the picture, then click **Format**, **Picture**, **Wrapping**). Leaving this box unchecked (which I strongly recommend, unless you specifically need to position the picture with the mouse, or wrap text around it in odd ways) puts the picture in the document itself. Inside the document, it's treated just like a character, albeit a big character. You can attach captions to pictures inside documents and refer to those captions elsewhere in the document.

☞ I talk about the drawing layer on page 124.

Freehand (AutoShapes and the Drawing Toolbar)

If you're going to do extensive freehand drawing for a picture in an Office document, you'd be crazy to use the tools built in to Office 97. They simply aren't robust enough to support any serious drawing effort.

Microsoft has a far more capable, ree drawing program called Draw 98 that you should consider if you're going to do more than a few simple callouts. I talked about it on page 37.

CALLOUTS?
What is a *callout*? Good question. In the World According to Word, a call-out is a line that points to a picture, usually with some explanatory text attached. You'll see a Word-style callout in the next Exercise. Unfortunately, terminology for these things vary, so don't be too surprised if your favorite graphics artist has a different definition for the term callout.

On the other hand, for the occasional quick drawing or picture call-out, Office 97's AutoShapes and Drawing toolbar may suffice. Let me show you how.

XERCISE

Picture and a Callout

1. Start with a new, clean document.

2. Let's take a screen shot, using the current screen, and put that in the document. (Cool, huh?) Press the Print Screen key on your keyboard (the Print Screen key may be marked PrtScr, or some variation on that theme). That puts a shot of the current screen on the clipboard. To put it into your document, click the **Paste** ⊡ icon. Your document should look something like Figure 12.22.

3. The picture is pasted into the drawing layer. At this point you can move or resize the picture almost any way you like. Simply click it once, then click and drag a corner to resize the picture without distorting it; drag an edge to resize and squish; or use the four-headed arrow to move the picture any place you like. You can even click **Format**, then **Picture**, and really change things around.

4. Click **Insert**, **Picture**, **AutoShapes**. Word responds by putting the Drawing toolbar at the bottom of the screen and setting up an AutoShapes toolbar. We want the kind of AutoShape called a Callout, so click the **Callout** icon, as shown in Figure 12.23.

5. The type of callout I like to use for most pictures is the one Word identifies as **Line Callout 3 (No Border)**. Look for it in the third column, fourth row of the various callouts Word offers. Click it, and Word sets you up with a callout AutoShape.

FIGURE 12.22
Using Word's built-in capabilities to put a screen shot in a document.

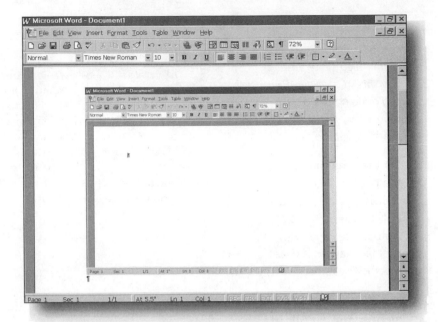

FIGURE 12.23
The AutoShapes toolbar organizes Office's extensive collection of prebuilt shapes.

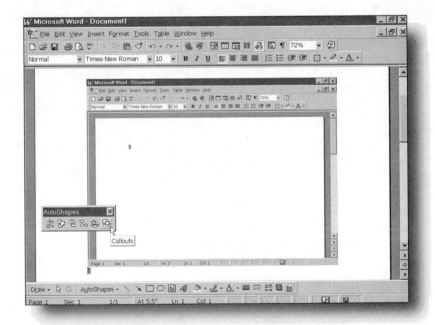

6. Move your cursor next to the paragraph mark in the screen shot and press the mouse button down. Then, holding the button down, draw to the bottom and right. When you have something that looks like Figure 12.24, let go of the mouse button. It's a little hard to describe, but very easy to do.

FIGURE 12.24
Drawing a
Line Callout 3
(No Border)
AutoShape.

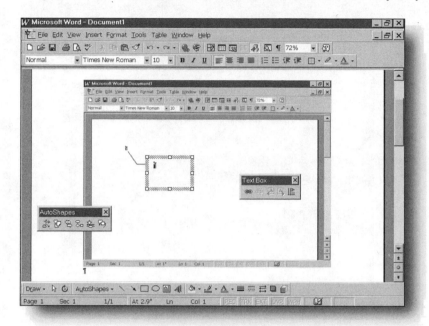

7. Here's the easy part. Type `This is a paragraph mark`, then click outside the text box. Your document should look like Figure 12.25.

8. I won't take you through all the various formatting options available at this point, but they are extensive: colors, backgrounds, shapes, lines, all sorts of things.

WHO SHOT THAT ARROW?
Okay. Just one formatting option. Click once on the callout, then right-click on the callout's line, and choose **Format AutoShape**. Use the **Colors and Lines** tab to, oh, put an arrow head on the callout. It's amazingly easy to do.

9. You can spend days playing with AutoShapes and the Drawing toolbar. When you figure you've had enough, close the document and don't save changes. To get rid of the Drawing toolbar, right-click anywhere on the toolbar and uncheck the box marked **Drawing**.

FIGURE 12.25
The finished callout.

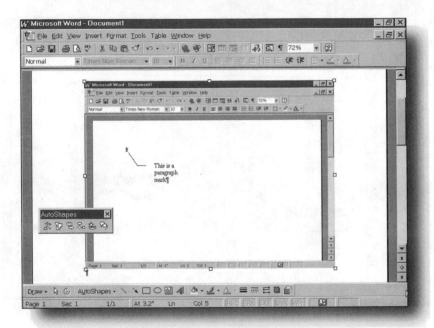

I've only touched the surface of the formatting options available with pictures. If you want to explore a little deeper—say, adjusting the contrast of pictures, or changing them from color to grayscale—click **Tools**, **Customize**, check the **Picture** box, and then **OK**. From that point, the Office Assistant can take you on a fantastic journey.

WordArt

Word 97 hosts a program called WordArt, which can be used to create all sorts of fancy font effects; see, for example, Figure 12.26. You can use WordArt in any Office 97 application.

I won't go into any detail here, except to say that you get to WordArt by clicking **Insert**, then **Picture**, then **WordArt**. Microsoft has written an extensive help system for WordArt. To get to it, click **Help**, **Contents and Index**. On the **Index** tab, type WordArt, and follow help from there.

FIGURE 12.26
WordArt
Works!

Scanned Art

If you have a scanner attached to your PC, you can access it directly from inside all the Office applications by clicking **Insert**, **Picture**, **From Scanner**. That brings up Microsoft's surprisingly capable Photo Editor.

I talked about the Photo Editor on page 38.

Charts

Word and PowerPoint both support an older Microsoft application called Microsoft Graph. If you have very simple charting requirements and you have all the data already calculated, and you want to avoid linking to Excel (for, say, performance reasons), you might want to try Microsoft Graph.

To set up a chart, click **Insert**, **Picture**, **Chart**. Word responds by bringing in a dummy spreadsheet—Microsoft calls it a *datasheet*, no doubt so you don't think that you have access to all of Excel's spreadsheet capabilities. Word also draws a graph on the page, tied to the numbers in the datasheet (see Figure 12.27).

Once again, I'm not going to bore you with the details, as Microsoft has provided a thorough Microsoft Graph tutorial. It's a little hard to find, though—the 'Softies didn't put it in the Help Index. Bring up the Office Assistant by pressing F1, then type chart. Follow the links from there.

FIGURE 12.27
Microsoft Graph provides limited, but sometimes useful, charting capabilities.

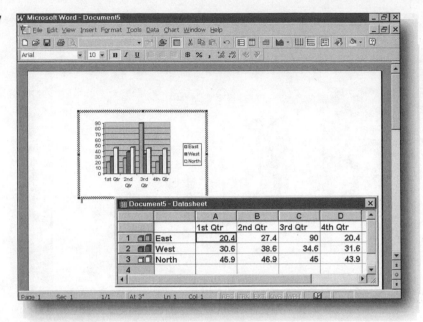

Inserting Files

Some of you construct Word documents by assembling them from prebuilt pieces of boilerplate text, mixing and matching as the need arises. That can be a very efficient way to churn out enormous quantities of Word documents.

To put an entire file into your current document, simply put the insertion point wherever you want the file to go, then click **Insert**, **File**, choose your file, and click **OK** (see Figure 12.28).

There are a few tricks to inserting files (aren't there always). Here are the ones you need to be aware of:

- There's no real limit to the size of the file you import. You can create files than contain just a single sentence, or one picture. On the other end of the spectrum, you can assemble documents from files that are megabytes in size. If you have a high tolerance for pain and infinite patience, anyway.

FIGURE 12.28
Put an entire file inside your document.

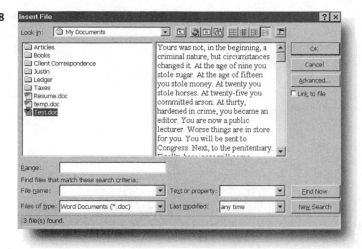

● At the same time, though, you have to realize that when you perform a File Insert, everything in the inserted file goes into your current document. So, in particular, if you're inserting a Word document into a Word document, you will *always* bring the paragraph mark at the end of the inserted file into your current document. (Remember, every document contains at least one paragraph mark!)

● If you insert a Word document into a Word document, sometimes Word brings across formatting that you don't want. The best way I've found to defend against this problem is to avoid inserting Word documents at the very end of other Word documents. It only takes a moment to put a few "virgin" paragraph marks at the end of a document, then back up before clicking **Insert**, then **Paragraph**.

Follow those little suggestions, and you can build documents from documents from documents.

On the Shoulders
of Giants

*L*ITERALLY TENS OF MILLIONS OF PEOPLE HAVE gone before you, trying to get

work done with Word 97. No matter what problem you've encoun-

tered, what word processing crosses you've had to bear, rest

assured that somebody, somewhere has confronted the same prob-

lem. With any luck at all, they might've found a solution, too.

This chapter concentrates on leveraging the solutions others have

found and setting up Word so you don't have to repeat many of

the mundane tasks you press every day.

Templates and Wizards that Work

If you need to create and work with a document that you've never encountered before, you should spend some time looking to see if there's a template in existence that paves the way. So much of Word's useful genetic memory lives inside templates and Wizards that were assembled by experts to tackle specific problems.

The Web abounds with templates—admittedly of varying quality—some free, some expensive, which can be useful in tackling specific Word jobs. A few minutes spent with your favorite Web browser can yield dozens, even hundreds, of Word templates for almost any imaginable project.

Office 97's own Valupack includes several templates and Wizards you may have overlooked. Here's how to retrieve them, and an example of how well one of them—the Calendar Wizard—works. The Calendar Wizard creates catchy, free-form calendars, ready for you to type whatever suits your fancy. Because the resulting calendars are 100% Word 97 documents, you can doctor them up with pictures, fancy fonts, or just about anything you can imagine. Hard to believe that Microsoft buried such a useful piece of software in the backwaters of the Valupack, but there it sits, ready for you to discover.

XERCISE

The Valupack's Calendar Wizard

1. Start with a clean, new document.

2. Copy the Calendar Wizard from the Office 97 Valupack onto your hard drive. To do so, right-click **My Computer**, and choose **Explore**. Inside Windows Explorer, navigate to the CD-ROM drive and find **\Valupack\ Template\Word**. Those are the files you want to copy. In the left pane, just using the **+** folder expansion icon, locate **c:\My Programs\Microsoft Office\Templates\Other Documents**. In the right pane, click **agenda.wiz**, then press **Ctrl+A** to select all the templates and Wizards in the folder. Then drag the whole she-bang (see Figure 13.1) to the **\Other Documents** folder. Click the **x** in the upper-right corner of the Explorer window to get rid of it.

3. Back in Word, click **File**, then **New**, then the **Other Documents** tab. (See how all the templates you copied now appear on the **Other Documents** tab?) Double-click **Calendar.wiz** (see Figure 13.2).

4. The Calendar Wizard kicks in (see Figure 13.3). Follow the steps in the Wizard to place a calendar in your new document.

FIGURE 13.1
Retrieving the Word templates in Office 97's Valupack.

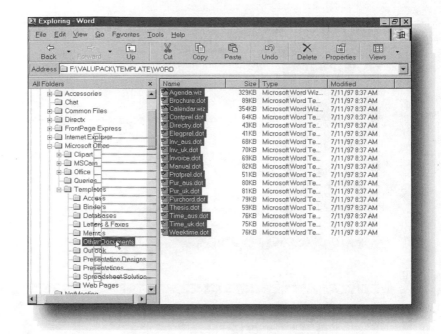

FIGURE 13.2
All the new templates appear under the Other Documents tab.

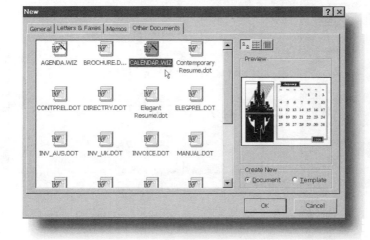

5. It's important to realize that the resulting document is a normal, everyday (sometimes very fancy!) Word document. If you poke around a bit, you'll find that the calendars produced by this Wizard (see Figure 13.4) primarily consist of tables.

FIGURE 13.3
The Calendar Wizard is one of Word's most powerful Wizards—and it's free.

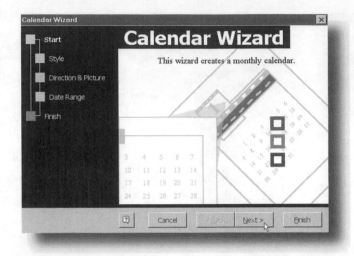

FIGURE 13.4
A banner calendar, demonstrating an innovative way to use tables.

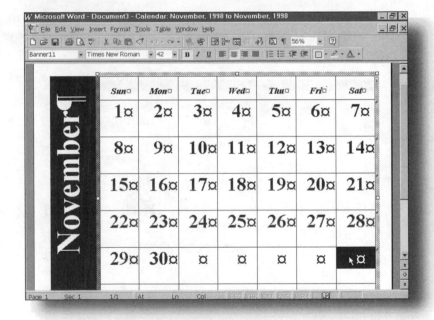

6. Feel free to change the tables around—resize the boxes by clicking and dragging, change the fonts, whatever you like. When you're done, close the file and don't save changes.

I hope that this exercise has shown you how a well-designed template or Wizard can save you hours, even days, of frustrating, nit-picking work. Whenever you tackle a new type of document, seriously consider downloading—even buying!—a template that's customized to solve your specific problems.

Doing It with Styles

I don't know why people get all sweaty when they hear the term *styles*. It's as if folks are convinced that Word styles are some sort of programmer's mumbo-jumbo, a feature that only advanced Word users or absolute loonies would even consider.

Well, that simply isn't the case. Word styles, which appear in the **Style** box `Heading 1 ▾`, amount to nothing more (or less) than formatting shortcuts. They let you set up formatting just once, after which you can easily apply that formatting, consistently, throughout your document. There's nothing remotely mysterious or off-putting about them. Styles solve all sorts of problems.

Let me give you an example, a little thought-experiment.

You're creating a report for The Boss, and The Boss has determined that the company name is to appear throughout the report as **Tremulous Tribbles, Inc**., bold, just like that. You spend a lot of time making sure the name gets typed in correctly, and alert everyone who reads the manuscript to make sure it shows up precisely the way The Boss wants. You hand in the report a couple of days before a Board meeting, and all is well.

Now tell me this hasn't happened to you. The day of the Board meeting, The Boss's Boss's Boss hits the fan, suddenly deciding that the company name must show up as ***Tremulous Tribbles, Inc.***, but in bold italic. And you have all of about two minutes to make the change and re-print the reports.

If you had typed in all those **Tremulous Tribbles** and applied the formatting by hand, dutifully clicking the **Bold** `B` icon as you typed, you could run a search and replace, and stand a fair chance of picking up most of the **Tribbles**. (That's the trouble with tribbles, eh?) If it's a long report, running through the replace, and double- and triple-checking it, could take quite a while.

On the other hand, if you had set up a *character style* for the company name and applied the style as you typed, it would take just a few seconds to update the style, and thus change the appearance of ***Tremulous Tribbles, Inc.*** throughout the document. Of course, it might still take all morning to get the report out of the printer, but I think you understand where I'm coming from.

Styles are good. Styles let you control your documents with a minimum of fuss.

Character Styles

Word's character styles allow you to apply a bunch of character formatting in one simple step. Let me show you how they work by going through the kind of ohmigosh last-minute changes that you saw in the Tribbles thought-experiment.

XERCISE

Apply Character Styles

1. Open test.doc.

2. Pick a word or phrase in test.doc that you'd like to emphasize, and select it. In Figure 13.5, I've selected the word **Congress**.

FIGURE 13.5
Start by choosing a word or phrase you would like to make different from the surrounding text.

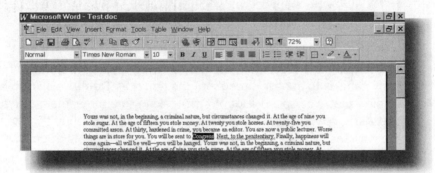

3. Let's create a new character style, one that we can use throughout the document to provide similar treatment to any text. Click **Format**, then **Style**. Click **New**. You'll see the New Style dialog box, as shown in Figure 13.6.

4. In the **Style type** box, in the upper-right corner of the New Style dialog box, choose **Character**. Then type a name for your new character style. In Figure 13.6, I've called the new style **Emphasize**.

5. Click **Format**, then **Font**. Then set up the font you want for the **Emphasize** style. In 7, I've decided that **Emphasize** should be Arial, bold, 18 point.

6. Click **OK**, then **Apply**. Word sets up the new character style and applies it to whatever you've selected. In Figure 13.8, note how the word **Congress** has taken on the new formatting—but also note how the **Style** box in the upper-left corner now says **Emphasize**. That's how Word tells you that you're working with a different style.

FIGURE 13.6
Setting up a
new character
style.

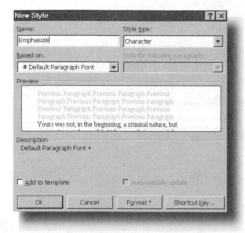

FIGURE 13.7
Specify font
formatting
for the new
style.

FIGURE 13.8
The
Emphasize
style is
applied to
the selected
text.

7. Next, select some other text in the document (it needn't be the same text that you originally set to the **Emphasize** style). In Figure 13.9 I've selected **public lecturer**. Apply the **Emphasize** character style to what you've selected by clicking the down-arrow next to the **Style** box, and picking **Emphasize**.

FIGURE 13.9
Applying the Emphasize character style to other text in the document.

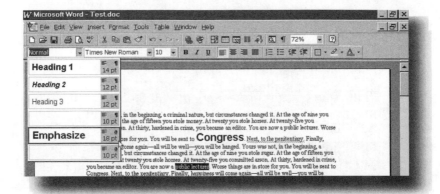

8. The text you've selected turns into the **Emphasize** style, and takes on all the formatting characteristics embodied in that style.

9. To see how changing a character style can ripple modifications throughout a document, let's make a change to the **Emphasize** style. To do so, click **Format**, then **Style**. On the left, click **Emphasize**, and at the bottom click **Modify**. Once again, you'll see the Font dialog box. Choose something outrageous. In Figure 13.10 I redefined **Emphasize** so it becomes Arial, bold italic, 28 point, all caps. That's pretty outrageous.

10. Click **OK** a couple of times and you'll see how **Emphasize** has changed. Each of the pieces of text in the document that have the **Emphasize** character style applied change to conform to the new **Emphasize** style (see Figure 13.11).

11. As you might imagine, there are lots of options available in these dialog boxes. If you use character styles fairly frequently, you should take a look behind the **Shortcut Key** button on the New Style dialog box in Figure 13.6, earlier in this chapter. That lets you set up a simple keystroke—say, Ctrl+Alt+E, for **Emphasize**—to apply character styles quickly and easily.

12. When you're done, close test.doc, and don't save changes.

FIGURE 13.10
Change the font for the Emphasize character style.

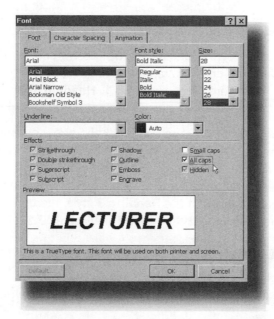

FIGURE 13.11
The new Emphasize character style formatting ripples all the way through the document.

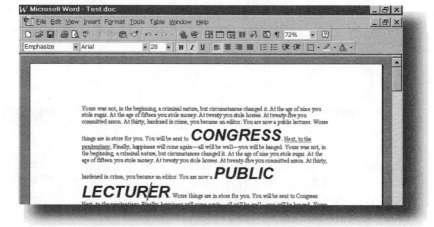

Character style formatting can come in very handy. Learn to use them, and the neck you save may be your own.

Paragraph Styles

Paragraph styles control both paragraph formatting and character formatting. That's a bit hard to grasp, but once you've used paragraph styles a few times you'll see what's happening.

*E*XERCISE

Modify Word's Heading Paragraph Styles

1. Start with a clean, new document. Word ships with quite a few built-in paragraph styles. The ones you're most likely to see if you pull down the **Style** `Heading 1 ▾` box are called **Heading 1**, **Heading 2**, and **Heading 3**. They appear, for example, in Figure 13.9.

2. Type `This is a level 1 heading`, click the arrow on the **Style** `Heading 1 ▾` box and choose **Heading 1**, then press Enter a few times. Type `This is level 2`, and again using the **Style** box, format it with the **Heading 2** style, then press Enter a couple more times. Finally, type `This is level 3` and apply to it the **Heading 3** style, then press **Enter** a few more times. Your document should look like Figure 13.12.

FIGURE 13.12
The standard, built-in Heading 1, 2, and 3 paragraph styles.

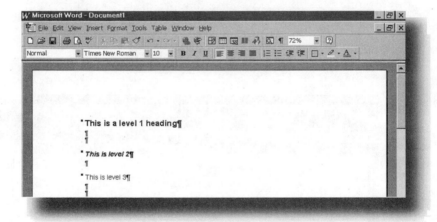

3. These built-in heading styles are a bit garish. Level 1 shows up as Arial 14 point bold, which is all right, but level 2 comes out Arial 12 point bold italic. To most graphic artists, that's a mortal sin. Bold italic is what you expect to see on ransom notes, for heaven's sake!

4. Let's say you want to change level 2 headings so they're Arial 12 point italic, but not bold. Easily done.

5. Click once anywhere inside the **This is level 2** line. Click **Format**, **Style**, make sure **Heading 2** is showing on the left, and click **Modify**. If you want to permanently change Word's definition of the **Heading 2** style, check the box marked **Add to template** (see Figure 13.13).

FIGURE 13.13
Checking
Add to template ensures that all new normal documents will use your modified definition for Heading 2.

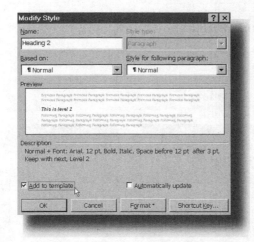

6. Click **Format**, then **Font**, and change the **Bold Italic** setting to just plain **Italic**. Click **OK**, then **OK** again, and finally **Apply**. From this point on, every time you use the **Heading 2** style, Word makes the heading Arial 12 point italic, but not bold.

7. Feel free to play with other changes to your built-in Word headings, but be aware of the fact that whenever you check that **Add to template** box you're making permanent changes to the way Word works.

8. If you want to change the **Heading 2** style back to Word's built-in setting (there's no overwhelming need to do so, unless you feel more comfortable trusting Microsoft's experts than your own eye), click **Format**, **Style**, choose **Heading 2** on the left, check **Add to template**, click **Modify**. Then click **Format**, **Font**, and set the font back to Arial 12 point Bold Italic. Blecch. A couple of **OK**s and you're back to normal.

9. When you're done, keep the document open for the next exercise.

Although we didn't explicitly go through it all, paragraph styles can include any sort of paragraph formatting—from alignment to tabs, bullets to borders. If you want to center all your **Heading 1** styled paragraphs, for example, simply choose **Modify**, **Format**, **Paragraph**, and set **Alignment** to **Center**.

Setting the paragraph style, as you've seen, also changes all the character formatting in the paragraph. You can go back and apply your own character formatting on top of the paragraph style, so to speak. Here's a quick exercise to show you how.

Character Formatting on a Paragraph Style

1. Start with the document you just created in the previous exercise.

2. Select a few characters from the level 1 heading. In Figure 13.14, I've selected the phrase **is a level**.

FIGURE 13.14
Choose some characters in the paragraph that are formatted as Heading 1.

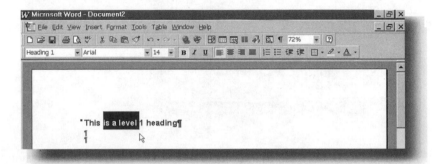

3. Apply some weird character formatting to the selected characters. In Figure 13.15, I've made them 28 points tall by clicking the **Font Size** [14 ▼] icon.

FIGURE 13.15
Change the character formatting of the selected characters.

4. See how you can change character formatting by going in and manually applying the formatting over the top of a paragraph that has already been formatted with a different style?

5. Keep the document up there. We'll use it one last time, in the next exercise.

You'd probably expect that you could even apply a character style over the top of a paragraph style—and you'd be right. The character style takes precedence over the underlying paragraph style, just as manually applied character formatting takes precedence over a paragraph's style.

One last little, nagging question. What if you make a mistake? For example, what if you apply manual formatting to some characters in the middle of a paragraph, but later you decide that you really want to make those characters normal?

The easiest way to unformat characters is to undo the formatting with the **Undo** button immediately after you screw up the formatting. Unfortunately, sometimes you don't catch your mistake in time to undo and you really need a reset button, to turn the character formatting back to its original state.

Ah, your wish is Word's command. Well, sometimes anyway.

EXERCISE

Using the Default Paragraph Font

1. Start with the document you created in the preceding exercise.

2. Select the text that's been incorrectly formatted—the text that you want to change back to normal text for the paragraph's style.

3. Click the down arrow to the right of the **Style Box** `Heading 1 ▼` and choose **Default paragraph font** (see Figure 13.16).

FIGURE 13.16 Resetting text to the default paragraph font—the font dictated by the paragraph's style.

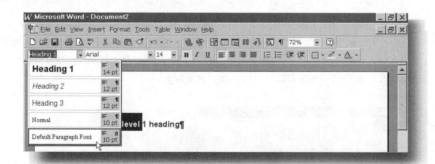

4. You can think of Default paragraph font as being a kind of *reset* character style—one that removes all manually applied formatting. Try applying character formatting to paragraphs with other styles (even the **Normal** style) and see how Default paragraph font resets things.

5. Close the document—don't save changes.

That's what I wanted to show you about styles. Get accustomed to them and you'll wonder how you ever lived without them.

Customizing Toolbars

Toolbars were originally designed to save you work: Instead of having to wade through a series of menus, you could simply click a toolbar icon and *poof!* Word would respond to your every desire. Obviously, you can't put all Word's commands on toolbar buttons. (Well, I guess you could, but trying to figure out what all those tiny pictures mean would drive you nuts.) So there's a natural give-and-take between having too few toolbar buttons—thus limiting your choices and forcing you to the menus, slowing things down—and having too many toolbar buttons, far more than you could ever grasp.

WHY CAN'T I HIDE THE MENU BAR? I just knew you'd try to do that. Geeks are so predictable. Word's menu—the **File**, **Edit**, **View**, **Insert**, etc., thing up at the top of the window—stands sacrosanct. Even though you see a check mark in a box in front of menu bar on the **Toolbar** tab, Word won't let you uncheck it; in other words, there's no way you can get rid of Word's menu. (At least, not by using this dialog box.) Don't mess around with it, OK? You need your menu.

Word 97 comes with 18 built-in toolbars. The two you see on your screen right now—the so-called Standard and Formatting toolbars—merely scratch the surface. To see the other toolbars available to you, click **Tools**, then **Customize**, and make sure the **Toolbars** tab is showing (see Figure 13.17).

FIGURE 13.17
The 18 toolbars Word has available for you, right now.

If you want to see a specific toolbar, just check the box next to its name. To hide a toolbar, uncheck the box.

Word 97 lets you put your own icons on toolbars. (It also lets you put your own commands on the menu, but I won't talk about that here.) I firmly believe this feature rates as one of Word's most powerful capabilities, yet the feature is so rarely discussed you'd think that it had the plague.

Let me show you how customizing toolbars can save you gobs of time.

Did you ever notice how Word 97's Standard toolbar has icons for creating new documents, opening and saving documents—but no icon for closing them? That's one of the most amazing oversights in all Word-dom. I mean, you're going to close at least as many documents as you open, right?

Here's how to add a **Close** button to your Standard toolbar.

XERCISE _____

Close on the Toolbar

1. Click **Tools**, **Customize**, and click the **Commands** tab. Make sure the **Save in** box shows **Normal.dot** (that ensures this toolbar change appears in all new, clean documents). On the left, under **Categories**, choose **File**. On the right, under **Commands**, click **Close** once (see Figure 13.18).

FIGURE 13.18
Choosing the File Close toolbar button from the options that Word offers.

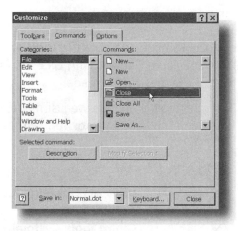

2. Drag the **Close** command up to the standard toolbar. In Figure 13.19 I've dragged it up to a point immediately to the right of the **Save** 🖫 button. As you can see, Word puts a big I-beam pointer on the toolbar, to indicate where this **Close** button will get dropped.

FIGURE 13.19
Click the command and drag it to any desired location on a toolbar.

3. Release the mouse button, and congratulations! You now have a **File Close** icon on your standard toolbar (see Figure 13.20). Play with it a bit and assure yourself that it behaves precisely the same way as clicking **File**, then **Close**.

FIGURE 13.20
The brand new File Close icon appears on your Standard toolbar.

4. Word lets you make these toolbar changes with impunity. If you ever get to the point where you want to restore the original buttons on all your toolbars, simply click **Tools**, **Customize**, and click the **Toolbars** tab. When you see the dialog box shown earlier in Figure 13.17, click the **Reset** button. Word resets all the toolbar changes you've made.

5. I went back in and Reset the toolbar change we just made, just to make the screen shots in this book look like typical Word. You can make your own decision.

Note that Word lets you do much more than place menu commands on the toolbars. If you scroll down the **Categories** list shown earlier in Figure 13.18, you'll find three very interesting entries.

HOW DO I CHANGE AN ICON'S PICTURE?
Choose **Tools, Customize, Toolbars.** As shown earlier in Figure 13.17, you can right-click any toolbar icon and change the picture, name—or just about anything else you can imagine— on that toolbar icon (see Figure 13.21).

FIGURE 13.21
Right-click an
icon to
change its
name or
picture.

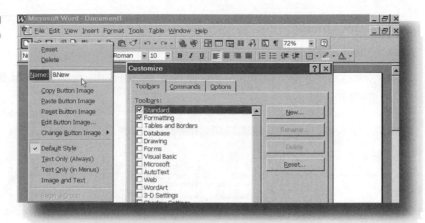

● The **Fonts** category lets you put a single button on a toolbar that changes the font of the selected text. That icon behaves a lot like scrolling down the **Font** box, and picking the font—but it's very quick and easy.

● The **Autotext** category lets you put entire Autotext entries on a toolbar— just click the icon and the chosen Autotext appears in your documents. (This is one of the very few occasions where Autotext beats AutoCorrect.)

● The **Styles** category lets you apply styles with a single click. Just like icons in the **Fonts** category, this one behaves the same as shuffling through the **Style Box**, but it works very quickly.

Bookmarks

With all the fancy ways I've shown you for getting around documents, you might think that the old-fashioned concept of bookmarks might be passé. Not so. Bookmarks remain one of the easiest and fastest ways to get around a Word document. They also form the cornerstone of hyperlinking, a topic we'll explore in the next section.

Out in the real world, you stick a piece of paper in a book so you can get back to the indicated location. Simple enough. In the Word world, a bookmark consists of a location and a name. The location covers just about anything you can select: a single point, a few words or paragraphs, even many pages of text. The name may only contain letters and numbers (no spaces).

*E*XERCISE

Create a Bookmark

1. Open test.doc.

2. Select some text. In Figure 13.22, I've selected the first word of the second paragraph.

FIGURE 13.22
Start setting up a book-mark by selecting text (or simply clicking some-place interesting).

3. To create a bookmark, click **Insert**, then **Bookmark**. Type a meaningful name—in Figure 13.23, I've chosen Kilroy—and click **Add**. That places a bookmark named Kilroy over the first word in the second paragraph.

FIGURE 13.23
Creating a new book-mark called Kilroy.

4. Click anywhere else in the document. Now let's see how to get back to **Kilroy**. There are several ways to navigate around a document's bookmarks. Probably the easiest is to click the **Select Browse Object** icon on the bottom of the vertical scrollbar, the one where **Find and Replace** lives (remember talking about it in Chapter 9, "Getting Around"?), and click the **Go To** → arrow in the upper-left corner.

5. In the box marked **Go to what?** click **Bookmark**. As shown in Figure 13.24, **Kilroy** should be there.

FIGURE 13.24
Jumping straight to a bookmark, compliments of the Go To dialog box.

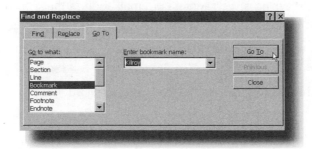

6. Make sure **Kilroy** is highlighted, then click **Go To**. Your cursor should spring to whatever location you chose for the **Kilroy** bookmark.

7. Add as many more bookmarks as you like. Note in particular how a bookmark can be a simple insertion point, or any selected characters you like.

8. Don't close the document just yet. We'll use it for hyperlinking in the next section.

Bookmarks are quite flexible, and very useful. Bookmarks can overlap—you can create bookmarks inside of bookmarks, overlap them partially to the left or right, or just about any way you can imagine. You can put as many bookmarks as you like in a document. You can even bookmark the same selection with as many different names as you might desire.

Hyperlinks

Hyperlinks are just hot buttons inside Word documents. Click a hyperlink, and you're magically transported somewhere else—onto the Web, into another document that's on your PC (or your network, if you have one), or even to another location inside the current document.

☞ *Way back on page 95, I showed you how to turn off Word's annoying tendency to automatically identify Web references and email addresses, and turn them into hyperlinks.*

I recommended you turn them off for all sorts of reasons:

- Word users rarely want a Web address in a document to be hot—usually you're just typing a Web address or email address that you want to print on a piece of paper

- It's easy to accidentally click a hyperlink in one of your own documents and be hurled onto the Web

- Sometimes Word mis-identifies Web and email addresses

- Even when Word gets everything right, the formatting of hyperlinks leaves a lot to be desired

Still, hyperlinks can be quite useful in two very specific situations: when you plan to distribute a document for other people to look at, using Word 97; and, when you use Word 97 to create Web pages. I won't address the latter topic until the very last chapter in this book. But, with Word 97 becoming more and more ubiquitous, you may find the former intriguing.

ℰXERCISE

Create a Hyperlink Inside a Document

1. Start with the version of test.doc you used in the previous exercise. It has a bookmark called Kilroy. We're going to create a hyperlink inside the document that jumps to Kilroy.

2. A hyperlink has two parts: the stuff the reader is supposed to click, and the place the link is supposed to jump to. We're going to put a picture inside test.doc and hook it up so that, when you click the picture, you're whisked away to the Kilroy bookmark. Cool, eh?

3. Let's start by putting a suitable picture in the document. Click inside the document somewhere. Click **Insert**, **Picture**, **From File**, and navigate to the c:\Windows folder. In Figure 13.25, I've chosen the **Black Thatch.bmp** picture for no particularly good reason. Make sure the box marked **Float over text** is not checked, then click **Insert**.

4. We're going to convert that picture into a hyperlink, so click once on the picture, then click the **Insert Hyperlink** icon on the Standard toolbar (see Figure 13.26).

FIGURE 13.25
Inserting a
picture into
test.doc.

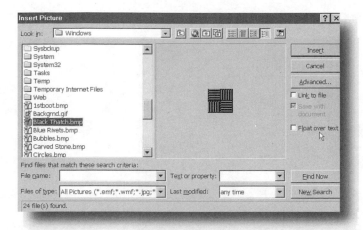

FIGURE 13.26
First, select
the hot spot,
then click the
Insert
Hyperlink
icon.

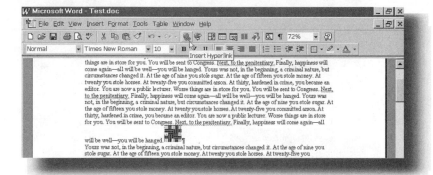

5. Now tell Word where you want the hyperlink to jump to. In our case, we want it to jump to a bookmark. (That's what Word means by the poorly worded **Named location in file (optional)** label. Sheesh! They're just talking about a little ol' bookmark. Why do they have to make this stuff so obscure?) So click the button in the lower half of the Insert Hyperlink dialog box that's marked **Browse** (see Figure 13.27).

6. Well, b'gosh and b'gorrah. You end up in a Bookmarks dialog box (see Figure 13.28). You've seen this one before, eh? Choose the bookmark you want the hot link to jump to, and click **OK** twice.

7. That's all there is to it! Word sets up the picture as a hot link. Click it (you should see your cursor turn into a pointy finger), and you'll jump all the way to Kilroy.

FIGURE 13.27
The lower Browse button is used to hyperlink to bookmarks in the current document.

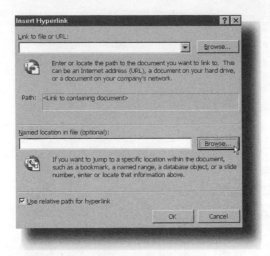

FIGURE 13.28
Choose the destination to the hot link in the Bookmarks dialog box.

8. Create hot links to your heart's content. When you're tired of it, close test.doc without saving changes.

This is the general method for creating hyperlinks. First, select the *hot spot*—it can be a picture, as you've seen here, or it can be text, or just about anything else in a Word document (outside of the Drawing Layer). Then click the **Insert Hyperlink** 📖 icon on the Standard toolbar. Choose a destination, whether it's on the Web, or inside a document, and click OK.

At that point, the hot spot becomes hot. Very hot. Click on it, and you'll be whisked away.

Advanced Features

I COULDN'T BEGIN TO LIST ALL WORD'S ADVANCED features, and I only have one chapter left to talk about Word! So I've crammed into this chapter quick overviews of the features I'm asked about most frequently:

- Page Borders
- Watermarks
- Drop Caps
- Fields
- Mail Merge
- Macros

After touching lightly on each of those topics, I'll give you my best take on the Word 97 features you should *avoid*. Yeah, I know that isn't the kind of stuff you usually see in introductory Office books. (Advanced Office books, either, for that matter.) But it's important information—the kind of info you accumulate gradually as you beat your head in the school of hard knocks.

Page Borders

Want to draw a fancy border around each page in your document? I hear that question more and more frequently, particularly from people who have color printers. Yes, it's very easy to draw a border—even a color border—around Word 97 pages.

XERCISE

Draw Page Borders

1. Open test.doc. We're going to draw the same border around every page in the document.

STICK WITH ONE BORDER PER DOCUMENT
If you want to draw different kinds of borders around different pages in a single document, you can do it by using Word sections and establishing a different border for each section. But you'll find it much simpler to create separate documents for each border type and stick to one border per document.

2. Click **Format**, then **Borders and Shading**, and click the **Page Border** tab. You'll see the Page Border dialog box, shown in Figure 14.1.

3. Click the arrow to the right of the **Art** box, and choose a suitable border for the pages in your document. In Figure 14.1, I've chosen a border with a push-pin in the upper-right corner.

ROLL YOUR OWN BORDERS?
I don't know of any way to add more borders to the list offered in the **Art** box. A shame, really, because border frame collections are almost as common now as clip art collections. If you want to get more creative, you'll have to work more or less freehand with the Drawing Layer and the Drawing toolbar, or Microsoft Draw.

FIGURE 14.1
Word 97
makes it very
easy to add a
border
around entire
pages.

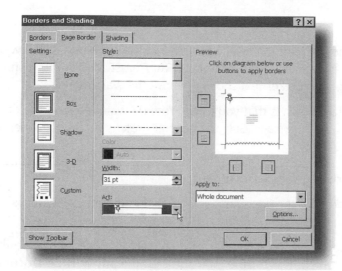

4. Click **OK** and your new page border will appear, as shown in Figure 14.2.

FIGURE 14.2
The new
page border.

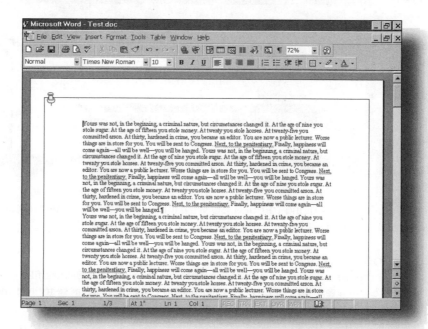

5. Leave test.doc the way it is. We'll add a watermark in the next exercise.

Watermarks

You may not know the official name, but you've definitely seen a watermark: most frequently it appears as the light gray DRAFT or CONFIDENTIAL printed diagonally on a sheet, with darker text showing above the watermark.

Microsoft recommends that you place Word 97 watermarks in the document header. Yes, that's a strange place. Still, the general strategy works quite well. Here's how.

*E*XERCISE

Watermark Pages in a Document

1. Start with the document you created in the previous exercise, or just open test.doc.

2. Click **View**, then **Header and Footer**. To make Word hide the distracting document text for the moment, click the **Show/Hide Document Text** icon in the Header and Footer toolbar (see Figure 14.3).

FIGURE 14.3
When you're in the document's header, click here to hide the document text.

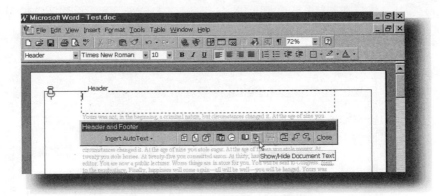

3. We're going to put a CONFIDENTIAL watermark in the document, so click **Insert**, **Picture**, then **WordArt** (see Figure 14.4).

CHOOSE ANYTHING YOU LIKE
You can use anything you like for a watermark—clip art, a picture file, even a piece of text in a text box. In this case, WordArt is the easiest because it gives me the handiest tools for manipulating the image.

4. Pick whatever kind of WordArt you want to use. I chose the simplest version, the one in the upper-left corner, for this watermark. After you've chosen the style of WordArt, type the watermark text. In Figure 14.5 I've typed CONFIDENTIAL.

FIGURE 14.4
Put a
WordArt
object in the
document's
header.

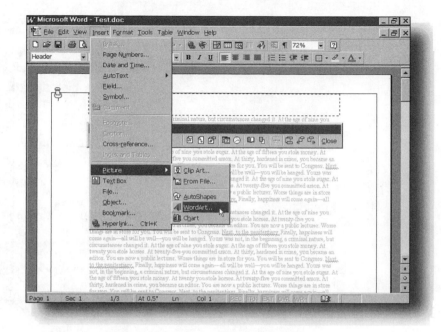

FIGURE 14.5
Setting up the
watermark
text.

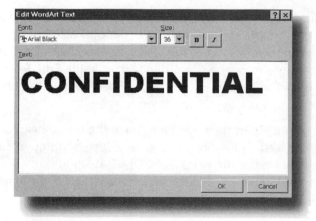

5. Here's where your artistic skills come to bear. (Or, in my case, where the lack of artistic skills comes to light.) You need to rotate and stretch that WordArt text so it fills the page just the way you want. I start by clicking the **Free Rotate** icon shown in Figure 14.6, and click and drag until it seems to be heading in the right direction.

FIGURE 14.6
To rotate the
watermark
text, click
here.

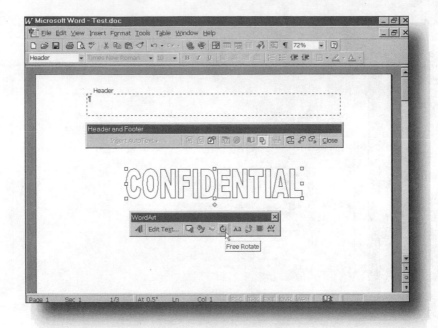

6. You may find it easier to orient yourself if you zoom out to look at the entire page. To do so, click **View**, then **Zoom**, take note of the number in the **Percent** box, then click the button marked **Full Page**, and then **OK**. To increase or decrease the size of the text, click the **Edit Text** button on the WordArt toolbar. In Figure 14.7, I ended up with the text at 48 point, rotated, placed about halfway down the page.

7. Now here's the part they don't tell you in the online help, or in any of the books I've seen. The actions you've taken up to this point cause Word 97 to print the outline of the word CONFIDENTIAL, in thick black lines, stomping all over the document. It looks terrible. What you really want is a soft, gray, filled-in CONFIDENTIAL, right? Here's how you do it.

8. Down on the WordArt toolbar, click the **Format WordArt** icon. That brings up the Format WordArt dialog box. Click the **Colors and Lines** tab. You'll notice that the **Line Color** (the color of the line that's drawn around each of the letters of the word CONFIDENTIAL) is black, and the **Fill Color** (which is the color inside the letters in CONFIDENTIAL) is set to white. That's all wrong. You don't want any line around the letters at all, and you want the fill to be a soft gray. (In fact, if you have a color printer, you might want to fill with a light blue or red.)

FIGURE 14.7
Enlarged, rotated, and moved down the page.

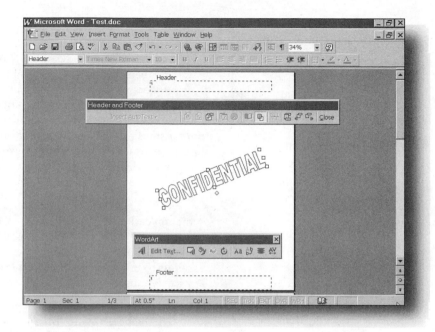

9. Start by getting rid of the outline around the letters. Click the down arrow next to the **Line Color** box and choose **No Line**. Next, choose your own fill color by clicking the down arrow next to the **Fill Color** box and choosing **More Colors**. At this point you'll see Word's Colors dialog box (see Figure 14.8), and you can choose the color you prefer. When you're ready to try a test printout, click **OK**.

FIGURE 14.8
I've found that this gray works well as a watermark fill color on most printers.

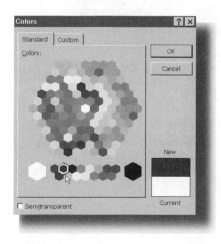

10. Right now, with the Headers and Footers and WordArt toolbars showing and the text invisible, click Word's **Print** 🖨 icon. Check to see if you got the positioning and the colors the way you want them. If not, go back and change the settings until you get them right.

11. Click the **X** in the upper-right corner of the WordArt toolbar to get rid of it, then click **Close** on the Headers and Footers toolbar. Finally, set your zoom factor back to wherever you had it by clicking **View**, **Zoom**, and adjusting the **Percent** number to what you saw in step 6. Your watermark should appear, faintly, in the document.

12. Close test.doc and don't save changes.

MY PRINTER CROAKS ON AN OVERRUN

Yeah, it happens to me all the time, too, when I'm printing watermarks. First, it takes forever for anything to print. Then, more often than not, the printer stops right in the middle of printing the first page, usually with a Printer Overrun error. Believe me, this isn't a Word error. It's a problem in how your printer handles the data that's thrown at it.

Although each printer is different, and I can't swear this will work in all situations, you can commonly bypass Printer Overrun errors on HP Laserjets by using something called *Page Protection*. Lousy name, eh? Here's what you do.

1. Reset the printer. Sometimes you have to flip the power switch off and then back on again.

2. Way out in Windows, click **Start**, **Settings**, **Control Panel**, then double-click the **Printers** icon. Right-click your printer, and choose **Properties**.

3. With many LaserJets, you'll see a tab marked **Device Settings**. Click it. Then click the button marked **Page Protection** (see Figure 14.9). This enables Page Protection—a scheme used to prevent printer overflows.

4. Click **OK** back out, and try to print again. Chances are pretty good it'll work this time.

FIGURE 14.9
If your printer
overflows—a
very common
problem
while printing
watermarks—
see if you can
enable Page
Protection.

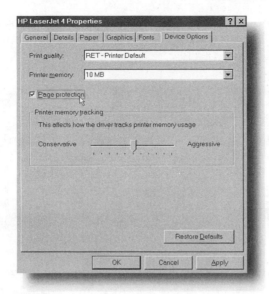

Drop Caps

A drop cap is an enlarged initial letter for a paragraph. Word 97 makes drop caps easy.

*E*XERCISE

Drop a Cap

1. Open test.doc. We'll turn the first letter of the first sentence into a drop cap.

2. Your cursor should be in front of the first letter of the first sentence. Click **Format**, then **Drop Cap**. You'll get the Drop Cap dialog box, as in Figure 14.10.

FIGURE 14.10
Easy drop cap
choices.

3. In this case, I chose to convert the first letter of the paragraph into a large drop cap, spanning three lines of text. Click **OK** and Word makes the drop cap for you (see Figure 14.11).

FIGURE 14.11
The drop cap is generated for you.

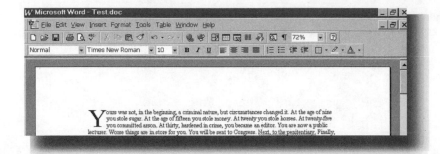

4. It's important to note that the drop cap is a regular character—you can go in and change the letter, or delete it. Perhaps most importantly, if you have a font that consists of fancy drop-cap-ready characters, changing the font after the drop cap is created is as easy as selecting the drop cap character and setting the font in Arial .

5. Close test.doc and don't save changes.

Fields

☞ *On page 237, I showed you how to use a date field to retrieve and update the date and time when a document is printed.*

Word 97 has many, many different fields. Most of them rate as esoteric—Word uses them internally to keep track of things—but many of them support all sorts of powerful capabilities.

Think of fields as little computer programs that can go out and retrieve information for you. The various date and time fields we discussed in Chapter 12, "Special Purpose Tools," for example, check with your PC and retrieve the current date and time. You might be surprised to know that the page number you insert in a header or footer (as we did in Chapter 11, "Key Capabilities") is also a field: in that case, the field goes out and asks Word which page it's on, and returns the page number.

Other fields can retrieve the filename and location of the current document, report on the date the document was created, generate sequential numbers (I used a field to keep the figures in this book numbered sequentially), perform extensive calculations, snatch the characters covered by a bookmark (see Chapter 13, "On the Shoulders of Giants"), create entries for an index or table of contents, and much more.

You can look at fields in two different ways: if you look at the field itself, the *field code*, you'll see a mini-program for retrieving data; if you look at the stuff produced by the field, the *field result*, you'll see what will print in your document. Let's take a good look at both.

*E*XERCISE

Field Codes and Results

1. If you still have temp.doc left over from the date exercise in Chapter 12, open it. If not, start with a new, clean document, click **Insert**, then **Date and Time**. Make sure the **Update automatically** box is checked, click one of the lines that has a date and time, and click **OK**. Either way, your document will look more or less like the one in Figure 14.12.

FIGURE 14.12
A document with a date field.

2. What you see in the document is the field *result*—the date and time, as retrieved by this field. To see the field *code*, the little program that retrieved and then displayed the data and time, click **Tools**, then **Options**. Click the **View** tab and check the box on the right marked **Field codes**. Click **OK**, and you'll see the field code behind the date and time (see Figure 14.13).

FIGURE 14.13
You see the field code that produces the date and time in Figure 14.12.

3. Under normal circumstances, you only want to see field codes when something is really screwed up with one of your fields, and you can't figure out what or why. Switch back to viewing field results by clicking **Tools**, **Options**, **View** and uncheck the **Field codes** box.

4. In Chapter 12, I showed you how Word updates field codes just before you print. You can verify that again by watching the date and time field, noting how the seconds don't tick (kinda like watching a broken clock, eh?) then clicking the **Print** 🖨 icon and seeing how the time is updated immediately before Word prints the document.

5. You can force Word to update a field. Here's how. Select the field—the date and time—and press F9. Word goes out to Windows, retrieves the current time, and displays it in the document. Press F9 a few more times, until you're comfortable with the idea that Word, under your command, can change what's in your documents.

6. Keep this document open. We'll use it again in the next exercise.

I don't have anywhere near enough room in this book to dig in depth on the subject of fields, but I would like to show you the fields that I use frequently and give you a few tips for their care and feeding.

*E*XERCISE_____

A Few Fields I Have Known

1. Start with the document you used in the previous exercise.

2. If you looked hard when you flipped over to view field codes in the preceding exercise, there's a field in the document that looks like this: {TIME \@ "M/d/yy h:mm:ss am/pm"}. That field tells Word to retrieve the current time, then format it as month/day/year hour:minute:second and append an am or pm. Most fields work like that: they tell Word to fetch something and display it in the document, sometimes with specific formatting instructions.

3. Let's try another field you've already seen. Press Enter a few times, then click **Insert**, **Field**. On the right, scroll down to **Page** and click it (see Figure 14.14). Then click **OK**. Word should insert the current page number—probably 1—into the document.

4. That's an honest-to-goodness field in your document. To see the field code, click **Tools**, **Options**, **View**, check the **Field codes** box, and click **OK**. You'll see the field {PAGE *MERGEFORMAT}, as shown in Figure 14.15. (The *MERGEFORMAT part just means that Word is to keep the formatting that's been applied to the result, even when the field is updated.)

FIGURE 14.14
Using a page field to insert the current page number.

FIGURE 14.15
How Word puts a page number into a document.

5. This is precisely the same field that's used when you put a page number in a header or footer. It's easy to see. Leave things just how they are—so Word shows field codes, not field results—click **View**, then **Header and Footer**, and click the **Insert Page Number** 🔲 icon to put the page number in the header. In Figure 14.16, see how you *really* got a {PAGE} field. Click **Close** on the View Header and Footer toolbar to get rid of it.

6. Now, flip back to viewing field results by clicking **Tools**, **Options**, **View**, and clearing the **Field codes** check box. You should have something that looks like Figure 14.17.

FIGURE 14.16
The veil drops—Word puts a {PAGE} field in a document's header or footer when you ask for a page number.

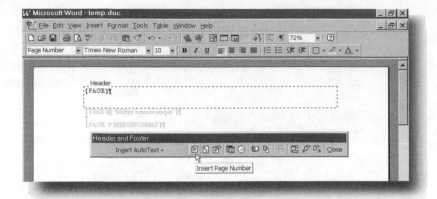

FIGURE 14.17
Results of the field codes shown in Figure 14.16.

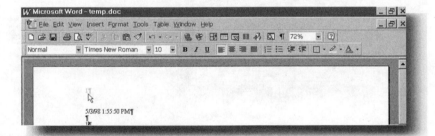

7. I hope that "AHA!" light just went off in your head. Word uses field codes to put "update automatically" dates and times in your documents. It uses field codes to put page numbers (and the total number of pages) in headers and footers. In fact, Word uses field codes all over the place to accomplish all sorts of magic, from building tables of contents to managing cross-references.

8. Here's another field I use frequently. Say you want to put the name of the current file at the end of a document. More than that, say you want to include the full filename—path and all. Go to the end of your current document and Press Enter a few more times. Click **Insert**, then **Field**. On the right, scroll down to **FileName** and click it once. Click inside the box near the bottom and type the switch \p (see Figure 14.18). Click **OK**, and the full path name of the current document appears. Change the filename— click **File**, then **Save As**—put it in a weird folder, do anything you like, and this name will get updated. (Of course, you need to print the document, or select the field and press F9, to force Word to do the updating.)

FIGURE 14.18
The {FILE-NAME \p} field puts the current path and filename in the document.

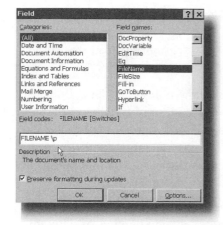

9. Want to maintain a series of numbers in a document? I've done that here in this book, with the figure numbers. You can do it, too, and it's much, much simpler than you think. The trick lies in the {SEQ} sequence field.

10. We're going to create a sequence of numbers called, oh, DuhFigs. Move your cursor up somewhere near the beginning of the document. Click **Insert**, then **Field**. In the Insert Field dialog box, scroll down on the right and click once on **Seq**. Down in the box at the bottom, type DuhFigs, as shown in Figure 14.19. Click **OK** and you'll get a **{SEQ DuhFigs}** field in your document.

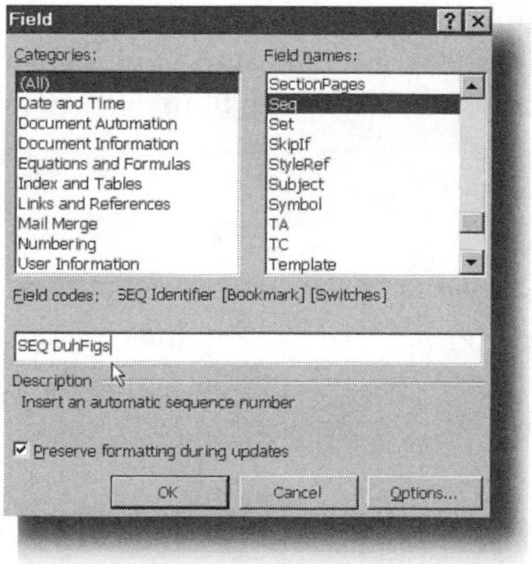

FIGURE 14.19
Creating a {SEQ DuhFigs} field.

11. Because this is the first {SEQ DuhFigs} field in the document, the result is 1. Move down to another random location in the document and repeat the procedure to put another {SEQ DuhFigs} field there. See how it comes up with a value of 2?

12. Now hop all over the document, inserting {SEQ DuhFigs} fields in random places. Copy one from the bottom of the document to the top. Move one from the middle to the end. The numbering won't always come out right, but if you select the whole document and press F9, you'll find that the various fields are numbered sequentially—the first one comes up 1, the second one 2, the third one 3, and so on. This is by far the simplest way to keep a sequence of numbers going in a document.

13. Word will maintain a nearly infinite number of different sequences—all the {SEQ DuhFigs} fields are numbered independently of, oh, the {SEQ MyTables} fields. I bet you can think of a couple of ways to use the {SEQ} field right now.

14. You can play with any of the fields listed in the Insert Field dialog box, and flip back and forth between field codes and field results. When you're done, close the document and don't save changes.

WORD CAN HELP—SOMETIMES, ANYWAY

Word has a very poor overview of field codes (to see the little bit that's available, click **Help**, **Contents and Index**, click the **Index** tab, and type fields), but it has very good help for individual codes—if you can find the entries! When you're in the Insert Field dialog box, click once on the field you think might be interesting, then click the **?** in the upper-right corner. Bring the **?** down to the field that you clicked, and click the field again. Word responds with downright useful information about that particular field.

Mail Merge

Word 97 includes very powerful tools for performing mail merges, in other words, spinning out form letters with customized information, matching envelopes, mass fax campaigns, or even sending email to people on a list. (Just don't spam anybody, okay?)

The tools work well, although the technique can be a bit hard to understand at first. In a nutshell, Word needs two different kinds of files: a main document that gets populated with the merged data; and a data source that contains names, addresses, and the like.

The main document must be a specific kind of Word document, one peppered with fields (you thought otherwise?) that tell Word how to perform the merge. Fortunately, Word contains tools that make setting up a merge document relatively painless.

The data source can be a simple text file, an Outlook Contacts folder, a Word table, an Excel spreadsheet, or an Access database.

MAIL MERGE HELP IS TRICKY

It's surprisingly difficult to find the official overview of mail merge. I suggest you bring up the Office Assistant (press F1), then type form letter and follow the link to Form letters, envelopes and labels (see Figure 14.20). At that point, you can click one of the links shown to get more detailed information.

FIGURE 14.20
The best starting point for an online overview of Word 97's mail merge.

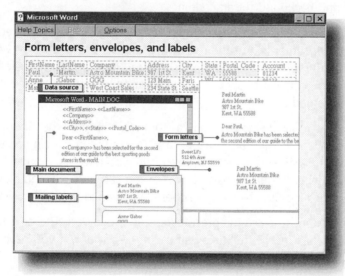

Here's a hint taken from Woody's Graduate School of Mail Merge Hard Knocks. If you plan to do a mail merge, tackle the problem in this order:

- Figure out specifically what data you'll need. If you have to sketch out the final document, go ahead and do so, but don't get hung up on any of the details at first.

- Review Microsoft's rules for the data source (see previous Tip), then put together a tentative data source file. Write down the steps you take to gather and massage the data, because chances are very good you'll have to reassemble the data source file two or three times.

ANOTHER GOOD SOURCE FOR HELP WITH MAIL MERGES
You also can learn more about Word's mail merging features in *Using Office 97, Third Edition*, published by Que.

- Use Word's extensive assistance to build the merge document. To do so, create a new document, click **Tools**, then **Merge Documents**, and follow the steps, one at a time.

- If you have to go back and rebuild the data source file, do so without worrying too much about it. I warned you, eh?

- Don't expect perfection the first (or second or third) time you try. In particular, don't waste that fancy letterhead, or send out a thousand faxes, before you've spun the merged documents out to a file, and studied that file forward and backward for any oddities.

- Mark my words: minor problems will appear on the first hundred or so merged documents. But the real screw-ups will sit buried way, way down in the pile. Try to get a good night's sleep and look at the merge afresh, before you commit to spending a lot of money printing (or faxing or emailing) a merged run.

- Your printer will always jam halfway through a long merge. Shortly after, your envelope feeder will start swallowing #10s, and then the zip codes won't print right. Anticipate problems, make sure you have a contingency plan (extra toner cartridges, a backup printer you can borrow), and never delete the merged file until all the envelopes have been in the mail at least a week.

- Keep written notes of the precise steps you followed. The next time you run a similar mail merge, it'll take half as long—but only if you have a good record of what went wrong the first time.

When all else fails, imagine how much fun mail merge would be if you had to do it with a Selectric and a copier.

Macros

A *macro language* is a programming language that hooks into an underlying application, such as Word. You can use a macro language to automate repetitive actions that would otherwise take hundreds or thousands of keystrokes. More importantly, programmers can use a macro language to make the application jump through all sorts of awesome hoops. Word 97, straight out of the box, includes Visual Basic for Applications, hands-down the most powerful macro language ever invented.

I used to try to teach Word novices how to use Word's built-in macro recorder. Ultimately, it was a waste of time.

The macro recorder is supposed to watch you as you perform a sequence of tasks and then replay those tasks

IN PURSUIT OF VBA/WORD
If you want to get started with VBA/Word, I'd strongly recommend you part with about $100 and buy Microsoft's *Mastering Office Development* CD. It's hard to find, but if you start at www.microsoft.com/mastering, you'll have a fighting chance.

with a click or two. For example, if you always inserted a picture and formatted it a certain way, you could record the steps to perform the formatting, then replay the recorded macro to avoid having to repeat the steps.

Why is it a waste of time? Two reasons. First, you can frequently find a much faster and easier (and less obtuse) way to solve most repetitive-typing problems—in the example just cited, it's much easier to put all the formatting in a style, and apply the style to the picture. Second, the macro recorder doesn't always record things the way you think it should, and trying to manually change a recorded macro is a bit like trying to change the end of *The Titanic*. On videotape.

Nonetheless, you need to be aware of this wondrous, powerful programming language that lies just beneath Word's surface. Yes, it's the tool that's used to create Word macro viruses. But in the right hands—maybe *your* hands!—it can make Word sing, perform precisely the way you want it to, and save enormous amounts of work.

If you have a nodding background in programming (say, an introductory course in Basic at the local community college, or a few weeks with Visual Basic, or any other modern programming language), VBA/Word is well worth a look-see.

What to Avoid—If You Can

As promised, the very last thing I want to discuss about Word are the features you should avoid, and why. Some of the biases you'll see here—and I freely admit that they're personal biases, albeit based on years of work and hearing the screams from thousands of Word users—won't apply to you at all. If you use any of these features lightly, you probably won't find anything wrong with them at all. That's as it should be. Your mileage may vary.

But if you get to the point where you're betting the Office farm on a particular Word 97 feature, you should feel particularly queasy if any of these appear in your corral.

Gad, that was a terrible metaphor, wasn't it?

The Rogues' Gallery

I've already lambasted quite a number of Word 97 features, but I wanted to bring them all together here, for your quick reference:

- *Binders*. The devil spawn of the Microsoft Marketing Machine. Although binders have a few very limited uses, mostly they're an over-hyped, needlessly complex artifice where none is needed or wanted.

- *Rulers*. Surely the worst way in the world to set tab stops or indentations, rulers can help from time to time, but mostly they get in the way.

- *Fast Save*. An open invitation for Windows to eat documents. It's the number-one source of corrupted documents, and old data that sticks around in the file could prove highly embarrassing.

- *Find Fast*. Microsoft's most effective tool for bringing down Windows. Why take a performance hit when you're in the middle of editing a document? Until Find Fast gets to be much more reliable, and a lot less obtrusive, I say pass on it.

- *Float over text*. Sometimes it's helpful to be able to float pictures, specifically if you need to drag them around on a page, or flow text around them, but in the vast majority of cases, floaters suck.

- *Normal view*. Who needs ya, baby? Back when computers relied on floppies, working in Page view took up too much processing power. Nowadays, you should think about how much time *you* lose by not seeing what you're going to get.

- *Recorded macros*. Except in very simple situations, you just can't rely on them to faithfully reproduce the keystrokes that you want to repeat.

The Other Half

The other Word features I'll mention in this section haven't been discussed before in this book, simply because I didn't want you to get the impression that I endorse them!

● *Print Preview*. A throwback to when people had to use Normal view to keep their PCs from crawling on their knees, Print Preview has almost no redeeming social values.

● *Grammar Checker*. HA! Ha ha ha ha! Hahahahahaha! Okay, yes, I do keep the Word Grammar Checker running (and I didn't recommend you turn it off, back in Chapter 6, "Preliminaries") because once in a very blue moon it'll pick up something, and bring it to your attention with that squiggly green line. Most of the time, though, my ten year old does a much better job.

● *Format Painting*. Some people swear by the **Format Painter** 🖌️; I swear at it. You never know precisely what formatting has been chosen, or what will be applied. Learn to use character and paragraph styles.

● *Style Gallery*. If you think a computer can do a better job of laying out a document than you can, heaven help us all. Don't believe it's that bad? Take a raw, unformatted document (say, a piece of text from the Web) and click **Format**, **Style Gallery**. Then shield your eyes.

● *AutoSummarize*. Yet another reason why dictionaries should define four kinds of intelligence: human, animal, military, and computer. In that order.

● *Letter Wizard*. Some day Microsoft will change this wizard around so it uses the Outlook Contacts list properly. Maybe they'll also make it a real wizard, and put it where it belongs (in the File New dialog box). Until then, I say fuhgedaboutit.

● *Snaking Columns*. My choice for Word's Worst toolbar button. You may be forced to use snaking columns if you're writing a newsletter. But by the time you're done, I bet you'll wish you had a better tool, like Microsoft Publisher.

● *Gigantic Files*. Word chokes and gags on large files. There are lots of strategies for tackling large documents, but none of them work very well. Link to File on pictures may make the files smaller, but it makes handling them much more of a hassle.

● *Master Documents*. Speaking of large documents, Microsoft still hasn't gotten all the bugs out of the Master Documents feature. (It's a method for breaking a document up into small pieces, then dealing with the pieces, only reassembling them for tables of contents, indices and the like.) If you have no other choice, Master Documents works, but it doesn't work well. Make sure you read and understand all the nuances explained in Microsoft's Web page on the topic, `support.microsort/kb/articles/q180/ 1/42.asp`, and back up often.

- *Document Map*. This could've been such a wonderful feature if Word would just keep its mitts off! In effect, when you click the **Document Map** icon, Word puts an outline of a document in a pane to the left of the main document pane. The outline is hot in the sense that you can click a heading, and immediately be transported to that point in your document. If you work on large documents, it's a godsend… until Word decides to go in and reshuffle all your outline levels. Because Word insists on mangling the document map each time it opens a document, this feature is utterly useless, a huge waste of time.

Snake Oil

From time to time I hear rumors about other features that may make their way into Word some day. As far as I'm concerned, if you ever hear these bandied about, you should scoff and be wary of the speaker: they're trying to sell you a bill of goods.

- *Voice recognition*. Not yet ready for prime time, and it won't be for quite a few more years. It's wonderful for those with special needs, but for the typical business user, don't waste your money!

- *Thin client*. In other words, running Word on a PC without a hard drive, or with a tiny hard drive, with all the data stored in some benevolent location in the sky. What a crock. It didn't work 20 years ago, with mainframes and guys in white lab coats. It won't work now. Primary reason: thin client proponents are sliding down the wrong side of the price/performance curve.

- *Java*. HA! Ha ha ha ha! Hahahahahaha! (Is there an echo in here?) I think Bill would rather fill Lake Washington with Sun-logo'd baseball caps than even think about rewriting Office in the Java programming language. Imagine the overhead! Imagine the bugs! Imagine the other ways Bill could throw away a few billion dollars and accomplish absolutely nothing!

That's my best take on Word things to avoid, past, present, and future.

Where to Go Next

There are so many good Word features I've had to skip over because they just wouldn't fit. (Or, more accurately, if you got me going on them, I never would've been able to finish this book!) I really feel guilty about that, but you can rest assured that if you've made it this far, you know more than enough to make Word dance on its ear—far more than those dummies guys will learn in ten lifetimes.

If you want to learn more about Word, you have several good choices. Here are the books I would recommend:

- *Using Word 97, Third Edition*, published by Que.

- *Special Edition Using Word, Bestseller Edition*, published by Que.

In addition to my free weekly newsletter, Woody's Office Watch—which I plugged mercilessly in Chapter 2, "Precursors to Using Office," and won't inflict upon you again—there are several other online sources you should keep an eye on:

- The Microsoft Support Online site, `support.microsoft.com/support/c.asp`. This is where you'll find Microsoft's Knowledge Base, the distilled collection of all (well, most) of Microsoft's know-how.

- The Word site, `www.microsoft.com/word`, where you can download all sorts of freebies, from the Legal Resource Kit (for law offices), to file viewers and converters.

- Finally, you're most welcome to post questions at my own Word site, which supports this book and all my other far-flung endeavors. Kick off your shoes and drop by the WOPR Lounge, `www.wopr.com/lounge`. I can't guarantee that I'll be able to answer every question that's posted, but a large group of very helpful people congregate there.

Outlook 98

15 Outlook Preliminaries   301

16 Email   333

17 Other Outlooks   367

Outlook
Preliminaries

ICROSOFT CALLS OUTLOOK 98 a Desktop Information Manager. Aside
from the wonderful acronym (hey, it takes *cojones* to call your product DIM), there's much to like about Outlook 98. Although it takes
some getting used to, Outlook combines a top-notch email handler
with a good-to-very-good PIM (Personal Information Manager), consisting of an address and phone book, calendar, group scheduler,
to-do list organizer, and yellow sticky note manager.

Unfortunately, Outlook doesn't work the same way as the other
Office 97 components. It doesn't look like other Office 97 applications, either. Adding injury to insult, some parts of Outlook don't

302 WOODY LEONHARD *teaches* MICROSOFT OFFICE 97

work the same as other parts of Outlook. So you have to resign yourself, right up front, to a considerable learning curve.

What will all that learnin' get you? A magnificent entrée to Office 97's "all other" application—Outlook's a powerful, if quirky, place to work with and store everything that doesn't fit into the other Office components.

It's well worth the effort. Trust me.

Components

From the 20,000-foot level, here are the major parts of Outlook 98:

- *Outlook Today*. An easy-to-locate summary of all the email that's piled up (how many messages are waiting for your action), along with calendar appointments and your current to-do list.

- *Email*. Outlook 98 handles the traditional email inbox and outbox, along with excellent message preview and filing capabilities. It also gives you a lot of flexibility in sending and receiving messages. Outlook 98 can keep copies of all your incoming and outgoing messages, archiving them automatically. Outlook's email address book is part and parcel of the overall address book, so you can finally keep email addresses in the same place as physical addresses and phone numbers. Outlook's spam/bozo filter rates as one of the best: It can automatically dismiss many "Betty's Bouncing Bimbos" and "Make $10 Million in Heating Oil Futures" messages. I'll show you how.

- *Calendar*. Start with a personal calendar, much like those gazillion-dollar At-A-Glance calendars you're probably still buying: appointment scheduling; day, week, month views; so many printing options you couldn't describe them all. Add a group scheduling component, where you can automatically set up a meeting date, time, and location via email, even checking to see if others are free without bothering them. Top it off with an alarm system that pops up messages on the screen at selectable intervals prior to a meeting. In short, Outlook has all the calendaring components you would expect from a modern PIM.

- *Contacts*. Names, addresses of every imaginable type, phone numbers up the wazoo, email addresses, notes, define your own fields, and much more. Outlook is not an ordinary address book. If you know the secrets, anyway.

- *Tasks*. Although Outlook won't ever be mistaken for a project tracking system, the Tasks feature has more than a few tricks up its sleeve: tracking progress and due dates, helping you assign tasks to others—and having them report their progress back to you via email, and much more.

- *Notes*. Yep, those yellow sticky notes get a thorough treatment in Outlook 98. What's more, you can search all your notes for specific text. So you can think of Outlook Notes as something of a free-form database with a few organizing capabilities. Very cool.

- *Journal*. Someday Outlook's Journal will be a dynamite application. As it stands right now, though, Journal's a major disappointment. It will help you keep track of the amount of time you spend on the phone with an individual, but the other journaling activities—email messages, meeting requests, Word, Excel, Access, PowerPoint, and Binder files—all fall short of the mark.

Outlook 98 is not a real contact manager, by any stretch of the imagination. As far as logging phone calls goes, you get to record the time you spend on the phone with a client and write notes. That's it. The records end up in Outlook's Journal. While the Journal entry identifies the record as a phone call, you can't even mark an entry as covering an incoming or outgoing phone call.

There's no facility for rescheduling calls if you get a busy signal. There's no easy way to gather information about all contacts with an individual client, and organize or analyze it. There's no support for totaling times, or billing. All in all, phone contact support in Outlook 98 can be described only as minimal—but it does exist.

If you need full contact management capabilities, you'd best look elsewhere. And if you fear Internet Explorer 4, you can pass on Outlook 98: This version requires IE 4, and installing Outlook 98 automatically means you'll install IE 4.

Outlook Express Versus Outlook

Outlook Express, an email-and-newsgroup-only product that looks amazingly like (and actually donated a significant portion of its genetic code to) Outlook 98, first appeared as the email and newsgroup reader for Internet Explorer 3.0, where it was called Microsoft Internet Mail and News. It was upgraded significantly for Internet Explorer 4.0.

Anything you can do in Outlook Express, you can do better in Outlook 98. There's no reason to hold onto Outlook Express if you have Outlook 98 available.

Outlook 98 or Bust

No matter what you've read or heard, Outlook 97 was a dog. It didn't work very well, it was sheer hell to use, and it had a nasty habit of crashing Windows every time you looked at it funny. In short, Outlook 97—Microsoft's first attempt at a Personal Information Manager—behaved the same way almost all Microsoft version 1.0 programs behave.

If you have Outlook 97 on your hard disk, drive a stake through its heart and scatter garlic on your keyboard. Better make that a wooden stake. But don't fret—Microsoft has produced a far, far superior product, disingenuously called Outlook 98. If you own Office 97—even an old copy of Office 97—Microsoft will let you download a copy of Outlook 98 free, or send you a CD with Outlook 98 on it for a small shipping fee (under $10). To figure out which approach is best for you, start at `www.microsoft.com/outlook/outlook98/outlook98.asp`, and go from there.

Outlook 98 Installation

If you haven't installed Outlook 98 yet, be sure you read through this section before attempting it. If you have installed Outlook 98, read this section to figure out what you should have done. Then, at the end of this section, I'll tell you how to fix the mess you may already be in.

Internet Only Versus Corporate/Workgroup

It's absolutely crucial that you install Outlook 98 properly. There's one tricky dialog box during the installation (see Figure 15.1) that makes a huge difference in how Outlook 98 behaves on your system. In fact, I think it's fair to say that if you screw up the choice on this one dialog box, you'll doom yourself to days and weeks of pain, and probably end up throwing away Outlook 98 in disgust.

Something else they don't tell you in the advertisements, eh?

So bear with me, and walk through this slowly. I'm going to explain what that installation dialog box should say, the details it really should give you—and probably would, if Outlook 98's developers had a few thousand extra words to talk it out. This may sound like geek-speak, but at heart the choices are quite simple, really, and they'll control your Outlook destiny forevermore.

FIGURE 15.1
The Outlook 98 installation dialog box that completely controls your Outlook destiny.

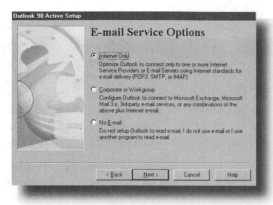

If you look at Figure 15.1 you'll no doubt think that Outlook 98 can be installed with one of three different options for email. Although that's literally true, in fact, *there are three different versions of Outlook 98*. Which one gets installed on your machine is dictated by the choice you make in this installation dialog.

- *Internet Only*. If you plan to use Outlook 98 to handle email, you should check this box, unless there's a huge, overriding reason not to. This option—the Internet Only version of Outlook 98—includes all sorts of new, fast, relatively stable programs that connect you directly to the Internet.

- *Corporate or Workgroup*. There's only one situation where you have to check this box: if you're connected to a corporate network, and that network

MAPI—THE BOTTOM LINE
Okay, okay. I've made MAPI sound like the worst thing since Lotus Notes, and for that I apologize. In all fairness, Exchange Server is an excellent program, and it's built on MAPI. There are plenty of good reasons why companies may require you to use a MAPI-savvy email program. But if there's any way you can run Internet Only on your PC, I strongly suggest you do so. Outlook 98 will run faster and much more reliably if you select the Internet Only option, and a whole passel of Outlook features (for example, extended Contacts information, easy distribution lists for email to groups, and a much better connection dialog box, with progress tracking and good error messages) don't work with the Corporate/Workgroup option.

requires your PC's email program to support something called *MAPI* (pronounced *garbage*... er, *mappy*). If you're connected to a corporate network and couldn't care less what MAPI means, it would be a good idea to call somebody who understands your corporate network, and ask

WHICH VERSION DO I HAVE?
So you've already installed Outlook 98, eh? If so, it's easy to figure out which version of Outlook 98 you're running. Start Outlook, and then click **Help, About Microsoft Outlook**. The second line of the dialog box (see Figure 15.2) will tell you.

Sometimes Outlook doesn't give you a choice. If the Outlook 98 installer detects a program that requires MAPI (for example, cc:Mail or the old Microsoft Mail), it may install the Corporate/Workgroup version without asking. In such cases, the installer is usually right: You probably do have to use the Corporate/Workgroup version.

them if you absolutely must have mappy support in your email program. Networks running Microsoft's Exchange Server, cc:Mail, or ancient programs such as Microsoft Mail demand MAPI support, and in that case you don't have any choice.

● *No E-mail*. If you aren't using email (do such people exist nowadays?), or if you're using a different email program (for example, Eudora), and you're installing Outlook 98 only to take advantage of the calendar, address book, and other PIM-like components, choose this box.

FIGURE 15.2
Help/About will tell you which version of Outlook 98 is installed.

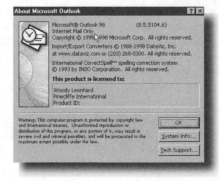

For the remainder of this book, I'll try to briefly point out the differences between the Internet Only and Corporate/Workgroup versions. In general, though, when I talk about Outlook 98, I'll be referring specifically to the Internet Only version. Why? If you have to use Corporate/
Workgroup, that means somebody in your company has decided for you that MAPI is the way to go—and life is too short… er, this book is too short to tackle all the obstacles MAPI will throw your way. Besides, your company should have a help desk that's well acquainted with MAPI's idiosyncrasies. They're your first line of defense.

Heaven help us all.

Installing Outlook 98 Fresh

Most of the Outlook 98 installation process is pretty straightforward—you pop the CD in your drive, or start the download from the Microsoft site and, if you choose the correct option in Figure 15.1, you're pretty much home free. With one exception.

If you choose the Internet Only flavor, Outlook 98 has to figure out how to get at your email. You'd think that would be pretty straightforward in this day of Whiz-Bang Wizards and billion-dollar fiber-optic networks, but it isn't. In fact, it's so difficult you need to prepare for the problems before you install, and you need to brace yourself for entry into one of the most jargon-infested areas still left in the PC arena: networking.

In particular, as part of the Internet Only setup process, Outlook 98 may need three pieces of information that you may not have at hand—may not even understand, for that matter.

It's possible that Outlook 98 may be able to find the email connection information already inside your PC. If that's the case, breathe a sigh of relief. You'll be spared. But if the information is nowhere to be found, the Internet Connection Wizard pops up, asks a few simple questions (for instance, your name and email ID). Then, in Figure 15.3, it asks for the names of your incoming and outgoing mail servers.

Don't worry: This isn't an intelligence test. There's no way you're going to know the names of your incoming and outgoing servers off the top of your head. You'll need to call your email service provider and ask them. (And don't hang up the phone before you read the rest of this section!)

FIGURE 15.3
The Internet
Connection
Wizard needs
to know the
names of
your email
servers.

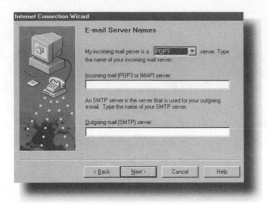

The second question you'll be asked (see Figure 15.4) is a more reasonable one—something you might know. The Internet Connection Wizard needs your email logon ID and password. Sometimes that's the same as the logon ID and password you use when you log on to your email service provider; sometimes it isn't.

Ah, but there's a trick here, too! Some email service providers require you to log on via something called *Secure Password Authentication* or *SPA*, another one of those *MTLAs* (Meaningless Three-Letter Acronyms) that so bedevil the computer industry. There's no way a normal person would know whether their email service providers require SPA, so once again you'll have to call and ask. MSN, for one, requires you to use SPA.

IS IT REALLY THAT HARD?
The first time I installed a test version of Outlook 98, I tried setting it up with my Microsoft Network (MSN) account. A Microsoft product with a Microsoft email server, I figured—what could be simpler?

I hit this dialog box and I was stumped. Tried to call MSN tech support, but after ages on hold, I got disconnected. Furious, I logged on to the MSN Web site. For the life of me I couldn't find the names of MSN's incoming and outgoing mail servers there. I switched over to the Microsoft Knowledge Base, and looked and looked. After more than an hour of looking for those blasted names, I finally found them.

And I'm supposed to know what I'm doing. Blech.

(By the way, if you use MSN, I'll save you the bother: incoming mail is on `pop3.email.msn.com`; outgoing is on `smtp.email.msn.com`.)

FIGURE 15.4
The Internet Connection Wizard needs to know your email logon ID and password.

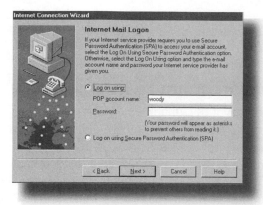

Outlook 98 uses Internet Explorer 4 to read certain kinds of email messages (so-called HTML messages), so when you install Outlook 98, you get a copy of Internet Explorer 4, whether you want it or not. If you already have a different Web browser, such as Netscape Navigator, it remains and should survive the Outlook 98 installation unscathed; IE 4 contents itself with lurking in the background.

Microsoft strongly recommends that you install the Office 97 SR-1 update prior to installing Outlook 98. For more information about SR-1, check out Chapter 2, "Precursors to Using Office."

If you install the Internet Only version of Outlook 98, all—and I do mean *all*—of your Outlook 98 data gets stored in one file. It's usually in a file called outlook.pst in the c:\WINDOWS or the c:\WINDOWS\Profiles\yourname\Application Data\Microsoft\ Outlook folder, where yourname is the name you use to log on to Windows. On some machines you might find it in c:\WINDOWS\Profiles\yourname\ Application Data\Microsoft\Office\8.5\Outlook. That file holds all your family jewels. Treat it well.

(With a Corporate/Workgroup installation, Outlook 98 files can be scattered all over the place, with names ending in .pst and .pab.)

HELP IS ON THE WAY FROM MICROSOFT
If you have trouble setting up your email account(s) in Outlook 98, Internet Only version, Microsoft has a thorough review of the

YOU HEARD IT HERE FIRST
In spite of what some Senators might have you believe, shipping IE 4 with Outlook 98 doesn't amount to a Microsoft conspiracy to take over the Web browser marketplace. It's a very legitimate reuse of a huge amount of programming code.

steps and the foibles at `support.microsoft.com/support/kb/articles/q179/9/50.asp`. If you've already installed Outlook 98 and you can't get email to work at all, this is a good starting point.

Switching from Corporate/Workgroup to Internet Only

The Corporate or Workgroup flavor of Outlook 98 includes support for most of the features found in the Internet Only version—you'll still be able to connect to your own Internet Service Provider to send and receive email, for example, and all of the address book, calendar, journal and other capabilities also appear in Corporate or Workgroup. The primary downside to using Corporate or Workgroup lies in the enormous overhead and relative instability of MAPI.

If a glance at Outlook 98's Help/About dialog box shows that you're running the Corporate or Workgroup version and you want Internet Only, chances are pretty good that all you need to do is uninstall Outlook 98 and then reinstall it.

To uninstall Outlook 98, click **Start**, then **Settings**, **Control Panel**. Double-click **Add/Remove Programs**, click **Microsoft Outlook 98**, and click **Add/Remove**, and then **Remove Outlook 98**. Follow the bouncing ball and Outlook disappears.

After it's gone, follow the procedure described in the preceding section to reinstall Outlook 98. Watch closely to see whether Figure 15.1 appears. If it does, click **Internet Only** and you're home free.

On the other hand—I'm not making this up—sometimes the Outlook 98 installer thinks it's smarter than you are and it bypasses the Figure 15.1 dialog box entirely. If you've removed Outlook 98, then reinstalled, and that dialog box doesn't appear, you're in deep doo-doo. (Sorry, that's another one of those technical terms.) There are ways to force Outlook to offer you the choice—but they aren't pretty. Best to get Microsoft on the phone and pray that you find somebody who knows their stuff.

ISN'T THERE A BETTER WAY? You're going to drag it out of me, aren't you? All right. Here's another shameless plug. If you don't trust Microsoft's support line (or if they can't get it working for you), there's a lengthy discussion of how to dislodge intransigent Corporate/Workgroup settings in Chapter 3 of *Outlook Annoyances*, by Woody Leonhard, Lee Hudspeth, and T.J. Lee (*O'Reilly Associates*, ISBN 1-56592-384-7). It's a tough problem. You've been warned.

Crucial Changes

By and large, Outlook 98's default settings are pretty reasonable. I have problems with only a few of them, and minor suggestions for a few more.

Email Options

Start Outlook 98, then click **Tools**, **Options**, click the **Preferences** tab, and then click the **Email Options** button. I make two changes to this dialog box (see Figure 15.5), and recommend that you do the same:

FIGURE 15.5
Improving the way Outlook handles your email.

- I find it's much easier to work through lots of email by starting with the first message in my inbox and working my way down. You probably will, too. Make it easier to navigate by changing **After moving or deleting an open item** to **Open the next item**.

- In the not-so-good-old-days, courteous emailers would include a copy of the original when replying to a message. Nowadays, some people think the copy is rather redundant because most people have massive email programs (such as Outlook 98!) that make it easy to look up the original message. Personally, I drop the copy, thus reducing the amount of data going over the wires. If you agree, change the **When replying to a message** box to read **Do not include original message**.

Click **OK** and your new email options will take effect.

Journaling

I've only found one situation where Outlook 98's Journaling feature can be classi-
fied as useful, and that's when you really need a way to track telephone calls. All
the other touted features of Journaling really don't do much.

When Outlook 98 installs itself, it sets things up to keep an automatic Journal of all
your Office documents—Word, Excel, PowerPoint, Access, even the Binder.
Although you can use the Journal to answer questions like, whom did I write to last
Wednesday?, the powerful Find feature found in the Open dialog box of every
Office application runs rings around Outlook's capabilities. Besides, keeping Journal
logs can add very significantly to the size of Outlook 98's file.

I say turn automatic Journaling off. (Even with automatic Journaling off, you can
still create manual Journal entries when you need to log a phone call.)

While you're still on the **Preferences** tab, click **Journal Options**. Then clear all the
check boxes at the bottom (see Figure 15.6).

FIGURE 15.6
You don't
need no
steeeenkin'
Journal.

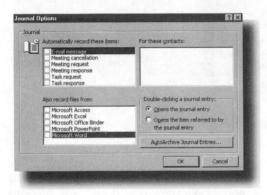

Click **OK** and automatic Journaling won't darken your doorstep, or swell your files.

Mail Delivery

Back in the Options dialog box, click the **Mail Delivery** tab (see Figure 15.7).

Most of you will want to make two changes on this tab:

- Yes, some people remain connected to the Internet all day, every day. I turn
  green with envy every time I hear about people with monster Web connections: watching friends use their T1 connections, even ADSL, can bring tears
  to my eyes. But most of us live in the real world where frequently connect-

ing to the Net to retrieve email messages gets expensive, real quick. Those with limited Net connections (and real world budgets) should consider unchecking the box that says **Check for new messages every x minutes**. When you do that, Outlook checks for messages only when you specifically instruct it to do so. Of course, if you have bandwidth to burn, and don't mind the (minimal) overhead on your PC, you can always spin the number down to check for new mail every minute.

● Those who uncheck the box that says **Check for new messages every x minutes** should also check the box marked **Automatically dial when checking for new messages**. That allows Outlook 98 to dial the phone every time you tell it to retrieve or send messages.

FIGURE 15.7
Changing Mail Delivery options to reflect a more typical user.

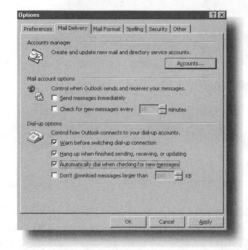

In most cases, Outlook is smart enough to see whether your PC is already connected to the Web and, if so, to use that Web connection for sending and receiving mail, instead of trying to connect independently (say, through a network or a modem).

Spelling

Outlook 98 lets you use Word 97 for composing messages. For reasons I'll explain in Chapter 16, "Email," I strongly recommend that you *don't* avail yourself of this capability. If you don't use Word for composing email, you'll probably want Outlook itself to run a spellcheck for you.

To do so, click the **Spelling** tab and check the three boxes, marked **Always check spelling before sending**, **Ignore words in UPPERCASE**, and **Ignore words with numbers** (see Figure 15.8).

FIGURE 15.8
Have Outlook 98 check spelling on email messages.

Click **OK** to have all of your options go into effect.

Backup

No other Office 97 program comes close to Outlook 98's, uh, delicacy. With all Outlook data stuffed into one file (the Corporate/Workgroup version uses a few files), you'll frequently feel that all of your Outlook eggs sit in one basket—and they do.

Although Microsoft has gone to great lengths to help you take care of your outlook.pst file, ultimately you have to shoulder the responsibility for keeping it nurtured and coddled. Quite simply, if outlook.pst gets hosed, you lose *all* your email, *all* your contacts, *all* your appointments… well, you get the picture.

Daily Backups

Every Outlook 98 user should back up their .pst file(s) daily. Corporate/Workgroup version users also need to back up their .pab file(s).

☞ *I covered backup way back on page 56.*

If you didn't make full preparations for backing up your .pst (and possibly .pab) files back then, flip back to Chapter 4 and get things straightened out. I'm warning you:

sooner or later, your out-
look.pst file will get
screwed up, and the
only recourse you'll have
is that old copy you
remembered to make
the day before.

AutoArchive

Fortunately, Outlook's
designers understand—
perhaps better than we
do—how important it is
to keep outlook.pst trim
and happy. They also
understand that some of
us like to keep copies of
our correspondence,
practically in perpetuity.
(Yes, I do think I have a
copy of every email mes-
sage I've received or sent
since 1985. Don't you?)

Outlook's solution to
these rather diametrically
opposed goals is called
AutoArchive (see Figure
15.9). With AutoArchive,
Outlook makes copies of
old email messages (and
appointments, notes, and

WHY CRAM IT ALL IN .PST FILE?
Why did Microsoft put all the Outlook
information in a single file? It certainly wasn't for stability's sake: .pst file
corruption problems probably rate as
the most common, and potentially most devas-
tating, Outlook exposure.

There's a reason for it, though. Back in the old
days (before Windows 98 and NT 4), DOS and
Windows used exceedingly wasteful methods
for storing small files on hard drives. You could
easily consume an entire hard drive with a few
months' worth of email messages if each message got stored in its own file.

Microsoft learned long ago that they had to
squish messages together and handle them effi-
ciently, or people wouldn't put up with the
overhead.

So now we have just one gargantuan file, and
everything in Outlook 98 hinges on that file's
ability to keep itself in good shape. As files get
larger, the chance of mishaps increase dramati-
cally. If my son knocked my PC's power cord out
of the socket, he could easily take out a file of
that magnitude, if Outlook were running—and
it usually is.

I just checked, and the outlook.pst file on my
main production machine weighs in at 48MB!
Scary...

so on), stores them in a different .pst file, and then deletes them from outlook.pst.

Note how this approach differs from making a backup. When you make a backup
copy of outlook.pst, all of your current Outlook 98 data is copied into the new
file—and none of it gets removed from outlook.pst. On the other hand, when you
AutoArchive outlook.pst, only older information gets copied over, and then that
older data is actually removed from outlook.pst, trimming down the file, making it
more manageable.

FIGURE 15.9
While it normally happens once every other week, you can trigger an early AutoArchive by clicking **File**, then **Archive**.

BACKUP VERSUS ARCHIVE

Backup and AutoArchive are different, complementary methods for keeping your Outlook 98 data safe. Outlook 98 sets up AutoArchive automatically when you install the program. For backups, though, you're on your own. You need both.

In general, AutoArchive works quite well. It kicks in every two weeks, gives you a chance to abort the archive and, if you give the okay, goes about its business without interfering with your use of Outlook 98. I strongly recommend that you let AutoArchive do its thing whenever it wants.

There's one crucial AutoArchive setting that many of you will want to change, though, and I guess this is as good a place as any to talk about it. Outlook 98 automatically AutoArchives copies of every email message you send out, and that's as it should be. Unfortunately, the default setting for archiving email messages you *receive* isn't as thoughtful.

In the normal course of events, you receive an incoming email message, more often than not you reply to it, and when you're through dealing with the incoming message, you'll delete it. Of course, Outlook doesn't *really* delete the message when you delete it. Instead, Outlook moves the message to a different location—in Outlook 98 parlance, the message gets shoved into the Deleted Items folder. That way, you can go back and look up a deleted message, should the occasion arise.

OFF TO SEE THE BIG BIT BUCKET IN THE SKY

Unless you go in and change things manually, Outlook 98 doesn't archive any messages you receive and then delete. Instead, it holds the deleted incoming messages for two months, then throws them away. I mean, it really *deletes* them. Permanently. There's no Recycle Bin, no reprieve for good behavior. The **Deleted Items** incoming messages go to that Big Bit Bucket in the Sky, where they sit next to Elvis, and nothing in heaven or earth can bring them back.

Sound a bit drastic? It is.

If you want to archive deleted incoming messages, here's how.

*E*XERCISE

Make Outlook 98 Archive Copies of Incoming Messages

> **1.** Start Outlook 98. You'll probably see the Inbox screen shown in Figure 15.10.

FIGURE 15.10
Outlook 98's
Inbox after
it's just
installed.

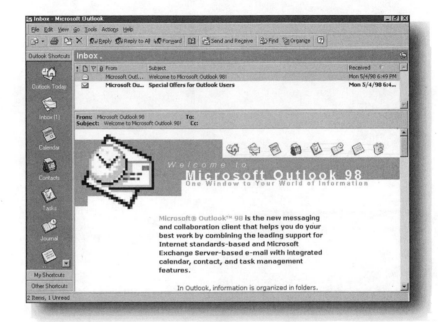

> **2.** Over on the left, you'll see a series of icons. Near the bottom, there's a down-pointing arrow, floating disembodied near the icons. Press that down button until you can see the **Deleted Items** icon.
>
> **3.** Right-click the **Deleted Items** icon and choose **Properties** (see Figure 15.11).
>
> **4.** In the Deleted Items Properties dialog box, click the **AutoArchive** tab. If you want to force Outlook 98 to automatically archive email messages that you receive, click the button marked **Move old items to** (see Figure 15.12).

READ THIS! YOU'LL BE GLAD YOU DID

If you want to keep copies of old messages that other people have sent to you, it's very important that you not choose the **Permanently delete old items** button. As the name implies, this choice tells Outlook to completely delete the old messages—and there's no way to recover them once they're gone.

FIGURE 15.11
The right-
click context
menu for
Deleted
Items.

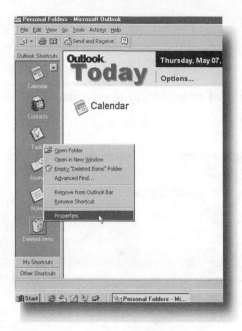

FIGURE 15.12
Setting up
Outlook 98 to
AutoArchive
Deleted Items
(primarily
incoming
email mes-
sages you've
deleted).

5. Click **OK** and Outlook starts AutoArchiving deleted email messages during the next AutoArchive round. That can be as much as two weeks away, so don't hold your breath.

Manual Archive

I'm not sure why, but Outlook 98 doesn't have the capability to AutoArchive your Contacts, the people in your address book. From time to time, you should archive your Contacts by clicking **File**, **Archive**, choosing **Contacts**, and clicking **OK**, as shown in Figure 15.13.

ROTATING ARCHIVES

I bet you've been sitting back, thinking to yourself, "Well, Woody, if you keep shoveling all this old Outlook data into the same archive file, what happens when the archive file gets so big it goes POP?"

You got me there.

The fact is, Outlook 98 doesn't have an elegant way to cycle archives: it sticks all the old data into the same file and, just as sure as Kenny meets his doom in South Park, some day the file's going to get overwhelming. I mean, as in incredibly huge.

Here's how I handle the problem. Every few months, right after Outlook goes through its AutoArchive cycle, I close Outlook 98 and rename the archive.pst file to something more informative: `Outlook Archive 99lQ.pst`, for first quarter, 1999 data, for example. Outlook will create a new archive.pst when it requires one. If I ever need to look back at that data, I open the Outlook by choosing **File**, **Open**, **Personal folders file**.

FIGURE 15.13
From time to time, be sure you manually archive the Contacts folder.

Ancillary Programs

Outlook 98 contains two auxiliary programs that you need to use from time to time.

Inbox Repair Tool

The Inbox Repair Tool scans your outlook.pst file (or any other .pst file you feed to it), searching for inconsistencies and bad entries. You'll know when you need to use it—Outlook will put a message up on the screen, telling you that errors have been detected in the file (see Figure 15.14).

FIGURE 15.14
The telltale sign of a hosed outlook.pst file.

There are two, uh, minor problems with that error message. First, it doesn't tell you how to *find* the Inbox Repair Tool. Second, as you'll no doubt discover some day, the Inbox Repair Tool doesn't always work!

If you get the message shown in Figure 15.14, make a note of the .pst file's name and location, and then shut down Outlook 98. Then click **Start**, **Accessories**, **System Tools**, and then **Inbox Repair Tool**. You'll see the tool, as shown in Figure 15.15.

FIGURE 15.15
The Inbox Repair Tool works most of the time.

Click **Browse**, find the file that caused Outlook dyspepsia, and click **Start**. The Tool asks whether you want to make a backup of your current .pst file, and you should always answer **Yes**. If you have a large .pst file, the repair could take ten minutes or more, so grab a cup of coffee and relax. As soon as the Tool finishes repairing, restart Oulook immediately and see whether the problem persists.

Compacting

As your .pst file(s) grows older, and you delete items from the file—really delete them, as opposed to moving them to the Deleted Items folder—the .pst file gets flabby. Although Outlook 98 is supposed to compact the .pst file from time to time, you might want to compact it manually, especially if you've just gone through a lengthy archive.

WHAT IF THAT DOESN'T FIX THE PROBLEM?
If you see the Figure 15.14 message again, immediately after running the Inbox Repair Tool, you're in for some exciting times. First, try renaming the offending .pst file (never delete it), and then copying your backup version over to replace the bad original. If that doesn't work, brace yourself, get a copy of *Outlook 98 Annoyances*, and follow the discussion in Chapter 3 for restoring .pst files. It's complicated.

If you're running the Internet Only version of Outlook 98, here's how to compact your main .pst file.

*E*XERCISE

Compact mailbox.pst

1. Start Outlook 98. If you're just starting out, the screen should look more or less like Figure 15.10.

2. Right-click the big **Outlook Today** icon, in the upper-left corner. Then choose **Properties** (see Figure 15.16).

FIGURE 15.16
I have no idea why the Compacting program is hidden under Outlook Today's Properties.

3. On the Personal Folders Properties dialog box, click the **Advanced** button.

4. The Personal Folders dialog box appears (see Figure 15.17). Click **Compact Now** and Outlook 98 will start compacting your primary .pst file.

FIGURE 15.17
Here is where the Compacting program hides.

For those of you running the Corporate/Workgroup flavor of Outlook 98, you'll find a similar dialog box by clicking **Tools**, **Services**, then clicking **Personal Folders** on the **Services** tab, and finally clicking **Properties**.

The Screens and Views

Outlook 98 uses more screens than all the other Office 97 applications put together, and each of those screens can be modified by myriad so-called *Views*. The bad news is that each of the screens looks so different that you can expect to spend some time getting used to them. The good news is that you can change parts of many of them to reflect the way you work. In fact, Outlook 98 has so many customizing options that you can easily get lost in the mire.

The Outlook Shell

Outlook itself takes over the top and left side of the screen. It leaves most of the screen for the Outlook application that happens to be in charge at the moment—Email Inbox, Calendar, Contact list, and so on—but the prime screen real estate at the top and left side remain firmly in control of Outlook 98 itself. I call that reserved area at the top and left the *Outlook Shell*.

FIGURE 15.18
The anatomy of Outlook's Inbox screen.

Outlook Bar

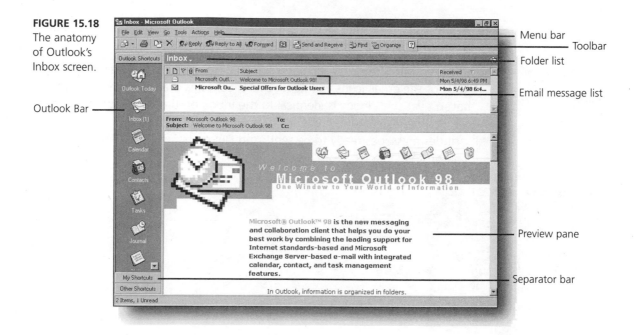

Working from top to bottom, and left to right, here's what the Outlook Shell offers:

- Just below the window title sits Outlook 98's menu bar. This menu bar resembles other Office 97 menu bars in that it can be modified, should you feel so daring. But it's different in one important aspect: When you change the Outlook application—in other words, move from the Email Inbox, to the Calendar, to the Contacts list, and so on—the contents of the menu bar change. The top-level menu items (**File**, **Edit**, **View**, **Go**, **Tools**, **Actions**, and **Help**) remain the same, but almost *everything* underneath changes. Most confusing.

- Under the menu bar sits the toolbar. It, too, changes when you change applications, but you'll see the toolbar change immediately, and that's less confusing.

- Over on the left sits the Outlook Bar, Microsoft's sop to pretty pictures, er, a more friendly user interface. I won't dwell on its obvious deficiencies, but I should point out that you can get to the Outlook Today screen, the Inbox, Calendar, Contacts list, Tasks list, Journal, Notes and Deleted Items by pushing the up and down arrows and single-clicking on the related icon.

● At the bottom of the Outlook Bar squat two separator bars, one marked My Shortcuts, the other marked Other Shortcuts.

● Click the **My Shortcuts** separator bar (see Figure 15.19). Here you'll find most of the email icons you need. Drafts contains drafts of messages you haven't yet sent. Inbox is identical to the Inbox on the Outlook Shortcuts list. Sent Items contains copies of all messages you've sent out. Outbox includes messages ready to be sent. And Deleted Items duplicates the same icon on the Outlook Shortcuts list.

FIGURE 15.19
My Shortcuts contains most of the folders you need for email.

● Click the **Other Shortcuts** separator bar and Outlook displays three icons that you probably won't use: My Computer, My Documents, and Favorites. Someday, it might make sense to get at your files from inside Outlook 98. For now, I think it's more effort than it's worth.

● If you click **Inbox**, Outlook shows you its Folder List (see Figure 15.20)—a very compact, easily accessible list of all the locations that correspond to those pretty icons over in the Outlook bar.

FIGURE 15.20
The Oulook
98 Folder
List.

RECLAIMING SCREEN SPACE
Personally, I reclaim a lot of screen space, get rid of the Outlook Bar (click **View**, then
uncheck **Outlook Bar**), and use this Folder List when I need to navigate around
Outlook's folders. I realize that many of you won't be comfortable with that
approach while you're growing accustomed to Outlook 98, so I left the pretty icons
showing while taking screen shots for this book.

Inbox

If email controls your life, as it does mine, you will find yourself spending much of
your working day sitting inside Outlook's Inbox screen. Click the **Inbox** 📧 icon, if
the Inbox isn't already visible, and you should see a screen much like Figure 15.18.

The vast majority of the screen, the part outside the Outlook Shell (Microsoft calls
this application-specific area the *Information Viewer*), contains information about
your email:

- Just below the Inbox folder list, you'll see yet another bar starting with an
  exclamation point (!). That bar (which doesn't seem to have an official
  Microsoft name) tells you what information Outlook is currently displaying
  about your email messages. You can change what information appears by

changing the Inbox View—a topic we'll explore in the next exercise. Below the bar sits a list of all the messages in your Inbox—that is, all the messages you've received, but haven't deleted as yet.

● Reading from left to right, the ! column contains a picture only if the person who sent the message took the extra effort to mark the message as high or low priority. The envelope icon tells you whether you've looked at the message or not. (It's redundant, usually, because the messages you haven't looked at are listed in bold.) The next column shows a flag if you've, uh, flagged the message. There's a paper clip showing next if the message has an attached file. Most of those fields don't mean much, unless you really go hog wild with Outlook email.

● Now comes the important stuff. The **From** field lists the person who sent you the message (note how Microsoft has kindly sent you at least two messages, automatically). Then there's the **Subject** field the sender typed into the message, and the date and time your Internet email service provider received the message.

● Although you wouldn't know it to look at them, those column headings are *hot*. Click the **Subject** box, for example, and Outlook re-sorts your messages alphabetically by subject. Click **From**, and they're sorted based on the text in the **From** field (which occasionally bears some semblance to the sender's name). Click once again and they're sorted in reverse order.

● You can even adjust the width of the columns by clicking and dragging the vertical bars that appear between the field names. Or right-click a field and choose **Best Fit** to have the column width vary dynamically, making itself just wide enough to cover the widest item in the list.

● Below the list of email messages you'll find one of Outlook 98's nicest features— the Preview Pane. Whenever you choose a message from the list above, a preview of the message appears below.

YOUR GUESS IS AS GOOD AS MINE
Heaven only knows why it's called a preview—scroll up and down and you'll see the whole message. Occasionally, you have to open a message (for example, if you want to save a file attached to a message somewhere else on your hard drive), but most of the time the preview works just fine.

We'll go through the ins and outs of email in the next chapter, but for now I want to show you how to change an Outlook View. This general approach works no matter which application you're using. When you change a view, you tell Outlook that you want to look at the data in a different way: Say, you want to see the time messages were sent, instead of received. That's done by creating a View that includes time sent. As the name implies, changing a View doesn't change any of the underlying data—for example, in the Inbox, your messages aren't modified in any way. Outlook just changes the way you look at them.

Microsoft has created some extraordinarily fancy Views. Let's take a look at what's available in the Inbox.

XERCISE

Check Out Inbox Views

1. Start Outlook 98 and click the **Inbox** 📧 icon.

2. Up on the toolbar, click **Organize**, and then click **Using Views**.

3. In the **Change your view** box, click once on **Messages with Auto Preview** (see Figure 15.21). Note how Outlook has changed the way you look at your messages—with this View, it shows the first three lines of each message directly below the message itself, and it ditches the Preview Pane.

FIGURE 15.21
Setting up the messages with AutoPreview view for the Inbox.

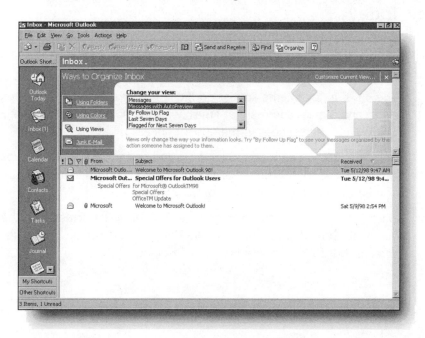

4. I, for one, don't like the AutoPreview mode; I greatly prefer the Preview Pane. But you can make up your own mind. Scroll up and down the **Change your view** box, clicking as you go, and you can see all the different Views the Inbox has to offer.

5. If you're really feeling adventurous, click the **Customize Current View** box in the upper right. Outlook lets you add new columns, delete and move existing ones around , and generally transmogrify any existing View to your heart's content. If you create a new View, make sure you give it a new name so you can get back to the default setting if/when you get tired of it.

6. As soon as you've found a View you like, click the **Organize** button again and Outlook shows the View you've chosen.

7. You might want to close Outlook 98 (**File**, **Exit**), to make sure your changes take.

With one exception—the Contact list—I won't go through the Views available in the other applications. Suffice it to say that the defaults Microsoft has chosen for you are pretty good, but you might be able to find something that better suits your needs by plunking around a little bit.

Outlook Today

If you click the **Outlook Today** icon, at the top of the Outlook Bar, Outlook presents you with a summary of the items in your most important folders (see Figure 15.22).

The day's appointments appear on the left, your unfinished tasks appear on the right, and a quick summary of email (with the number of unread messages appearing in parentheses) goes in the upper right.

You can click just about anything here and be transported to the appropriate part of Outlook: Click **Inbox**, for example, and you end up in Inbox. (Click **Mail**, and you end up in Inbox, too.) Ho-hum.

Microsoft built a lot of power into the Outlook Today screen, but they didn't use it very well. Someday, independent developers will come up with much better screens, but for now it's pretty yawn-inspiring.

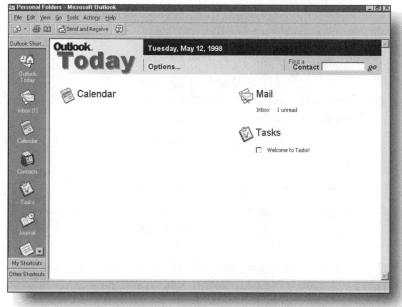

FIGURE 15.22
Outlook
Today doesn't
do much.

Calendar

Click the **Calendar** icon in the Outlook Bar. Outlook's Calendar application appears, as shown in Figure 15.23.

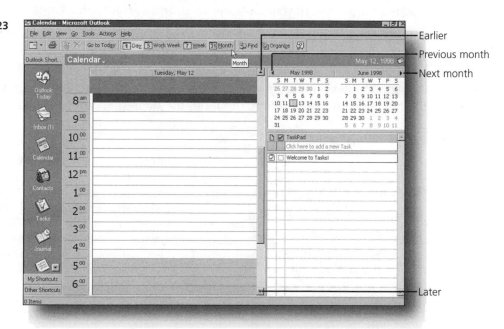

FIGURE 15.23
The bone-
stock
Calendar.

Earlier

Previous month

Next month

Later

The Calendar's toolbar actually focuses on views, with 1-day, 5-day, week, and month options available with just a click.

You can probably figure out what most of the screen elements in Figure 15.23 do, but here are a few pointers:

- The up and down (vertical) scrollbar on the day calendar lets you switch to times before 8:00 a.m. or after 6:30 p.m.

- Click the left or right arrows on the calendar thumbnail to show the previous or next month.

- Click a day in the calendar thumbnail to show that day's activities.

- The TaskPad in the lower-right corner contains Task information—the same info you'll see if you click the **Tasks** icon on the Outlook Bar.

Details for each of the major views differ—for example, the TaskPad appears only if you're looking at a single day—but by and large these are the main components of the Calendar application.

Contacts

As far as I'm concerned, this is the only Outlook 98 application that misses the boat in its default View. Click the **Contacts** icon in the Outlook Bar. You should see the Address Cards View of your Contacts, as shown in Figure 15.24.

Bah. Humbug. The Address Cards View takes up a lot of room, so you can't see very many contacts at a time. Yes, it's pretty. But it won't let you sort your Contacts by, oh, company name. (At least not very easily.) It won't let you visually scan lots of contacts at a time—your eyes have to go down one column, then up and over to the next, then the next. And to top it off, the Address Cards View is so… wasteful. Look at all that wasted space! Shameful.

*E*XERCISE

Get Contacts in Shape

1. Start Outlook 98 and click the **Contacts** icon in the Outlook Bar.

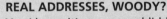

REAL ADDRESSES, WOODY?
Yes, I know it's a no-no publishing real addresses in books. Oh well. That really is Bill Gates' business address. Good luck getting through to him Bill employs living Bozo filters (see the next chapter). And, yep, that really is my business address. Feel free to write!

FIGURE 15.24
The Address
Cards View in
Contacts.

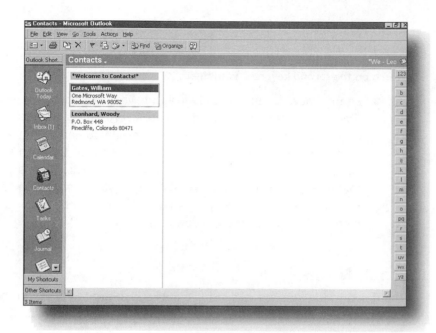

2. Click **Organize** on the toolbar, and then **Using Views**. In the **Change your view** box, click **Phone List**. Then click the **Organize** button once again. You should see something like Figure 15.25.

FIGURE 15.25
The Phone
List View for
Contacts.

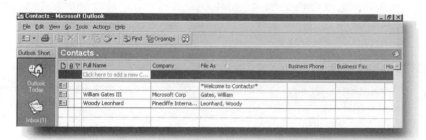

3. As it stands, Phone List View won't let you type a letter and zoom you to the appropriate place in the list. If you want that capability—so you can type an **L**, say, and go straight to the beginning of the Ls, click **View**, **Current View**, and then **Customize Current View**. Click **Other Settings** and clear the box marked **Allow in-cell editing**. Click **OK** all the way back out, and Contacts will jump to whatever letter you type.

KEEP THOSE FINGERS MOVING
If you type two letters quickly—say, Le—Contacts hops down to the beginning of the
Les. Step lively, though; if you dawdle, Outlook assumes that you want to start a new
search on the second keypress, with the Es.

4. I don't know about you, but I like to have my Contacts list available all the
   time, even when I'm working on email. Fortunately, Outlook keeps a copy
   of the Contacts folder open all the time—if you know the trick. Right-click
   the **Contacts** icon in the Outlook Bar, and choose **Open in new window**.
   Outlook creates a new window with your Contacts list, and you can place
   that window anyplace you like. As long as you're careful to use **File**, **Exit** to
   leave Outlook every time you restart it, the Contacts list appears as a running application on the Windows taskbar.

Tasks, Journal, Notes

The default Tasks screen looks just like the TaskPad that appears on the Calendar
views available by clicking **Organize** may come in handy, particularly if you use
Tasks to manage small projects.

The Journal screen won't do much for you, either, until you start keeping track of
telephone conversations via the Journal. Skip it for now.

Finally, the default Notes screen is just a single sticky note. Very uninspiring. To take
advantage of Notes' flat-file database and organizing capabilities, you'll have to
switch to a different View.

The Oops Switch

If you start monkeying around with different Outlook 98 views, sooner or later
you'll make a mistake—things will be so totally messed up you'll wish all the customizing would go away.

Have I got a switch for you!

If you ever want to completely wipe out all of your custom views, set them back to
the Outlook 98 defaults, click **Start**, then **Run** and type `Outlook/CleanViews`.

Note that there's a space after Outlook, but no space after the /.

Outlook 98 starts with absolutely pristine views, and you can take it from there.

Email

FOR MANY PEOPLE, OUTLOOK EMAIL rates as the second-most-frequently used Office 97 application, second only to Word. It won't be long before millions of people will rely on Outlook email every day. Astounding.

As the saying goes, "Know thy ass well, for it bears thee." This is one of those big-payoff topics you've heard about. Learning to use Outlook email—and using it well—will pay untold dividends every day. I'm going to assume that you have Outlook 98 running, and that you've clicked the **Inbox** icon on the Outlook Bar, so Outlook is using its email application. Follow along here and I'll have you up and using email like a pro in no time flat.

Setting Up Email Accounts

☞ *If you already have an email account and you followed the directions I gave on page 307, there's a better-than-middlin' chance that Outlook 98 is ready to send and receive your email.*

The easy way to check whether Outlook is ready to handle your email: Click the **Send and Receive** button on the toolbar. If your PC dials in to your email service provider (or connects to your company network), and completes its mission without giving you any sort of weird error messages, you're home free. Breathe a sigh of relief and move down to the next section, "New, Reply, Reply to All, Forward."

Not so lucky, eh? Don't worry. Email problems may be the most common PC problems of all.

If you're using the Internet Only version of Outlook 98 and you can't get Outlook 98 to connect to the outside world, you should first go back and double-check your account information.

XERCISE

Set Up an Internet Only Mail Account

1. Start Outlook 98, click the **Inbox** icon on your Outlook Bar, and make sure you're running the Internet Only version of Outlook by clicking **Help**, then **About Microsoft Outlook**. The second line of that dialog box should say Internet Mail Only. (If it doesn't, see the following discussion for some alternatives.)

2. Click **Tools**, **Accounts**, and in the Internet Accounts dialog box, click the **Mail** tab. You should see something like Figure 16.1.

FIGURE 16.1
Add or modify email service information here.

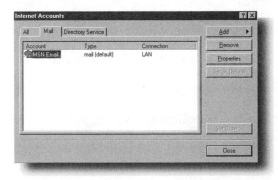

3. If you want to review the settings for an existing email service connection, click the Account, and then click **Properties**. In the Properties dialog box (see Figure 16.2), try clicking the **Servers** tab.

FIGURE 16.2
Server information for the selected email service.

4. Verify that the server names you typed in here are correct: It will take a call to your email service provider to confirm that they're right. (The server name may be a weird Internet name, as you see in Figure 16.2, or a set of four numbers, such as 123.123.123.1.)

GET THOSE SERVER NAMES RIGHT
Here's a weird one. If your connection isn't working right, check to make sure all the letters in the server name are lowercase. Yes, it can make a difference. If the server name is a bunch of numbers, each of the four numbers, separated by periods, should be between 1 and 255.

5. If Outlook 98 can't even get a phone line (frequently you can tell just by listening for a dial tone, coming from your PC's modem), click the **Connection** tab (see Figure 16.3) and try to get the **Modem** box set up correctly. You may have to click the **Add** button and tell Windows how to connect to the outside world.

6. Click **OK** all the way back out and see whether Outlook will connect by clicking the **Send and Receive** icon on the toolbar.

FIGURE 16.3
Wrestle with
phone line
access prob-
lems on the
Connection
tab.

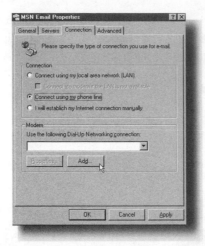

MORE WAYS TO GET HELP

There's more information about this approach available on the Web at

support.microsoft.com/
support/kb/articles/
q179/9/50.asp. It doesn't
work all the time, but it's a
decent place to start.

(If you're using the
Corporate/Workgroup ver-
sion of Outlook 98, the
procedure is quite drasti-
cally different. Refer to
support.microsoft.com/
support/kb/articles/
q179/9/50.asp.)

For help installing specific
mail services—at this
moment, there are very
detailed instructions for
Microsoft Network (MSN
2.5), AT&T WorldNet,
Sprynet, CompuServe, and
others—log on to the
Microsoft Knowledge Base
site at support.microsoft.
com/support/c.asp, specify

DON'T TWEAK WITH YOUR EMAIL SETTINGS

After you've got your email set up
and working, don't mess around with
it! Email is fraught with all sorts of
problems—your PC might not be able to establish a phone connection with your service
provider, the provider's computers (*servers*) may
crash and burn, key programs may get flaky—
and the worst thing you can do is monkey
around with Outlook's settings, trying to com-
pensate.

If your email has been working fine and all of a
sudden it stops working, get on the phone and
complain to your email service provider!
Whatever you do, resist the temptation to
blame Outlook 98 and go hunting for a setting
gone awry. If email suddenly goes belly up,
there's at least a 99% chance that your email
service provider is to blame.

that you want to **Search About** Outlook, and type o198 followed by the name of your service, for example, o198compuserve.

If that doesn't solve the problem for you, hop onto the Web, go to the Knowledge Base site at support.microsoft.com/support/c.asp, **Search About** Outlook, and try searching on o198 mail setup.

And if that doesn't yield results, get on the horn to your email service provider (don't bother calling Microsoft; they won't have the information you need) and tell them you need help setting up your email account to work with the Internet Only version of Outlook 98.

For those of you stuck with the Corporate/Workgroup version of Outlook 98, if you can't get email going with all of this heavy artillery at hand, you have no choice but to call your company's help desk. Good luck.

REAL WORLD VERSUS WOODY

Lemme tell you a story. I was working with an early beta test version of Outlook 98. Email worked fine for a day or two. All of a sudden, I started getting these weird error messages from Outlook, saying "Unable to establish Dial-Up Network connection. Please go to Dial-Up Networking and make sure your connections are configured properly." I clicked OK, and Outlook even provided a dialog box for me to do precisely that. I scratched my head, and wasted hours trying to pacify Outlook, changing this setting and that, dialing and redialing.

Know what the problem was? Dear old MSN wasn't putting through any calls that day! Outlook 98 was working fine. It dialed MSN, and MSN's computers picked up the phone. But for reasons only known in Redmond, on that particular day MSN in Denver wasn't establishing a connection between its phone-answering computers and its network-connecting computers.

I called MSN, of course, but the tech support people assured me that everything was just fine. I hunted and sweated and swore and pecked, and finally decided that the problem *had* to be on MSN's side. I hopped over to a friend's house (he didn't have Outlook 98), used his PC to dial in to MSN, and sure enough—I couldn't get onto MSN from his machine, either.

Moral of the story: It doesn't pay to futz with Outlook settings.

Get your Outlook settings right once, write 'em down so you can go back to a bunch of settings that work should something go awry, then leave 'em alone. If you suddenly have email problems, even if Outlook itself makes you think they're Outlook problems, blame your email provider and you'll be right 99% of the time.

New, Reply, Reply to All, Forward

So how do you create a new email message? You'll be happy to know (particularly if you've gone through a lot of hassles to get Outlook 98 connected) that it's like falling off a log.

*Ɛ*XERCISE

Talk to Yourself

1. Your very first Outlook 98 email message should be a message to yourself, eh? If Outlook is working, and you know your own email address, you have all you need to talk to yourself. Start Outlook 98, and then click the **Inbox** icon.

2. Click the **New Mail Message** 📧 icon on the toolbar. Outlook responds by creating a new mail message, and placing your cursor in the **To** box (see Figure 16.4).

FIGURE 16.4
Message to myself.

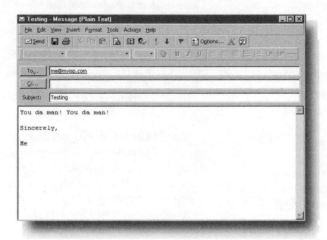

3. Type your email address in the **To** box. Then press Tab, down to the **Subject** box. Type an appropriate subject line, and then press Tab again. Type the message that you want to send to yourself. Click the **Send** 📧Send icon at the top of the message.

4. You might think that clicking **Send** would send your message. If you're permanently connected to the Internet (and some of you may be, through your corporate network), that's probably what happens. For most people, though, clicking **Send** merely puts the message in Outlook's Outbox.

5. To see what's in your Outbox, you have several choices. The simplest method is to click the **My Shortcuts** separator bar, at the bottom of the Outlook Bar, and then click the **Outbox** icon (see Figure 16.5). Much faster: Click the **Inbox** icon to reveal the Folder List, and then choose **Outbox** from that list.

FIGURE 16.5
Switch over
to the
Outbox.

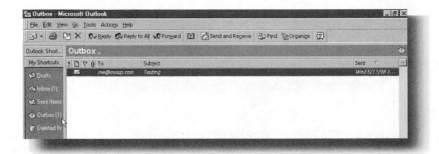

6. Note that you have one message in your Outbox, the one you just wrote. You can open that message and modify it, if you like, by double-clicking it.

DON'T LEAVE ORPHANED MESSAGES
If you open the message in the Outbox, make sure you click **Send** at the end of your editing. Otherwise, the message will be stuck in your Outbox, and it will sit there forever—or at least, until you go back in and click **Send** again. Weird, eh?

7. To truly send the message, click the **Send and Receive** icon on the toolbar. Outlook 98 should dial the phone (or connect to the local network), and send the message.

8. Depending on the speed of your email service provider, the state of the Internet, and the phase of the moon, it may take anywhere from a few seconds to a few hours for that message to make its way through the Internet and back to your email service provider, where it's available for you to download. Check every-so-often to see whether the message has come back by clicking the **Send and Receive** icon.

9. When the message comes back, it'll be deposited in your Inbox (see Figure 16.6). At this point, you would normally read the message, then delete it by clicking the message in the upper pane and pressing the Del key, or by clicking the **Delete** ⊠ icon on the toolbar. Don't delete the message just yet, though. In the next exercise, I'll show you how to reply to yourself.

FIGURE 16.6
The message goes all the way through the Internet and comes back to you.

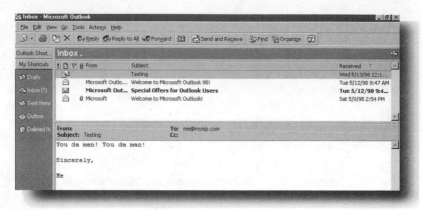

WHEN DELETE REALLY MEANS DELETE
Remember, deleted messages aren't really deleted—they're just moved to the Deleted Items folder. You can see any messages that you've deleted by clicking the **Deleted Items** icon in the Outlook Bar. (At least, you can find them there until you archive your Deleted Items. See the preceding chapter for details.)

Outlook 98 really does make the standard email functions easy, quick, and (relatively) easy to understand. In this exercise, we'll reply to the message you just received and then forward it, just for fun.

XERCISE

Reply and Forward to Yourself

1. You should have the message you sent to yourself showing in the Inbox's Preview Pane, as shown in Figure 16.6.

2. To reply to this (or any other) message, simply click the **Reply** button on the toolbar. Outlook fills out the **To** field with the ID of the person who sent you the message. It fills out the **Subject** field with **RE** (presumably meaning Regarding:) followed by the subject of the incoming message. Finally, it puts your cursor down in the body of the message, where you can type your reply. Go ahead and type something erudite (see Figure 16.7).

3. When you're through typing your message, click **Send**, and the outbound message is deposited in your Outbox.

4. Now let's forward the message to a friend of yours. Do you have their email ID? Good. With the original talk-to-yourself message showing in the Preview Pane, as shown in Figure 16.6, click the **Forward** button on the toolbar.

5. Outlook fills in the **Subject** field with **FW** (as in *Forward*), then the subject of the incoming message. It then creates a copy of the original message, puts it in the body of this new message, and sticks the delivery information at the top of that copy, as shown in Figure 16.8.

6. All you have to do is type the email address for your friend, add whatever text you like on top of the forwarded message, and click the **Send** button.

7. Both of those messages should've been placed in your Outbox (unless you're directly connected to the Internet). To send the messages, click the **Send and Receive** button.

RULES FOR THE EMAIL NEWCOMER
If you're new to email, you should be cognizant of the fact that it's a totally different medium—unlike any you've used before. Start out slowly and study the messages that come in. There are a few simple cardinal rules:

- Don't type all capitals. IT MAKES YOU LOOK LIKE YOU'RE SHOUTING.

- Don't compose an emotional message hastily and send it out before thinking about it. So-called flames always come back to haunt you. In 15 years of using email, I've sent out four flames—maybe five—and I've deeply regretted every one of them.

- Remember that email messages can end up in the strangest places. If you use your company's email account, your company owns your messages. If you forward a copy of a message to someone else, make sure the originator of the message won't be offended.

- Don't get too cute (for instance, use emoticons such as :-) and <G>) before you get the hang of it. Patience, patience.

People tend to think out loud when they type email messages, so give them the benefit of the doubt. Even good friends misread messages from time to time.

Congratulations. You now know enough to do serious damage as an email maven.

FIGURE 16.7
Outlook sets up Reply messages with the important fields filled in.

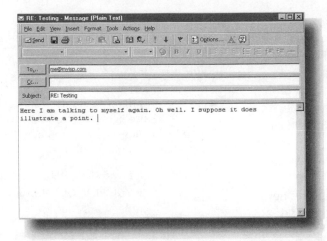

FIGURE 16.8
Outlook takes care of all the dirty work in a Forward.

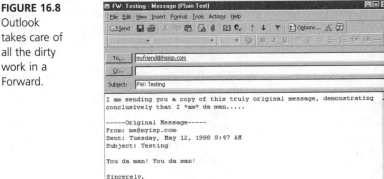

Using Email Addresses

In this section, we're going to look at Outlook's ways for managing and using email addresses: adding them to the Contacts list, then using them in email messages.

Can't remember your correspondents' email addresses? Not to worry. Neither can I. Outlook offers myriad ways to get at all your Contacts, via shortcuts to the Contacts application.

XERCISE _____

Retrieve an Email Address from Contacts

1. If you haven't already, add a few names to your Contacts list. Click the **Contacts** icon in the Outlook Bar, then click the **New Contact** ⬚▾ icon on the toolbar. When you're done with a specific entry, click **Save and Close** to have Outlook save your new Contact. Make sure you have at least one Contact with an email ID. In Figure 16.9, I've constructed a Contact for a fellow you've no doubt heard of, complete with his (real) email ID, billg@ microsoft.com. I'll use this Contacts entry for various exercises in this book.

FIGURE 16.9
Creating a Contacts entry for BillG.

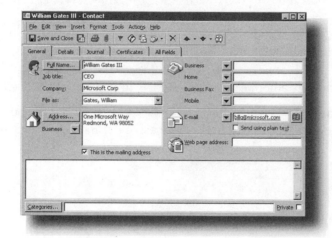

2. I'm going to show you how Outlook can pluck out email IDs with almost no effort on your part. Go back to the Inbox, and click the **New Mail Message** 🗎 icon on the toolbar. Type just part of your intended recipient's name in the **To** box. In Figure 16.10, I've typed only ga. Then press Tab twice and start typing the **Subject**.

FIGURE 16.10
A new message with only "ga" in the To: box.

3. *Boom!* As soon as you press the Tab key to get out of the **To** box, Outlook runs out to your Contacts list and tries to match what you've typed with any entry in the list. If only one entry matches—in this case, the let-

WHAT DOES OUTLOOK REALLY LOOK FOR?
When Outlook looks for matches in the To and Cc boxes, it scans the names and email addresses in your Contacts list. In this example, ga matched on Gates. But if I had typed icr, Outlook would've looked at the email address billg@microsoft.com, and come up with a match on that.

ters ga only appear in the entry for William Gates—and that entry has an email address, it's automatically filled into the **To** box. You don't need to lift a finger.

4. Go ahead and type a message to Bill, as in Figure 16.11, but don't click the **Send** key just yet. We'll use this message in the next exercise.

FIGURE 16.11
Message to Bill, ready to send.

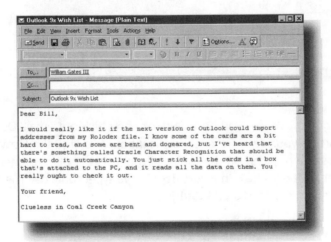

You're probably asking yourself two questions right now:

- What if I don't know whom I'm going to send the message to? For example, "I think the guy's name is Jim or Harry or something, but I need to look in my Contacts list to jog my memory."

- What if two (or more) Contacts entries match the bit of text I typed in the box? Say, I typed micr, but I have six entries that match, ranging from Micron Corporation to wishlist@microsoft.com.

Answers coming right up…

𝓔XERCISE

Contacts in To, Cc, and Bcc Boxes

1. You should still have a message similar to the one shown in Figure 16.11 on your screen.

2. Click the **To** button immediately to the left of Bill's name. You should see the Select Names dialog box, as shown in Figure 16.12.

FIGURE 16.12
Outlook runs out to the Contacts list for you and presents names for your plucking.

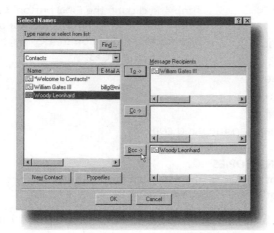

3. You can add as many recipients to the message's **To** or **Cc** list as you like. Just click once on a name, and then click the **To** or **Cc** button in this Select Names dialog box. The name gets added to either the **To** or the **Cc** list, depending on which button you press.

4. Outlook 98 allows you to send blind copies (that's the **B** in **Bcc**). A blind copy recipient receives a copy of the message, but their name

WHAT'S THE DIFFERENCE BETWEEN TO: AND CC:?
There isn't any. The message gets sent to everybody on the **To** list, and to everybody on the **Cc** list, precisely the same way. Some people like to differentiate between **To** and **Cc** simply to show whom they expect to follow up on the message. But from Outlook's point of view, there's really no difference at all.

and ID don't appear anywhere on the **To** or **Cc** lists. Thus, other people receiving copies of the message have no idea the **Bcc** person also received a copy. In Figure 16.12, I've clicked once on **Woody Leonhard**, then clicked **Bcc**. That puts, ahem, Woody Leonhard on the blind copy list.

THE SELECT NAMES DIALOG BOX
As you probably noticed in Figure 16.12, the Select Names dialog box has all sorts of buttons. If you're curious, try adding a new Contact directly from this dialog box by clicking **New Contact**. Narrow down the list of Contacts by typing selection criteria up at the top and clicking the **Find** button. Look up all the information you have about a particular Contact by clicking on that Contact, and then clicking **Properties**.

UNDERSTANDING BLIND COPIES

The blind copy recipient can see all the names on the **To** and **Cc** list, but they can't see the names of any other blind copy recipients.

5. When you've finished using the Select Names dialog box, click **OK**. You should have a message similar to the one shown in Figure 16.13. Note how the **Bcc** recipient appears, in a new box marked (of all things!) **Bcc**.

FIGURE 16.13
A new message, complete with blind copy recipient, ready to go.

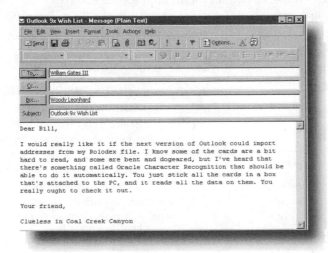

6. If you want to send this message to Bill, by all means, click **Send**. Otherwise, you can delete the message by clicking the **X** in the message's upper-right corner and replying **NO** when asked if you want to save changes.

Resolving multiple matches in the Contacts list is a piece o' cake, if you know the trick. This rates as a very important trick—Outlook behaves very strangely if you don't do it right—so pay attention!

*E*XERCISE

Choosing the Right Contact

1. In Outlook's Inbox, start a new message by clicking the **New Mail Message** icon on the toolbar.

2. I want you to type something in the **To** box that will trigger matches on two or more items in your Contacts list. One possibility: If you have two or more entries in the Contacts list that have email IDs ending with .com, you can type **com** in the **To** box, as I have in Figure 16.14.

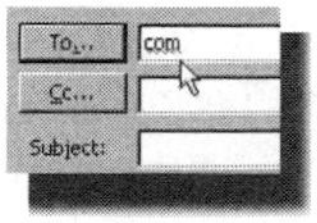

FIGURE 16.14
Type something in the To box that will trigger multiple matches in your Contacts list.

3. Press Tab a couple of times to move down to the **Subject** box. Outlook scurries out to the Contacts list, trying to match what you've typed with what exists in the list. If Outlook finds more than one match, it puts a red squiggly line under the entry in the **To** box. In this case, as you can see in Figure 16.14, Outlook found two or more matches for com, so it stuck a red squiggly line under com in the **To** box.

4. If you remember your Word 97 experiences, you might be tempted to right-click the text with the red squiggly under it and choose the correct email ID. (After all, that's what you do when Word identifies a misspelled word and puts a red squiggly line underneath it: You right-click the word and choose one that's spelled correctly.) DON'T DO IT! I'll explain why at the end of this exercise.

5. Instead, finish typing your message. When you're ready to send it, click the **Send** button. Outlook pops up a Check Names dialog box, as shown in Figure 16.15. From the list offered here, you can choose the person you meant to receive the message, then click **OK**. The message goes out properly.

FIGURE 16.15
If you click Send for a message with multiple Contacts matches, Outlook presents you with a list.

6. Why shouldn't you right-click the text with the red squiggly line? In point of fact, you *can* do it—and Outlook presents you with a list quite similar to the one that Word 97 offers. But after you choose a recipient this way—say, if you tell Outlook that *com* really means *Woody Leonhard*—it remembers the association. After you do it once, every time you type **com** in the **To** box, Outlook automatically substitutes Woody Leonhard. Believe me, you don't want to do that.

Resolving multiple matches in the Check Names dialog box works fine every time. But after you resolve a match using the right-click method, Outlook *knows* that you always want to make that same association.

I just hate it when programs think they're smarter than I am.

This particular Outlook 98 oddity is very poorly documented. I don't know of any other introductory book that mentions it. Even the official documentation buries the description way down in the fine print. Watch out!

Adding Contacts

It's probably become crystal clear to you, at this point, that you're going to want to put all of your email correspondents' names in your Contacts list. Outlook 98 imports that information from just about every email package imaginable, and most address books, to boot. If all else fails, you can always type all of them into the Contacts list. Blecch.

There's one trick for adding Contacts quickly, directly from email, though, and you should take advantage of it to add new email addresses whenever new people send you email messages.

XERCISE

Add Email Address to Contacts—Correctly

1. In the Outlook Inbox, the Sent Items folder, or the Deleted Items folder, choose an email message that was sent to you by someone whom you'd like to include in your Contacts list. Open the message by double-clicking the message in the upper pane, so you can see the full message, as shown in Figure 16.16.

FIGURE 16.16
Right-click to look up a Contact before adding it.

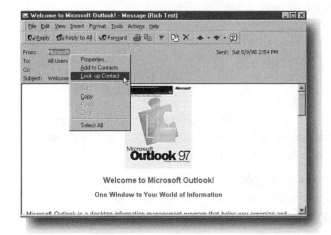

2. Immediately after the word **From** in the message itself, you'll see the sender's name, although it's grayed out. Everywhere—I do mean *everywhere* —in Windows, a grayed-out field is dead, in the sense that you

WHY NOT? I WANT TO ADD THE ADDRESS TO MY CONTACTS LIST...
Well, yes, but if you click **Add to Contacts**, Outlook doesn't automatically check to see whether this Contact is already in your Contacts list, before adding it. Dumb, eh? If you blindly click **Add to Contacts** at this point, you could end up with two—or three or four or ten—entries for Microsoft in your Contacts list. Bummer.

can't do anything with it. Outlook decided to do things differently. (Aren't we the lucky ones?) Not only is this grayed-out name "live," it's the only easy way to get a sender's email ID added to your Contacts list!

WHAT DO YOU MEAN "CLOSE MATCHES"?
Ah, you caught me again. Thought I could finesse that one. In fact, Outlook's Contact application searches for an exact match on the email ID that's in the message. Outlook doesn't care one whit what the name might be: it only looks for identical email ids.

3. Right-click the sender's name. In Figure 16.16, I right-clicked **Microsoft**.

4. Resist the temptation to click **Add to Contacts** right away. You don't want to do that.

5. Instead of clicking **Add to Contacts**, click **Look Up Contact**. Outlook's Contact application scans the list of Contacts and lets you know if there are any close matches.

6. If Outlook finds that it already has that Contact in the Contacts list, it presents you with that entry from the list. Ho-hum. If it doesn't find that the Contact already exists, it tells you so.

7. If the Contact doesn't exist in your Contacts list, right-click the From: name again and choose **Add to Contacts**.

If you want to keep your Contact list from getting clogged with dozens of duplicated entries, you must click the **Look Up Contact** choice before running an **Add to Contacts**. Bizarre. Sloppy programming on Microsoft's part. Not very well documented. But crucial to maintaining a decent Contacts list.

Something else they didn't tell you on the Office 97 box, eh?

ADDING CONTACTS WORKS THE SAME WAY EVERYWHERE
You can use this same technique to add Contacts that appear in any From or CC field, in any message. Just open the message, check to see whether you already have the Contact and, if you don't, click **Add to Contacts**.

Attaching Files

Once upon a time, attaching files to email messages—the procedure you need to use to send a file to somebody else over the Internet—owed more to black art and luck than rational thought and science. Things are much better today than they were just a year ago, but you'll still encounter some sporadic problems sending and receiving files. Such is the state of the art in the waning hours of the twentieth century.

Outlook 98 makes it easy to attach a file to a message.

XERCISE

Sending and Receiving Files

1. Start in Outlook's Inbox. Click the **New Mail Message** 📧 icon on the toolbar to start a new message. You'll be sending a message, with an attached file, to yourself.

2. Type your email ID in the **To** box, add any **Subject** you like, and when you're ready to attach a file to the message, click **Insert**, and then **File** (see Figure 16.17).

FIGURE 16.17
Attaching a file to an email message.

A NOTE ABOUT ATTACHED FILES
Files are always attached to the end of the message, so it doesn't matter where your cursor sits when you insert the file.

3. When the message and attached file are to your liking, click the **Send** icon on the message's toolbar. Then click **Send and Receive** on the Inbox toolbar, to send the message (with attached file) to yourself.

4. After a few minutes, or a few hours if you're exceedingly unlucky, your message should be ready for you to retrieve. Clicking the **Send and Receive** icon on the Inbox toolbar should bring it in to the Inbox.

5. You'll be able to tell that this message has an attached file because of the paper clip icon that appears to the left of the message. (You can see just such an icon on the bottom message in the Inbox list of Figure 16.6.)

6. Similarly, a paper clip icon appears at the top of the Preview Pane. Click it and you'll see a list of the files attached to the message. Click one of the files and you'll get the dialog box shown in Figure 16.18.

FIGURE 16.18
Outlook asks what you would like to do with the file attached to a message.

7. When you're done with this message, click it once in the upper pane, and press the **Delete** ☒ icon on the toolbar. Your message, along with its attached file(s), will be sent to the Deleted Items folder.

Note that you can attach as many files as you like to a particular message, but as the message size goes up, the chances of it surviving the trip through the Internet go down. That isn't the fault of the files, necessarily: Long messages always have a harder time getting through the Net than smaller messages. Some email service providers even refuse to send (or receive) messages larger than a predetermined size!

LIMIT THE FILE SIZE FOR YOUR EMAIL ATTACHMENTS
Some files are just huge, and there isn't much you can do about it. Even after you zip a file, it may still be so huge (say, over 1MB, or 1,000,000 bytes) that you'll have trouble getting it sent, or your correspondent may not be able to download it.

If that's the case, consider breaking the file into smaller pieces, if that's possible. (On some files it

ZIP IT UP
While files up to, oh, 50KB (about 50,000 bytes) in size work just fine over the Net, after you get much above that point, it pays to compress the file. Compression removes redundant data from the file. You compress the file on your end, and the person receiving the file has to uncompress it on the other end.

While there are many programs that compress and uncompress files, I've long used a utility called WinZip, and it's served me well. Check out www.winzip.com for details.

isn't.) Word documents, for example, can be broken into pieces, with each segment stored in a separate file.

Finally, note that you don't have to use the **Insert, File** menu to get a file into an Outlook 98 message. Outlook supports drag and drop just like most other Windows programs. Try dragging files and dropping them onto messages. Most of the time, it works like a charm.

AutoSignature

Have you ever noticed how many advanced email users tack a *signature* onto the end of their messages? Some of them are pretty simple—their name, maybe their email address or Web site, perhaps some personal information or a witty saying. Some of them include cute drawings, or even designs straight from a Grateful Dead poster—kinda makes you wonder what the sender's been smoking. If you set up a signature properly, it can be a real time saver for the people who read your messages.

XERCISE

Create an AutoSignature

1. Once again we'll start in Outlook's Inbox.

2. Click **Tools**, **Options**, and click the **Mail Format** tab. Click **Signature Picker**, then **New**. You should see the Create New Signature Wizard, as shown in Figure 16.19.

FIGURE 16.19
Give your new AutoSignature a name.

3. Outlook lets you create all sorts of different AutoSignatures, so type a name for this one (in Figure 16.19 I've called it WoodyStandard), then click **Next**.

4. Now type whatever you want to appear in your AutoSignature, being careful to add paragraph marks (in other words, press the Enter key) only where you want Outlook to force an end of paragraph. In Figure 16.20 I've typed in an AutoSignature that lists my email ID, Web site, and a shameless plug for WOW.

FIGURE 16.20
Enter your
AutoSignature
here.

5. Resist the temptation to format the AutoSignature for now. (If you ever decide to use HTML Mail—I talk about it at the end of this chapter—you may want to add some formatting; for now, don't get yourself confused with it.) Click **Finish**, then **OK**.

6. Back in the Options dialog box, make sure your new signature appears in the **Use this Signature by default** box, and uncheck the box that says **Don't use when replying or forwarding** (see Figure 16.21). Click **OK**.

7. Test your AutoSignature. If you create a new message, as shown in Figure 16.22, the AutoSignature should appear at the bottom of the message. If you reply to a message, the AutoSignature appears similarly. If you forward a message, the AutoSignature shows up before the forwarded copy.

ADDING A SIGNATURE ANYWHERE YOU LIKE
If you ever want to stick your AutoSignature into the middle of a message, click **Insert**, then **Signature**, and choose the AutoSignature you want.

That's all there is to the AutoSignature shtick. If you want to dig into the formatting question a bit more, check out `support.microsoft.com/support/kb/articles/q179/4/36.asp` on the Web.

FIGURE 16.21
Setting up the AutoSignature to work on new messages, replies, and forwards.

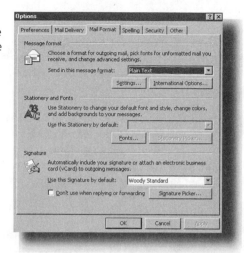

FIGURE 16.22
A new message with the "Woody Standard" AutoSignature.

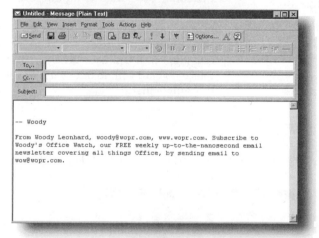

vCard

The electronic version of a business card, vCards (short for *Virtual Cards*) provide a convenient, fast way to send a correspondent your name, address, phone number, email ID, and just about anything else you would normally think of putting on a business card.

Outlook 98 supports vCards, but more importantly other email packages do as well. In particular, if you send a vCard to somebody using Netscape, they can add the information to their Netscape address book. Look for all the major email packages to support vCards soon. It's just too good an idea to ignore.

*E*XERCISE

Create and Send a vCard

1. To create a vCard, you have to flip over to the **Contacts** application, so click the Contacts icon in the Outlook Bar.

2. If you haven't yet created an entry for yourself, do so now. Include all the information you want people to have. At the same time, exclude any information (say, home phone number) you *don't* want people to have. I've completed an entry for myself in Figure 16.23.

VCARD AS AUTOSIGNATURE
If you hand out business cards like confetti on Fifth Avenue, you might want to send out your vCard with every email message. I *don't* recommend it, but if you want to, click **Tools**, then **Options**, then choose the **Mail Format** tab. Click **Signature Picker**. Either select an existing AutoSignature and click **Edit**, or click **New** to create a new AutoSignature.

On the Edit Signature dialog box (see Figure 16.24), click **New vCard from Contact**. Choose the Contact you want to include, click **Add**, then click **OK**. Back on the Edit Signature dialog box, in the Attach this business card (vCard) to this Signature box, select the vCard you want to add, then click **OK**. Click **OK** again and the selected vCard will go out every time you use this AutoSignature.

FIGURE 16.23
To create a vCard, start by filling out a Contact entry for yourself.

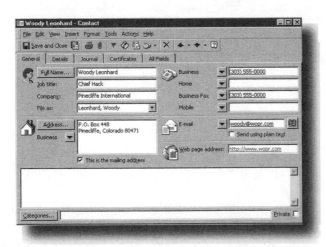

3. Next you need to save this information as a .vcf file. Click **File**, **Save As**. When Outlook presents you with its Save As dialog box, in the **Save as type** box, choose **VCARD Files (*.vcf)**. Outlook chooses an appropriate file name for you—in this case, it suggested Woody Leonhard.vcf. Save the vCard in a convenient location.

4. This .vcf file can be treated the same as any other file. In particular, you can attach it to an email message. Try it by flipping over to the Inbox, creating a new email message, clicking **Insert**, then **File**, and inserting the .vcf file you just saved.

5. When you receive a message with an attached .vcf file, simply click the paper clip icon at the top of the Preview Pane, and select the file. Outlook responds by presenting you with a Contact entry, precisely as you saw in Figure 16.23. If you then click **Save and Close**, Outlook adds this new entry to your Contacts list.

FIGURE 16.24
This is where you specify that a vCard should be included in a given Auto-Signature.

Find

Outlook's Inbox, Outbox, Sent Items, and Deleted Items folders all support a very powerful Find function. As the name implies, Find lets you search through messages (either the subject lines, or all the text in all the messages) for specific words.

*E*XERCISE

Find a Deleted Item

1. Say you want to find a message you deleted from your Inbox last week. No problem. Bring up the Deleted Items folder by clicking the **Deleted Items** icon in the Outlook Bar.

2. Click the **Find** button on the toolbar. Outlook responds by tacking a Find panel at the top of the message list (see Figure 16.25).

FIGURE 16.25
Outlook 98's powerful Find function is just one click away.

3. Type whatever text you want to search for in the **Look for:** box. In Figure 16.25, I typed clueless. If you want Outlook to look inside the body of all the messages, check the box marked **Search all text in the message**. (If you don't check that box, Outlook only searches the **To**, **Cc**, **Bcc**, and **Subject** contents.) Click the **Find Now** button.

4. Outlook will present you with a list of all the messages that match your search criteria. Rummage through those messages and see if you found what you were looking for.

5. Outlook also puts a few lines up on the Find panel, saying "Did you find it? If not, try: Go to Advanced Find… / Clear Search." Although that text is grayed out (sheesh!), it is nonetheless hot. Click **Advanced Find** to see all the extensive search options available to you. Click **Clear Search** to start out fresh.

6. When you're done searching through the messages, you can click the **Find** icon on the toolbar again to clear away the Find panel. The Find panel also clears out if you switch to any other Outlook folder or application.

Organize

Outlook 98 also includes very powerful capabilities for organizing your email. While organizing is certainly in the eye of the beholder, the ability to highlight mail from important colleagues, customize the views, and perhaps most importantly, shuffle junk email to a special holding area, puts Outlook 98's email handling among the very best.

All of these Organize features apply equally well to Outlook's Inbox, Sent Items, and Deleted Items folders. You'll probably use them most within the Inbox, and that's what I'll focus on in these exercises.

Folders

$\mathcal{E}$XERCISE

Organize with Folders

1. Move to Outlook's Inbox, and click the **Organize** button on the toolbar. Outlook presents you with the Using Folders dialog box, as shown in Figure 16.26.

FIGURE 16.26
Organizing
your email
with folders.

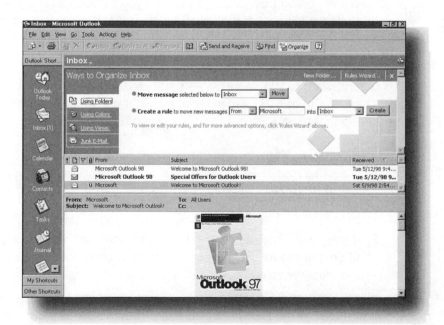

2. The first option in the **Using Folders** pane lets you move a selected message from one folder to another. That's a real yawner: you can move messages much more readily by clicking and dragging them.

3. The second option is much more powerful. You can create rules that Outlook will automatically apply to all incoming mail. In this particular case you can create a rule that will move any email message coming in from a specific person (actually, from a specific email ID) to any folder you choose. You can even create a new folder to receive all of those messages—simply click the **New Folder** text at the top of the **Using Folders** pane, or choose **Other folder** in the **into** box.

4. There's more. You can create rules that will move messages sent to a specific ID into a particular folder. If you commonly get messages from more than one email service provider, or if you receive email addressed to all sorts of different IDs, this option lets you organize the mail according to the intended receiver.

5. If you really want to see an amazingly powerful (and quite complex!) message filtering system, click the **Rules Wizard** text at the top of the Using Folders dialog box. I won't try to step you through all the nuances here. Suffice it to say that the Office Assistant (**F1**) does a pretty good job of it.

Colors

If you don't want to shuffle messages to different folders, you should certainly take advantage of Outlook 98's capability to highlight messages coming from people most important to you. Believe me, when a red message shows up in your Inbox, you'll take notice!

*E*XERCISE _____

Highlighting Important Messages with Color

1. Go into Outlook's Inbox.

2. If you have a message sitting there from someone who's important to you (a boss, a spouse, a significant other, even your stock broker!), click once on the message so it appears in the Preview Pane.

3. Click the **Organize** button on the toolbar, then click **Using Colors**. You should see the Using Colors dialog box, as shown in Figure 16.27.

4. Choose a color for all the messages from this particular person by choosing one from the **in** box. When you're happy with the choice, click **Apply Color**.

FIGURE 16.27
Use color to
flag mes-
sages from
important
people.

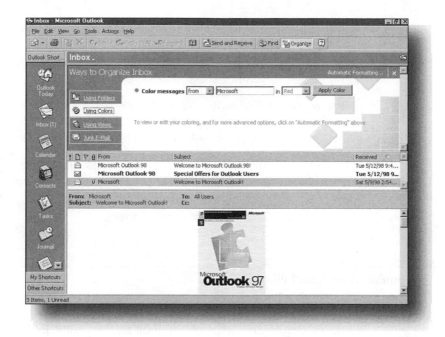

5. If you really want to feel like you've fallen down the rabbit hole, click
Automatic Formatting at the top of the Using Colors dialog box. You'll
discover that Outlook 98 can color code messages based on the content of
the message, the size of attachments—just about anything you can imagine. The Office Assistant doesn't provide much help with these choices, but
there's limited help available by clicking the **?** in the upper-right corner of
the appropriate dialog boxes.

Views

☞ I covered views on page 325.

We took a look at the various views in the earlier exercise. Check it out if you want
to modify your Inbox, Outbox, Sent Items, or Deleted Items views.

Junk Mail

This is quite possibly Outlook 98's most compelling feature—every email user
should set up Outlook to filter out junk mail.

I tend to lump junk mail into three categories:

● *Mail from Bozos*. Some Bozos are people you know; they just can't quit sending you mail that you don't want to read. These Bozos are easily handled—you know their IDs, and you can deal with their mail via the Using Folders dialog box shown in Figure 16.26.

● *Spam, which is email sent indiscriminately to everyone on a mailing list.* Typically the mailing lists are huge, and the ID of the sender changes with every message. Outlook's Junk filter will help you bypass much spam.

● *XXX messages*. Microsoft calls these Adult messages though I fail to see anything adult about them. Prurient maybe. Usually XXX messages are a form of spam, but sometimes they're more targeted. Outlook's Adult Content filter will take care of most of them.

XERCISE

Enable Junk Email Filters

1. Go into Outlook's Inbox.

2. Click the **Organize** button on the toolbar, then **Junk E-Mail**. You should see the Junk E-Mail dialog box shown in Figure 16.28.

FIGURE 16.28
Outlook's built-in junk email filters.

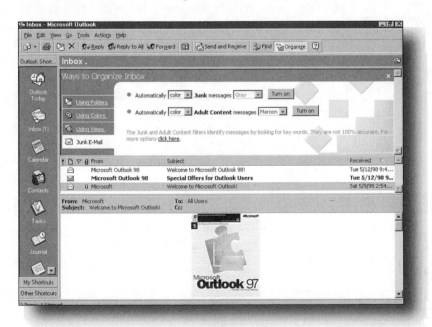

3. Outlook scans the content of each message to see if there are any matches on a specific set of words. These keywords, and Outlook's method for searching for the keywords, are described in a file called filters.txt, which is in your c:\Program Files\Microsoft Office\Office folder. You might want to use Word or Notepad (**Start**, **Programs**, **Accessories**, **Notepad**) to open that file and study it. The one that shipped with my system is shown in Figure 16.29.

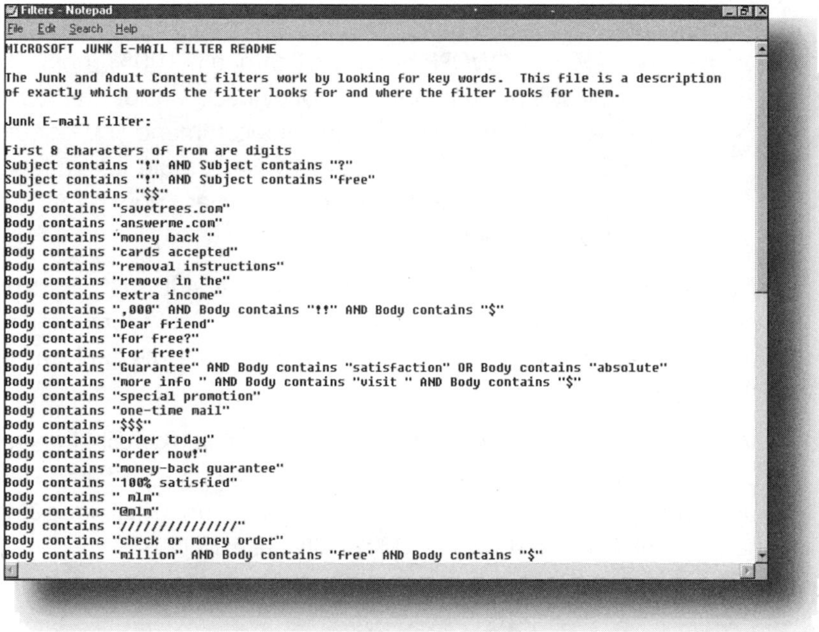

```
MICROSOFT JUNK E-MAIL FILTER README

The Junk and Adult Content filters work by looking for key words.  This file is a description
of exactly which words the filter looks for and where the filter looks for them.

Junk E-mail Filter:

First 8 characters of From are digits
Subject contains "!" AND Subject contains "?"
Subject contains "!" AND Subject contains "free"
Subject contains "$$"
Body contains "savetrees.com"
Body contains "answerme.com"
Body contains "money back "
Body contains "cards accepted"
Body contains "removal instructions"
Body contains "remove in the"
Body contains "extra income"
Body contains ",000" AND Body contains "!!" AND Body contains "$"
Body contains "Dear friend"
Body contains "for free?"
Body contains "for free!"
Body contains "Guarantee" AND Body contains "satisfaction" OR Body contains "absolute"
Body contains "more info " AND Body contains "visit " AND Body contains "$"
Body contains "special promotion"
Body contains "one-time mail"
Body contains "$$$"
Body contains "order today"
Body contains "order now!"
Body contains "money-back guarantee"
Body contains "100% satisfied"
Body contains " mlm"
Body contains "@mlm"
Body contains "///////////////"
Body contains "check or money order"
Body contains "million" AND Body contains "free" AND Body contains "$"
```

FIGURE 16.29
Outlook's junk mail filter rules, in filters.txt.

4. Although Outlook's default settings for Junk and Adult messages (shown in Figure 16.28) assigns them colors, I find it much more effective to move the messages out to a folder created specifically for junk mail. If you would like to do the same, change the **Automatically** boxes to say **move** (see Figure 16.30). Outlook creates a new folder called Junk E-Mail for you, and shuffle messages that match the Junk and Adult definitions in filters.txt into that folder.

FIGURE 16.30
How to make
Outlook
move junk
mail into its
own folder.

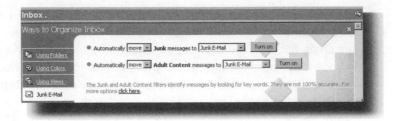

5. Mail filtering isn't a perfect science. For example, if I send you a message that says, oh, "WOPR has always carried a 100% money back guarantee," Outlook will see the phrase "money back" inside the message and assume it's junk mail! That's why I strongly recommend you *not* direct junk mail to your Deleted Items folder, and why you should take a look at your Junk E-Mail folder from time to time. You never know—you might have a message from me hiding in there!

If you constantly get junk mail sent from the same ID, it's easy to tell Outlook 98 that you want all messages from that ID to go in your Junk Mail folder. Just right-click the message (in the upper pane, where all the messages are listed), and choose **Junk E-mail**.

Microsoft is constantly refining and updating its junk mail filters. If you click the underlined phrase **click here** in the Junk E-Mail pane (refer to Figure 16.28), Outlook offers several alternatives for handling junk mail, including an automatic tie-in to the Web to download Microsoft's latest filters.

What to Avoid—If You Can

So much for the high points of email in Office 97. I hope you agree with me that Outlook 98 contains one humdinger of an email program, and that you have a chance to use it to help tame the onslaught of email that seems destined to engulf us all.

That said, there are two Outlook email options that I think you should avoid.

WordMail

Outlook 98 allows you to use Word 97 as your email editor. That feature is known as WordMail, and it stinks.

Yes, I know how nice it is to have all of Word's power available when composing email messages. (Hey, remember, you're talking to Mr. Word here.) Yes, I do hate to give up the red squiggly underline on misspelled words, and the simple right-click correction routine that Word 97 offers. Yes, I realize that Document Map—which doesn't work worth beans on Word documents—can make traversing long email messages a snap.

There's just one problem. For the vast majority of people, WordMail doesn't work. It causes all sorts of strange, indescribable problems with Word itself and it frequently makes Windows so unstable you'll see *GPFs* (general protection faults) on top of GPFs. If Outlook crashes, you'll have a hidden instance of Word running in the background. If Word crashes, it'll probably take Outlook along with it. Sorry, but as much as I love Word 97, it still doesn't work well inside Outlook 98.

If you're using WordMail right now, turn it off. Click **Tools**, **Options**, the **Mail Format** tab, and switch the **Send in this message format** box to **Plain Text**.

I know, I know. Some of you won't give up on WordMail until Microsoft pries it from your cold, dead fingers. If you fall into that camp, I wish you luck. Back up often, back up well!

HTML Mail

Notice how I just recommended that you send messages in Plain Text, and not HTML (one of the other options in the Mail Format tab's Send in this message format: box). There's a reason for that.

Using HTML mail doesn't carry with it the huge overhead and instability inherent in WordMail. For that we can all be thankful. But, in my experience, it isn't a good choice for beginning Outlook users, for two reasons:

IDENTIFYING HTML MESSAGES IN THE WILD
If you've never heard pf *HTML*, don't worry about it. It's just another computer buzzwork. Er, acronym. HTML is the lanquage of the Web—World Wide Web pages are all constructed in HTML.

Outlook 98 and the Netscape mail reader both allow you to create mesages in HTML format and to read them if you get one in your Inbox. If you've ever seen a message that includes more than plain, drab, old everyday text, it's probably an HTML message.

1. HTML just isn't appropriate for some kinds of messages, for example, any message that may receive wide distribution. At this point only a tiny fraction of all email programs recognize HTML mail, and the ones that don't can turn a perfectly beautiful HTML message into plain text mush.

2. New Outlook 98 users are more likely than most to be conversing with people who don't have HTML-speaking email programs. Starting out with email is hard enough without having to answer tough questions from novice email correspondents. "Why did your message come through all garbled, with a weird attached file?" The minute you stray from Plain Text, you invite those problems. By the droves.

That said, if you want to tackle the wacky but glorious world of HTML mail, go ahead and set the Send in this message format: box mentioned in the previous section to **HTML**.

After you get your bearings, try adding a background (Microsoft calls it *stationary*) to your email messages. Check the Microsoft Knowledge Base article at `support.microsoft.com/support/kb/articles/q182/2/22.asp` for all sorts of helpful tips.

Other Outlooks

ALTHOUGH THE MAJORITY OF OFFICE 97 users spend the bulk of their days with Word and Outlook's email component, there's lots more to like about Office in general, and Outlook in particular. In this chapter, I'll hit the high points of the other, non-email, parts of Outlook.

Contacts

No doubt you've struggled with Windows-based telephone and address books before. If you're lucky, you used one of the easy ones (such as Sidekick or Metz Phones) that sit back and get out of the way while you go about your business. If you aren't so lucky, you probably struggled with one of the heavy-duty contact management packages, where it helps to have a Ph.D. in Computer Science before you make your first entry.

Outlook 98's Contacts application takes a little more effort than the bone-simple address books: There are some tricks you can employ to make retrieving names, addresses, and phone numbers faster down the road. Still, most people find it remarkably easy to use straight out of the box, and amazingly flexible.

Contacts is far from perfect, of course, and we'll delve into some of its idiocies here. (More idiocy will become apparent in Chapter 28, "Making Presentations Look Better," where we look at how the Contacts application interacts with Word 97.) For now, though, it will behoove you to take a moment and think through the way you're going to use Contacts. A little time spent now will greatly speed up things as you become more adept.

USE CONTACTS!
If you're new to computerized address/phone books—or if you've tried to use them in the past but come away with a very bad taste in your mouth—give Outlook Contacts a chance. It's a lot easier to use than you might think, and there are great benefits to having all your contacts' names, addresses, phone numbers and email addresses in the same location.

Whenever you think about bypassing Contacts, even for a moment—say, you have a new address you're going to type into a letter, or you're sending out an email message to somebody new—take a moment and create a contact, particularly if you think there's a chance you'll ever write to that person again. Yes, there's a certain amount of overhead involved in switching over to Outlook and typing the name and address, and if you use the address only once it's overkill. But the second time you need that address you'll come out ahead because it's already in Outlook. By the third time you use the address, it's all gravy.

Creating a Contact

You'll be amazed at how well Outlook 98 analyzes the information you type. Let's start by putting an entry in your Contact list for little ol' me. (Okay, okay. *Big* ol' me. Never mind.)

*E*XERCISE

Make Me a Contact

1. Start Outlook 98. If you followed the instructions in Chapter 15, "Outlook Preliminaries," you should have a separate Contacts program running down on the Taskbar. Click it to bring up the Phone List view of your Contacts. (If you didn't follow Chapter 15, you'll have to click the **Contacts** 🔲 icon on the Outlook Bar, and then click **Organize** on the toolbar and then **Using Views**. In the **Change your view** box, click **Phone List** and click the **Organize** button again.) In either case, you should be in Phone List view, as shown in Figure 15.25 (Chapter 15).

2. Start by getting rid of that **Welcome to Contacts!** contact by clicking it once, then clicking the **Delete** ⊠ icon on the toolbar.

3. Create a new contact by clicking the **New Contact** icon on the toolbar. You should see the standard Contact entry form, shown in Figure 17.1.

FIGURE 17.1
Name and company information is extracted and presented so you can choose how Contacts sorts names.

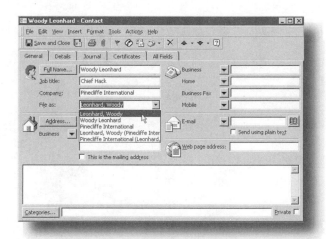

4. Type my name and company information, and watch carefully to see how Outlook's Contacts program handles much of the work for you. When you finish typing the **Name**, Outlook takes a first guess at the **File as** entry (that's what Outlook uses to alphabetize the list). Type a **Job Title** and

Company, and then click the drop-down list next to **File as**. See how Outlook has created five entries for you to choose from? In the case of my contact information in Figure 17.1, you can file me away as Woody Leonhard or Leonhard, Woody or Pinecliffe International or Leonhard, Woody (Pinecliffe International) or Pinecliffe International (Leonhard, Woody). It's an amazing bit of wizardry that can save you all sorts of time— the hallmark of a very well designed computer program.

5. In most cases, you'll want to file away names of individuals in Lastname, Firstname order. That makes it easy to see your contacts alphabetized by last name. In some cases, though (for example, if you have only a contact name at a company, but all the other information is for the company itself), you might want to use the Company Name or Company Name (Lastname, Firstname) for sorting. For now, let's file me under Leonhard, Woody.

6. Now type my business address, as shown in Figure 17.2. (You also could type my home address by clicking the down-arrow next to the word **Business** and choosing **Home**.) When you're done typing the address, click the **Address** button, and see how the Contacts application has interpreted the address. It's uncanny how well Outlook interprets most addresses, picking up many tough European addresses where the postal code precedes the city name.

FIGURE 17.2
Type my address, and Outlook interprets it correctly—as can be verified by clicking the Address button.

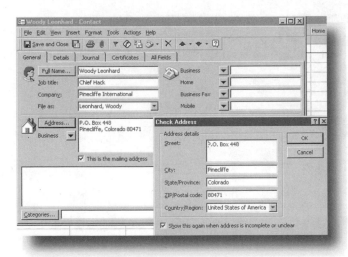

7. You can easily enter up to four different phone numbers for this contact. (Simply click the down-arrow next to Business, Home, Business Fax, or Mobile if you have other kinds of phone numbers to enter.)

HOW TO ENTER PHONE NUMBERS

It's important to enter phone numbers correctly. Otherwise, Outlook won't be able to dial the phone for you properly. Even if you never use Outlook to dial voice calls, you probably will use it for faxes, so listen up!

For each entry, the primary question is whether you have to dial a country code prior to dialing the phone number. If you don't need to dial a country code, type the area code followed by the local number, in other words, 3035550000, *even if it's a local call*. (Force your fingers to ignore spaces, hyphens, parentheses, and the like; it's much faster.) Outlook will interpret the number correctly.

SOURCE OF THE COUNTRY

There's an important detail to note in Figure 17.2. If you don't type a country name (or at least, if Outlook doesn't recognize a country name in the **Address** box), Outlook assumes you want to use the country name that was stored away when you first installed Windows. If you live in the USA and said so when you installed Windows, *every single* entry in your Contacts list will be marked **United States of America**, even though you can't see it, unless you explicitly type a country name. When we get to Chapter 29 you'll see how incredibly frustrating that little detail can be.

If you do need to dial a country code, type the number like this: +country code (area code) local number, for example, +61(02)12345678. Again, Outlook will interpret the number correctly.

If you follow these simple instructions, you'll be ready to dial even if your phone company goes to ten-digit dialing, or if your area code changes. I'll talk about the details at the end of this exercise.

EXTENSIONS AND NOTES

Outlook ignores any letters you type in a phone number box, so typing an entry like 800-OK-WINWORD gives the Contacts program heartburn. You'll be asked to retype the number.

But you can put any free-form notes you like at the end of the phone number itself. For example, 3035550000X1234 will be interpreted as **(303) 555-0000**, the number that Outlook should use when it's dialing the contact, followed by the characters **X1234**, which appear on the Contact form and on the Phone List, but aren't actually used by Outlook.

8. Outlook lets you store up to three email addresses for each contact. Type the one you want to use most frequently in the **E-mail** box, or click the **Address Book** 📖 icon to retrieve an email address that already exists in your Contacts list. For the second and third email addresses, click the down arrow next to the **E-mail** box (see Figure 17.3).

FIGURE 17.3
Add phone numbers, up to three email addresses, and a Web page URL.

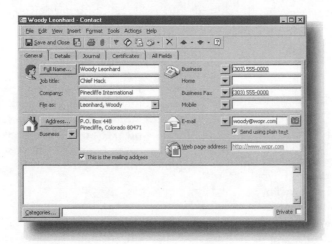

THE FLEETING THREE EMAIL ADDRESSES

It's nice that the Contacts application lets you save three email addresses. Really, it is. But Outlook's Email program—the one we tore to pieces in Chapter 16—doesn't yet handle multiple email addresses very well.

Say you have three email addresses stored in the contacts entry for, oh, **Woody Leonhard**. If you start a new email message—look back at Figure 16.4—and type Woody, you might expect Outlook to ask you which email address for **Woody** you'd like to use.

Unfortunately, it doesn't work that way. You have to wait for the Email program to find the name and then, after it's in the **To** box, right-click the name to be able to pick the correct email address.

You can't even get at the multiple addresses by clicking the **To** button, where you normally choose recipients' names. The Email program doesn't even list the alternate addresses. Amazing how a really neat feature in one part of Outlook can be negated by lousy design in another part, eh?

9. Type the contact's Web page address, if they're so endowed, and any comments you like in the big box at the bottom. You're just about ready to click **Save and Close** to add the contact to your Contacts list, but first there's a very important decision you have to make. It's called a **Category**, and it's so important that I'll cover the topic, all by itself, in the next section.

DIALING CONVENTIONS

How does Outlook know when to dial a 1 before an area code—or whether to dial an area code at all? When the phone company changes your area code, how do you tell Outlook? What happens when the phone company changes to ten-digit dialing (where you have to dial the area code, but not a 1, before dialing any number)? When you're on the road and try to send a fax from your portable to the home office, how do you tell Outlook to start dialing the 1 and area code?

WHAT IS TEN-DIGIT DIALING?

In some locations in the USA, the telephone company requires you to punch in an area code, even for a local call. For example, I live in the 303 area code. If I want to call my neighbors down the street, I have to dial 303-555-1212; the old 555-1212 doesn't work any more. Another neighbor might have the number 277-555-1212, and to call them I cannot precede the number with a 1. It gets confusing quickly. Outlook 98 handles these kinds of telephone company oddities with aplomb.

The answers to all these questions are buried so deep inside Outlook you could spend ages hunting them down. In brief, here's where they all sit...

Back out in the Contacts application, click **Actions**, **Call Contact**, **New Call**, and then click the **Dialing Properties** button. You should get the dialog box shown in Figure 17.4.

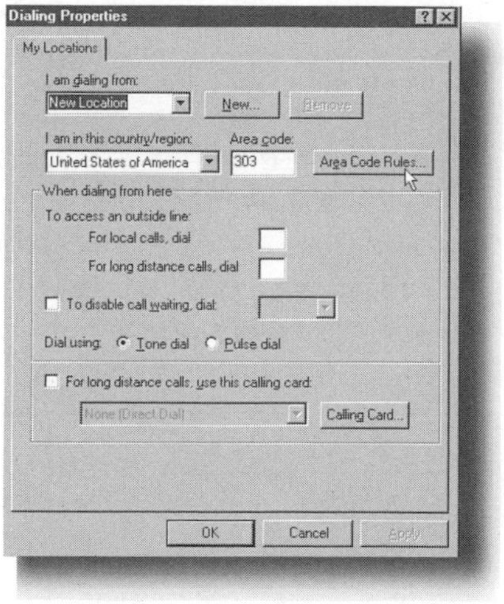

FIGURE 17.4
Dialing Properties, where you tell Outlook which area code you're dialing from and how to get an outside line.

You can set up collections of settings and assign them a name in the **I am dialing from** box. For specific help on each setting, click the **?** icon in the upper-right corner and click the appropriate box.

To set the rules for dialing a 1 before the number, or dialing the area code at all, click the **Area Code Rules** button on the Dialing Properties dialog box to get the dialog box shown in Figure 17.5. These entries should be pretty self-explanatory, after you find them!

FIGURE 17.5
Tell Outlook when to dial a 1 and when to dial the area code by using these settings.

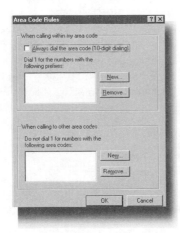

Categories

Plan from the get-go for your Contacts list to grow very large. Trust me. Before long you'll be putting the Cub Scout roster in here, along with your holiday card mailing list, the addresses of all your elected representatives, and the name of the local dog catcher.

Outlook's Contacts application includes a marvelous way to help you sort out the various groups of people, without forcing you to create (and manage) ten different Contact lists. It's called *Categories*. You have to take the initiative to get the categories set up and maintained, but when your Contacts list grows to 100 entries (or 1,000 or 10,000!), you'll thank the day you started out on the right foot.

*E*XERCISE

Set Categories for Contacts

1. You should have the Contacts entry form we were working on in the previous exercise open and ready for action.

2. Click the **Categories** button. Outlook presents you with a list of categories that it has predefined for your use (see Figure 17.6).

FIGURE 17.6
Outlook's pre-
defined cate-
gories.

3. In this case, I want to assign Woody Leonhard to three different categories: **Business** and **Hot Contacts**, as shown in Figure 17.6, but I also want to assign him to a category called **TCF** (for Tibetan Children's Fund, of course).

4. The **TCF** category doesn't exist. To create it you need to click **Master Category List**. Outlook responds by showing you the list of all available categories, as shown in Figure 17.7.

FIGURE 17.7
Outlook's list
of all avail-
able cate-
gories.

5. Simply type the name of the new category—in this case **TCF**—into the **New Category** box, and click **Add**.

WHEN AN ADD DOESN'T
You might assume that clicking **Add** at this point would **Add** the contact called **Woody Leonhard** to the **TCF** category. It doesn't. The **Add** here signifies only that you want to **Add** a new category to Outlook's overall list. Careful!

6. After you've added the new category called **TCF** you have to go back into the **Categories** dialog box, check the box marked **TCF**, and then click **OK** (see Figure 17.8).

FIGURE 17.8
The contact is added to the new category only after you check it in this dialog box.

7. Click **Save and Close**, and **Woody Leonhard** is added to your Contacts list.

Although it's possible to type categories down in the Contact form's Categories box, I strongly recommend against it. You'll find it much simpler—and more accurate—to click the **Categories** button and check off the appropriate categories as you add new contacts.

So now that you have your contacts assigned to categories, what can you do with them? Good question...

Invariably, whenever I want to look up a contact quickly, one of two situations applies: Either I know the person's (or business's) name; or I can't remember the name, but I certainly know the category. You're probably the same way. Outlook's Contact application gives you some powerful tools to make your look-up job easier.

Exercise

Two Views of Contacts

1. You have your Contacts list open, and it's in Phone List view, as shown in Figure 15.25. Good. This is an excellent general-purpose view, the one you should use when you look up a name.

2. You can make this view even better, though, by changing the font of select Contacts, based on their categories. Say I want to make all of my Business category contacts bold, so they'll stand out on in the Phone List view. (It's more dramatic, but harder to see in this book, if you actually color code them—say, make them all blue and bold.) Start by clicking **Organizer**, and then **Using Views**. You should see **Phone List** in the **Change your view** box. Click **Customize current view**, as shown in Figure 17.9.

FIGURE 17.9
Color code
the various
categories by
clicking
Customize
Current View.

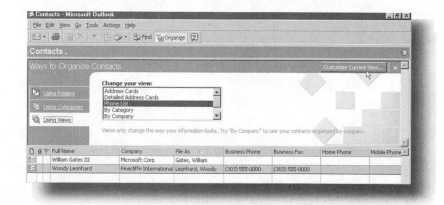

3. When Outlook asks you which View component you want to change, click the **Automatic Formatting** button. You'll see the **Automatic Formatting** dialog box, as shown in Figure 17.10.

FIGURE 17.10
Outlook has
names for its
various auto-
matic format-
ting rules.

4. We need to add a new automatic formatting rule, so click **Add**. Type a name for the new formatting rule; I chose Business. Then click the **Font** button, and apply whatever formatting you like. In this case, I chose 8 pt. bold Tahoma. You may well want to assign a color to these particular contacts. Click **OK** and your new automatic formatting rule will appear, checked, in the **Automatic Formatting** dialog box (see Figure 17.11).

FIGURE 17.11
The new automatic formatting rule called Business has been added.

5. Now you have to tell Outlook that you want to apply this formatting to any contact in the Business category. To do so, click **Condition**, and then in the **Filter** dialog box, click the **More Choices** tab. Click **Categories** and, in the **Available Categories** dialog box, check the box marked **Business**. Click **OK** and you'll have your new filtering rule set, as shown in Figure 17.12.

FIGURE 17.12
Set the filter to catch any contacts in the Business category.

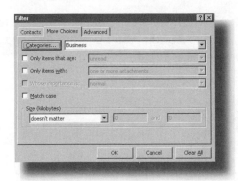

6. Click **OK** twice, and then click the **Organize** icon to get rid of the Organize box. Your custom Phone List view should now show all Business contacts in bold, as shown in Figure 17.13. Neat!

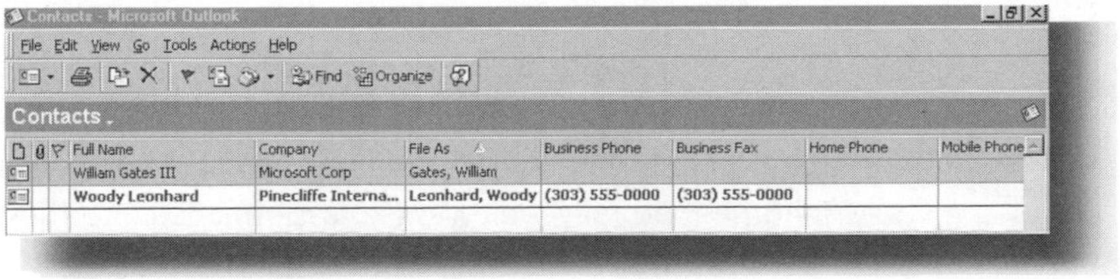

FIGURE 17.13
The new Phone List view puts Business contacts in bold.

7. But what if you know the category—or want to restrict your attention to a single category—and you don't want to deal with all the other contacts, whether they're blue and bold or green and italic? That's pretty easy, too.

WHAT IF THERE'S MORE THAN ONE CATEGORY?
If a particular contact belongs to more than one category and each category has a different font treatment, Outlook makes a game attempt to combine the fonts. For example, if you have Business contacts set up for bold, and Hot Contacts set up as red, a contact that's both Business and Hot shows up in bold red.

8. Back in Phone List view, click the **Organize** button, and then click **Using Views** (no, not **Using Categories**!). In the **Change your view** box, choose **By Category**. Suddenly, all of your contacts appear grouped by category, as shown in Figure 17.14. Click the **+** sign in front of the category that interests you, and only those contacts show up on the grid.

FIGURE 17.14 Outlook will also gladly group contacts by category.

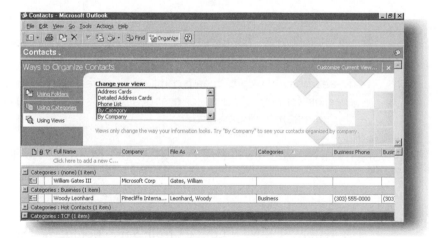

MULTIPLE CATEGORY PROBLEM SOLVED
When you're in By Category view, Outlook will put separate copies of each contact in every appropriate category. Because I put **Woody Leonhard** in **Business, Hot Contacts,** and **TCF** categories, the contact will actually show up in three different places in the By Category view, as you can probably surmise from Figure 17.14.

9. You can either flip back to Phone List view by clicking **Phone List** in the **Change your view** box, or stay in By Category view by clicking the **Organize** icon again.

HOW WOULD YOU KNOW THAT?
I have no idea why Microsoft put this under **Actions**. It isn't under **File**, **New**, where most Office users would expect it; nor is it an option under the **New Contact** icon. It isn't accessible when you're filling out a new contact form, either via a tunnel button or the Insert menu. In short, you just have to learn about this feature by osmosis.

BY CATEGORY VIEW SHOWS ALL
Note that you have all the usual tools at your disposal while in By Category view: click **Company**, for example, and the displayed contacts are sorted by company.

Copying

For such a clearly brilliant program, Outlook 98 can be awfully dumb at times.

Two important capabilities are nowhere to be seen in the Contacts application:

● It's impossible to put a contact's name and address on the Clipboard so you can use it in some other program.

● There's no easy way to type a company's address once and have it readily available for new contacts (or change it once and have the change ripple throughout my contacts list).

I wish I had a nickel for every time I've typed "One Microsoft Way/Redmond, WA 98052."

That said, Outlook 98 does have one rather anemic method for minimizing the amount of typing involved in setting up a new contact. If you select a contact, and then click **Actions**, and **New Contact from Same Company**, Outlook fills in the company name, address, and business phone numbers from the selected contact, then presents the new Contact form for you to complete.

You can also right-click a Contact and choose **New Contact from Same Company**.

From my point of view, anyway, that's the bare minimum of what you need to understand about Contacts. Keep your categories straight and Outlook's Contacts application will serve you well. Ignore them and you'll end up with a jumbled mess.

Calendar

Outlook 98's Calendar application rates right up there with the best calendar/ scheduling packages available on the market. In fact, for most people, much of Calendar rates as wishful thinking and overkill. I'll show you what I mean.

The Outlook Calendar tracks three kinds of activities: Events, Appointments, and Meetings. There's a very easy way to tell which is which:

- An Event is an all-day or multiple-day activity, such as a birthday, holiday, or convention. There's no beginning or ending time.

- An Appointment, on the other hand, has a starting and (at least projected) ending time. Appointments are, well, appointments.

- Meetings are Appointments where you contact the participants *electronically* to ascertain whether they can attend.

Let's deal with Meetings first.

Meetings

As you can probably guess, it takes a lot of discipline to get good-sized Meetings— in the Outlook sense of the term—off the ground. Just for starters, everybody attending the meeting has to be running software compatible with Outlook 98. Those needed for a Meeting must maintain accurate calendars online so the Meeting planner software can check to see whether the participant has the time slot free. All the attendees have to be in your Contacts list, and they all must have email IDs. Then everybody has to answer the query email messages in a timely manner to say whether they'll be going to the meeting. If one key person finks out, another round of email is necessary to change times (or locations). And on and on.

Personally, I don't know of anybody who's ever kept their electronic appointment calendar updated, accurately, more than a few minutes in advance. (Present company included.) I figure Meetings are more hassle than they're worth. As anyone who's put together a Meeting—in the Outlook sense of the term—will tell you, it almost never works the way it's supposed to; and if there are more than three or four participants, you can kiss the whole electronic effort good-bye from the start.

Anyway, I'm not going to talk about Meetings in this book. If you work with people disciplined enough to maintain their electronic calendars, conscientious enough to respond to email rapidly, and organized to the point that they can make Meetings work, I salute you. I also direct you to your corporate Help Desk for assistance in setting up Meetings with Outlook.

Events

The easiest way to learn about Events is to see how one looks inside the Calendar. Let's set up a week-long Event and take a gander.

XERCISE

A Convention

1. Click the **Calendar** 📆 icon in the Outlook Bar to bring up Outlook 98's Calendar application.

2. This particular Event, Microsoft's TechEd conference (a big annual conference that many Office fans try to attend), runs five days from June 1 through June 5. So start by selecting all five days in the calendar in the upper-right corner, as shown in Figure 17.15.

FIGURE 17.15
To set an Event, start by selecting the day it encompasses.

3. As you select the days, you'll notice that your calendar automatically changes from a one-day view to a five-day view. That's to give you a visual reminder that you've selected five days.

4. Click the **New Appointment** 📅 icon on the toolbar. You'll get the Calendar's **New Appointment** form (see Figure 17.16). Type the Subject and Location, check the box marked **All day event**, and set the **Start time** (which is just a date) and the **End time**. Uncheck the **Reminder** box (you

don't want a reminder to pop up on the screen 15 minutes before midnight on Sunday night!). Add a note in the big box at the bottom and click **Save and Close**.

FIGURE 17.16
The
Calendar's
New
Appointment
form, set to
an all-day
(actually, all-
week) Event.

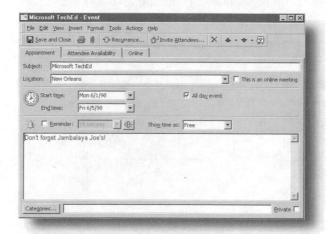

5. When you get back to the Calendar (see Figure 17.17), note how Outlook puts the name and location of the Event up at the top of the five-day calendar. That keeps it out of the way so you still have room add Appointments, even during the Event.

FIGURE 17.17
The Event
appears at
the top of
the calendar.

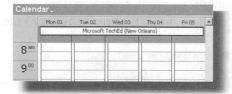

Appointments

Outlook 98's Calendar makes it very easy to add appointments during the day. Let's add an appointment at 10:00 Monday morning, during TechEd.

*E*XERCISE

Making—and Breaking—an Appointment

1. Start with the five-day view of TechEd that you created in the preceding Exercise.

2. Put your cursor in the 10:00 box on Monday morning, and double-click. Outlook responds with the New Appointment form, much as you would expect (see Figure 17.18). Outlook initially assumes you want to set up a 30-minute-long appointment, starting at 10:00.

FIGURE 17.18
Set up a new appointment.

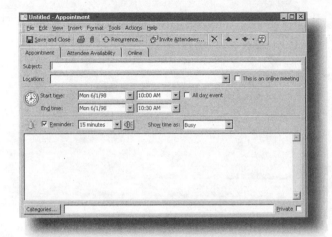

3. Fill in the **Subject**, **Location**, and adjust the **End Time** to something a bit more reasonable, as shown in Figure 17.19. Keep the **Reminder** box checked—this time you want a warning to pop up on the screen and a little sound to go off 15 minutes before the meeting. Finally, type any notes you need in the big box and the bottom and click **Save and Close**.

FIGURE 17.19
Filling out the details on a one-hour appointment.

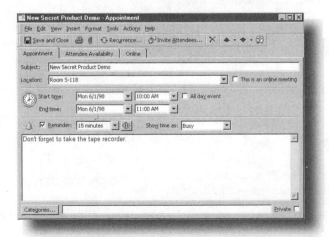

4. Back you go to the five-day calendar. Outlook shows a one-hour appointment starting at 10:00 for New Secret Product. The bell in front of the appointment title reminds you that a reminder alarm will go off before the meeting.

5. Sure enough. It's 9:45 on Monday morning, and you overslept. Your portable (which you left on, plugged into the wall) is wailing like Bo-Peep's sheep, and there's no way you can make the 10:00 appointment. You get on the horn and reschedule for 11:00. (Try doing *that* with an Outlook-style Meeting!) How to change the appointment in Outlook? No sweat. Hover your cursor over the 10:00 appointment. It'll turn into a four-headed arrow. Click and drag the appointment down to 11:00, as shown in Figure 17.20.

FIGURE 17.20
Rescheduling an appointment is as simple as a click and drag.

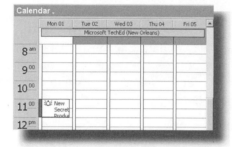

6. Outlook reschedules everything—including the 15-minute warning reminder beep. Go back to sleep. You've got plenty of time.

Recurring Activities

Some events happen on the same day every year: birthdays, anniversaries, and the like. Many appointments also recur: the traditional weekly staff meeting or monthly sales meeting. As long as the activities recur daily, weekly, monthly, or annually, chances are pretty good Outlook 98 can set up your calendar automatically. (Nope, it isn't smart enough to figure out "the third Thursday of every month.")

To set up a recurring appointment or event, just bring up the Appointment form (as shown in Figure 17.19), and click the **Recurrence** icon. Outlook presents you with the Appointment Recurrence dialog box, shown in Figure 17.21.

The choices here are pretty self-explanatory. Note that if you want to get rid of a recurring appointment, you merely click it, click the **Recurrence** icon, and then press the **Remove Recurrence** button at the bottom of this dialog box.

FIGURE 17.21
Set recurring appointments and events here.

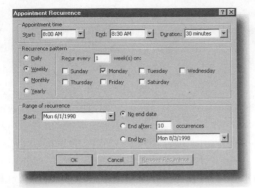

Printing Calendars

I won't say that Outlook's capability to print calendars will win any awards, but I'm frequently surprised by how few Outlook users realize the option exists. In fact, the Calendar application contains a host of options for printing daily, weekly, and monthly calendars, both on a single page, and tri-folded.

The printed calendars are generally quite good, and they can be customized very easily.

To see the options available, just click **File**, and then **Print**. Outlook's calendar Print dialog box (see Figure 17.22) is considerably more complex than those in other Office 97 applications, but it's ideally suited to the job.

SQUISHED PRINTING

Many people complain when they see that Outlook doesn't wrap lines when printing. Instead, it chops long appointment descriptions off in midsentence. You can't change the wrapping behavior, but you can make the font smaller. To do so, click **File**, **Print**, click **Define Styles**, choose **Calendar Details Style**, and click **Edit**. From that point, you can make the font as small as you please.

The customizing options you'll most likely want sit under the **Page Setup** button. Click it and have fun!

Tasks: It's What to Do

Outlook's To-Do List (Microsoft calls them *Tasks*) feature offers much more than first meets the eye. If you get in the habit of keeping your Tasks inside Outlook (instead of, oh, jotting them down on the back of envelopes, as I usually do), Outlook can help you with a number of memory-joggers.

FIGURE 17.22
Outlook prints calendars 10 ways from Tuesday.

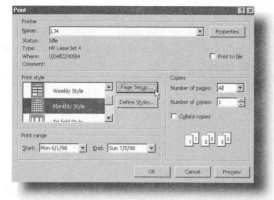

_E_XERCISE

Set a Task

1. Go into Outlook's Tasks application by clicking the **Tasks** 🗒 icon on the Outlook Bar.

2. Underneath the **Subject** heading, click once on the grayed-out text that says **Click here to add a new Task**. Type a description of the Task, press the Tab key, and type a due date (see Figure 17.23).

WHAT'S IN A DATE?
Note how, in Figure 17.23, I typed next Tuesday for a due date. In general, any time you're asked to type a date, you have a great deal of flexibility in what Outlook 98 will recognize as legitimate. Try playing with it a bit and you'll come away impressed.

FIGURE 17.23
Creating a new Task from the Tasks application.

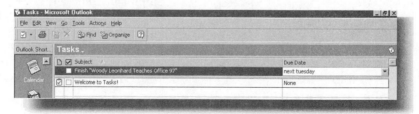

3. That sequence of actions creates a simple Task; if you do nothing more, Outlook shows you a reminder (and plays a little song) at 8:00 on the morning the Task becomes due. If the Task falls past due, it will start appearing in red on all the Task screens.

4. It probably won't surprise you to know that Outlook has quite a few additional options for Tasks. To see the first level of embellishment, double-click the Task you just created. The Task application shows you a Task form, as shown in Figure 17.24. (Note how "next Tuesday" has been translated into a more conventional date.)

FIGURE 17.24
The Task form, where you can gussy up Tasks.

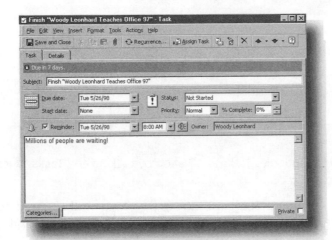

5. Most of the entries on the Task form are self-explanatory, but you should take note of a few options. The Status box is limited to five choices (Not started, In progress, Completed, Waiting on someone else, and Deferred). **Priority** can be set only to High, Normal, or Low.

INFORMATION AT SOME FINGERTIPS
Surprisingly, different Task information shows up in different locations. As you've seen, the due date appears in the Task list and in Outlook Today, but not on the TaskPad. (Not surprising, as the TaskPad doesn't have a whole lot of spare room.)

What *is* rather amazing: Changing a Task's Priority doesn't change the Task's icon. Thus, you won't be able to distinguish high priority Tasks when looking at them in the Tasks list, or the Calendar's TaskPad. High priority Tasks do get an exclamation point, though, when they show up on the Outlook Today page.

Go figure.

6. The **Details** tab in Figure 17.24 may be helpful. It contains built-in fields where you can list how many hours you worked on the Task, Contacts and Companies involved, mileage, and billing notes. Don't get too excited, though: there's no easy way to group and total this information or export it to, say, Excel for billing or other analysis.

7. The **Assign Task** icon on the toolbar in Figure 17.24 is another option worth exploring, particularly if you commonly assign tasks to other people via email. It automatically generates email to inform the stuckee, er, assignee, and there are additional hooks to work with status reports, completion tracking, and the like. Hardly a full-blown Project Management package, but if your needs aren't particularly demanding, it can be handy— and it works much better than the Outlook Meetings feature. For more information, look in Chapter 5 of *Outlook Annoyances*.

8. Your new task appears not only in the Tasks list, but in the Calendar's TaskPad. Click the **Calendar** icon in the Outlook Bar, and you'll see the task in the lower-right corner (see Figure 17.25).

FIGURE 17.25
The new task appears in the TaskPad corner of the Calendar.

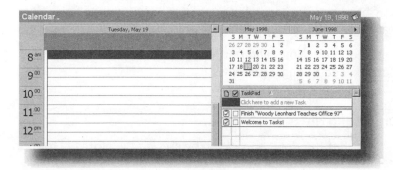

9. Finally, the new task also appears on the Outlook Today page (see Figure 17.26), along with the due date, which doesn't show up in the Calendar's TaskPad. From Outlook Today, you can click the task, and the full **Task** form appears to show all the task's details.

FIGURE 17.26
More information about the Task also appears in Outlook Today.

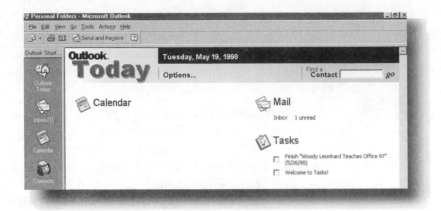

Notes

The great unsung hero of Outlook's back pages, you might think of Notes as the electronic equivalent of little yellow sticky-notes. But if you do, you'll be selling this amazing flat-file database program short. All you have to do is kind of stand on your head and squint real hard, and you'll see how the lowly Notes application can really help you organize all the flotsam and jetsam that crosses your desk every day.

Trust me. Learn Notes and start using it, even if you don't use any other part of Outlook. Let me show you how.

*E*XERCISE

Organizing Notes

1. Start the Notes application by clicking the **Notes** icon on the Outlook Bar.

2. Microsoft has a pre-fab Note waiting for you, which starts out "Notes are the electronic...". You can click that Note and drag it onto the Windows desktop, as shown in Figure 17.27, to see how the yellow sticky-notes function works. That's cool, I guess, but it doesn't show you what Notes can do.

3. Click the **New Note** icon to create your own new Note. In Figure 17.28 I've created a couple of new Notes, both of which contain quotes from famous (or at least infamous) sources. I collect quotes to use in my writing. So I started both of these Notes with the word Quote to show that they're both quotes.

FIGURE 17.27
Click the
preconstructed
Note and drag
it onto the
Windows
desktop, just
to see that it
can be done.

FIGURE 17.28
Creating a
couple of
new Notes,
both Quotes.

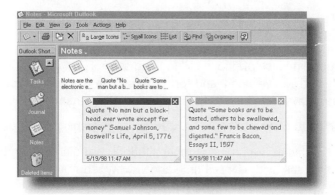

4. Why did I start these Notes with the word Quote? Figure 17.29 should give
you a hint. When you click the **List** button, the Notes application sorts all
the Notes alphabetically. Because I had the foresight to begin each quote-
related Note with the word Quote, they all sort together—making them
easy to identify and track.

FIGURE 17.29
The List view sorts Notes in alphabetical order.

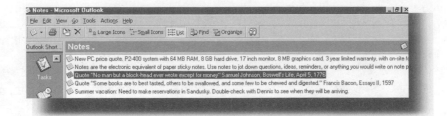

5. If you want to get a little fancier and don't mind spending the time, you can even color code the Notes (five different colors are available by right-clicking the Note and choosing **Color**), or assign them to Categories, just as we did with Contacts. If you use these more advanced organizing techniques, click the **Organize** button to get customized views of your Notes sorted every which way.

6. You also have Outlook's full **Find** capability available, up on the toolbar. That means you can search for any text, in any Note, with just a click. Very powerful.

Journaling Phone Calls

Although Outlook 98 has many screaming lapses, none scream more energetically than its astounding lack of phone call logging support. Many people depend on phone calls for their livelihood, and for those people the poor support of this one feature alone may force them to use a package other than Outlook.

When it comes to phone calls, Outlook 98 has two feeble capabilities:

● If a Contact has a phone number, Outlook will dial the number for you and log that call, with elapsed time and your typed notes.

● If you receive a call from someone on your Contacts list, you can bring up a form that lets you time the conversation and keep notes about it.

CAN THE COMPUTER DIAL MY PHONE?
To use a PC to dial outbound calls, you need to have a suitably capable modem, plus a microphone or telephone handset that works with the modem to let you talk on the phone, after the number has been dialed by the computer.

XERCISE _____

Log an Outbound Call

1. Start in the Contacts application; click the **Contacts** [icon] icon in the Outlook Bar.

2. Choose the Contact you want to call. Right-click the name, and click **Autodialer**. Outlook responds with the New Call dialog box, as shown in Figure 17.30.

FIGURE 17.30
Have the computer dial the phone with this dialog box.

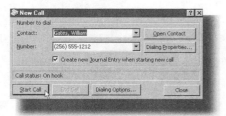

3. Make sure the Create new Journal Entry when starting new call box is checked, and then click Start Call.

MODEM SETUP PROBLEMS
If you haven't set up your modem properly, Outlook will complain. This is pretty common, so don't be too worried about it, but you're pretty much at the mercy of your PC (or modem) manufacturer. Contact them and tell them you're trying to use Outlook 98 to dial an outbound voice call.

4. If all works as it should, Outlook will show a Call Status dialog box that lets you switch over to the microphone or handset when somebody answers.

5. When you're done with the call, click the **Save and Close** button. The call will appear in the Journal—and we'll talk about that in the next exercise.

To reliably log inbound calls, you need to be right next to your PC, and should probably have your Contacts list (in Phone List view!) already showing. Even then it takes some fancy footwork to get the logging mechanism working.

*E*XERCISE

Log an Inbound Call

1. Start in Outlook's Contacts application.

2. Double-click the Contact who's calling you. You'll get the standard **Contact** form, as shown in Figure 17.3, way back at the beginning of this chapter.

3. Click the **Journal** tab in the **Contact** form. Then, at the bottom, click the **New Journal Entry** button. You'll get the **Journal Entry** form, as shown in Figure 17.31.

FIGURE 17.31
Creating a Journal entry for an incoming phone call.

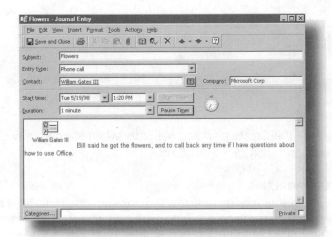

4. Quickly, before you do anything else, click the **Start Timer** button. Then, at your leisure, as the conversation unfolds, fill in the **Subject** box, and type whatever notes you may desire in the big box on the bottom.

5. When your conversation ends, click **Save and Close**. That stops the timer and saves the new Journal entry. You'll be propelled back to the Contact form for this particular Contact, but now you can also see the Journal entry for this phone call (see Figure 17.32).

6. In general, you can find all the Journal entries for all your phone calls in Outlook's Journal application (see Figure 17.33). Simply click the **Journal** icon on the Outlook Bar, and your phone log can be viewed in many different ways by using the Organize button.

That's the only use I've found for the Journal.

FIGURE 17.32
The Contact form, showing this most recent phone call.

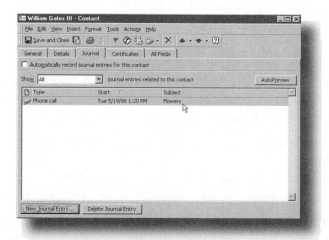

FIGURE 17.33
Inbound and outbound phone logs can be found in the Journal.

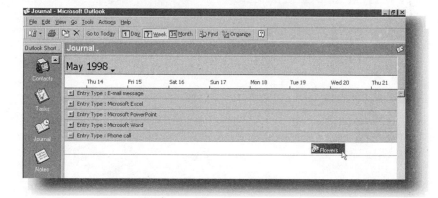

Add-ins

I wanted to conclude this discussion of Outlook 98 with some indication of how it can be made better. Just as the ascendancy of Word generated a host of Word add-ons to make the operation of Word faster, easier, and more reliable, so, too, will the inevitable success of Outlook bring more and better add-ons, spelling relief to all of us long-suffering users.

After all, there's a reason why Personal Information Managers are called *Personal*. Everybody does things a little differently. That's what makes life interesting, eh?

At this point, I know of two Outlook 98 add-ons that may be worth your perusal.

The first one, called Integrated File Management, which adds an Advanced Find capability to search for files from inside Outlook, comes from Microsoft. While its highfalutin' name might overstate the capabilities a bit, the price is right—it's free. You can read about it and download it from `support.microsoft.com/support/kb/articles/q181/8/21.asp`.

The second package is a commercial add-on that holds great promise, I think. It's called Lightning, and it adds all sorts of features to Outlook 98: quick Contact look-up, easier entry for Tasks ("Call Jim next Thursday at 8:00"), and far simpler access to Contacts, Categories, and much more.

If you find yourself spending a lot of time in Outlook, it's definitely worth a look. There's a description and download instructions for a free trial version at `www.catalystinnovations.com`.

Excel 97

18   Excel Preliminaries 399

19   Working with Workbooks 413

20   Building Spreadsheets 427

21   Getting Around 467

22   Making Spreadsheets Look Good 479

23   Excel-lent Charts 507

24   Advanced Features 517

Excel
Preliminaries

E'VE COME A LONG WAY FROM THE days of green eyeshades, columnar pads, pencil sharpeners, and mechanical pull-down-the-handle calculators. With Excel 97 you can make more calculation errors in a second than an experienced accountant used to be able to make in weeks.

That's why I'm going to approach Excel differently here than in the other introductory books, videos, online help systems, and the like. They want you to think of Excel as a wonderfully capable upgrade of the old columnar pad, with a fast and savvy built-in calculator. I want you to think of Excel as a loaded shotgun aimed directly at your foot, with the safety off.

If you're accustomed to looking at computer-generated spreadsheets and believing the numbers are correct just because "they were done on the computer; they have to be right," think of the following chapters as a much-needed dose of reality. Mathematical errors in Excel spreadsheets are almost as common as spelling errors in Word documents. It isn't enough that Excel (and Word for that matter) gives you the tools to avoid most of the problems. You have to learn how to use the tools and then apply what you've learned religiously. Otherwise, one twitch and the Excel shotgun goes *kaboom!*

Welcome to Excel Boot Camp, recruit.

Heh heh heh.

Terminology

What is the difference between a worksheet and a workbook? Is a spreadsheet the data I see on the screen, the stuff that prints on a page, or the computer program responsible for both? Is a printed spreadsheet the same as a worksheet?

Just accept it right from the get-go. Excel terminology sucks. In fact, terminology throughout the spreadsheet industry (there's that s word again!) runs all over the map. In Excel 97 if you click **File**, then **New**, you'll see a tab marked **Spreadsheet Solutions**. Yet if you click **File**, then **Print**, you'll be

GOSPEL ACCORDING TO WOODY
Throughout this book I'll use the term *spreadsheet* (or occasionally *sheet*) to refer to a single grid with rows and columns and cells.

One or more spreadsheets make a *workbook*. In fact, a workbook is just an .xls file, and I will use that term occasionally as well.

given the option to print the **Active sheet**. If you look in the Help index, you'll find some reference to *sheets*, a lot of reference to *worksheets*, but nothing at all about *spreadsheets*. When you create a new .xls file, Excel calls it Book1. Yet if you look in the Help index, you'll find lots about *workbooks*, but the only entries about *books* refer to bound paper books, like the one you're holding in your hand. And on and on.

The beast that I call a *spreadsheet* has an official name in Microsoft-speak. It's called a *worksheet*, but Microsoft uses the name so cavalierly, and you'll hear worksheet used so infrequently, that I'm going to use the common, vulgar term.

OH REALLY?
OK. Yeah, I *do* know why Microsoft doesn't activate AutoSave automatically. Advanced Excel users tend to play around with their spreadsheets quite a bit, and they use Save as a safety net. Instead of relying on Undo to back out of a series of mistakes, Excel users frequently Save when they've reached a steady point in a spreadsheet's development, then go back and open the saved file if something major goes awry. (It's important to note that Excel doesn't have anywhere near the Undo capabilities that are embodied in Word, and that all Undo information disappears whenever a workbook is saved; I'll talk about that more in the next chapter.)

I don't like that approach for two reasons. First, running without AutoSave leaves you incredibly vulnerable to a power outage or other system screw-up: if you've been playing with a spreadsheet for a couple of hours without saving and the power goes bye-bye, your only option may be cyanide.

Second, Excel should be set up to help novices, right out of the box. That includes AutoSave. More advanced users should be able to figure out how to cycle through several backups using Save As. Novices' spreadsheets shouldn't be sacrificed for the convenience of advanced users, who can generally fend for themselves.

Crucial Changes

Excel 97's settings, straight out of the box, are certainly more than adequate if you don't intend to use it very much. On the other hand, if you really want to take advantage of what the product has to offer, I'd strongly recommend you make these simple changes.

AutoSave

For the life of me, I have no idea why Excel 97 doesn't install AutoSave automatically.

The very first thing you should do before you start relying on Excel 97 is to install and activate the AutoSave feature. Just as with Word 97, AutoSave automatically saves a copy of your open workbooks, at intervals you can set. Unlike Word 97, though, AutoSave is considered an add-in and you have to go hunting for it. Bah!

Although Microsoft's implementation of AutoSave in Excel leaves much to be desired—for example, you have to specify a filename for any previously unsaved workbook, which is ludicrous—running with AutoSave still beats the devil out of working without a net. Get AutoSave going now.

XERCISE

Enable AutoSave

1. Start Excel. (Click Start, Programs, Microsoft Excel.)

2. Click Tools, then Add-Ins. You should see the Add-Ins dialog box, as shown in Figure 18.1.

FIGURE 18.1
The Add-Ins
dialog box,
where you
can find
AutoSave.

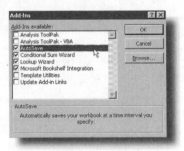

WHAT IF IT ISN'T THERE?

If you did something very weird when you installed Office 97, it's possible that you don't have AutoSave listed in the Add-Ins dialog box. If that's the case, dig out your Office 97, and click **Start**, **Settings**, **Control Panel**. Double-click **Add/Remove Programs**, click **Microsoft Office 97**, then click **Add/Remove**. When you get the Microsoft Office 97 Setup screen, click **Add/Remove**. At the Microsoft Office 97 Maintenance dialog box, click once on **Excel**, then click **Change Options**. Choose **Add-Ins** from the list, then click **Change Options** again. Finally, check the box marked **AutoSave**, then **OK**, and continue with the Add Programs options.

3. Check the box marked **AutoSave**, then click **OK**. That activates the AutoSave Add-In.

4. To set AutoSave options, click **Tools**, then **AutoSave**. You'll see the AutoSave dialog box, as shown in Figure 18.2.

FIGURE 18.2
AutoSave settings become available under the Tools menu.

5. Personally, I feel comfortable having the active workbook saved every ten minutes, but your impressions may differ. (Just don't set it too low, if you're going to be using large workbooks—the delay from too many AutoSaves will drive you nuts.) I also don't want to be asked if I want to save every time AutoSave kicks in, so I unchecked that box.

If you haven't yet given a new Excel workbook a filename when AutoSave kicks in, you'll have to type a name and put up with AutoSave's nonsense. And I can hardly believe that Excel deletes all Undo information whenever a workbook is saved. Those are two of the worst design glitches in Office 97 today, in my opinion, and the people who are responsible for them should be banished to the seventh level of Excel Hell.

Even given AutoSave's myriad problems, using it is still better than losing all your data if Excel crashes or locks up. And it does. Oh, yes, it does.

Stay Put After Enter

When you type in Word, the program just puts whatever you type up on the screen. Simple. But when you move to Excel, you have to be able to tell Excel when you're done typing things into a cell. Although there are lots of ways to do that, most people simply press the Enter key.

Unfortunately, Excel 97 does strange things when you press Enter. Generally it moves the cursor down to the next cell, the one directly below the one you've been typing in. (There are circumstances where pressing Enter can trigger even more bizarre behavior.) Personally, I rarely want to go down to the next cell when I press Enter. Mostly I just want Excel to acknowledge the fact that I've typed a number or a formula, and show the result in the spreadsheet. Sometimes I want to move on to the next cell—right, left, up, or down, but when that happens I'm perfectly content to use the arrow keys on my keyboard to specify precisely where I want to go.

If you want Excel to simply stay put after you type something into a cell and press Enter, it's easy to change.

Click **Tools**, **Options**, and click the **Edit** tab. Remove the check mark in front of the **Move selection after Enter** box, as shown in Figure 18.3.

FIGURE 18.3
Make Excel behave normally when you enter data into a cell and press Enter.

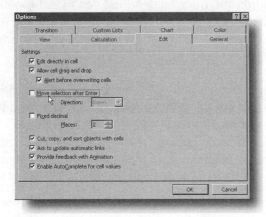

Click **OK** and Excel drops one of its most irritating predispositions.

Max Out the Most Recently Used List

Excel, like Word, keeps a list of most recently used files at the bottom of the **File** menu. If you have a very tiny screen and run Excel at 640 x 480 resolution, you might want to succumb to Excel's anemic default setting, showing only the four most recently used files on the list. Most of us, though, would like to see all that Excel can offer. In this case, the maximum number Excel will show is nine files.

Click **Tools**, **Options**, and click the **General** tab. Make sure the **Macro virus protection** box is checked, then run the **Recently used file list** spinner up to **9** (see Figure 18.4).

FIGURE 18.4
Check the Macro virus protection setting and run the MRU list up to 9 entries.

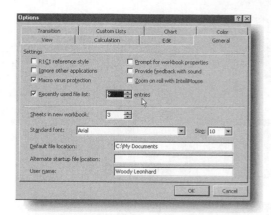

Click **OK** and Excel will start showing nine files on the **File** menu.

Add Auditing Toolbar

Get ready for the most controversial recommendation you'll find in this book.

Excel 97 ships with one of the most sophisticated set of error-tracking tools available in any computer program, anywhere. For some reason, though, most people don't know they exist, and only a tiny fraction of all Excel-ulites ever use them.

I say "for some reason" as if I didn't know why the tools are never used. Fact is, I *do* know why. First, they're buried in a weird Excel backwater and if you didn't already know they existed, you'd never find them. (Try bringing up Office Bob and typing, oh, `audit` or `check formulas`.) Second, none of the introductory books even *mention* them, much less show you how to use them. Third, even if you did know they existed, there's only one way (far as I know, anyway) to get to them—through an obscure toolbar that isn't referenced anyplace in the menus, and only rarely in Help.

Here's how you get at Excel's auditing tools, the gizmos that will catch a very large percentage of all your mistakes—before your boss does.

Click **Tools**, **Customize**, and click the **Toolbars** tab. Check the box marked **Auditing**. It's way down on the list, but that's the one you need. Click **Close** and the Auditing toolbar appears. Personally, I click the double vertical lines at the front of the Auditing toolbar and drag it down to the bottom of the screen, as shown in Figure 18.5.

I'll show you how to use the Auditing toolbar in the beginning of Chapter 20, "Building Spreadsheeets." Think of it as an integral part of your Excel arsenal. Some day it'll save your tail.

FIGURE 18.5
Bring the
Auditing
toolbar onto
the screen
and position
it someplace
handy.

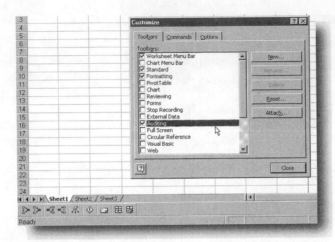

The Screen

Let's take a look around the Excel screen. You don't need to get too hung up on any of this terminology, but you might want to mark this page and refer back to Figure 18.6 if you get bogged down at some future point.

FIGURE 18.6
The Excel 97
screen.

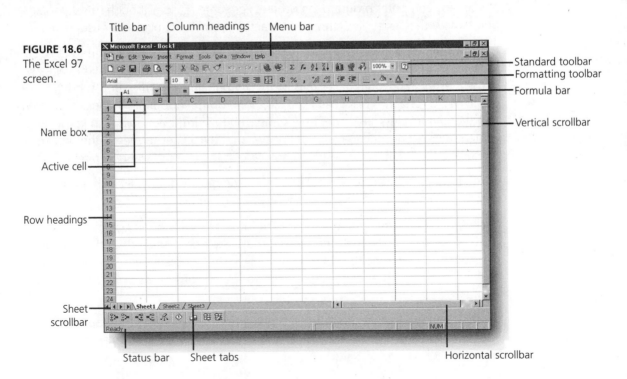

Title Bar

☞ *The Excel 97 title bar is virtually identical to Word 97's. I talked about the Word 97 title bar on page 97.*

Menu Bar

Right below the title bar, Excel has a menu bar. The top-level menu items look remarkably similar to those in Word. We'll have a chance to use them all in the next few chapters.

Toolbars

Excel 97 ships with two toolbars showing: the top one is called the Standard toolbar and the second one is known as the Formatting toolbar. Again, similarities with Word pop up all over the place.

I also had you add the Auditing toolbar, in the preceding Exercise. It's probably sitting at the bottom of your screen.

Formula Bar

The Excel 97 Formula bar, on the other hand, is quite unique to Excel. On the left side you'll see the Name box, which lets you navigate to different places in your spreadsheets. On the right side Excel has room for you to type things into cells and edit the stuff that already exists in cells.

The Spreadsheet

The major part of the Excel 97 screen is devoted to the spreadsheet, of course.

As you've probably guessed already, each of those little rectangles you see is a *cell*. The cell is the atomic particle of Excel spreadsheets, the basic building block that will ultimately hold all the numbers and formulas.

Every Excel 97 spreadsheet is limited to 16,777,216 cells, arranged in 256 columns (which run from A to IV), and 65,536 rows (numbered 1 to 65536). That's a *lot* of cells.

The active cell—the one that has contents currently displayed in the Formula bar—gets outlined with a heavy black line. In Figure 18.6, cell A1 is the active cell.

The horizontal and vertical scrollbars let you navigate through the spreadsheet, much as you would expect. Click the up or down arrows, and the spreadsheet moves up or down. Grab the *thumb* to slide around long distances. Click in the blank area on the scroll bar to move up, down, left, or right a page or so at a time.

CELL NAMES

If you're new to spreadsheets, you need to get used to the naming convention. It's a lot like the naming system you'll find in chess, or on most maps—or if you've ever played Battleship.

Each cell in a spreadsheet has a name, called an *address*. The cell in the upper-left corner is called A1. (You can tell because it's in the A column, and in the row marked 1.) The cell below it is called A2. The cell to the right of A1 is called B1. Then, working left to right, you'll see C1, D1, E1, and so on. Get the picture?

When Excel runs out of letters, it doubles-up. So, for example, the cell to the right of Z1 gets the moniker AA1, then AB1, AC1, and so on. To the right of AZ1 sits BA1, then BB1, then BC1.

If you're ever in doubt, look at the Column headings and Row headings to get your bearings.

Sheet Tabs and Scrollbar

Unless you tell Excel to do something differently, every time you create a new workbook you get three spreadsheets in that workbook. When you start Excel 97, it creates a new workbook called Book1. And, lo and behold, Book1 contains three spreadsheets.

Near the bottom of Figure 18.6, you'll see three tabs, marked Sheet1, Sheet2, and Sheet3. If you click each of those tabs in turn, you'll jump from the first spreadsheet (called Sheet1) to the second and then the third.

The Sheet scrollbars to the left of the Sheet tabs just give you a way to cycle through the tabs. Imagine a workbook with 20 sheets. Only a few Sheet tabs can show at once, so the Sheet scrollbars let you move left-to-right among the 20 Sheet tabs.

Status Bar

Down at the very bottom of Figure 18.6 you'll find a status bar not unlike the one in Word 97. It's here that you'll see visual cues about what Excel is up to. There's also a very neat feature called AutoCalculate that uses the status bar.

☞ *We'll play with AutoCalculate on page 437.*

Zoom

More than any other Office 97 application, working effectively with Excel 97 entails a lot of moving back and forth. As your spreadsheets get larger and larger, navigation gets tougher. Many times life would be much easier if you could see your entire spreadsheet—or at least a big chunk of it—at one time.

That's why Excel has a **Zoom** `100% ▾` icon on the Standard toolbar. Click the icon and see what your screen looks like at, oh, 50%, as I have in Figure 18.7.

FIGURE 18.7
The Excel screen at 50% zoom factor.

Zoom from the Standard toolbar is OK. If you can't live with the built-in percentages shown in Figure 18.7, you can click once on the icon and type whatever zoom percentage you like. But Zoom really comes into its own with the Microsoft IntelliMouse, or competing roller mice—the ones that have a roller in between the two buttons. (Implementations vary. I've seen roller mice with the roller under the thumb position, and several other locations as well.)

Zoom is so important in getting around a spreadsheet that you may well want to splurge and get an IntelliMouse (or finally figure out how to use the one you already have).

IntelliMouse

☞ *I talked about using the IntelliMouse with Word 97 on page 140.*

The roller mouse received a lukewarm endorsement in Chapter 9, "Getting Around," at least in my opinion, it's of limited value if your major Office preoccupation extends no further than word processing. If you do a bit of spreadsheet work—particularly with fairly large spreadsheets—the nature of the problem changes, and the IntelliMouse becomes a reasonably cost-effective addition to your bag of tricks.

Unless there's a roller mouse installed on your PC, you'll have to go out and buy one, then install it with the software using the manufacturer's recommendations.

Inside Excel 97, the IntelliMouse gives you three significant capabilities:

WHICH ROLLER MOUSE IS BEST?
Every hand is different, and for that reason I strongly recommend that you try a mouse before paying for it. If you can, use the mouse in some sort of real world environment, where you're sitting down in front of a PC and working with applications you use every day.

My experience with Microsoft's IntelliMouse has been uniformly excellent: it's a high-quality beast that keeps rolling and rolling and... well, you get the idea. Even my ten-year-old son, who has a habit of destroying mice while playing intense simulation games, has a hard time going through an IntelliMouse.

MORE MOUSING
Microsoft has quite a few IntelliMouse capabilities buried, of all places, inside its (unsupported) TweakUI Windows application. TweakUI lets you modify all sorts of strange Windows settings; the mouse support is just a tiny piece.

You can get Windows 95 and NT versions of TweakUI from www.microsoft.com/windows95/info/powertoys.htm. The Windows 98 version is on the Win98 CD, in the folder \tools\reskit\powertoys; you can install it by right-clicking tweakui.inf and choosing install.

Microsoft won't support TweakUI—it would put quite a strain on their phone support system, as parts of it don't work on every PC—but I've found it to be quite stable and, in some cases, indispensable.

● Roll the wheel up or down and the spreadsheet moves up or down, much as it would if you clicked the vertical scrollbar.

● Click the roller, then move the mouse. Excel moves the spreadsheet in sync with the mouse—up, down, right, or left. Move the mouse farther, and the spreadsheet moves more quickly.

● This is the feature I use most. Hold the Ctrl key down and roll the wheel. Excel responds by zooming in and out, from 10% to 100% zoom factor, in 15% increments.

There are lots of little features that Microsoft threw in with the IntelliMouse, but by and large I find them bothersome. You can play with them by clicking **Start**, **Settings**, **Control Panel**, then double-clicking the **Mouse** applet.

I'm not going to assume that you're going to run out and buy yet another Microsoft product, so I won't explicitly talk about the IntelliMouse in the rest of this book. Suffice it to say that any time you need to zoom, the IntelliMouse offers substantial benefits.

Working with
Workbooks

*T*HE BASICS OF FILE MANIPULATION IN Excel 97 closely resemble those in Word 97. If you survived the Word file-manipulation examples earlier in this book, these should come as second nature.

The only conceptual tripping point seems to be terminology. Once again, for emphasis: an Excel workbook is just an *.xls* file. Workbooks can have many spreadsheets. If you don't do anything to change how Excel works, a new workbook contains three spreadsheets.

Got that?

New, Close, Open

Let's start out easy.

*E*XERCISE

Start a Test Workbook

1. Start Excel. (Click **Start**, **Programs**, and choose **Microsoft Excel**.) Your screen should look like the one shown in Figure 19.1. Excel starts out with a new workbook called Book1. This workbook has three Spreadsheets, called Sheet1, Sheet2, and Sheet3.

2. Create a new workbook by clicking the **New** ⬜ icon on the Standard (top) toolbar. Excel responds by creating a workbook called Book2 (do you detect a pattern here?), as shown in Figure 19.1. It, too, has three spreadsheets.

FIGURE 19.1
Creating a
new work-
book called
Book2.

3. We're going to build a very simple test workbook. Click cell A2, then type `Apples`. Press the down arrow on your keyboard and type `Oranges`. Then press down, type `Grapes`, press down again and type `Mangoes`. (Rocket science, eh?) Click cell B1 and type `Q1` (that's my shorthand for "first quarter"). Press down, type a number in B2, and similarly fill in dummy numbers for the cells B3, B4, and B5. If you press down one last time, your Book2 will look much like mine, in Figure 19.2.

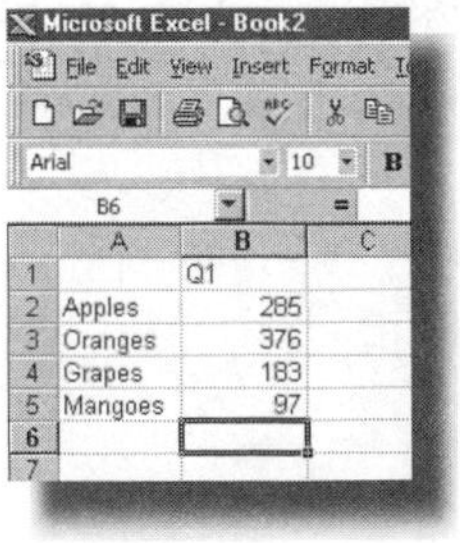

FIGURE 19.2
The begin-
nings of a
test work-
book, with a
few columns
entered.

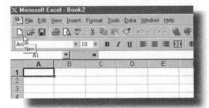

4. To close this workbook, click **File**, then **Close**. When asked if you want to save changes to Book2, click **Yes**. You'll see the Save As dialog box, as shown in Figure 19.3.

FIGURE 19.3
Excel asks you to give the test workbook a name.

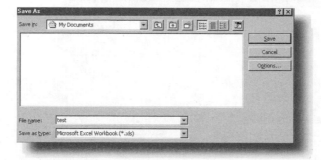

5. Type a name like test in the **File Name** box, and press **Save**. The workbook with all the fruits and numbers that you just created has been saved as the file test.xls, in the folder called c:\My Documents.

The other Excel 97 file manipulation methods work much like Word 97, too.

XERCISE

Open an Existing Workbook

1. With Excel running, click the **Open** icon on the toolbar. You should see Excel's Open dialog box, as shown in Figure 19.4.

2. Choose the workbook you want to open—in this case test.xls—and click **Open**. Excel opens the workbook and

WHAT ABOUT PREBUILT FANCY SPREADSHEETS?
Word 97 ships with lots and lots of templates, so you can take advantage of all sorts of prebuilt documents, modifying them to your specific situation. By contrast, Excel 97 only ships with eight usable templates (.xlt files), and a handful of pretty boring workbooks (.xls files). You can play with a couple of them by clicking **File**, **New**, and choosing the **Spreadsheet Solutions** tab (the **Village Software.xlt** template is an ad for the company that made these few samples). For the rest of them, use Windows Find (**Start**, **Find**, **Files** or **Folders**) to look for *.xlt and *.xls files on the Office 97 CD.

presents it to you precisely as it was when you last saved it (see Figure 19.5).

FIGURE 19.4
Opening a workbook.

FIGURE 19.5
The opened test.xls, identical to how it was when you saved it—note how the Active Cell hasn't even changed.

3. Of course, there are many ways to skin the Open cat: you could've opened test.xls by choosing it from the bottom of the **File** menu, or by clicking **File**, then **Open**. All the tricks in Word 97 work with Excel, too.

YOU DON'T MEAN ABSOLUTELY IDENTICAL, RIGHT?

Nope. Er, yes. The Word 97 and Excel 97 file handling routines are identical. I mean absolutely, totally, 100% identical.

This really is one of the great advances in Office 97, one that you'll only start to appreciate as you gain experience in Office's more advanced features. It's called *common code*. Office 97 uses the very same program to open and save files, no matter which Office application you're in. So if you mastered the Search or the Advanced features in Word's Open dialog box, you can use *precisely* the same features in Excel.

If this whole series of exercises has you yawning, there's a good reason why. The Save, Save As, and Open dialog boxes in Word 97 and Excel 97 are identical. Don't believe it? Double-check Figure 7.8. The only difference is in the **Files of type** box, and that only changes because you're looking for .xls files (that is, Excel workbooks), not .doc files (Word documents).

Sheets

There's nothing worse than an unnamed sheet, eh? Just ask the sheet.

Anyway, one of the first things you're likely to do with a new workbook is to give the first sheet, at least, a name. Here's how.

XERCISE

Renaming Sheets

1. In your test.xls workbook, right-click the tab marked Sheet1. You should see several options, as shown in Figure 19.6.

FIGURE 19.6
The right-click context menu for a Spreadsheet Tab.

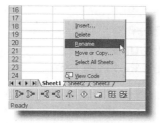

2. Choose **Rename**. Excel grays out the name Sheet1, inviting you to type something over the top of it. In Figure 19.7, I've typed `Fruit Sales by Quarter`, then press Enter.

FIGURE 19.7
Renaming Sheet1.

3. Now let's insert a new sheet into this workbook. Right-click Sheet2 and choose **Insert**... When Excel shows you the Insert dialog box, click the **General** tab, and double-click **Worksheet**. You should get a new spreadsheet, automatically called Sheet1, between Fruit Sales by Quarter and Sheet2 (see Figure 19.8).

FIGURE 19.8
Inserting a new sheet into test.xls.

4. Click the **Fruit Sales by Quarter** tab. Then save this latest version of test.xls by clicking the **Save** 🖫 icon on the toolbar.

Undo/Redo

The Undo capability in Excel 97 works much like the same feature in Word 97, except it's limited to a measly 16 undo's. In other words, you can undo your last 16 actions, but that's it, that's all she wrote.

To undo your most recent action, click the **Undo** ↺ icon on the toolbar. And then to redo whatever you've undone, click the **Redo** ↻ icon.

As always, the undo information remains as long as the workbook is open—even when you save it. But the information disappears as soon as the workbook is closed.

Print

Printing in Excel rates as a full sub-discipline. You can spend half your workday setting up a spreadsheet to print legibly. The fundamental reason seems pretty clear: whereas Word documents exist (pretty much) simply to be printed, and printing in PowerPoint comes as a natural byproduct of producing a presentation, printing in Excel is almost an afterthought, something you worry about after the spreadsheet is cranking out good numbers.

It shows.

I'll go into specific tricks for making your printed spreadsheets look good in Chapter 22, "Making Spreadsheets Look Good." We'll cover headers and footers, setting page breaks, and the like. What I'd like to tackle here are general, overall strategies for printing spreadsheets so you can kind of stick them in the back of your mind while you're working through the coming exercises.

The job ain't over till the paperwork's done—and in Excel, that usually involves printing a spreadsheet.

Print Area

Excel 97 spreadsheets tend to get real big, real fast. Quite commonly all you want to do is print a bottom-line summary of all the calculations performed in a spreadsheet: the boss doesn't want to drown in the detailed lists of component numbers when a simple set of totals will do. That's where Print Area comes in.

XERCISE

Set and Clear the Print Area

1. Open test.xls, if it isn't already staring at you.

2. Print test.xls by clicking the **Print**  icon. So far it's pretty easy, eh?

3. Now say the boss only wants her printouts to cover apples and oranges; she couldn't care less about grapes and mangoes. That's easy to do in Excel with something called the Print Area.

4. Start by selecting the range that you want to print—in this case, click the cell A1, hold down the mouse button, and drag it down to B3. (You can also click **A1**, hold down the Shift key, and then click **B3**.) As you see in Figure 19.9, you'll end up with six highlighted cells, the ones between A1 and B3 (Excel calls that the range A1:B3).

FIGURE 19.9
Selecting the range A1:B3.

5. Because this is the area you want to print, click **File**, then **Print Area**, then **Set Print Area** (see Figure 19.10). Excel 97 turns the range A1:B3 into the print area.

FIGURE 19.10
After the print area range has been selected, you tell Excel about it with this menu item.

6. Now click the **Print** 🖨 icon again. See how Excel only prints the cells in the Print Area?

7. Remove the Print Area by clicking **File**, **Print Area**, then **Clear Print Area**.

If Excel has no defined Print Area, it prints everything between cell A1 and the very last (bottom-right-most) cell in your spreadsheet. That can cover quite a bit of territory, as you'll see in the next section.

Page Sequence

When Excel can't print all of your spreadsheet on one page, it follows a very simple series of rules for determining where to print what:

● If you've set up a Print Area, these rules are applied to the Print Area. If there's no defined Print Area, Excel takes the entire area between cell A1 and the last cell in your spreadsheet and considers that to be the Print Area.

● Excel prints the upper-left page in the Print Area. It then moves down and prints the next page-full. It continues downward until it's printed all the left-most pages in the Print Area. Then it starts at the top of the next column of pages. It continues that way, working top to bottom, and then left to right, until all the pages are printed.

- If there isn't enough room on a page to fit an entire row, that row is pushed down to the next page. Similarly if there isn't enough room on a page to fit an entire column, that column gets shifted to the next page to the right.

Let's take our little test.xls and make it big enough to demonstrate how Excel prints a four-page spreadsheet.

*E*XERCISE

Print a Big Spreadsheet

1. Start with test.xls.

2. We don't want to screw up the main test file, so let's make a copy of it. Click **File**, **Save As**, and type `test2` in the **File name** box. Click **Save** (see Figure 19.11). That saves a copy of test.xls; the new copy is called test2.xls.

FIGURE 19.11
Saving a copy of test.xls as test2.xls.

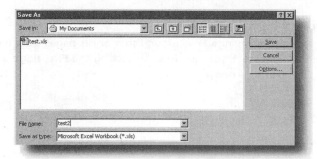

3. You should be working on test2.xls. Verify that by looking up at the title bar. It should say Microsoft Excel – test2.xls.

4. Click once in cell K4. Type `Far right` and press Enter. Your screen should look like Figure 19.12.

FIGURE 19.12
Putting the text Far right in cell K4.

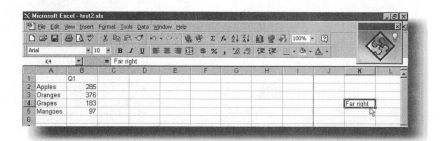

I CAN'T SEE K4!
If you have a smaller screen, at lower resolution than the one shown in Figure 19.12, you may need to use the horizontal scrollbar or the right arrow key on your keyboard to get all the way over to cell K4.

5. Use the vertical scrollbar and click once in cell C56. Type `Down below` and press Enter.

6. Then use the horizontal scrollbar to move all the way over to cell L68. Click once on it and type `Right and Below`. Press Enter.

7. Now click the **Print** 🖨 icon one more time. You should get four pages printed, covering the range A1:L68. Excel first prints the upper-left page, which is the one with our Fruit Sales by Quarter figures. Then it prints the page below that one, so page 2 should say Down below. Next, it hops up to the upper-right page, and thus page 3 should say Far right. Finally, it goes down one more time, to print the Right and Below page.

IS THAT ENGRAVED IN STONE?
Nope. If you ever need to change Excel around so it prints pages from left to right, and then from top to bottom, you can do so by clicking the **File**, **Page Setup**, **Sheet** tab, and changing the **Page order**.

Portrait and Landscape

Frequently, Excel pages print better if they're turned on edge so the long side of the paper is at the top.
That's called *Landscape* printing.

What happens when we print test2.xls in Landscape? I bet you can guess...

WHY LANDSCAPE?
Printers have been using these terms for centuries. A Portrait page is the normal way for printing word processing documents—with the short edge of the paper at the top. Think of a drawing of a person's portrait: typically it's taller than it is wide.

Similarly, Landscape refers to pages printed on their side, with the long side of the sheet on top. Think of a drawing of a landscape.

*Ɛ*XERCISE

Print Landscape

1. Start with test2.xls, the test page you just created.

2. Click **File**, then **Print**. Make sure the **Page** tab is showing, and click the button marked **Landscape**, as shown in Figure 19.13.

FIGURE 19.13
Setting test2.xls to print Landscape.

3. Click the **Print** button. Now you'll see the same information coming out the printer, this time printed on just two pages.

Wait. It gets better.

Fit to Page

The people who created Excel know that sometimes you just want to print the blasted spreadsheet and you couldn't care less if it's pretty. For those times, they've invented a magical shrinking machine.

*E*XERCISE

Just Print the Blasted Thing

1. With test2.xls up on the screen, the Page Setup dialog box showing, and the **Landscape** button pressed, click the **Fit to** button, as shown in Figure 19.14.

2. You can spin the buttons to tell Excel how many pages to squish down to. In our case, I think you'll find it instructive to see how small a squished single page comes out. Click **Print**.

3. You'll get one page coming out of the printer. Take a close look at it. Can you read the information? On some printers the text will be quite legible; on others it'll be totally inscrutable. Only you can decide for sure.

FIGURE 19.14
Forcing Excel to print it all on one page.

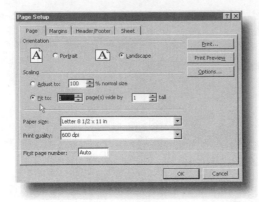

4. Keep this trick in your hip pocket if you ever need to simply get the data printed, damn the torpedoes, full speed ahead.

Gridlines

Excel will print spreadsheet gridlines—light horizontal and vertical lines that make it easier to pick out individual cells. You almost always want gridlines to appear onscreen; entering data without them can be monstrous. But whether or not they appear on printouts depends very much on your predilections.

WHEN GRIDLINES HELP
I've found that printing gridlines helps when you're shrinking a spreadsheet down, so text appears at less than 10 point. It's also useful for sparse spreadsheets—ones that have few entries.

*E*XERCISE _____

Print Gridlines

1. Using test2.xls as it appears now, with the Page Setup dialog box on the screen, click the **Sheet** tab. Down in the **Print** section, click the box marked **Gridlines** (see Figure 19.15).

TRULY ADVANCED PRINTING
If you ever get stuck printing really, really hairy reports from Excel—particularly ones that include certain parts of the spreadsheet and exclude others, perhaps for multiple "what if" scenarios—make sure you look at the Report Manager. You can get a rudimentary introduction to Report Manager by calling up the Office Assistant and typing `report manager`.

FIGURE 19.15
Tell Excel to print horizontal and vertical gridlines with this option.

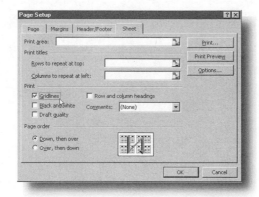

2. Click the **Print** button, and then **OK**. The cells on the printout will be clearly identified with gridlines. Do they help or hinder? It's very much up to you.

That will do for a quick introduction to the major print options. I'll go into much greater detail when we talk about making your spreadsheets look good.

Building Spreadsheets

OKAY, OKAY. I HAVE A LITTLE CONFESSION to make. I tricked you. Most introductory books make a big deal about Excel values and labels and ranges and whatnot, going into excruciating detail about how you have to click in a cell before typing a value or a label, how values differ from labels, and all sorts of folderol.

Bah! Humbug!

In the previous two chapters I introduced you to all those things and more, and I bet you didn't even blink an eye. The simple fact is that you can do an awful lot in Excel if you don't get bogged down in the details, and go ahead and do what comes naturally.

Let me show you what I mean.

Data

Excel understands data. You'd be amazed at how frequently Excel guesses exactly what you mean, just because of the way you type.

*E*XERCISE

Excel's Automatically Recognized Data Types

1. Start with a new, clean workbook by clicking the **New** 🗋 icon.

2. In cell A1, type $12.34 and press Enter (see Figure 20.1). Excel interprets the number as 12.34, and understands that you want to display the number as a dollar amount.

3. In cell A2, type 15%. Excel interprets that as, uh, 15%.

4. In cell A3, type –17.95. Excel interprets that as a negative 17.95. Stop yawning. It gets better.

5. In cell A4, type (17.95). Excel is smart enough to know that a number in parenthesis is negative. Hey, that's better than some accountants I've known.

6. In cell A5, type 3,000. See how commas don't give Excel fits?

7. Here's a fun one. In cell A6, type 1:30 p. As soon as you press Enter, Excel turns that into 1:30:00 PM up in the Formula bar, and puts 1:30 PM in the active cell. Pretty smart, eh?

8. In cell A7, type 9/1/98. When you press Enter, Excel realizes that's a date, and converts it into 9/1/1998, which you can see in the Formula bar. Down in the active cell, you'll see 9/1/98, just as you typed.

9. Now for the grand finale: in cell A8, type Aug 20 and press Enter. Excel recognizes that as a date, attaches the current year to it (as I write this, that's 1998), converts it to 8/20/1998 in the Formula bar, then shows 20-Aug down in the active cell. Don't applaud. Throw money.

10. Close the workbook (click **File**, **Close**). No, you don't want to save changes.

All of those are pretty cool, but if you think about it a bit, there's no great leap of faith involved. When Excel sees you type Aug 20, for example, it doesn't take a whole lot of imagination to figure that you wanted to type a date.

In fact, in 1998, you can type any of these on the keyboard and get the same date, 8/20/1998, put in a cell:

FIGURE 20.1
Excel 97 correctly interprets Aug 20 as a date.

● 8/20/98 (no surprise with that one)

● Aug 20

● 8/20

● 8-20

…and I bet you can see the problem right there. What if you *want* Excel to calculate 8 divided by 20, or 8 minus 20? This automatic recognition of data types is all good and well, but how do you tell Excel when to stop interpreting what you wrote, and just go do the calculation? That's where formulas come in to play.

Formulas

What's a formula? Good question.

There's a lot of mumbo jumbo associated with formulas—the Office Assistant spouts a lot of it—but it all boils down to one thing. In Excel, a formula is an entry in a cell that starts with an = equal sign. It's that simple.

You write a formula—that is, you start by typing an = sign in a cell—when you want Excel to calculate something for you. Type = and Excel does the calculation. No = sign, no calculation. Nothing to it.

XERCISE

A Simple Formula

1. Open the test workbook, file test.xls.

2. Click cell B6 and type this formula: **=B2+B3+B4+B5** (see Figure 20.2). That tells Excel to add the values in B2, B3, B4, and B5, and to put them in the current cell, which is B6.

FIGURE 20.2
A simple for-
mula for
adding the
contents of
four cells.

3. Press Enter. Excel takes the formula, which is displayed in the Formula bar, calculates the result, which is 941 (if you don't believe it, grab a calculator!), and puts the result in cell B6 (see Figure 20.3).

FIGURE 20.3
The result of
=B2+B3+B4+
B5 gets
placed in
cell B6.

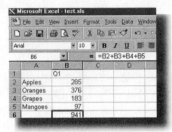

4. In Figure 20.4, I've filled in three more columns of data, to start fleshing out test.xls. Please do the same. You can use my numbers or choose some of your own; doesn't matter.

FIGURE 20.4
Completing
the sales fig-
ures for Q2,
Q3, and Q4.

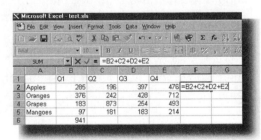

5. Now that you're an old pro at entering formulas, click cell F2 and type =B2+C2+D2+E2, as shown in Figure 20.4. Press Enter and the total Apples sales for the four quarters appears in F2 (see Figure 20.5). You expected something different?

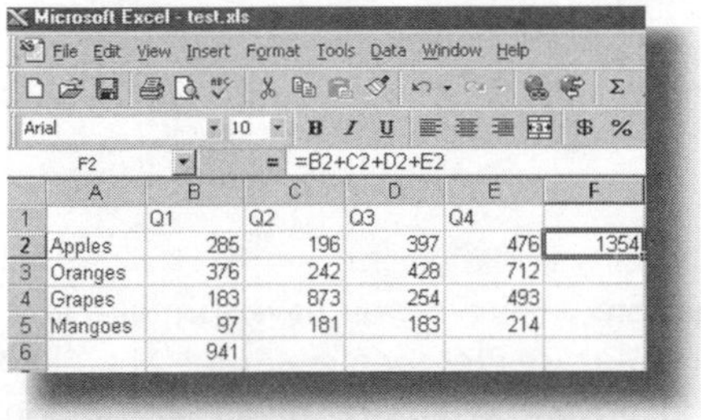

FIGURE 20.5
Total Apples sales, the sum of four quarters.

6. Here's the most important step, the one most people miss, the one where you double-check and make sure you got things right. With F2 still the active cell, click the **Trace Precedents** 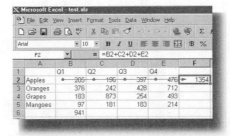 icon down on the Auditing toolbar. Excel shows you, quite visually, *precisely* which cells have been used to calculate the number in F2. Take a close look at Figure 20.6 and verify that there are dots in the cells you expected to be used in the calculation of F2.

FIGURE 20.6
Trace Precedents shows you which cells go into the calculation of cell F2.

7. In fact, wherever you have a formula the Trace Precedents icon shows you which cells go into the calculations for a given cell. In Figure 20.7 I've clicked cell B6 and then the **Trace Precedents** icon, to verify that B6 refers to the correct cells.

FIGURE 20.7
Tracing prece-
dents for the
other formula
in the spread-
sheet.

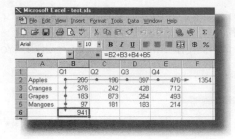

USE IT!

I can't emphasize this often enough: whenever you have formulas in a spreadsheet, you should verify them with Excel's Trace Precedents feature. Yes, I know that Trace Precedents is considered to be an advanced feature, something you only need when auditing a spreadsheet. But if you use it, and use it well, from the very beginning, you'll greatly reduce the chances of messing up a formula and nip calculation problems in the bud.

8. Remove the Trace Precedents line for B6 by clicking the cell once, then clicking the **Remove Precedent Arrows** icon. Click cell F2 and do the same. Then, just to make test.xls a little more legible, click A6 and type **Total**, then click F1 and do the same. Your test.xls should look something like Figure 20.8.

FIGURE 20.8
Cleaning up
test.xls.

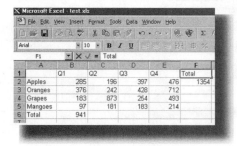

9. Click the **Save** icon to save the changes you've made to test.xls.

There are lots and lots of ways to enter formulas. Each of the methods has its own advantages and drawbacks. The method you just used, where you type a mathematical formula and the cell names, rates as the slowest and most error prone method—but the easiest to see and understand.

I'm going to take you through six more methods for adding columns or rows of numbers, just to expose you to the major tricks and concepts. This list is far from exhaustive, but I think you'll find it instructive.

NOT JUST FOR ADDING

Although I'll use addition for my examples here, you aren't limited to sums—not by any stretch of the imagination. Most of the techniques adapt to almost any mathematical combination you can imagine, and there are functions far, far more sophisticated than the Sum( ) function I'll be using. In fact, built-in Excel functions can calculate everything from the number of days between two dates, to the net present value of a series of financial transactions, to sophisticated statistical analyses you've never heard of and wouldn't dare touch without a textbook in hand.

WHAT'S A FUNCTION?

Gulp. I thought I'd be able to finesse that question. You're pretty sharp, you know?

When you get down to it, a *function* is just a formula that's built into Excel itself. For example, once you get good at Excel formulas, you could write a formula to figure out the largest number in a list of numbers. (Yeah, it might take a while before you're at that stage, but it can be done.)

Microsoft realizes that there are lots and lots of calculations people need to use all the time, so instead of forcing you to write and rewrite a formula to calculate the maximum number in a list, they've created a function called *Max()* that does all the work for you.

Excel has hundreds of built-in functions. I'll talk about some of them later in this chapter.

To learn more about Excel's functions, see the following:

- *Office 97 User Manual*, **published by Que**

- *Using Excel 97*, **published by Que**

- *Special Edition Using Excel 97*, **published by Que**

Pointing and Clicking

You don't need to type the names of the cells in your formulas. Excel is smart enough to pick them up, if you click the cell. Here's how.

Building a Formula by Pointing

1. Click cell F3. We want to put the sum of B3, C3, D3, and E3 in there, adding up the numbers in row 3.

2. Type =, then click cell B3. Magically, as you can see in Figure 20.9, B3 appears in the Formula bar, starting out the formula =B3. It also appears down in cell F3. And, just for emphasis, Excel sets off cell B3 with "marching ants" that scroll around the cell.

FIGURE 20.9
Click the cell where you want to add to a formula, and Excel picks it up.

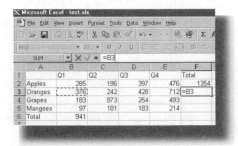

3. Type + and click cell C3. The Formula bar now reads =B3+C3, and the ants now march around cell C3.

4. Type another + and click D3. Now the formula sits at =B3+C3+D3, and the ants are running around D3.

5. Finally, type one last + and click cell E3. Then press Enter. As you can see in Figure 20.10, the correct formula appears in the Formula bar, and the total sits in F3.

FIGURE 20.10
The finished click and peck formula sits in F3.

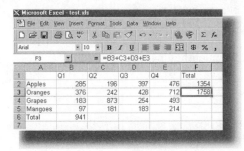

6. That's how you can construct a formula by clicking and typing.

The Sum() Function

One of the simplest Excel functions, *Sum()* takes in a bunch of cells and spits out the total of all the values in those cells. Simple, once you see how to do it.

*E*XERCISE

Sum() the Total

1. Click cell F4 once. This is where you want to put the sum of cells B4, C4, D4, and E4, right?

2. Type =sum(b4,c4,d4,e4). That just tells Excel to add up the numbers in cells B4, C4, D4, and E4. Note that you can type lowercase; Excel understands.

3. Press Enter, and you'll see the sum in cell F4, along with the formula up in the Formula bar, as shown in Figure 20.11.

FIGURE 20.11
Using the Sum() function to calculate a sum.

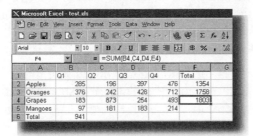

AutoSum

This method rates, far and away, as the best way to calculate the sum of a row or column of numbers.

*E*XERCISE

Sigma: The Fastest Way to Add

1. Click cell F5. This is where we want to put the sum of B5, C5, D5, and E5.

2. Click the **AutoSum** Σ icon on the toolbar. The result should look like Figure 20.12. Whoa!

FIGURE 20.12
Excel's
AutoSum
tool, run
from the
cell F5.

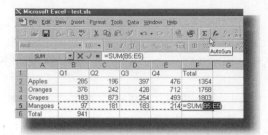

3. A whole bunch of things kicked in, all at once. First, Excel's AutoSum tool realized that you wanted to calculate a sum. It guessed that you want to sum the cells between B5 and E5. (Pretty good guess, eh? AutoSum usually guesses right.) Second, it put the formula =SUM(B5:E5) up in the Formula bar. Third, it drew those marching ants around the cells B5 through E5.

4. Play with those marching ants a little bit. Tease them, er, click one of the edges and drag the rectangle around. See how the AutoSum tool lets you adjust which cells are included in the sum by simply moving around the marching ants? Pretty cool.

5. When you're done playing with the tool, make sure the marching ants cover cells B5 through E5 and press Enter. You should get the sum in cell F5, along with the formula you see in Figure 20.13.

FIGURE 20.13
Press Enter to
freeze the
marching
ants and put
the sum in
cell F5.

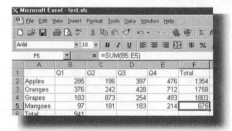

Sum() on the Range

Aha! You were watching closely in that last Exercise, weren't you? If so, you probably noticed that Excel understands the abbreviation B5:E5 to mean *all the cells between B5 and E5.*

In fact, that's an example of Excel's shorthand for any range of cells. The colon does the trick. If you type A1:D4, you're referring to all the cells between A1 and D4. C2:R23 means all the cells between C2 and R23, and so on.

That leads us to yet another way to enter sums.

*E*XERCISE

Sum() Using Ranges

1. Click the cell C6. This is where we'd like to have the sum of all the numbers in the range C2:C5, correct?

2. Type =sum(c2:c5) and press Enter. Sure enough, the correct sum appears in cell C6, and the formula shows up in the Formula bar, as shown in Figure 20.14.

FIGURE 20.14
Using =Sum(Range) to calculate a sum.

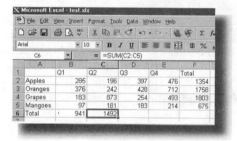

RANGES RULE

Many operations in Excel work on ranges. As you've just seen, a (contiguous) range is specified by its upper-left and lower-right cells, with a colon in between. It's quite simple, really.

We'll be working a lot with ranges. In fact, we already have. Believe it or not, when you set the Print Area for printing a spreadsheet back in the previous chapter you were actually defining a range that's used by Excel's print routines.

Titles

Excel boasts a really cool trick that will astound your friends and neighbors but probably won't help you much at all. It can recognize certain labels—row and column headings, mostly—and let you substitute the names in the headings for cell references.

As far as I'm concerned, this qualifies as a parlor trick, best suited for quick demos and flashy salespeople, but you might be able to use it at some point.

$\mathcal{E}$XERCISE

Formulas with Labels

1. Click cell D6. This is where you want the total of Apples, Oranges, Grapes, and Mangoes sold in the third quarter, okay? (Trust me. In the hands of a good salesdroid, this looks very, very cool.)

2. Type `=Apples+Oranges+Grapes+Mangoes` and press Enter. Excel recognizes that you want to sum the row, so it places the total in D6 and leaves the odd formula in the Formula bar, as shown in Figure 20.15.

FIGURE 20.15
Apples and
Oranges and
Grapes and
Mangoes,
oh my!

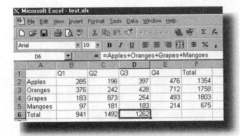

I never use this particular method for typing in formulas, for at least two reasons:

- You never know exactly when Excel is going to recognize some titles, and not others. For example, in this very spreadsheet if you had tried to calculate one of the horizontal totals in F2, F3, F4, or F5 using the formula `=Q1+Q2+Q3+Q4`, you would've received a 0 (zero) for your efforts. Why? Excel interprets Q1 as being cell Q1, not the column with the heading Q1.

- The spellings must match exactly. If you spelled Apples as Appels, you would've missed the last row.

Excel's Formula Checker sometimes picks up minor spelling errors, as shown in Figure 20.16, but if you're more than a few letters off using this method for typing formulas can result in all sorts of garbage.

FIGURE 20.16
Excel's
Formula
Checker
catches the
misspelled
word.

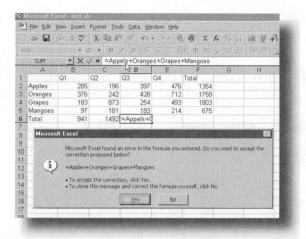

Using Parentheses

I don't want to dredge up bad memories of high school algebra. So I'll make this section very short. Although some might take issue with my assertion, the laws of mathematics apply, even in Excel. And at some point or another, in spite of your successes or failures in algebra class, that might actually work in your favor.

I'm talking about parentheses. When you group a bunch of numbers together and place them in parentheses, Excel evaluates them before it evaluates the stuff outside the parentheses. And then the stuff outside the parenthesis is evaluated from left to right. So, for example:

- =2*(3+4) evaluates to 14, whereas
- =(2*3)+4 comes out 10, and
- =2*(3+4)+5 is 19, but
- =(2*3)+4+5 is 15.

Note how Excel uses the asterisk for multiplication.

If you have problems with formulas like that, I'll just refer you to your local math teacher. Heh heh heh.

Our final excursion into writing sums shows how you can put parentheses in Excel formulas.

*E*XERCISE

In Loco Paren-tis

1. Click cell E6.

2. Type =(e2+e3)+(e4+e5) and press Enter. Note how this, mathematically, is the same as e2+e3+e4+e5. You'll get the result shown in Figure 20.17.

FIGURE 20.17
A total using (totally redundant) parentheses.

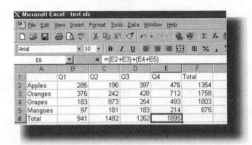

3. Click **File**, then **Save**. We're going to use this version of test.xls for a while.

Verifying

And now, after that heavy dose of typing and clicking, it's time to verify all your calculations. (In fact, I repeated these verification steps while I was performing the original calculations, just because I knew that about ten million of you would write to me if I added up a column of numbers wrong!)

XERCISE

Trace Dependencies

1. Start with the test.xls you just saved in the previous Exercise.

2. Let's double-check the precedents for cell B6. Click B6, then click the **Trace Precedents** 📊 icon on the Auditing toolbar. You should have a precedent list like that shown in Figure 20.6.

3. Now click cell C6, then click the **Trace Precedents** 📊 icon. This trace looks a little different, because the cell C6 relies on the entire range C2:C5. In Figure 20.18, Excel is showing you two things: first, it draws a box around the range C2:C5 to show you that the whole range is involved; then, second, it draws that arrow from the top of the range down to cell C6. Between the two visual clues you should get the impression that the range C2:C5 is used in cell C6.

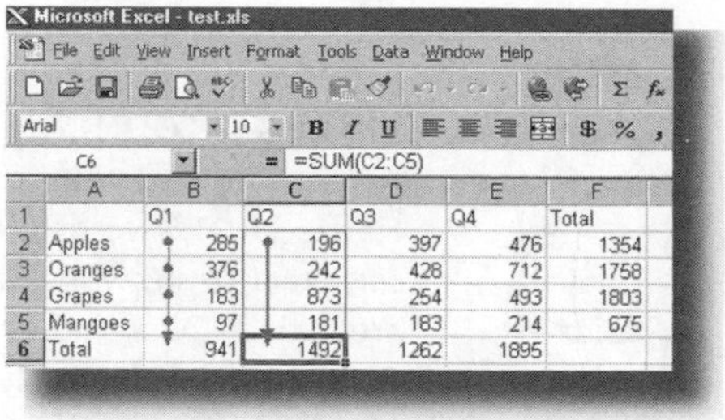

FIGURE 20.18
Showing that the entire range C2: C5 is used in cell C6.

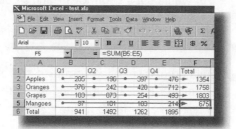

4. Continue tracing precedents for cells D6, E6, then F2, F3, F4, and F5. Note how F5 is another one of those range precedent cells (see Figure 20.19).

FIGURE 20.19
Double-checking the formulas at the end of each row.

5. Got 'em all checked out? Good. Click those cells, and remove the arrows by clicking the **Remove Precedent Arrows** icon on the Auditing toolbar.

There's one other popular way of verifying formula interconnections like these. If you double-click, oh, cell F2, you'll see how it works. Excel presents you with color-coded references to each of the cells in the formula (see Figure 20.20). You can then click, drag, move, or otherwise manipulate the individual cells and make changes in the formula. Press Enter to go back to normal.

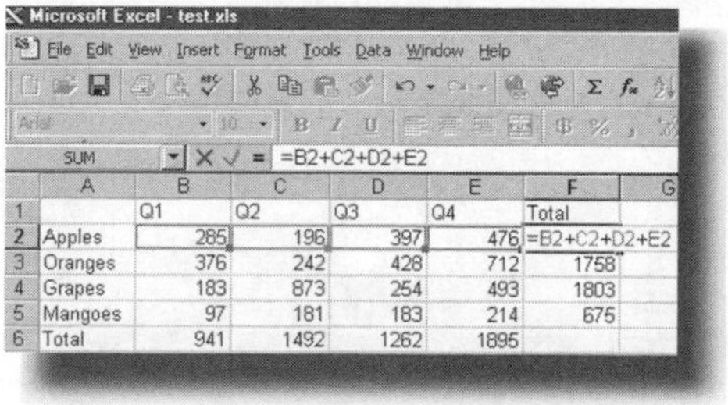

FIGURE 20.20
Excel's color-coded formula verifier.

Although this approach certainly works—and it beats the living daylights out of not verifying at all—I find it harder to use than the trace precedents capability. If you accidentally click inside the spreadsheet before you click Enter, or otherwise disturb the color coded cells, you can really mess up your formula.

WHAT'S A COUNT?
Ah, you noticed that, did you? In Figure 20.21, two of the values you can elect to show in AutoCalculate are called *Count* and *Count Nums*. The Count number is simply the number of cells with something in them that is selected (blank cells don't, uh, count). Count Nums tells you how many of the selected cells contain valid numbers. So, for example, if you selected cells A2 through B6 in test.xls, you would get a Count of 10, and a Count Nums of five.

AutoCalculate

While we're on the subject of building and verifying formulas, there's one more trick you should know about. It's called AutoCalculate, and neither the Office Assistant nor the Help Index will tell you a thing about it.

Every time you select a range of cells, Excel quickly calculates the sum of the values in those cells and puts the number down on the status bar. If you right-click the AutoCalculate panel, as you see in Figure 20.21, you can even tell Excel that you'd rather see the average, maximum, minimum, and so on.

This little number can come in very handy to quickly cross-check the answers you're getting in your spreadsheet.

FIGURE 20.21
AutoCalculate sits unobtrusively on the status bar.

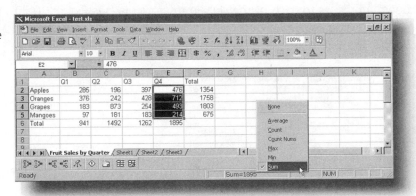

Entry Tricks

Let's take a few minutes right now to look at the ways Excel helps you enter data in a spreadsheet. Learn these tricks well, and you'll save enormous amounts of time—and improve your chances of getting the spreadsheet right the first time.

Enter and Cancel

Have you noticed how you need to press Enter every time you type a formula so Excel knows that you're through typing? In fact, there are several alternatives to pressing Enter when typing formulas:

- If you press any of the four directional keys (up, down, left, right arrows) on the keyboard, Excel understands that you're done typing the formula, and that you want to move on to the next (up, down, left, or right) cell.

- Ditto for the tab and back tab keys: the formula is finished, and you move left or right one cell.

- If you press Escape (the Esc key on most keyboards), Excel understands that you want to throw away whatever you've typed and revert to whatever was in the cell before you started typing. Esc is the Ooops! key.

If you're severely addicted to using the mouse you can mimic the behavior of the Enter key by clicking the **Enter** ☑ icon on the Format bar: Clicking that icon makes Excel behave precisely the same way it would if you pressed Enter. Similarly, the **Cancel** ☒ icon on the Format bar produces precisely the same result as pressing the Esc key.

DON'T LEAVE 'EM DANGLING
It's important that you realize new entries in cells don't "take" until you press Enter (or, equivalently, click the **Enter** ☑ icon). Until you press Enter, Excel thinks you're still editing the entry and it will refuse to do all sorts of things—most of the menu items are grayed out—until the editing is done.

If Excel ever seems to be stuck or frozen, first check to make sure you aren't in the middle of editing a cell. The easy way to do that, in most cases, is to press Enter.

Correcting Misteaks

What if you've entered something in a cell, and it's wrong? You have three choices:

- Click once on the cell and press Del or the Backspace key. That wipes out the entry and lets you type a new value or formula.

● Click once on the cell, then click in the Formula bar at whatever point you want to start editing. I don't use this approach very much, because the next approach is much faster.

● Double-click the cell. When you do that, Excel makes a pretty good guess where you put the mouse cursor and lets you edit the entry starting at that point. You'll end up editing right there in the cell. This method isn't per-fect—it's a little hard to see where the cursor will go before you do the double-click, because it's usually a thick plus-sign, and formatted entries flip-flop like a dying fish when you edit in the cell—but it tends to be the fastest, easiest way to make changes to the contents of a cell.

PARAMETERS, THE BANE OF MY EXISTENCE

Most functions require you to give them information to get an answer back. For example, Excel's WEEKDAY() function tells you the day of the week for a particular date. You feed it a date, and WEEKDAY() returns a number between 1 and 7 that represents the day of the week. (That isn't precisely correct—there are a few additional things the function can do—but it's close enough for our purposes.)

Because different people have different ideas about which day of the week is the first day of the week, you also need to tell WEEKDAY() which day of the week should come back as the number 1.

These two things you need to feed WEEKDAY() are called *parameters* and remembering precisely how to feed those parameters to WEEKDAY()— or any other Excel function—can be a monu-mental pain in the brain.

Excel's Paste Function capability will help you keep your parameters straight, whether you're entering a new formula or modifying an old one. Simply click the cell that's going to receive the formula and click the **Paste Function** f_{*} icon. After you pick the function, or if you're editing an existing function, Excel provides a handy form that sorts out, defines, and man-ages the function's parameters (see Figure 20.23). It's a godsend. If you ever need to use functions, don't forget the **Paste Function** f_{*} icon.

Entering Functions

Functions intimidate a lot of people because there are so many of them, and some of the functions sound like they're from a different planet. (Tell me the truth: Even if you know how to use a hyperbolic arctangent, how frequently do you need one?)

That's too bad, really, because Excel includes a remarkable support system for functions. Any time you think Excel may be able to help you calculate something—whether it's the monthly payment on a mortgage, or the day of the week (Monday, Tuesday, and so on)—click the **Paste Function** $f*$ icon on the toolbar. Excel responds with its Paste Function dialog box (see Figure 20.22), which lists all the available functions, along with brief descriptions of what the function will calculate and what kind of information you need to feed it.

FIGURE 20.22
Excel's amazingly detailed Function support system.

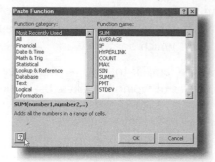

If you click the **?** icon in the lower-left corner, Office Bob, er, the Office Assistant pops up, ready to search for the specific function you want.

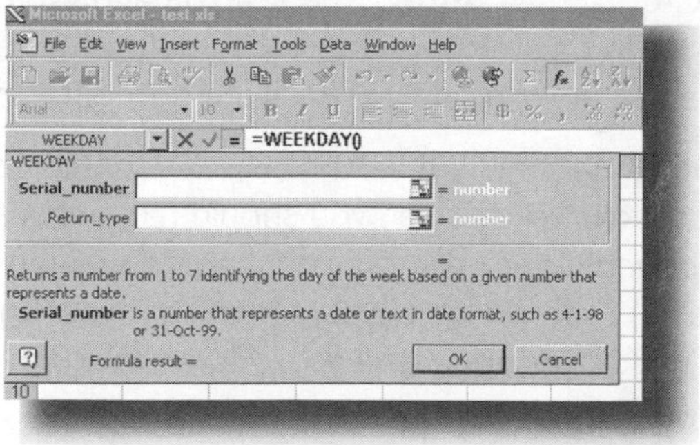

FIGURE 20.23
Excel's parameter support for the WEEKDAY() function.

AutoComplete

Whenever you start typing characters in a cell, Excel takes a quick look at all the text entries in the current column. If it finds a match on the characters you've typed, it offers to fill in the rest of the cell for you.

XERCISE_____

AutoComplete

1. Start with a clean, new spreadsheet.

2. In cell B3 type `Microsoft Corporation`.

3. In cell B4 just type `M`. See how Excel offers to fill in the rest of the entry? Press Enter to accept it.

Excel can't read your mind, of course, so if you have entries for Microsoft Corporation and for Micron Electronics in the same column, you'll have to type all the way out past Micro for Excel to guess which one you want.

This AutoComplete feature (which will be familiar to anyone who's used Quicken) not only saves time, it reduces the chances of typing mistakes. Use it well.

AutoCorrect

Excel 97 shares Word 97's AutoCorrect feature: if you type `teh`, Excel, too, will correct it to *the*.

☞ *I talked about AutoCorrect on page 216.*

The care and feeding of Excel's AutoCorrect mirrors Word's precisely, down to its location on the menu (click **Tools**, then **AutoCorrect**). Excel and Word even use the same list of corrections, with one minor exception: formatted AutoCorrect entries in Word 97 do not show up in Excel 97. That's the only difference.

If you aren't yet familiar with AutoCorrect, it would behoove you to go back to Chapter 11 and take a close look. In particular, you should remember that AutoCorrect *isn't just for spelling errors!* You can use it to store and expand abbreviations of your own choosing. For example, if you commonly type, oh, `Sub-Total for this Division of Woody's Widgets Inc.`, you can set up AutoCorrect so you only need to type a very short string, like `st#`, to get the full text put in your spreadsheets.

AutoFill

There's one last data entry trick you need to know about. It's called AutoFill and, when the situation's right, it can save you all sorts of time.

XERCISE _____

AutoFill as Copy

1. Start with a new, clean spreadsheet.

2. Type **10** in cell B2. Note how there's a little thickening in the lower-right corner of the box around cell B2 (see Figure 20.24). That tiny thick part is called a *fill handle*.

FIGURE 20.24
The fill handle in the lower-right corner of the active cell.

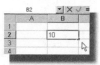

3. Click the fill handle and drag the resulting dotted line (see Figure 20.25) down to cell B10. Watch the little Tooltip, in yellow, as you drag the fill handle. See how it says 10? That's a little visual clue to tell you that all of these cells will be set to 10 as soon as you release the mouse button. Let go of the fill handle, and you'll see it happen.

FIGURE 20.25
Dragging the fill handle down to B10.

4. At this point, cells B2 to B10 are highlighted, and there's a fill handle at the lower-right corner of B10. Click that fill handle, and drag it over to the D column (see Figure 20.26). All the while you drag, the yellow Tooltip says 10 and, when you release the mouse button, you'll see that the entire range B2:D10 has been filled with 10s.

FIGURE 20.26
The fill handle works in all four directions, for individual cells and for ranges.

5. Push and pull the fill handle until you get the feel for how Excel will copy data from a cell or a region into adjacent cells or regions.

That's pretty cool if you need to copy the same data through a spreadsheet, but it gets much better. AutoFill has some native intelligence you can exploit to generate sequences of numbers and labels. Let me show you what I mean.

*E*XERCISE_____

AutoFill a Sequence of Numbers

1. Start with a clean, blank spreadsheet.

2. Type 1 in cell B2.

3. Right-click the fill handle and drag it down to cell B9. Let go of the mouse button, and you'll see the list shown in Figure 20.27.

WHAT HAPPENS IF I CLICK SERIES
If you're curious, go ahead and choose **Series** from the list of options offered in Figure 20.27. You'll discover that Excel can create a wide variety of series, based on your choices, including trend lines under various regression models. The mathematics gets a bit hairy, so if you're interested in such things, bring up the Office Assistant and type growth trend.

FIGURE 20.27
Various options available when you right-click the fill handle.

4. Click **Fill Series**. That instructs Excel to construct a series of numbers in the filled area. When you click **Fill Series**, you'll get the sequence shown in Figure 20.28.

FIGURE 20.28
The sequence formed by choosing Fill Series.

AutoFill's smarts aren't limited to simple sequences of numbers. Take a look at this.

$\mathcal{E}$XERCISE

AutoFill Sequences of Labels

1. Start with a new, clean spreadsheet.

2. Type Jan in cell B2.

3. Click B2's fill handle, and drag it out to column I, as shown in Figure 20.29. See how the Tooltip changes from Feb to Mar to Apr, and so on, until in column I it turns into Aug?

FIGURE 20.29
Creating a sequence of months with the fill handle.

4. If you release the mouse button over column I, Excel fills in the first row with Feb, Mar, Apr, May, Jun, Jul, and Aug.

5. That isn't the only label sequence Excel will AutoFill for you. In Figure 20.30, I've put together quite a few AutoFills, and they're all available in bone-stock Excel 97.

Excel follows some strange rules when deciding if it should just copy, or fill in a full series, when you use the fill handle on a range. (For example, if you AutoFill starting with a row of numbers, the numbers are simply copied. But if you put just one formula in that row, the numbers will be incremented. Weird, but true.) So be careful when you AutoFill starting with more than one original cell.

ROLL YOUR OWN AUTOFILL LIST
If there's a series of entries you commonly type into your spreadsheets—say, a bunch of account numbers, or a list of expense categories—you can have Excel do all the dirty work for you.

To see how it works, bring up test.xls and select cells A2 through A5. Click **Tools**, **Options**, and click the **Custom Lists** tab. If you then click the **Import** button (see Figure 20.31), and **OK**, Excel adds the list "Apples, Oranges, Grapes, Mangoes" to the AutoFill feature. From that point on, you can type Apples, grab the fill handle, and get the whole list inserted into your spreadsheets.

FIGURE 20.30
A wide variety of AutoFill labels, created by simply dragging the fill handle.

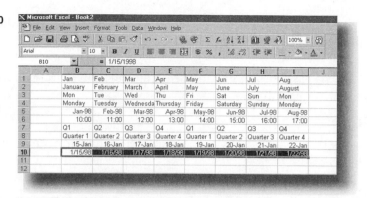

FIGURE 20.31
Make your own AutoFill lists.

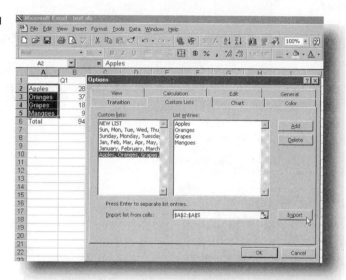

Copy/Move Data

You would think that cut, copy, and paste—the mainstays of all Windows applications, not just the Office crew—would be incredibly simple in Excel 97. And you would be wrong. Way wrong.

Copying and moving data in Excel get down-right confusing for two simple reasons:

● Excel doesn't behave the way any normal Windows application behaves when you paste data from the clipboard.

● Excel tries to help you by altering formulas behind the scenes when they're copied or moved.

Let's start with the easiest case, then tackle each of those two tough points in turn.

Simple Copy, Move

By far the fastest and simplest way to move data around in an Excel spreadsheet is to just click and drag.

*E*XERCISE

Move and Copy

1. Open test.xls. Drag your cursor over cells A1:F6 to select them (or click A1, hold down Shift, and click F6).

2. Move your mouse so the pointer hovers just below the range you just selected, as shown in Figure 20.32. The pointer turns into an arrow, indicating that Excel is ready to move or copy the range.

FIGURE 20.32
Select a range and move the mouse pointer to the bottom of the range, to prepare for a move.

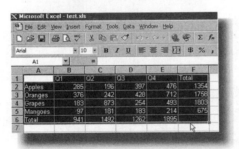

3. Click and drag the whole range to some other location on the spreadsheet. In Figure 20.33, I've moved it to C10:H15.

4. That's all it takes to move a range using the mouse. Practice for a bit, and note in particular that you don't have to

CLICK A SIDE, ANY SIDE
While I tend to click the bottom line of a range when I want to move or copy it, in fact you can click any of the outside lines, except the fill handle. It takes a little manual dexterity, but the other edges can come in handy, particularly when you're moving or copying a big range.

move the range to a completely virgin location on the spreadsheet; Excel has no trouble at all moving the range just a few cells. When you're done practicing, click the **Undo** ↶▾ icon enough times to put the range back in the upper-left corner of the spreadsheet, where it started, at A1:F6.

FIGURE 20.33
Drag the selection to move it.

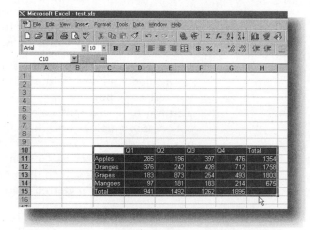

FIGURE 20.34
Copying by holding down the Ctrl key.

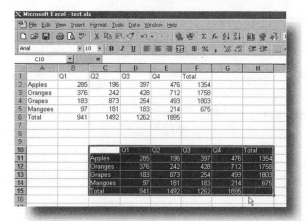

5. Copying is very similar to moving, except you hold down the Ctrl key while clicking and dragging. In Figure 20.34, I started by selecting A1:F6. Then I held down the Ctrl key and clicked the bottom of the range. (A visual cue that you're copying: the arrow gets a small **+** sign next to it.) When I had moved the range to C10:H15, I released the mouse button, and then the Ctrl key, in that order. The result: Excel copied the range to the new location.

6. Again you can practice copying until you're comfortable with it. When you're done, click **Undo** to restore test.xls to its original condition.

Excel lets you click and drag ranges anywhere in a spreadsheet. If you want to drop a range of cells down below the bottom of the current screen, just hold your cursor at the bottom and Excel will scroll the spreadsheet for you. All in all, click and drag is the best way to go. You'll see why in the next section.

MORE MOVE AND COPY OPTIONS
Sometimes you want to move a row, but when you're through dragging it, you don't want to over-write an existing row, you want to stick it between two other rows.

Excel supports this option and many more. You can memorize a lot of weird key combinations to insert, copy, bump, and grind, but the simplest way to take advantage of Excel's multiple options is to simply right-click, drag, and then pick what action you want to perform. In Figure 20.35, I've selected A5:F5 in test.xls, right-clicked, dragged, then released the mouse button to select my preferred action.

FIGURE 20.35
Right-click and drag to uncover a host of options for shifting, copying, and moving.

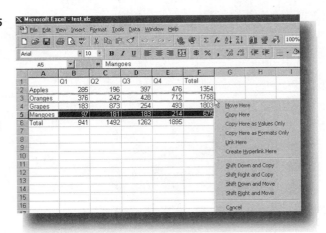

How Excel Pastes

If you can't use the mouse to move or copy ranges in your spreadsheet—perhaps you need to move the range a long distance, or you're afraid you might miss the destination area by a cell or two—you need to be aware of the strange way Excel handles cut, copy, and paste.

XERCISE

Copy and Paste

1. Open test.xls, if it isn't already open.

2. Click a cell, say C4, then click **Edit**, **Copy**. (Equivalently, if you're accustomed to Windows' shortcut keys, you can press Ctrl+C.) Excel responds by placing the contents of C4 on the Clipboard, the common Windows procedure, and it adds a bit of lagniappe by showing the marching ants around cell C4, as shown in Figure 20.36.

FIGURE 20.36
Cell C4 is copied to the Clipboard.

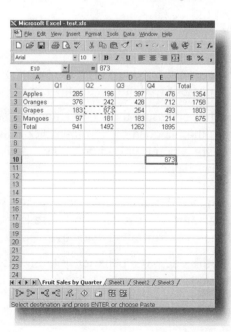

3. Excel is capable of performing a fairly normal paste. Click in, oh, cell E10, then click **Edit**, **Paste** (or press Ctrl+V, the Windows shortcut key combination). As you can see in Figure 20.37, that puts a copy of cell C4 in cell E10.

FIGURE 20.37
A standard paste with Edit/Paste or Ctrl+V.

4. Notice two things that are very odd about Figure 20.37: even after the paste, Excel keeps the ants marching around cell C4, and it continues to show the message Select destination and press Enter or choose **Paste** in the status bar. That's where the problem arises.

5. Say you've performed a copy in this manner, but you get to scrolling to some obscure part of your spreadsheet, and you've forgotten that the ants are still marching around cell C4. You end up somewhere in your spreadsheet—in Figure 20.38, I just happened to get to cell B19—and you press Enter.

FIGURE 20.38
While the ants are marching around a cell, the Enter key is still hot and will copy the contents.

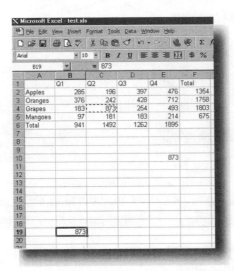

6. *Boom!* For no apparent reason, Excel copies the contents of cell C4 into cell B19. That's a real bummer. But wait. It gets stranger.

7. After you've completed a copy using this weird Enter key method, Excel removes the value from the Clipboard! If you then click **Edit**, as you can see in Figure 20.39, the **Paste** action is grayed out. Excel has literally thrown away the contents of the Clipboard.

Some people shrug off this odd (and decidedly un-Windows-like!) behavior as another Excel anomaly. Personally, when I was learning to use Excel for the first time, I found it to be one of the most frustrating inanities in Excel.

Anyway, whether you think of this odd paste behavior as another ho-hum stupidity or a major stumbling block to understanding what's going on, the conclusion comes out the same: Use the mouse to copy and move cells, unless you absolutely *have* to resort to the **Edit** menu or keyboard shortcuts.

FIGURE 20.39
When you use the Enter key to paste into a spread-sheet, Excel nukes the value on the Clipboard.

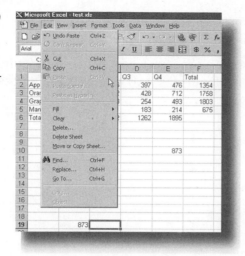

Absolute and Relative Addresses

I was astounded to discover that some introductory Office books don't even mention the difference between absolute and relative cell addresses. When you see how important they are, you'll be astounded as well.

The whole problem stems from a simple fact: sometimes when you copy (or move) formulas, you want them to change, and sometimes you don't. Let me show you what I mean.

XERCISE

When You Want Formulas to Change

1. Start with a new, clean spreadsheet. We're going to calculate some sales-people's commissions.

2. Put some numbers in cells B4:C5. In Figure 20.40, I've built a small spread-sheet to hang the numbers in, and give them some context.

FIGURE 20.40
The beginning of a small commission calculator.

3. In cell D4, type the formula =B4+C4. In the example in Figure 20.40, that just calculates Ed's total sales for the first two quarters.

4. Copy the formula in D4 to D5. You would expect this new formula in D5 to calculate Barry's total sales for the first two quarters—and it does (see Figure 20.41).

FIGURE 20.41
Copy Ed's total sales formula to Barry's line, and you would expect the total to reflect Barry's sales.

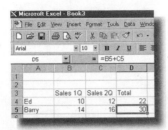

5. Something strange happened when Excel copied the formula from D4 to D5, though, and you can see what happened in the Formula bar of Figure 20.41. Excel changed the cell references around, so the total now refers to Barry's numbers on row 5, and not Ed's numbers on row 4. Cell D5 now reads =B5+C5, which is as it should be.

6. If you subsequently move or copy the A3:D5 range to some other place on the spreadsheet, you would expect the total for Ed's line to stay 22, and the total for Barry's line to stay 30. They do—but Excel changes the underlying formulas as the range moves around, so these two formulas refer to the correct cells, no matter where the A3:D5 range might sit.

That's an example of *relative* addressing: when you move or copy formulas around, you let Excel take care of the details and switch the formulas to fit the situation.

Sometimes, though, you don't want Excel to change the formulas—or part of the formulas.

*E*XERCISE

When You Don't Want Formulas to Change

1. Continue with the spreadsheet you were just using.

2. Let's figure out how much commission I owe Ed and Barry for the first two quarters' sales. I'll put the commission rate in cell A1, as you can see in Figure 20.42.

FIGURE 20.42
Commission
rate goes into
cell A1.

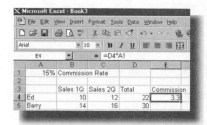

3. To calculate Ed's commission, I need to multiply his total sales (cell D4) by the commission rate (cell A1). That's why I put the formula **=D4*A1** in cell E4. Sure enough, his commission comes up 3.3, which is 15% of 22.

4. Now copy the formula in cell E4 to calculate Barry's commission, in cell E5. As you can see in Figure 20.43, Barry would be a bit, uh, perturbed to learn that his commission is 0!

FIGURE 20.43
Copy the
commission
calculation
formula
down one
cell, and all
hell breaks
loose.

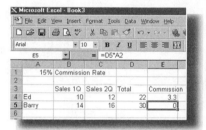

5. What happened? Let's trace the precedents to see. Click cell E4, and click the **Trace Precedents** icon on the Auditing toolbar. You'll see in Figure 20.44 that the precedents for E4 look fine.

6. But when you run a Trace Precedents on cell E5, as shown in Figure 20.45, you'll see immediately that the formula in E5 refers to cell A2—and that isn't where the Commission Rate is located!

FIGURE 20.44
Precedents
for cell E4
look fine.

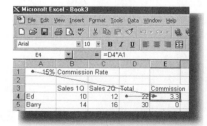

FIGURE 20.45
Trace Precedents on cell E5 reveals the culprit—Excel has changed the formula, incorrectly.

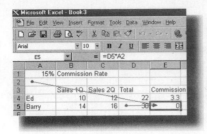

This is one of those occasions when you want Excel to keep its mitts off your formula. More accurately, you want these commission calculations to continue to refer to cell A1, no matter where the formula may be moved or copied.

When you want Excel to change a cell address as a formula gets copied or moved, you use the regular cell addressing method we've been using all along: A1, C3, D5, and the like. Those are relative addresses.

When you want Excel to refrain from modifying a cell address, you have to use something called an absolute address. You specify absolute addresses by putting $ dollar signs in front of the row and column: A1, C3, D5, for example. The dollar signs don't have any celestial significance. They're just Keep Off signs, warning Excel not to change the addresses.

XERCISE

Using Absolute Addresses

1. Go back into the commission spreadsheet we've been using, and click cell E4.

2. This time, instead of using the (relative) address A1 in the formula, try using the (absolute) address A1. I've modified the formula in E4, as you can see in Figure 20.46.

FIGURE 20.46
A modified commission calculation formula, using an absolute address for the Commission Rate.

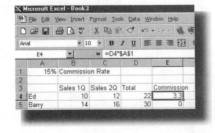

3. Now copy the formula in cell E4 down to E5. Sure enough, the new formula, =D5*A1, refers to the correct location for the Commission Rate, and the commission gets calculated properly (see Figure 20.47). Barry should be a happy guy.

VARIATIONS ON A THEME
Things aren't quite as neat as I made them out to be. In addition to relative and absolute addresses, Excel also recognizes hybrid addresses, such as A$1 and $A1. As you might imagine, the part of the address preceded by a $ dollar sign is the absolute part, while the other half of the address can be modified by Excel when you copy or move formulas. I'll leave it as a, uh, exercise for the reader to work out the nuances of those puppies.

FIGURE 20.47
The formula copies across correctly because you used an absolute address.

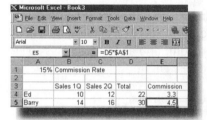

If you start copying formulas and they go haywire, run a quick Trace Precedents. If the Trace shows that the formulas aren't referring to the correct cells, chances are very, very good that you need to use an *absolute* address.

Add/Delete Rows and Columns

If you knew exactly what your spreadsheet was going to look like at the time you started, you'd never have to add or delete rows or columns.

'Course if you knew exactly what your spreadsheet was going to look like, you wouldn't need me to help, would you?

$\mathcal{E}$XERCISE

Insert a Column

1. Start with test.xls.

2. Let's say you want to add a new column between the existing columns A and B. As shown in Figure 20.48, you would start by clicking the B column heading, thereby selecting all of column B.

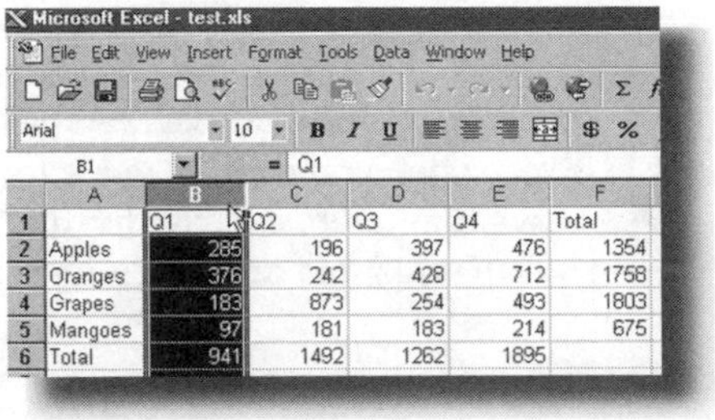

FIGURE 20.48
To insert a column to the left of column B, first select column B.

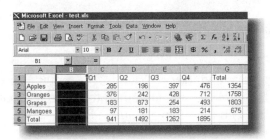

3. Up on the menu, click **Insert**, then **Column**, and viola, a new column B appears, as shown in Figure 20.49. Remarkably, all the other columns in test.xls are shifted to the right, and all the formulas still work. (Such is the wonder of relative addresses, eh?)

FIGURE 20.49
Click Insert, then Column, and a new column appears to the left of the selected column.

That was easy. Now, what if you want to insert more than one column or row?

$\mathcal{E}$XERCISE

Insert Multiple Rows

1. Continue with test.xls, as in the previous exercise.

2. Say you want to insert three rows directly above the row marked Oranges. Here's the trick: select the Oranges row, plus two additional rows, for a total of three rows, by clicking and dragging on the row headings 3, 4, and 5. See Figure 20.50, where I've selected rows 3, 4, and 5.

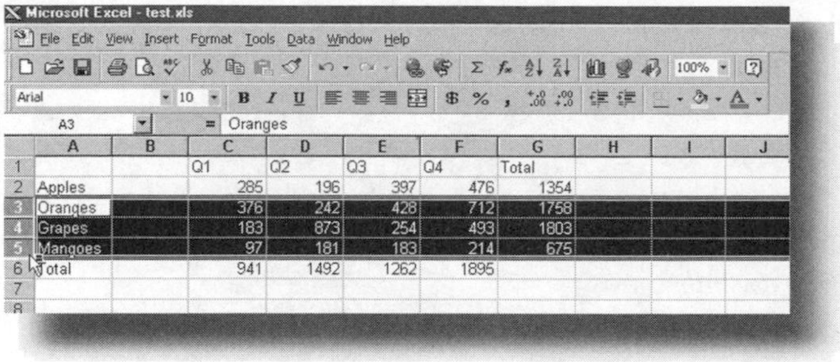

FIGURE 20.50
Select a number of rows equal to the number of rows you want to insert.

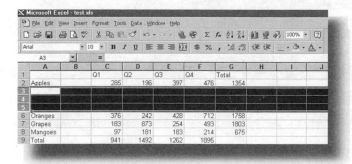

3. Now click **Insert**, then **Rows**. Excel responds by adding three rows—a number equal to the number of rows you selected—and placing them above the top selected row. In Figure 20.51 you can see how the other rows have been moved down, and once again all of the formulas remain intact.

FIGURE 20.51
Click Insert, Rows and Excel inserts an equal number of rows above the one at the top of the selected range.

If adding rows and columns is so easy, deleting rows and columns must be easy, too, right?

Well, it is… if you know the trick. (Have you heard that one before?)

*E*XERCISE

Delete Rows

1. Start with the modified version of test.xls you just created in the previous exercise. Type a number—say **123**—in cell B4. Your spreadsheet should look like Figure 20.52.

2. Let's say you want to get rid of rows 3, 4, and 5. Select the rows by clicking and dragging on the row headings 3, 4, and 5.

3. You want to delete the rows? OK. Press the Del or Delete key on your keyboard.

WHY DOESN'T EXCEL DO WHAT WINDOWS DOES?
Why doesn't the Del key delete? Probably the same reason why Excel uses the Enter key for Paste: Excel has always worked that way, and Microsoft is afraid to change it. Funny, though, that the Redmondians don't let you change this very un-Windows-like behavior in the **Tools** menu.

FIGURE 20.52
Type some data in one of the new rows.

	A	B	C	D	E	F	G	H	I	J
1			Q1	Q2	Q3	Q4	Total			
2	Apples		285	196	397	476	1354			
3										
4		123								
5										
6	Oranges		376	242	428	712	1758			
7	Grapes		183	873	254	493	1803			
8	Mangoes		97	181	183	214	675			
9	Total		941	1492	1262	1895				

4. Guess what? The rows don't disappear. Only the data goes away, and you end up with a spreadsheet that looks just like Figure 20.51!

5. To delete the rows, you have to click **Edit**, then **Delete**. Similarly, to delete a column, you must first select the entire column, then click **Edit**, and **Delete**.

6. Return test.xls to its original condition by deleting the three rows and one column we added in this section.

#Bad Data

When Excel looks at a number and has a problem, it invariably uses some variation of the # sign to alert you to the problem.

The simplest situation is when a number is too big to fit in a cell. In that case, Excel shows ####### in the cell, just to warn you that you need to make the cell wider to display the number. I'll talk about adjusting column widths in Chapter 21, "Getting Around"—and if you haven't already adjusted a column width, Excel should be smart enough to automatically adjust the width to hold your widest entry—but if you hit the problem before you read the next chapter, just double-click the vertical bar to the right of the column heading and the column will expand, growing wide enough to accommodate the widest entry in the column.

Other # warning values aren't so benevolent. These are the ones you're most likely to encounter, in "normal" business spreadsheets:

- #VALUE! appears when you try to use a text string in an arithmetic formula. For example, if cell B1 contains the text Apples, and you type the formula =B1*3, you'll get the #VALUE! error.

- #NAME! will pop up if you forget to put the colon in a range name. For example, the formula =SUM(B2F6) will trigger a #NAME! error.

- #REF! usually happens when you delete a cell that's needed for a formula. Say cell B4 contains the formula =B3+7, and you delete the B3 cell. B4 will come up with #REF!.

To get more details on these and the other error values, #DIV/0!, #N/A!, #NUM!, and #NULL!, bring up the Office Assistant and type `formulas error values` (for some reason, error values isn't good enough!).

Show Formulas

Most of the time you want to look at the results of all the formulas in your spreadsheet. But sometimes it makes more sense to look at the formulas themselves. In Figure 20.53, I've switched test.xls over to show formulas.

FIGURE 20.53
Showing formulas in test.xls.

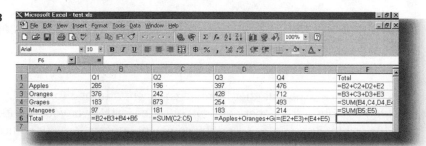

Fortunately, it's easy to switch back and forth between seeing formulas and seeing results. Unfortunately, the key combination is so weird you'll probably have to write instructions down on your monitor to remember it: hold down the Ctrl key and press the single open quote key, which is usually underneath the tilde, to the left of the number 1 on most keyboards. (On some it's way down near the spacebar.) To bring back the results, press Ctrl+` once again.

Comments

A couple of good friends of mine, Lee Hudspeth and T.J. Lee, like to call Excel spreadsheets the largest undocumented computer programs in existence. They have a good point. Spreadsheets that start out as little 8 × 10 cell quick calculators frequently end up a hundred times that size, and more often than not many such spreadsheets can be found running important parts of major corporations. True fact.

Just as programmers know how important it is to put comments in their programs (present company, ahem, excluded), it's vitally important that you put comments in your spreadsheets to show anything even remotely out of the ordinary, and to document when and why changes were made.

To put a comment in a cell, just click the cell, then click **Insert**, **Comment**. Excel responds with a little box (see Figure 20.54) where you can type whatever you feel is appropriate.

FIGURE 20.54
Comments are easy to insert and can save your neck.

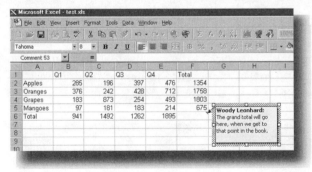

Excel gives you a visual cue that there's a comment attached to a cell by placing a small red triangle in the upper-right corner of the cell. Hover your mouse pointer near the cell for just a second, and the comment appears for your edification.

Getting Around

OU'VE ALREADY SEEN HOW TO GET around a spreadsheet by using the mouse and the directional keys on the keyboard (up, down, left, right). Those all come naturally; they're pretty much the same in every Windows application. Now I'd like to explore navigation a little further and introduce you to one of Excel's most important concepts along the way: named ranges.

Worthwhile Shortcut Keys

Gad, I hate shortcut keys in all the Windows applications. They're hard to memorize, and they almost never do what I expect them to do.

Excel 97, though, is a little different. At least there's some logic to the key combinations: Just remember to use the Ctrl and End keys and you can save quite a bit of time, particularly when you're trying to navigate large spreadsheets.

Here are the two key combinations I find useful. Your results may vary, of course:

- Ctrl+Home takes you to cell A1.

- Ctrl+End takes you to the last cell in your spreadsheet. Actually, it's a little more complicated than that. Say the last row in your spreadsheet that has any data in it is, oh, line 2345. And say the last column that has any data in it is CD. Pressing Ctrl+End would take you to cell CD2345, even if there's nothing in that cell.

- If you have a very dense spreadsheet with values in most of the cells, the End key can be helpful. Press End, then one of the arrow keys, and you'll be transported to the end of the current column (or row) of data.

And the way we have things set up, if you ever want to get back to the active cell (say you've scrolled into the lower forty and aren't quite sure where the active cell went), just press Enter.

There are other keys, of course, but most of them are too esoteric for my blood. You can get a list of them by calling up the Office Assistant and typing `shortcut keys`.

Named Ranges

Word 97 has bookmarks. Excel 97 has named ranges. The concepts are very similar, and the uses for both go far beyond what you might imagine. When you start to hyperlink workbooks, connect the various Office 97 applications together with features such as

WHY SUCH A WEIRD NAME?
Range names can take on only a very specific form. They can contain only letters, numbers, periods, and the underscore (_) character. Capital letters get treated the same as lowercase. No spaces are allowed. Worse, the name can't start with a number or a period, and the name can't look like a cell name. So _KilroyWasHere is a valid range name, while 52Skidoo and IV17 are not.

Paste Special, or move your spreadsheets onto the Web, named ranges are the anchor points within workbooks that you can access, retrieve data from, or go to.

What is a named range? Well, it's a range that has a name. (Rocket science again, eh?) You can assign almost any name you want to any range you like.

*Ε*XERCISE

Assign a Name to a Range

1. Start with our trusty test workbook, test.xls.

2. Select the guts of the spreadsheet, range B2:E5, by clicking B2 and dragging down to E5, or clicking B2, holding down the Shift key, and clicking E5 (see Figure 21.1).

FIGURE 21.1
To define a named range, start by selecting the range.

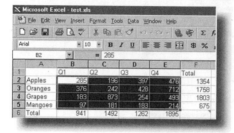

3. Now click in the **Name** box on the Formula bar. Excel responds by highlighting the current name in the box, inviting you to change it. In Figure 21.2, I typed the name `FruitSales`, thus giving the selected range a name.

FIGURE 21.2
Type a new name for the range in the Name box.

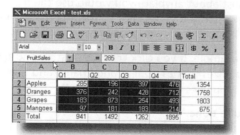

After a range has been given a name, navigating to it couldn't be simpler.

$\mathcal{E}$XERCISE

Go to a Named Range

1. In test.xls, click a random cell.

2. To go to the range called **FruitSales**, click the down-arrow to the right of the **Name** box

GO TO UNNAMED RANGES
Have a hankering to jump to, oh, cell F49? Use the **Name** box. Just click the **Name** box, type F49, press Enter, and you're off.

[A1 ▼], and choose **FruitSales**, as shown in Figure 21.3.

FIGURE 21.3
Using the Name box to go to FruitSales.

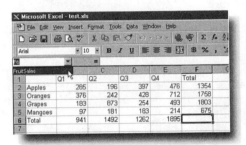

3. Excel selects the entire range called **FruitSales**, and the result looks precisely like Figure 21.2.

OTHER USES FOR NAMED RANGES

You can use a named range just about anyplace you would use the more traditional kind of range (that is, a range indicated by two cell addresses separated by a colon, such as A1:D5).

Take the Sum() function, for example. If you click cell F8 in test.xls and type =sum(fruitsales), Excel recognizes that as a valid range name and gives you the sum of all the cells located in the FruitSales range (see Figure 21.4).

Delete the formula when you're done.

Although creating and using named ranges is quite easy, getting rid of a range name involves a few extra steps.

$\mathcal{E}$XERCISE

Delete a Range Name

1. Start with test.xls.

FIGURE 21.4
Using the named range FruitSales to calculate a sum.

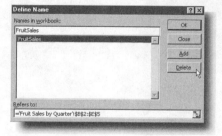

2. This is a little weird (like clicking **Start** to turn off your PC, eh?), but click **Insert**, **Name**, **Define**. You'll see Excel's **Define Name** dialog box, as shown in Figure 21.5.

FIGURE 21.5
The only way to delete a range name is via the Define Name dialog box.

3. Click **FruitSales**, then click **Delete**. That gets rid of the **FruitSales** name (note that it doesn't touch the range itself!). Click either **OK** or **Close** and you can verify through the Name box that **FruitSales** is gone.

Find

Excel 97, like Word 97, has a Find feature that enables you to scan spreadsheets for words and characters. Surprisingly, though, Excel Find isn't anywhere near as capable as the Word find.

XERCISE

Find Apple

1. Start with test.xls.

2. Click **Edit**, then **Find**. Excel puts the **Find** dialog box on the screen. In the **Find what** box, type apple, as shown in Figure 21.6.

FIGURE 21.6
Looking for "apple."

3. Click **Find Next**. As you can see in Figure 21.7, Excel finds **Apples** in cell A2. (Note that if you had checked either **Match case** or **Find entire cells only** in the Find dialog box, Excel wouldn't have stopped in cell A2. **Match case** is for upper- and lowercase; **Find entire cells only** forces Excel to look for whole cells that precisely match the text in the **Find what** box.)

FIGURE 21.7
A match on "Apples" in cell A2.

4. Click **Find Next** again. Lo and behold, Excel stops in cell **D6** (see Figure 21.8)!

FIGURE 21.8
Another match on "apple"—but this time it's in the formula.

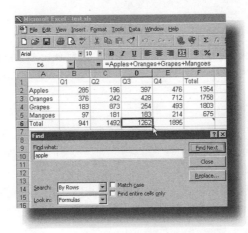

5. It may seem strange for Excel to match the word "apple" with the value "1262," but if you look in the Formula bar, you'll see why. The string "apple" is part of the formula that sits in cell D6. That's why you got a match.

6. You can limit Excel's searching to Formulas, Values, or Comments, as you can see in Figure 21.9.

FIGURE 21.9
Limiting Excel's searching to Formulas, Values, or Comments.

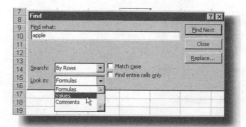

WHEN IS A VALUE NOT A VALUE?

These terms in the Find dialog box are awfully misleading. Excel has a very specific definition for the term *Value*, and it's blown completely away in this dialog box. (In fact, in this book I don't use the term Value in the same strict way that Excel does, precisely because of this dialog box!)

Comments, as you might imagine, are the Comments put inside cells, as we have in cell F6. That's fine.

But in this context, *Formulas* means anything that you typed into the cell, whether what you typed is a real formula, or any other kind of data, including text and numbers. Here, a Formula is anything that appears in the Formula bar, whether it's an Excel formula or not.

Values in this context means whatever you normally see on the screen, whether that's text you've typed, or a number that's been typed or calculated via a formula.

Excel's designers desperately need to differentiate between formulas and formula results, just as Word's designers differentiate between field codes and field code results.

WHAT ABOUT WILDCARDS?

Ah, you remember those from Word, don't you?

Excel supports two wildcards: the **?**, which stands for any single character, and the *****, which stands for any string of characters. Thus, searching for "a*le" will match apple, argyle, and ale, while searching for "gr?pe" will match grape, gripe, or grope.

7. Anyway, if you change the **Look in** box to look only for **Values**, you'll get a match on "apple" for A2, but not for D6. That's probably what you expected, and why you're usually best off looking for **Values**.

Excel can also perform a Find and Replace, just like Word. If you click **Edit**, then **Replace** (or click the **Replace** button on the Find dialog box, as in Figure 21.9), you'll get Excel's Replace dialog box, shown in Figure 21.10.

FIGURE 21.10
The options available to perform a replace in Excel.

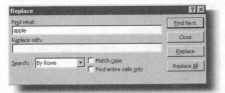

Replace proceeds much as you would expect, as it closely mimics the Find/Replace cycle in Word, but there are all sorts of strange gotchas and a great deal of caution is warranted.

WHAT DOES REPLACE REPLACE?
Replace will replace only text and numbers you've typed into the spreadsheet—it won't even go near formulas.

For example, if you replace "apple" in test.xls with some other string, the Replace touches only cell A2; it won't even look at cell D6. If you replace "12" with some other string, the number in E3 gets changed, but again D6 won't be touched.

Go figure.

All of this adds up to an enormously confusing situation. (To me, anyway.) Make sure you go slowly when you use Excel's Replace feature.

SOAPBOX ON
While I'm taking Microsoft to task over its inconsistent Value terminology and the strange way it scans for Replace strings, I want to throw one more barb in the direction of Redmond. Why oh why are Excel's Find and Replace capabilities so wimpy? Word can Find and Replace 'til the cows come home, with all sorts of patterns, style matches, formatting changes, and the like. Excel can't even perform a simple Replace without some sort of convoluted definition of what it's replacing.

Go To

Excel's Go To dialog box (click **Edit**, and then **Go To**) works much like the Name box: Type a cell address, or the name of a region in the box, press Enter, and you move to that location.

The Go To dialog box, though, has two additional capabilities that you won't find in the Name box. They can come in handy for getting around a spreadsheet.

First, it keeps a list of the locations you've jumped to most recently. (Whether or not you used Go To or the Name box.) As you can see in Figure 21.11, returning to a spot you recently visited is as easy as clicking the location, then clicking **OK**.

FIGURE 21.11
The Go To dialog box lists the most recently "jumped to" locations.

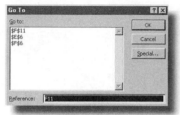

Second, Go To lets you cruise through an entire spreadsheet, looking for certain types of entries. If you click the Special button in Figure 21.11, you'll get the Go To Special dialog box shown in Figure 21.12. From this dialog box you can look for Formulas, Precedents, and much more.

FIGURE 21.12
Go To Special hops through a spreadsheet looking for specific kinds of entries.

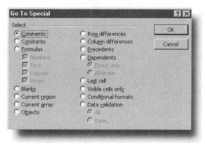

Multiple Sheets

Although all the Excel work in this book concentrates on a single spreadsheet, you can pull data from other spreadsheets in a workbook, or even other workbooks.

Welcome to the bang.

*E*XERCISE

Multiple-Sheet Formulas

1. Start with a clean, new workbook by clicking the **New** icon on the tool-bar. This new workbook should have three spreadsheets, identified as Sheet1, Sheet2, and Sheet3.

2. Type some numbers in Sheet1's A1:B2 range. In Figure 21.13, I've typed 2, 3, 4, and 5.

FIGURE 21.13
Type numbers on Sheet1.

3. Click the tab, down near the bottom of the screen, and type some more random numbers, this time in Sheet2's A1:B2 range. In Figure 21.14, I've typed 6, 7, 8, and 9.

4. Click the **Sheet3** tab. I'm going to make this a *total* sheet. For example, in Sheet3's cell A1, I want the total of Sheet1's A1 and Sheet2's A1.

5. Nothing to it. Click **Sheet3**'s cell A1. Then type an **=** sign, as if you were going to write a formula. In fact, that's precisely what we're going to do, using the old point-and-click method.

6. Click the **Sheet1** tab, and then click cell A1 on Sheet1. The Formula bar should read =Sheet1!A1. Now type a **+** sign.

7. Click the **Sheet2** tab, and then click cell A1 on Sheet2. The Formula bar should now say =Sheet1!A1+Sheet2!A2. That's the formula we want, so press Enter.

FIGURE 21.14
Put more
numbers on
Sheet2.

8. You're propelled back to Sheet3, where you started, and the number
   appearing in cell A1 is, indeed, the sum of A1 on Sheet1 and A1 on Sheet2
   (see Figure 21.15). Nifty, eh?

FIGURE 21.15
Cell A1 on
Sheet3 is the
sum of the
A1s on
Sheet1 and
Sheet2.

9. You could repeat this laborious procedure for Sheet3's B1, A2 and B2, but why bother? Hold the Ctrl key and click and drag to copy the formula in Sheet3's A1 into Sheet3's B1. Do the same for A2 and B2. Excel understands perfectly what you want to do, and modifies the (relative) addresses accordingly. As you can see in Figure 21.16, the formula it puts into Sheet3's B2 is =Sheet1!B2+Sheet2!B2.

FIGURE 21.16
Copied formulas mutate properly.

See how the Sheetname!Cellname address is such a straightforward extension of the cell addresses you've already used? Sheet1!A6:D8, for example, refers to the range A6:D8 on Sheet1. Nuthin' to it.

Care to take a guess what Sheet1:Sheet3!A1:B2 refers to, in this example? Right. It's the twelve-cell range, four cells on each of three sheets, that contains numbers. In fact, it's a three-dimensional range.

3D ranges can be named, used in functions (try =sum(Sheet1:Sheet3!A1:B2) in your spreadsheet), cut, copied, moved, sliced, and diced just like any other range. All you need is a little gumption and a big bottle of Excedrin—good-sized 3D worksheets will drive you crazy in no time flat.

I won't try to incorporate 3D calculations (or ranges) into the rest of this discussion. You'll have your hands full formatting and charting single spreadsheets without the added distraction. But remember that anything you can do with a single spreadsheet can probably also be done with a 3D range, although the details may prove, uh, challenging.

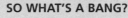

SO WHAT'S A BANG?

I'm not sure where it comes from, but for many, many years UNIX programmers have called the **!** exclamation point a *bang*. Somehow the pronunciation has carried over to the PC world in general, and Excel in particular. So, for example, =Sheet1!B2 is pronounced "equals sheet one bang bee two."

New Excel users tend to emphasize the bang when reciting a name like that, but experienced users generally pronounce all of the syllables with the same, flat tone.

I'll have you talking like an old Excel salt in no time.

Making Spreadsheets Look Good

THE TRIUMPH OF APPEARANCE OVER SUBSTANCE. Such is the fate of the formatted spreadsheet. But let's face it. If you need to use your numbers to get a point across, you'll end up spending an amazing amount of time formatting and reformatting those cells, borders, headings, and whatnot.

Format on, I say.

Resizing Columns and Rows

All in all, Excel 97 does a pretty good job of adapting automatically to most column width challenges. In most cases, you don't need to do a thing.

XERCISE

The Limits of Column Width

1. Start with a new, clean spreadsheet.

2. In cell A1, type eleven 5s, or **55555555555**. Press Enter. On most spreadsheets, Excel automatically adjusts the width of column A to accommodate the entire number.

3. Now try typing twelve 5s in cell B2. Excel is smart enough to realize that the number is too wide for column B. Further, it decides that you really don't want to expand the column width all *that* much, so it converts your number into scientific notation, widens the column, and displays as many decimal places as it can in the allotted space (see Figure 22.1).

FIGURE 22.1
Excel 97 adapts column widths to accommodate reasonably large numbers.

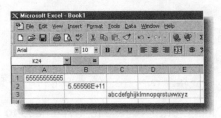

4. Excel doesn't try to change column widths when confronted by text that's too large for a cell. Instead, it flops the excess text into the next cell. You can see that in Figure 22.1, where I've typed abcdefghijklmnopqrstuvwxyz in cell C3. The part that doesn't fit into cell C3 shows up where D3 and E3 would appear.

5. As soon as something else occupies one of those "flop over" cells, though, the excess text disappears. Look at Figure 22.2, where I've put abc in cell D3. See how the extra text in C3 no longer flops over?

6. Hold onto this spreadsheet. We'll use it in the next exercise.

FIGURE 22.2
Putting any-thing in a cell stops the long text "flop over."

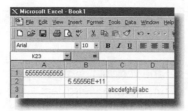

Excel 97 starts out with each column about as wide as 8.5 numbers, in the standard font (in this case, Arial 10 point). It then automatically expands up to a little over 11 numbers wide, should you type a large number, but it doesn't get narrower if you type smaller (in other words, shorter) numbers. Different auto width-adjustment rules apply for formulas, but let's ignore that for the moment.

In many cases you'll want to make column widths narrower so your spreadsheet will fit on a single printed page, or on a screen, and that brings me to an important point.

NARROW TO PRINT

If you're only going to adjust column widths to fit a spreadsheet on a single printed page, consider modifying the print settings instead of changing the column widths.

As you saw in Chapter 19, "Working with Workbooks," you can turn the page hori-zontal (*Landscape*). You can also have Excel automati-cally shrink the page so it will fit, no matter what. Using print settings is far, far easier than laboriously slogging through spread-sheet columns. The built-in printer options usually cre-ate a better-looking spreadsheet, too.

With that bit of warning, here's how you can adjust the width of the columns in your spread-sheet.

WHAT'S SCIENTIFIC NOTATION?
It's shorthand for big numbers. Excel uses the letter E to represent *times ten to the following power*. So, for example, 4E+3 is 4 times ten to the third power—or 4,000. (Remedial les-son: 10 to the xth power is 1 followed by x zeroes.)

In this case, 5.55556E+11 is 5.55556 times ten to the eleventh power, or 5.55556 * 100000000000, or (roughly) 555556000000. Excel actually knows the number is 555555555555, but it saves your eyes by show-ing the number on the screen as 5.55556E+11.

XERCISE _____

Widening a Column

1. Let's adjust the width of Column C in the spreadsheet we just created.

2. Hover your mouse pointer over the vertical line that separates the C and D column headings. The pointer turns into a weird Janus-like thing that points both forward and backward at the same time.

3. Click the vertical line, and drag it to the right (see Figure 22.3).

FIGURE 22.3
Adjusting the
column width
by dragging.

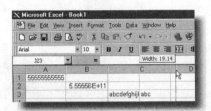

4. The Width: number you see in the yellow ToolTip is something of a fantasy. It's approximately how many numbers will fit in the column without over-flowing. (Note that all numbers, in most fonts, are the same width.) It has very little use when you're trying to scope out the size of a cell containing proportionally-spaced characters.

5. When you figure you're out beyond the z in cell C3, let go of the mouse button. Play with it a bit until you're happy with the width.

Sometimes you want a bunch of columns to all have the same width. Excel makes that easy, too.

XERCISE _____

Adjusting Multiple Column Widths

1. Continue with the spreadsheet we've been using.

2. Let's say you want to make columns D, E, and F wider—and you want them all to have the same width, when you're done. It's actually quite simple.

3. Select the D, E, and F column headings by clicking and dragging across all three, or by clicking D, holding down the Shift key, and clicking F.

4. Hover your mouse pointer over any of the vertical bars to the right of D, E, or F. When you get the two-headed arrow, click and drag the column to your desired width (see Figure 22.4).

FIGURE 22.4
Setting the
width of
three
columns
simultan-
eously.

5. Even if Columns D, E, and F all started out with different widths, they'll finish this operation all the same size.

There's one more column width trick you need to know—how to adjust a column's
width, automatically, so it's just wide enough for the widest entry.

*E*XERCISE
_____

AutoWidth

1. Continue with the spreadsheet we've been using.

2. Let's say we want to make column D just wide enough to cover the widest
entry in the column. Hover your mouse pointer on the vertical bar to the
right of the D column heading.

3. When you get the double-headed arrow, double-click. Excel makes column
D very narrow, just wide enough to accommodate the one, short entry in
cell D3 (see Figure 22.5).

FIGURE 22.5
Double-click
to adjust the
width auto-
matically.

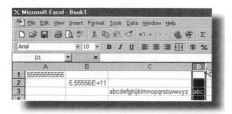

4. There's no need to save this spreadsheet. We won't be using it again.

If there's no data in a column, and you try to auto-adjust the width, Excel does
nothing.

Row height works much the same way as column width: Click and drag the horizontal line beneath a row heading to adjust the row's height; select multiple rows to adjust all the heights at once; and double-click to auto-adjust. (One small difference for the row height auto-adjust: if there's no data in a row, Excel

CAN I MAKE A COLUMN AUTOWIDTH ALL THE TIME?
Nope. After you adjust a column's width—even if you use this double-click trick to make it just as wide as the widest entry—the column stays the same size until you change it again. There's no way to say, "Excel, just take care of the width for me" and have it adjust the column's width dynamically, as you enter new data.

returns the row to standard height instead of leaving it untouched.)

AutoFormat

Although I love to deride Word 97's AutoFormatting capabilities, Excel 97 does a very commendable job of putting a large number of formatting options together—particularly options appropriate to smaller tables—and making them available to you with just a few clicks.

XERCISE

Format a Table

1. Open test.xls. We're going to put a pretty new face on the old Fruit Sales by Quarter spreadsheet.

2. Click once inside the main part of the spreadsheet. Excel is very good about snagging the whole spreadsheet, as long as you start inside of it.

3. Click **Format**, then **AutoFormat**. Bring down the **Formats to apply** box by clicking the **Options** button. You'll see the AutoFormat dialog box, as shown in Figure 22.6.

4. Click the various options in the **Table format** box. Watch as Excel shows you a sample of the particular format, each in turn, in the **Sample** pane.

FIGURE 22.6
Excel's handy-
dandy
AutoFormat
dialog box.

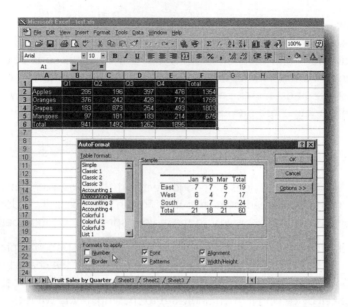

5. Note that you can modify Excel's built-in formats by the simple expedient of clearing the check box next to the type of formatting that you don't want. For example, the Accounting 2 format, which you can see in Figure 22.6, usually puts dollar signs in front of all the numbers. I didn't want the dollar signs, so I unchecked the **Number** box—and Excel refrained from formatting the numbers.

6. When you find a format you like, click OK. Figure 22.7 shows you how test.xls looks with the Accounting 2 format, but no Number formatting.

FIGURE 22.7
Fruit Sales
formatted
with the
Accounting 2
AutoFormat.

7. Go ahead and save test.xls. This one looks cooler than the previous version, doncha think?

After you've AutoFormatted a table, chances are pretty good you'll go back in and change some of the data. When that happens, column widths may change, you might have additional rows or columns that come up—all sorts of things can (and will) change. Fortunately, it's easy to reapply AutoFormatting. Just click once inside the new table of data, click **Format**, then **AutoFormat**, and apply the same formatting style you chose previously.

Formatting Cells

Where AutoFormatting does a good job with small tables, sometimes you just can't avoid formatting a spreadsheet manually. Fortunately, Excel 97 includes a wide variety of tools designed exclusively to make your spreadsheets look better.

The general rule in Excel is the same as in Word: select first, then apply the formatting. If you want to format a few characters inside a cell, select the characters first. (Do this by double-clicking the cell to go into Edit mode.) If you want to format an entire cell, select the cell by clicking it, then apply the formatting. If you want to format a whole column, click the column heading. To format a row, click the row. For multiple columns or rows, select all of them before formatting (use the Ctrl key to select rows or columns that aren't next to each other). To format an entire spreadsheet, click the rectangle to the left of the A column heading and above the 1 row heading.

Always, always select before applying the formatting.

WHERE'S THE FORMATTING STORED?
Except for formatting applied to individual characters, all the formatting in Excel is stored in the cell. If you select a column and apply formatting to it, *every* cell in the column gets that particular formatting.

If you subsequently select a few cells in that column and apply different formatting, that new formatting supersedes the old.

If you want to clear formatting out of a cell—whether the cell has any data in it or not—click the cell, then click **Edit**, **Clear**, **Formats**.

WHAT YOU SEE VERSUS WHAT YOU GET
Some of the AutoFormat formats listed in the Table format: box look great onscreen, but don't print worth beans. In particular, I've found the background colors on the Colorful versions wash out black-and-white printed text.

If you're going to print the spreadsheet some day, take a moment at this point and test print your AutoFormatted spreadsheet, to make sure you'll be able to read the results.

Number

Excel lives and dies by numbers, and the formatting options available for numbers only emphasize their central nature.

Format Numbers

1. Start with a new, clean spreadsheet.

2. Type a column of numbers that could be dollar amounts. In Figure 22.8, I've typed **6**, **7.5**, and **8.25** in column B.

FIGURE 22.8
Column B is meant to be a series of dollar amounts.

3. Let's have the numbers in column B appear as dollar amounts. Start by selecting the entire B column by clicking the B column header.

4. The easiest way to format numbers as dollar amounts is to select the appropriate cells, then click the **Currency Style** 💲 icon on the Formatting toolbar. When you do, the result is as in Figure 22.9.

FIGURE 22.9
Currency Style formatting applied to column B.

5. Keep this spreadsheet. We'll use it in the next Exercise.

Similarly, you can click the **Percent Style** % icon to show numbers as percentages, with no decimal places.

The **Comma Style** 〔,〕 icon on the Formatting toolbar formats selected numbers so commas appear to separate thousands, millions, and so on. The **Increase Decimal** 〔〕 and **Decrease Decimal** 〔〕 icons increase and decrease (respectively) the number of decimal places shown.

WHY DON'T MY PERCENTAGES COME OUT RIGHT?
Remember that percentages are fractions: if you type 1 in a cell and apply the Percent Style, you'll get 100%; type 0.5 and you get 50%. If you have a hard time remembering that percentages are fractions, get in the habit of typing a **%** percent sign after the number you're entering. Typing 1%, for example, will always result in a value of 1%, or 0.01.

Although the Formatting toolbar buttons come in handy, they can't hold a candle to Excel's mother lode of number formatting. To see that, choose the cells you want to format, then click **Format**, **Cells**, and click the **Number** tab (see Figure 22.10).

FIGURE 22.10
Hundreds of number formatting options are built in to Excel.

I think it's fair to say that if you can't find the right number formatting here, it just doesn't exist. Well, almost.

Alignment

Excel includes some very fancy options for aligning data within cells.

*E*XERCISE

Center Text in a Column

1. Use the spreadsheet you had in the previous exercise.

2. Let's center the peoples' names in their cells. Click the A column heading to select the whole column, as shown in Figure 22.11.

FIGURE 22.11
Select the entire A column for centering.

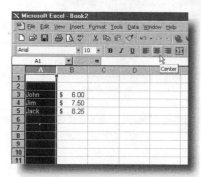

3. Click the **Center** ▤ icon on the Formatting toolbar. All of the names in the A column should appear centered in their cells, as shown in Figure 22.12.

FIGURE 22.12
Center everything in the A column by clicking the Center icon.

4. Play with the left, center, and right align buttons on the toolbar, and when you're done, click the **Align Left** ▤ icon to return the spreadsheet to its original state.

Excel 97 has a new alignment tool that has many long-time Excel users swinging from the rafters. It's known as Increase/Decrease Indent. Prior to Excel 97, indenting text was a real pain in the neck. Now it's one-click simple.

*E*XERCISE

Indent Cells

1. Use the spreadsheet from the preceding Exercise.

2. Select cells A4 and A5. These are the cells we want to indent, so Jim and Jack appear slightly indented below John. Click the **Increase Indent** ▤ icon on the Formatting toolbar, as shown in Figure 22.13.

FIGURE 22.13
First select the cells you want to indent.

3. Excel responds by indenting the text in the selected cells, as you can see in Figure 22.14.

FIGURE 22.14
Click the Increase Indent button, and Excel indents the chosen cells.

4. Try increasing and decreasing the indent a few times. You'll find that the text will never run out the left end of the cell, but it can be indented by almost any amount. When you're done, click **Decrease Indent** until the cells are back to where they started.

Although the centering options you've seen so far are just fine for most cells in the body of a spreadsheet, Excel users frequently want more control over headings. These last two alignment options apply more to headings than to normal cells.

*E*XERCISE

Center a Heading Over Multiple Rows

1. Continue working with the spreadsheet we've been using.

2. Say I want to center the heading Hourly Wages over the names and dollar amounts in our little table. None of the alignment options we've hit so far will do that—many people resort to typing spaces and jury-rigging things so they look right. Sorta. If they only knew how simple this centering trick can be!

3. Start by typing `Hourly Wages` in cell A1. I want to center that heading in cells A1 and B1, so I select both A1 and B1, as shown in Figure 22.15, then click the **Merge and Center** ▦ icon on the Formatting toolbar.

FIGURE 22.15
Type the
heading in
the leftmost
cell, then
select all the
cells you
would like to
include in the
centering.

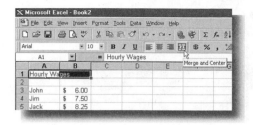

4. Excel obliges by merging together all the cells you've selected—in this case, A1 and B1—and then centering the title text (from the first selected cell) in the newly merged cell. See the result in Figure 22.16.

FIGURE 22.16
The Merge
and Center
button takes
care of both
merging the
cells and
centering
the title.

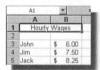

5. Hold onto the spreadsheet.

There's one last ultra-cool alignment feature in Excel 97's bag o' tricks. It's very easy to rotate text within a cell.

*E*XERCISE

Rotate Text

1. Continue with the spreadsheet we've been using.

2. Say you want to put in a couple of column headings, one each over the names and the amounts. And let's say those column headings are either a bit too long to fit nicely into the allotted space, or perhaps that you want to call attention to them by making them different. Easily done.

3. Type `Name` in cell A2, and `Hourly Amount` in cell B2. Then select row 2 by clicking the 2 row heading, as shown in Figure 22.17.

FIGURE 22.17
Lengthy column headings are in place, and row 2 is selected.

4. Click **Format**, then **Cells**, then the **Alignment** tab. We want to rotate the text in row 2 by 45 degrees. So grab the **Text** line in the **Orientation** box and twist it until it lines up at the 45 degree mark, as shown in Figure 22.18.

FIGURE 22.18
Rotate all the text in row 2 by 45 degrees.

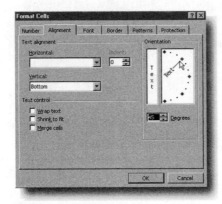

5. Click **OK** and Excel dutifully rotates the titles in row 2 by 45 degrees, as shown in Figure 22.19.

FIGURE 22.19
The titles in row 2 get rotated.

6. The text you see rotated onscreen may not look very good; typically the jaggies take over, and sometimes you can barely read the result. But if you're printing on a laser printer, or a good ink jet, I bet you'll be impressed by the quality of the printing. Go ahead and print a test page, just to see how it comes out.

WHAT, NO MARQUEE?
Surprisingly, Excel 97 doesn't have anywhere near the number of font formatting options available in Word 97. Aside from Word's Animation effects, which exude coolness with no redeeming social value, it's surprising that Excel gives you no fine control over subscripting or superscripting.

7. When you're done, keep the spreadsheet around.

The actions of all the Formatting toolbar shortcuts we've been using can be duplicated by choosing the appropriate combination of settings on the Alignment tab, as seen in Figure 22.18. If you're curious about the capabilities of a particular setting, click the **?** in the dialog box's upper-right corner, then click the setting that puzzles you.

Font

The font choices available to you are similar to those in Word 97, so I won't belabor the point here. Simply select the text you want to format, then choose the font name, point size, bold, italic, or underline from buttons on the Formatting toolbar. Or you can click **Format**, **Cells**, then click the **Font** tab to get the choices shown in Figure 22.20.

To change the default font, the one used in all spreadsheets, click **Tools**, **Options**, and click the **General** tab. On the **Standard Font:** line, choose the font name and size. Click **OK**.

Your choice will take effect in all spreadsheets you create from that moment on.

FIGURE 22.20
Rather hum-drum font formatting choices.

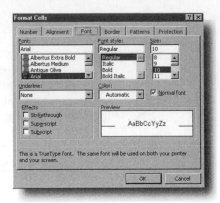

Border

Every new Excel user wants to know the best way to draw lines under columns of numbers. Somehow, a total isn't a total unless there's a line above it, right?

The answer: Borders.

*E*XERCISE

Draw a Total Line

1. Continue using the spreadsheet you've been working on.

2. Let's say you want to draw a double-line (all together now: "Oooooh! Aaaaaah!") under cell B5. Presumably you would then put the total of all the hourly wages in cell B6.

3. Start by clicking cell B5. Then click the down arrow next to the **Borders** ⊞· icon on the Formatting toolbar, as shown in Figure 22.21.

FIGURE 22.21
To draw a line under a cell, select the cell, then go for the Borders icon.

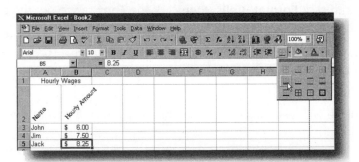

4. Choose the double-underline icon, which is the first icon in the second row of the Borders list. As you can see in Figure 22.22, Excel places a double-underline at the bottom of cell B5.

FIGURE 22.22
Choose the double-underline icon, and a double-underline appears on the selected cell.

5. When you're done drawing lines, nuke the spreadsheet. We don't need it any more.

Excel has a large number of Border formatting options, located on the **Border** tab of the Format Cells dialog box (see Figure 22.23). Although the choices are similar to those in Word, it's surprising that Excel doesn't support full-page borders, or easy methods for constructing watermarks.

FIGURE 22.23
All the Borders options under Format, Cells, Border.

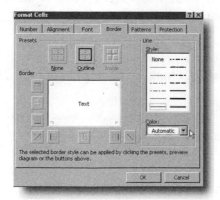

Patterns

Excel lets you apply background colors and designs to cells. To see the variety of options Excel offers, select the cells you want to change, click **Format**, **Cells**, and choose the **Pattern** tab, as shown in Figure 22.24.

FIGURE 22.24
Patterns you can apply to the back-ground of cells.

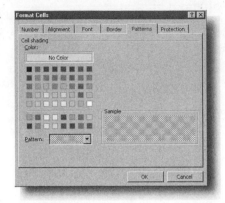

Insert Picture

One of the easiest ways to add some visual diversity to your ever-boring long rows of numbers is to add a picture.

☞ *I discussed Word 97's ability to insert pictures (Files, AutoShapes, WordArt, and Scans) in Chapter 12, "Special Purpose Tools," on page 239.*

Excel's capabilities are identical to Word's for all of those kinds of pictures: the picture gets placed in a *drawing layer* that floats over the top of the spreadsheet, and a full range of drawing tools are available. Refer to Chapter 12 for all the gory details.

Excel also includes a great, if limited, organization chart drawing tool. To get at it, click **Insert**, **Picture**, **Organization Chart**. You'll see an entire Org Chart application in Figure 22.25.

"Microsoft Organization Chart," as it's called, was developed by Banner Blue Software, the makers of Org Plus for Windows—a much larger, but extra-cost, organization charting program. The Office Assistant isn't available inside the Org Chart application, but if you click **Help**, then **Index**, you'll find a complete description of the program and its capabilities.

FIGURE 22.25
Excel includes a capable organization chart drawing tool.

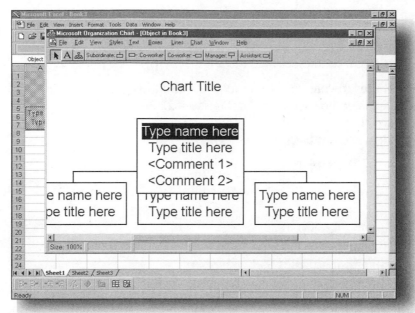

Hide Rows and Columns

Sometimes the best thing you can do to an ugly column is to hide it. That may sound a bit flippant, but frequently spreadsheets look better with less data in them, not more. Other times, you just don't want prying eyes to see where all the data came from.

Hiding a row or column couldn't be simpler. Just right-click the heading of the row or column you want to hide, then choose **Hide**.

Unhiding rows and columns takes a trick. If you've hidden a row, select both the row above and the row below the hidden row, then click **Format**, **Row**, **Unhide**. If you've hidden a column, choose the column to the left, and the column to the right, and click **Format**, **Column**, **Unhide**.

WHAT IF YOU HID ROW 1 OR COLUMN A?
There's always one in every crowd.

If you've hidden column A, click the **Name Box**, type A1 and press Enter. Then click **Format**, **Column**, **Unhide**.

Spell Check

Before you print an important spreadsheet, or send it out for review, you'll always want to check the spelling. In Excel, that's easy: click **Tools**, then **Spelling**.

Excel uses the batch spelling tool that's also available in Word 97. It consists of a single dialog box, which looks like Figure 22.26.

FIGURE 22.26
The Excel spell check-ing dialog box.

You can change, ignore, or retype a word. You can also add words that weren't found to your own personal dictionary.

☞ *You can edit your custom dictionary using the tools Word provides. Check out page 214 for details.*

Keep Titles Onscreen

Sometimes you want to keep column or row titles on the screen so that you can see what the columns or rows mean as you scroll through reams and reams of data. The means for doing so is quite simple, if you realize that Microsoft calls this capability *Freeze Panes*.

*E*XERCISE

Keep Column and Row Titles Onscreen

1. Let's go back to our old standby. Open test.xls.

2. Imagine that test.xls contains thousands of cells of breathtakingly interest-ing information. (That's a stretch, eh?) Further, imagine that both the first column and the first row of test.xls contain titles that you'd like to remain onscreen while you flip through that vast quantity of information. (This part's true!)

3. Click cell B2. Then click **Window**, **Freeze Panes**, as shown in Figure 22.27.

FIGURE 22.27
Freezing the first row and the first column so they remain on-screen.

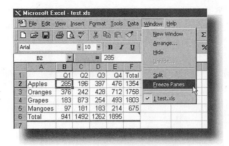

4. Now try scrolling, up, down, left, right. See how column A and row 1 stay on the screen, no matter what other rows or columns may appear? That's what Freeze Screen does. It lets you specify which rows and columns should stay put while the rest of your data scrolls on by.

5. To undo the Freeze, click **Window**, **Unfreeze Panes**.

There are many variations on this technique, as you might imagine. For help, bring up the Office Assistant and type `freeze panes`.

Print Titles

These last three "Look Good" topics only apply if you're printing your spreadsheet. The goodies you add here never (well, hardly ever) show up on the screen.

Print Titles is just like Freeze Screen, except it applies to printouts. The intent is precisely the same: show the contents of rows or columns on every page of the printout. That way you can set up your column titles in row 1, say, and have them print on every page.

XERCISE

Print Column Titles on Every Page

1. Let's set up row 1 in test.xls to print on every page. Open test.xls, if it isn't already.

2. Click **File**, **Page Setup**, and click the **Sheet** tab (see Figure 22.28).

3. Back in the spreadsheet, select row 1 by clicking the 1 row heading, as shown in Figure 22.29. Excel fills the correct value in the **Rows to repeat at top** box.

FIGURE 22.28
Tell Excel which rows or columns repeat on every printed page on the Sheet tab.

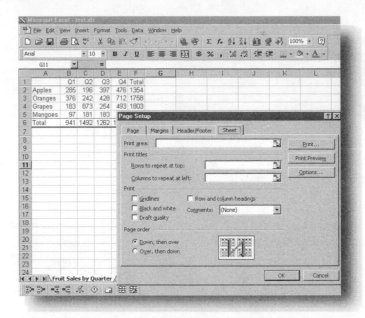

FIGURE 22.29
Go back to the spread-sheet and choose the row that's to be repeated.

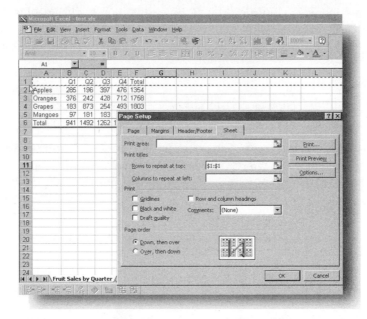

4. Click **OK** and the row (and/or column) you've selected will print on every page.

5. When you've had a chance to experiment with this, go back to the **File**, **Page Setup**, **Sheet** tab and delete this entry in the **Rows to repeat at top** box. Leave test.xls in good shape; we'll use it again in the next Exercise.

PRINT AREA
The row and column you choose to print on every page will print on the first page, too! So adjust the spreadsheet's Print Area, per Chapter 19, to exclude whatever row or column you have printing on every page.

Headers, Footers

Most of the time you'll want to print a header or footer on your spreadsheet pages. (Remember, a header is the text that appears at the top of each printed page; a footer appears at the bottom.)

This is yet another one of those situations where Word 97 and Excel 97 tackle precisely the same problem in completely different ways. So don't bother looking back at the Word section on headers and footers; it won't help you a bit.

XERCISE

Headers and Footers

1. Start with test.xls. We're going to gussy it up so it will print with a header and a footer.

2. Click **File**, **Page Setup**, and click the **Header/Footer** tab.

3. Click the down-arrow to the right of the **Header** box (see Figure 22.30). One of the choices there is precisely what I want to print in the header—it says Fruit Sales by Quarter—so I chose it.

4. I tried looking in the **Footer** box, but couldn't find what I wanted, so I decided to make a custom footer. To do so, I clicked the button marked **Custom Footer**. When I did, I got the Footer dialog box you see in Figure 22.31.

A HEAD LIKE A FOOT
Don't expect to get much out of this Footer dialog box. The buttons don't even have ToolTips! Whatever you type in the **Left section** box is left-justified at the bottom of each page. The stuff in **Center section** gets centered, and the text in **Right section** gets right justified.

To change the font, select the text you want to change, then click the A icon. From left to right, the remainder of the icons insert the following into the footer: page number, total number of pages, date (short form, as in, 8/19/98), time (AM/PM format, as in, 4:35 PM), the name of the current workbook (for example, book1.xls), and the name of the current sheet (for instance, Sheet1).

5. In my case, in the **Left section** I typed `Printed at`, then clicked the fifth icon (which looks like a clock), typed `on`, then clicked the fourth icon (the calendar). In the **Right section** I typed `Page`, then clicked the second icon, typed `of`, and clicked the third icon (##). You can see the results in Figure 22.32.

FIGURE 22.30
Choose a header from the drop-down list, if you find one you like.

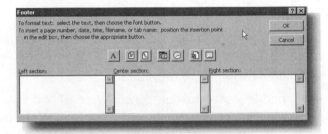

FIGURE 22.31
Excel's poor excuse for a custom footer helper.

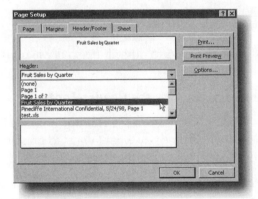

FIGURE 22.32
The custom footer I created for test.xls.

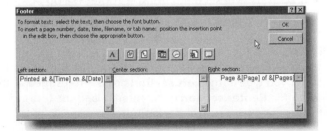

6. You can see the results of the typing in Figure 22.33, which shows test.xls in Page Preview (click **File**, then **Page Preview**). Actually, the print is so small I'd better spell it out for you. The header, centered, says Fruit Sales by Quarter. The footer, on the left, says Printed at 4:42 PM on 5/24/98. On the right, it says Page 1 of 1.

FIGURE 22.33
How the final
page looks.

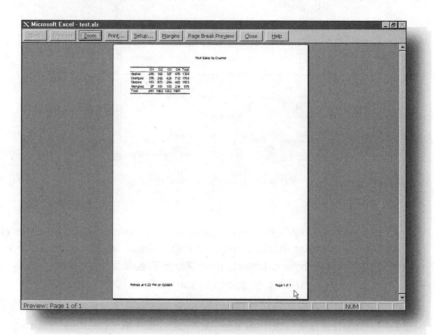

7. Save test.xls. It keeps getting better and better, eh?

Page Break Preview

There's one last spreadsheet formatting trick that you need to know about, if you ever get to the point where you're printing big spreadsheets. It's called Page Break Preview, and it's the best thing since sliced bread. Unfortunately, the online documentation for Page Break Preview consists of two paragraphs, with no real instructions.

To go into Page Break Preview, click **View**, then **Page Break Preview** (see Figure 22.34). That part's easy.

FIGURE 22.34
Page Break
Preview.

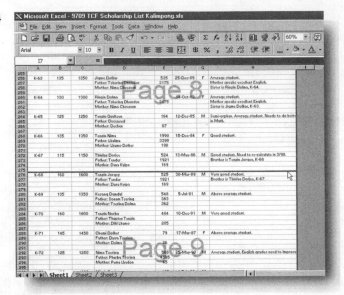

Page Break Preview lets you set page breaks manually by clicking and dragging a dark blue line that marks off where pages begin and end. You can always set a page break by clicking **Insert**, then **Page Break**, but that method can be mighty tedious when you have to precisely paginate a 100-page report.

As you can see in Figure 22.34, Excel offers you a preview of how the pages will break, with a heavy dotted horizontal line signifying where the page will end. Changing the page breaks is as easy as dragging that horizontal line to where you want the page break to occur. Excel then reshuffles everything for you, quickly, and you can continue scanning for the next page break.

HOW TO WORK PAGE BREAK PREVIEW

There's a trick. When working in Page Break Preview, you should always, always move the dotted line *up*! If you move a dotted line down, Excel gets all confused because you're telling it to print more data on a page than the page can hold.

Keep moving the dotted lines up and you'll have your report properly paginated in no time.

Sometimes when you set page breaks manually, the whole document seems to get screwed up, and you really want to start all over again. If you ever want to have Excel remove all your manual page breaks, right-click anywhere inside the spreadsheet, and choose **Reset All Page Breaks**, as shown in Figure 22.35.

FIGURE 22.35
To reset all the manually inserted page breaks, right-click inside the spread-sheet.

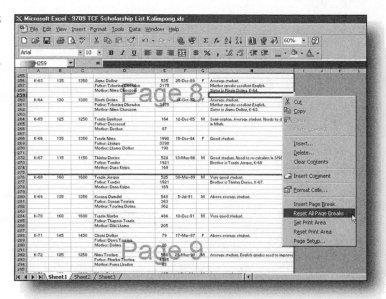

As far as I know, Reset All Page Breaks isn't mentioned anywhere in the documentation.

23

Excel-lent Charts

QUITE POSSIBLY THE COOLEST PART OF Office 97, Excel's charting feature lets you convert all those boring numbers into whiz-bang pictures. The most remarkable part? You need to understand only a few simple concepts, and click the right button. Excel does all the heavy lifting. It's amazing.

Making a New Chart

Before you start to create a new chart, you have to ask yourself one simple question: Do you want the chart to appear on the spreadsheet along with the data, or would you rather have it on a special kind of sheet, called a *chart sheet*, all by itself? If the chart goes on the sheet with the data, you can see the data at the same time that you see the graph. If the chart sits on a chart sheet, you won't have to look at that (yech!) dirty data, or the gridlines that usually accompany the numbers.

The choice is up to you.

XERCISE

The Chart Wizard

1. We're going to make a chart out of test.xls, so open it up.

2. First, you must select the data you want to chart. In almost all situations, that means you want to select the raw data, including row and column titles, but *without totals*. In Figure 23.1, I've selected the range A1:E5, which meets those criteria.

FIGURE 23.1
Select the basic data, plus row and column titles, but without totals.

HOW MUCH IS TOO MUCH?

Although there are no hard and fast rules, you need to be careful that the data you select in the initial step is pretty well consolidated. In most kinds of charts, if you get too much data the chart starts looking like an abstract painting of a pig pen.

3. When you have the data selected, click the **Chart Wizard** ![icon] icon on the Standard toolbar. That awakens the Chart Wizard, one of the most sophisticated pieces of software in Office 97.

4. First, the Chart Wizard wants to know what kind of chart you want to create. Take your time, because there are hundreds of choices—and you can make up your own chart types on the **Custom Types** tab. In Figure 23.2, I wanted to check out the 3D Stacked Column chart, which is the Column chart shown in the second row and second column of the Chart sub-type box.

FIGURE 23.2
Choose a Chart sub-type of 3D stacked columns.

5. Any time you want to see how your data will look when poured into a particular type of chart, click the **Press and hold to view sample** button, as I have in Figure 23.3.

FIGURE 23.3
Previewing the Fruit Sales data in 3D stacked column format.

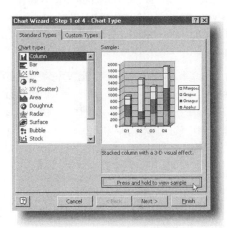

6. When you're satisfied that you have the right kind of chart, click the **Next** button. The Chart Wizard advances to the next step, where it verifies that you've selected the data you really want to show in the chart. In my case (see Figure 23.4), I was careful to select the data properly. But if you flubbed your choice, click the **Collapse Dialog Box** icon next to the **Data Range** box, and then go back to your spreadsheet and make the right selection.

FIGURE 23.4
Verify that
you selected
the correct
data when
you started
the Chart
Wizard.

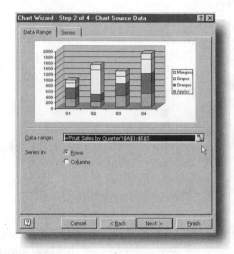

7. When you have the correct data selected, click the **Next** button. The Chart Wizard now presents you with a fascinating array of options. I won't go through all the details (you'd be sitting here till next Tuesday), but I would like to show you some of the high points.

8. Under the **Titles** tab, the Chart Wizard lets you type titles for your x-, y-, and z-axes. (Remedial lesson: The x-axis runs horizontally across the bottom; the y-axis runs vertically up the left side, and the z-axis is a weird thing that's hard to visualize, but for most 3D graphs the z title goes in the same general place as the y title.) In Figure 23.5, I've given my chart a title of Fruit Sales by Quarter, I've identified the x-axis as **1998**, and the z-axis as **Metric Tons**.

9. Skipping lightly over to the **Data Labels** tab, I wanted to point out that you can put labels—that is, actual values—at various points on the chart (see Figure 23.6). I didn't want to put data labels on this chart because it looks very cluttered. But if you want to show actual values to support the numbers on the gridlines, this is the place you set them up.

FIGURE 23.5
Assign titles
to the chart,
and the axes
on the Titles
tab.

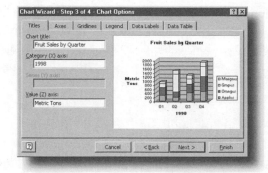

FIGURE 23.6
The Data
Labels tab
lets you put
actual data
values in your
chart for
emphasis or
clarity.

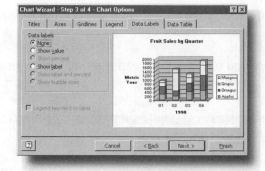

10. Behind the **Data Table** tab, you can actually have the Chart Wizard show a
small table on the chart that lists all the data. To do so, check the **Show
data labels** box (see Figure 23.7). Again, to avoid clutter, I didn't end up
putting Data labels on the Fruit Sales by Quarter chart, but this preview
should give you a good idea of what could have been.

FIGURE 23.7
The Chart
Wizard will
put all the
data on the
chart, if you
ask it.

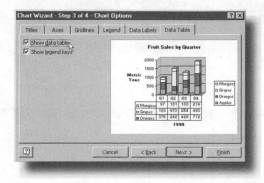

11. When you're done playing with the option tabs, click **Next**. The Chart Wizard asks you its last question: Where do you want to put the chart? In Figure 23.8, I've chosen to put the chart on a new sheet called Chart1.

FIGURE 23.8
The final
Chart Wizard
question:
Where to
put it?

12. Click **Finish** and the Chart Wizard sets up the chart precisely the way you've described it.

The Chart Wizard dumps you out in your spreadsheet, or in your new chart sheet if you chose to put the chart on a new sheet. In Figure 23.9, my chart is almost done.

FIGURE 23.9
First stab at
the Fruit
Sales by
Quarter
chart.

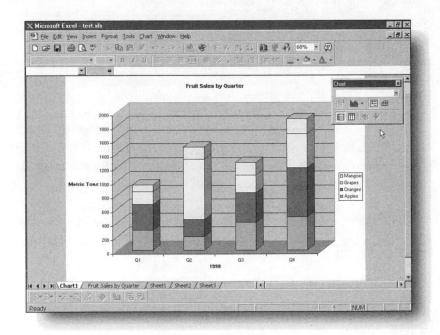

Note the Chart toolbar, which I've placed in the upper-right corner of Figure 23.9. You can change any part of a chart—including any or all the choices made in the Chart Wizard—by twiddling with settings on this toolbar.

Editing an Existing Chart

Now that the basic chart's in place, it's time to tweak things a bit. I'll start by changing one of the titles on the chart.

*E*XERCISE

Change a Chart's Appearance

1. We'll continue working with the chart on sheet Chart1 in test.xls.

2. See the axis title over on the left, the one that says Metric Tons? (It's actually a z-axis title, but that's only because I decided to use a 3D stacked bar chart; in any 2D chart it would be the y-axis title.) Let's rotate that title by 90 degrees.

3. Click the title you want to change. Then click the **Format Selected Object** icon on the Chart toolbar. Excel presents you with the Format Axis Title dialog box, as shown in Figure 23.10.

FIGURE 23.10
Select the part of the chart you want to change, and then use the Chart toolbar to change it.

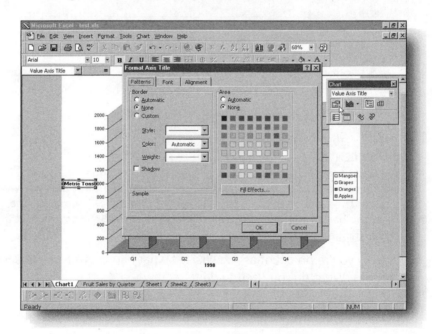

4. In this case, you want to change the alignment of the title, so click the **Alignment** tab (see Figure 23.11). Excel shows its alignment dialog box.

FIGURE 23.11
To align the title, click the Alignment tab.

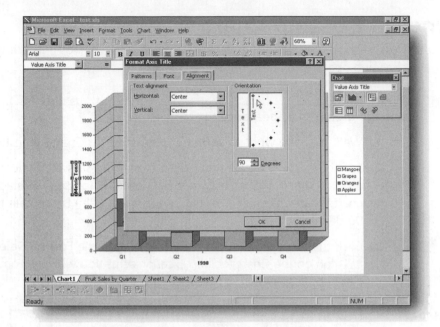

5. To rotate the text by 90 degrees, click the Text- graphic handle and rotate it upward. Click **OK** and note how the Metric Tons title has been rotated.

6. Save test.xls. It only gets better and better, eh?

CHART CENTRAL

The Chart toolbar holds the key to all your charting options. In general, it's easiest to modify part of a chart by first picking the object on the chart that you want to change. The name of that object will appear in the drop-down list at the top of the Chart toolbar. At that point, you can click the **Format Selected Object** icon and make changes.

By now you're no doubt asking yourself what happens when the underlying data changes. What do you need to do to redraw the chart?

There's a surprise answer: You don't need to do a thing. Excel goes in and updates the chart without your lifting a finger.

*E*XERCISE

Change Chart Data

1. Keep working with test.xls.

2. Let's see what happens when the underlying data—the data feeding a chart—changes. Click the **Fruit Sales by Category** tab; and change one of the data points. In Figure 23.12, I've changed cell C4—the number of metric tons of grapes sold in the second quarter—to 0.

	A	B	C	D	E	F
1		Q1	Q2	Q3	Q4	Total
2	Apples	285	196	397	476	1354
3	Oranges	376	242	428	712	1758
4	Grapes	183	0	254	493	930
5	Mangoes	97	181	183	214	675
6	Total	941	619	1262	1895	
7						

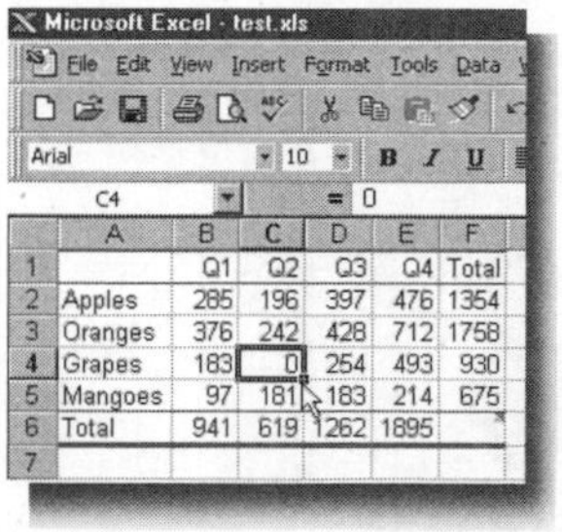

FIGURE 23.12 Change the chart's underlying data.

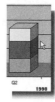

3. Now flip back to the chart by clicking the **Chart1** tab. Guess what? The bar for the second quarter (see Figure 23.13) shows that no grapes were sold!

FIGURE 23.13 No grapes in the second quarter—the data change worked.

4. Just to prove that this trick wasn't done with smoke and mirrors—fingers never leave the hands—click the **Fruit Sales by Quarter** tab again and change cell C4 back to 873. Flip back to Chart1 and let your mouse pointer hover over the Grapes portion of the bar for the second quarter. As you can see in Figure 23.14, the value of 873 has been restored.

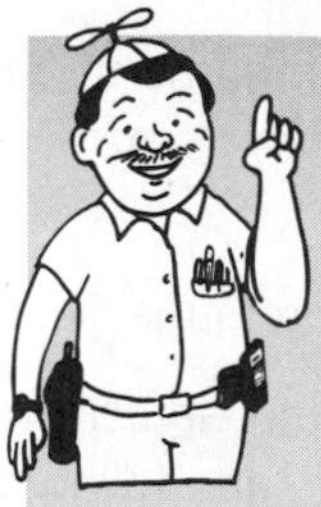

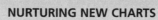

NURTURING NEW CHARTS

Many advanced Excel users place charts on their own sheets until the chart looks right, then copy or cut the sheet onto the main spreadsheet. That's a particularly useful technique because, if you have the foresight to put your chart on a new chart sheet, you can delete the whole sheet by right-clicking the sheet's tab and clicking **Delete**. That's a clean way to get rid of your old, failed experiments.

FIGURE 23.14
Restore the value of 2Q grapes sales, and it appears back in the chart.

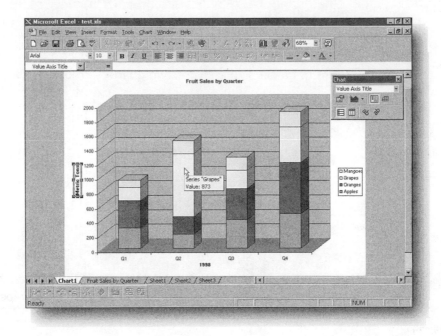

5. Save test.xls. We'll use it again.

Deleting Charts

Charts can be moved, resized, or deleted, just like other pictures in the Excel drawing layer. Simply click once on the chart's border:

- To move the chart, click in the middle and drag it.

- To resize the chart, grab one of the resizing handles (the little squares) and push it around. To keep from squishing the chart, use the resizing handles in the corners.

- To delete the chart, press the Del or Delete key.

You can move, resize, or delete elements of a chart similarly. Just click once on the element you want to mangle, and follow the usual procedure.

Entire charts can also be copied, cut, and pasted: Select the chart and use the **Cut**, **Copy** and **Paste** items on the **Edit** menu, or the appropriate shortcut keys.

24

Advanced
Features

Excel 97 has more ways to slice and dice data than a county fair huckster. If you know, or can guess, the name of a particular data analytical tool, try typing it into the Office Assistant and see what comes up. Failing that, log on to Microsoft's support site, www.microsoft.com/support, and see whether you get any hits there.

In this final Excel chapter, I wanted to take a look at some of the more widely used, general-purpose advanced features, just to make sure you know they exist.

Scenarios

What if?

That's the question you always hear when working with spreadsheets. What if Jimmy sells 20 percent more widgets next month? What if the weather gets bad in Kenya and the price of coffee goes up 35 percent? What if Long Term T-Bill yields drop by 2 basis points? What if my Adjustable Rate Mortgage goes up half a point next year?

Excel does "What if" like Carter does liver pills. You can create all sorts of scenarios, and compare and contrast them—if you know the tricks.

XERCISE

Create a Scenario

1. Start with our old standby, test.xls.

2. When you create different scenarios—different "what if?" situations—you have to figure out which numbers in which cells will change from scenario to scenario. Before you start the Scenario Manager, select those cells.

SELECTING RANDOM CELLS

The cells you select need not be contiguous—that is, they don't have to be next to each other. To select cells anywhere in a sheet, click the first cell, hold down the Ctrl key, click the next cell, keep the Ctrl key down, click the third, and so on.

3. In Figure 24.1, I've decided to create scenarios based on fourth quarter sales of all four fruits. Accordingly, I've selected E2:E5. Then I brought up the **Scenario Manager** dialog box by clicking **Tools**, **Scenario**.

BACK TO THE STARTING POINT

I've found it much, much simpler to use the Scenario Manager if I first create a scenario that reflects the current state of the spreadsheet—in other words, a Baseline scenario. I strongly recommend that you do the same because switching to alternate scenarios and then going back to the Baseline is so easy.

4. To create a Baseline scenario, click the **Add** button. Excel presents you with the Add Scenario dialog box. In Figure 24.2, I've created a scenario called `Baseline`. With the name chosen and the changing cells specified, click **OK**.

5. Next, you have to tell Excel what values this scenario will use for the chosen cells. In the case of a Baseline scenario, as in Figure 24.3, you don't want to change the values, so simply click **OK**.

FIGURE 24.1
Scenario
Manager
starts with
fourth quar-
ter fruit sales
selected.

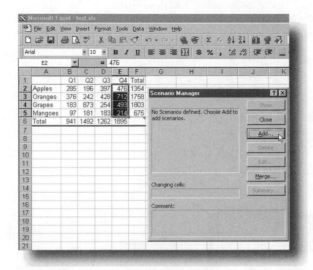

FIGURE 24.2
Adding the
Baseline
scenario.

FIGURE 24.3
Set values for
the changing
cells in the
Baseline
scenario.

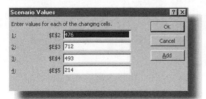

6. Excel hops back to the **Scenario Manager** (see Figure 24.4). This time, you have the Baseline scenario firmly established, so you can switch to it (by clicking the **Show** button) at any time.

7. Click the **Add** button in the **Scenario Manager** to add your first scenario. In Figure 24.5, I've called this scenario **Fourth Quarter Goes to the Dogs**. With the scenario name and changing cells specified, click **OK**.

FIGURE 24.4
Scenario
Manager
now contains
a Baseline
scenario.

FIGURE 24.5
Creating a
new scenario,
Fourth
Quarter Goes
to the Dogs.

8. Tell Excel which values to use for this scenario. In Figure 24.6, I've typed numbers that are half of the Baseline numbers. When you're done, click **OK**.

FIGURE 24.6
The Fourth
Quarter Goes
to the Dogs
scenario
posits sales in
the fourth
quarter that
run half the
baseline.

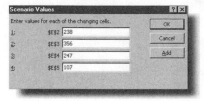

9. The Scenario Manager now contains two scenarios: **Baseline**, and **Fourth Quarter Goes to the Dogs** (see Figure 24.7). To see how the two scenarios stack up against each other, click the **Summary** button.

FIGURE 24.7
Two scenarios
are now avail-
able.

10. In the Scenario Summary dialog box, you have to tell Excel what kind of report you want, and which cells interest you—that is, which ones you're looking at, in the various scenarios. In Figure 24.8, I've chosen a summary report (we'll get to PivotTables by the end of this chapter), and I've specified that I want to look at total sales for the fourth quarter, which is cell E6.

FIGURE 24.8
Choose the
kind of report
you like, and
point Excel to
the cells that
interest you
in the various
scenarios.

11. Click **OK** and Excel presents you with a **Scenario Summary**, created on a new spreadsheet with a tab of that name. In the simple example we've been using, Figure 24.9, the Scenario Summary says that the **Fourth Quarter Goes to the Dogs** scenario drops total fourth quarter sales by about half. (Not surprising, eh?)

12. Scenarios can do much more than summarize. You can trace through all the details of each scenario by clicking **Tools**, then **Scenarios**, choosing the scenario you like, and clicking **Show**. In Figure 24.10, I've chosen the Fourth Quarter Goes to the Dogs scenario, then popped over to the Chart1 tab to see the sales chart.

FIGURE 24.9
Excel's
Scenario
Summary lists
the scenarios,
their depen-
dent cells,
and the
results.

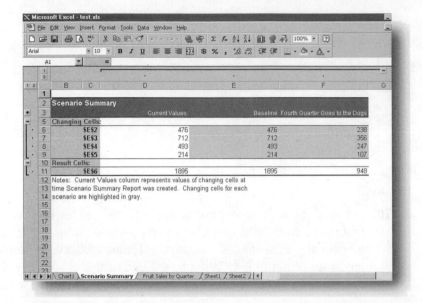

FIGURE 24.10
The Fruit
Sales by
Quarter
chart, using
the Fourth
Quarter Goes
to the Dogs
scenario.

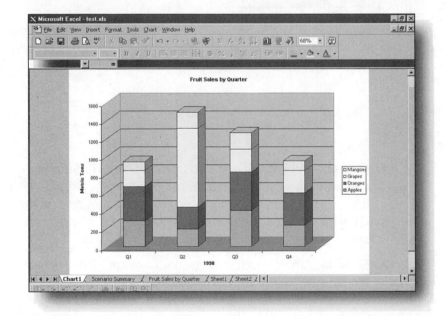

13. Explore a bit and create as many scenarios as you like. When you're done,
return to the Baseline scenario by clicking **Tools**, **Scenarios**, choosing
Baseline, and clicking **Show**. Save test.xls.

Audit Techniques

After a spreadsheet gets to a certain size—certainly, by the time it's more than a page long—the chances for errors grow enormously. I like to think of errors as falling into three categories:

- *Errors where somebody put a bad number into the spreadsheet.* For example, if the unit price for an item is negative, you can pretty much bet somebody made a mistake.

- *Errors where the spreadsheet doesn't calculate correctly.* The most common example I've seen of this kind of error is where a Sum() function doesn't cover the first or last cells in a series.

- *Errors generated by flaws in Excel.* These are quite rare, compared to the other two, but they do exist. You need to make sure you're using the most recent version of Excel, as I discussed in Chapter 2, "Precursors to Using Office."

Although no sizable spreadsheet is certain to be error-free, you can greatly increase your chances of creating a good spreadsheet by using some of the tools Excel provides.

You already have the number one bug-killing weapon available—that's the Auditing toolbar, which you've used numerous times in this book to trace precedents and nail down formulas. In this section, I'd like to talk about two more features that can save your tail: data validation and conditional formatting.

Data Validation

Sometimes it's easy to tell when data is good, and when it's bad. For example, if you type a person's name in a cell that's supposed to contain a date, you probably screwed up. Excel has a very easy-to-use feature called *data validation* that can help you keep data entry errors to a minimum.

FOR MORE INFO...
I don't have anywhere near enough room in this book to introduce you to all of Excel's auditing tools. If you get to the point where you are creating and maintaining sizable, important spreadsheets (say, where your money is involved!), I'd strongly recommend that you pick up a copy of *Excel 97 Annoyances* and devour the Auditing discussion that starts on page 215.

*E*XERCISE

Validate a Date

1. Start with a new, clean spreadsheet.

2. I've created a very simple expense report spreadsheet that uses column A for the date, B for the amount, and C for a description (see Figure 24.11). Let's set up the spreadsheet so it checks the date entries to make sure they're valid. Start by selecting column A (by clicking the A heading), then click **Data**, **Validation**. Excel responds with the Data Validation dialog box.

FIGURE 24.11
Setting up data valida- tion for col- umn A.

3. In the **Allow** box, you can choose from several different kinds of valid data. In our case, we want to check for dates, so the **Allow** box gets set to **Date**. More than that, as you can see in Figure 24.12, we want to ensure the dates fall between January 1, 1998 and December 31, 1999. When the criteria look good, click the **Input Message** tab.

4. Excel lets you write a custom ToolTip, which will appear whenever the user clicks a cell in column A, even before they type the data. In this case (see Figure 24.13), I've constructed a friendly message with details about the kind of data I want to see in column A.

5. What happens if the user types invalid data? That's what you get to decide on the **Error Alert** tab. In Figure 24.14, I've set up a rather terse message to prompt the user (even if the user is me!) to enter only valid dates. Click **OK** and the data validation restrictions go into effect for Column A.

FIGURE 24.12
Tell Excel to accept dates only between 1/1/98 and 12/31/99.

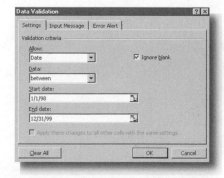

FIGURE 24.13
Create a message for the column A ToolTips.

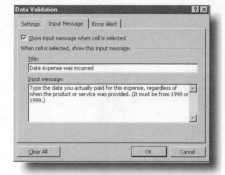

FIGURE 24.14
Use the Error Alert tab to compose a message for those who dare to enter invalid data.

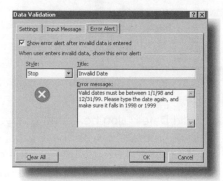

6. To see how the data validation routines work, click a cell in column A. In Figure 24.15, I've clicked A2. The ToolTip I wrote in Figure 24.13 shows up in yellow.

FIGURE 24.15
The ToolTip appears whenever the user clicks a cell in column A.

7. If I try to type an invalid date, number, name or otherwise—anything other than a date between 1/1/98 and 12/31/99—Excel pops up the dialog box I created in Figure 24.14. In Figure 24.16, I tried to get away with 12/31/97. It didn't work.

FIGURE 24.16
Type an invalid entry and Excel won't let you put it in the spreadsheet.

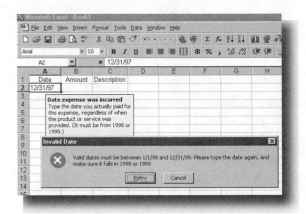

8. The two buttons in the Invalid Date dialog box don't give you much choice: Click **Retry** and Excel puts you in the cell, with the original entry highlighted so you can edit it; click **Cancel** and Excel wipes out the cell entirely. Either way, you can't get past the data validation routine until the number satisfies the validation criteria.

9. Hold onto this spreadsheet. We'll use it in the next exercise.

That's how you can use Excel to keep bad data from getting posted in the first place. Now let's take a look at how Excel can help you highlight iffy entries.

Conditional Formatting

We spent a lot of time in Chapter 22, "Making Spreadsheets Look Good," discussing formatting: You can make text in cells big, bold, italic, red, even draw boxes around the cells, or change their background colors.

Now imagine being able to do much of that based strictly on the value of what's in a particular cell. That's the concept behind conditional formatting—and the reason why conditional formatting can be such a powerful auditing tool. It can draw your attention to values that just don't look right and make it much simpler to catch data errors with a glance.

XERCISE

Highlight Big Expenses

1. Use the spreadsheet you just finished in the previous Exercise.

2. Management has declared that no single expense line item may exceed $250. (Do you have Management like that? I sure did, back in the days when I worked in the real world. Dilbert's got nothin' on this ol' boy.) By Management Dictate, we're going to set up this expenses spreadsheet so any amount—that is, any value in column B—over $250 appears in red, bold.

3. Start by selecting column B. (Real quick, go over and click the **Currency Style** $\boxed{\$}$ icon, so numbers in this column appear in dollars-and-cents form.) Then click **Format**, **Conditional Formatting**. Excel responds as shown in Figure 24.17, with the Conditional Formatting dialog box.

FIGURE 24.17
Select the cells that you want to have conditional formatting, and then click Format, Conditional Formatting.

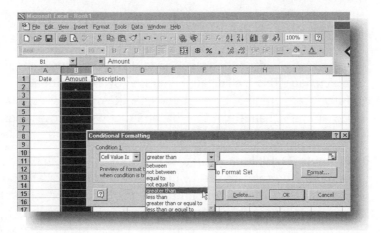

4. We want to make entries over $250 stand out, so click the down arrow next to the middle box and choose **greater than**.

5. In the third box, type **250** (see Figure 24.18).

FIGURE 24.18
Set your
selection
criteria.

6. Now choose the way you want to format all entries greater than 250, by clicking the **Format** button. Excel gives you the Format Cells dialog box, as shown in Figure 24.19.

FIGURE 24.19
Choose for-
matting for
cells that
match the
selection
criteria.

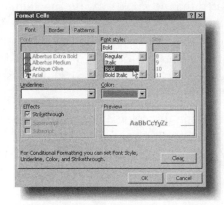

7. Note that you cannot change the font, size, or super/subscript for a conditional flag. (This is a limitation imposed by Excel, probably to simplify row height formatting; if Excel let you change fonts or sizes, it would have to dynamically change row heights, and that would pose a significant programming problem.)

8. In Figure 24.19, I told Excel to format numbers greater than 250 as bold and red. You can also specify borders (to draw a box around the cell) or patterns (that is, a background shading or color) for values that match the criteria. With the formatting set, click **OK**. Excel gives you a preview of the formatting chosen in the Conditional Formatting dialog box (see Figure 24.20).

FIGURE 24.20
Formatting
for cells that
meet the
criteria now
appears in the
lower box.

9. Click **OK** one more time and the conditional formatting criteria are set. Test it out by typing a number greater than 250 in the B column. In Figure 24.21, I've had the audacity to file an expense report with a $275 dinner at Chez Chez. Excel has responded by turning cell B3 red and bold.

FIGURE 24.21
Any number
greater than
$250 in
column B
now gets the
treatment.

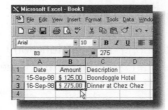

10. Try other criteria, in other cells. You needn't select an entire column or row, for example—you can choose just one or a few cells for special treatment. You can also specify different treatment for different values (for example, red if the number's too big, blue if it's too small) by clicking the **Add** button in Figure 24.20.

11. When you're finished, nuke this spreadsheet. We won't need it anymore.

I hope this excursion into creative auditing has given you a few ideas you can use in your spreadsheets, even if you're the only user.

IF in a Crossfoot

Bet you've been wondering when we were going to put that grand total in test.xls.

It's time.

One of the most common problems in spreadsheet land—no, make that *the* most common problem in spreadsheet land—is validating crossfoot totals.

It happens all the time. You have a rectangle of numbers, with totals to the right, and totals at the bottom, just as we have in test.xls. The grand total better be equal to the sum of the totals on the right. It also better be equal to the sum of totals at the bottom. If it isn't, something is out of whack.

There's an easy way to make crossfoot totals self-validating. And you now have all the tools at your disposal to do the job properly.

XERCISE

A Robust Grand Total

1. Open up test.xls.

2. Click cell F6, the place where the grand total should go.

3. You want to compare SUM(F2:F5) with SUM(B6:E6)—the totals on the right and the totals on the bottom—to make sure they're equal. The way to do that is with Excel's IF function. So bring up the IF function by clicking the **Paste Function** 𝑓ₓ icon on the Standard toolbar. You'll see the Paste Function dialog box, as shown in Figure 24.22.

FIGURE 24.22
Start validating crossfoot totals by bringing up the Paste Function.

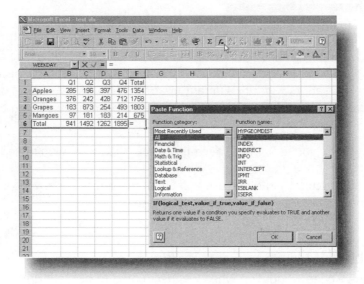

4. On the left, under **Function category**, choose **All**. Then on the right, choose **IF**. Click **OK** and Excel presents the IF formula construction kit shown in Figure 24.23.

FIGURE 24.23
Excel's built-in support for the IF function.

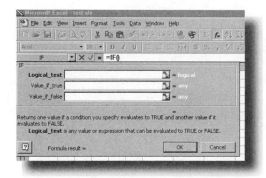

"TUNNELING" OUT OF THE DIALOG BOX

Figure 24.23 has three Hide Dialog Box buttons, at the right end of each input box. If you need to refer back to the spreadsheet itself to retrieve data, click one of those buttons. The big dialog box shrinks down to a single line. Choose up the data you need (perhaps by pointing at cells) and when you're done, click the **Show Dialog Box** button to get the dialog box back.

5. We need to retrieve some cell locations from the spreadsheet itself, so click the **Hide Dialog Box** button to the right of the box marked **Logical_test**. The entire IF formula construction kit turns into a single line, shown in Figure 24.24, which floats above the column headings.

FIGURE 24.24
Click the Hide Dialog Box button and the IF construction kit backs off to let you retrieve data from the spreadsheet.

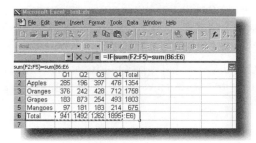

6. We want to see whether the sum of the right side totals equals the sum of the bottom totals, so start by typing SUM(and then click the range F2:F5. Type)=SUM(and click the range B6:E6, and then type). You're building the formula shown in the Formula bar, so you can use that for guidance.

7. When the IF formula is complete, click the **Show Dialog Box** button, which appears in Figure 24.24 immediately to the left of the J column heading. The IF construction kit reappears, this time with the Logical_test box filled out.

8. We want a formula that says something like, "If SUM(F2:F5) is equal to SUM(B6:E6), the crossfoots match, so put SUM(F2:F5) in the grand total cell; If they aren't equal, though, something is wrong, so put ERROR! Totals don't match. in the cell." I've filled out the entries necessary to do precisely that (see Figure 24.25).

FIGURE 24.25
The key test for matching crossfoot totals.

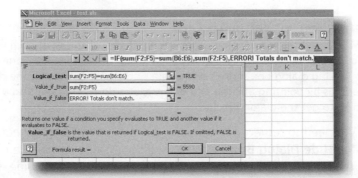

9. Before you click **OK** to get out of the IF construction kit, select the text **ERROR! Totals don't match.** and press Ctrl+C to copy it to the Clipboard. We'll use it in the next exercise.

10. When you click **OK**, the Fruit Sales by Quarter spreadsheet finally, finally has a grand total, sitting in cell F6, as you can see in Figure 24.26. Congratulations!

FIGURE 24.26
The Fruit Sales spreadsheet gets a grand total.

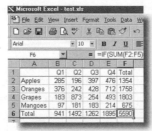

11. Don't close test.xls just yet. There's one final embellishment you might want to add.

Whenever I use an IF() formula to verify cross-footing in a spreadsheet, I like to toss in one little enhancement—I want to make that ERROR! Totals don't match. warning stand out. With conditional formatting, it's easy.

WHAT IF SOMETHING GOES WRONG?
If you get that ERROR! Totals don't match. message, there's no reason to panic. One of your crossfoot totals isn't right—either the formula for calculating the total got screwed up, or somebody (not *you*, of course) typed a number over the top of one of the subtotal formulas.

The simplest way to find where the error occurred is to break out the Trace Precedents program on the Auditing toolbar. You'll have the spreadsheet back together in no time.

*E*XERCISE

Emphasize Botched Crossfoot Totals

1. You should still be working on test.xls, from the previous Exercise.

2. Click cell F6, the grand total cell.

3. Click **Format**, then **Conditional Formatting**. In the Conditional Formatting dialog box (see Figure 24.27), set things up so the criterion matches when the cell is equal to ERROR! Totals don't match., the text you used in the IF construction kit in the previous exercise.

FIGURE 24.27
Setting up the criterion for conditional formatting of the grand total.

How to Get a Match

If you paste the text in that third input box precisely as it appeared in the IF construction kit, you'll be sure you get a match when you want it. That's why I had you copy the text at the end of the previous exercise.

4. Click the **Format** button and choose whatever formatting you feel is appropriate. In Figure 24.27, I chose bold red, which stands out pretty well. Click **OK** and your conditional formatting rules take effect.

5. To test the conditional formatting, go back into the spreadsheet and change one of the crossfoot totals. In Figure 24.28, I've changed B6 to 1. Press Enter and the message should appear—in bold red or whatever other formatting you may have chosen.

FIGURE 24.28
Trigger an
error by over-
writing one
of the cross-
foot totals.

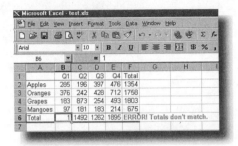

6. Click the **Undo** icon to fix the messed up cell B6. Then save test.xls. It's one robust spreadsheet now.

That's the technique I use for putting grand totals in spreadsheets. It's relatively easy and fast, once you get the hang of it. And it double-checks and triple-checks all the subtotals, automatically, with very little fuss on your part.

I hope that's given you a good feel for the steps you can take to make sure your spreadsheets are solid, and that they'll continue to work for years and years. A little bit of precaution in the Excel world can save you lots and lots of frustration. In fact, it may save you lots and lots of money. Don't skimp on the audits.

Conditional Sums

As we finish with Excel 97, I want to take you through two key features that can help you analyze data in ways you might not imagine possible. Both of these features, conditional summing and PivotTables, work on a specific kind of spreadsheet, one where some of the same data gets repeated. Rather than flapping my gums and beating my arms trying to describe what that kind of spreadsheet looks like, let me show you an example.

*E*XERCISE

Total Sales by Salesperson

1. Start with a new, clean spreadsheet.

A LIST

The kind of spreadsheet that best lends itself to conditional summing is called a *list*. There's no formal definition of a list (at least, not as far as I'm concerned), but it has several characteristics. Typically, a list contains a lot of raw data, usually without totals or subtotals. The text entries generally repeat a lot: You see the same text over and over again. The numbers, though, can be just about anything.

2. I've concocted a rather typical (if short) list in Figure 24.29. It's supposed to show sales by product by salesperson, for four quarters. You can make up a list of your own liking, or just copy the one here.

FIGURE 24.29
List of fruit sales, by product and salesperson.

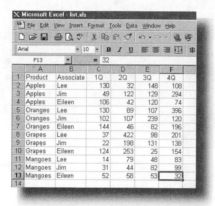

3. Excel implements conditional sums via something called the Conditional Sum Wizard, which gets thrown into the mix in a typical Office 97 install. The Conditional Sum Wizard lets you specify what kinds of data you want to add, and then calculates sums based on those specifications. Click one of the cells in the list, and then click **Tools**, **Wizards**, **Conditional Sum**. You'll get the first dialog box in the Wizard, as shown in Figure 24.30.

4. Excel does a very good job of guessing which data you want to use in the conditional sum. In Figure 24.30, it chose A1:F13, which happens to be the entire list. When you have the data chosen, click **Next**.

5. In the wizard's Step 2, you have to set the criterion for summing, and choose the column you want to sum. In Figure 24.31, I've told the wizard that I want to sum all of the first quarter sales numbers for the salesperson named **Lee**.

FIGURE 24.30
First step in
conditional
summing—
select the
data.

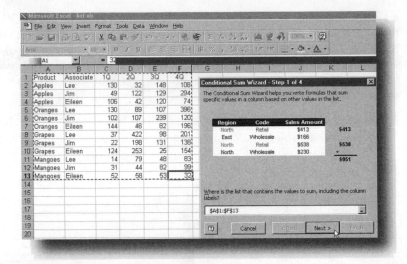

FIGURE 24.31
Choose the
column you
want
summed and
establish the
selection
criteria.

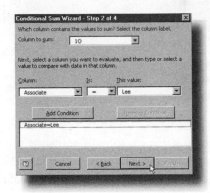

6. The wizard does much more than add up all the first quarter sales numbers for Lee. In fact, it creates a formula (a very convoluted formula!) that *calculates* the total first quarter sales for Lee. That's a very important distinction because it means you can paste the formula into your spreadsheet and, even if the data changes, the formula will continue to give the correct answers. In Figure 24.32, I've specified that I just want the formula to be placed in the spreadsheet.

7. Finally, you have to tell the wizard where you want it to put the formula—in this case, the formula that calculates total first quarter sales for Lee. In Figure 24.33, I've told it to put the formula in cell C15.

FIGURE 24.32
Tell Excel you want only the formula.

FIGURE 24.33
Choose a cell to hold the formula that calculates the conditional sum.

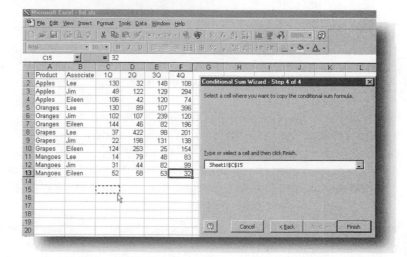

8. I went back and used the Conditional Sum Wizard to calculate second, third, and fourth quarter totals for Lee, and similar totals for Jim and Eileen. It took a few minutes, but not much more than that. Then, just to double-check all the totals, I added the crossfooting and grand total fields that I spoke about in the previous section, making good use of the **AutoSum** Σ icon to generate totals, and Excel's Fill Handles to copy formulas. You can see the result in Figure 24.34.

9. Go ahead and save this spreadsheet. Call it, oh, list.xls. We'll use it in the next exercise.

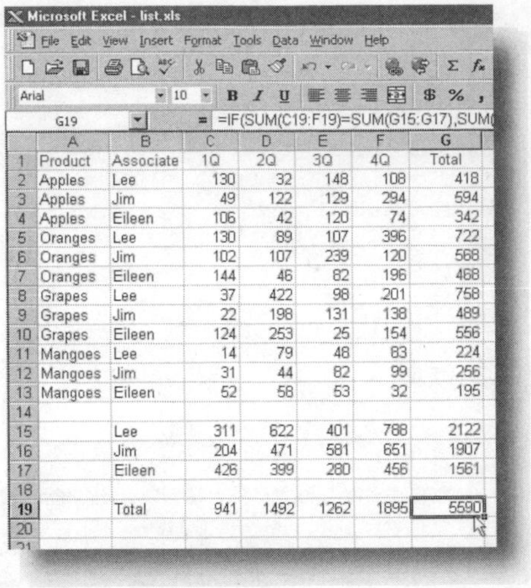

FIGURE 24.34
The filled-out
list, with
subtotals by
salesperson
and crossfoot
totals up the
wazoo.

PivotTables

Here's the one Excel feature everyone talks about and, for the life of me, I don't understand why people think it's complicated. I think it's fair to say that PivotTables rate as the premiere data analysis tool, certainly in Excel and possibly for most business situations, period. If you have a bunch of data and you're trying to understand it, PivotTables let you look at the numbers in many different ways. You provide the insight; Excel provides the spectacles.

What's a PivotTable? Sounds mysterious, but it isn't. Usually when you think of spreadsheets, you think in two dimensions: quarterly sales by product, as we've just seen, or inventory levels by location. There's a series of "things" going across the top of the spreadsheet, and a different series of "things" going down the side. That's fine and dandy; most people think in two dimensions (when they're dealing with data anyway), and spreadsheets are ideally suited to that kind of analysis.

Unfortunately, real data is rarely two dimensional. Reality strays from the spreadsheet ideal in two very different ways.

First, you might want to change the things going across the top or down the side—looking at different things might give you some insight into what the numbers are saying. For example, while you're looking at quarterly sales by product, it may suddenly strike you that what you really should be looking at is quarterly sales by salesperson. So instead of wondering why, oh, oranges sold so well in the third quarter, you might flip the data around and suddenly realize that the important point is that Lee's total sales in the third quarter went through the roof.

Second, you may want to flip into three dimensions. So instead of looking at quarterly sales by product, you may decide that the nugget of information you seek will best show up if you concentrate on, oh, how well each salesperson sold a specific product in a given quarter, and then step through the information quarter by quarter. Thus, you might discover that most of your salespeople sold a lot of oranges in the third quarter, but that Jim just didn't keep pace. That's how things go with real data. You can take a static two-dimensional view with predefined buckets and hope that the meaty information jumps up and punches you in the face. Or you can go digging for information and insight by varying the things you examine, and by jumping from two to three dimensions and back again.

PivotTables, uh, excel at allowing you to quickly and easily change things in a two-dimensional view. PivotTables also make it easy to arrange data three-dimensionally, with the third-dimensional slices appearing on separate spreadsheets.

That's why PivotTables are so powerful. They put you in the driver's seat so you don't have to sit back and passively take the data in predefined two-dimensional ways. Instead, you can dig into the data with both hands and, with a bit of luck, come up with an elusive bit of insight.

HOW HARD ARE PIVOTTABLES, REALLY?
If you know enough to construct a very basic spreadsheet—say, one on a par with the version of list.xls shown in Figure 24.29—you know enough to use PivotTables. Yes, it may take an hour or two to get the hang of it. But if you follow along here—even if you skipped all the rest of this book—you should be able to construct, analyze, and understand PivotTables in an afternoon. Maybe less.

PivotTables work best with lists. As explained in the previous section, lists are just spreadsheets with lots of raw data, repeating text entries, and numbers by the gazillion.

*E*XERCISE _____

From List to Pivot

1. Start with a usable list, containing data similar to that shown in Figure 24.29. The first row should include titles for all the columns, and there shouldn't be any blank rows. If you saved list.xls in the previous exercise, open it and delete all the totals. When you feel comfortable with the list, click a cell inside of it, then click **Data**, **PivotTable Report**. The first step of the PivotTable Wizard kicks in (see Figure 24.35).

2. We're going to use the list that you can see in Figure 24.35, so make sure **Microsoft Excel list or database** is checked, and choose **Next**.

FIGURE 24.35
The
PivotTable
Wizard can
work off
almost any
kind of data,
if need be,
but it eats
spreadsheets
for breakfast.

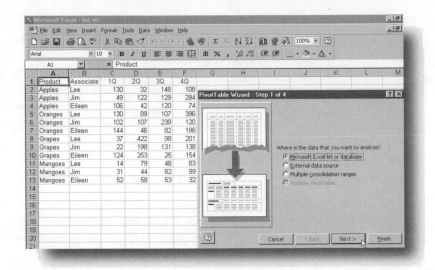

3. In Step 2, the wizard wants to verify that it has your data selected properly (see Figure 24.36). If you have a good list—particularly one without any completely blank rows—it will. Make any changes necessary, then click **Next** again.

FIGURE 24.36
Next, the
PivotTable
Wizard
verifies that
it has the
correct data.

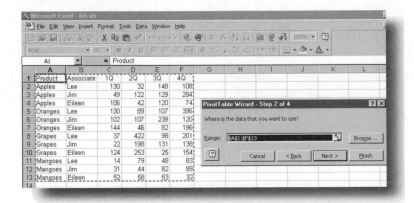

4. Step 3 is where things start getting interesting (see Figure 24.37). You set up your first PivotTable by dragging the field buttons (which contain the names that the PivotTable Wizard scarfed up from the first row of your list) into one of four locations: **Page**, **Row**, **Column**, or **Data**. This screen looks intimidating, but it isn't as bad as you think—and no matter how you start, you'll end up changing things when you pivot your PivotTable.

FIGURE 24.37
Set up the
initial pivot of
the PivotTable
in Step 3.

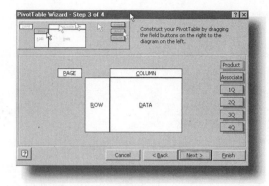

WHICH FIELD GOES WHERE?

In general, the columns in your spreadsheet come in two different flavors: the text columns, where you have many repeating entries; and the data columns, which usually (but not always) contain numbers.

As a first approximation, I like to drag one of the text columns to **Row** and all the rest to **Column**. Then I'll drag all the data columns to **Data**. That doesn't always work real well—and it ignores **Page** entirely—but it's usually a good starting point.

5. In Figure 24.38, I've dragged the **Products** onto **Row**, the **Associates** onto **Column**, and all four data categories—**1Q**, **2Q**, **3Q**, and **4Q**—onto **Data**. When you've made a first stab, click **Next**.

FIGURE 24.38
A first
attempt at
arranging the
components
of the
PivotTable.

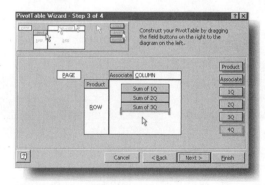

6. The final Step in the PivotTable Wizard, Figure 24.39, just asks whether you want to put the PivotTable in a new worksheet. I always do because it's easy to delete an entire sheet if I really screwed up. Click **Finish**, and Excel constructs your PivotTable.

FIGURE 24.39
Have Excel put the PivotTable in a new worksheet, and click Finish.

7. Your first glance at a PivotTable is bound to be a little overwhelming, so let's take the one in Figure 24.40 slowly and see what kind of conclusions you can draw.

FIGURE 24.40
The newly constructed PivotTable.

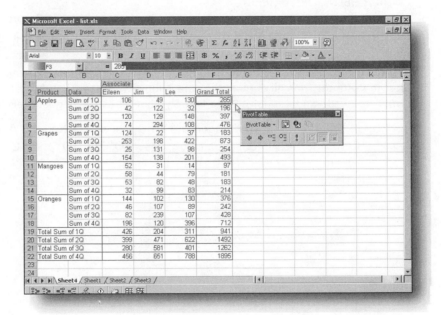

8. Looking at the information in Figure 24.40, you can tell at a glance that Apple sales in the fourth quarter beats the second quarter by a wide margin (which won't surprise any apple growers out there), and that a lot of that swing is due to Jim's salesmanship in the fourth quarter. Grapes go way up in the second quarter, thanks largely to Lee's efforts. Mangoes go way down in the first quarter, but Eileen somehow manages to keep her numbers up even then. And Eileen does a good job of selling Oranges in the fourth quarter, but Lee does better. Pretty neat, huh?

9. Now let me explain what a pivot does by flipping this table over. The numbers you see on the screen won't change, but you should start to get an idea of what we're dealing with in a PivotTable.

10. Click cell C1, where it says **Associate**, and drag that cell over to the right of cell A2, the one that says **Product**. Then drag the A2 cell, which says **Product**, and drop it just below the C column heading. You should have a PivotTable that looks a lot like Figure 24.41.

FIGURE 24.41
Swapping the Associate and Product categories.

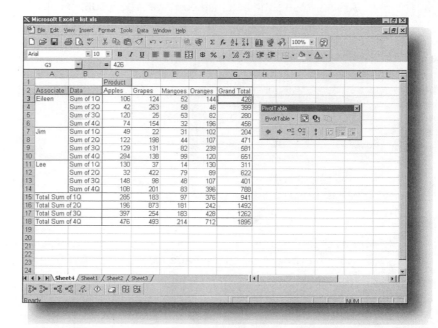

SCRUNCHING

Sometimes it's hard to drop these category headings precisely where they belong. In those cases, try clicking the **PivotTable Wizard** icon on the **PivotTable** toolbar. That icon opens up the wizard at the point in Figure 24.38, and you can easily drag and drop from there.

11. What you've just done is a pivot. Admittedly, it isn't terribly interesting because the data is the same in both Figure 24.40 and Figure 24.41, as you can readily verify by looking at the numbers while cocking your head at a 90-degree angle. But now you're in a position to understand what happens next.

12. Pivot the table back to where it stood in Figure 24.40. You may be able to do that by clicking and dragging. If that gets to be too much of a, uh, drag, use the **PivotTable Wizard** 🔲 icon on the **PivotTable** toolbar and drag **Products** to **Row**, and **Associates** to **Column**, as shown in Figure 24.38.

13. Now let's collapse all the **Associate** entries. The easiest way to do that is to click **Associate**, in cell C2, and drag it on top of the A column heading. Alternatively, you can click the **PivotTable Wizard** icon and drag **Associates** to the box marked **Page**. The result, collapsing all the salesperson information, should look like Figure 24.42.

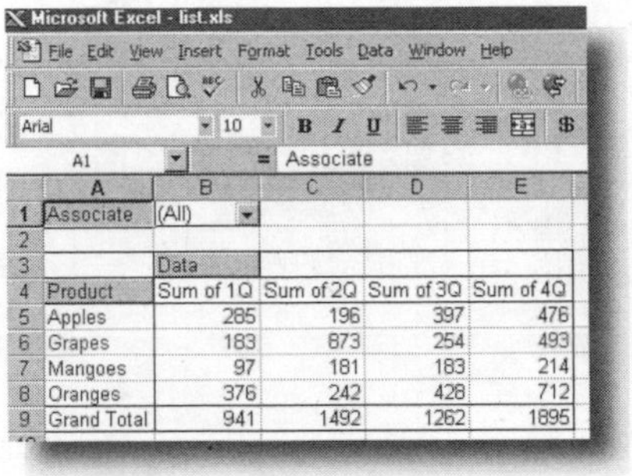

FIGURE 24.42
Collapsing the PivotTable on Associate by moving Associate to the "Page" block.

14. Play with this a bit. No. Play with this a lot. Try collapsing by Product, moving the **Product** cell to the **Page** location (cell A1). The result should look like Figure 24.43.

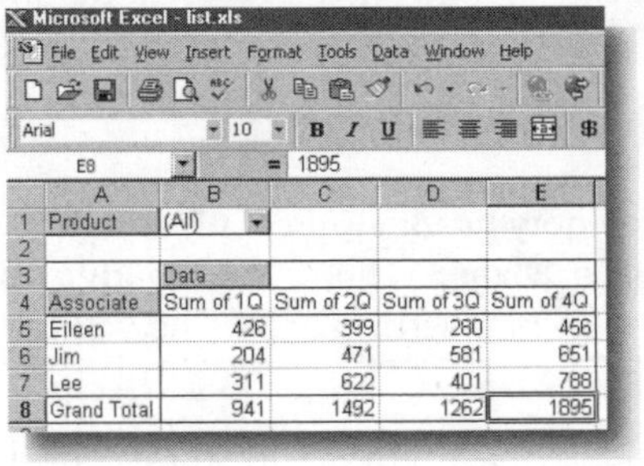

FIGURE 24.43
Collapsing the PivotTable by Product.

YES, VIRGINIA, IT IS A SPREADSHEET

These PivotTables look really cool, but you need to keep in mind that they are *real* spreadsheets, too! If you want to run a quick total, click a cell and then click the AutoSum icon. Insert a picture. Create a chart. Do anything you can do with any other spreadsheet. Knock yourself out!

15. I guarantee this gets positively addictive, especially if you have a stack of real-world data that's been bugging you with unseen and unanalyzed relationships. You can look at the data in so many different ways, so easily, you'll wonder how you ever lived without PivotTables.

Wait a minute! Wait a minute!

Take another glance at those PivotTables. Don't the numbers look familiar?

Compare Figure 24.42 with, oh, Figure 24.26. Compare Figure 24.43 with Figure 24.34. Is that little light going off in your noggin'?

If Excel can come up with PivotTables that generate all these reports from the raw data, why would you want to digest the data in the first place? Why not feed everything into PivotTables, and let Excel do all the hard work?

Why, indeed.

PowerPoint

25   PowerPoint Preliminaries   549

26   Working with Presentations   563

27   PowerPoint's Auto Support   587

28   Making Presentations Look Better   617

PowerPoint
Preliminaries

HERE'S A REASON WHY POWERPOINT TAKES up less room in this book than
the other Office 97 applications. To put it bluntly, there isn't as
much *to* PowerPoint as the other applications. Most PowerPoint
users never venture beyond the AutoContent Wizard, and the ones
who do frequently expect PowerPoint's concepts and terminology
to be similar to Word and Excel's.

Guess what? They aren't.

In fact, experienced Word, Outlook, and Excel users are going to
find the hardest part of PowerPoint lies in just finding things.
PowerPoint presents an unfamiliar terrain to Office adepts,

and you'll be battling that problem from the minute you start the
program and find that you have to make a choice (see Figure 25.1),
up front, before PowerPoint will even run!

So I'm going to approach the next few chapters as if you knew a
bit about the other Office apps—fonts, centering, inserting pictures,
and the like—but need to come up to speed on PowerPoint quickly.

Don't worry. You'll survive.

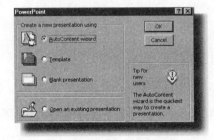

FIGURE 25.1
PowerPoint's
in-your-face
opening
screen.

A Note on Terminology

PowerPoint creates presentations. You knew that.

Presentations consist of *slides*, but these have nothing to do with the slides you put
in a slide projector. Each PowerPoint slide is really a computer screen. When I talk
about a PowerPoint slideshow, I'm really talking about a series of computer screens,
one after another, that together make up your presentation.

Although it's possible to have PowerPoint slides reproduced on 35mm slide film or
overhead projection transparencies—indeed, there are companies that specialize in
doing precisely that—you'll only be able to take advantage of the vast majority of
PowerPoint's powerful capabilities if you deliver your presentation straight from a
computer.

So when I say slide, I really mean *one screen in the presentation*. Got that?

Crucial Changes

PowerPoint's initial settings are an odd mixture of overly protective handholding with one resource-conserving but dangerous default. Very schizophrenic. Let me show you what I mean.

Exercise

Set PowerPoint Options

1. Start PowerPoint. You'll get the in-your-face screen shown in Figure 25.1. Click **Cancel**. You can get rid of that obnoxious screen, but if you do, PowerPoint replaces it with an even more obnoxious screen, demanding that you choose an AutoLayout. So I guess we'll have to learn to live with it.

2. Click **Tools**, then **Options**, and bring up the **View** tab. Click the **General** tab. Run the **Recently used file list** up to **9** entries, the maximum (see Figure 25.2). You might also consider checking the **Provide feedback with sound to screen elements** box, if you appreciate squeaks and squawks to confirm that your work is actually being recognized by PowerPoint.

FIGURE 25.2
Roll the
Recently used
file list up to
9, as you did
with all the
other Office
programs.

3. Here's one of those resource-conserving, penny-wise but pound-foolish settings I mentioned. Click the **Edit** tab, and roll the **Maximum number of undos** box up to **100**, as shown in Figure 25.3. I have no idea why Microsoft sets this initially at 20; the performance hit seems minimal on any reasonably powerful PC.

FIGURE 25.3
Give yourself
lots of Undo
breathing
space—cheap
insurance.

4. Finally, click the **Save** tab. Fast saves are always a bad idea; they don't add that much to performance, they make file sizes swell and, worst of all, they can corrupt files. Drive a stake through Fast save's heart by unchecking the **Allow fast saves** box (see Figure 25.4). While you're here, consider changing the AutoRecover (known as AutoSave in Excel) interval. If you don't often save your files manually, you might want to run this setting down to 5 minutes, or less.

FIGURE 25.4
Get rid of
Fast save.

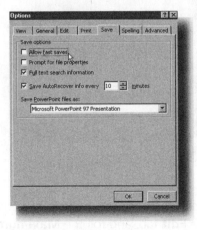

5. That sets your Options straight. Click **OK** and that splash screen will never darken your door again.

PowerPoint has one toolbar that you'll use rather frequently. It's called the Common Tasks (catchy name, eh?) toolbar, and I don't understand why Microsoft left it off the default screen. If you're running your monitor at anything more than 640 x 480 resolution, you really should put it on the screen.

XERCISE

Show Common Tasks Toolbar

1. With PowerPoint running, right-click any blank space on any toolbar. In Figure 25.5, I've right-clicked to the right of the Drawing toolbar. Check the box marked **Common Tasks**.

FIGURE 25.5
Making the Common Tasks toolbar appear.

2. The Common Tasks toolbar starts out floating, as you see in Figure 25.5. It tends to get in the way if you let it float. So click the window title bar (the part that says Common Tasks), drag the toolbar down to the right, and dock it to the right of the Drawing toolbar (see Figure 25.6). It fits there nicely.

FIGURE 25.6
Dock the Common Tasks toolbar to the right of the Drawing toolbar.

With those changes in effect, you're ready to start building a presentation with PowerPoint.

The Screen

There's no such thing as *the* PowerPoint screen. In fact, PowerPoint has five different screens, called views, each of which provides a different insight into a given presentation.

Let me show you the different screens, and what they contain. Let's start by creating a very simple presentation.

XERCISE _____

Create a Dumb Dummy Presentation

1. If PowerPoint is running, click **File**, then **New**, and click the **Presentations** tab. We're looking for the AutoContent Wizard, which should be the first icon in the **Presentations** area (see Figure 25.7). Click the **AutoContent Wizard** and click **OK**.

FIGURE 25.7
The AutoContent Wizard, first among equals.

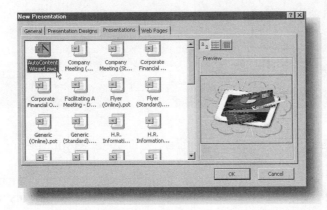

2. If PowerPoint is not running, start it, make sure the **AutoContent Wizard** button is pressed, and click **OK**.

3. The AutoContent Wizard kicks in. Just keep clicking **Next** until you can't any more, and at that point click **Finish**.

4. Let's save this presentation; we'll work with it. Click **File**, then **Save**, type `Dumb Dummy Presentation`, and click Save (see Figure 25.8).

The AutoContent Wizard leaves you in Outline view, one of the five views I was talking about. That's as good a place to start as any.

FIGURE 25.8
Saving the
Dumb
Dummy
Presentation.

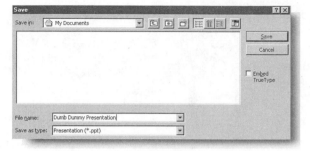

Outline View

If you think of a presentation as a big outline, where each high-level entry and the
text below it goes on a single slide, you'll have captured the essence of Outline
view (see Figure 25.9).

FIGURE 25.9
The Dumb
Dummy
Presentation
in Outline
view.

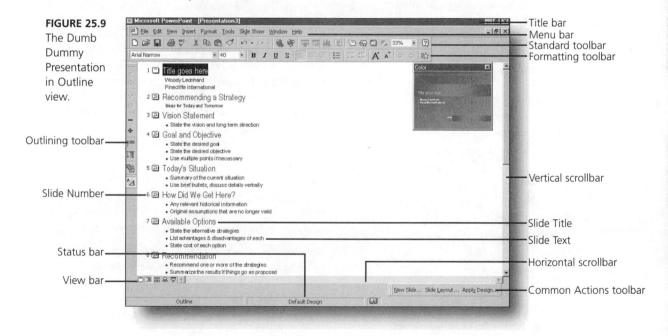

Working from the top in Figure 25.9, we have the title bar, menu bar, then the
Standard and Formatting toolbars. Except for the Slide Show menu item and a few
icons on the ends of the Standard toolbar and Formatting toolbar, you've seen all
this before.

Similarly, the horizontal and vertical scrollbars and status bar behave much like their counterparts in Word and Excel.

The View bar lets you select among the different views we're discussing here. Clicking the **Slide View** ⬚ button puts you in Slide view; the **Outline View** ▤ hops into Outline view, subject of the current discussion; similarly, **Slide Sorter View** ▦, **Notes Page View** ▣ and the **Slide Show** itself ▣.

The main part of the screen shows your presentation in Outline view. Again, you have to think of your presentation as an outline, where each line at the highest level of the outline marks the beginning of a new slide. If you think about it a bit, you'll understand why the Slide Number changes with each highest-level entry, and why the text at each highest level is called the Slide Title. The Slide Text—which is to say, all the text under a given Slide Title—appears on the slide.

TEXT IN OUTLINE VIEW

All the text you type into the Outline view appears on the appropriate slide. However, it's possible to put text on a slide and *not* have the text appear in Outline view.

Yeah, it's confusing, but the problem stems from the infamous Drawing Layer—the same Drawing Layer we had to deal with in Word and Excel.

☞ *I talk about the Drawing Layer extensively on page 124. You might want to look back there if the term Drawing Layer doesn't immediately trigger moans and make you break out in a cold sweat.*

If you put text in a slide's Drawing Layer—typically by using Text Box from the Drawing toolbar, or the **Insert**, **Text Box** menu item—that text floats above the slide itself and, even though it appears when the slide is shown, the text isn't really stuck inside the slide. Because it isn't really inside the slide, text in the Drawing Layer won't appear in Outline view.

If you think that's confusing, you should read the official (and unofficial) documentation on the subject. I swear, if you didn't know what the Drawing Layer was, you'd *never* understand what the references were talking about.

Anyway, the only text that appears in Outline view, as far as I can tell, is text that you type while in Outline view, plus text you type directly on the slide, inside the predefined areas for the slide's title and body text. Everything else floats above, in the Drawing Layer never-never world.

Down the left side of the Outline view screen sits the Outlining toolbar. The left ⬅ and right ➡ arrows at the top *Promote* and *Demote* selected lines—*Promoting* a line moves it to a higher level in the outline hierarchy, and *Demoting* moves the line lower in the hierarchy.

DON'T OVER-PROMOTE
It's very, very easy to accidentally promote a line to the highest level in the outline, and thus create a new slide. Keep a close eye on the Slide Numbers to make sure you don't fall into that trap.

The remaining icons on the Outlining toolbar are rather ho-hum. The up ⬆ and down ⬇ arrows just move selected text toward the beginning or end of the presentation—an action just as easily accomplished by clicking and dragging. The next four icons expand and collapse outline levels, so you can hide the Slide Text underneath a particular Slide Title. And I never use the last two.

Finally, as you move from slide to slide by clicking the text at the left, PowerPoint shows you a little thumbnail of the slide in the upper-right corner.

Some people like to work almost exclusively in Outline view, only flipping over to the slides themselves for fine tuning. Personally, although I spend some time in Outline view ironing out the general flow of a presentation, I like to work directly on the slides, in Slide view, to get the details ironed out.

As they say, the devil's in the details, eh?

Slide View

Flip over to Slide view by clicking the **Slide View** 🔲 icon on the View bar (see Figure 25.10).

Several screen actions should strike you immediately: PowerPoint has dropped the Outlining toolbar and put the Drawing toolbar down at the bottom of the screen. It's also shifted things around to leave more room on the screen for the slide. Those are pretty obvious.

What's not so obvious is the change in font—I have no idea why PowerPoint shows Times New Roman 24-point at the top of Figure 25.10; there's no Times New Roman text anywhere in sight. I think this is a bug, pure and simple.

FIGURE 25.10
The first slide
of the Dumb
Dummy
Presentation
in Slide view.

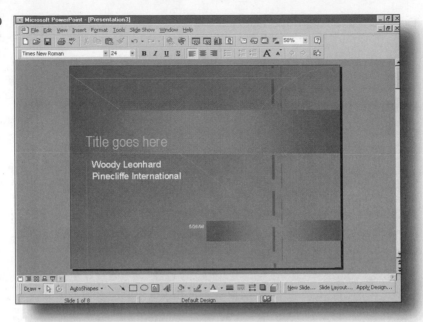

Also not obvious: Where did that date come from, the last line on the slide? Ends up it originates in something called the Title Master, which is sort of an uber-slide that affects all the real slides in the presentation. We'll wrestle with the Title Master in Chapter 27, "PowerPoint's Auto Support."

Finally, if you have the slide on your screen, try clicking the text. Although the slide may appear to be a solid piece of work, in fact it contains two areas—called placeholders—where you can easily click and type your own data. One placeholder has the text **Title goes here**. The other has my name and company name. Clicking and typing into a slide directly is a great way to make sure that what you see is what you get in the presentation.

Slide Sorter View

Click the **Slide Sorter View** 🔡 icon, down on the View bar. PowerPoint shifts to Slide Sorter view (see Figure 25.11), where you have a chance to see thumbnails of all your slides, in order.

While working in Slide Sorter view, you can click a slide and move it to a different place in the presentation. That's probably how you'll use Slide Sorter view most often.

FIGURE 25.11
The Dumb
Dummy
Presentation
in Slide Sorter
view.

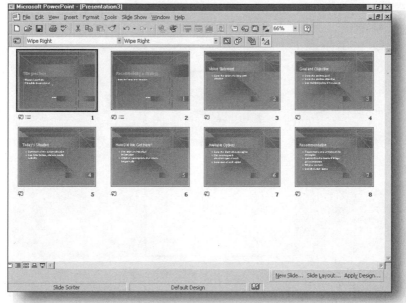

This is also the most logical place to work on transition effects—the way one slide transforms into the next (called a *wipe*), sounds that should be played when moving from one slide to another, even whether the slide should be changed automatically, not under the presenter's control. We'll look at Transitions in Chapter 28, "Making Presentations Look Better."

Notes Page View

And you thought PowerPoint only did slides.

Attached to each PowerPoint slide is a freehand text page which PowerPoint refers to as Notes or Presentation Notes. If you click the **Notes Page View** ▣ icon in the View bar, you'll get a series of pages like those shown in Figure 25.12.

At the top of each Notes Page sits a copy of the associated slide. You can enter any text you like in the lower Notes area. This can be handy if you need to develop notes along with your presentation, or if you want to hand out written notes to accompany your presentation.

I don't use it very much.

FIGURE 25.12
Presentation
Notes Pages
are visible in
Notes Page
view.

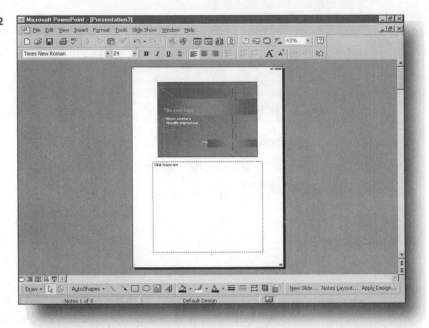

Slide Show

The final view is the slideshow. Click the **Slide Show** ⬛ icon in the View bar, and PowerPoint launches into the presentation you're currently working on (see Figure 25.13). Slides in the slideshow appear one at a time, starting with the slide you've been working on.

THE WHOLE ENCHILADA
If you want to see the entire slideshow, from start to finish, click **View**, then **Slide Show**.

In most cases, you advance to the next slide by simply clicking the mouse on the screen. There are several exceptions to that general rule, though. You can program the slides to appear at predefined intervals, whether you click the slide or not. More than that, though, if you click the small graphic in a slide's lower-left corner (or if you right-click anywhere on the screen), a host of navigational aids pops up, as shown in Figure 25.14.

GET BACK
To quit the slideshow at any point, press the Esc key. You'll go back into whatever view you had been using before sliding into Slide Show view.

Now let's take a look at how you can handle PowerPoint presentations.

FIGURE 25.13
The presentation, the so-called Slide Show view.

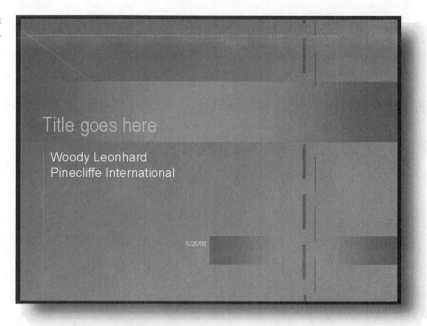

FIGURE 25.14
Navigate by clicking the graphic in the lower-left corner.

Working with Presentations

HEN YOU START OUT CREATING PowerPoint presentations, you'll feel mighty proud just being able to put together a presentation that gets your point across. That's as it should be.

Then, if you're like most people, you'll gain enough confidence to start doing fun things with your presentations—add video clips, hot links, multiple customized presentation sequences, fancy wipes, and other effects. And you'll soon discover that, instead of making your presentations better, they'll get *worse*.

With all due apologies to Marshall McLuhan, when it comes to PowerPoint presentations, the medium is *not* the message.

When people start paying more attention to your whiz-bang effects than they do to the message you're trying to convey, it's time to take stock. In PowerPoint, more than in any other Office 97 application, it's best to keep things relatively simple.

The View from 10,000 Feet

So how does PowerPoint hang together? Excellent question, and one that's relatively easy to answer. I'll spend the next few chapters going into details, but here's what you really need to understand about what's going on behind the PowerPoint scenes.

PowerPoint sports one of the best wizards Microsoft has ever built. It's called the *AutoContent Wizard*, and in the vast majority of cases it's more than adequate for just about any kind of presentation you can imagine. Answer a few questions, make a few choices, and out pops a presentation skeleton, complete with title slide, decent selections for colors and fonts, and even a few suggestions for what you might want to say. You add the content, and the presentation is ready to go very quickly.

There's much more to PowerPoint than one wizard, though, and sooner or later you're going to bump into a situation that the wizard can't handle directly. When that happens, you need to know about PowerPoint's, uh, eccentricities.

The other slides in the presentation are just called *slides*. (Whew!) Typically, each slide has a background of some sort, plus room for a title (there's that word again), a body (bullet points, pictures, and the like), a date, a number (for automatic slide numbering), and a footer. In addition, you can use the Drawing Layer above each slide to add whatever you like.

Behind each of the slides sits something called a *Slide Master*. There's only one Slide Master for each presentation. Anything that appears on the Slide Master appears in all the slides (except title slides). So if you want to change the background on all your slides, move the

THE POWERPOINT FAMILY JEWELS
This is critical information, and as far as I know nobody has ever put it all together in one place at one time. If you have to use PowerPoint but you don't want to spend time learning about the nuances, you need to read the rest of this section. At least it'll get you started and point you in the right direction when you inevitably get frustrated.

title, change fonts in the body, add text that will appear in the Drawing Layer in all the slides, or even change the whole appearance of your presentation, you need to work on the Slide Master.

TITLE SLIDES
The very first slide of a presentation is usually a *title slide*. You're going to hear the term title in many different contexts, so don't get confused. Designated title slides are treated differently from the other slides in a presentation. I'll explain all about title slides later in this section. Don't worry about them. Yet.

WHAT'S A MASTER SLIDE?

Confusingly, the Slide Master is frequently referred to as *the Master Slide*. In common parlance they're one and the same, but PowerPoint lingo is so confusing that your head is probably swimming by now anyway, so I'll try hard to stick with the official term, Slide Master.

I just told you that anything appearing on the Slide Master appears on all the slides. I lied. It's a little more complicated than that. Take a look at the typical Slide Master in Figure 26.1.

FIGURE 26.1
The Slide Master for the Dumb Dummies presentation.

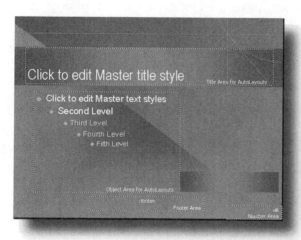

If you change any of these things in the Slide Master, the changes are reflected in every slide in your presentation:

- *Background*. Whatever background you choose for this slide appears on all the slides in your presentation (except on the title slides).

- *Floating Text and Pictures.* If you put text on the Slide Master—typically by clicking **Insert**, **Text Box**, or by clicking the **Text Box** 🖼 icon on the Drawing toolbr—that text shows up on all the slides. Similarly, if you put a picture on the Slide Master (with **Insert**, **Picture**), the picture goes on all the slides.

- *Title formatting.* Click once on the box marked **Title Area for AutoLayouts**. Then apply whatever formatting you like—fonts, size, color, centering—and that formatting gets applied to the titles on all the normal slides. If you want to move the title on all your slides to a different location, click and drag this box to whatever location you like. To make the title area bigger on all your slides, click and drag the sizing handles on this box.

- *Body formatting.* Click once on the box marked **Object Area for AutoLayouts** (I just love the way this terminology ping-pongs all over the place, don't you?), and apply the formatting you want for body text. Typically that includes fonts, color, and the like. Frequently, people like to change the bullet character used on their slides, and that's easy, once you know the trick. To change the third-level bullet, for example, click inside the line that says **Third Level**, click **Format**, **Bullet** and choose your favorite bullet. That bullet will be used for third-level text throughout the presentation.

- *Footer formatting.* Click the box marked **Footer Area**, and format away. Again, you can relocate the box, make it larger or smaller, or click once and apply any formatting you like.

WHY CAN'T I PUT TEXT IN THESE BOXES?

I dunno. You'd think that PowerPoint would let you type text in the title, body, or footer boxes, and have that text appear on all the slides. It doesn't work that way. Nothing you type in the **Title** or **Body** boxes appears anywhere else in the presentation. And PowerPoint won't even let you type in the Footer box!

I'll go into some detail on the **Footer Area**, **Number Area**, and something called the **Date Area** (which doesn't even appear in Figure 26.1), in Chapter 28, "Making Presentations Look Better." They're weird. Don't worry about them for now.

These examples for modifying the Slide Master point out an important difference between PowerPoint and the other Office 97 applications: All the text in PowerPoint appears inside boxes. The easiest way to change formatting for all the text in a box is to select the box by clicking it once, and then applying the formatting. So, in PowerPoint, you don't have to select text before formatting it—merely selecting the box that surrounds the text is sufficient.

Changes made to the Slide Master are reflected in all the slides in your presentation (except title slides). In addition to those changes, you can make changes to individual slides—change formatting for a title, or the bullets in the body, or move the footer. In those cases, the formatting you've applied manually to an individual slide takes precedence over the Slide Master. Thus, if the Slide Master says the title should be in 20-point Arial bold, and you go into an individual slide and make the title 14-point Gotham Condensed, the slide will show the title in Gotham. Subsequent changes to the Slide Master will still be overridden by the changes you've applied manually. The only way to force an individual slide to go back to the Slide Master settings is by selecting the slide, clicking **Format**, **Slide Layout**, and clicking the **Reapply** button, as shown in Figure 26.2.

FIGURE 26.2
To remove manual changes applied to an individual slide, click Reapply here.

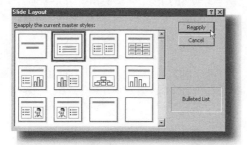

This bears repeating: If you want to change *all* the slides in your presentation, except for title slides, change the Slide Master. Don't play around with individual slides. I'll show you how to change the Slide Master in Chapter 27, "PowerPoint's Auto Support."

Whenever you create a new slide, PowerPoint presents you with the Slide Layout dialog box. As you can see in Figure 26.3, if you choose the first layout that's offered, PowerPoint tells you (in the box in the lower-right corner) that you're creating a title slide.

If you click **OK** at this point, the slide that's added to your presentation is a title slide. It's really that simple: You create a title slide at any point in your presentation by creating a new slide and choosing the

BUT THAT DOESN'T CHANGE EVERYTHING BACK!
True. This Reapply trick resets only manually applied formatting—it doesn't change any text you've typed into the slide.

first layout. I don't know of any way to change a normal slide into a title slide, or vice versa.

In many respects, title slides are just like normal slides—you can move them, delete them, copy them—but there's one big exception. Whereas the Slide Master sits behind normal slides, the title master controls the appearance of all title slides. If you change the

WHAT'S WITH THE TITLE SLIDE?
First of all, there's no such thing as *a* title slide. Your presentation can have one, many, or no title slides. The AutoContent Wizard puts a title slide at the beginning of all the presentations it generates. But you don't have to limit yourself to just one.

In fact, you don't have to have any title slides at all. You can get rid of a title slide just like any other slide—go into Slide Sorter view, click the slide, and press the Delete key.

Slide Master, all normal slides change, but none of the title slides do. If you change the Title Master, all the title slides change, but the normal slides stay the same.

FIGURE 26.3
How to create a new title slide.

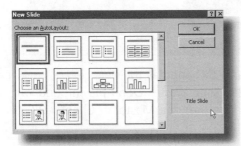

The fact is that PowerPoint behaves strangely in many respects. For example, Outline view doesn't really show an outline. It doesn't even show all the text on the slides—it just slaps an outline-like format onto the text in the Text and Body boxes. Another example: You can specify only footer text in a dialog box, and you can specify only the formatting of that text on the Slide Master! That's okay. The dialog box you type the footer into is called the Header and Footer dialog box—and there are no headers in PowerPoint. Meshugge.

(Yiddish/Hebrew lesson for the day: *meshugge* = "crazy, nuts, absurd." Leon Rosten, in *Joys of Yinglish*, says, "Perhaps the soundest insight into human behavior is this folk saying: 'Every man has his own *mishegoss*.'")

Even with the inconsistent terminology, the woefully inadequate Help (I dare you to come up with a coherent description of the Slide Master, based on the online Help), and the tendency to flaunt other Office applications' long-standing traditions, PowerPoint still has a lot of capability. It's remarkably easy to use once you know the secrets. And it has some features that are nothing short of amazing.

That's about it for the way PowerPoint hangs together. It's considerably simpler than Word, Excel, or Outlook (in fact, I'm not certain even now that I understand how those applications hang together!). The rest of the PowerPoint story is all embellishment and technique.

WHAT'S AN OBJECT?
I thought I knew the answer to that question before I started digging deep into the PowerPoint documentation. The term *object* has a very specific meaning to grizzled old programmers like me. The term has been, uh, adopted by Microsoft in several interesting ways, but I'll have to admit that PowerPoint takes the cake.

As best I can tell, in PowerPoint, an object is a thing. And that's about as specific as the documentation gets. I'm not going to use the word object when referring to PowerPoint.

The minute you start getting confused by a discussion (in the official documents, or in other books) about text boxes as opposed to text box objects as opposed to text objects and on, and on... don't feel bad, just bail out. I can't follow them either. I get the distinct impression that a lot of people who write about PowerPoint get confused, too, and start swinging around a lot of meaningless drivel to throw you off the track.

General Strategy

Which PowerPoint tools should you use to build presentations? Here's my school-of-hard-knocks series of recommendations:

- Use the AutoContent Wizard. If everybody at your company is using the AutoContent Wizard and management is getting tired of slide shows that all look the same, use the AutoContent Wizard, and then change one simple item (a color, say, or a piece of art) on the Slide Master.

- If you (or your boss) get so sick of presentations generated by the AutoContent Wizard that you're considering throwing all your ThinkPads out the tenth-floor window, use one of the pre-fab presentations provided with PowerPoint. You'll find those pre-fab presentations in the Presentations folder of the File New dialog box.

- When you (or your boss) get so sick of those presentations that you're considering throwing the next presenter out the tenth-floor window, use one of the pre-fab presentations in the Presentation Designs folder of the File New dialog box to change the format of a presentation. You can do that regardless of whether you start with the AutoContent Wizard or the pre-fab presentations in the Presentations folder, or if you build your presentation slide-by-slide.

- And when those get stale, get a new job. Nobody except a full-fledged card-carrying graphics designer should attempt to build a new PowerPoint design scheme from scratch.

You think I'm joking? Hey, if you'd suffered through the kind of presentations I've seen, you wouldn't be laughing. PowerPoint makes it easy to create good presentations—if you stick to the designs provided with the product, and add top-notch content. PowerPoint also makes it easy to make execrable presentations, in spite of the quality of the content. The difference between the two boils down to something called artistic talent—and that's a rare commodity.

Content, content, content. Stick to the substance and leave the design to PowerPoint.

Making a New Presentation

PowerPoint gives you three choices for creating a new presentation: AutoContent Wizard, the pre-fab presentations in the Presentations folder, and building a presentation one slide at a time.

Starting AutoContent

To use the AutoContent Wizard when you first start PowerPoint, click the **AutoContent wizard** button and click **OK** (see Figure 26.4).

To use the AutoContent Wizard when PowerPoint is running, click **File**, then **New**, click the **Presentations** tab, **AutoContent Wizard**, and **OK**. I'll talk about the AutoContent Wizard extensively in Chapter 27, "PowerPoint's Auto Support."

FIGURE 26.4
The initial
PowerPoint
screen.

Using Pre-Fab Presentations

Surprisingly, you can't use the pre-fab presentations in the Presentations folder (which cover topics as diverse as Company Meetings, Financial Reports, Strategy Recommendations, and much more) directly from the initial PowerPoint screen, shown in Figure 26.4. To get at it, you have to cancel out of the initial screen, click **File**, **New**, click the **Presentations** tab, and select from the proffered presentations.

Going It Alone

If you want to build your presentation screen by screen, you can check *either* **Template** or **Blank Presentation** in the initial PowerPoint screen.

If you choose **Template**, PowerPoint lets you choose a so-called *template*, which is simply a collection of Slide Master, Title Master, Notes Master (which controls how presentation notes are printed), and Handout Master (which controls how handouts appear). You're then responsible for creating your own slides one at a time.

TERMINOLOGY ALERT!

It's important that you realize a PowerPoint template isn't anything at all like a Word template or an Excel template. Not even close.

In PowerPoint, a template, or a .pot file, is a collection of Slide Master, Title Master, Notes Master, and Handouts Master, which can be applied to a presentation. That's it.

Whereas Word templates and Excel templates are somewhat different, the differences with PowerPoint are like night and day. So don't be confused! The closest PowerPoint gets to a Word or Excel template is in those pre-fab presentations in the Presentations folder.

I will try to avoid using the term template when discussing PowerPoint, simply because the term is so completely different here than in other parts of Office.

Man, PowerPoint's odd terminology gets confusing!

The only difference between Template and Blank Presentation in Figure 26.4 is in choice of Masters. If you choose Blank Presentation, PowerPoint doesn't let you choose the template, or master files, before you build your presentation. Everything else is the same.

If you're running PowerPoint and want to roll your own presentation, click **File**, then **New**. Choosing **Blank Presentation** from the **General** tab does precisely the same thing as choosing **Blank Presentation** from PowerPoint's initial screen, shown in Figure 26.4. And clicking the **Presentation Designs** tab inside **File New** does precisely the same thing as clicking the **Template** button on the initial screen.

Go figure.

Page Setup

If you use the AutoContent Wizard, PowerPoint asks what kind of output you're going to use for your presentation. If you use pre-fab presentations or build your presentation one screen at a time, you need to tell PowerPoint whether the presentation is destined to be output to 35mm film, overhead transparencies, and the like. (If you're just going to use the computer's screen, there's no need to change anything: PowerPoint assumes you're going to do the presentation onscreen unless you tell it otherwise.)

WHAT'S A .PPS FILE?
PowerPoint stores files in two forms. The first form, the one you're accustomed to because it's just like all the other Office 97 forms, simply contains the presentation. Open one of these .ppt files and you can edit, save, and otherwise work with the presentation. Double-click a .ppt file (in Windows Explorer, say, or on the Desktop) and PowerPoint comes up with the file loaded and ready to go. Typical for an Office file.

The other form, called a *.pps* form, is the slideshow: If you double-click a .pps file and PowerPoint is available on the PC, the presentation begins. On the other hand, if you open a .pps file from inside PowerPoint, you can edit, save, and work with that version, too.

To avoid the all-too-common problem of having different versions of a file with essentially the same name ("Gee, which one has the more recent version, foo.ppt, or foo.pps?"), I strongly recommend you *not* open .pps files from the Open dialog box. If you absolutely must open a .pps file—perhaps because you lost the original .ppt file, or because somebody gave you the .pps but not the .ppt—you should immediately save the file as a .ppt (click **File**, **Save As** and in the **Save as type** box choose **Presentation (*.ppt)**), and work on the .ppt version.

It's important that you tell PowerPoint about these alternate output devices, because they'll affect the size (actually, the aspect ratio) of your slides. If you build the perfect onscreen presentation, the 35mm version of that same presentation can flop all over the place.

To tell PowerPoint that you're going to use an output device other than the computer screen, click **File**, **Page Setup**, and set the **Slides sized for** box.

Opening a Presentation

☞ *On page 554, you created a presentation called the Dumb Dummy Presentation. If you somehow skipped that exercise, pop back there now and get a presentation saved on your disk.*

PowerPoint starts out differently from all the other Office 97 applications. PowerPoint's handholding may be a little cloying to most of you, but it could be worse. At least it works.

*E*XERCISE   **Opening a Presentation**

1. If PowerPoint isn't running, get it going (**Start**, **Programs**, **Microsoft PowerPoint**). When the PowerPoint dialog box opens, as shown in Figure 26.4, click the **Open an existing presentation** button and click **OK**.

2. If PowerPoint is running, just click **File**, then **Open**.

3. In either case, you'll get the Open dialog box, as shown in Figure 26.5, which looks like all the other Office Open dialog boxes, with one exception—in the **Files of type** box, PowerPoint lists both .ppt and .pps files.

FIGURE 26.5
PowerPoint's
Open dialog
box—just like
all the others,
but with one
important
twist.

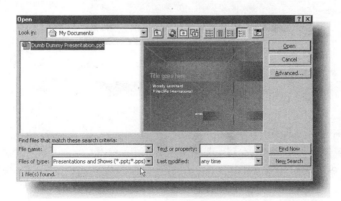

4. Simply click **Dumb Dummy Presentation.ppt**, click **Open**, and you're in the fast lane. Leave Dumb Dummy up on the screen; we'll use it in the next exercise. (Dumb Dummy Presentation.ppt was created in the previous chapter. Use it if you want to follow along closely here. Or, if you prefer, create a new presentation.)

Save, Save As, Close, Exit

PowerPoint's Save, Close and Exit routines are identical to those in the rest of Office.

Save As, however, holds one important wrinkle: This is where you create .pps or slide show files.

*E*XERCISE

The Dumb Dummy Slide Show

1. Let's save the Dumb Dummy Presentation, which should be on your screen, as a slide show or .pps file.

2. Click File, then **Save As**. You'll get the Save As dialog box, shown in Figure 26.6. In the Save as type box, click the down arrow and choose **PowerPoint Show (*.pps)**. Click **Save** to save a copy of the Dumb Dummy Presentation as a PowerPoint slide show.

FIGURE 26.6
Saving Dumb Dummy as a PowerPoint slide show.

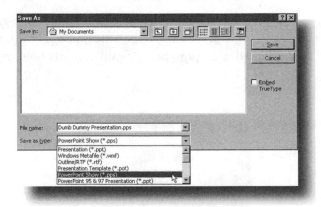

3. Right now you're in a very delicate position, so *follow these instructions very carefully!* If you look in the Window title, you'll see that you're currently editing the file Dumb Dummy Presentation.pps (see Figure 26.7). You do *not* want to edit the .pps file—the minute you do, the .ppt presentation file will be different from the .pps slide show file, and there's no way you'll ever get them synched up again.

FIGURE 26.7
CAREFUL!
You're editing
the .pps file.
Close it
before you
make
changes.

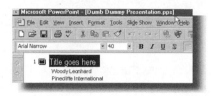

4. Immediately after saving a file as a .pps slide show file, you should close the .pps file and open the original .ppt file. To do that in this case, click **File**, then **Close**. Then click the **File** menu item and choose **Dumb Dummy Presentation.ppt** from the list of files at the bottom of the menu. Make sure you're working with the .ppt file, shown in Figure 26.8, before you continue.

FIGURE 26.8
Make very
sure you're
using the
.ppt file
before you
continue.

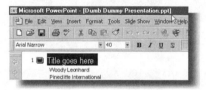

THIS IS CONFUSING...
As my son says, "No DUH!" Whoever designed PowerPoint to work this way should be forced to spend the rest of his life reconciling users' incompatible changes to .ppt and .pps files. I have a few they can start working on right now!

The general rule: .pps files are nice as self-contained slide shows, but never, ever, ever edit a .pps file. As soon as you create one (using File, Save As), close the .pps file and open the associated .ppt file.

5. If you want to view the slide show, find the file (using Windows Explorer, or **Start**, **Find**), and double-click the **Dumb Dummy Presentation.pps** file. The slide show is displayed on your screen; click each slide, in turn, to advance to the next slide.

6. Make absolutely, totally, 100% sure that you have the Dumb Dummy Presentation.ppt file showing on the screen before you continue.

Organizing Slides

After you have a presentation going, adding, copying, moving and deleting slides couldn't be easier.

*E*XERCISE

Adding a New Slide

1. Make absolutely, totally, 100% sure that you have the Dumb Dummy Presentation.ppt file showing on the screen before you continue. Yeah, I know I said that already. I mean it.

2. When you need to organize slides, there's only one place to be: Slide Sorter view. So click the **Slide Sorter View** ⬅ icon on the View bar, and your presentation should look like Figure 26.9.

FIGURE 26.9
Slide Sorter view of the Dumb Dummy Presentation, with eight slides.

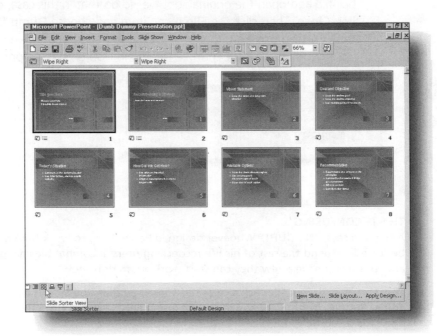

3. Let's say you want to put a new slide in your presentation, immediately after the title slide. Click in the blank area between slide 1 and slide 2. You should see a solid black vertical line appear between the two slides, as shown in Figure 26.10.

FIGURE 26.10
Click where
you want
your new
slide to go.

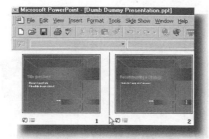

4. To add a new slide to the presentation, click the **New Slide** button in the
lower-right corner, on the Common Tasks toolbar. PowerPoint responds with
the New Slide dialog box, as shown in Figure 26.11. I'll talk about the
meaning of each of those 12 thumbnails in Chapter 27.

FIGURE 26.11
PowerPoint
needs to
know what
kind of layout
you want for
your new
slide.

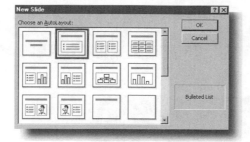

5. I chose a simple bulleted slide, the second thumbnail in the New Slide dialog
box, and clicked OK. When PowerPoint came back to my presentation, Slide
Sorter view showed a new slide, number 2, had been inserted, and the subsequent slides had all been bumped down by one slot (see Figure 26.12).

6. I double-clicked slide 2. (I also could've clicked the **Slide View** 🔲 icon on
the View bar, to get the same effect.) Up pops slide 2, per Figure 26.13,
ready for my captivating prose.

7. Following the displayed instructions, I clicked in the upper box (the Title
box) and typed a new title. Then I clicked the lower box (the Body box) and
started adding bullet points. The first point I typed was at the top level.
When I started the second line, I pressed the Tab key to indent the line and
move in to the second level. On the third line, I pressed Shift+Tab (or the
backwards Tab) to return to the top level. From there, I used the Tab and
Shift+Tab keys to move back and forth from first, to second, to third levels
(see Figure 26.14).

FIGURE 26.12
The new slide takes on position 2, displacing the others by one position each.

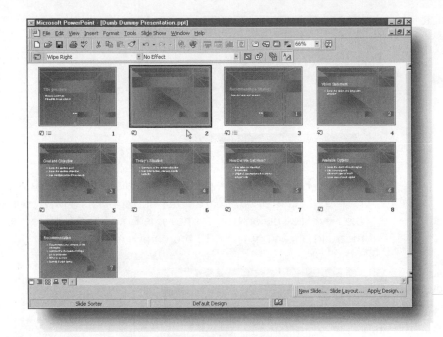

FIGURE 26.13
The new slide 2 needs text.

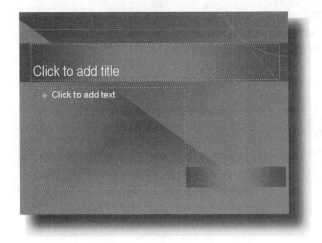

8. Because I carefully added all this text to the defined Text and Body boxes, all the stuff I typed should appear in Outline view. Clicking the **Outline View** icon on the View bar, I verified that, indeed, PowerPoint had picked it all up (see Figure 26.15).

FIGURE 26.14
Use the Tab and Shift+Tab keys to move between the various levels of bulleting.

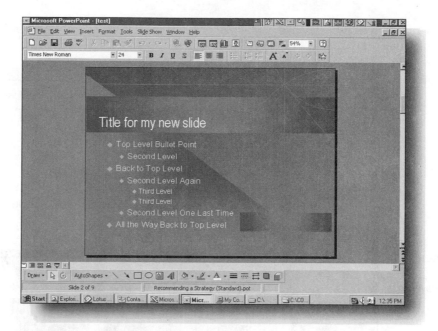

FIGURE 26.15
This new text appears in Outline view because it was typed in the predefined Title and Body boxes.

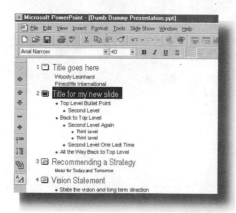

9. At this point, you should try to select individual lines in this new slide and click the **Promote** ⬅ or **Demote** ➡ icons to move them in or out in the outline levels. You'll not only see the result of your actions in the outline, but they'll also appear in the thumbnail of the slide in the upper-right corner.

10. When you're finished mangling the new slide, leave Dumb Dummy Presentation.ppt showing on the screen.

If you thought adding a slide was easy, you'll be amazed at moving, copying, and deleting. Couldn't be simpler.

*Ɛ*XERCISE_____

Move, Copy, Delete Slides

1. You should have Dumb Dummy Presentation.ppt open and visible.

2. Managing slides is always easiest from the Slide Sorter, so click the **Slide Sorter View** 🔡 icon on the View bar.

3. Say you decide that the new slide, number 2, really belongs between slides 7 and 8. To move it, click slide 2 and drag it to the space between slides 7 and 8, as shown in Figure 26.16.

FIGURE 26.16
Click and
drag to move
a slide.

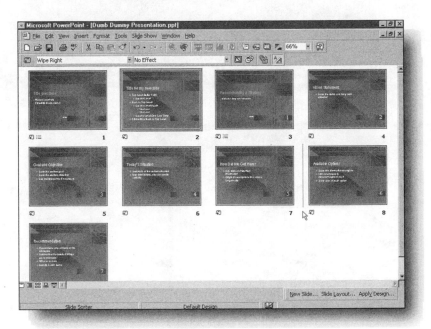

4. When you let go of the mouse button, the old slide 2 turns into slide 7, rearranging the numbering on all the intermediate slides (see Figure 26.17).

FIGURE 26.17
Drop the slide and all the others get reshuffled.

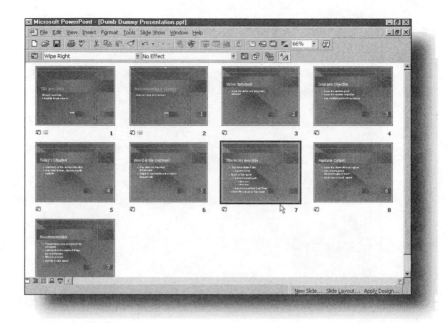

MOVE LONG DISTANCES
If you need to move a slide for a long way, and you can't see both the slide and the destination at the same time, you have three choices. First, you can click the slide, **Cut** [✂] it, move to the destination, and **Paste** [📋] the slide. Alternatively, you can click the slide and drag it to the top or bottom of the screen; PowerPoint scrolls along with you. Finally, you can zoom (click **View**, and then **Zoom**) so both source and destination are visible.

5. Copying slides is just as simple. Say you need to make a copy of this new slide. (Hey, the content's so good you gotta say it twice!) Click the slide, and then click the **Copy** [📋] icon on the Standard toolbr. Then click wherever you want the slide to go—in Figure 26.18, I clicked between slides 5 and 6—and click the **Paste** [📋] icon.

6. When the copy of the slide gets inserted, all the appropriate slides are renumbered and rearranged on the screen (see Figure 26.19).

7. Finally, to delete a slide, you select it and press the Del key. (Difficult, eh?) To delete the two new slides in Dumb Dummy Presentation.ppt, click slide 8 and press Del, and then click slide 6 and press Del.

8. We've come full circle.

FIGURE 26.18
To copy, select the slide you want copied, click the Copy icon, click where you want it to go, and click Paste.

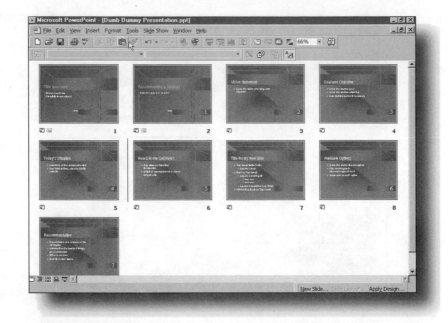

FIGURE 26.19
When you paste, all the other slides move around.

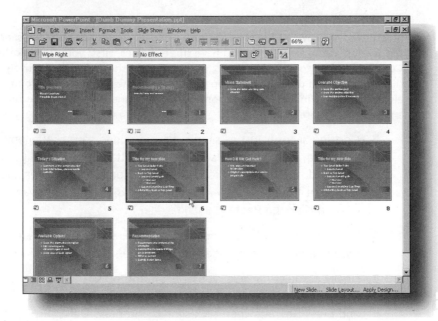

Notes and Handouts

PowerPoint lets you type notes for each slide. They're freeform and, as the name implies, they're primarily intended as speaker's notes. Unfortunately, the only way you'll be able to read them when you're making a presentation is by printing them out and reading from the hardcopy, flipping from page to page as you go from slide to slide. Not a very elegant solution. You get one slide on a page, plus whatever text you've typed, and that's it.

To type notes for a slide, click the **Notes Page View** 🖳 icon on the View bar (see Figure 26.20).

FIGURE 26.20
Notes can be entered in the usual PowerPoint fashion, in Notes Page view.

If you have a very morbid curiosity, you can see the layout of notes pages on the Notes Master (**View**, **Master**, **Notes Master**). Modify the Notes Master, and notes pages change in lockstep. To print notes pages, click **File**, **Print**, and choose **Notes Pages** in the **Print what** box (see Figure 26.21).

FIGURE 26.21
Printing notes.

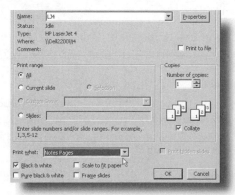

In PowerPoint parlance, handouts are just thumbnails of the slides, with no ancillary text. You can have two slides to a page, three-up (along the left side of the page), or six-up (two columns of three each). Layout of the pages is controlled by (what else?) the Handout Master, which sits under **View**, **Master**, **Handout Master** (see Figure 26.22).

FIGURE 26.22
The Handout
Master for
six-up
thumbnails of
your slides.

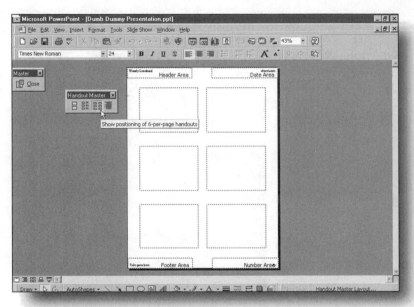

OUTLINE MASTER

Yes, you can print the Outline view—but (wonder of wonders!) you *don't* specify the form of the printing in an Outline Master. Instead, you have to go into the Handout Master and click the last button on the Handout Master toolbr, which is marked Show positioning of outline.

Now there's a trivia question for you.

Finally, you choose which set of thumbnails you want (two-up, three-up or six-up) in the File Print dialog box, as you can see at the bottom of Figure 26.23.

WHEN ARE NOTES HANDOUTS?

Just because Microsoft calls the notes printout *speaker's notes*, there's no reason why you should feel constrained. If you want to hand out copies of your slides with supporting text and a bit of room for viewers to jot down their ideas, you should definitely consider printing the notes and distributing them.

FIGURE 26.23
The place to go for thumbnails.

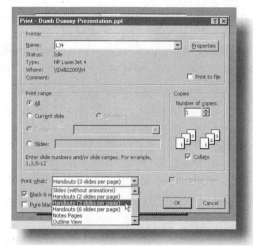

Print

To print your presentation, click **File**, and then **Print**, just as you would with any other Office application.

The latest generation of color inkjet printers do an exceptionally good job printing color handouts and overhead transparencies. The usual precautions apply: If you need good color definition, use the expensive paper; don't expect color pages to print anywhere near as fast as black and white; and remember that the ink is water soluble, so don't spill coffee on your overheads!

35MM SLIDES

If you're going to print your presentation on 35mm slides, you have three basic choices:

- *Genigraphics.* Long a specialist in turning PowerPoint presentations into 35mm slides, Genigraphics knows what they're doing, although they're rarely the least expensive alternative. To send your presentation to Genigraphics, have them turn it into 35mm slides, and deliver the slides back to you via FedEx, get your presentation together, and then click **File**, **Send To**, **Genigraphics**. Have your credit card handy.

- *Service Bureau.* Many communities around the country have service bureau companies that know PowerPoint inside and out. If you can find a service bureau that will work with you, they can save you money and get the slides back to you fast. To find a local company, check the Yellow Pages under Graphics or Computer Graphics.

● *Film Recorder.* The ultimate do-it-yourself output device, a film recorder acts just like a printer, except it prints on 35mm film. Pop the film canister out of the recorder, take it to your local 1-hour photo shop, and you're in business. If you can't find any locally, check out Publishing Perfection at www.publishingperfection.com.

As for other kinds of presentation hardware, you're on your own. The market for projection boxes changes daily (see *PC Week* for lots of ads). LCD panels that sit on top of overhead projectors delight some people, but leave others swearing. Portable panel and screen technology can take your breath away—and relieve you of a substantial amount of capital at the same time. All in all, anything I write today about presentation hardware will be obsolete by the time you read it. So watch the magazine reviews, and put off buying hardware as long as you can, secure in the knowledge that the prices will always go down.

So much for dealing with presentations. Now let's take a look at what kinds of auto goodies PowerPoint provides for your edification and entertainment.

PowerPoint's Auto Support

ORE THAN ANY OTHER OFFICE APPLICATION, PowerPoint abounds with auto

tools that help you put together whiz-bang presentations—and you

hardly need to get your fingers dirty. In this chapter I'm going to

introduce you to the Auto features, one at a time, and show you

how to use them to create an effective presentation.

AutoContent Wizard

The granddaddy of all PowerPoint wizards, the AutoContent Wizard (what a weird name!) churns out presentations. The presentations that come out of this wizard look good, hang together well, and they even include hints for creating and organizing content. Unless you're going up against a very jaded audience—one that has seen hundreds of PowerPoint presentations—chances are pretty good that the AutoContent Wizard has all you need to get your point across.

Wizard Options

Let's step through the wizard, one point at a time. I'd like to give you an idea of the kind of choices available, and what you can expect when you run the AutoContent Wizard.

XERCISE

A Generic Presentation

1. If PowerPoint isn't running, start it and choose **AutoContent Wizard** on the initial screen. If PowerPoint is running, click **File**, then **New**, bring up the **Presentations** tab, and double-click **AutoContent Wizard**.

2. The AutoContent Wizard presents its splash screen (see Figure 27.1). If you want help from the Office Assistant, click the **?** icon at the bottom. Otherwise, click **Next**.

FIGURE 27.1
The
AutoContent
Wizard starts.

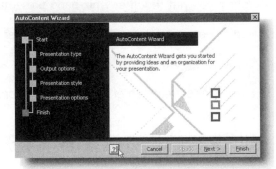

3. In the next wizard panel, you have to make a key decision: what kind of presentation do you want to create? Click the buttons on the left side to see the presentations grouped by category, or scroll through the left box to see what comes closest to your ideal. In Figure 27.2, I've chosen **Generic** to create a presentation we can play with. When you're done, click **Next**.

FIGURE 27.2
The key
AutoContent
question—
what kind of
presentation
do you want
to build?

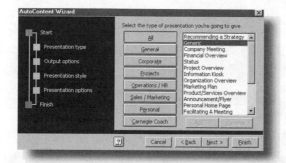

4. You need to tell the wizard whether you're going to use the presentation on the Internet (actually, the Web) or in a kiosk, for free-standing viewer-directed presentations (see Figure 27.3). If so, PowerPoint inserts forward and backward viewing buttons, and other support details helpful for navigating the presentation.

FIGURE 27.3
Will the pre-
sentation go
on the Web,
or in a kiosk?

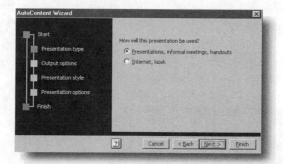

POWERPOINT ON THE WEB

I've had nothing but problems trying to put PowerPoint presentations on the Web. Your mileage may vary, but don't even try it until you've read Chapter 30, "Office on the Web."

POWERPOINT IN KIOSKS

Typically a kiosk presentation runs itself, or at least restricts what the observer can do while the presentation is running. Kiosk presentations also frequently start over again once they're done. PowerPoint has extensive kiosk support. To get more information, crank up the Office Assistant, type `self-running`, and click Search. (Amazingly, typing `kiosk` doesn't work.)

5. If you don't choose the Internet/kiosk option, PowerPoint wants to know how you'll be presenting the show, and whether you'll want handouts (see Figure 27.4). These settings are used to adjust the size (aspect ratio) of the slides, and set certain printing options.

FIGURE 27.4
Choose the type of output you need, so PowerPoint can adjust the slide size accordingly.

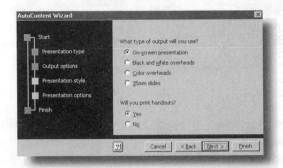

6. In the last informational panel, the wizard wants data for the Title Slide and the File Properties box (see Figure 27.5). The AutoContent Wizard invariably creates a single title slide and puts it at the beginning of the presentation. Don't be too worried about getting this right; you can always go back and change what you typed on the slide itself.

FIGURE 27.5
The wizard generates the presentation's title slide from this information.

7. Click **Next,** then **Finish**, and the AutoContent Wizard creates your new presentation, then dumps you out in Outline view. Note in Figure 27.6 how the wizard has created a fairly good skeleton, onto which you can hang your own content.

8. We're going to use this presentation, so click **File**, then **Save**, type Generic Presentation, and click **Save**.

FIGURE 27.6
The generic
presentation
ready to edit.

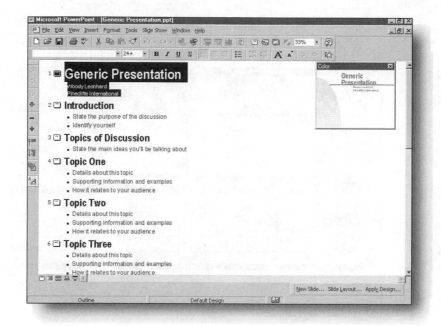

Summary Slide

Let's take that generic presentation and make it a little better.

*E*XERCISE

Summary Slide

1. Start with the
generic presenta-
tion from the
previous exercise.
Click the **Slide
Sorter View**
on the View bar
to flip into Slide
Sorter view.

2. Slide 3 in that presentation, titled
Topics of
Discussion,
doesn't say
much—and, I

HOBGOBLINS
Although it may be true that a foolish
consistency is the hobgoblin of little
minds, this PowerPoint inconsistency is
hard to fathom. Every single Office
application—and most Windows applications,
for that matter, including Windows Explorer—
let you select several items by holding the Ctrl
key while clicking the items you want.

Not PowerPoint. The Ctrl key doesn't do a
thing. Instead, you have to remember to hold
down the Shift key to select these slides.

That's ludicrous. Get a clue, Redmond.

would argue, duplicates what should go in the Introduction slide, number 2. Let's get rid of that slide by clicking it (see Figure 27.7), and pressing the Delete key.

FIGURE 27.7
Give slide 3
the deep six.

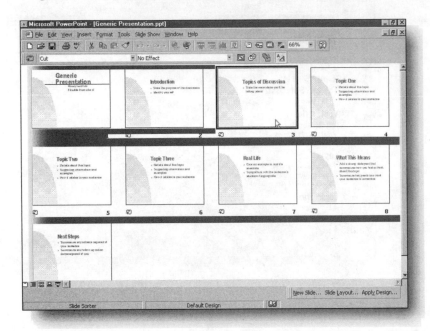

3. There's a nifty PowerPoint feature called *Summary Slide*, which creates a new slide based on the titles of all selected slides. Here's how to use it. Hold down the Shift key and click slides 3, 4, 5, 6, 7, and 8. When they're all selected, click the **Summary Slide** 🖼 icon on the Outlining toolbar, as shown in Figure 27.8.

4. PowerPoint creates a new slide, with the title Summary Slide, and inserts it at the beginning of the selected slides—in this case, as slide 3. Note how the body of Summary Slide is composed of bullet points, each of which comes from the titles of the chosen slides (see Figure 27.9).

5. I've found that the summary slide often works best as a review slide— sometimes called a snooze slide—that is, a slide at the end of your presentation that reviews all the most excellent points you made during the presentation. So click and drag slide 3 to the end of the presentation, as shown in Figure 27.10.

6. Save it as Generic Presentation.ppt. We'll keep using it.

Now let's see what other goodies await our generic presentation.

FIGURE 27.8
The Summary Slide icon creates a new slide based on titles from all the selected slides.

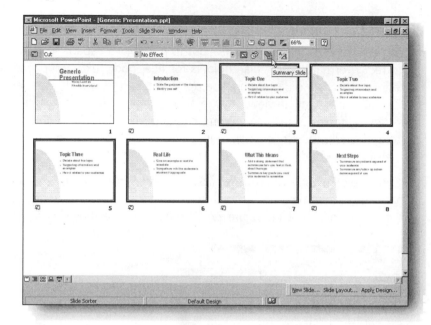

FIGURE 27.9
The summary slide gets put into the presentation ahead of the selected slides.

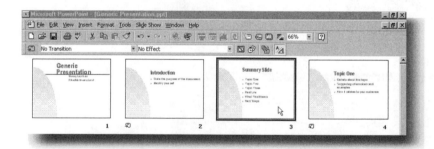

FIGURE 27.10
Move the summary slide to the end to help wrap up your presentation.

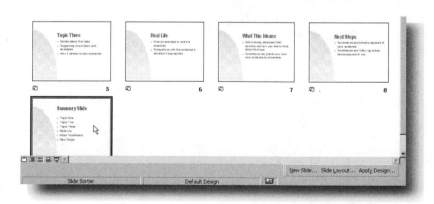

AutoLayout/New Slide

PowerPoint uses the term *AutoLayout* to refer to its capability to insert new slides—correctly formatted with placeholders for title, body text, and pictures—into presentations. The new slides are hooked up so you can type text into them and have the text appear in Outline view. They're also capable of more-or-less automatically retrieving tables of text from Word, creating Microsoft Chart charts (which don't hold a candle to Excel charts), or inserting clips—pictures, sound, or movies—from the outside world.

If you have PowerPoint running, click the **New Slide** icon on the Common Tasks toolbar. PowerPoint presents you with the New Slide dialog box, which has 24 options; the first 12 are shown in Figure 27.11, the last 12 are shown in Figure 27.12.

FIGURE 27.11
The first 12 prototypical slides in the New Slide dialog box.

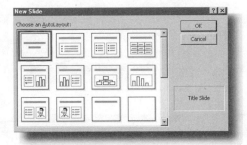

FIGURE 27.12
The last 12 prototypes in the New Slide dialog box.

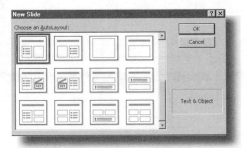

Although that seems like a lot of options, in fact there are just a handful of unique types of slide placeholders. (*Placeholders* are those boxes on slides that you fill with your own content.)

You can see names of the placeholders listed in the bottom right of the New Slide dialog box. For example, the first slide in Figure 27.12 says Text & Object, while the second slide in the same figure says Object & Text. The Text and Object placeholders, in that case, are just reversed.

The following list shows the different kinds of slide placeholders, with their names as they appear in the box at the bottom right, and what they really mean:

- *Title Slide*. Has room for a title and subtitle. Click this icon to create a genuine designated title slide.

- *Bulleted List*. By far the most common type of slide, the bulleted list has room for a title and body text. The **2 column text** slide is identical, except that it has two separate placeholders for body text, laid out side by side.

- *Table*. This kind of slide contains one large Word 97 table. Only use it when a Word table would be appropriate, for example, for text.

- *Chart*. The chart placeholders are hard-wired into Microsoft's Chart application, which I discussed way back in Chapter 12, "Special Purpose Tools." Unless you specifically need a very simple, quick and dirty chart, avoid Chart and use Excel.

- *Organization Chart*. This is identical to the Excel Organization Chart application, which I discussed in Chapter 22, "Making Spreadsheets Look Good." Only use it if you want to spend a while drawing an org chart in your presentation.

- *Clip Art*. This is a real misnomer. Clip Art placeholders are hardwired into Microsoft's Clip Gallery, which I discussed in Chapter 12. The Clip Gallery includes sounds and video clips, but it's pretty limited in scope.

- *Object*. By far the most powerful placeholder, Object lets you put anything inside the slide that you can retrieve using **Insert/Object**—parts of Excel spreadsheets (including charts), Word documents, almost any kind of image, sound, or clip, including those from the Clip Gallery. If you want to put a picture or sound into your presentation, this is the kind of placeholder to use.

- *Media Clip*. If you know that you specifically want a movie clip on a slide, use this kind of placeholder. Otherwise, use Object, because it will enable you to choose movies as one of the options.

Make your choice in New Slide based on the number and type of placeholders on the icon. Don't get hung up about size or location of the placeholders—those are easy to change, once the slide is under construction.

Global Changes

In this section I want to go over the auto features PowerPoint includes to change all the slides in a presentation. I've talked about masters, those phantom slides that sit in the background, affecting all the slides in your presentation, and we'll work with those. There's also a way to apply a set of PowerPoint masters to an existing presentation, and that's done through a command called Apply Design.

TERMINOLOGY ALERT!
I don't know why PowerPoint can't get its terms straight. If you look through the official documentation and the various menus, you'll see this very simple concept—four masters in a .pot file—referred to as a template, a design template, and, as in Figure 27.13, a design, a Presentation template, and a Presentation design.

That's at least five different names for the same thing.

Far as I'm concerned, you'd be crazy to try to understand the official terminology. I'll call it Four Masters in a .pot, and be done with it.

Apply Design

 I talked about PowerPoint templates on page 571.

PowerPoint templates, as you may recall, aren't really templates in the usual Office sense of the term. Instead, they're collections of four masters in a single .pot file. When you tell PowerPoint to apply a design, what you're really doing is telling PowerPoint to throw away its current set of masters and to bring in a different set from a .pot file.

Exercise

Apply a Design to the Generic Presentation

1. Open Generic Presentation.ppt, and click the **Slide Sorter View** 🔳 icon to flip into Slide Order view.

2. Click **Format**, then **Apply Design**. Flip through the list of designs in the box on the left. In Figure 27.13 I've chosen **Dads Tie.pot**. Click **Apply**.

3. PowerPoint gets rid of all the masters it was using, and replaces them with the masters stored in the .pot file you've just chosen. In Figure 27.14 you can see how the Dads Tie masters look when applied to the generic presentation.

FIGURE 27.13
Apply the
Dads Tie
design to
your generic
presentation.

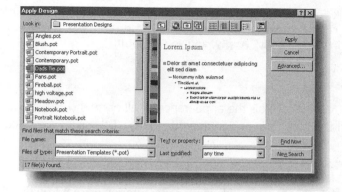

FIGURE 27.14
PowerPoint
applies the
design by
swapping out
masters.

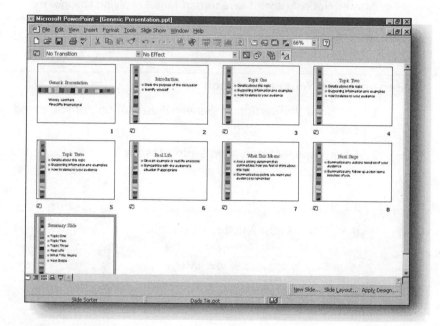

4. Go ahead and save this new version of Generic Presentation.ppt. We'll keep plugging away on it.

STEAL A SET OF MASTERS

Do you know somebody who's created a really, really cool presentation? If you have a .ppt or .pps file of that presentation, you can steal their masters—and along with them, the backgrounds, font settings, bullets, and everything else that can be set in the masters—and use them in your presentation.

Simply click **Format**, **Apply Design**, and in the Apply Design dialog box's **Files of type** box, choose **Presentations and Shows (*.ppt, *.pps)**. Navigate to the presentation in question, click **Apply**, and you've got it.

Slide Master

The Slide Master controls the appearance of all normal slides in your presentation—that is, all the slides except genuine title slides. (Title slides are discussed in the next section.)

USE THE SLIDE MASTER!

If you want to change every slide in your presentation (except title slides), use the Slide Master. Not only does it save tons of time—applying changes manually to every slide in a presentation can take forever—it also ensures that the changes appear uniformly on every single slide.

XERCISE

Personalizing Your Presentation

1. Start with the version of Generic Presentation.ppt you saved in the previous Exercise.

2. Click **View**, **Master**, then **Slide Master**. You should see the Slide Master for generic presentation, as shown in Figure 27.15.

FIGURE 27.15
Click View, Master, Slide Master to see the Slide Master for this presentation.

3. This slide master has titles set up in the Times New Roman font. Pardon me, but gag me with a RAMDAC; Times New Roman is soooo boring. I want to change that font. So I clicked once on the Title box—that is, the box surrounding the title—and used the Formatting toolbar to change the title to Arial Narrow, bold. You can see the result in Figure 27.16.

FIGURE 27.16
Change the title font to something a little less, uh, boring than Times New Roman.

4. Next, let's change the bullet for second-level lines down in the body boxes on all the normal slides. Start by selecting a second-level line in the Body box, as shown in Figure 27.17.

5. Click **Format**, then **Bullet**, and choose a bullet you like. In Figure 27.18 I've chosen a Wingdings wheel of life symbol as my second level bullet. Click **OK**.

6. The Slide Master is updated to show you the new bullet (see Figure 27.19). Simultaneously, all the second-level text in your presentation is updated to have this new bullet appear in front of it.

YATA—YET ANOTHER TERMINOLOGY ALERT!
The first time I saw the Title box up at the top of Figure 27.15 I just about croaked. What is a "Master title style?" If you ask Office Bob, he doesn't have any answers. Nor does the Help Index.

PowerPoint is just trying to tell you that, if you change the formatting of the Title box up there—as we just did—your new formatting will ripple through all your normal slides.

I've already complained about the nonsense labels Title Area for AutoLayouts and Object Area for AutoLayouts. Just ignore them. The box on top is the Title box; the box on the bottom is the Body box. Anything else is pretentious garbage.

FIGURE 27.17
To change a bullet for a specific level in the body, start by selecting text at that level.

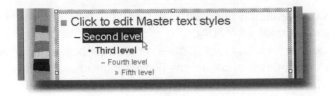

FIGURE 27.18
Choose your new bullet from the Bullet dialog box.

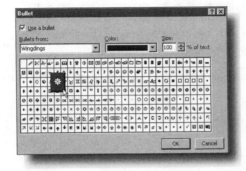

FIGURE 27.19
The new bullet appears on the Slide Master—and thus in the presentation.

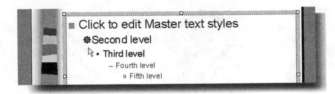

7. One last embellishment. I'm constantly running out of room at the bottom of the body boxes in my slides, so I'd like to enlarge the area. I could reduce the size of the fonts in the Body box, but that would make a lot of people squint. Besides, I only need an extra line or two, so it makes sense to simply make the Body box bigger.

8. Start by moving the Date, Footer, and Number boxes out of the way. This isn't strictly necessary, but it makes it easier to see how far you can enlarge the Body box without falling off the slide. Simply click once on the Date box, and drag it to the top of the slide. Then repeat the action with the Footer and Number boxes, ending up with the result shown in Figure 27.20.

9. Finally, click once on the Body box and drag the lower sizing handle to the bottom of the slide (see Figure 27.21).

FIGURE 27.20
Move the Date, Footer, and Number boxes out of the way.

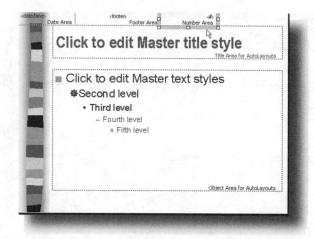

FIGURE 27.21
Click and drag the edge of the Body box to expand it.

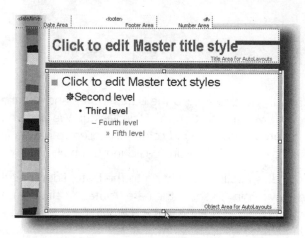

10. To see how the presentation has changed, simply click the **Slide Sorter View** ⬅ icon on the View bar, and PowerPoint stores away the changes to the Slide Master, reflecting them in all the normal slides in the presentation (see Figure 27.22).

11. We'll continue to use this presentation, so save Generic Presentation.ppt.

That exercise only covers a small part of what you can do with the Slide Master.

FIGURE 27.22

The new, (slightly) improved generic presentation.

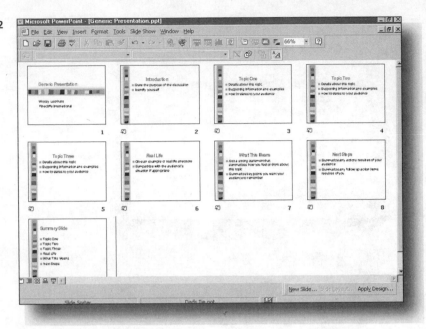

For example, although we only moved the Date, Footer, and Number boxes, we could've resized or moved any box on the Slide Master. We also could've specified a fill color (in other words, a background color) or chosen to have a line drawn around any of the boxes simply by double-clicking the box.

In addition, we could've applied formatting to the Date, Footer, and/or Number boxes. If we told PowerPoint to show the date, footer, or slide number—I'll show you how in the next section—that formatting would be applied to all the Date, Footer, and/or Number boxes in the normal slides.

COMPANY LOGO

Many companies want to put their logos on all their presentations. It's very easy. Bring up the Slide Master (**View, Master, Slide Master**), then click **Insert, Picture, From File**, and bring in a picture file that contains your company's logo. Then click and drag the logo to resize and position it wherever you like.

From that point on, all the normal slides in your presentation will include the logo. PowerPoint sticks it in the Drawing Layer, floating above the text in your slides.

One final note on the Slide Master. The changes you make to the Title box and the Body box—including formatting, bullets, and the like—are reflected in the title boxes and body boxes of your normal slides (in other words, slides that are not designated as title slides). If you have other boxes on your normal slides, they aren't affected at all. And if you put text on one of your slides using the **Insert, Text Box** menu or the **Text Box** icon on the Drawing toolbar, none of that text will be changed by modifications to the Slide Master.

Title Master

Now let's turn our attention to changing title slides. Real, honest-to-goodness title slides come from three places:

- They can be placed in your presentation by the AutoContent Wizard.
- They can be copied in when you create a new presentation based on one of the pre-fab presentations on the **File**, **New**, **Presentations** tab.
- You can put them in your presentation manually, using the New Slide dialog box (see Figure 27.11) and choosing the first prototypical slide.

Most presentations only have one title slide. When you only have one title slide, it doesn't much matter if you change that slide directly, or if you change the Title Master and let PowerPoint roll those changes onto the title slide.

On the other hand, if you have more than one title slide—or if it's possible that you might want more than one sometime in the future—changing the Title Master makes sense. That way, you'll know that all the title slides will look the same.

*E*XERCISE

Change Generic's Title Master

1. We're going for overkill. Some day we might want to add a second title slide to Generic Presentation.ppt, so instead of just manually changing the title slide in the presentation, we're going to change the Title Master.

2. Start by taking a good look at the title slide in Generic Presentation.ppt. If you're in Slide Sorter view, click the first slide in the presentation, then click the **Slide View** 🔲 icon on the View bar (see Figure 27.23).

3. Let's say you want to move that picture (it's supposed to be "Dad's Tie") from the middle of the slide to the top, and shuffle the generic presentation heading lower. More than that, let's say you want to make those changes to all the title slides in the presentation—even new ones, which you might create at a later date.

4. That's a job for Title Master. Click **View**, then **Title Master**. You should see a Title Master that looks like Figure 27.24. Because you want to move the tie, click it once to reveal the sizing handles.

FIGURE 27.23
The original title slide for generic presentation.

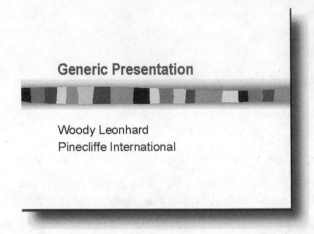

FIGURE 27.24
Click the graphic on the Title Master.

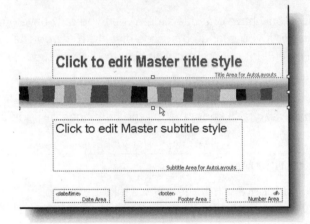

5. Move your cursor until it turns into a four-headed arrow. Then click and drag the tie up toward the top of the slide. When you have it in position, let it go. Then, because you want to move the Title box downward, click once on it, as shown in Figure 27.25.

6. Again, jockey around until the mouse pointer turns into a four-headed arrow, then click and drag the Title Box down. When you're happy with its new location, let go of the mouse (see Figure 27.26).

7. That's all the changes you wanted to make, so click the **Slide View** 🔲 icon on the View bar. You'll see how your Title Slide has been changed (see Figure 27.27).

FIGURE 27.25
Drag the graphic up, then select the Title box.

FIGURE 27.26
Click and drag the Title box down.

FIGURE 27.27
The new title slide.

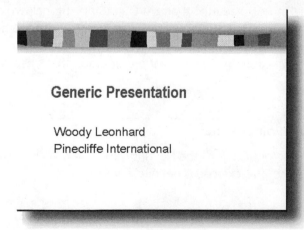

8. Save Generic Presentation.ppt. We'll use it again in Chapter 28, "Making Presentations Look Better."

That's how PowerPoint supports global changes. All the strings are being pulled by the masters, and you can find four masters in a .pot.

Easy, huh?

Footer, Date, Slide Number

Every Slide Master has boxes set up for a footer, date, and slide number. You can format those boxes, add text to them (for example, put the text Slide in front of the <#> marker in the Slide Number box), move them, resize them, and so on.

Oddly, though, you don't use the Slide Master to tell PowerPoint that you want to see the footer, date, or slide number on slides. In fact, you can't even use the Slide Master to type a footer that will appear on all the slides—PowerPoint won't let you get in to edit the Footer box.

To get footers, dates, and/or slide numbers going on your slides, click **View**, then **Header and Footer**. There you can pick and choose which you want to see. If you click **Apply to All** on the way out, the changes are made to the Slide Master. If you just click **Apply**, the change is only made to the current slide.

PowerPoint Central

Microsoft's PowerPoint Central is another one of those odd Microsoft mixtures of the truly useful with the utterly useless. Speaking of the former, did you know that you have 150 fonts—*good* fonts—on your Office 97 CD? All you have to do is install them. Speaking of the latter, there's a QuickStart tutorial, which is really a PowerPoint presentation that attempts to explain how to put together PowerPoint presentations. (Say that ten times quickly.) The QuickStart tutorial rates as an excellent example of a typical flashy PowerPoint presentation that's nearly devoid of content.

XERCISE

Connect to PowerPoint Central

1. If your PC is connected to the Net and you have a Web browser working on your machine, this exercise is definitely worthwhile.

2. Click **Tools**, then **PowerPoint Central**. You'll get a message (see Figure 27.28) scolding you for not coming here sooner. If you have a Web connection that works, click **Yes** and PowerPoint downloads the latest version of PowerPoint Central.

FIGURE 27.28
PowerPoint Central wants to know if you want to get the latest version.

3. PowerPoint Central appears (see Figure 27.29, although the version you get may differ slightly from this one). When you have an extra day or two you can browse through the flotsam and jetsam on this screen. For now, we want the free stuff, so click the link marked **FREE**.

FIGURE 27.29
PowerPoint Central, updated version.

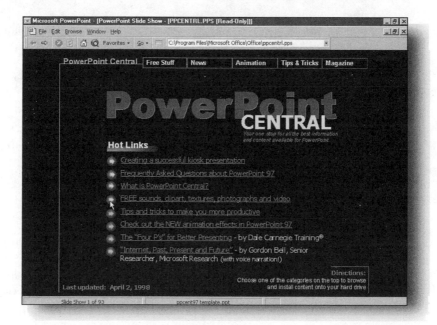

4. The first three links at the top of the Free Stuff page (see Figure 27.30) include worthwhile stuff. The fourth link heads to the Microsoft Help site on the Web. And the **Start** button at the bottom puts you in the utterly useless QuickStart tutorial. Click the first link.

FIGURE 27.30
Try the first
three links,
but avoid the
QuickStart
tutorial.

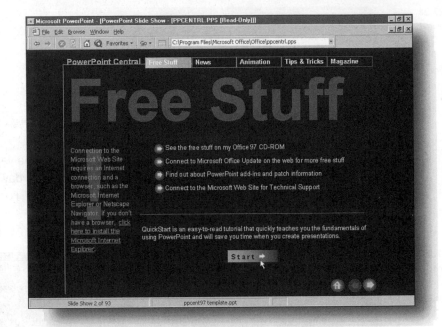

5. Most of the items listed on the ValuPack slide (see Figure 27.31) have been covered elsewhere in this book. In particular, the Audio, Clip Art, Photographs, Textures, Video, and Custom Soundtracks buttons just point to items you'll find in the Office 97 Clip Gallery. But you might find products that interest you under the Fonts, RealAudio, ActiveMovie, Wizards, and Templates links. Take a few minutes and check them out.

6. If you click the second link in Figure 27.30, PowerPoint Central puts you on the Web, bounces you around once or twice, and finally ends up on a Microsoft Web page that offers a wide variety of free add-ins (see Figure 27.32). I've found the Weblinks Help file to be particularly worthwhile. Try downloading it and any other add-ins that strike your fancy.

FIGURE 27.31
The only definitive list of products available in the Office 97 ValuPack.

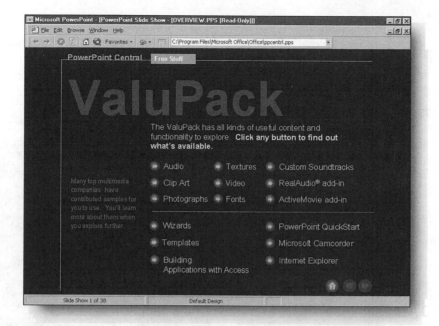

FIGURE 27.32
Microsoft's free add-ins for PowerPoint.

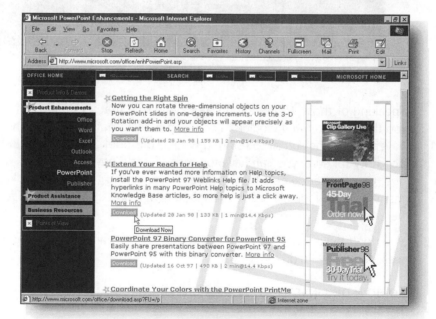

7. Clicking the third link in Figure 27.30 brings you to the most important PowerPoint information you'll find anywhere: a list of bug fixes and updates (see Figure 27.33). Make sure you get the latest and, when you're done, get out of the PowerPoint Central presentation by clicking **File**, then **End Show**.

FIGURE 27.33
PowerPoint's bug fixes and updates.

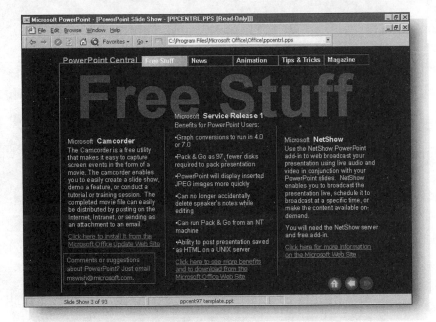

Speaking of those 150 free fonts. It may be true that you can never be too young, too thin, or too tan. I wouldn't know. I'm old (er, mature), fat (uh, huggable), and I haven't seen the sun since I started writing this book months ago. But one thing I do know for sure: you *can* have too many fonts. They can be awful hard to manage, you'll never be able to remember the names of the ones you like, and all too many of them look alike. So don't go hog-wild and install all those fonts just because they're there.

You don't believe a word I said, did you? The free part is what caught your eye. Oh well. Don't say I didn't warn you.

SO HOW DO I INSTALL ALL THOSE FONTS?

There are more than 150 fonts from well-known foundries included free on the Office 97 CD. PowerPoint Central shows them to you, but never really tells you how to install them. Here's how.

Out in Windows, click **Start**, then **Settings**, then **Control Panel**. Double-click the Fonts applet. Click **File**, then **Install New Font**. Navigate to the \valupack\msfonts folder on your Office 97 CD, and twiddle your thumbs while Windows' Font installer sucks up the names of all the fonts.

Pick and choose the fonts you'd like to install from the **List of fonts** box (see Figure 27.34). Or, if you must, click **Select All**. When you have the fonts you want selected, click **OK**.

FIGURE 27.34
Add a few of the free fonts, but don't go overboard.

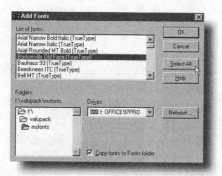

Multiple PCs

Sometimes when you're making a presentation, you want the same presentation to show on two different machines—typically the first one is a portable you're using, and the second is hooked up to the projector. If you have a null modem cable it's easy. Just click **Slide Show**, then **View on Two Screens**, and follow the wizard.

PowerPoint also includes an amazingly powerful conferencing capability that's rarely mentioned. How often do you want to show your presentation to somebody who isn't sitting down right next to you, or in a conference room with you? PowerPoint has the solution. As long as you and your contact have PCs running PowerPoint 97, you can get a voice phone connection going (so you can talk while giving your presentation). If you're both connected to a corporate network or can get on the Internet, you can deliver your presentation without being physically present.

*E*XERCISE

Tele-Presentation

   1. Make sure you and your audience are all running PowerPoint 97, and you all have a way to connect your PCs.

   2. Get the presentation you want to deliver open in PowerPoint. Then place a conference call that connects you with all the members of the audience.

3. Have everyone start PowerPoint 97, then click **Tools**, then **Presentation Conference**. You need to follow the Presentation Conference Wizard (see Figure 27.35) to get connected.

4. In Figure 27.36, PowerPoint needs to know whether you're the presenter or a member of the audience. You should click **Presenter**; all the other folks on the conference call should click **Audience**.

WHAT'S A NULL MODEM CABLE?
It's a special kind of computer cable that fakes out two computers to think that they're both connected via modem—but without the modem. Both ends of a null modem cable (sometimes known as a *laplink* cable, in honor of the software package Laplink, which connects PCs and makes it easy to transfer files) have nine-pin female connectors, but the wires don't go straight through; they're swapped around in a specific way. They plug into serial ports or (sometimes) parallel ports on both of the PCs.

You can pick up a null modem cable at any computer shop. Just make sure you get a cable that's specifically called a Null Modem Cable.

Laplink, by the way, is still a great way to quickly transfer files, via a null modem cable, from your desktop PC to your portable. Think about it the next time you dash off to the airport to make your presentation.

FIGURE 27.35
PowerPoint's powerful Presentation Conference Wizard.

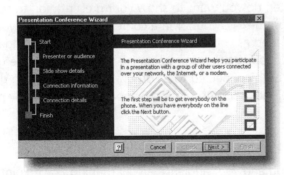

5. Next, everyone needs to get connected (see Figure 27.37).

FIGURE 27.36
Tell PowerPoint that you're the Presenter.

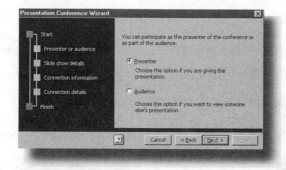

FIGURE 27.37
This is the time to connect.

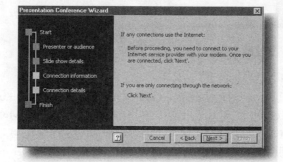

6. At this point, members of the audience will see a computer name or Internet address appear on their screens, compliments of the Presentation Conference Wizard. Each of them needs to tell you, via the conference call, the name or address, so you can enter it on the screen in Figure 27.38.

FIGURE 27.38
The connection is made when you tell PowerPoint which computers or addresses to look for.

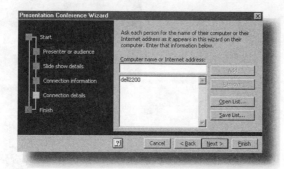

7. There's a little timing glitch at this point; the Audience needs to click **Finish** to end their copies of the Presentation Conference Wizard before you do (see Figure 27.39). They'll see a message that tells them to wait while the presentation is being loaded.

FIGURE 27.39
Don't click
Finish until
everybody
else has.

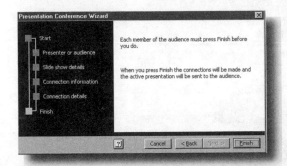

8. Now you're in the driver's seat. PowerPoint shows you the current screen (upper-left corner in Figure 27.40) and gives you a Stage Manager for the common screen controls, a Slide Navigator for moving directly from one slide to another, and a Meeting Minder window for taking notes.

FIGURE 27.40
A bevy of
tools for
making your
presentation,
long
distance.

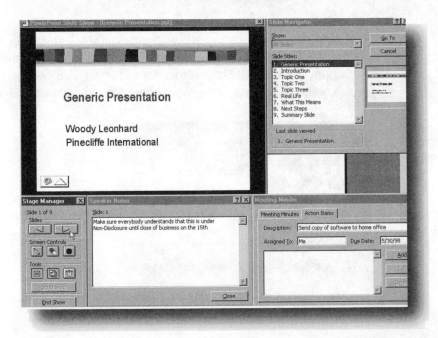

   9. When you're done with the presentation, click **End Show** in the Stage Manager window.

While this method of making presentations requires a voice phone line independent of the computer connection, it's fast, easy, and relatively foolproof. I recommend it highly.

Pack and Go

I wish all the Office applications had this feature.

PowerPoint's designers realize that it's a PC jungle out there. When you take your presentation to an unfamiliar site, you have no idea if the computers there will have the latest version of PowerPoint available. You don't even know if they'll have the right fonts installed. About all you can depend on is the availability of a 3.5 inch floppy disk drive. Beyond that, you're taking chances.

That's why PowerPoint includes something called Pack and Go. This feature packs up everything—and I do mean *everything*—you need to take your presentation on the road. It'll scarf up the fonts you've used. It can even pack up a PowerPoint viewer that will run on Windows 3.1!

GET THE LATEST
Make sure you install Office 97 Service Release-1 (mentioned in Chapter 2, "Precursors to Using Office") before you try to use Pack and Go; also, drop by PowerPoint Central in case there's a later version. The old version has a nasty habit of not working with Windows NT installations. The latest version not only cures that problem, it can reduce the number of diskettes necessary to hold an entire presentation.

Pack and Go lets you put your presentation on any media you choose, including 3.5 inch floppy disks. (Fair warning: Presentations with graphics of almost any sort will fill several floppies.) When you get to the other site, you insert the first diskette into the presentation PC, run a program called pngsetup.exe, watch it all unpack, then run the PowerPoint viewer, ppview32.exe, and choose your presentation.

To use Pack and Go, get your presentation ready and, with the presentation open, click **File**, then **Pack and Go**. Follow along with the wizard (see Figure 27.41) and you'll be done in no time.

FIGURE 27.41
The Pack and
Go Wizard
makes trans-
porting a pre-
sentation
easy.

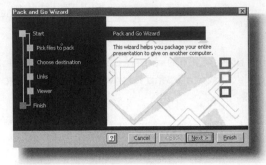

Making Presentations Look Better

CONTENT, CONTENT, CONTENT.

I assume you're only reading this chapter because you have stellar content in your presentation, and you want to jazz things up a bit visually. Okay. I can understand that. But don't lose focus on your content. A presentation with lousy content and a zippy presentation may keep your audience awake, but it won't do much more.

In this chapter I'm going to assume you have a presentation pretty much put together, but you want to add a few bells and whistles to some of the slides, maybe stick a chart someplace, or add a few transition effects.

Charts

Let's say that we're pretty happy with Generic Presentation.ppt (Generic Presentation.ppt was created in Chapter 27, "PowerPoint's Auto Support"), except we want to add a chart on the slide marked Topic One. You have an amazing array of tools available to you. In particular, if you know the trick, you can take advantage of Excel's powerful charting tools to draw the perfect chart.

THE ADVANCED COURSE

Most books step you through using Microsoft Chart in PowerPoint slides, but I refuse to do it. You don't want to use Chart if you have Excel handy. Yes, I know, this is a topic that should go in the next chapter, where we discuss tying parts of Office 97 together. But you're almost ready for more advanced topics, and you might as well learn how to do this right.

It's true that you can animate a Microsoft Chart, that is, you can set things up so bars on the chart fly in from the left or right, with appropriate whooshing sounds, and the like. But in every other respect, Excel is superior to MS Chart and should be your first weapon of choice for graphing data on a PowerPoint slide.

*E*XERCISE

Put a Chart in a Slide

1. Open **Generic Presentation.ppt**. The slide we want is the third slide in the presentation, so click the **Slide Sorter View** ▦ icon on the View bar, click slide number 3, then click the **Slide View** ▣ icon.

2. Although there are lots of ways to add a chart to this simple bullet slide, by far the best way is to change the Slide Layout. That ensures that all the text on the slide remains intact, and that the precious link between this normal slide and the Slide Master isn't broken. To change the Slide Layout, click **Format**, then **Slide Layout**. You'll see the Slide Layout dialog box (see Figure 28.1), which is identical to the New Slide dialog box we saw in Figure 27.11 and Figure 27.12.

3. Although it's true that you can change the layout to Text & Object (reading in the lower-right box in Figure 28.1), a quick check of the New Slide discussion in the previous chapter will remind you that "Chart" refers to that stunted Microsoft Chart application. You don't want that. You want to connect with the mother lode, Excel 97.

FIGURE 28.1
PowerPoint
offers to
change the
layout of the
slide, in a
dialog box
that's identi-
cal to the
New Slide
dialog box.

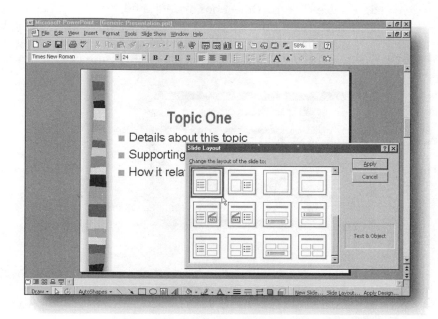

4. So scroll down in Figure 28.1 until you get to the **Text & Object** layout.
Click once on the layout, and click **Apply**. PowerPoint responds by
rearranging the text on your slide and putting a placeholder for an Object
on the right side, as shown in Figure 28.2.

FIGURE 28.2
The Body box
stays on the
left, but a
new Object
box appears
on the right.

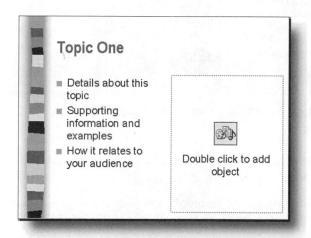

5. Double-click the Object box, as indicated, and PowerPoint goes to the Insert Object dialog box (see Figure 28.3). This Insert Object dialog box is identical to the one you'll see in all the Office applications. We want to insert an Excel Chart, so choose it from the **Object type** box, and click **OK**.

FIGURE 28.3
PowerPoint
lets you
choose what
kind of object
you want to
put in the
Object box.

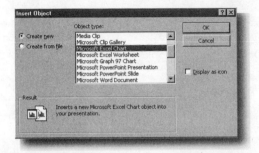

6. Excel responds with a dummy chart attached to a spreadsheet called Sheet1 (see Figure 28.4).

FIGURE 28.4
Excel's initial
chart, with
attached
spreadsheet.

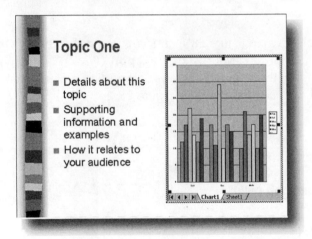

7. Click the **Sheet1** tab and Excel shows you what data it's using to draw that dummy chart (see Figure 28.5).

8. Replace the data with some of your own devising. In Figure 28.6 I've used the numbers from test.xls, our test spreadsheet from the Excel chapters.

FIGURE 28.5
The data that corresponds to the initial chart.

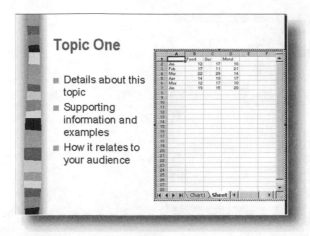

FIGURE 28.6
Type or copy your own data into the spreadsheet.

9. Click the **Chart1** tab again and get to work on the chart. Right-click the chart and choose **Source Data** to reset the cells used to draw the chart. Then right-click the chart again and choose **Chart Type**, to let you choose the kind of chart you'd like to see, as shown in Figure 28.7.

10. After a few more right-clicks to reset the axis labels and a little futzing here and there, I came up with the chart shown in Figure 28.8. You should try it, too. It's easy, and if you run into problems you can always check back in the Excel chapters in this book.

11. Save Generic Presentation.ppt.

FIGURE 28.7
Right-click
the chart and
start modify-
ing it.

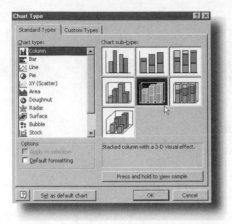

FIGURE 28.8
The final
chart in slide
number 3.

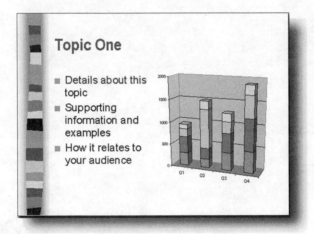

Text Boxes

The next common modification most people want to make with their slides involves adding more text to a slide—but not in the main bullet-ridden Body box. (There's something eerie about that phrase, but never mind.)

If you want to add a second column of bullets on one slide, that's easy: click **Format**, **Slide Layout**, and choose the layout with two columns of bullets. (It's the third layout in Figure 27.11.) Your existing bulleted text ends up scrunched in the left side Body box, and a new Body box appears on the right.

But if you want to add free-form text to a slide you have to use a text box.

XERCISE

Text Floating Above a Slide

1. Let's say you know that your audience will be tired and grouchy by the time you finish the Generic Presentations slide called Topic Two. You want to put some text at the bottom of the slide that says, "Let's take a break!" so they know that there's some relief in sight.

2. Open up **Generic Presentation.ppt**. The slide called Topic Two is the fourth slide in the presentation, so click the **Slide Sorter View** ▦ icon on the View bar, click slide number 4, then click the **Slide View** ▣ icon. You'll get slide 4, which is shown in Figure 28.9.

FIGURE 28.9
Slide 4, where we want to put the text "Let's take a break!"

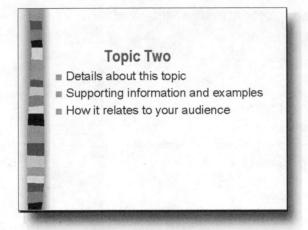

3. There are several ways to put a text box on a slide, but the easiest is to click the **Text Box** 🔳 icon on the Drawing toolbar. Your mouse pointer turns into a weird vertical-line-thingy with a crosshatch. Figure out where you want to put your text, then click and drag to create a box to hold it (see Figure 28.10).

4. You can immediately start typing text. In Figure 28.11, I've typed `Let's take a break!`

5. You can format the text directly by using the usual formatting tools (font, size, color, centering, and so on), either the ones on the Formatting toolbar, or the ones buried in the menus. You can also format the box. If you right-click that new text box and choose **Format Text Box**, PowerPoint responds with the Format Text Box dialog box shown in Figure 28.12.

FIGURE 28.10
Click and drag to insert a text box on top of your slide.

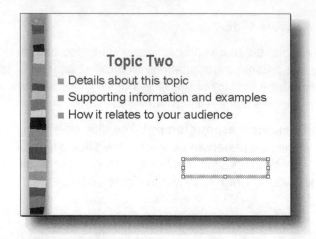

FIGURE 28.11
Type the text that goes into the box.

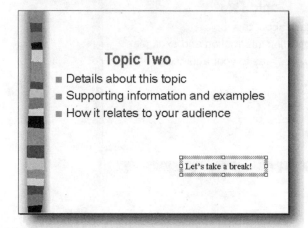

FIGURE 28.12
You can even apply formatting to the text box, by right-clicking.

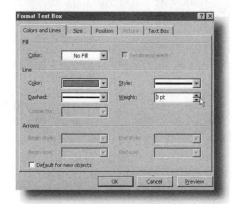

6. Per Figure 28.12, I've chosen to have the text box appear with a dark line around it. After setting the formatting, click **OK** and your text will appear on the slide (see Figure 28.13).

FIGURE 28.13
The text box appears with a thick line.

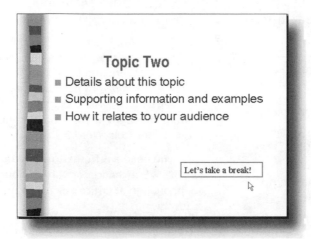

7. Save **Generic Presentation.ppt.**

It's important to realize that this text is "floating" above the slide, in PowerPoint's Drawing Layer. As such, the text won't appear in Outline View, nor will it be changed should you change the Body box in the Slide Master. In fact, nothing you do in the Slide Master will influence this floating text.

Pictures

Pictures, pictures, everybody wants pictures in their presentations. If they help prove your point, there's much to be said about pictures—worth a thousand words and all that. But if they merely adorn, you're running dangerously close to producing an airhead presentation.

By far the simplest way to put a picture on a particular slide is to change the layout. Click **Format**, **Slide Layout**, and choose the layout marked **Text & Clip Art**, or the one marked **Clip Art & Text**, the two layouts in the lower-left corner of Figure 27.11. The current bulleted text shows up either to the left or right of the picture placeholder. Double-click the picture placeholder and you end up in Office's Clip Gallery. From there you can bring any picture you like into the Clip Gallery and, from there, into the picture placeholder.

Most of the time, though, you want to put a picture on a slide without moving around the text that's already there.

*E*XERCISE

Paste a Picture on a Slide

1. Let's put a picture on the slide titled Topic Three. In Generic Presentation.ppt, the slide called Topic Three is the fifth slide in the presentation, so click the **Slide Sorter View** ⊞ icon on the View bar, click slide number 5, then click the **Slide View** ▢ icon.

2. Click **Insert**, **Picture**, then **From File**, as in Figure 28.14.

> **WHOA! THAT INSERT PICTURE MENU LOOKS FAMILIAR!**
> Oh no. The cat's outta the bag.
>
> Yes, PowerPoint has the same **Insert Picture** menu that you've seen in Word and Excel. Yes, you can use it in precisely this way to put AutoShapes in your presentations—or Org Charts, WordArt, scanned images (if you have a scanner), even text tables from Word 97.
>
> ☞ If you need a refresher on those options, see page 239. But chances are pretty good you're adept enough at Office's picture handling by now to just dive in.
>
> Don't go overboard, though, okay? Chances are awfully good that any WordArt you put on a slide will be just that...awful.

FIGURE 28.14
PowerPoint's Insert Picture menu looks familiar, eh?

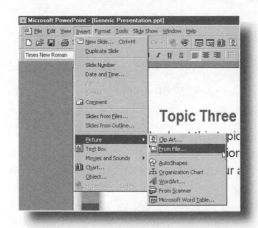

3. Anyway, when you click **Insert**, **Picture**, **From File**, PowerPoint responds
with the now-familiar Insert Picture dialog box, as shown in Figure 28.15.
I found a picture of a globe worth snagging in the Windows 98\Windows
folder. You can hunt around for your own favorite picture. When you've got
it, click it and click **Insert**.

FIGURE 28.15
Look for a
decent
picture.

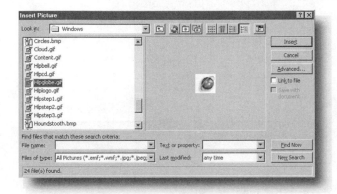

4. The picture—no doubt way too big, or way too small, as in Figure 28.16—
appears in your slide along with the Picture toolbar.

FIGURE 28.16
The picture
appears at a
random loca-
tion inside
your slide.

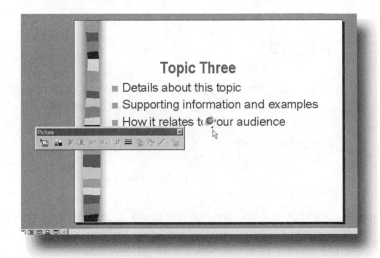

5. Click and drag the picture to whatever location you like. Click the square box
sizing handles to make it bigger or smaller (see Figure 28.17). And apply
whatever picture-mangling options suit your fancy from the Picture toolbar.

FIGURE 28.17
Click and drag the picture, and resize it to fit the location.

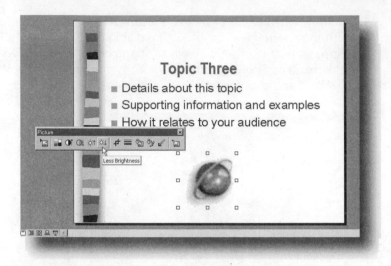

6. Save **Generic Presentation.ppt**.

Once again, it's important to realize that pictures you put on a slide using **Insert Picture** (or the Drawing toolbar, for that matter) float above the slide itself. Nothing you do to the Slide Master will change them.

Movies and Sounds

PowerPoint lets you put movie files and sounds in your slides. Many major video file formats are supported, including .avi, .mpg, .flc, and .fli. And sounds can be played directly from a CD in the PC's CD drive. Office 97 comes with a few video clips and sounds in the Clip Gallery. You can pick up many, many more on the Web. (Just make sure you get permission from the owner to use them!)

XERCISE _____

Self-Starting Video

1. This time we'll put a self-starting video of a PC going up in smoke on the slide called Real Life. In Generic Presentation.ppt, that's the sixth slide in the presentation, click the **Slide Sorter View** icon on the View bar, click slide number 6, then click the **Slide View** icon.

2. Click **Insert**, **Movies and Sounds**, **Movie from Gallery**. You'll get the Clip Gallery, open to the **Videos** tab, as shown in Figure 28.18. Choose the video called **blowup**, and click **Insert**.

FIGURE 28.18
When you
Insert from
the Gallery,
Microsoft's
Clip Gallery
comes up.

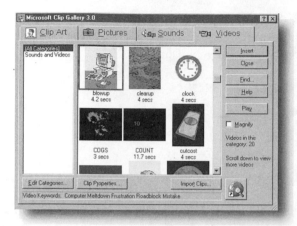

3. PowerPoint puts the video clip in slide 6. Resize it, then click and drag it to a convenient corner, as shown in Figure 28.19.

FIGURE 28.19
Resize and
move the clip.

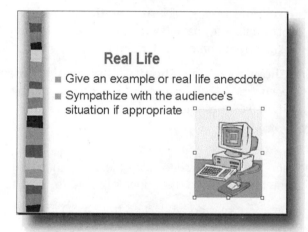

4. Here's the trick. When you insert a video clip into a PowerPoint presentation, it's set up so you have to click the video before it will start running. So, when you have a presentation running you must have the presence of mind to click the video—otherwise it just sits there, looking like a simple unanimated picture. But we want to set things up so the video clip runs automatically, as soon as the slide appears onscreen.

5. Right-click the video clip (in this case, right-click the picture of the PC in the lower-right corner of slide 6), and choose **Custom Animation**. Then click the **Timing** tab, as shown in Figure 28.20.

FIGURE 28.20
The self-starting setting sits buried in this dialog box.

6. In the **Start animation** box, click **Automatically**. You can run the spin number up if you like, to make PowerPoint delay just a bit after it shows the slide on the screen, before it starts running the video. Click **OK**.

7. Click **Slide Show**, then **View Show**. Go through the presentation normally by clicking each slide in turn. When slide 6 appears, the **blowup** video runs by itself, and the PC goes into meltdown. Cool!

8. Save Generic Presentation.ppt.

Sounds work the same way as this video clip: Unless you change the Custom Animation setting you'll have to click the sound's picture to get it to work.

For more information about playing a selection from a CD in a slide, bring up the Office Assistant (in other words, press **F1**) and type `play cd`.

Transitions and Builds

When used in moderation, transitions and builds can add a lot to your presentations without becoming overly distracting.

What's a *transition*? It's the way that PowerPoint moves from one slide to the next. You can have PowerPoint simply cut—move from one slide to the next, with no animation in between—or you can make the new slide arrive in a blaze of checkerboard patches, wiping across the screen, zooming in from the top, bottom, lower right, or any of dozens of additional animation techniques.

A *build*, on the other hand, controls how elements of the slide are placed on the slide. For example, you can have the title appear, and then make each bullet point appear, one at a time, when you click the screen, or at predefined, timed intervals.

MORE CONTROL

If you want to see the transition effect in greater detail, or if you want to control how quickly the transition takes place, click **Slide Show**, then **Slide Transition**. In the Slide Transition dialog box you can also tell PowerPoint that you want the slides to advance automatically—without a mouse click—and if you want a sound triggered as the slides change. *Whoosh! HOOORAY! Gimme a break…*

In short, the options would befuddle a movie director, and the potential for visual over-stimulation looms greatest right here.

*E*XERCISE

Generic Transitions and Builds

1. Open **Generic Presentations.ppt** and go into Slide Show Preview.

2. Usually you'll want to set the same transition for all the slides in a presentation. It can be distracting having some explode out from the middle, others fly in from the bottom, and still others checkerboard! To set one transition for all the slides in a presentation, click **Edit**, then **Select All** to select all the slides. You can then set the transition effect by selecting them from the **Slide Transition Effects** drop-down box on the left of the Slide Sorter toolbar (see Figure 28.21).

FIGURE 28.21
Select a transition effect by choosing it from this drop-down list.

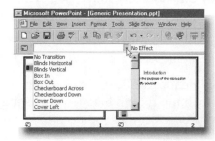

TRANSITION FOR ONE
If you want to set the transition for just one slide, select the slide, then choose the transition from the **Slide Transition Effects** drop-down box. This is the transition that takes effect when the slide appears on the screen—it has nothing to do with the way the slide goes away.

3. If you watch closely, the first selected slide will show a miniature animation of whichever transition effect you choose, so you can get quick visual confirmation of the effect.

4. In Figure 28.22, I've chosen the **Cover Left** transition, which shuffles new slides in from the right to the left. It's a reasonable animation that isn't too distracting.

FIGURE 28.22
Applying the
Cover Left
transition to
all the slides
in the presen-
tation.

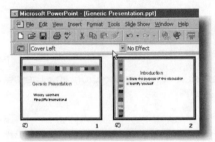

5. Let's also put together a build for the last slide, the one marked Summary Slide. I'm particularly impressed by the Spiral build, which adds each bullet item by spiraling it in from the top, gradually making the item bigger, until it ends up at the correct size in the right location.

6. To apply the Spiral build technique to the final slide, just click the slide (in Figure 28.23, that's slide 9). Then choose **Spiral** in the **Text Preset Animation** drop-down list on the Slide Sorter toolbar.

7. Start the presentation by clicking **Slide Show**, then **View Show**. Each slide arrives on the screen from left to right. And the final slide, shown in Figure 28.24 in mid-spiral, builds the bullet points one at a time.

8. Keep Generic Presentation.ppt around just to wow your friends.

That's about all I have to say on the topic of PowerPoint. There are a few features I didn't cover, but they're all pretty obvious from the menus and they don't really go to the heart of how PowerPoint works, or what you need to know to get a good presentation up on the screen.

FIGURE 28.23
Have PowerPoint build the Summary Slide by spiraling in each bullet item when you click the mouse.

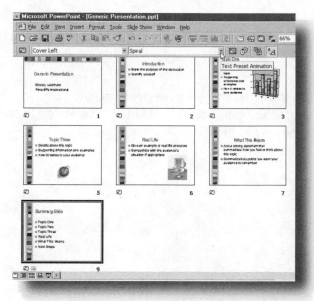

FIGURE 28.24
The Summary Slide build, caught in mid-spiral with one of the bullet items.

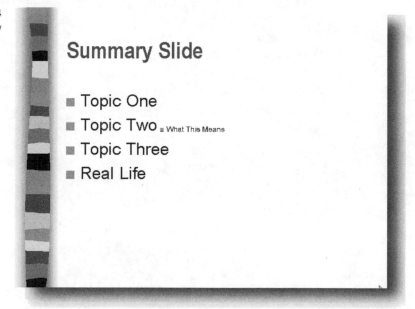

If you have a microphone on your PC, you can record narratives to go with the slides. In fact, it's quite possible to record your entire presentation, and never speak a word. (Audiences will just love it, eh?) To find out how to do that, bring up Office Bob and type `voice`.

You can also use PowerPoint to time your presentation, and warn you if you're running too fast or too slow, using something called the Slide Meter. To see details on that feature, type `rehearse` in the Office Assistant.

Advanced Topics

VII

29   Tying the Parts Together   637

30   Office on the Web   667

Tying the
Parts Together

ONE OF OFFICE 97'S STILL-NASCENT CAPABILITIES, the possibility of making all

the Office 97 applications work together in harmony, rates as the

Holy Grail of Office suite programmers. Sadly, we're still a long,

long way from the time when all the parts of Office work similarly,

and all work together. Until that time comes we're going to hear a

lot of marketing hype about how the parts of Office interconnect—

the logo on the box shows the pieces coming together as in a

jigsaw puzzle, for heaven's sake—whereas the real-world inter-

connections consist of little more than broad tips and a handful

of very obscure tricks.

That's why I put this chapter in the advanced topics category. If you're still a little green behind the ears (as were we all at one time!), tread lightly. You can't expect all the interconnections to work precisely as advertised all the time—your system will lock up unexpectedly every now and then, you'll face weird errors with even weirder error messages, and sooner or later things will go wrong and you'll never figure out why.

That said, Office 97 has much stronger, more capable, and more reliable interconnections than any previous version of Office—or any other collection of computer applications that I know about. Working with the glue that holds them together can be exciting, challenging, and ultimately make your working day go much more smoothly.

Once you figure out the tricks, of course.

Copying, Embedding, Linking

There are three ways to put data from one Office 97 application into another Office 97 application:

- *Copying.* Office supports copying through the Clipboard, just like every other Windows application. When you copy data into one of the Office applications, there's no memory of where the data came from: The application just scarfs up the data and goes on its merry way.

● *Embedding*. Depending on the applications involved, you may be able to embed data from one Office application into another. When you embed, the data is actually moved from one application to the other, but the receiving application remembers where it came from.

● *Linking*. Similar to embedding, but the data doesn't get shuffled around. Instead, Office sets up a link to the data so it can retrieve the data when it's needed.

Yeah, those definitions seem kind of loosey-goosey at the moment. Cut me a little slack, though, and I'll show you how each of the interconnection methods works.

In the remainder of this chapter, I'm going to look at specific pairs of Office 97 applications, and show you how to get data from one into the other. I'll clearly identify whether the data is going from one application to another by copying, embedding, or linking, and thereby help tighten up the loose definitions.

I hope.

Word and Outlook

When you think of moving data from one Office 97 application to another, what's the first thing that comes to your mind?

Of course. You want to be able to retrieve names and addresses from your Outlook 98 Contacts list and use them in Word 97. At least to a first approximation, *everybody* needs to do that. You'd think it would be the major focus of Microsoft's Office interconnection efforts.

And, of course, you'd be wrong.

Retrieving Names and Addresses

You can try to do it manually—get Outlook 98's Contacts list running, find the person in question, copy their address to the Clipboard, flip back to Word 97, paste the address information, but oh! wait!

Guess what? You can't even copy the name and the address from Contacts to Word in one round-trip. You can pick up one or the other, but not both.

Fortunately, there are a couple of stopgap measures you can take to make it much easier to copy Outlook 98 Contacts into Word 97.

XERCISE

Retrieve a Name and Address in Word

1. Start Word 97.

2. We're going to put a new icon on the Standard toolbar (that's the toolbar on top) that will insert a name and address from Outlook 98 into the current document. Click **View**, **Toolbars**, **Customize**, and click the **Commands** tab (see Figure 29.1).

3. Make sure the box marked **Save in** says Normal.dot. On the left side, in the **Categories** box, scroll down to **Insert**. Then, in the **Commands** box scroll down to **Address Book**.

WHY DID THEY SCREW UP?
You ought to be able to retrieve a name and address directly while you're inside Word, without having to worry about flipping over to Outlook's Contacts, copying, pasting, or anything else. Surely, this is one of the major shortcomings of Office 97. How could Microsoft have overlooked such an obvious feature?

The short answer, I'm convinced: timing. When Office 97 originally shipped, Outlook 97 was such a dog that nobody at Microsoft wanted to build good hooks between Word 97 and that bow-wow of a program. If the hooks were good enough, they'd only highlight how deficient Outlook 97 really was. Then Outlook 98 came out, and suddenly—within a month of its release—there's more than a million people using Outlook for its Contacts management. By that time, though, it was too late to change Word 97.

COPY, EMBED, OR LINK?
This is copying, pure and simple. After Word 97 snags the name and address from Outlook 98's Contact list, that data gets pasted into the document at the current insertion point (in other words, where the cursor is sitting). There's no link back into Outlook, or even any memory that the data originally came from Outlook.

FIGURE 29.1
Put a new
icon on a
toolbar by
clicking View,
Toolbars,
Customize.

4. Next, you're going to create a new icon on the Standard toolbar. Click **Address Book** and drag it up to a convenient location on the toolbar. In Figure 29.2, I've chosen to put the new icon to the right of the **Spelling** icon, but you can put it wherever you like.

FIGURE 29.2
Click and
drag Address
Book onto a
handy tool-
bar.

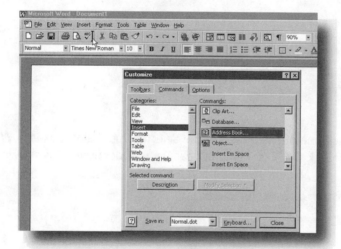

5. Let go of the mouse button, and you'll have a new icon on the toolbar, as shown in Figure 29.3. Close the dialog box. If you hover your mouse over the icon, you'll note how the ToolTip says Insert Address. And that's precisely what this icon does. Sorta.

FIGURE 29.3
Drop the new
icon on the
toolbar.

6. Let's take the new icon out for a spin. Click **Insert Address**. Word chunks
and whirrs for a little bit—it has to wake up Outlook 98 to get the
names—and when it's done, Word presents a list of names in the Select
Name dialog box, shown in Figure 29.4.

FIGURE 29.4
Word lets
you select a
name from
Outlook's
Contacts list.

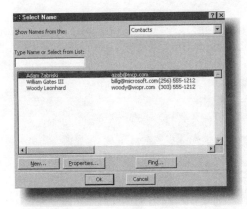

7. Click one of the names in the Select Name dialog box, say **William Gates
III**. Click **OK**. The name appears in your document, as shown in Figure 29.5.

FIGURE 29.5
When Word
retrieves a
name from
Contacts, it
never includes
the company
name, but
always
includes the
country
name.

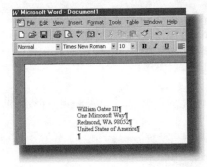

8. Yes, what you see is what you get. Word never brings in the company name, and it always brings in the full country name—even if the country name is United States of America.

Fortunately there's a way to get around the problem, although you won't find any documentation for this solution anywhere in the Office 97 package.

WHAT'S WRONG WITH SELECT NAME?
Just about everything.

The names only appear in alphabetical order—sorted by first name. (It doesn't matter how you sort them in Outlook.) Only the names of people appear, no business names. You can't see addresses, so if you have two separate entries for a person or company, you have to guess which one includes the correct address. You can't sort. And on and on. In short, the only thing worse than this dialog box that I can imagine would be no dialog box at all.

But wait. It gets worse.

On Useful Information

Word uses a hidden AutoText entry called AddressLayout to determine what name and address fields it should retrieve, and how to put them in your documents. Don't bother trying to find it. You won't see AddressLayout anywhere in the AutoText list, or anyplace else in Word, for that matter.

This is a difficult exercise—quite likely the most difficult one in the whole book—so follow along carefully. There's no inherent danger; you won't mess up your machine if you flub some of the typing, for example. But to get a decent name and address imported into your documents from the Insert Address icon, you have to follow these instructions exactly.

*E*XERCISE

Make the Name and Address Useful

1. Word 97 is running. Click the **New** ▢ icon to create a new, blank document.

2. Carefully type this information into the document (see Figure 29.6):

```
<PR_DISPLAY_NAME>
<PR_COMPANY_NAME>
<PR_STREET_ADDRESS>
<PR_LOCALITY>, <PR_STATE_OR_PROVINCE> <PR_POSTAL_CODE>
```

FIGURE 29.6
Type these weird formatting commands in a new document, and be careful to spell everything correctly.

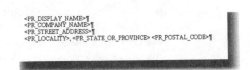

3. Select all the information that you typed, then click **Insert**, **AutoText**, **New**, as shown in Figure 29.7.

FIGURE 29.7
Select the entire document and set it up as an AutoText entry.

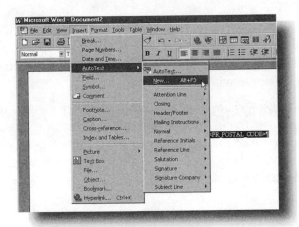

4. When asked for the name of the AutoText entry, type `AddressLayout` (all one word), as shown in Figure 29.8. Word replaces the existing AddressLayout AutoText entry—the one you can't see—with this new one.

5. Before you delete the document with all those weird formatting commands, test out your new setup. Click the **New**  icon to crank out a new, blank document. Then click the **Insert Address** icon. Choose one of your contacts, per Figure 29.9, and click **OK**.

ARE THOSE FIELD CODES?
Nope. These formatting directives are complete gibberish, unlike anything I've ever seen in Word (and, believe me, I've seen a lot of strange stuff in Word!). As far as I know, you'll never come across anything quite like this anywhere else in Office.

FIGURE 29.8
Call this AutoText entry Address-Layout.

FIGURE 29.9
Test the new formatting commands with one of your contacts.

6. The name and address should be inserted in your document, along with the company name, but no country name, as shown in Figure 29.10.

7. Now that you've seen how these new commands work, you might want to change them. For example, you might want to delete the line that says <PR_COMPANY_NAME>. Or you might want to go back to always printing the country name, in which case you need to add an extra line at the end that says <PR_COUN-TRY>. If you make either of those changes,

WHAT IF I DON'T HAVE A COMPANY NAME?
The way I set up the formatting codes, if there's no company name associated with a particular contact, you get a big, ugly empty line where the company name should go.

Unfortunately I haven't found any way to make those commands conditional, so they can give different results based on the contents of the fields. For example, I don't know how to tell Word "Insert the company name if there is one, but if there isn't, just forget it." I also don't know of any way to say "Insert the country name if it isn't United States of America," or even "Use USA instead of United States of America." My guess is that the people who invented these bizarre formatting codes never thought anybody would be interested in doing anything with them!

make sure you select all the lines and go back through steps 3 and 4 to update the AddressLayout AutoText entry.

FIGURE 29.10
The new commands have Word insert the name, company name, and address (but no country name).

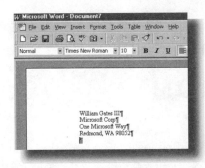

There are several other formatting commands that you might want to use:

- <PR_TITLE>—Job title
- <PR_DEPARTMENT_NAME>—Department name
- <PR_OFFICE_TELEPHONE_NUMBER>—Business phone number
- <PR_BUSINESS_FAX_NUMBER>—Business fax number
- <PR_HOME_TELEPHONE_NUMBER>—Home phone number
- <PR_EMAIL_ADDRESS>—Email address

Go ahead and experiment. If you get to the point where you'd just as soon go back to Word's original weirding ways, simply click **Insert**, **AutoText**, **AutoText**, select **AddressLayout**, and click **Delete**. Word automatically restores its hidden version of the AddressLayout AutoText entry.

Word and Excel

More time, effort, and money have been devoted to tying together Word and Excel than any other two programs in the Office 97 pantheon. That's surprising to me because I'll put an Excel spreadsheet or chart in a Word document once or twice a week, but I need to use the brain-dead Word to Outlook Contacts connection many times a day. And I doubt that I'm unique.

Anyway, the Word-to-Excel connection gives us a good chance to look at all three of the methods for interconnecting Office applications: copying, embedding, and linking.

Copy Excel Data to Word

Office 97 offers not one but three genuinely useful ways to copy spreadsheet data from Excel into Word. Let's try each one.

*E*XERCISE _____

Excel Spreadsheet to Word Table

1. Start Excel. Open a handy workbook. If you have test.xls available, it will do nicely.

2. Select some spreadsheet data. In Figure 29.11, I've chosen the range A1:F6 in test.xls. Click **Edit**, then **Copy** (or press Ctrl+C) to copy the data to the Windows Clipboard.

FIGURE 29.11
Select a range in the spreadsheet.

3. Start Word. You should have a new, clean document visible.

4. Paste the Excel spreadsheet into Word by clicking **Edit**, then **Paste** (or Ctrl+V). The result should look something like Figure 29.12.

FIGURE 29.12
A spreadsheet range copied from Excel and pasted into Word.

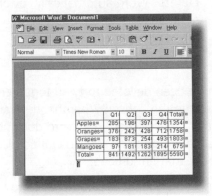

IS THAT A SPREADSHEET IN WORD?

Nope. What you have in Figure 29.12 may have originated as a spreadsheet. It may look like a spreadsheet. It even has all the formatting you applied to it in Excel. *But it is not a spreadsheet!* What you see in Figure 29.12 is a Word Table. You can resize the rows and columns. You can format it with the Table AutoFormat feature. You can change the text and numbers any way you like. But you have to be very cognizant of the fact that totaling no longer works.

Word does have a few formula functions that will total columns and rows, and do a little bit of arithmetic, but I hesitate to bring it to your attention because the capabilities (built into obscure fields) are so pathetic they'll only lead to madness. If you're going to need the ability to update numbers and get totals to reflect the new numbers, embed or link the spreadsheet (detailed later in this chapter), don't paste it in.

5. Try it. Click the Oranges/Q1 cell, and change the number to zero. Then press Enter or tab out of the cell. As you'll notice in Figure 29.13, none of the totals change—horizontally, vertically, or even the Grand Total.

FIGURE 29.13
It's a Word
Table, and as
such there are
no calculation
smarts.

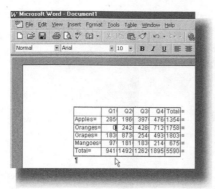

That's the most common way to copy data from an Excel spreadsheet into Word. The next most common way brings the data across without any formatting, so the resulting text doesn't look at all like a table—much less a spreadsheet.

XERCISE

Excel Spreadsheet to Raw Data

1. If you're continuing from the previous exercise, you have some spreadsheet data in the Windows clipboard. (If not, start Excel and copy some data.)

2. In Word, click **Edit**, then **Paste Special**. Word shows you the Paste Special dialog box, where most fancy application interconnection takes place. In Figure 29.14, I've chosen to paste the data from Excel into Word as unformatted text.

FIGURE 29.14
Paste as
unformatted
text.

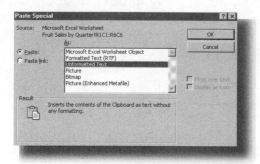

3. When Word pastes a spreadsheet as unformatted text, each row comes across as its own paragraph. Then, within each paragraph, the columns are separated by tabs. You can see the effect in Figure 29.15.

FIGURE 29.15
Unformatted spreadsheet data is separated by tabs and paragraph marks.

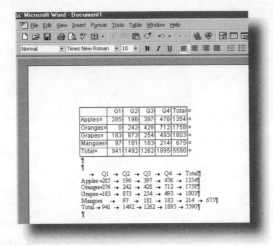

This method of bringing across data as unformatted text is a good choice if you want to apply formatting to the data inside Word, and don't want to carry across any formatting that was applied back in Excel.

XERCISE

Excel Spreadsheet to Word Picture

1. If you're continuing from the previous exercise, you have some spreadsheet data in the Windows Clipboard. If not, start Excel and get some.

2. Inside Word, click **Edit**, then **Paste Special**. Again, the Paste Special dialog box comes up. In Figure 29.16 I've chosen to treat the spreadsheet data as a picture. Note that I've unchecked the **Float over text** box.

FIGURE 29.16
Paste a spreadsheet as a picture in Word.

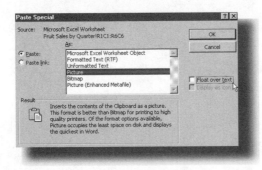

3. A picture, as you might imagine, is precisely that (see Figure 29.17). You can't go in and change the data (which may be a very good thing if you'd be tempted to think that this was a live spreadsheet). You can format the picture: make it larger or smaller, move it around, crop it, and so on.

FIGURE 29.17
Spreadsheet data inserted as a picture.

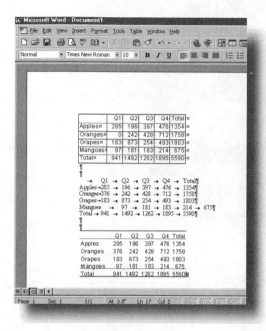

So there you have three powerful methods for copying data from Excel into Word. In each case, there's no memory of where the data came from. Word hasn't the slightest idea that the table, raw data, or picture originated with its sibling application.

Embed a Spreadsheet in a Word Document

Now we get to go beyond the amnesia stage. When you embed a spreadsheet in a Word document, Word is fully cognizant of the fact that the data came from Excel, and can be manipulated in Excel. The data stays inside the Word document, but it's treated in a special way, as you'll see.

*E*XERCISE

Embed a Spreadsheet

1. Start Word.

2. To create a new, blank spreadsheet at any point in a Word document, click **Insert**, then **Object**. You'll see the Object dialog box, as shown in Figure 29.18.

FIGURE 29.18
Word wants to know what kind of object you want to insert.

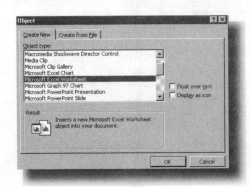

3. If you scroll through the list, you'll discover that Word can insert a couple dozen kinds of objects into documents. In our case, we're interested in an Excel Worksheet, so click **Microsoft Excel Worksheet** and click **OK**.

4. Word undergoes a significant transformation. It takes a while, so be patient. By the time Word comes up for air you'll discover that a spreadsheet has been inserted in your document (see Figure 29.19). More than that, though, the Standard and Formatting toolbars suddenly revert to the Excel toolbars of the same name, the menus have turned into Excel menus, and even your Auditing toolbar appears at the bottom of the screen.

WHY JUST ONE SPREADSHEET?
Actually, Word lied to you. It didn't exactly insert a spreadsheet into your document. It really inserted an entire workbook. You only see one sheet in Figure 29.19 because Word only sets up one sheet initially. But if you poke around a bit, you'll discover that you have an entire workbook on your hands—you can add more sheets, run Scenarios, create charts, the whole nine and a half yards.

FIGURE 29.19
Word as werewolf, taking on all the aspects of an Excel window.

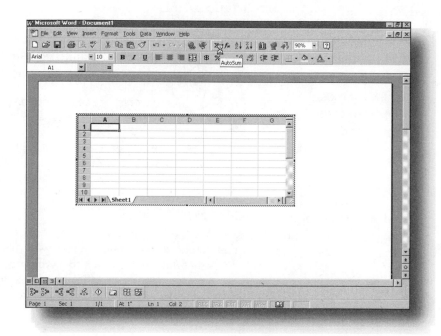

5. Go ahead and create your own little spreadsheet. In Figure 29.20 I've charted sales of widgets and wombats, in two designer colors.

FIGURE 29.20
Anything you can do in an Excel .xls file, you can do right here, inside Word.

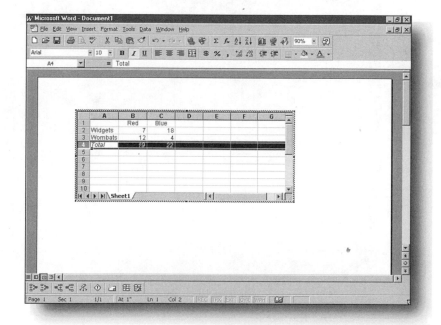

6. When you tire of spreadsheeting, click anywhere in the document outside the spreadsheet area, and Word returns. You can type sentences (as shown in Figure 29.21), bring in pictures, do everything you normally do in a .doc file.

DOES IT WORK THE SAME WAY?
No, it doesn't. When you use Paste Special to paste a Microsoft Excel Worksheet Object into a Word document you don't get a worksheet object pasted in your document, in spite of what the dialog box says. You actually get a copy of the whole workbook—the equivalent of the entire .xls file! (Yet another example of Microsoft's inconsistent use of the terms worksheet, workbook, and spreadsheet.)

So if you select a small part of a spreadsheet in a big .xls file and try to use Paste Special to get that data embedded into a Word document, you're going to be in for an unpleasant surprise. The Word .doc will grow huge, simply because it has to hold all the data.

FIGURE 29.21
Click in the document, outside the spreadsheet, and the Word persona returns.

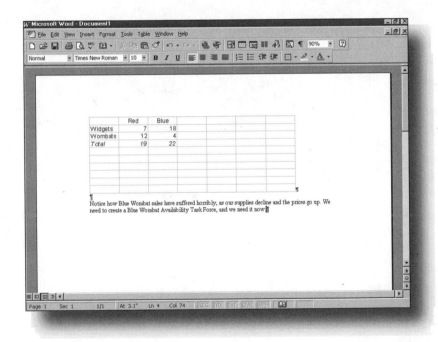

7. Any time you want to return to the spreadsheet, just double-click it. The Word wrapper fades away and Excel takes over once again, as shown in Figure 29.22.

FIGURE 29.22
Double-click to bring back Excel.

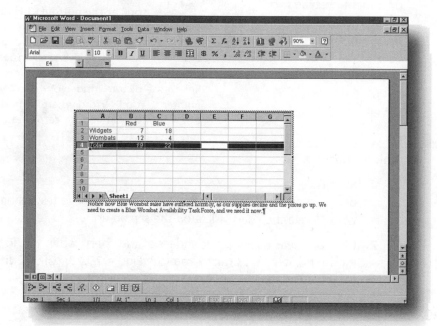

That's how embedding works. Word keeps the data in the document, but it knows that you want to use Excel to manipulate the numbers. This werewolf-like ability of Word to give way to Excel when you're editing the embedded data is, in fact, an enormously complex capability that took Microsoft years to make usable.

You can embed a spreadsheet in a Word document going the other way—by selecting the data inside a spreadsheet, doing a copy, moving to Word, and running a Paste Special, choosing **Microsoft Excel Worksheet Object**, as shown in Figure 29.16.

Now let's look at the fanciest way to put Excel data in a Word document.

Link to a Chart from a Word Document

I don't recommend that you try linking unless you have at least 32MB of memory on your machine. Windows has to keep copies of both Word and Excel running at the same time when the links are updated, and that's a bit like feeding Shamu and Willy, simultaneously, from the same bucket.

Linking is a little bit like embedding, except the data doesn't sit in the document. Instead it stays where it came from—in this case, in an Excel spreadsheet—and Word only retrieves the information when it's needed.

I THOUGHT YOU SAID THE PICTURE WASN'T PUT IN THE DOCUMENT
Look at the bottom of Figure 29.24, where it says this action "Inserts the content of the Clipboard as a picture." That isn't really true. When you run a Paste Link, Word puts a link to the picture inside your document, a pointer that tells Word where to find the picture when Word needs to retrieve it. The picture isn't there at all.

XERCISE

Link a Chart

1. Start Excel, and open a workbook that contains a chart. If you have test.xls handy, it will work. Make the chart visible on the screen (in test.xls, click the **Chart1** tab).

2. Click out near the outer boundary of the chart, when the ToolTip on your mouse pointer says **Chart Area** (see Figure 29.23). Click **Edit**, then **Copy** (or press Ctrl+C).

FIGURE 29.23
Select the entire chart and copy it to the Clipboard.

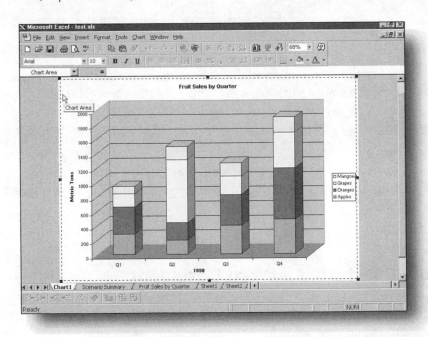

3. Start Word. Put your cursor wherever you want the Excel chart to appear. Then click **Edit**, **Paste Special**. As in Figure 29.24, click **Microsoft Excel Chart Object**, make sure **Paste link** is chosen on the left, and uncheck the box next to **Float over text**.

FIGURE 29.24
Pasting a link inside Word, using Paste Special.

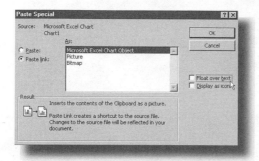

4. Click **OK**, and you'll see the chart inside your Word document (see Figure 29.25). Even though you can see and print the picture, Word only stores a little pointer to the picture. It takes up almost no space. Even better, if the picture changes out in test.xls, it'll change in the Word document, too.

FIGURE 29.25
The chart appears, even though it's linked and doesn't actually exist inside the document.

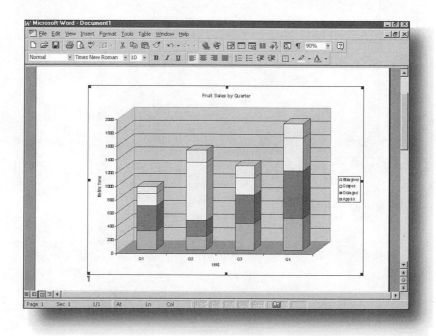

5. Let me show you how that works. Close this document and give it a name like, oh, temp.doc. Flip back over to Excel and change the number in cell B3 to zero (see Figure 29.26).

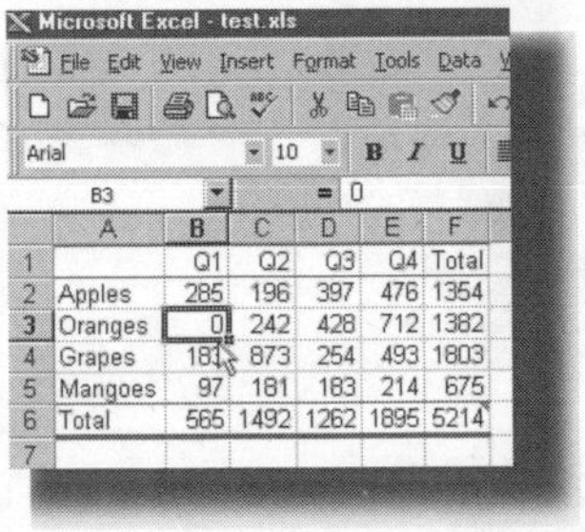

FIGURE 29.26
Change the data in test.xls.

6. Click the **Chart1** tab to see how the new data changes the chart (see Figure 29.27). The first column looks short, right?

FIGURE 29.27
The new data takes effect in Chart1.

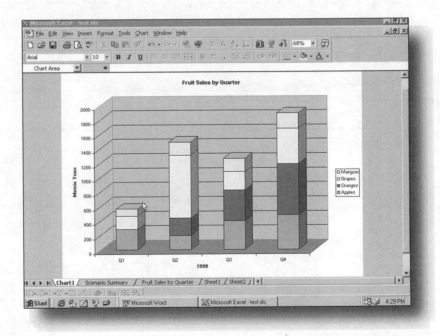

7. Now go back to Word and open temp.doc. Voila! The first column gets chopped off here, too (see Figure 29.28).

FIGURE 29.28
Open the document in Word and the link gets updated, bringing in the latest version of the chart.

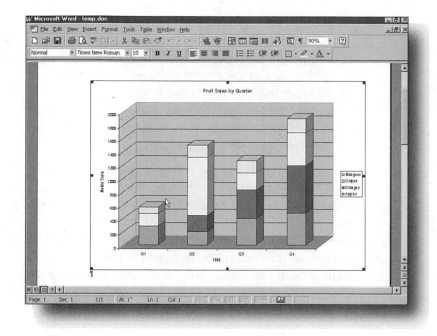

8. There's another big difference in the way Word behaves when it has linked—as opposed to embedded—data. Try double-clicking the chart in Figure 29.28. You might expect Word to pull a werewolf and bring in the Excel menus and toolbars. It doesn't. Instead, Word actually shifts over to Excel and presents you with the chart, as it did in Figure 29.23.

And that pretty well shows you the relative benefits of copying, embedding, and linking.

Which Is Best?

Ah, you ask such tough questions...

The best way to bring Excel data into Word documents is the way that creates the fewest headaches for you! Here are the salient points:

- When you copy data, there's no memory of where it came from, so it's hard to change any calculated numbers. If you keep a copy of the original spreadsheet around, though, making changes isn't too hard, and copying isn't difficult at all. Copied data doesn't take up much room at all, and it always travels with the document, so any program that can read Word documents will be able to see the copied data.

● Embedding spreadsheets adds the convenience of having Excel a double-click away for modifying data. Other people will be able to read the data with any program that can view Word documents, but if they want to change the data in any way, they have to have Excel running on their PC. The data is in the document, so the .doc file can get quite big, particularly if you use Paste Special to do the embedding. But because the data is in the file, you don't have to worry about sending multiple files to anybody who wants to read your document.

● Linking is very cool, but has several drawbacks. You have to send the linked file along with the document. Worse, the linked file has to be in precisely the same location on the disk, or Word won't be able to find it. (For

example, if you originally linked data from the workbook c:\someplace\ mysheet.xls, that workbook has to be in the same location on another machine before the other user will be able to see the data.) Most of all, Word and Excel have to run simultaneously to make linking work—and that requires a fairly powerful machine.

Ya pays yer money and ya takes yer chances...

Word and PowerPoint

There's a special tunnel between Word and PowerPoint, which, at least in theory, allows you to create presentations directly from Word documents.

The trick lies in formatting your Word document so PowerPoint can figure out what in the world to do with the text in the document. PowerPoint looks for paragraphs formatted with these specific styles:

● Heading 1 paragraphs in Word, when transferred to PowerPoint, start new slides. PowerPoint puts the contents of Heading 1 paragraphs in the Title box, up at the top of the slide. So, when you want to start a new slide, just format your Word paragraph with the Heading 1 style.

● Heading 2 paragraphs become the highest-level bulleted text down in the Text box, at the bottom of the slide. (PowerPoint calls these *Second level* bullet points, but they're actually the highest level text on the slide, aside from the slide title.)

● Similarly, Heading 3 paragraphs become *Third level* bullet points, Heading 4 paragraphs become *Fourth level*, and so on.

If you already have a Word document formatted with those specific styles, you're way ahead of the game. If you don't, you'll have to create a document and apply those styles. (In fact, if you're starting from scratch, you may well find it easier to use PowerPoint directly—forget about Word—and work in PowerPoint's Outline view.)

Here's an interesting way to use the tunnel to quickly generate a Q&A slide show, based on a great idea I pilfered from Paul Somerson at *PC Computing*.

*E*XERCISE

Turn a Document into a Presentation

1. Start Word.

2. Create a document with the appropriate styles. In Figure 29.29, I've written a document with three Heading 1 paragraphs, and three Heading 2 paragraphs, interlaced. Alternatively, if you have a nicely formatted Word document with those styles already applied, open it.

FIGURE 29.29
The Word document must have Heading x styles applied in the appropriate places.

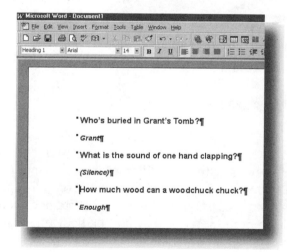

3. When the document looks right, click **File**, **Send To**, **Microsoft PowerPoint** (see Figure 29.30).

4. PowerPoint comes up in Outline view, with each of the Heading 1 paragraphs identified as titles of their own slides. Note that PowerPoint hasn't created a title slide for the beginning of the presentation. Nor has it applied any sort of formatting. This (see Figure 29.31) is one bare-bones presentation.

FIGURE 29.30
Send the
document to
PowerPoint.

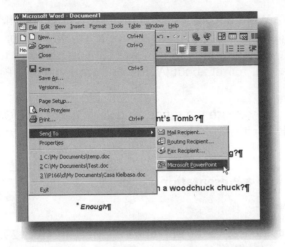

FIGURE 29.31
The three
Heading 1
styles trans-
late into three
slides.

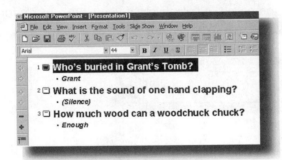

5. These slides really need a lot of cosmetic surgery, but I'll only work on the basics. Click **View**, **Master**, then **Slide Master** to bring up the one slide that controls how all the slides in this presentation will appear. I want the title (the Heading 1 questions in the original Word document) to appear near the middle of the slides, and I want the body (the Heading 2 answers in the .doc) to appear at the bottom. So I clicked and dragged a bit, and came up with what you see in Figure 29.32.

6. I want some text to appear at the beginning of each slide. (I'd call this a title, but that name's already been taken, and I'd only confuse you!) I clicked on the **Text Box** 🖻 icon on the Drawing toolbar, clicked and dragged to create a location for this text, then typed CRRRRAZY QUES-TIONS in the new text box, as shown in Figure 29.33. Because that text box appears on the Slide Master, it will also appear on all the slides.

FIGURE 29.32
The Slide Master for this presentation.

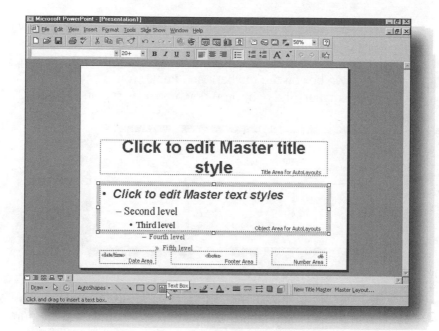

FIGURE 29.33
Use a text box in the Slide Master to put text on all slides.

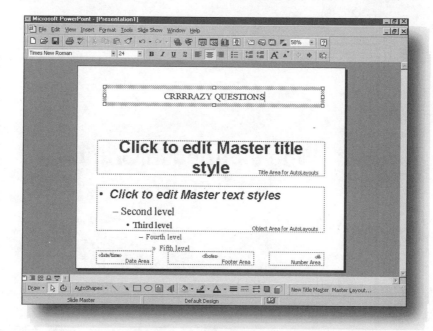

7. Next, I clicked the **Slide Sorter View** ▦ icon on the View bar, to flip PowerPoint over to Slide Sorter view. I then selected all three slides (**Edit**, **Select All**) and chose **Box In** for a Slide Transition Effect (the left drop-down box on the toolbar), and **Peek From Bottom** for a Text Preset Animation (the right drop-down box), as shown in Figure 29.34.

FIGURE 29.34
Go into Slide Sorter view to select transitions and build effects.

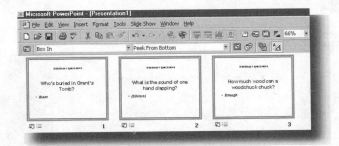

8. Click **Slide Show**, then **View Slide Show**, and PowerPoint runs through the presentation. Each slide with a question appears, in turn. Then, when you click the slide, the answer to the question slides into view (see Figure 29.35).

FIGURE 29.35
The presentation, including a boxy transition between slides and answers appearing at the click of a mouse.

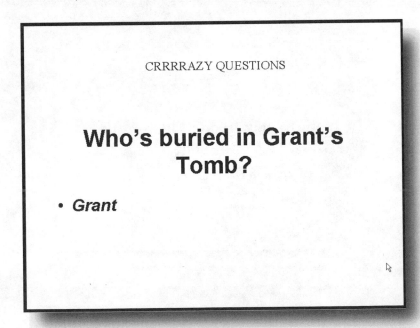

CRRRRAZY QUESTIONS

Who's buried in Grant's Tomb?

• *Grant*

Conversely, there's another tunnel from PowerPoint back into Word that will dump a presentation out in a Word-friendly format. To use it, bring up the presentation you want to move in PowerPoint, then click **File**, **Send To**, **Microsoft Word**. You'll have a few options—you can even run a Paste Link to link the Word document back to the presentation—but they're pretty self-explanatory.

PowerPoint and Excel

☞ *I covered this link on page 618 simply because I couldn't bear to tell you how to use a cheap Excel substitute with PowerPoint when the real thing works much better.*

30

Office on the Web

MICROSOFT GOT INTERNET RELIGION RATHER late in the game. By the time Office 97 arrived on the scene, everybody knew the Web was the way to go—but nobody was quite sure how to handle it. Office 97 contains Microsoft's quick and dirty response to the Web challenge. The Web components you'll find in Office 97 aren't so much integrated features as they are slapped-on last-minute modifications.

If you're going to do any serious Web work, you're much better off with Web-specific packages like FrontPage, or any of its many competitors. (A stunted but eminently usable version of FrontPage, called FrontPage Express, comes free with Windows 98 and Internet Explorer 4.) Office 97 doesn't even come close. On the other hand, if you have an existing document or spreadsheet that you'd like to publish on the Web and don't want to spend much time in the effort, Office's rudimentary tools make it possible. I'll show you how.

WHAT'S THE DIFFERENCE BETWEEN NET AND WEB?

The Internet (commonly called *The Net*), as you probably know, is a massive collection of computers and the phone lines that connect them. Yes, this is the information superhighway you've read about, but it doesn't really work like a superhighway.

The World Wide Web (also known as *The Web*) sits on top of the Net. It consists of another massive collection of computers, called Web servers, interconnected via the Net, that contain Web pages. The Web pages, as you've probably discovered, refer to each other via links; click a link and you move to a different Web page, whether it sits on the same Web server or halfway around the world.

For more information about the Internet and the World Wide Web, see the following texts:

● *Using the Internet, Fourth Edition*, published by Que.

● *Sams Teach Yourself the Internet in 24 Hours, Second Edition*, published by SAMS.

Get HTML Support

Before you try using any Office 97 Web features, it would be a good idea to make sure that you have Web support for Office 97 installed on your PC. The easiest way to do that is to start Excel and check to see if the File menu has an entry called Save As HTML (see Figure 30.1).

FIGURE 30.1
Excel's Save as HTML entry doesn't appear if you don't have full Web support installed.

If Save as HTML does not appear on Excel's File menu, don't worry. You probably went through a Typical installation, which doesn't include HTML support.

To get full HTML support in your copy of Office 97, put the Office 97 CD in your PC and run Setup. When asked if you want a Typical, Custom, or Minimal installation, click **Custom**. Then check the box marked **Web Page Authoring (HTML)**, as shown in Figure 30.2, click **Continue** and sit back while Office installs all the appropriate programs.

FIGURE 30.2
To pick up full Web support, reinstall using the Custom button and click this component.

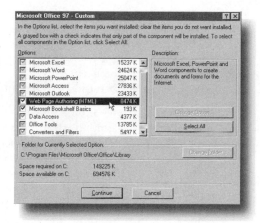

With all your HTML support in hand, it's time to check out the Web—Office style.

Open, Save on Net

Brace yourself for some weird new terminology.

The most common way to pull files off the Internet, or to put them on the Internet, is via something called *FTP*, or *File Transfer Protocol*. You don't need to understand what FTP actually entails. All you need to know is that when you see FTP, you're looking at something that lets you read and write files on the Internet.

Word, Excel, and PowerPoint all have the capability to open and save files on the Internet, using FTP. Here's how.

*E*XERCISE
_____

Open a File on the Net

1. Start Word 97. Click **File**, then **Open**.

2. In the Open dialog box, click the down-arrow to the right of My Documents. As you can see in Figure 30.3, the entries at the bottom of that list refer to Internet Locations (FTP) and FTP Locations. An Internet Location or FTP Location (which is the same thing, in this case) is just a place on the Internet where you can pick up or drop off files.

WHAT'S HTML
HTML (Hypertext Markup Language) is the language used on the Web, the language understood by Web browsers such as Internet Explorer and Netscape. When Excel saves a spreadsheet as HTML, that means it converts the spreadsheet to HTML code and saves the HTML code. The process is amazingly similar to printing a spreadsheet: When you have Excel print a spreadsheet, it converts the spreadsheet into a code that can be understood by your printer, then ships that code to the printer.

After Excel has saved a spreadsheet as HTML, you can take the resulting HTML code and put it on a Web page. When a Web browser sees that HTML code, it should interpret the HTML so the stuff that shows up on the screen looks just like your original spreadsheet. Again, it's quite similar to a printer, where the intelligence inside the printer interprets the code sent to it by Excel.

The terms *Web page* and *HTML file* can be used interchangeably: Any HTML file can be used as a Web page, and every Web page is an HTML file.

For more information on HTML, see *Using HTML 4.0*, published by Que.

3. Choose **Add/Modify FTP Locations**. Word responds immediately with the Add/Modify FTP Locations dialog box, as shown in Figure 30.4.

4. If you have a favorite site on the Net for storing files, enter it here. If you're just learning, try using Microsoft's main file storage site, known as `ftp.microsoft.com`.

5. Click **OK** and you're back in the Open dialog box, as shown in Figure 30.5. Now this is the most important part of this Exercise: BACK UP EVERYTHING BEFORE YOU PROCEED!

FIGURE 30.3
The Open dialog box directly supports retrieving files from the Net.

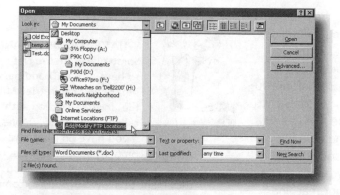

FIGURE 30.4
You must tell Office, in advance, which Net locations you want to use to retrieve or store data, and how to log on to the location.

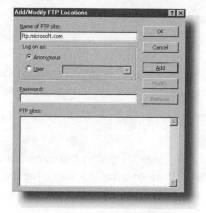

FIGURE 30.5
The Microsoft FTP site has been added to the Open folder list.

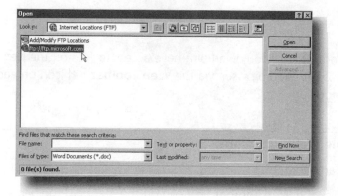

6. At the risk of repeating myself, make sure you back up *everything* before you try to connect to the FTP site. There's a fairly good chance Word will lock up your machine when you try to connect. Don't say I didn't warn you!

WHAT'S LOG ON AS ANONYMOUS?
Some places on the Net require you to have a user ID and password before you can retrieve files or store files in that location. Other sites, called *Anonymous FTP sites*, don't care if you have an ID or password. Most software company support sites, such as `ftp.microsoft.com`, are anonymous because they want to allow anybody to come in and download files.

7. Double-click `ftp://ftp.microsoft.com`. If you're lucky, Office will connect to the FTP site and show you a list of folders and files available on the site.

8. You're pretty much on your own at this point. Just navigate the site as if it were your hard drive.

The Word, Excel, and PowerPoint File, Save As dialog boxes contain similar facilities for letting you save files on the Net. They, too, have a nasty habit of locking up your machine, so be careful to save everything (on your hard drive, or on your local network) before trying to connect.

Browse

Just as Word, Excel, and PowerPoint have access to files on the Net, they can also flip over to your Web browser, via the **Web Toolbar** 🌐 icon on each application's Standard toolbar.

*E*XERCISE _____

Search the Web from Word

1. Start Word 97.

2. Click the **Web Toolbar** 🌐 icon on the Standard toolbar. Word responds by placing the Web toolbar below the Formatting toolbar, as shown in Figure 30.6.

FIGURE 30.6
The Web toolbar makes an appearance.

3. While you would think, just looking at the toolbar in Figure 30.6, that Word would be able to leap out to the Web, reality isn't quite so wonderful. Yes, you can use the Web-style navigation buttons to move forward or backward among open documents, or to jump to a document. But if you try to do anything that requires the Web, such as clicking the **Search the Web** icon, Word just brings up your Web browser, as you can see in Figure 30.7.

FIGURE 30.7
Click Search the Web from inside Word and you're propelled to your Web browser, which goes to a predefined Microsoft Web site.

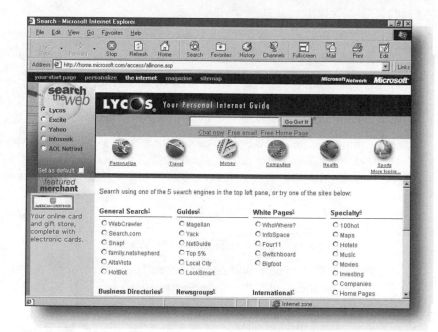

4. If you poke around a bit, the rest of Office 97's Web browsing support proves equally underwhelming. For example, although all the Office 97 applications (including Outlook 98, shown in Figure 30.8) have Microsoft on the Web entries on their Help menus, clicking any of them merely launches your Web browser. There's no connection between the application and the Help topics, so you'll find yourself frequently flipping back and forth between Web page and application.

FIGURE 30.8
Microsoft on
the Web
entries all
lead to your
Web browser,
with an
appropriate
page loaded.

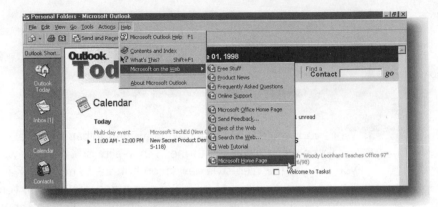

Hyperlinks

☞ *I discussed some forms of Word 97 hyperlinks back on page 271. You might want to look over that section again to refresh your memory on hyperlinking and hot spots.*

Word, Excel, and PowerPoint all support hyperlinking. In particular, it's very easy to create a hot hyperlink from your document to a Web page—and if you then post your document on the Web, the hyperlink continues to work.

Let's put a hyperlink on a PowerPoint presentation slide. The link will be hot, so if you click it while giving a presentation, and the presentation PC is connected correctly to the Net, the Web page you specify will appear on the screen during the presentation. Cool, no?

*E*XERCISE

Hyperlinking a PowerPoint Slide to the Web

1. Start PowerPoint, and open Generic Presentation.ppt. If you aren't in Slide Sorter View, click the **Slide Sorter View** 🔡 icon on the View bar (see Figure 30.9).

2. Let's put the hot link on slide 8, the one marked **Next Steps**. Click that slide, then click the **Slide View** 🔲 icon on the View bar.

3. In Figure 30.10, I've used **Insert, Picture** to put a picture from the Clip Gallery in the lower-right corner. Then I used the **Text Box** 📧 tool on the Drawing toolbar to stick the text Check Que's Web page on the slide, and the **Arrow** 🢒 icon to draw an arrow from the text to the picture.

4. Click once on the picture. We're going to set up the picture so it's hot.

FIGURE 30.9
Open Generic
Presentation.
ppt and
navigate to
slide 8.

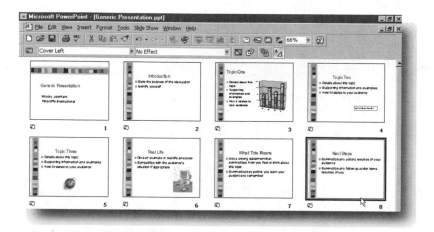

FIGURE 30.10
A clip art pic-
ture, a text
box, and an
arrow placed
on the slide.

5. Click the **Insert Hyperlink** 🔳 icon on the Standard toolbar. PowerPoint knows that what you've selected—in this case, the picture—is supposed to be hot, and it presents you with the Insert Hyperlink dialog box, as shown in Figure 30.11.

6. Type a favorite URL (that is, a Web address) in the **Link to file or URL** box. In Figure 30.11, I've set the picture up to link to the Macmillan Computer Publishing Web page, `www.mcp.com`.

7. Now run the slide show by clicking **Slide Show**, then **View Show**. When you get to slide 8, let your cursor hover over the picture. You'll see a ToolTip advising you of where the hot link leads—in this case, to `http://www.mcp.com` (see Figure 30.12).

FIGURE 30.11
Type the URL (Web address) to which you want to link.

FIGURE 30.12
The picture is hot; clicking it will lead to www.mcp.com.

8. Click the hot picture. Your Web browser should come up, with the indicated page loaded, as shown in Figure 30.13.

Anything you can select in any Word document, Excel workbook, or PowerPoint slide can become a hot hyperlink. That includes text, pictures, ranges, charts—just about anything you can imagine. Simply select whatever you want to turn into a link, then click the **Insert Hyperlink** icon, and type the Web address.

FIGURE 30.13
Clicking the hot picture brings up your Web browser, with the indicated page loaded.

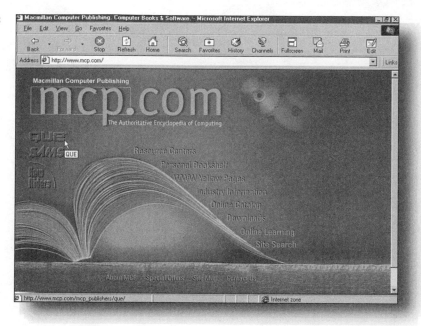

Excel has quite a few quirks when dealing with hyperlinks—for example, if you put a hyperlink on a range, it'll insist on putting the location for the link in the first cell in that range. Excel also insists on saving the document before inserting or using a hyperlink—but Word and PowerPoint are quite straightforward.

Word Document to Web Page

If you aren't too picky about how your Web pages look, by far the easiest way to create a Web page inside Office 97 is with Word's Web Page Wizard. To get the wizard going, start Word, click **File**, **New**, and look for a tab marked **Web Pages**. If you find it, double-click **Web Page Wizard.wiz**. If you don't find it, get out your Office 97 CD and look in the file \Templates\Web Pages and double-click the file **Web Page Wizard.wiz**.

The wizard takes you through a few simple questions, then dumps you in Word, with the skeleton of a Web page going (see Figure 30.14). From that point it's pretty easy to click and replace text, customizing the page to your heart's content.

As soon as you have a Web page (or even a traditional Word document) ready for publishing on the Web, you need to go through three steps.

FIGURE 30.14
A simple
Web page
generated by
Word's Web
Page Wizard.

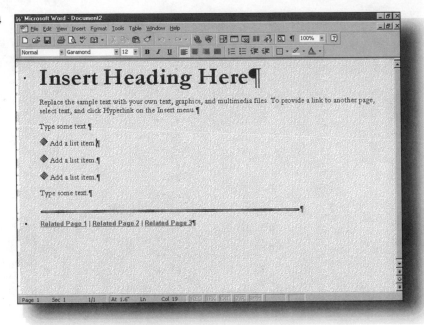

1. Save your document normally, as a regular old everyday Word .doc. That way, if something goes wrong, it'll be easy to recover your work.

2. Save the document in HTML format. If you have a Save as HTML item on your File menu, use that. If not, click File, Save As, and in the Files of type box, choose HTML document (*.html; *.htm).

3. Post the HTML document (along with any associated picture files) to the Web. The easiest way to do that, by far, is with Microsoft's Web Publishing Wizard. The Web Publishing Wizard is located on the Office 97 CD, in the \Valupack\ Webpost folder. Run the program webpost.exe to install the Web Publishing Wizard, then click Start, Programs, Accessories, Internet Tools, Web Publishing Wizard. You'll have to gather the files you need to go on the Web (see Figure 30.15), but much of the grunt work is handled by the wizard.

That, in a nutshell, is an easy way to publish a so-so Web page on the Web. When you're ready for a much better Web page, learn how to use FrontPage or FrontPage Express, or learn HTML.

FIGURE 30.15
Transferring all necessary files to the Web is easier with the Web Publishing Wizard.

Excel Spreadsheet to Web Page

Yes, you can use a technique similar to the one in the previous section to publish Excel spreadsheets on the Web. No, the results aren't much, and I can pretty much guarantee you'll be disappointed by the result of the **Save as HTML** option on Excel's **File** menu, if you use it to create a free-standing Web page.

On the positive side, you can copy an Excel chart and put it in a Word document, or any Web page (that is, any HTML file under the control of a decent HTML editor), and the picture comes out, uh, picture-perfect.

The problem—or should I say the opportunity?—arises when you want to copy a portion of an Excel spreadsheet onto a Web page. You might think that you could simply select a range on an Excel spreadsheet, copy it to the Clipboard, then paste that into a Web page. Sorry, but for now at least, that doesn't work. The stuff you get off the Clipboard is a jumble of strange codes and embedded data.

But don't give up! If you have access to a Web page editor, such as FrontPage, there's a strange but effective way to copy your Excel spreadsheets directly onto a Web page, and the results (in HTML) will be readily legible to any Web browser.

Let me use Windows 98's free FrontPage Express to show you how.

*E*XERCISE

Put an Excel Range on a Web Page

1. Start by creating a new Web page to hold the piece of the Excel spreadsheet that interests you. If you're running Windows 98, click **Start**, **Programs**, **Internet Explorer**, **FrontPage Express**.

FIGURE 30.16
Put some text in the new Web page, then save it.

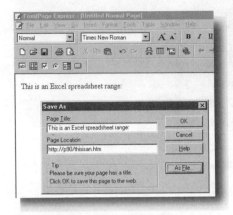

2. Type a sentence or two in the new file. In Figure 30.16, I've typed `This is an Excel spreadsheet range:`.

3. FrontPage Express has a, uh, unique way of saving documents. Click **File**, then **Save**, and you'll get the Save As dialog box, shown in Figure 30.16. You want to save this new Web page as a file, so click **As File**. FrontPage Express presents you with the Save As File dialog box shown in Figure 30.17.

FIGURE 30.17
Choose a name for the new HTML file, er, Web page.

4. Choose a good location and type a filename, then click **Save**. In Figure 30.17, I've decided to call the new file Spreadsheet Test.htm, and put it on my Windows Desktop.

5. Leave FrontPage Express running, with Spreadsheet Test.htm open, for the moment.

6. Start Excel. Bring up the workbook that contains the range you want to put on the Web page. In Figure 30.18, I've opened our old standby, test.xls, and clicked the **Fruit Sales by Quarter** tab.

FIGURE 30.18
Open an interesting spreadsheet, such as test.xls.

7. Select the range that you want to copy over to the Web page. In Figure 30.18, I've selected A1:F6. When you've selected the right data, click **File**, then **Save as HTML**. Excel pops up its Internet Assistant Wizard, as shown in Figure 30.19.

FIGURE 30.19
Clicking File, Save as HTML brings up this wizard.

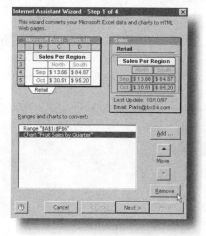

8. The Internet Assistant Wizard takes a look at the data you've selected and lists that as a range in its **Ranges and charts to convert** box. As you can see, the range we want, A1:F6, is one of the choices in Figure 30.19. We don't want to convert the chart, so click once on **Chart "Fruit Sales by Quarter"** and click the **Remove** button. Then click **Next**.

9. Excel offers to convert the selected range in one of two ways: You can turn it into a free-standing Web page, or you can add it to an existing Web page (see Figure 30.20). We want to add the range to Spreadsheet Test.htm, so click the second button and click **Next**.

FIGURE 30.20
Have Excel insert the range's data into an existing Web page, er, HTML file.

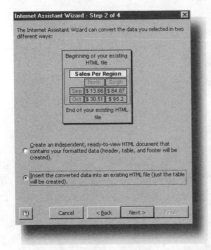

10. Here's the really hokey part of this exercise. The next Internet Assistant Wizard dialog box (see Figure 30.21) tells you to put a line in the HTML file that says—I swear I'm not making this up!—<!--##Table##-->.

FIGURE 30.21
The Internet Assistant Wizard wants you to put a very strange line in your Web page.

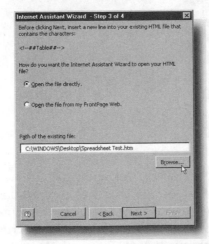

11. So drop Excel for a minute, and switch back to FrontPage Express, where Spreadsheet Test.htm should be open and waiting. To see the HTML code behind the page, click **View**, then **HTML**. FrontPage Express shows you the HTML code lurking behind the scenes (see Figure 30.22).

FIGURE 30.22
Tell FrontPage Express you want to see the HTML code by clicking View, HTML.

12. Put your cursor between the two blank paragraphs (that <p> </p> stuff means "put a blank paragraph here"). Then type the weird stuff that the Internet Assistant Wizard wants, <!--##Table##-->. You can see the result in Figure 30.23.

13. Click **OK** to get rid of the HTML code window. Then, back in FrontPage Express, click **File**, then **Close** to close Spreadsheet Test.htm and save the new, odd line that the Internet Assistant Wizard demands.

14. Flip back to Excel, where you should see Step 3 of the Internet Assistant Wizard, as shown in Figure 30.21. Click **Next** and, if you did everything right, the Internet Assistant Wizard moves forward to Step 4 (see Figure 30.24).

FIGURE 30.23
Give the
Internet
Assistant
Wizard the
funny line
that it wants.

FIGURE 30.24
As a final
step, the
Internet
Assistant
Wizard needs
to know
where to put
the updated
Web page.

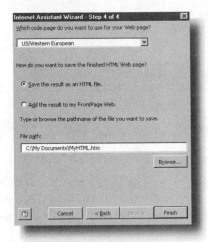

15. Choose a location and a filename for the new Web page, the one that includes the spreadsheet range. In Figure 30.24 I've just accepted the filename suggested by the wizard.

16. Click **Finish** and the new Web page (uh, HTML file) contains your spreadsheet range. Go back to FrontPage Express, open the new file, and you'll be able to see the spreadsheet range, as shown in Figure 30.25.

FIGURE 30.25
Open the new page in FrontPage Express, and the spread-sheet range appears.

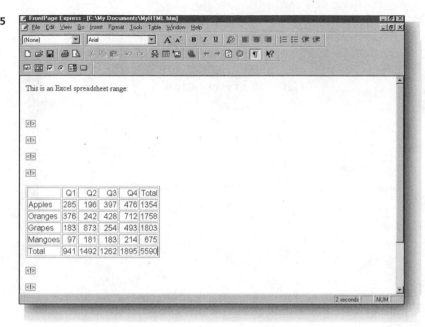

I think you'll agree that's an enormous amount of work to accomplish what is, in essence, a simple copy. Still, the wonder is that Excel can do it at all!

PowerPoint Presentations on the Web

Just to end the book on a cautionary note...

Microsoft claims that PowerPoint can pump out presentations that will go up on the Web. According to the marketing hype, you can take a slide-based presentation and turn it into a Web-page-based presentation, with just a few clicks.

Well, I've tried it several times—even wrote an article about it in *PC Computing*—and I'm here to tell ya that there are all sorts of mine fields awaiting anyone who tries.

If you have a very simple presentation—all text, with few if any effects—you can take that presentation and put it on the Web relatively easily. Stick to the AutoContent Wizard choices for the Internet, don't add anything but text boxes and arrows, and you'll be okay. Transitions and builds won't work, animations may or may not, and the first screen (see Figure 30.26) can best be described as gawd-awful. But in most cases, you'll be okay.

FIGURE 30.26
The opening screen for a PowerPoint presentation transferred to the Web.

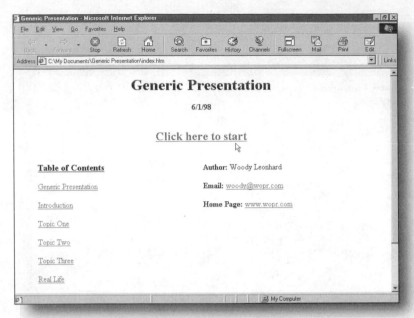

That's the best case situation. If your Web site has naming standards for files—and many do—you can expect to spend hours trying to trace down links that don't work and pictures that won't load. Help is minimal at best. Few Web masters know anything about putting a PowerPoint presentation on the Web, and fewer still want to learn how. You're definitely fighting an uphill battle.

There's a little bit of good information: PowerPoint automatically generates clickable icons for First Slide, Previous Slide, Next Slide and Last Slide, Index (which takes you back to the Web page shown in Figure 30.26), Home, and View as Text.

The presentation looks okay after you get to it (see Figure 30.27), but if a person keeps clicking the **Next Slide** button after the last slide appears in the browser, nothing happens.

If that didn't scare you off, bring up PowerPoint, open your presentation, then click **File**, and **Save as HTML**. PowerPoint's Save as HTML Wizard takes you through the steps, producing a new folder that contains all the component files. When it's done, navigate to that folder, and double-click index.htm. Your Web browser should kick in and show you the way the presentation should look on the Web.

FIGURE 30.27
A PowerPoint slide seen through Internet Explorer.

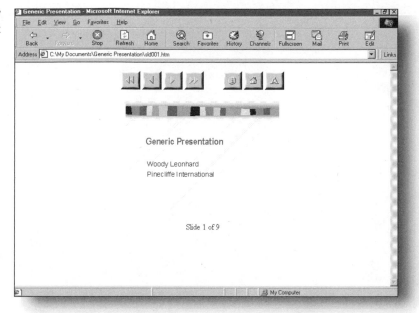

The operative word: *should*. It's easy to run a presentation off your hard drive. Getting it transferred to a real live Web server is an altogether different kettle of red herrings.

Good luck!

Index

Symbols

 # (bad data warning), spreadsheets, 464

! (bang), description of, 478

3D ranges, using in functions, 478

35mm slides, printing presentations on, 585

A

absolute addresses for spreadsheets, 460
changing formulas, 457-458
preserving formulas, 458-459

accounts, email, 334, 336-337

acl files, 57

Actions menu commands (Outlook 98), New Contact from Same Company, 380

active cells in spreadsheets, 408

active window, definition of, 138

add-ins (PowerPoint), downloading, 608

Add-Ins dialog box (Excel), AutoSave, 402

add-ons (Outlook 98)
Integrated File Management, 385, 396
Lightning, 385, 396

Add/Modify FTP Locations dialog box (Word), 670

adding
drop caps, 283
email addresses to Contacts, 348-350
watermarks, 278-279, 282
see also inserting

Address Cards view (Contacts), 330

address/phone books
categories, setting, 374, 376
copying, 380
creating entries, 369-370
Dialing Properties dialog box, 373
multiple email addresses, 372
phone numbers, 371
ten-digit dialing, 373
deciding how to use, 368
overview of, 368
views
customizing, 376, 378-379
Phone List, 376

addresses
absolute and relative in spreadsheets, 457-460
copying Outlook Contacts into Word, 640-641, 643, 645
email
Contacts, adding to, 348-350
multiple name matches, 347-348

retrieving from Contacts, 343-346
To list versus Cc list, 345
hybrid in spreadsheets, 461

AddressLayout (AutoText entry), formatting, 643, 645, 647

After Spacing option (Paragraph formatting dialog box), 176

Align Left icon (Formatting toolbar), Excel, 489

aligning
data within cells of spreadsheets
centering text, 488
indenting cells, 489
headings in spreadsheets, 490
rotating text in cells of spreadsheets, 491-492
tabs and, 188

Alignment dialog box (Excel), 513

Alignment tab (Format Cells dialog box), Excel, 492

Alt+Print Screen keys (Word), 138, 140

anonymous FTP sites, 672

anti-virus programs, 16

applications
anti-virus, 16
Binders, *see* Binders
bugs, *see* bugs
Camcorder, 37-38

common code, 416

copying, embedding, and linking data into other applications, 638

Exce, *see* Excel

hyperlinks, 674

integration, 39

interconnectedness of, 637

Office Assistant, *see* Office Assistant

Outlook, *see* Outlook

performance speed and stability, 67

Photo Editor, 38

PowerPoint, *see* PowerPoint

scheduling, *see* Calendar

viruses, *see* viruses

Word, *see* Word

Appointment Recurrence dialog box (Calendar), 385

appointments, making and breaking, 383, 385

archiving
Contacts, 319
deleted incoming email messages, 317
rotating archives, 319

arrow keys (Word), 138

Assign Task icon (Task form), 385, 389

asterisk (*) strop character, 167

attaching files to email messages, 351-352

auditing techniques
conditional formatting, 527-528
data validation, 523-524

Auditing toolbar
Excel, adding, 405
Remove Precedent Arrows icon, 441
Trace Precedents icon, 431-432
crossfoot total errors, 533
verifying calculations, 440

AutoArchive feature (Outlook 98), 315-316
copying deleted incoming messages, 317
rotating archives, 319

AutoCalculate feature, 442

AutoComplete feature (Excel), 446

AutoContent Wizard (PowerPoint), 554, 564
options, 588, 590
page setup, 572
presentations, building, 569-570
Summary Slide feature, 591-592

AutoCorrect feature, 216-217
adding entries to menu, 218
Excel, 446

AutoFill feature (Excel)
copying, 447
customizing list, 450
sequence of labels, 449
sequence of numbers, 448

AutoFormat As You Type command (Tools menu), Word, 96

AutoFormat dialog boxes (Excel), 484

AutoFormat feature
printing problems, 486
spreadsheets, 484-486
tables (Word), 235-236

AutoLayout feature, 594-595

Automatic Formatting dialog box (Contacts), 377

AutoRecover feature (Word), 111

AutoSave dialog box (Excel), 403

AutoSave feature
Excel, installing and activating, 402-403
Word, 111

AutoShapes command (Insert menu), Word, 245

AutoSignature, 353-354

AutoSum, 435-436

AutoSummarize, avoiding use of, 295

AutoText command (Insert menu), Word, 644

avoiding tabs, 195

axes of charts, titling, 510

B

backing up files
backup systems, 59, 61-62
LANs (local area networks), 56
Outlook 98
archiving Contacts, 319
AutoArchive, 315-317
daily, 314
selecting files, 57-58
Windows 98 Backup, 59, 61-62

Backspace key to delete characters (Word), 125

bad data warning (#) in spreadsheets, 464

bar codes on envelopes, 224

baseline scenarios, creating, 518

Before Spacing option (Paragraph formatting dialog box), 176

Binders
avoiding use of, 294
overview, 36-37

Blank Presentation command (PowerPoint), 572

blind copies of email messages, 345

body box, enlarging in presentations, 600

bookmarks, 269-271

Bookmarks dialog box (Word), 273

borders
drawing around paragraphs, 173
page, drawing, 276
paragraphs, formatting, 180-181
spreadsheets, 494

Borders and Shading command (Format menu), Word, 276

Borders icon (Formatting toolbar), Excel, 494

Borders tab (Format Cells dialog box), Excel, 495

Break command (Insert menu), Word, 226

browsers, 672

bugs, 3
anti-virus programs, 16
defined, 4-6
Excel patches, 14-15
Outlook patches, 15-16
SR-1, 12-14
see also viruses

builds
definition of, 631
presentations, adding to, 632

Bullet command (Format menu), PowerPoint, 599

Bulleted List slide placeholder, 595

bulleted lists
formatting paragraphs, 172, 196-197
auto bullets, 200
bullet options, 198

buttons
Shortcut bar, customizing, 66
toolbars, adding to, 267-268

buying roller mouse, 410

By Category view (Contacts), 379

C

calculations (Excel), verifying, 440-442
See also Formulas

Calendar (Outlook)
appointments, making and breaking, 383, 385
events, setting up week-long, 382-383
meetings, 381
overview of, 302
printing, 385-386
screen, 329
TaskPad, 385, 389

Calendar Wizard, 254-255

callouts, definition of, 245

Camcorder, 37-38

cat character (Earl), 74

categories (Contacts)
By Category view, 379
setting up, 374, 376

CDs
installing
fonts, 610
SR-1, 14
templates and wizards, 107
Web Page Authoring (HTML), 669
Mastering Office Development, 39, 293

cells, 407
active, 408
formatting, 486
names, 408
rotating text in, 491-492
selecting for scenarios, 518

Center icon (Formatting toolbar), Excel, 489

centering
headings over multiple rows in spreadsheets, 490

text in cells of spreadsheets, 488

character formatting on paragraph styles, 264

Character Spacing dialog box (Word), 162

characters
in documents, 122
formatting, 156
editing and, 166-167
fonts, changing from dialog box, 160, 162-163
fonts, changing from toolbar, 157, 160
highlighting, 158
kerning, definition of, 162
Office Assistant, changing, 73-74
stropping, 167
styles, applying, 258, 260

chart sheets, using, 508, 515

Chart slide placeholder, 595

Chart toolbar (Excel), 512, 514

Chart Wizard (Standard toolbar), Excel, 508, 512
Data Labels tab, 510
Titles tab, 510

charts
creating with Chart Wizard, 508, 510, 512
cutting, copying, and pasting, 516
editing, 513-514
Excel, 31
linking from documents, 655-656, 658
Microsoft Graph, 249
moving, resizing, and deleting, 516
presentations, adding to, 618, 620-621
updating data, 514

Check Names dialog box (Contacts), 348

clip art (Word)
inserting, 240-241
own, inserting, 242, 244

Clip Art slide placeholder, 595

Clipboard, 128-129

Clippit, 70-71
changing character of, 73-74
size, 75
tactics for using, 74-75
toggling on/off, 72

closing Word, 113-114

color, highlighting email messages with, 360-361

color-coded formula verifier, 441

columns (spreadsheets)
hiding, 497
inserting, 462
keeping titles onscreen, 498
printing titles for, 499, 501
resizing, 480
adjusting multiple column widths, 482-483
AutoWidth, 483
widening, 482

Comma Style icon (Formatting toolbar), Excel, 488

commands
Actions menu (Outlook 98), New Contact from Same Company, 380
Data menu (Excel)
PivotTable Report, 539
Validation, 524
Edit menu (Excel)
Clear, Formats, 486
Delete, 464
Find, 471
Go To, 475
Paste, 455
Replace, 474

Edit menu (Word)
Copy, 132
Cut, 130
Find, 142
Paste, 130
File menu (Excel)
Page Preview, 503
Save As HTML, 668
Set Print Area, 420
File menu (Outlook), Archive, 319
File menu (PowerPoint)
Pack and Go, 615
Page Setup, 572
Print, 585
Save As, 572, 574
Save as HTML, 686
File menu (Word)
Close, 113-114
Exit, 113
New, 107
Open, 115
Print, 118
Save, 133
Format menu (Excel)
AutoFormat, 484
Cells, 488
Conditional Formatting, 527
Format menu (PowerPoint)
Apply Design, 596-597
Bullet, 599
Slide Layout, 567, 618
Format menu (Word)
Borders and Shading, 180, 276
Bullets and Numbering, 198
Drop Cap, 283
Font, 160
New, 258
Paragraph, 175
Tabs, 187
Wrapping, 244
Help menu
Contents and Index, 76
Microsoft on the Web, 79
Index menu, Delete Index, 21
Insert menu, WordArt, 248

Insert menu (Excel)
Column, 462
Comment, 466
Organization Chart, 496
Page Break, 504
Rows, 463
Insert menu (Outlook 98)
File, 351
Signature, 354
Insert menu (PowerPoint)
Movie from Gallery, 628
Object, 595
Picture, 566, 626
Text Box, 566
Insert menu (Word)
AutoShapes, 245
AutoText, 644
Bookmark, 270
Break, 226
Chart, 249
Clip Art, 240
Date and Time, 237-239
Field, 286
File, 250
Format, 201
From File, 242
From Scanner, 249
Object, 652
Symbols, 221
New menu (Explorer), Folders, 48, 50
Start menu
Files or Folders, 58
System Tools, 59
Table menu (Word)
AutoFormat, 235
Delete Rows, 230
Draw Table, 231
Insert Table, 228
Tools menu (Excel)
AutoSave, 403
Conditional Sum Wizard, 535
Options, 8
Scenario, 518
Spelling, 498
Tools menu (Outlook 98), Accounts, 334

Tools menu (PowerPoint)
PowerPoint Central, 606, 608
Presentation Conference, 612
Tools menu (Word)
AutoCorrect, 217
AutoCorrect to disable strop characters, 168
AutoFormat As You Type, 96
Customize, 248, 266
Envelopes and Labels, 222
Merge Documents, 292
Options, 8, 89
Spelling and Grammar, 216
Thesaurus, 220
View menu (Excel), Page Break Preview, 503-504
View menu (FrontPage Express), HTML, 683
View menu (PowerPoint)
Header and Footer, 606
Slide Master, 598
Slide Show, 560
Title Master, 603
View menu (Word)
Headers and Footers, 209
Online and Outline, 102
Page Layout, 86
Rulers, 86
Zoom, 103
Window menu (Excel)
Freeze Panes, 499
Unfreeze Panes, 499

comments, adding to spreadsheets, 466

common code applications, 416

Common Tasks toolbar (PowerPoint)
docking, 553
New Slide icon, 594-595
showing, 553

compacting .pst files, 321

compressing files to attach to email messages, 352

Concept.A virus, 7

conditional formatting, 527-528

Conditional Formatting dialog box (Excel), 527, 533

Conditional Sum Wizard (Excel), 535

conditional summing, 534

conferencing feature (PowerPoint), 611, 613

contact managers, comparing to Outlook, 303

Contacts feature (Outlook)
adding email addresses to, 348-350
archiving, 319
categories, setting, 374, 376
copying, 380, 639-641, 643, 645
creating entries, 369-370
Dialing Properties dialog box, 373
multiple email addresses, 372
phone numbers, 371
ten-digit dialing, 373
overview of, 303, 368
retrieving email addresses from, 343-344
multiple name matches, 347-348
Select Names dialog box, 345-346
screen, organizing, 330
views
customizing, 376, 378-379
Phone List, 376

Contents (help), 76, 78

Contents and Index command (Help menu), 76

Copy icon (Standard toolbar), PowerPoint, 581

copying
charts, 516
Contacts, 380, 639-641, 643, 645
data
from one application to another, 638
spreadsheets, 451-454
Excel data
into documents, 659
into Word, 647-649
into Word pictures, 650
slides in presentations, 580-581
text in documents, 132

Corporate or Workgroup version of Outlook 98, 305
Help articles Web site, 336
switching to Internet Only, 310

Count number (AutoCalculate), 442

country names, defaults in address/phone book, 371

Mike Craven Web site (right-click Thesaurus program), 220

Create New Signature Wizard (Outlook 98), 353

creating
address/phone book entries, 369-370
Dialing Properties dialog box, 373
multiple email addresses, 372
phone numbers, 371
ten-digit dialing, 373
charts
Chart Wizard, 508, 510, 512
selecting data for, 508
documents (Word), 106, 110
email messages, 338
Inbox, checking, 339
netiquette, 341
Outbox, checking, 339

folders, 48, 50
résumés, 107-108
scenarios, 518, 521
slides, 567
vCards, 356
workbooks, 414-415

crossfoot totals in spreadsheets
emphasizing errors, 533-534
tracing errors, 533
validating, 529-532

Ctrl key
navigation keys, 138
PowerPoint, 591

Currency Style icon (Formatting toolbar), Excel, 487

cursors, 99

custom dictionary, 215

Customize command (Tools menu), Word, 248

customizing
bullets for bulleted lists, 198
My Documents folders,
42-43, 45-46, 55-56
creating, 48, 50
deleting, 51-52
moving, 54
multiple, creating, 52
naming, 51-52
numbering for numbered
lists, 199
Office, 41-42
toolbars (Word), 266-268
views
Contacts, 376, 378-379
restoring original, 332

cutting
charts, 516
text from documents, 130

D

data
aligning in cells of
spreadsheets
centering text, 488
indenting, 489
copying and moving in
spreadsheets, 451
*clicking and dragging,
452-454*
entering into spreadsheets
*alternatives to Enter
key, 443*
AutoComplete, 446
AutoCorrect, 446
AutoFill, 447-450
mistakes, correcting, 443
pasting in spreadsheets,
454-456
three dimensional and
PivotTables, 539
two dimensional and
PivotTables, 538

Data menu commands (Excel)
PivotTable Report, 539
Validation, 524

data types (Excel), automatically recognized, 428

data validation, 523-524

Data Validation dialog box (Excel), 524

databases, Excel spreadsheets as, 32

Date and Time dialog box (Word), 237

dates
automatically recognized
data types, 428
inserting (Word), 237-239
Tasks, setting, 385, 387
updating in headers and
footers when printing, 211

deactivating vertical scrollbar, 141

Decrease Decimal icon (Formatting toolbar), Excel, 488

Decrease Indent icon (Formatting toolbar), Excel, 490

default paragraph font, 265

default settings
address/phone book, country
name, 371
fonts, changing, 165
Excel, 493
Outlook 98
changing, 311
*email options,
changing, 311*
Journal feature, 312
Mail Delivery tab, 312
Spelling tab, 313
restoring views to, 332

Delete Index command (Index menu), 21

Delete key (Excel), 464

Delete Rows command (Table menu), Word, 230

deleting
charts, 516
in documents, 125
email messages, 316, 340
folders, 51-52
named ranges, 470
paragraph marks, 184
rows from spreadsheets, 463
Shortcut bar, 64
slides from presentations,
580-581

Desktop, saving Word documents to, 5

Details tab (Task form), 385, 389

dialing outbound calls, 392

Dialing Properties dialog box (Contacts), 373

dialog boxes
Calendar, Appointment Recurrence, 385
Contacts
Automatic Formatting, 377
Check Names, 348
Dialing Properties, 373
Select Names, 345-346
Excel
Add-Ins, 402
Alignment, 513
AutoFormat, 484
AutoSave, 403
Conditional Formatting, 527, 533
Data Validation, 524
Find, 473
Footer, 501
Format Axis Title, 513
Format Cells, 488, 492-493, 495, 528
Go To, 475
Internet Assistant, 682
Invalid Date, 526
Open, 415
Paste Function, 445, 530
Replace, 474
Scenario Manager, 518
Scenario Summary, 521
formatting paragraphs, 175-176, 179
FrontPage Express, Save As File, 680
modeless, 145
Outlook 98
installation, 304-305, 307
Internet Accounts, 334
Junk E-Mail, 362
New Call to Log Outbound Calls, 385, 393
Print, 385-386
Properties, 335
Using Colors, 360
Using Folders, 359-360

PowerPoint
File New, 570-571
File Print, 584
Format Text Box, 623
Insert Hyperlink, 675
Insert Objects, 620
Insert Picture, 627
New Slide, 577, 594
Open, 573
Save As, 574
Slide Layout, 567, 618
Slide Transition, 631
Word
Add/Modify FTP Locations, 670
Bookmarks, 273
Character Spacing, 162
Date and Time, 237
Drop Cap, 283
Envelopes, 222
File Open, 114
Find and Replace, 142, 145-147, 149, 153-154
Font, 160, 165-166
Format Font (Word), 160, 162-163
Insert Field's Help System, 290
Insert Picture, 242-243
Insert Table, 228
Label Options, 225
New Style, 258, 260
Open for Opening Files on Internet, 670
Page Borders, 276
Page Setup, 202-204
Paragraph formatting, 175
Paste Special for copying Excel data, 649-650
Print, 118
Replace, 151
Save, 94
Save As, 116
Spelling and Grammar, 216
Thesaurus, 220
View, 89

.dic files, 57

dictionary, 215, 220

Different First Page concept, 211

disabling strop characters, 168

displaying filename extensions, 19-20

.doc files, 57

Document Map, avoiding use of, 296

documents (Word), 105
AutoCorrect, 216-218
bookmarks
creating, 270-271
navigating with, 269
borders and shading, 180-181
building
characters, 122
drawing layer, 124
paragraphs, 122-123
sections, 124
clip art
inserting, 240-241
own, inserting, 242, 244
Clipboard, 128-129
closing, 113-114
copying between, 134-135
copying text, 132
creating, 106, 110
from presentations, 665
presentations from, 660-662
test documents, 131, 133
cutting text, 130
dates, inserting, 237-239
definition of, 121, 124
deleting, 125
drop caps, adding, 283
embedding spreadsheets into, 651-652, 655
envelopes and labels, printing, 222-223, 225-226
Fast Save, 93-94

files
  inserting, 250-251
  list length settings, 90
formatting, 155-156
  editing and, 166-167
  fonts, changing from
    dialog box, 160,
    162-163
  fonts, changing from
    toolbar, 157, 160
freehand drawing,
  244-245, 248
headers and footers, 210
  different first page,
    211-213
  standard, 208
hiding text in, 162
hyperlinks, 271
  creating in, 272-274
  disabling, 96, 272
  problems with, 95-96
linking to charts,
  655-656, 658
macro virus protection,
  6-8, 90
maintaining series of
  numbers in, 289
Microsoft Graph for
  charts, 249
navigating
  Find, 142, 145-147,
    149-150
  Go To tab, 154
  IntelliMouse Wheel,
    140-141
  keys, 138
  Replace, 150, 153
  Replace All option, 153
opening, 114
overstrike mode, disabling,
  91-92
page breaks, forcing, 226
page numbers, inserting, 286
Page Setup dialog box
  options
    Layout tab, 204
    Margins tab, 202
    Paper Size tab, 203
    Paper Source tab, 204

paragraphs, 169
  auto bullets and
    numbers, 200
  bulleted and numbered
    lists, 196-198, 200
  dialog box, 175-176, 179
  fill-in-the-blank forms,
    191-192, 194-195
  paragraph marks and, 88,
    182, 185
  tab stops, propagating,
    189-190
  tabs, 185-187, 191, 195
  toolbar, 169, 171, 173
pasting text, 130
pictures, inserting, 239
placing names at end of, 288
printing, 118
  duplex printing, 119
  uncollated copies, 120
rulers, removing, 85
saving, 5, 93-94, 110, 133
scanned art, inserting, 249
sections, 201
selecting and moving
  text, 126
Spell Check, 214-215
spreadsheets,
  incorporating, 659
starting over, 116
styles, 257
  applying, 258, 260
  character formatting on
    paragraph styles, 264
  default paragraph
    font, 265
  paragraphs, applying,
    261-263
symbols, inserting, 221
tables
  AutoFormat feature,
    235-236
  creating and formatting,
    228
  free-form, 231-232
  preformatted, 228-229
  ways of using, 236
templates, 106-107, 254-255

Thesaurus and
  Dictionary, 220
Undo and Redo commands,
  117-118
watermarks, adding,
  278-279, 282
wizards, 106-108, 254-255
Word, 99
WordArt, 248
dog character (Rocky), 74
.dot files, 57
dragging and dropping
  files into email
    messages, 353
  text into documents, 126
Draw 98, 37, 245
**Draw Table command
  (Table menu), Word, 231**
drawing page borders, 276
Drawing layer
  in documents, 124
  text
    adding to slides, 625
    in PowerPoint's Outline
      view, 556
**Drawing toolbar
  (PowerPoint), Text Box
  icon, 623**
**Drop Cap dialog box
  (Word), 283**
drop caps, adding, 283

E

**Earl Office Assistant
  (cat character), 74**
Edit menu commands
  Excel
    Clear, Formats, 486
    Delete, 464
    Find, 471
    Go To, 475
    Paste, 455
    Replace, 474

Word
  Copy, 132
  Cut, 130
  Find, 142
  Paste, 130
editing
  charts, 513-514
  formatting documents,
    166-167
  presentations, .pps versus
    .ppt files, 574
email
  accounts, setting up, 334,
    336-337
  attaching files, 351-352
  AutoSignature, creating,
    353-354
  Contacts
    addresses, adding to,
      348-350
    multiple addresses, 372
    multiple name matches,
      347-348
    retrieving addresses from,
      343-344
    Select Names dialog box,
      345-346
  Find function, 357-358
  Inbox screen, 325-328
  messages
    creating, 338-339
    deleting, 340
    netiquette, 341
    Outbox, checking, 339
    replying and forwarding,
      340-341
  options to avoid
    HTML Mail, 365-366
    WordMail, 364
  organizing
    filtering junk mail,
      361-362, 364
    folders, 359-360
    highlighting with color,
      360-361
  Outlook 98, 302, 333
    installing, 307-308
    messages, deleting, 316

  service providers, 336-337
  To list *versus* Cc list, 345
  vCards, 355
    as AutoSignatures, 356
    creating and sending, 356
embedding
  data from one application
    into another, 639
  spreadsheets into documents,
    651-652, 655, 660
End key (Word), 138
end of cell markers, 229
enhancing performance of
  Office, 66-67
Enter key
  Excel, staying put after
    hitting, 403
  spreadsheets, alternatives
    to, 443
entering in spreadsheets
  data
    alternatives to Enter
      key, 443
    AutoComplete, 446
    AutoCorrect, 446
    AutoFill, 447-450
    mistakes, correcting, 443
  functions, 445
Envelopes dialog box
  (Word), 222
envelopes, printing, 222-225
errors
  crossfoot totals, 533-534
  preventing Printer Overrun
    error message, 282
  spreadsheets
    conditional formatting,
      527-528
    data validation, 523-524
    types of, 523
Escape key
  dropping and dragging text
    (Word), 127
  quitting slide shows, 560
etiquette in email
  messages, 341

Events, setting up week-long,
  382-383
Excel
  Auditing toolbar
    adding, 405
    Trace Precedents icon,
      431-432
  automatically recognized
    data types, 428
  AutoSave feature, installing
    and activating, 402-403
  bugs and patches, 14-15
  calculations, verifying,
    440-442
  changing settings, 401
  charts, *see* charts
  as database program, 32
  Enter key, staying put after
    hitting, 403
  Formula Checker, 438
  formulas
    AutoSum, 435-436
    building by pointing and
      clicking, 433-434
    labels, 437-438
    methods for entering, 432
    parentheses, 439-440
    simple, 429, 431
    Sum( ) function, 435-437
  functions, definition of, 433
  hyperlinks, 677
  IntelliMouse, 410
  maximizing most recently
    used list, 404
  overview of, 26, 31-32, 399
  printing, 418
    Fit to page, 423
    gridlines, 424
    landscape orientation,
      422
    page sequence, 420
    portrait orientation, 422
    Print Area, setting and
      clearing, 419
    Report Manager, 424
    spreadsheets, 421-422

screen elements, 406
Formula bar, 407
menu bar, 407
sheet tabs and scrollbars, 408
spreadsheets, 407-408
status bars, 409
title bar, 407
toolbars, 407
Zoom icon, 409
starting, 414
terminology, 400
Undo feature, 418
Word, interconnection with
copying data, 647-648
embedding spreadsheets, 651-652, 655
evaluating methods, 659
linking, 655-656, 658
spreadsheet to picture, 650
spreadsheet to raw data, 649

exiting Word, 113

extensions, displaying, 19-20

F

F1 key (Word), 139

Fast Save
avoiding use of, 294
Word, problems with, 93-94

field codes, Help system for, 290

Field command (Insert menu), Word, 286

fields, 286-287, 290
codes and results, 285-286, 289
functions of, 284

File Find utility, 58

file list length settings, Word, 90

File menu commands
Excel
Page Preview, 503
Save As HTML, 668
Set Print Area, 420
Outlook, Archive, 319
PowerPoint
Pack and Go, 615
Page Setup, 572
Print, 585
Save As, 572, 574
Save As HTML, 686
Word
Close, 113-114
Exit, 113
New, 107
Open, 115
Print, 118
Save, 133

File New dialog box (PowerPoint), 570-571

File Open dialog box (Word), 114

File Print dialog box (PowerPoint), 584

File Transfer Protocol (FTP), 669

files
attaching to email messages, 351-352
backing up
backup systems, 59
LANs (local area networks), 56
Outlook 98, 314-316
selecting files to be, 57-58
Windows 98 Backup, 59, 61-62
documents, definition of, 121
Excel, maximizing most recently used list, 404
inserting into documents, 250-251

Internet, opening on, 669-670
large, avoiding using in Word, 295
names
extensions, 19-20, 57-58
sorting by, 112
PowerPoint
.pps versus .ppt, 572, 575
.pps, editing warning, 574
.pst
backing up daily, 314
compacting, 321
Outlook 98, 315
saving prior to connecting to FTP sites, 672
searching for in Word, 115
signature, 16
storing data in
Outlook 98, 309
types of, 57
.vcf, 357

Files or Folders command (Start menu), 58

fill-in-the-blank forms, 191-192, 194-195

film recorders, printing presentations on 35mm slides, 586

filtering junk mail, 361-362, 364

Find and Replace dialog box (Word)
basic searches, 142, 145-146
complex searches, 147, 149
Go To tab, 154
sticky settings, 153

Find dialog box (Excel), Values, Comments, and Formulas, 473

Find Fast
avoiding use of, 294
turning off, 20-21

Find feature
Excel
limitations of, 474
spreadsheets,
navigating, 471
wild cards, 473
Word
complex searches, 147, 149
navigating documents,
142, 145-146, 150
wildcard characters , 150

**Find function (Outlook),
357-358**

**First line indentation option
(Paragraph formatting
dialog box), 176**

**Fit to button (Excel),
printing, 423**

**Flat-file database programs
(Notes), 385, 390, 392**

Float over text
avoiding use of, 294
check box, 244

**floating text (Drawing
layer), 625**

Folder List (Outlook 98), 324

folders
My Documents
creating, 48, 50
deleting, 51-52
moving, 54
multiple, creating, 52
naming, 51-52
organizing, 45-46
organizing email with,
359-360
Windows Explorer,
sorting, 53

**Folders command (New
menu), Explorer, 48, 50**

**Font command (Format
menu), Word, 160**

Font dialog box (Word)
accessing, 165
highlighting and, 166

**Font tab (Format Cells
dialog box), Excel, 493**

fonts
animation effects, 163
changing
default, 165
from dialog box, 160,
162-163
from toolbar, 157, 160
formatting when editing,
166-167
installing from CD, 610
spreadsheets, 493

Footer dialog box (Excel), 501

footers, 210
different first page, 211-213
formatting presentations,
566
printing on spreadsheets,
501-502
standard, 208

forcing page breaks, 226

**Format Axis Title dialog box
(Excel), 513**

**Format Cells dialog box
(Excel), 528**
Alignment tab, 492
Borders tab, 495
Font tab, 493
Number tag, 488
Patterns tab, 495

**Format Font dialog box
(Word), 160, 162-163**

Format menu commands
Excel
AutoFormat, 484
Cells, 488
Conditional Formatting,
527
PowerPoint
Apply Design, 596-597
Bullet, 599
Slide Layout, 567, 618

Word
Borders and Shading,
180, 276
Bullets and Numbering,
198
Drop Cap, 283
Font, 160
New, 258
Paragraph, 175
Tabs, 187
Wrapping, 244

**Format Painter, avoiding use
of, 295**

**Format Text Box dialog box
(PowerPoint), 623**

formatting
AddressLayout AutoText
entry, 643, 645, 647
borders and shading,
180-181
cells in spreadsheets, 486
characters, 156
editing and, 166-167
fonts, changing, 157,
160, 162-163
documents, 155
footers in presentations, 566
numbers in spreadsheets,
487
paragraphs
auto bullets and
numbers, 200
bulleted and numbered
lists, 196-198
dialog box, using,
175-176, 179
fill-in-the-blank forms,
191-192, 194-195
paragraph marks and,
182, 185
tab stops, propagating,
189-190
tabs, 185-187, 191, 195
toolbar, using, 169,
171, 173
percentages in
spreadsheets, 488

styles, 257
  character formatting on paragraph styles, 264
  character, applying, 258, 260
  default paragraph fonts, 265
  paragraph, applying, 261-263
  text in presentations, 566
  titles in presentations, 566
  undoing mistakes, 265
Formatting toolbar (Excel), 488
  Align Left, 489
  Borders icon, 494
  Center icon, 489
  Currency Style icon, 487
  Decrease Indent, 490
  Increase Indent, 489
  Merge and Center icon, 490
  Percent Style icon, 487
formatting Web sites, 354
Formula bar (Excel), 407
Formula Checker, 438
formulas
  Excel, 429
    AutoSum, 435-436
    building by pointing and clicking, 433-434
    Find dialog box, 473
    labels, 437-438
    methods for entering, 432
    parentheses, 439-440
    simple, 429, 431
    Sum( ) function, 435
    Sum( ) function with ranges, 436-437
    Trace Precedents icon, 431-432
  multiple sheets, 476
  show formulas in spreadsheets, 465
  see also calculations
formulas error values, 464
forwarding email messages, 340-341

freehand drawing (Word), 244-245, 248
Freehand drawing tool, 231-232
Freeze Panes feature, spreadsheets, 498
From File command (Insert menu), Word, 242
From Scanner command (Insert menu), Word, 249
FrontPage Express, publishing spreadsheets as Web pages, 679, 681-683
FTP (File Transfer Protocol), 669
fully justified, definition of, 171
functions
  3D ranges, using in, 478
  definition of, 433
  entering in spreadsheets, 445
  WEEKDAY( ), 444
  see also calculations; formulas

G

genigraphics, printing presentations on 35mm slides, 585
Go To dialog box (Excel), navigating spreadsheets, 475
Go To tab, navigating documents, 154
GPFs (general protection faults), WordMail, 365
Grammar Checker, avoiding use of, 295
graphic images
  inserting into spreadsheets, 496
  Photo Editor, 38

graphing data on slides, 618, 620-621
graphs (Excel), 31
gridlines (Excel), printing, 424

H

Handout Master, 584
handouts, preparing for presentations, 584
hanging indentation, Paragraph formatting dialog box, 176
Header and Footer command (View menu), PowerPoint, 606
headers, 210
  different first page, 211-213
  printing on spreadsheets, 501-502
  standard, 208
headings, centering over multiple rows in spreadsheets, 490
Help menu commands
  Contents and Index, 76
  Microsoft on the Web, 79
Help system
  Clippit, 70-71
    changing character of, 73-74
    size, 75
    tactics for, 74-75
    toggling on/off, 72
  contents and index, 76, 78
  disadvantages, 69-70
  field codes, 290
  Mail Merge, 291
  searches, 77
  tips, 72
  see also online help
hiding
  rows and columns in spreadsheets, 497
  text in documents, 162

highlighting
characters, 158
email messages with color,
360-361
Font dialog box and, 166

Home key (Word), 138

horizontal rulers
avoiding use of tabs
with, 195
viewing hidden, 86

**horizontal scrollbars
(Word), 102**

**HP Laserjet printers,
preventing Printer
Overrun errors, 282**

htm files, 57

**HTML (Hypertext Markup
Language), description
of, 670**

**HTML command
(View menu), FrontPage
Express, 683**

HTML files, 57

HTML Mail, avoiding, 365-366

HTML support, 668

**HTML Wizard (PowerPoint),
686**

**hybrid addresses in
spreadsheets, 461**

**hyperlinking slides to Web,
674-675**

hyperlinks, 271
applications, 674
creating in documents,
272-274
disabling, 272
Excel, 677
Word, problems with, 95-96

**Hypertext Markup Language
(HTML), description of, 670**

I

**icons, changing on
toolbars, 268**

**IF formula construction kit
(Excel), 530**

import filters, 243

**inbound phone calls, logging,
385, 394**

Inbox (email)
checking for messages, 339
screen, 325-328

**Inbox button
(Outlook 98), 324**

**Inbox Repair Tool feature
(Outlook 98), 320**

**Increase Decimal icon
(Formatting toolbar),
Excel, 488**

**Increase Indent icon
(Formatting toolbar),
Excel, 489**

indenting
cells of spreadsheets, 489
definition of, 172
paragraphs
*Paragraph formatting
dialog box, 176*
toolbar, 172

**Index menu commands,
Delete Index, 21**

indexes, Help system, 76, 78

infection (virsues), 7

**Insert Field dialog box
(Word), Help system, 290**

**Insert Hyperlink dialog box
(PowerPoint), 675**

**Insert Hyperlink icon
(Standard toolbar),
PowerPoint, 272, 675**

Insert key (Word)
overstrike mode,
disabling, 91
pasting text, 130

Insert menu commands
Excel
Column, 462
Comment, 466
Organization Chart, 496
Page Break, 504
Rows, 463
Outlook 98
File, 351
Signature, 354
PowerPoint
Movie from Gallery, 628
Object, 595
Picture, 566, 626
Text Box, 566
Word
AutoShapes, 245
AutoText, 644
Bookmark, 270
Break, 226
Chart, 249
Clip Art, 240
Date and Time, 237-239
Field, 286
File, 250
Format, 201
From File, 242
From Scanner, 249
Object, 652
Symbols, 221
WordArt, 248

**Insert Object dialog box
(PowerPoint), 620**

Insert Picture dialog box
PowerPoint, 627
Word, 242-243

**Insert Table dialog box
(Word), 228**

inserting
columns into spreadsheets,
462
pictures into spreadsheets,
496

rows into spreadsheets, 462
sheets into workbooks, 418
see also adding

insertion point (Word), 99

installing
AutoSave feature (Excel),
402-403
Camcorder, 38
fonts from CD, 610
mail services, Help articles
Web site, 336
Outlook 98, 304
*changing default
settings, 311*
*email and networking,
307-308*
email options, 311
Journal feature, 312
Mail Delivery tab, 312
Spelling tab, 313
*switching to Internet Only
version, 310*
*versions of program, 305,
310*
SR-1 release, 14
templates and Wizards from
CD, 107
Web Page Authoring (HTML)
from CD, 669

**Integrated File Management
Web site, 385, 396**

**integration of
applications, 39**

IntelliMouse
Excel, capabilities in, 410
navigating documents,
140-141

**interaction of applications,
39, 637-638**

Internet
description of, 668
files, opening on, 669-670

**Internet Accounts dialog box
(Outlook 98), 334**

**Internet Assistant Wizard
(Excel), 681**

**Internet Assistant Wizard
dialog box (Excel), 682**

Internet Connection Wizard
email logon ID and
password, 308
installing Outlook 98, 307

**Internet Explorer 4.0 and
Outlook 98, 303, 309**

**Internet Only version of
Outlook 98, 305**
changing default settings
email options, 311
Journal feature, 312
Mail Delivery tab, 312
Spelling tab, 313
Help articles Web site, 336
installing, help Web site, 309
setting up email accounts,
334-335, 337
storing data, 309
switching to from Corporate
or Workgroup version, 310

**Invalid Date dialog box
(Excel), 526**

J

Java and Word, 296

Journal feature (Outlook)
logging phone calls,
385, 394
overview of, 303, 312
screen, 332

**Journal Entry form, logging
inbound calls, 385, 394**

**Junk E-Mail dialog box
(Outlook 98), 362**

**junk mail, filtering,
361-362, 364**

justifying paragraphs, 170

K

**Keep lines together option
(Paragraph formatting
dialog box), 179**

kerning, definition of, 162

**key combinations,
recommended, 139**

key number, 17-18

**keys, navigating
documents, 138**

kiosk presentations, 589

L

**Label Options dialog box
(Word), 225**

labels
formulas, 437-438
printing, 222, 225-226

landscape orientation, 422

**languages, Visual Basic for
Applications, 38-39**

**LANs (local area
networks), 56**

**Laplink cables and
software, 612**

launching, *see* **starting**

**Layout tab (Page Setup
dialog box), 204**

**left-justifying, definition
of, 170**

**Letter Wizard, avoiding use
of, 295**

Lightning Web site, 385, 396

**Line and Page Breaks tab
(Paragraph formatting
dialog box), 179**

**line spacing in paragraphs
when formatting, 178**

**Line Spacing option
(Paragraph formatting
dialog box), 178**

linking
data from one application to another, 639
documents to charts, 655-656, 658
spreadsheets with documents, 660

List view (Notes), 392

lists, spreadsheets
conditional summing and, 535
PivotTables, 545
creating, 539, 541
viewing, 542, 544

local area networks (LANs), 56

logging phone calls, 392
inbound, 385, 394
outbound, 385, 393

logos, inserting into presentations, 602

M

Macmillan Computer Press Web site, 675

macro language, definition of, 292

macro recorders
avoiding use of, 294
overview of, 293

macros
VBA, 38
viruses, 6
Concept.A, 7
protection, 8, 10, 90
reproduction, 7

Mail Delivery tab, setting options in Outlook 98, 312

Mail Merge, 290-292

mail services, Help articles on Web about installing, 336

MAPI, installing Outlook 98 and, 306

Margins tab (Page Setup dialog box), 202

Master Documents, avoiding use of, 295

Mastering Office Development CD, 39, 293

masters, applying from other presentations, 597

maximizing screens (Word), 86

.mdb files, 57

Media Clip slide placeholder, 595

meetings, overview of, 381

menu bars
Excel, 407
Outlook 98, 323
Word, 98, 266

Merge and Center icon (Formatting toolbar), Excel, 490

Merge Documents command (Tools menu), Word, 292

messages
archiving deleted incoming, 317, 319
attaching files, 351-352
AutoSignature, creating, 353-354
Contacts
addresses, adding to, 348-350
addresses, retrieving from, 343-344
multiple name matches, 347-348
Select Names dialog box, 345-346
creating, 338-339
deleting, 340
Find function, 357-358
netiquette, 341
organizing
filtering junk mail, 361-362, 364

folders, 359-360
highlighting with color, 360-361
replying and forwarding, 340-341
To list *versus* Cc list, 345
vCards, 355-356

Microsoft
Chart, 618
Draw 98, 125, 245
Graph, charts for Word and PowerPoint, 249
Network, incoming and outgoing servers, 308
Office, *see* Office
Web sites, 37, 107
AutoSignature information, 354
backgrounds, adding to email messages, 366
Corporate or Workgroup version of Outlook 98, 336
file storage, 670
Integrated File Management, 385, 396
Internet Only version of Outlook 98, 309, 336
mail services, installing, 336
Mastering Office Development CD, 293
Outlook 98, 304
support, 517
Support Online, 297
TweakUI, 410
Word, 297

Microsoft Knowledge Base (MSKB), 79

Microsoft on the Web command (Help menu), 79

***mirabile dictu*, definition of, 122**

mistakes, correcting in spreadsheets, 443

modeless dialog boxes, 145

modems, problems dialing outbound calls, 385, 393

Most recently used (MRU) file list
Excel, maximizing, 404
opening documents from, 115

mouse
advancing slides, 560
Intellimouse 140-141, 410
pointer (Word), 99

Movie from Gallery command (Insert menu), PowerPoint, 628

moving
charts, 516
data in spreadsheets, 451-454
folders in My Documents, 54
slides in presentations, 580
text in documents, 126-, 127

MSKB (Microsoft Knowledge Base), 79

multiple documents, copying between, 134-135

multiple email addresses, entering in address/phone book, 372

multiple sheets (Excel), spreadsheets,navigating, 475-476, 478

My Documents folders, customizing, 42-43, 45-46, 55-56
creating, 48, 50
deleting, 51-52
moving, 54
multiple, creating, 52
naming, 51-52

My Shortcuts separator bar (Outlook 98), 324

N

named ranges in spreadsheets, 468, 470

#NAME! warning, 465

names
cells, 408
copying Outlook Contacts into Word, 640-641, 643, 645
of documents, placing at end of, 288
files, names, *see* files
folders (My Documents), 51-52
sheets in workbooks, 417

navigating
documents
bookmarks, 269-271
IntelliMouse Wheel, 140-141
keys, 138
slide shows, 560
spreadsheets
Find feature, 471, 473-474
Go To dialog box, 475
multiple sheets, 475-476, 478
named ranges, 468-470
shortcut keys, 468

Net, *see* Internet

netiquette, 341

New Call dialog box (Outlook 98), 385, 393

New command (File menu), Word, 107

New Contact from Same Company command (Actions menu), Outlook 98, 380

New menu commands (Explorer), Folders, 48, 50

New Slide dialog box (PowerPoint), 577, 594

New Slide icon (Common Tasks toolbar), PowerPoint, 594-595

New Style dialog box (Word), 258, 260

No E-mail version of Outlook 98, 306

Normal view
avoiding use of, 294
Word, 85

Notes feature (Outlook)
organizing, 385, 390, 392
overview of, 303, 385, 390
presentations, preparing for, 583
screen, 332

Notes Master, viewing and modifying, 583

Notes Page view (PowerPoint), 559, 583

null modem cables, 611-612

Number tab (Format Cells dialog box), Excel, 488

numbered lists
formatting paragraphs and, 196, 198
auto numbering, 200
numbering options, 199
formatting paragraphs as, 171

numbers
formatting in spreadsheets, 487
maintaining series of in documents, 289

O

.obd files, 57

Object command (Insert menu), Word, 652

Object slide placeholder, 595

objects (PowerPoint), definition of, 569

.obt files, 57

Office 97
advantages of, 28
applications, *see* applications
Developer Edition, 34
development of, 27
disadvantages of, 28
integration of
applications, 39
patches
Excel, 14-15
Outlook, 15-16
SR-1, 12-14
performance, improving, 66-67
registration, 17-18
Small Business Edition V1, 34
Small Business Edition V2, 34
Standard Edition, 33
starting, 63
upgrades, 15
versions, 12-14

Office Assistant (Clippit), 70-71
changing character of, 73-74
formulas, error values, 465
overview of, 35
shortcut keys (Word), 137
tactics for using, 74-75
toggling on/off, 72

Office Clip Art Gallery, 240

Office Pro, 34

OfficeArt, 37

.oft files, 57

online help, 69
Clippit, 70-75
contents and index, 76, 78
disadvantages of, 69-70
searches, 77
tips, 72
see also help system

Online view (Word), 102

Open dialog box
Excel, 415
PowerPoint, 573
Word, opening files on
Internet, 670

opening
documents in Word, 114
files on Internet, 669-670
presentations, 573-574
workbooks, 415

Options command (Tools menu)
Excel, 8
Word, 8, 89

Organization Chart command (Insert menu), Excel, 496

Organization Chart slide placeholder, 595

organizing
email
filtering junk mail, 361-362, 364
folders, 359-360
highlighting with color, 360-361
My Documents folders, 42-43, 45-46
creating, 48, 50
deleting, 51-52
moving, 54
multiple, creating, 52
naming, 51-52
notes, 385, 390, 392
slides for presentations, 576-578

orphans, definition of, 179

Other Shortcuts separator bar (Outlook 98), 324

outbound phone calls, logging, 385, 393

Outbox, (email)checking for messages, 339

Outline view
PowerPoint, 555-557
organizing slides, 578
printing, 584
Word, 102

Outlining toolbar (PowerPoint), 557, 591-592

Outlook 97, comparing to Outlook 98, 304

Outlook 98
add-ons, 395
Integrated File Management, 385, 396
Lightning, 385, 396
annoyances, 310
backing up files
archiving Contacts, 319
AutoArchive, 315-317
daily, 314
bugs and patches, 15-16
compacting .pst file, 321
comparing to contact
managers and Outlook
Express, 303
comparing to
Outlook 97, 304
components of, 302-303
Corporate or Workgroup
version, Help articles Web
site, 336
email, overview of, 333
Inbox Repair tool, 320
installing, 304
changing default settings, 311
email and networking, 307-308
email options, 311
Journal feature, 312
Mail Delivery tab, 312
Spelling tab, 313
switching to Internet Only version, 310
versions of program, 305

Internet Only version
  *Help articles Web
    site, 336*
  *setting up email accounts,
    334-335, 337*
mail services, installing, Help
  articles Web site, 336
options to avoid
  HTML Mail, 365-366
  WordMail, 364
overview of, 26, 30, 301
screens and views, 322
storing data, 309
uninstalling, 310
upgrade, 15
versions of
  *Corporate or Workgroup,
    305*
  determining, 306
  Internet Only, 305
  No E-mail, 306
Web sites, 304
Word, interconnection with,
  639-641, 643, 645

**Outlook Express, comparing
to Outlook, 303**

**Outlook Shell screen,
322, 325**

Outlook Today
  overview of, 302
  screen, 328
  Task form, 385, 389

**overruns when printing,
preventing, 282**

**overstrike mode, disabling
(Word), 91-92**

P

**Pack and Go feature
(PowerPoint), 615**

**Page Border dialog box
(Word), 276**

page borders, drawing, 276

**Page Break command (Insert
menu), Excel, 504**

**Page Break Preview
command (View menu),
Excel, 503-504**

page breaks, forcing, 226

Page Down key (Word), 138

**Page Layout command (View
menu), Word, 86**

**page numbers, inserting into
documents, 201, 286**

**Page Preview command
(File menu), Excel, 503**

**page setup, presentations,
572**

**Page Setup dialog box
(Word)**
  Layout tab, 204
  Margins tab, 202
  Paper Size tab, 203
  Paper Source tab, 204

Page Up key (Word), 138

paper clip character,
  see Clippit

**Paper clip icon, email
messages with
attached files, 351**

**Paper Size tab (Page Setup
dialog box), 203**

**Paper Source tab (Page Setup
dialog box), 204**

**Paragraph formatting dialog
box (Word), 175**

paragraph marks
  bulleted and numbered lists
    and, 196
  deleting, 184
  documents, 122
  formatting paragraphs
    and, 182, 185
  tab stops and, 188
  Word, 90
    showing, 88

paragraphs
  borders and shading,
    180-181

definition of, 122
documents, 122-123
formatting, 169
  *auto bullets and
    numbers, 200*
  *bulleted and numbered
    lists, 196-198*
  dialog box, 175-176, 179
  *fill-in-the-blank forms and
    tabs, 191-192, 194-195*
  paragraph mark, 182, 185
  *tab stops, propagating,
    189-190*
  tabs, 185-187, 191, 195
  *toolbar, using, 169,
    171, 173*
styles
  applying, 261-263
  *character formatting on,
    264*
  *default paragraph font,
    265*

parameters (Excel), 444

parentheses, 439-440

**Paste Function dialog box
(Excel), 445, 530**

**Paste Function icon (Excel),
444-445**

**Paste Special dialog box
(Word), 649-650**

pasting
  charts, 516
  data into spreadsheets,
    454-456
  text in documents, 130

patches, 12
  Excel, 14-15
  Outlook, 15-16
  SR-1, 12-14

patterns in spreadsheets, 495

**Patterns tab (Format Cells
dialog box), Excel, 495**

Pause key (Word), 138

PCs
dialing outbound calls, 392
multiple for presentations, 611-612

Percent Style icon (Formatting toolbar), Excel, 487

percentages, formatting in Excel, 488

performance, improving, 66-67

phone books, *see* **address/phone books**

phone calls, logging, 392
inbound calls, 385, 394
outbound calls, 385, 393

Phone List view (Contacts), 331, 376

phone numbers
entering in address/phone book, 371
Office upgrades, 14

phone registration, 18

Photo Editor, 38

Picture command (Insert menu), PowerPoint, 566

pictures
adding to slides, 625-627
inserting
into spreadsheets, 496
into Word documents, 239

PivotTable toolbar (Excel), PivotTable Wizard icon, 543

PivotTable Wizard (Excel), 539

PivotTable Wizard icon (PivotTable toolbar), Excel, 543

PivotTables
creating from lists, 539, 541
overview of, 538
uses of, 545
viewing, 542, 544

placeholders
description of, 558, 594
types of, 595

points, definition of, 157

portrait orientation, definition of, 422

.pot files, 57

PowerPoint
differences from other applications, 568
options, setting, 551
overview of, 26, 33, 549
Word, interconnection with, 660-662, 665

PowerPoint Central command (Tools menu), PowerPoint, 606, 608

.pps files (PowerPoint)
editing warning, 574
versus .ppt, 572, 575

.ppt files, 57

pre-fab presentations (File New dialog box), 570-571

prebuilt documents, 415

Presentation Conference Wizard (PowerPoint), 613

presentation hardware, overview of, 586

presentations
AutoContent Wizard, 564
options, 588, 590
Summary Slide feature, 591-592
AutoLayout, 594-595
building
AutoContent Wizard, 569-570
screen by screen, 571
charts, adding to, 618, 620-621
conferencing feature, 611, 613
creating, 554
documents from, 665
from documents, 660-662

description of, 550
footer, date, and slide number, 606
getting message across, 563
global changes to slides
Apply Design command, 596-597
Slide Master, 598-599, 601-602
handouts, preparing for, 584
kiosk option, 589
macros, viruses in, 10
masters, applying from other presentations, 597
modifying individual slides, 567
multiple PCs, 611-612
Notes Page view, 559
notes, preparing for, 583
opening, 573-574
Outline view, 555-557
Pack and Go feature, 615
page setup, AutoContent Wizard, 572
PowerPoint Central, 606, 608
pre-fab, File New dialog box, 571
printing, 585
recording narration for, 634
Slide Master
logos, inserting, 602
modifying, 566
using, 565-566
slide shows, 33, 550, 560
Slide Show view, 560
Slide Sorter view, 558
Slide view, 557
slides, 33, 564
creating, 567
free-form text, adding to, 622-623, 625
moving, copying, and deleting, 580-581
organizing, 576-578
pictures, adding to, 625-627
timing, 634

title slides
  definition of, 565
  Title Master, 603-604
transitions and builds, adding
  to, 630-632
videos, adding to, 628, 630
Web pages, creating from,
  685-686

**Preview Pane feature
(Outlook 98), 326**

Print dialog box
Outlook 98 calendar,
  385-386
Word, 118

**Print Preview, avoiding use
of, 295**

**Print Screen key (Word),
138, 140**

**printer overrun errors,
preventing, 282**

printing
AutoFormat formats, 486
calendars, 385-386
envelopes, 222-223, 225
Excel, 418
  Fit to page, 423
  gridlines, 424
  *landscape orientation,
    422*
  page sequence, 420
  portrait orientation, 422
  *Print Area, setting and
    clearing, 419*
  Report Manager, 424
  *spreadsheets, large,
    421-422*
labels, 225-226
notes, 583
Outline view
  (PowerPoint), 584
presentations, 585
resizing columns to fit
  spreadsheets on one
  page, 481

spreadsheets
  column titles, 499, 501
  *headers and footers,
    501-502*
  *Page Break Preview,
    503-504*
updating times and dates in
  headers and footers, 211
Word, 118
  duplex printing, 119
  uncollated copies, 120

programs, see applications

**Properties dialog box
(Outlook 98), Servers
tab, 335**

protection from viruses
Excel, 8
PowerPoint, 10
Word, 8

.pst files, 57
backing up daily, 314
compacting, 321
Outlook 98, 315

**publishing pages on the
Web, 677**

Q

**Quick Launch toolbar,
starting Office from, 63**

quitting slide shows, 560

R

ranges
3D, using in functions, 478
specifying, 437
spreadsheets, assigning
  names to, 469

**recommended reading
(Word), 296**

**recording narration for
presentations, 634**

**recurring activities or
appointments, setting
up, 385**

**Redo command (Word),
117-118**

#REF! warning, 465

registration, 17-18

**relative addresses in
spreadsheets**
changing formulas, 457-458
preserving formulas, 458-459

**Remove Precedent Arrows
icon (Auditing toolbar), 441**

renaming, see names

Replace dialog box
Excel, 474
Word, 151

Replace feature
Excel, limitations of, 474
navigating documents,
  150, 153

**replying to email messages,
340-341**

**Report Manager (Excel),
printing, 424**

resizing
charts, 516
columns and rows in
  spreadsheets, 480
  AutoWidth, 483
  *multiple column widths,
    482-483*
  row height, 484
  widening columns, 482

résumés
creating with Word, 107-108
tables, using to design, 236

**retrieving email addresses
from Contacts, 343-344**
multiple name matches,
  347-348
Select Names dialog box,
  345-346

right-justifying, definition of, 170

Rocky Office Assistant (dog character), 74

roller mouse, buying, 410

rotating
archives for deleted incoming messages, 319
text in cells of spreadsheets, 491-492

rows
deleting from spreadsheets, 463
hiding in spreadsheets, 497
inserting in spreadsheets, 462
keeping titles onscreen, 498
resizing in spreadsheets, 480, 484

rulers
avoiding use of, 294
horizontal, avoiding use of tabs with, 195
Word, removing, 85

running, *see* **starting**

S

Save As command (File menu), PowerPoint, 572

Save As dialog box
PowerPoint, 574
Word, 111, 116

Save As File dialog box (FrontPage Express), 680

Save As HTML command (File menu)
Excel, 668
PowerPoint, 686

Save dialog box (Word), 94

saving
documents, 110, 133
Fast Save, disabling, 93
Fast Save, problems with, 93-94
to Desktop, 5
files prior to connecting to FTP sites, 672
incoming email messages, 317
Undo command and, 118
Word
AutoSave feature, 111
Save versus Save As commands, 113

scanned art, inserting (Word), 249

Scenario Manager dialog box (Excel), 518

Scenario Summary dialog box (Excel), 521

scenarios, creating, 518, 521

scheduling applications, *see* **Calendar**

scientific notation, definition of, 481

screen shots (Word), 138

screens
Calendar, 329
Contacts, 330
Excel elements, 406
Formula bar, 407
menu bar, 407
sheet tabs and scrollbars, 408
spreadsheets, 407-408
status bars, 409
title bar, 407
toolbars, 407
Zoom icon, 409
Inbox, 325-326
Journal, 332
maximizing, 86
Notes, 332

Outlook 98, 322
Outlook Shell, 322
Outlook Today, 328
presentations, creating, 554
Notes Page view, 559
Outline view, 555-557
Slide Show view, 560
Slide Sorter view, 558
Slide view, 557
reclaiming screen space, 325
Tasks, 332
views, changing and customizing, 327-328
Word elements
documents, 99
horizontal scrollbars, 102
menu bars, 98
status bars, 100
title bars, 97
toolbars, 99
vertical scrollbars, 101
zoom factor, 103

Scroll Lock key (Word), 138

scrollbars (Excel), 408

scrolling
IntelliMouse Wheel, 140-141
moving text, problems in Word, 127

search engines (Word), 115

searching
help, 77
Web from Word, 672
Word, 147, 150

sections
description of, 123
in documents, 124, 201

Select Names dialog box (Contacts), 345-346

selecting
cells in scenarios, 518
characters (Word), 128
multiple items (PowerPoint), 591
text in documents, 126, 156

self-starting video clips, creating, 630

Send and Receive icon, 339

sending vCards, 356

separator bars (Outlook 98), 324

servers
incoming and outgoing
  installing Outlook 98, 307
  Microsoft Network, 308
names of, setting up email accounts, 335

service bureaus, printing presentations on 35mm slides, 585

service providers (email), solving problems, 336-337

Set Print Area command (File menu), Excel, 420

setting up
categories for address/phone book entries, 374, 376
email accounts, 334, 336-337
Events, week-long, 382-383

shading for paragraphs, formatting, 180

Sheet tabs (Excel), 408

sheets
inserting, 418
renaming, 417

Shift+F5 (return to last place edited), Word, 140

shortcut bar, 35
customizing, 65-66
deleting, 64

shortcut key combinations
spreadsheets, navigating, 468
Word, 137, 139

show formulas, spreadsheets, 465

signature files, 16

signature lines for email messages, 353-354

sites, *see* Web sites

size of Clippit, 75

Slide Layout command (Format menu), PowerPoint, 567

Slide Layout dialog box (PowerPoint), 567, 618

Slide Master, 565-566
global changes to presentations, 598-599
  boxes, moving, 601
  formatting changes to boxes, 602
logos, inserting, 602
modifying, 566
overview of, 564
versus Title Master, 568

Slide Numbers, Outline view, 556

Slide Show view (PowerPoint), 560

slide shows, 33
description of, 550
quitting, 560
see also presentations

Slide Sorter toolbar (PowerPoint)
Slide Transition Effects drop-down box, 631
Text Preset Animation drop-down box, 632

Slide Sorter view (PowerPoint), 558
moving, copying, and deleting slides, 580
organizing slides, 576

Slide Transition dialog box (PowerPoint), 631

Slide Transition Effects drop-down box (Slide Sorter toolbar), PowerPoint, 631

Slide view (PowerPoint), 557

slides, 33
35mm, printing presentations on, 585
advancing, 560
creating, 567
description of, 550
footer, date, and slide number, 606
free-form text, adding to, 622-623, 625
global changes to
  Apply Design command, 596-597
  Slide Master, 598-599, 601-602
graphing data on, 618, 620-621
hyperlinking to Web, 674-675
logos, inserting with Slide Master, 602
modifying individual, 567
moving, copying, and deleting, 580-581
organizing, 576-578
pictures, adding to, 625-627
placeholders, 594-595
presentations, 564, 571
title slides, Title Master, 603-604

Snaking Columns toolbar button, avoiding use of, 295

software, Laplink, 612

sorting
files by name, 112
folders using Windows Explorer, 53

spam, definition of, 362

speed of performance, improving, 67

Spell Check, 214-215

Spelling and Grammar dialog box (Word), 216

Spelling command (Tools menu), Excel, 498

Spelling tab, selecting options in Outlook 98, 313

spreadsheets (Excel)
absolute and relative addresses
changing formulas, 457-458
preserving formulas, 458-460
active cell, 408
assigning names to ranges, 469
auditing techniques
conditional formatting, 527-528
data validation, 523-524
AutoFormat feature, 484-486
automatically recognized data types, 428
bad data warning (#), 464
borders, 494
bugs and patches, 14-15
calculations, verifying, 440-442
cells, 407
formatting, 486
names, 408
rotating text in, 491-492
columns
hiding, 497
inserting, 462
keeping titles onscreen, 498
comments, adding to, 466
conditional summing, 534
copying and moving data, 451-454, 647-650
crossfoot totals
emphasizing errors, 533-534
tracing errors, 533
validating, 529-532
data
aligning in cells, 488
indenting cells, 489
definition of, 31, 400
embedding into documents, 651-652, 655

entering data
alternatives to Enter key, 443
AutoComplete, 446
AutoCorrect, 446
AutoFill, 447-450
mistakes, correcting, 443
errors, types of, 523
fonts, 493
Formula Checker, 438
formulas
AutoSum, 435-436
building by pointing and clicking, 433-434
labels, using, 437-438
methods for entering, 432
parentheses, using, 439-440
simple, 429, 431
Sum( ) function, 435-437
Trace Precedents icon, 431-432
functions
definition of, 433
entering, 445
headings, centering over multiple rows, 490
hybrid addresses, 461
incorporating into documents, 659
macros and viruses, 8
navigating
Find feature, 471, 473-474
Go To dialog box, 475
multiple sheets, 475-476, 478
named ranges, 468, 470
shortcut keys, 468
numbers, formatting, 487
overview of, 399
pasting data, 454-456
patterns, 495
pictures, inserting, 496
PivotTables
creating from lists, 539, 541
overview of, 538

uses of, 545
viewing, 542, 544
printing, 418
column titles, 499, 501
Fit to page, 423
gridlines, 424
headers and footers, 501-502
landscape orientation, 422
large, 421-422
Page Break Preview, 503-504
page sequence, 420
portrait orientation , 422
Print Area, setting and clearing, 419
Report Manager, 424
resizing columns and rows, 480
AutoWidth, 483
multiple column widths, 482-483
row height, 484
widening columns, 482
rows
deleting, 463
hiding, 497
inserting, 462
keeping titles onscreen, 498
show formulas, 465
Spell Check, 498
templates, 415
Web pages, creating from, 679, 681-683
WEEKDAY( ) function, 444

SR-1 release, 12-14

stability of performance, improving, 67

Standard toolbar
Excel
Chart Wizard, 508, 510, 512
Zoom icon, 409
Insert Hyperlink icon, 272

PowerPoint
Copy icon, 581
Insert Hyperlink icon, 675
Web Toolbar icon, 672

Start menu commands
Files or Folders, 58
System Tools, 59

starting
Excel, 414
Office, 63
Word over, 116

status bars
Excel, 409
Word, 100

**storing data
(Outlook 98), 309**

strop characters, 167-168

**Style Gallery, avoiding
use of, 295**

styles, 257
character formatting on
paragraph styles, 264
character, applying, 258, 260
default paragraph font, 265
paragraph, applying,
261-263

Sum( ) function, 435-437

**Summary Slide icon
(Outlining toolbar),
PowerPoint, 591-592**

symbols, inserting, 221

**System Tools command
(Start menu), 59**

T

**Table menu commands
(Word)**
AutoFormat, 235
Delete Rows, 230
Draw Table, 231
Insert Table, 228

Table slide placeholder, 595

tables
AutoFormat feature
Excel, 484-486
Word, 235-236
Word
*creating and formatting,
228*
free-form, 231-232
preformatted, 228-229
from spreadsheets, 648
ways of using, 236

tabs
avoiding, 195
characters, 88, 90
fill-in-the-blank forms,
191-192, 194-195
formatting paragraphs,
185-187
rules for, 191
stops
definition of, 185-186
propagating, 189-190
setting, 188

Task form
Assign Task icon, 385, 389
Details tab, 385, 389
Outlook Today, 385, 389

TaskPad (Calendar), 385, 389

Tasks feature (Outlook)
overview of, 303, 385-386
priorities, 388
screen, 332
setting, 385, 387-388

**tele-presentations
(PowerPoint), 611, 613**

telephone numbers, *see*
phone numbers

**Template command
(PowerPoint), 571**

templates, 254
installing from CD, 107
Microsoft Web site, 107
PowerPoint, 571
spreadsheets, 415
Word, 106-107

ten-digit dialing, 373

text
centering in spreadsheet
cells, 488
copying in documents, 132
cutting from documents, 130
formatting in presentations,
566
free-form, adding to slides,
622-623, 625
hiding in documents, 162
pasting into documents, 130
rotating in cells of
spreadsheets, 491-492
selecting in documents,
126, 156

**Text Box command (Insert
menu), PowerPoint, 566**

**Text Box icon (Drawing
toolbar), PowerPoint, 623**

**Text Preset Animation
drop-down box
(Slide Sorter toolbar),
PowerPoint, 632**

Thesaurus, 220

**Thesaurus dialog box
(Word), 220**

thin client and Word, 296

**three-dimensional data,
PivotTables and, 539**

**thumb of vertical scrollbars
(Word), 101**

**times, updating in
headers and footers when
printing, 211**

timing presentations, 634

tips (help), 72

title bars
Excel, 407
Word, 97

**Title box, Master title
style, 599**

**title formatting for
presentations, 566**

Title Master
description of, 558
global changes to
presentations, 603-604
versus Slide Master, 568

Title Slide placeholder, 595

title slides
adding or deleting, 568
definition of, 565

**titles, printing for columns on
spreadsheets, 499, 501**

**Titles tab (Chart Wizard),
Excel, 510**

**toggling on/off, Office
Assistant, 72**

toolbars
Auditing (Excel), adding, 405
*Remove Precedent Arrows
icon, 441*
Trace Precedents, 533
*Trace Precedents icon,
431-432, 440*
AutoShapes, 245
buttons, adding to, 267-268
Chart (Excel), 512, 514
Common Tasks (PowerPoint),
553, 594-595
customizing, 266-268
Drawing (PowerPoint), Text
Box icon, 623
Excel, 407
fonts, changing from,
157, 160
formatting paragraphs,
169, 171, 173
Formatting (Excel), 488
Align Left, 489
Borders icon, 494
Center icon, 489
Currency Style icon, 487
Decrease Indent, 490
Increase Indent, 489
*Merge and Center
icon, 490*
Percent Style icon, 487
Outlining (PowerPoint), 557,
591-592

Outlook 98, 323
PivotTable (Excel), PivotTable
Wizard icon, 543
QuickLaunch (PowerPoint),
starting Office from, 63
Slide Sorter (PowerPoint)
*Slide Transition Effects
drop-down box, 631*
*Text Preset Animation
drop-down box, 632*
Standard
Insert Hyperlink icon, 272
Web Toolbar icon, 672
Standard (Excel)
*Chart Wizard, 508,
510, 512*
Zoom icon, 409
Standard (PowerPoint)
Copy icon, 581
Insert Hyperlink icon, 675
Word, 99
Headers and Footers, 209
versus menu bars, 98

Tools menu commands
Excel
AutoSave, 403
*Conditional Sum
Wizard, 535*
Options, 8
Scenario, 518
Spelling, 498
Outlook 98, Accounts, 334
PowerPoint
*PowerPoint Central,
606, 608*
*Presentation Conference,
612*
Word
AutoCorrect, 168, 217
*AutoFormat As You
Type, 96*
Customize, 248, 266
Envelopes and Labels, 222
Merge Documents, 292
Options, 8, 89
*Spelling and Grammar,
216*
Thesaurus, 220

total lines, drawing, 494

**Trace Precedents feature
(Auditing toolbar), crossfoot
total errors, 533**

**Trace Precedents icon
(Auditing toolbar),
431-432, 440**

**Transition effects, Slide
Sorter view and, 559**

transitions
definition of, 630
presentations, adding to,
631-632

troubleshooting
email problems, 336-337
modems, dialing outbound
calls, 385, 393

turning off Find Fast, 20-21

TweakUI Web site, 410

**two-dimensional data,
PivotTables and, 538**

U

**underscore (_) strop
character, 167**

**Undo button, correcting
formatting mistakes, 265**

**Undo command (Word),
117-118**

Undo feature (Excel), 418

**Unfreeze Panes command
(Window menu), Excel, 499**

**unhiding rows and columns
in spreadsheets, 497**

uninstalling Outlook 98, 310

updating
chart data, 514
field process, 238
PowerPoint, 610

upgrades to Outlook, 15
see also patches

Using Colors dialog box (Outlook 98), 360

Using Folders dialog box (Outlook 98), 359-360

V

validating crossfoot totals, 529-532

#VALUE! warning, 465

Valupack templates and Wizards, 254-255

VBA (Visual Basic for Applications), 38-39

vCards
as AutoSignatures, 356
creating and sending, 356
overview of, 355

.vcf files, 357

verifying calculations, 440
AutoCalculate, 442
color-coded formula
verifyer, 441

versions, 12
Corporate or Workgroup,
305, 310, 336
of Outlook 98,
determining, 306
saving, 117
SR-1, 12-14

vertical rulers, viewing hidden, 86

vertical scrollbars
deactivating, 141
navigation buttons
(Word), 101

videos
adding to presentations, 628
self-starting, 630

View dialog box (Word), 89

View menu commands
Excel, Page Break Preview,
503-504

FrontPage Express,
HTML, 683
PowerPoint
Header and Footer, 606
Slide Master, 598
Slide Show, 560
Title Master, 603
Word
Headers and Footers, 209
Online and Outline, 102
Page Layout, 86
Rulers, 86
Zoom, 103

views, 85
changing, 327
Contacts
Address Cards view, 330
By Category, 379
customizing, 376,
378-379
organizing, 330
Phone List, 331, 376
customizing, 328
Inbox View, 325-326
Information Viewer, 325
Notes, 332, 392
Outlook 98, 322
Outlook Shell, 322
reclaiming screen space, 325
restoring, 332
Tasks, 332

viruses, 3
anti-virus programs, 16
Concept.A, 7
defined, 6
protection
Excel, 8
PowerPoint, 10
Word, 8, 90
reproduction, 7
SR-1, 12-14
see also bugs

Visual Basic for Applications (VBA), 38-39

voice recognition and Word, 296

W

watermarks, adding, 278-279, 282

Web
addresses, converting to
hyperlinks in Word, 95
browsers, 672
components
HTML support, 668
overview of, 667
description of, 668
hyperlinking slides to,
674-675
putting presentations
on, 589

Web Page Authoring (HTML), installing from CD, 669

Web Page Wizard (Word), 677

Web pages
creating
Excel spreadsheets, 679,
681-683
PowerPoint presentations,
685-686
Web Page Wizard, 677
editors, 679
publishing, 677

Web sites
author's, 12
Mike Craven (free right-click
Thesaurus program), 220
Lightning, 385, 396
Macmillan Computer
Publishing, 675
Microsoft, 37
AutoSignature
information, 354
backgrounds, adding to
email messages, 366
Corporate or Workgroup
version of Outlook 98,
336
file storage, 670
help, 79-80

Integrated File
Management, 385, 396
Internet Only version of
Outlook 98, 309, 336
mail services,
installing, 336
Mastering Office
Development, 293
Outlook 98, 304
support, 297, 517
templates, 107
TweakUI, 410
Word, 297
WinZip, 352
WOPR Lounge, 297

**Web Toolbar icon
(Standard toolbar), 672**

WEEKDAY( ) function, 444

**What if? scenarios,
creating, 518, 521**

widows, definition of, 179

**wild card characters and Find
feature**
Excel, 473
Word, 150

**Window menu commands
(Excel)**
Freeze Panes, 499
Unfreeze Panes, 499

**Windows Backup, installing,
59, 61-62**

Windows Explorer
folders, sorting, 53
My Documents folders
creating, 48, 50
customizing, 55-56
deleting, 51-52
moving, 54
multiple, 52
naming, 51-52
organizing, 45-46

WinZip Web site, 352

wipes, definition of, 559

.wiz files, 57

wizards
AutoContent (PowerPoint)
page setup, 572
presentations, building,
569-570
Calendar, 254-255
Excel
Chart, 508, 510, 512
Conditional Sum, 535
Internet Assistant, 681
PivotTable, 539
installing from CD, 107
Internet Connection
email logon ID and
password, 308
installing Outlook 98, 307
Letter, 295
Outlook 98, Create New
Signature, 353
PowerPoint
AutoContent, 554, 564,
588, 590-592
HTML, 686
Pack and Go, 615
Presentation Conference,
613
Word, 106-107
creating résumés, 108
Web Page, 677

**Woody's Office Watch
(WOW), 12**

WOPR Lounge Web site, 297

Word, 84
advanced features, 275
AutoCorrect, 216-218
AutoRecover feature, 111
AutoSave feature, 111
bookmarks, 269-271
borders and shading,
180-181
clip art
inserting, 240-241
own, inserting, 242, 244
closing, 113-114
dates, inserting, 237-239
disadvantages, 29

documents
Clipboard, 128-129
copying between,
134-135
deleting, 125
description of, 124
opening, 114
saving, 110
selecting and moving
text, 126
documents, building, 121
characters, 122
drawing layer, 124
paragraphs, 122-123
sections, 124
test document, 131, 133
documents, navigating
Find, 142, 145-147,
149-150
Go To tab, 154
IntelliMouse Wheel,
140-141
keys, 138
Replace, 150, 153
Replace All option, 153
drop caps, adding, 283
envelopes and labels,
printing, 222-223, 225-226
Excel, interconnection with
copying data, 647-648
embedding spreadsheets,
651-652, 655
evaluating methods, 659
linking, 655-656, 658
spreadsheet to
picture, 650
spreadsheet to raw
data, 649
exiting, 113
Fast Save, 93-94
features to avoid, 293-295
fields
codes and results,
285-286, 289-290
functions of, 284
using, 286-287, 290
file list length settings, 90
files, inserting, 250-251

formatting characters, 156
  editing and, 166-167
  fonts, changing from
    dialog box, 160,
    162-163
  fonts, changing from
    toolbar, 157, 160
formatting documents, 155
formatting paragraphs
  auto bullets and
    numbers, 200
  bulleted and numbered
    lists, 196-198
  dialog box, 175-176, 179
  fill-in-the-blank forms,
    191-192, 194-195
  paragraph marks and,
    182, 185
  tab stops, propagating,
    189-190
  tabs, 185-187, 191, 195
  toolbar, 169, 171, 173
freehand drawing,
  244-245, 248
headers and footers, 208,
  210-213
hyperlinks, 271
  creating in documents,
    272-274
  disabling, 96, 272
  problems with, 95-96
macros, 90, 292
Mail Merge, using, 290-292
menu bar, 266
Microsoft Graph for
  charts, 249
novice versus advanced
  users, 84
Outlook, interconnection
  with, 639-641, 643, 645
overstrike mode, disabling,
  91-92
overview of, 25, 29
page borders, drawing, 276
page breaks, forcing, 226
Page Setup dialog box
  options
  Layout tab, 204
  Margins tab, 202

  Paper Size tab, 203
  Paper Source tab, 204
paragraph marks,
  showing, 88
pictures, inserting, 239
PowerPoint, interconnection
  with, 660-662, 665
printing, 118
  duplex printing, 119
  uncollated copies, 120
recommended reading, 296
recommended settings, 84
removing rulers, 85
rumored features, 296
Save *versus* Save As
  commands, 113
scanned art, inserting, 249
screen elements
  documents, 99
  horizontal scrollbars, 102
  menu bars, 98
  status bars, 100
  title bars, 97
  toolbars, 99
  vertical scrollbars, 101
  zoom factor, 103
screen shots, 138
search engine, 115
searching, 147
  limiting search, 150
  Web from, 672
sections, 201
shortcut key combinations,
  137, 139
Spell Check, 214-215
starting over, 116
styles, 257
  character formatting on
    paragraph styles, 264
  character, applying,
    258, 260
  font, 265
  paragraph, 261-263, 265
symbols, inserting, 221
tables
  AutoFormat feature,
    235-236
  creating and formatting,
    228

  free-form, 231-232
  preformatted, 228-229
templates, 254-255
Thesaurus and Dictionary,
  220
toolbars
  buttons, adding to,
    267-268
  customizing, 266-268
  icons, changing, 268
Undo and Redo commands,
  117-118
views, 85
watermarks, adding,
  278-279, 282
Web site, 297
wizards, 254-255
WordArt, 248
see also documents

word processors, defined, 29

WordArt, 248

WordMail, 364

words, formatting, 166

workbooks
  creating, 414-415
  definition of, 400, 413
  inserting sheets, 418
  opening existing, 415
  renaming sheets, 417

World Wide Web, 668

**WOW (Woody's Office
Watch), 12**

**Wrapping command (Format
menu), Word, 244**

WWW Microsoft Help, 79-80

X-Z

.xla files, 57

.xls files, 57

.xlt files, 57

zoom factor (Word), 103

Zoom icon (Excel), 409

**zooming, IntelliMouse
Wheel, 141**